A CHANCE TO LEARN

A CHANCE TO LEARN

The history of race and education in the United States

Meyer Weinberg

Professor of History, City Colleges of Chicago
Director, Center for Equal Education, Northwestern University

CAMBRIDGE UNIVERSITY PRESS

Cambridge

London - New York - Melbourne

Published by the Syndics of the Cambridge University Press
The Pitt Building, Trumpington Street, Cambridge CB2 IRP
Bentley House, 200 Euston Road, London NW1 2DB
32 East 57th Street, New York, NY 10022, USA
296 Beaconsfield Parade, Middle Park, Melbourne 3206, Australia

© Cambridge University Press 1977

First published 1977

Printed in the United States of America

Library of Congress Cataloging in Publication Data:

Weinberg, Meyer, 1920–
    A chance to learn.
    Bibliography: p.
    Includes index.
    1. Minorities – Education – United States – History.
2. Discrimination in education – United States – History.
I. Title.
LC3731.W44   370.19'342   76–4235
ISBN 0 521 21303 7   hard covers
ISBN 0 521 29128 3   paperback

Contents

To the memory of Horace Mann Bond

Believer in the right of every
child to learn and to grow

Historian of the travail in
protecting that right

Preface

This book is a history of the educational experience of black, Mexican-American, Indian-American, and Puerto Rican children in the United States. At the heart of the story is the unending attempt of minority parents to assure their children a chance to learn. Wherever possible, these efforts are documented from primary historical sources rather than through the screens and nets of second-hand commentary.

In this first book to comprehend such a broad scope, minority education is viewed in relation to the historic contours of the economic and political system. Economic subordination and political powerlessness are the presuppositions of public policy for minority education. These bitter facts have complicated immensely the efforts of minority communities to achieve educational equality for their children. Sustained efforts collided head-on with a deeply resistant economic-political structure. Yet from time to time, the structure gave way – only, however, under continued pressure.

Nearly two decades of participation in the civil rights movement in Chicago heightened my awareness of the subject of this book. As chairman of the education committee of the combined civil rights organizations in Chicago during the first six or so years of the 1960s, I came to know the abysmal conditions of segregated urban schools. I learned far more, however, from the parents who, despite their own meager schooling – often in the South but frequently in the very schools their children attended – were determined to change the schools. In addition, nearly thirty years of teaching young people in their first two years of higher education convinced me of the enormous creative potential they bear. Having taught young and old from every economic and ethnic condition in one of America's greatest cities, I strongly affirm the equality of all.

All this has informed, but not imprisoned, the history that follows. I have tried to tell the truth as far as I am able. In the course of the research and reflection, I have learned much. At numerous points I departed from various conventionalities and pieties, both of liberal historiography and the civil rights movement, some of which I had shared at an earlier time. It is up to the reader to judge the result.

A companion work to the present volume, *Minority Students: A Research*

Appraisal (Washington, D.C.: Government Printing Office, in press), is an analysis of the principal social science research literature of the subject.

I wish to thank the following persons who read part or all of the present work in first draft. A number of their suggestions were incorporated in the revision; few were considered and respectfully laid aside: Rodolfo Acuña, Allen Ballard, Hon. Robert Carter, John W. Caughey, Norman Chachkin, Robert Coles, Owen Fiss, Patricia Locke, James Neal, Gary Orfield, and Hon. John Minor Wisdom.

A grant from the Field Foundation was critical in permitting me sufficient time for writing; Leslie W. Dunbar, Executive Director of the Foundation, was most cooperative. The grant was administered by the Metropolitan Applied Research Center in the helpful persons of Kenneth B. Clark, Hylan Lewis, and Mary Strong. Jeannette Hopkins edited the first draft on behalf of MARC. Dorothy Obre, Cambridge copyeditor, proved to be a good friend of the reader's. I'm grateful for her close attention to the manuscript.

Research materials were consulted with the help of librarians at Northwestern University, especially Margery Carpenter; the University of Chicago; DePaul Law Library; Loop College; and Malcolm X College. I wish to thank Gertrude Martin for helping with the proofreading and preparation of the name index. The index was typed by Pearl Weiss.

Gladys Hamilton typed the manuscript with her usual care and skill. It is a fitting close to a number of splendid years during which she deciphered my handwriting and I wondered at her wizardry.

M. W.

Introduction:
race in American education

Since its earliest beginnings, the American public school system has been deeply committed to the maintenance of racial and ethnic barriers. Higher education, both public and private, shared this outlook. Philosophers of the common schools remained silent about the education of minority children. The most devout defenders of the common school from Horace Mann to John Dewey held their tongues when the subject of minority – especially black – children became a public issue. Exceptions were few, and the comfort they afforded minority children slight.

Public school authorities also all but deserted minority children. Federal, state, and local governments communicated the political imperatives of racial exclusion to the school. These became the guidelines for discriminatory school policies. Professional organizations of teachers and administrators collaborated actively in maintaining the racial order. The alum of privilege sealed many a lip. White educators profited from the enforced absence of black and other minority competitors for jobs. Planned deprivation became a norm of educational practice.

Deliberate racial and ethnic discrimination in schools followed a national, not a sectional, pattern. Nor did the discriminatory patterns flow northward. If anything, the direction of flow was southward. Before the Civil War, every important technique of discrimination was practiced in the North. These ranged from statutory exclusion of black children from the public schools to legally required separate schools to discriminatory school finance. After the Civil War, these practices – and more – made their appearance throughout the South. The development of a national educational profession facilitated the nationwide transfer of discriminatory techniques.

But nearly all this has escaped notice in the standard histories of the United States and of American education. Unfortunately, scholarly research sometimes bears the same relationship to truth as staring does to sight. All the mental equipment is at hand, but nothing much registers. The eyes may as well be closed.

Historians have fashioned a benevolent portrayal of constantly expanding opportunity. The creation of the common school system of public

1

education around mid-nineteenth century is equated with a national conviction that educational opportunity must be made universal. But such an ideal never existed in historical America. Racial and ethnic barriers were accepted by school people as inevitable limitations on educational opportunity. The tendency of historians to adopt the same view reflects an intellectual problem of far deeper import than simple individual prejudice.

A fundamental characteristic of modern life is not the existence of social problems but the effort to seek the aid of scientific thought in solving them. Basic to scientific inquiry is a habit of seeking the factual core of a subject. Indeed, modern industrial culture disciplines us to what Veblen long ago called the matter-of-fact mode of thought.[1] We tend to take things as they are, without such aids as superstition and the supernatural. Nature and society tend to be seen as matters of fact rather than as parts of a sacred order.

The authority of this mode of thought, as well as of science and scholarly research, rests on a foundation assumption that matters of fact are rooted in reality. Science is valued as a way of uncovering what is real. When, however, science becomes engaged with certain social problems, it may fail even to approach reality. Little defense is then left of its claim to intellectual authority.

American social science long ago adopted a live-and-let-live stance toward racial discrimination. Much effort was expended on explaining how deeply rooted in ancient traditions the folkways of segregation were. Interracial problems were defined in terms of white resistance to change. Negroes were regarded – when they were noticed at all – as passive victims of an inevitable process. Sociology and social psychology, the social sciences most directly relevant to the study of race conflict, virtually abdicated their responsibility. Pettigrew and Back note that "the major private foundations and governmental research agencies have been extremely reluctant to support social research on the desegregation process."[2] In time, "the expectation of funding rejection became self-fulfilling."[3] Even when sociological and psychological inquiry did occur, it tended toward investigation of "safer" aspects, such as the role of extremist thought or the impact of racist concepts on individual whites and blacks. Social science as a whole, however, simply failed "to explore the structural and power bases underlying segregation and racial discrimination."[4]

As a consequence of this failure to engage the mainsprings of racial discrimination, social and behavioral scientists condemned themselves to a superficiality frequently accompanied by astonishment at the course of events in the real world.[5] Reality threatened to become irrelevant.

But such a fate is not peculiar to the study of race. Blumer remarks that "'reality' for empirical science exists only in the empirical world, can be sought only there and can be verified only there."[6] He declares that "the prevailing mode in the social and psychological sciences is to turn away from direct examination of the empirical social world."[7] As a consequence, Blumer continues, "we have multitudes of studies of groups such as delinquents, police, military elites, restless students, racial minorities, and labor unions in which the scholar is unfamiliar with the life of the groups and makes little, if any, effort to get inside their worlds of meaning."[8] Only an occasional study holds out for more than a decent acquaintance with the everyday world of social reality.

In matters of race, America's ugliest reality, the tendency is widespread. We may even speak of a sweeping *suspension* of reality. Discussion and analysis often proceed as though many essential realities do not exist. *Denial* of reality is not adequate to describe the situation; there is no attempt to acknowledge a condition while denying its importance or to argue that a condition does not actually exist in the first place. To suspend reality is to render it invisible. The suspension of reality casts a pallor of unreality over many aspects of the racial situation in the United States. And it has utterly no special regional significance.

Historians also bear an important responsibility for the submergence of reality in the study of race. Not only have they failed to present a balanced factual account of minorities in American education, but they have portrayed minorities as suppliants and passive recipients instead of as parents and persons struggling and contriving autonomously to gain an equal chance for children. A contempt for minorities is expressed even in the most authoritative histories of education.[9] The failure of nineteenth century colleges to enroll minority youth is attributed even by recent authorities to the young peoples' insufficient secondary school training; no mention whatever is made of active discrimination by institutions of higher learning.[10] Many historians provide interpretations that effectively cloak the deliberate, conscious policy of racial discrimination of school authorities. This is done even when numerous expressions of discriminatory intent can be found in contemporary documents. Because historians tend to depend upon official records of school boards, they unwittingly reflect a bureaucratic approach to minority children. Frequently absent from these records are straightforward accounts of problems bearing especially on minority children. Secondary sources based on such records tend to reflect this bias. The critical use of school records by historians is in its infancy.

Historians have ignored the role of the parent. To be sure, even Anglo white parents are absent from the historical accounts, but this omission only slightly distorts the picture. These parents, because of their identification with ruling community groups, often succeeded in dominating school board policies. Minority parents, however, denied equal political rights in the larger community, were all but excluded from recourse to official government machinery. Responsibility for educating minority children was thrust back upon the minority community itself. With the slenderest financial resources, parents attempted to fashion private schooling comparable to the quality of public schooling. The practical impossibility of such an enterprise pressed minority parents into the political and legal arena to gain access to the public schools. Until recently, such actions were invisible as far as the standard histories of education were concerned. Detailed investigations of the subject are only about a decade old.

White academia ensured its ignorance by excluding eminent minority scholars from university faculties. Their work was discounted as special pleading and unworthy of notice. W. E. B. Du Bois, a graduate of Harvard University, whose doctoral dissertation on the slave trade became the first volume of the Harvard Historical Series, was one of the most prolific students of Negro education, in both its historical and contemporary aspects. Throughout a life of ninety-five years, he was never invited by his alma mater to deliver even a single lecture on this subject or any other.

In 1915, Carter G. Woodson, another black recipient of a Harvard doctorate in history, wrote the first connected history of black education, *The Education of the Negro Prior to 1861*. It was a pioneer work in the truest sense. Woodson saw farther than any author up to that time, and his book arose from his personal dedication and insight rather than from an accepted research tradition. No later historian has even tried to cover the same ground. Woodson was the first historian of education to use primary sources deriving from Negro people, especially correspondence and periodicals. But he was forced into the ghetto of black colleges and finally into a lonely life of immense productivity as an individual scholar. (In Washington, D.C., he was not permitted to join the Harvard Club when it was discovered he was black.)

In 1934, Horace Mann Bond – to whom the present book is dedicated – also wrote a pioneer work, *The Education of the Negro in the American Social Order*. He took up the story where Woodson had stopped, covering the years since the Civil War. Bond was a master not only of historical method but also of the theory and practice of education. As the title of his book indicates, he saw the education of the Negro within a broad social context. Accordingly, Bond attended to the role of political realities, class conflicts, and the economics of planned deprivation. Both he and his work were ignored by universities, which excluded him from employment. White scholars failed to incorporate his contributions into their own work.[11] Bond was compelled to teach an extremely heavy load in impecunious Negro colleges.

The submergence of Du Bois, Woodson, and Bond facilitated the suspension of reality in research on black educational history. Other minorities fared even worse. A generation ago Martha E. Layman wrote the first and only full-scale history of Indian education.[12] For whatever reason, this excellent work was never published, although it continues to be consulted by researchers. No general history of the education of Mexican-American and Puerto Rican children on the mainland has ever been written, nor are the topics mentioned in histories of American education.

This book is concerned almost wholly with four minority groups: blacks, Mexican-Americans, Indian-Americans, and Puerto Ricans. Together, their children make up about one-fifth of all public school students in the United States. In many local areas they constitute an overwhelming majority of enrollment.

The educational history of the children of the four minorities is marked by certain basic commonalities. First, their communities and families occupied a subordinate position in the American economy and society. Incorporated into the nation by force and violence, through enslavement and war, they bore the mark of conquered people. Second, by the consequent exclusion from a voice in government, public institutions were closed to them or made available only on a token basis. Schools fitted into this category. Third, because of their relative powerlessness, they were compelled to help pay for the very services they were forbidden to enjoy. In effect, their taxes often bore the character of tribute rather than of a proportionate share of an equal public burden. Fourth, the educational institutions – both common schools and colleges – adopted the prevailing social evaluation of the conquered peoples. Children were received grudgingly, when at all, and school personnel universally withheld from them the fullest resources available to the children of privileged groups. Fifth, they shared the fate of living in a country that was especially driven to deny the cultural distinctiveness of minority people. This drive to assimilate took on a special force when joined with other commonalities.

But each group also was distinctive. Enslavement was unique to black people and Indians, although varieties of oppression and exploitation were the lot of other minorities. The heritage of slavery was no mere memory of evil things. It was an active effort to salvage the privileges of the old order in a new context. The attempt succeeded for many years, in the classroom and in the wider polity. The designed annihilation of Indian culture was rare in its comprehensiveness and depth. It placed special limitations on the sparse formal education made available sporadically to Indian children. Until recently, a certain tentativeness characterized the Mexican-American's place in American society, in part because of the nearness of the mother country. This feature, too, facilitated the treatment of Chicano children as underprivileged tourists rather than as integral members of the larger society. The physical and cultural separateness and utter economic dependency of Puerto Rico created a setting for sharp deviations from American educational standards.

Children of Asian background shared many of the humiliations of minority status, and their parents suffered extreme material deprivation. Their schools were segregated by law, and during World War II many, even though they were citizens, were placed within concentration-camp-like reservations.[13]

Children of European immigrants experienced the difficulties of cultural strangeness and poverty. But these were remedied in rather short order. Even when explicit discrimination was enacted into law – which happened only rarely – it was quickly overcome. This was, for example, the case with German-speaking Catholics in Wisconsin, who were forbidden by the Bennett Act to conduct school instruction in the German language. The law was overturned in the course of a well-organized political campaign.[14] Neither the German nor any other European group saw its children consigned to deliberately inferior and segregated schools. Nor were they denied the political means to protect their group interests. If their traditions failed to escape ridicule, it occurred to nobody that their culture should be annihilated as was that of the Indians. When the children of European immigrants sought entry into schools and colleges financed in part by federal funds derived from land grants, they were beneficiaries of a bounty that was denied Puerto Ricans on the island, as well as the other three special minorities on the mainland.

Minority education has been presented conventionally as a tree without roots. Combining hardy growth with arrested development, the trunk as a whole persisted. Both its strengths and weaknesses, however, need to be more clearly related to the lights and shadows of the total environment and past.

In the present volume, each minority is first studied in the light of its earliest origins. The story of the education of black children begins with West Africa, that of Mexican-American children with preconquest Indian history. Attention is then directed to the historical conditions – primarily enslavement and conquest – under which the group was incorporated into American society. The economic and sociopolitical context of the group's participation or nonparticipation in community institutions is analyzed. Legal and other institutional constraints on the right of minority children to attend schools are examined, as are efforts of each group to overcome institutionalized obstacles and to provide schooling opportunities to minority children. Whenever possible, the children themselves are quoted in order to portray the fullest human impact of events in the strongest, most human terms.

Several issues repeatedly dealt with throughout the book include:

> 1. How did minority groups organize themselves to gain an
> effective voice in the education of their children?
> 2. Did entry into American society result in gains for each minor-
> ity in contrast with the source society?
> 3. What were the specific bases for antagonism against the
> minorities by the dominant American society?
> 4. How did the schools adapt themselves to these antagonisms?
> 5. In what ways did the relative political subordination of
> minorities permit them to be forced to finance majority schools?
> 6. To what degree were legal rights enforced by government and
> school authorities?

A history of minority education would lose cogency were its attention fixed only on the minority people. At an early point, two more questions must be asked: Where and why did the exclusory patterns originate in the dominant society? And how did the exercise of discrimination affect the educational structures provided for majority children? A society that asserted belief in universal values also withheld the benefits of those values from millions of children. Such paradoxical behavior greatly weakened the reality of the values even for the majority. It never proved possible to instruct white American children in the imperatives of democracy in social institutions where it was held imperative that democracy not be practiced. Without a clear understanding of these situations, racial and ethnic discrimination in education can only be seen as the consequence of irrational or mistaken policies adopted by misguided individuals.

Another problem in the study of minority education is the ease with which majority children are assumed to enjoy common privileges. America is a race-conscious society. But it is also a class-ridden society in which economic differences and conflicts have long regulated the volume and quality of community services children enjoy. American political history – of which the history of public schools is a subdivision – testifies amply to the manipulation of racial issues so as to convince disadvantaged whites of their stake in the perpetuation of the color line. The error is not less if minority people indulge in it. Discrimination by class and by race is double deprivation. We cannot avoid the destructive effects of one by denying the existence of the other.

Part I
Elementary and secondary education

1

The system of compulsory ignorance: black children to 1865

Alexander Crummell, whose father was a slave, said of slaveowners in the new world: "They began, at the first, a systematic ignoring of the fact of intellect in this abased people. They undertook the process of darkening their minds."[1] American educational policy for slave children was "compulsory ignorance."[2] Most never saw the inside of a school or received instruction. Ignorance was the primary instrument of enslavement. The minds of the slaves had not been darkened by ignorance when they were free men and women in their native lands. In West Africa, home of more than half the black slaves sold to America, formal education had existed at least since the sixteenth century.

During the sixteenth century, there was a great deal of formal education in traditional West Africa. But extensive institutionalized education appeared in large cities that came under Muslim influence. Islam meant literacy in Arabic and access to the broad range of Islamic scholarship. The Muslim universities in Timbuktu and Jenne, great cities of West Africa, were renowned throughout the Islamic world. Outside the royal and trading classes of the cities, in the great hinterland there was almost no formal education, but traditional education was common regardless of social divisions. Exclusion of anyone from the process of education was unthinkable. Instruction outside the Muslim world was conducted orally, with no reading or writing; it was available to all.

In eighteenth century West Africa, education ensured the continuation of traditional social and cultural life. Mastery of local customs and their religious significance was the universal goal: "Metal workers, weavers, boatmakers, drummers, warriors, and others had to be schooled not only in the material techniques of their respective crafts, but also in the spells, rituals, and other magic believed to be essential to success in their work."[3] Apprenticeship in a traditional craft followed family lines and extended from childhood to the eve of adulthood, when the new journeyman set himself up as a master craftsman.[4]

All this was destroyed under pressure of the world trade in slaves. During the eighteenth century alone, West Africa lost about 6.2 million people. Many were torn from their roots before they could be taught

11

customs and crafts. The supply of slaves included hundreds of thousands of children. While no strict minimum age limit was established or respected, ten years of age is frequently mentioned in the slavers' literature as a rough measure of minimum acceptability. Not all were as old as ten. Children took up less room on the ships and were cheaper.

Of the 697,624 slaves counted in the 1790 census in America, about 200,000 were under ten; some of these children had been born in West Africa.[5]

When, in 1788, the scandal of inhuman conditions on the slave carriers penetrated the British Parliament, a bill was presented to establish minimum space requirements on the vessels. Slave merchants in Liverpool called the standards "ruinous." The final text of the law provided that if more than two-fifths of the human cargo were made up of children shorter than 4 feet 5 inches, then space for every five such children could be reckoned by the slaver as equal to the space for four adult slaves.[6] A committee of the South Sea Company in 1717 noted that "children generally sell best on the Windward Coast [in the West Indies] where the people are very poor, and few can reach the price of a grown Negro."[7]

The African child arrived in the American slave market no longer a constructive member of a traditional local community, but an outcast-stranger whose role was to be used rather than to be useful. If he was taught to perform a task more effectively, it was because this would increase his economic value to someone else. The black minister H. Easton said, in 1830, that the slave's narrowly technical education was only "a collateral means by which he was rendered a more efficient machine."[8] The African heritage was more than a word or song or prayer that could be transplanted into the new earth. It could thrive only in a context of local, kinship-based community life. Under slavery, this was impossible. African heritage became a sacred remnant, and none suffered the loss more grievously than the children.

A slave might be taught to read and write if his work required such skills; less often he was taught by his owner out of kindly regard. The conscience of later generations has led to a belief that this benevolence was fairly widespread. No ground can be found for such belief.

The process of darkening minds was most often enforced by private vigilance. "In 1821, Levi Coffin and his cousin, Vestal, opened a Sunday School for the blacks at New Garden [North Carolina] and began to teach some slaves to spell; but when they could spell words of two or three letters they were withdrawn by their masters."[9]

In colonial South Carolina, missionaries of the Society for the Propagation of the Gospel (SPG) met deep resistance among slaveholders to efforts toward Christianization of the slaves. To minimize opposition, SPG agents stressed work with women and children, whose economic value was less compelling, and made definite progress, even organizing classes taught by slaves.[10] In 1740, South Carolina adopted the first compulsory ignorance law in America:

> *And whereas* the having of slaves taught to write, or suffering them to be employed in writing, may be attending with great inconveniences;

> *Be it enacted,* That all and every person and persons whatsoever, who shall hereafter teach, or cause any slave or slaves to be taught to write, or shall use or employ any slave as a scribe in any manner of writing whatsoever, hereafter taught to write; every such person or persons shall, for every offense, forfeith the sum of one hundred pounds current money.[11]

During the next century or so, this law was strengthened and duplicated in one state after another.

In 1823, Mississippi outlawed any gathering of six or more Negroes for educational purposes. A survey of the issue in Mississippi concluded that "the education of the slaves was almost entirely neglected."[12] An 1830 law in Louisiana prescribed imprisonment of from one to twelve months for anyone guilty of teaching a slave to read or write.[13] Virginia adopted laws in 1819 and 1831 forbidding meetings to instruct Negroes. In Alabama, an 1832 law made the teaching of slaves illegal. Sellers writes that "there is no record of a school Negro children could attend in Alabama before 1860."[14] The compulsory ignorance laws of North Carolina, enacted in 1831 and 1832, abruptly reversed a slight tendency toward slave literacy and precluded slaves freed after those dates from learning to read and write. The situation was not essentially different in the North wherever slavery was legal. The historian of Missouri slavery notes that "as late as 1820 . . . a slave who could read was something of a novelty."[15] Twenty-seven years later, the state legislature specifically forbade the instruction of all Negroes.

Against this wall of economic interest and legislative control, some slaves pursued the educational interests of their children through a series of secret schools. "Clandestine schools," Woodson says, "were in operation in most of the large cities and towns of the South where such enlightenment of the Negroes was prohibited by law."[16] In many of these schools, slave and free Negroes mingled. This very fact made attendance at the school dangerous.

Take the case of Susie King. She was born in 1848 on the Isle of Wight, near Savannah, Georgia. Along with her brother – the two eldest of nine children – she was sent to Savannah to live and study with a free Negro woman, the widow Woodhouse. She described the daily adventure:

> We went every day about nine o'clock, with our books wrapped in paper to prevent the police or white persons from seeing

them. We went in, one at a time, through the gate, into the yard
to the L kitchen, which was the schoolroom. . . . The neighbors
would see us going in sometimes, but they supposed we were
there learning trades. . . . After school we left the same way we
entered, one by one, when we would go to a square, about a
block from the school, and wait for each other.[17]

Mrs. Woodhouse and her daughter Mary Jane taught about thirty students at a time. Similar scenes were repeated all over the South, reflecting the affirmation of an oppressed people for a measure of freedom.

In 1834, James G. Birney, a slaveholder turned abolitionist, reported that day schools for free Negroes existed in Lexington and Louisville, Kentucky, but no slaves were enrolled.[18] Five years later, it became known that an African Sabbath school had been operating in Louisville since 1832. Headed by a Boston woman, Miss Bliss, the classes were housed in the basement of the Second Presbyterian Church. After a series of physical attacks against the school, it was moved to the teacher's own quarters. Only those slaves whose masters had given permission were taught.[19] In the state as a whole, one historian held, at least 10 percent of the runaway slaves read and wrote "tolerably well."[20] Under the guise of attending sewing classes, free Negro children received illegal instruction in Saint Louis, Missouri. Occasionally, some slave children joined in. In the District of Columbia, young slaves were regularly admitted into six Roman Catholic free primary schools.

In Deep South states such as Alabama and Mississippi, the vigilance of slaveowners triumphed. Virtually no record or even claim exists of a secret school for slaves in either state. In 1836 Birney wrote: "Of the 200,000 slaves now probably in Alabama, I confidently venture the assertion that there are not two hundred who can read understandingly a single tract published at the antislavery office."[21]

Court records reveal extremely few cases involving violations of the compulsory ignorance laws. Does this mean the laws were not generally enforced, as some historians contend? In 1850, Frederick Douglass, black abolitionist and escaped slave, acknowledged that some slaveowners ignored the laws; he knew this from personal experience. But experience also taught him that "there is the greatest unanimity of opinion among the white population of the South in favor of the policy of keeping the slave in ignorance." The lack of litigation reflects instead the lack of violations. It also, Douglass said, reflects the financial inability of the slave "to offer a temptation sufficiently strong to induce a white man to violate it." The few who dared teach the slaves, "usually white," did so out of a higher motive than money.[22]

Slaveholders' wills are melancholy evidence of their reluctance to educate their slaves. Few slaves, compared with the total, were promised literacy as a legacy, and any benefits conferred were frequently subject to a strict timetable. Jonathan Pleasants stipulated that his slaves were to be freed as they attained age thirty; meanwhile, he did "order and direct, as the most likely means to fit them for freedom, that they be instructed to read, at least the young ones as they come of suitable age." John Dunlap willed two slaves to his daughter; one of them, Jack, was to be taught to read and practice "the art and mystery of shoemaker," and he was to be freed upon attaining age twenty-six.[23]

Undoubtedly, the ubiquity of individual instruction of slaves meant that many unrecorded cases of slave literacy existed. These cases were certainly of deep personal significance both to slave and master, but viewed from the perspective of 4 million enslaved parents and children, they were few. (See Table 1 for numbers of Negro children in the United States during the pre-Civil War period.)

Table 1. *Number of Negro children in the United States, 1830–1860*

Year	Under 10 years of age	Aged 10–19 years	Total under 20 years of age
1830	797,167		
1840	955,461		
1850	1,138,455	889,576	2,028,031
1860	1,356,890	1,103,240	2,460,130

Source: U.S. Bureau of the Census, *Negro Population in the United States, 1790–1905* (Washington, D.C.: GPO, 1918), p. 166.

Free Negroes in the South

Even if all the free Negroes had become literate – which failed by far to happen – the net impact on black literacy as a whole would have been minor. During 1800–1860, in the South, where nearly all the slaves and somewhat over half the free Negroes in the country lived, the ratio of slaves to free Negroes was about 9:1 (Table 2). The free Negro's educational future lay outside the planter's direct authority. Regulation of his education, therefore, became a matter of legislation and public administrative action. The impersonal and distant nature of public regulation opened many avenues of accomplishment that were closed to the slave. Typically, free Negroes hastened to take advantage of the rare opportunities. In North Carolina, for example, 43 percent of the state's free black adults in 1850 were literate. At the same time, some 20 percent of Virginia's adult Negro population could read and write.[24] Undoubtedly, literacy rates were much lower in the Deep South.

Free Negroes in the South gained their education through one or more of the following: (1) public schools, (2) secret and other private schools, (3) Sabbath schools, (4) apprenticeship, and (5) special treaty requirements.

Table 2. *Negro population, slave and free, 1790–1860*

	Slaves		Free		
Year	Number	Percent of total	Number	Percent of total	Total
1790	697,624	92.1	59,557	7.9	757,181
1800	893,602	89.2	108,435	10.8	1,002,037
1810	1,191,362	86.5	186,446	13.5	1,377,808
1820	1,538,022	86.8	233,634	13.2	1,771,656
1830	2,009,043	86.3	319,599	13.7	2,328,642
1840	2,487,355	86.6	386,293	13.4	2,873,648
1850	3,204,313	88.1	434,495	11.9	3,638,808
1860	3,953,760	89.0	488,070	11.0	4,441,830

Source: Data in U.S. Bureau of the Census, *Historical Statistics of the United States, Colonial Times to 1957* (Washington, D.C.: GPO, 1960), pp. 11–12.

Public schools, secret schools, Sabbath schools, apprenticeship

Free Negroes in the sixteen slave states, but concentrated in the Upper South and border states, enrolled 4,114 children in public schools in 1850 and only 3,661 ten years later (Table 3).

Throughout the South, the national crisis of the fifties over slavery took its toll in a tightening of control over free Negroes. The compulsory ignorance laws were strengthened and applied more explicitly to free Negroes. Penalties were toughened. Several southern states set up free "common" school systems before the Civil War, but all excluded black children.

White philanthropy was of marginal importance in education of freedmen. Substantially excluded from public schools – although in many cases paying school taxes – free Negroes were forced to rely on their own efforts and resources. In Baltimore, New Orleans, Richmond, and Norfolk, free Negroes flocked to secret schools. In the principal cities of Virginia, a historian reports, "schools . . . were secretly maintained. . . . The colored aspirants after knowledge were constrained to keep their books and slates carefully hidden from every prying eye, and to assume the appearance of being upon an errand as they hurried along and watched their chance to slip unnoticed into the sedulously concealed schoolroom."[25] Children in the Richmond and Norfolk secret schools were generally taught by other free Negroes.

In the District of Columbia, free Negroes organized schools very early in the city's history; the first was built in 1807.

In Mississippi, Myrtilla Miner, a guileless young New Yorker, had come to teach daughters of planters, at Newton Institute in Wilkinson

Table 3. *School attendance of free Negro children, by state, 1850 and 1860*

State	Free Negroes in state 1850	Free Negroes in state 1860[a]	Free Negroes in school 1850	Free Negroes in school 1860	Percent in school 1850	Percent in school 1860
Alabama	2,265	2,690	68	114	3.0	4.2
Arkansas	608	144	11	5	1.8	3.5
California	962	4,086	1	153	0.1	3.8
Connecticut	7,693	8,627	1,264	1,378	16.4	16.0
Delaware	18,073	19,829	187	250	1.0	1.3
Florida	932	932	66	9	7.1	1.0
Georgia	2,931	3,500	1	7		0.2
Illinois	5,436	7,628	323	611	5.9	8.0
Indiana	11,262	11,428	927	1,122	8.2	9.8
Iowa	333	1,069	17	138	5.1	12.9
Kansas		625		14		2.2
Kentucky	10.011	10,684	288	209	2.9	2.0
Louisiana	17,462	18,647	1,219	275	7.0	1.5
Maine	1,356	1,327	281	292	20.7	22.0
Maryland	74,723	83,942	1,616	1,355	2.2	1.6
Massachusetts	9,064	9,602	1,439	1,615	15.9	16.8
Michigan	2,583	6,797	207	1,105	8.0	16.3
Minnesota		259		18		6.9
Mississippi	930	773	0	2	0.0	0.3
Missouri	2,618	3,572	40	155	1.5	4.3
New Hampshire	520	494	73	80	14.0	16.2
New Jersey	23,810	25,318	2,326	2,741	10.0	10.8
New York	49,069	49,005	5,447	5,694	11.1	11.6
North Carolina	27,463	30,463	217	133	0.8	0.4
Ohio	25,279	36,673	2,531	5,671	10.0	15.5
Oregon		128		2		1.6
Pennsylvania	53,626	56,949	6,499	7,573	12.1	13.3
Rhode Island	3,670	3,952	551	532	15.0	13.5
South Carolina	8,960	9,914	80	365	0.9	3.7
Tennessee	6,422	7,300	70	52	1.1	0.7
Texas	397	355	20	11	5.0	3.1
Vermont	718	709	90	115	12.5	16.2
Virginia	54,333	58,042	64	41	0.1	0.1
Wisconsin	635	1,171	67	112	10.6	9.6
District of Columbia	10,059	11,131	467	678	4.2	6.1
Territories	292	303	4	2	1.4	0.7
Total	434,495	488,068	26,461	32,629	6.1	6.7

[a]Total for this column has been corrected.

Source: Rearranged and calculated from basic data in Carter G. Woodson, *The Education of the Negro Prior to 1861* (Washington, D.C.: Associated Publishers, 1919), pp. 237–240.

County. Her first encounter with slaves was shattering, and she asked her employers if she might teach the slaves on her own time. "Why don't you go North and teach the 'niggers,' if you are so anxious to do it?" was the reply.[26] She left soon afterward. In 1851 Miss Miner came to the District of Columbia to start the Normal School for Colored Girls. Frederick Douglass had advised against it. He recalled: "To me, the proposition was reckless, almost to the point of madness."[27] Yet, Miss Miner persevered. Her two greatest problems were money and threats of violence. She bought a very large dog and became a practiced shot. Since the purchase and the practice, she wrote, "we have been left in most profound peace." A former student described Miss Miner at work: "Some rowdies came in the schoolhouse. She stood bravely at the window with a revolver, and declared she would shoot the first man who came to the door. They retreated at once."

Virginia's free Negroes educated their children under special handicaps. Because the law of 1831 forbade instruction of free Negroes, families who could afford it sent their children out of the state for schooling. After six years, free Negroes in Fredericksburg petitioned the state legislature to allow them to erect a school in that city. Their petition pointed out:

> Many of them are possessed of property, real as well as personal and have therefore an abiding interest in preserving the peace and good order of the community. They beg leave further to represent that so general has become the diffusion of knowledge that those persons who are so unfortunate as not to be in slight degree educated are cut off from the ordinary means of self-advancement and find the greatest difficulty in gaining a livelihood.[28]

The request was rejected, and the legislature vindictively passed a law preventing the return to Virginia of any child who left "the state for schooling."[29] The Fredericksburg Negroes emigrated to Michigan, where it was expected their children could learn without obstacles. In less than a decade, the educational opportunities of free Negro children in Virginia had suffered extraordinary reverses. Before 1830 they had by private means provided schooling in every city in the state. By 1839 all these projects had been effectively cut off, and free Negroes were forced to make exiles of their children or themselves if they wanted the children educated.

Sabbath schools were an acceptable evasion of the compulsory ignorance tendency, at least for a time, because learning to read and write was identified with religious practice and thus appeared to whites as nonpolitical. In many southern cities, especially, the Sabbath school was the primary school for thousands. But the same restrictive spirit that brought the compulsory ignorance laws ultimately undermined the Sabbath schools. As slaveowner sensitivity to abolition doctrine grew, so did fear of the revolutionary potential of literacy among slaves and free Negroes. The southern churches in which slaveowners were prominent – especially the Presbyterian and Episcopalian – stopped teaching reading and writing. The Sabbath schools became, in Woodson's phrase, examples of "religion without letters." He explained that oral instruction had become dominant by 1834 and that these denatured Sabbath schools also stressed "memory training of the blacks that they might never become thoroughly enlightened as to their condition."[30] After Nat Turner's slave uprising of 1831 in nearby Virginia, white residents of the District of Columbia were so unnerved that they excluded all black children from the Sabbath schools. This tragedy spurred black people to organize their own Sabbath schools. Three years later, an anti-Negro riot turned its fury against black schools and destroyed nearly all the Negro schoolhouses, furniture and all. The mob then marched on the home of John F. Cook, Negro organizer of schools, and burned his books and furniture. After a year, Cook reopened the school.

Free Negroes in the District of Columbia seemed to fare better in the Catholic Sabbath schools than in those of Protestant denominations. During the 1830s when the anti-Negro mob spirit was high, free Negro children were excluded from all the Protestant schools but retained in Catholic Sabbath schools.[31] By 1840, however, 1,459 blacks attended fifteen Negro Sabbath schools in the entire South.

American apprenticeship indentures or agreements usually stipulated that the master was to teach the apprentice the fundamentals of reading, writing, and arithmetic. Negroes made up the great majority of southern craftsmen, practicing skilled trades that required training, and potentially, therefore, apprenticeship should have been a major avenue of education. In North Carolina, it was. Franklin found that during the 1850s a majority of free Negro apprentices in Craven County were bound by indentures requiring instruction in reading and writing. Taking the state as a whole, he concluded, "what literacy there was among the free Negroes, came largely from the apprenticeship system."[32] This concern for teaching apprentices is clear from a review of colonial school legislation from 1642 to 1731.

During the eighteenth century, masters of black apprentices in Virginia were required by custom to teach them how to read and write, but in 1804, the state legislature outlawed the practice. In Delaware, an 1832 court decision involving an apprentice included sample forms of apprenticeship indentures. The form for black apprentices stipulated that "at the regular expiration of his servitude . . . [the master is] to pay to the said

Y.Z. the sum of _____ dollars in lieu of schooling, it being inexpedient to stipulate for education in reading and writing." The form for white apprentices read: "reasonable education in reading and writing, to wit: _____ years and _____ months schooling during his said apprenticeship." Some crafts placed a special premium on literacy. Barbers, for example, were, as ever, expected by their clients to pronounce on various public and philosophical issues as they worked, and so many were literate.[33] Free Negroes in the printing trades, who were unavoidably literate, were regarded with suspicion by whites. A Georgia statute specifically outlawed the employment of any black person "in setting up type or other labor about a printing office requiring a knowledge of reading and writing."[34] South Carolina enacted an even broader prohibition in 1834 against Negroes working in stores and offices.

The 1803 Treaty of Paris, including the conditions of the Louisiana Purchase between France and the United States, guaranteed to the inhabitants of the territory "all the rights, advantages, and immunities of citizens of the United States."[35] This was interpreted as protecting the right of Creoles to pursue their schooling through private means. A few such schools existed in New Orleans in the pre-Civil War period. In 1833, the Alabama legislature acknowledged the rights of Creole children under a similar provision, and a law permitted one or more private schools in Mobile City as well as Mobile and Baldwin counties. Hardly more than a handful of black children were affected by these rights.

The 260,000 free Negroes in the slave states in 1860 had fought a losing battle for basic human rights, and especially the right of their children to an education. Hershaw explained: "In actual practice the term 'free colored person' embraced the idea of freedom from personal service to a specified owner and little else, particularly in the slave-holding states."[36] Wherever possible, of course, free Negroes seized upon that "little else" and squeezed it dry – most successfully, perhaps, in North Carolina. Free Negroes in the Upper South did not profit from the southwestward movement of slavery, except in numbers. Even as the proportion of slaves fell in Virginia, the animus of the laws regulating black education intensified.[37] In Alabama, Sellers wrote, "education was almost as hard to come by for the free Negro as for his brother in slavery."[38]

Woodson, after the most probing examination of the matter, concludes that during the years 1825–1860 the percentage of Negro adults who had "the rudiments of education" fell to only 10 percent from a much higher level.[39] The compulsory ignorance laws had taken their toll.

Free Negroes in the North

On the eve of the Civil War, nearly 250,000 free Negroes lived in the North. They were concentrated in a small number of urban centers as well as in many scattered settlements. But wherever they dwelt, it was as an organized community, a distinctive feature of free Negro life. The search for educational opportunities was a communitywide project.

Black life in the North never wholly escaped the shadow of the plantation. Proscription and deprivation pursued Negroes everywhere. But in at least two respects, black life in the North was immeasurably enriched: (1) greatly increased physical mobility and (2) unprecedented communication. The first, aided by the growth of railroads in the pre-Civil War generation, destroyed the traditional physical isolation bred by plantation life. The second, embodied in the black and abolitionist press, helped create a sense of a national black community. Neither black nor abolitionist journalism had a chance in the South.

Black children were excluded from public schools throughout Pennsylvania. In Philadelphia, with the largest black population in the North, notorious for its racial discrimination and oppressive treatment of Negroes, ex-slaves nevertheless withstood the storm. During the 1830s, anti-Negro riots swept the city. Even during normal times it was dangerous for a free Negro to venture far from his home after dark, if only to attend night school.[40] Still, as nearly one-tenth the city's black population, the largest group of homeowners of the black community, ex-slaves sent more of their children to school than any other black group.

The Negro community as a whole developed a striking array of institutions to serve community needs. As abolitionist leader William Lloyd Garrison told a London audience in 1833: "In the city of Philadelphia alone, they have more than fifty different associations for their moral and intellectual improvement."[41] Five years later, the greatest leader of Pennsylvania Negroes and a close friend of Garrison, Robert Purvis, wrote that "there are among us in Philadelphia, Pittsburgh, York, West Chester, and Columbia, 22 churches, 48 clergymen, 26 day schools, 20 Sabbath schools, 125 Sabbath school teachers, 4 literary societies, 2 public libraries, consisting of about 800 volumes, besides 8,333 volumes in private libraries, 2 tract societies, 2 Bible societies, and 7 temperance societies."[42] Most of these facilities were in Philadelphia.

In New Bedford, Massachusetts, according to Garrison, "the colored man had always been permitted to mingle on terms of perfect equality. The result was seen in the comfort, respectability, wealth and education so diffused throughout the class, and making them the worthy peers of the best of their brethren in the United States."[43] New Bedford's schools were never segregated by race. But some states were less hospitable.

Connecticut was especially risky for Negroes. Richards called it "the most inhospitable of the New England states" for black people and doctrines of abolition.[44] As of 1790, a total of 3,763 slaves were owned in New England, and two-thirds of the total were in Connecticut. Fewer than a fifth of the region's free Negroes lived in the state. Nor was Rhode Island a haven. John T. Waugh, of Providence, Rhode Island, told the Convention of Colored Citizens of New England that "when he was a slave in the South, and attempted to gain his freedom, he had no idea of living to see his son excluded from a Rhode Island school."[45]

Cleveland, Ohio, known for its more prosperous black community, composed mostly of formerly free Negroes from the South, permitted black children to attend the common schools despite an explicit provision to the contrary in the city's charter of 1835.[46] Groups of blacks emigrated westward and established thriving communities. A group of twenty families, including a number of ex-slaves, who settled in Columbia County, Ohio, educated their children in the school kept by the Society of Friends. In Mercer County, Ohio, representatives of a black settlement reported: "We have had a good school most of the time for six years. Our children have learned to read and write and cipher."[47] Such opportunities in the West were not the usual experience of blacks, for if abolitionism was merely unpopular in New England, it was near to subversion in the Old Northwest.

Communication among black communities was extensive, along both informal and formal channels. When Robert B. Forten, the black sail-maker and abolitionist leader, refused to allow his daughter Charlotte to attend segregated schools in Philadelphia, he sent her instead to the nonsegregated schools of Salem, Massachusetts. There, she lived at the home of Forten's friend, black abolitionist Charles Lenox Remond. Through Remond, Charlotte met many abolitionist leaders, black and white.[48]

Numerous statewide and interstate meetings of free Negroes tapped lines of communication and protested the evils of slavery and discrimination against free Negroes. In 1839, an Education Convention of Colored People of Ohio met in Columbus. Delegates were present from nine cities. In 1856, a Colored People Convention convened in Sacramento, California, to deal with statewide political issues. When Pennsylvania was about to rescind the free Negroes' right to vote in 1838, blacks throughout the state organized petition campaigns. Despite these efforts on the part of blacks in Pennsylvania, the right to vote was annulled.[49]

The press was a vital communication link. An independent black press, which started to emerge during the 1820s, never succeeded to a firm financial basis prior to the Civil War.[50] However, during the first year of publication of the *Liberator*, in 1831, Garrison reported, 400 of the paper's 450 subscribers were Negro. Two years later, there were 1000 black subscribers. A teacher in Miss Miner's school for colored girls in the District of Columbia wrote Garrison: "We feel proud when we read in your paper the speeches delivered by *colored* men – proud because you respect them as men."[51]

Table 4. *Enrollment in Negro schools in Ohio, 1853–1865*

Year	Number of Negro schools	Number of Negroes aged 5–21	Number enrolled in Negro schools[a]	Percent enrolled
1853	22	6,862	702	10.2
1854	48	9,756	2,439	25.0
1855	88	10,516	4,110	39.1
1856	88	10,500	4,297	40.9
1857	93	11,582	4,685	40.5
1858	129	12,562	4,888	38.9
1859	131	13,487	4,820	35.7
1860	159	13,632	6,512	47.8
1861	168	14,247	6,902	48.4
1862	172	14,068	7,456	53.0
1863	167	15,312	7,229	47.2
1864	145	16,605		
1865	143	18,137	7,409	40.9

[a]These statistics do not include an unknown number of Negro children who attended nonsegregated schools.

Source: Calculated from basic data in Charles T. Hickock, *The Negro in Ohio, 1802–1870* (Cleveland: Williams Publ. and Electric Co., 1896), table facing p. 106.

Exclusion, discrimination, mobism

Nowhere in the North was systematic and widespread schooling a gift of whites to blacks. Statutory obligations to provide such instruction were often ignored by state governments. The 1784 Rhode Island Emancipation Bill, owing to Quaker influence, made it compulsory to teach freed Negro children to read and write. The provision was not enforced. During the colonial period, when New England provided public schools for its white children, few free black children attended them. Free Negroes in Missouri who were apprenticed lost significant legal protection in 1825 when that state followed Virginia in abolishing a requirement that black apprentices be taught to read and write. Public funds appropriated for black schooling were often withheld altogether or wrongfully diverted to the use of white children.

Negroes squeezed their resources and pressed their public authorities to provide schools for the young. Shortly after the American Revolution, black parents in the North established private schools for their children. In Philadelphia, as early as 1797, seven such schools existed. Thirty years later, ten Negro schools were reported in five northern cities. That same year, *Freedom's Journal*, the country's first black weekly newspaper, wrote proudly that African free schools operated in several cities: Portland, Maine – one school; Boston, Massachusetts – three schools; New Haven, Connecticut – two schools; Philadelphia, Pennsylvania – three schools; New York City – two schools. The editor noted: "We need not mention the names of any other places as we know of none other schools."[52] During the remaining years before the Civil War, private black schools were organized in many areas of the country.

The separate private schools were aided from time to time by white abolitionists. But the basic poverty of Negroes determined that the schools would offer only a minimal program. Often located in basements and spare rooms, lacking materials and books, and operating for as little as two months a year, the schools filled a small part of a great need. Publicly funded schools were the answer. Yet dominant white opinion was not ready for this step. Indeed, in many parts of the North, whites did not acknowledge widely the necessity or even desirability of educating black children.

Black schools were often fired by the torch of white mobs. In several towns in Ohio, whites destroyed schoolhouses as the blacks built them, but "if one house was burned another was put up in its place."[53] In Zanesville, Ohio, a school organized by blacks was sacked by whites the very night black citizens met to form a board to manage their school; the same building had also served as their church. White citizens of Canterbury, Connecticut, annoyed by the efforts of white teacher Prudence Crandall to operate a school for Negro girls, attacked the school with iron bars and smashed the windows. Miss Crandall was forced to close the school. In Noyes Academy, in Canaan, New Hampshire, the trustees announced black youth would be welcomed. After a year of harassment of the school, a white mob physically moved the academy building onto a vacant lot. That night, some of the mob fired into the homes of abolitionists.[54]

Black parents persisted, however. During the 1820s and 1830s, common school systems were opened – on a segregated basis – to increasing numbers of black children. In 1820, the Smith School opened in Boston as a citywide public school for black children. Its plant was unattractive and inadequate, but the school became the point of embarkation for many of Boston's future black leaders. While the school was "public," it was not "common." Not until 1849 were the children of Smith School allowed to march with white students in the citywide Fourth of July parade. Every year, the best students in the city received silver medals and dined with school board members and teachers at Faneuil Hall. Outstanding students at Smith were not eligible for this honor.

William C. Nell, a brilliant young black scholar at Smith, was one of four students whose tests showed them to be deserving of the highest science award, the Franklin Medal. Their counterparts in white schools received the medal and attended the dinner at Faneuil Hall. Nell and his classmates each received a small book about Benjamin Franklin; they were not permitted to participate in the dinner. But Nell convinced a Negro waiter to let him act as a waiter at the dinner, "while satiating my mental appetite, the physical being then with me subordinate."[55] A teacher who saw him whispered that Nell ought to have been honored. Nell reflected to himself: "If you think so, why have you not taken steps to promote it?" (Nell became the single most important leader in Boston's black community on school issues. With no children of his own, he once observed, he had adopted the city's black students as his "children.")

The Ohio law for a common school system, passed in 1829, explicitly excluded Negro children. By 1837, black citizens formed a School Fund Institution to finance a system of forty schools on a total budget of $40,000. Within two years, fourteen schools received some help from the fund, but the amount was tiny. The largest sum paid a single school for a year was $78.83.[56] Poverty underscored the Negro's stake in public education. With experience gained in organizing the statewide network of private schools, Negroes began legislative lobbying for publicly supported schools. After a decade of petitioning, black parents won several victories of a sort. In 1848, a law provided that twenty or more Negro children could constitute a school district, supported by school taxes paid by black residents. The taxpayers could elect their own school directors to build schoolhouses. If there were fewer than twenty children, they could attend a white school, provided no white parent or citizen in the district objected. Very few black children were, in fact, admitted. In response to black pressure, the next year the law was amended to omit any minimum number of children and to facilitate the election of black school trustees.

Continued black pressure brought additional changes in Ohio, each one resulting in opening school doors further – on a separate basis – to black children. Between 1853 and 1860, the number of Negro schools rose from 22 to 159 and the number of Negro children in school from only 702 to 6,512 (Table 4). The percentage of children enrolled in Ohio black schools in 1860 was 47.8, not far from the national average for white children, 59.6 percent. By 1860, the percentage of school attendance of black children in Ohio almost matched that of Massachusetts. In good measure, this was made possible when black taxpayers were allowed to elect their own school boards. It was all the more remarkable because before the Civil War blacks could not vote for any other public official in the state. In 1849, a meeting of Negro citizens in Oberlin, Ohio, had resolved: "That we very much doubt about paying any tax upon which representation is based, until we are permitted to be represented."[57] Changes in the school law during the next years legitimized the levying of school taxes upon Negroes.

In neighboring Pennsylvania, the blacks' right to vote, which had been exercised for many years, had been withdrawn in 1838. Without the vote, Negroes were unable to secure services like education provided to full citizens. Nevertheless, the law was bent to permit black public schools here and there. Not until 1854, however, did the basic school law provide for the organization of Negro school districts in situations where twenty or more children applied for school privileges. During the decade of the 1850s, the percentage of Negro children in school rose slowly in the state.

Parent revolt against segregated caste schools

Of small moment to black parents in the early part of the nineteenth century was the matter of segregation. Much more immediate was the provision of education in any setting. Thus, all over the North black parents during the first four decades strove for public schooling, even if it entailed segregation. But for the decade and a half before 1860, blacks in one northern city after another began to insist on desegregated schools. In 1860, of the 28,000 or so black children attending northern schools, perhaps 90 percent were in segregated schools.

In time, little was as galling to black parents as the imposed separation of their children into segregated schools. Whenever possible, they insisted upon nonsegregated facilities. Robert Purvis, who lived in a suburb of Philadelphia, refused to pay the town's school tax until black children were admitted to the public schools: "I object to the payment of this tax, on the ground that my rights as a citizen, and my feelings as a man and a parent, have been grossly outraged in depriving me, in violation of law and justice, of the benefits of the school system which this tax was designed to sustain."[58]

Segregation inside formally nonsegregated schools was also attacked. James L. Smith, an escaped slave, complained to Garrison of suffering racial discrimination in an "abolitionist" school in Springfield, Massachusetts. A daughter of William Wells Brown – himself an escaped slave – recalled: "And even after coming to Massachusetts, where we were allowed to receive instruction in the same school with white children, we had to occupy a seat set apart for us, and therefore often suffered much annoyance from the other children, owing to prejudice."[59] In another case, "there was one colored boy in a school who did not sit on a bench, like the rest, but on a block of wood that looked like a backlog turned endwise. Aunt Hannah [the teacher] often called him a 'blockhead.'"[60]

Frederick Douglass became enraged when he read a letter from his daughter, who was attending Seward Seminary in Rochester, New York: "I get along pretty well, but father, Miss Tracy does not allow me to go into the room with the other scholars because I am colored." He remonstrated and the principal asked the girl's white classmates where the girl could sit. All shouted "by me"! Then parents were asked whether they agreed. Except for one, they did. The only parent who refused to countenance desegregation was H. G. Warner, editor of the *Rochester Courier*. Douglass reminded Warner in a letter: "We are both worms of the dust, and our children are like us."[61]

The communitywide character of black opposition to segregation was demonstrated repeatedly. Basic to these campaigns was the presence of a functioning local antislavery society and "a propertied and educated black elite." Leadership exercised by an elite was not unlike the pattern in white communities. Rank-and-file support was astonishing, however. When a decision had been reached to boycott the all-black school until Negro children could attend the common schools, parents cooperated. Boycotting black parents kept students home in large numbers: "In Nantucket, Mass. 98 per cent of students took part in a boycott; in Salem, Mass., 71 per cent; in Boston, Mass., 71 per cent; in Rochester, N.Y., 80 per cent; in Buffalo, N.Y., 83 per cent, and in Lockport, N.Y. 67 per cent."[62]

Parents rallied support in regular mass meetings and door-to-door canvassing. Black lawyer Robert Morris described the process in Boston: "We went round to every parent in the city, and had all the children removed from the Caste Schools; we made all our people take their children away. And in six months we had it all our own way – and that's the way we always should act. Let us be bold, and they'll have to yield to us."[63] Without such boycotts, black protests would have remained rhetorical only.

Nantucket was the scene of a protracted campaign against separate schools. A black public school had been started in 1831 at the insistence of the Baptist African Society. Not until five years later was its school year as long as that of the white schools. In 1842, the black citizens of the town began a campaign to abolish the separate school, Negro parents asserting their equal right to educate their children. Negro children had only a single school, while white children were privileged to attend "a gradation of schools" on four age levels. To the assertion that blacks had *their own* school, the assembled citizens replied: "We are weary of this kind of honor or distinction; we want no exclusive school privileges; we are citizens of this great republic; our veins are full of republican blood; we contend not for, neither do we desire, any rights or privileges that are not common to the rest of the members of this community."[64] School board members resisted the appeal. The next year, abolitionists were elected to the school board, and the separate school was abolished.

In 1844, the issue arose again. Blacks and abolitionists protested against an impending reimposition of separate schools in these words: "They who have an execrable prejudice to indulge, who seek to perpetuate a petty aristocracy of the skin, should at least do so at their own expense, and not, for such a purpose, dip their fingers into the pockets of honest men, who

have no such prejudice to gratify, and who despise such an aristocracy."[65]
The matter was settled finally by another victorious election whereby
friends of integration won twelve of thirteen seats on the school board. In
1845, separatists had had a two-to-one margin on the board.

Boston was the scene of a long, bitter campaign against continued
operation of the Smith School. An early petition for desegregation, circulated in 1840 by William Lloyd Garrison, collected the grand total of three
signatures – his own and those of Wendell Phillips and Garrison's young
apprentice, William C. Nell! Four years later, a black clothier, Thomas
Dalton, petitioned for the same goal and gathered seventy signatures.
The document noted that, as in Nantucket, Boston's black children had
not the advantage of different grades of schools and that this system "robs
the more intelligent of a higher education." The petitioners declared: "Do
not say to our children that, however well behaved, their very presence
in a public school is contamination to your children."[66]

In less than two months during 1844, black parents of Smith School
carried on a probing study of conditions at the school, and especially the
role of Abner Forbes, the white principal. The report of the parents
reflected a deep respect for the rights of all concerned but especially care
for the interests of Smith students.[67] Parents found that Forbes punished
children on the basis of third-party reports. A standing rule he established
forbade, during recess, any "noise in the yard . . . not even a whisper, as
it tended to disturb a primary school, which was in the lower story of the
same building." Forbes was found to have been abusive of parents.
Clearly neglectful of his duties, especially in the past, he was guilty of
"absence in school hours, writing in school hours, reading newspapers,
and so forth, and allowing scholars of the first class to hear the lessons of
the younger children."

Forbes was found to have voiced, and possibly written about, his sentiments that blacks were intellectually inferior. One of the complaining
parents asked:

> Shall I send my child to a physician, who believes that the rem-
> edies applied to other children having a similar complaint, can-
> not benefit him, owing to his peculiar nature? Or shall I go to one
> who set resolutely to work, sure that the same remedies which
> cured the one will cure the other. Can an instructor ever be
> successful without FAITH – (the great mainspring of every good
> work) – without faith, that the means he uses are competent to
> effect the end at which he aims?

Parents asked that Forbes be discharged.

During the next eleven years, the struggle against caste schools persisted. Boston authorities tried to cut the movement short by selecting a
Negro principal for the Smith School. This was rejected by most parents.

In 1849 evidence was heard before the state supreme court in a challenge to segregation in Boston. When the court ruled against the plaintiff early in 1850, Benjamin F. Roberts waited two months and then announced that he was undertaking a statewide petition campaign to outlaw segregated schools. At the same time, a black boycott of the Smith School began. A number of black parents simply moved from Boston to nearby towns where school segregation was not the rule. In 1855, the legislature finally adopted a measure forbidding separate schools anywhere in the state. During the summer, black parents met to plan for the forthcoming desegregation. Nell reported: "It was stated at the meeting . . . that . . . the teachers had been advised to see that the colored youth were not imposed upon or annoyed by their white associates." At a great mass meeting of black citizens later in the year, Nell was honored for his leadership. He stressed the important part black women had played in the successful fight for equal schools. Scattered firsthand reports during the next years indicated that desegregation had occurred with favorable results.[68]

The many desegregation campaigns and actions in the North varied only in details. Providence authorities exceeded even Boston in stubbornness. In Rochester, New York, a lowly woman domestic, Phoebe Ray, started the move for desegregation; it took the arrival of Frederick Douglass the year following to stimulate a full-scale campaign. Wherever Negroes had the right to vote, a favorable outcome was more likely; in Boston the campaign took thirteen years; in Buffalo, forty-three.

Discrimination dominated the type of education available to Negro children. The issue of a practical vocational schooling versus an academic education rose early. In Philadelphia four out of five black males worked in unskilled occupations. More or less the same was true in New York, New Orleans, and other large cities. Black leaders never tired of attacking the discrimination that oppressed black youth and kept them out of skilled occupations. Martin Delany attacked efforts to give black youth a classical education: "What we most need . . . is a good business practical Education; because, the Classical and Professional education of so many of our young men, before their parents are able to support them, and community ready to patronize them, only serves to lull their energy, and cripple the otherwise praiseworthy efforts they would make in life."[69] Delany, who advocated emigration of blacks, wrote from the bitter experience of having been refused a chance to complete his medical course at Harvard Medical School. Delany replied to Garrison's criticism of the emigration policy: "We desire the *exercise* and *enjoyment* of these rights, as well as the *name* of possession. If there were any probability of this, I should be willing to remain in the country, fighting and struggling on, the good fight of faith."[70] To this, Garrison could offer only continued hope.

Boston lawyer John S. Rock was the first black admitted to practice before the U.S. Supreme Court. In an extraordinary address in 1862, he explained the essentials of why "there is no field for these young men."[71] Education limited black life chances, for black men appeared to suffer more the greater their education. Without the benefits of an education, what virtue was there in entering the schoolhouse? "You can hardly imagine," he declared, "the humiliation and contempt a colored lad must feel in graduating the first in a class, and then being rejected everywhere else because of his color." Boston was not different. In fact, Rock held: "We are colonized in Boston. . . . It is ten times more difficult for a colored mechanic to get employment [in Boston] than in Charleston [South Carolina]." Rock chided white abolitionists: "Colored men in business in Massachusetts receive more respect, and less patronage, than in any place that I know of." Speaking to the annual convention of the New England Anti-Slavery Society, Rock exclaimed: "This living entirely for posterity sounds well from the rostrum, but a loaf of bread today is worth a barrel of flour next year."[72]

Meanwhile, black parents sent their children to school wherever they could. In New York City, black leader Henry Highland Garnet, said that "most of our people belong to the laboring classes, and it is seen by our school reports that we have a larger number of children in the public schools, of the city than the same class have among the whites."[73] But some of the children were not swayed from everyday realities by their schooling. One day in 1858, the governor and state school superintendent of Florida visited the Negro school on Mulberry Street in New York City and complimented the children. In return, the music teacher asked the children to sing "Hail, Columbia" for the visitors. Very few did. As a newspaper reported: "Mr. Petit afterward explained that he had never been able to induce teachers and scholars to sing any of the patriotic tunes; they said that it wasn't a free country for black people, and they could not call it a 'happy land.'"[74]

Black children had to face up to the overwhelming efforts of the larger white community to inculcate feelings of self-depreciation. Dr. James McCune Smith, leading black intellectual in New York City and a graduate of the African Free School there, referred to "the free blacks, taught to believe themselves naturally inferior . . . and taunted with ignorance."[75] Alexander Crummell, a black contemporary of Smith and later a graduate of Cambridge University in England, explained the logic of the compulsory ignorance laws: "It was done . . . with the knowledge that the Negro had brain power. There was *then*, no denial that the Negro had intellect. That denial was an afterthought."[76] A black leader from Chicago, H. Ford Douglass, underscored the crucial role of equal opportunity: "Now, I want to put this question to those who deny the equal manhood of the Negro: What peculiar trait of character do the white men of this country possess, as a mark of superiority, either morally or mentally, that is not also manifested by the black man, under similar circumstances?"[77] The obverse point was made by Rock: "Abject as our condition has been, our whole lives prove us superior to the influences that have been brought upon to crush us."[78]

Negro youth, Rock explained on another occasion, required the encouragement of personal example: "The success of such a man as Frederick Douglass is worth more to the race than a pile of resolutions and speeches as high as Bunker Hill Monument. Had it not been for the Abolitionists, the brilliant genius of Mr. Douglass would probably have died with him."[79] A southern black newspaper noted a connection between self-concept and segregated schools, which were declared to "perpetuate from childhood the infatuation of the white, and prompt the black to retaliate by enmity or envy."[80]

Negro inferiority was sometimes placed in a patronizing framework, as educator Horace Mann did in 1851. In a letter to the central committee of an Ohio state convention of Negro people, Mann wrote approvingly: "In fine, I suppose the almost universal opinion to be, that, in intellect, the blacks are inferior to the whites; while in sentiment and affection, the whites are inferior to the blacks."[81] He advocated the voluntary repatriation of free Negroes to Africa, contending that it was "their place" to whose climate God had "adapted their organization." Few voices, black or white, rose to attack Mann for his theories, although Wendell Phillips conducted a searing critique in the columns of the *Liberator*, dwelling in detail on Mann's failure to use his office against school segregation in Massachusetts. Mann replied in equal detail, but evasively, nonetheless.[82] As far back as 1847, Phillips had criticized Mann for his silence about segregation: "He is a politic man, and stands weighing out the blood and morals of a despised class, buying, by his indifference thereto, well-ventilated school houses! new school books! physiological seats! broad playgrounds! and philosophical apparatus! . . . He never mars his pages with an allusion to color."[83]

In defense of segregation, school and public authorities called on everything but experience. Boston school board members alleged that black children were a different sort altogether:

> Their peculiar physical, mental and moral structure, requires an educational treatment, different, in some respects, from that of white children. Teachers of schools in which they are intermingled remark, that, in those parts of study and instruction in which progress depends on memory or on the imitative faculties, chiefly, the colored children will often keep pace with the white children; but when progress comes to depend chiefly on the faculties

of invention, comparison, and reasoning, they quickly fall behind.[84]

No specific teachers were cited as authority for the statement. Nor was it observed that plentiful testimony to the contrary was on record.[85] In any event, the majority of the school board prescribed more segregation rather than new methods of instruction to meet what was portrayed as an educational problem.

Financing of education: deprivation and taxation without representation

By 1860, the publicly financed common school was established in the North. Only the beginnings of the system were present in the South. Wherever it existed, however, the critical factor was federal aid in the form of land grants for common schools.[86] When a territory became a state, Congress awarded land grants specifically for support of the schools. Between 1803 and 1864, seventeen new states received more than 27 million acres of federal land for schools (Table 5).[87] Crucial to the receipt of land grants was certification that the territory had reached the minimum population for statehood established in the Northwest Ordinance of 1787. This number (60,000) consisted of all male adults. No distinction of race was drawn in the law.

Between 1812 and 1845 five new southern states received 4.5 million acres of federal land for common schools. A very slight portion of this total actually supported schools before the Civil War. None of it was used to finance public education of slaves and free Negroes in the South, although they had been enumerated for statehood purposes. In the North, twelve new states received 23.4 million acres of federal school lands. An undetermined but surely minuscule portion helped educate black children. In 1838, a legislative committee in Ohio noted formally that free Negroes were then excluded from public schools in the state: "They are deprived of all participation in the school fund arising from donations made by Congress for the support of schools."[88] The committee recommended repeal of all antiblack laws, but this proposal was rejected. In 1850, the Indiana Supreme Court rejected an argument that black children were entitled to attend common schools by virtue of the federal land grant for schools.[89]

Black children were effectively excluded from sharing in the federal bounty of public lands, North and South. As a rule free Negroes paid school taxes even if their children were not allowed to attend the schools. This was as true in Maryland and Virginia as in Illinois and Ohio. Blacks thereby helped finance the public education of white children. As a committee of the Michigan State Senate declared accusingly: "There is not a member of the present legislature who has not in his pocket the money of

Table 5. *Federal land grants for schools to new states, 1803–1864*

State	Date of admission	Extent of grant (acres)
North		
Ohio	1803	724,266
Indiana	1816	668,578
Illinois	1818	996,320
Missouri	1821	1,221,813
Michigan	1837	1,021,867
Iowa	1846	1,000,679
Wisconsin	1848	982,329
California	1850	5,534,293
Minnesota	1858	2,874,951
Oregon	1859	3,399,360
Kansas	1861	2,907,520
Nevada	1864	2,061,967
Total		23,393,943
Average		2,126,722
South		
Louisiana	1812	807,271
Mississippi	1817	824,213
Alabama	1819	911,627
Arkansas	1836	933,778
Florida	1845	975,307
Total		4,452,196
Average		890,439

Source: Calculated from basic data in Paul W. Gates, *History of Public Land Law Development* (Washington, D.C.: GPO, Nov. 1968), p. 804.

the disfranchised, and politically degraded taxpayer of color."[90] The Ohio legislature's judiciary committee explained the rationale for excluding black children from public schools in a frankly racist statement offered without apology:

> The security of our government rests and remains in the morality, virtue and wisdom of our free white citizens, and . . . by the education of them by means of a public fund, the government is only strengthening her own resources, and providing for her own security, honor and elevation; the fact will be readily yielded that the common school fund is not the offspring of the offices of charity; but the principal and interest is amply repaid by the

exercise of those functions which the government itself imposes upon all her free white citizens.[91]

Black spokesmen were bitter in their denunciation of such public finance. Douglass, as usual, got at the core of the matter: "In the Northern States, we are not slaves to individuals, not personal slaves, yet in many respects we are the slaves of the community."[92] Black abolitionist Remond recommended civil disobedience: "Let every colored man, called upon to pay taxes to any institution in which he is deprived or denied its privileges and advantages, withhold his taxes, though it costs imprisonment or confiscation. Let our motto be – *No privileges, no pay.*"[93] Robert Purvis had done just this when his child was refused admittance to the town's public school. After several years, the town gave in.

A more difficult kind of law to counter was the Nevada enactment of 1865 that revoked state school aid if a locality admitted black children into white schools.[94] Even when states were directed to provide public funds for educating black children, often the letter and the spirit of the law were violated. In 1829, the Ohio legislature forbade the attendance of blacks in white schools, directing that school taxes paid by Negroes be devoted exclusively to the education of blacks. Hickock comments: "The prohibition was vigorously enforced, but the second clause was practically a dead letter."[95] After years of collecting school taxes from black taxpayers but forbidding their children to attend public schools, the Illinois legislature in 1855 provided: "In townships where there are persons of color the Board of Trustees shall allow such persons a portion of the school fund equal to the amount of taxes collected for school purposes from such persons of color, in their respective townships."[96] This seemed to authorize the beginning of public schools for blacks. Harris cautions: "But no other provisions were made to secure such an end. Nor does the State ever appear to have seriously attempted any such movement."[97] Bremner notes that in those northern states allocating tax funds according to the race of the taxpayer "in no instance were funds divided according to the number of black and white children attending school, nor were other efforts made to assure that the separate schools . . . should be equal in length of the school term, pay of teachers, or expenditures for equipment."[98]

The role of the courts: enforcement of racial order

In general, the courts enforced the racial order in education. Sometimes the cause of court action seemed ludicrous, as when Samuel Jackson was found guilty of trespass when he entered Josiah Hughes's house to take his (i.e., Jackson's) two slave children who were owned by Hughes. The court noted that the children had a total market value of

$1,000.[99] A number of courts set aside wills made by white persons with bequests for the education of free Negroes. A bequest made in 1843 for "the education of free colored persons in the city of Baltimore" was found by the court to be "too vague and indefinite to be enforced."[100]

Many times white parents sued to eject individual black children who were enrolled in a white school. In the *Chalmers* case, which came to be cited in other states, the Ohio Supreme court equated black children with immoral persons. Chalmers, a white parent, withdrew his children from public school when Stewart, the teacher, illegally permitted black children to enroll. Judge Wood ruled:

> I have no hesitation . . . in laying it down as a general principle, in all cases, that a teacher of a public school is under the implied obligation to regard the morals of the youth entrusted to his care, and, should he so far disregard his duty as to admit the vicious and corrupt, controlled by no sense of moral obligation he fill his school with prostitutes or thieves, or those openly profane or licentious, such teacher would forfeit all claims to compensation.[101]

Eight years later, the Supreme Court of Indiana granted a white parent's request that black children – who were paying tuition – be excluded from a public school so that the parent might send his own children there. Judge Perkins explained the legislative exclusion of black children:

> This has not been done because they did not need education, nor because their wealth was such as to render aid undesirable, but because black children were deemed unfit associates of white, as school companions. Now, surely, this reason operates with equal force against such children attending the schools at their own, as at the public expense.[102]

Chalmers was cited as authority to exclude the "vicious and corrupt" from schoolrooms.

Courts regularly refused to recognize the existence of a proximity principle for assignment of black children to specific schools. When black parents sued to enter their children in the nearest school, courts held that school authorities were not bound by any such rule. In Boston, the chief justice of the state argued that it was no hardship for all the city's black children to attend a single school, while white children often attended schools nearest their homes. Justice Shaw explained: "In Boston, where more than one hundred thousand inhabitants live within a space so small . . . it would be scarcely an inconvenience to require a boy of good health to traverse daily the whole extent of it."[103]

The hue of a black child's skin was the subject of many legal actions. In

1853, a teacher in a Boston white school ejected a five-year-old Negro boy of very fair complexion. The boy's father, William T. Pindell, sued. At the trial two physicians examined the youngster and determined that he had one-eighth to one-sixth of African ancestry. He was thus sufficiently "colored" to be excluded from a white school. The court so found.[104] In Cincinnati, a teacher ordered a young Negro boy to transfer to a black school. The child described himself as a "quadroon," but his transfer was approved by the board of education.[105]

In Ohio the supreme court dealt with the question of the school and civil rights of light-skinned Negroes. In *Jeffries,* an older ruling was reaffirmed: "All nearer white than black . . . were entitled to enjoy every political and social privilege of the white citizens."[106] Dissenting in *Thacker,* a companion case, Judge Read insisted: "It is not the shade of color, but the purity of the blood, which determines the stock or race to which the individual belongs."[107] Anyone not "purely" white was black. After rejecting several later tests, the court in 1859 changed course and accepted the Read viewpoint. In *Van Camp* the court denied it was approving the exclusion of children from any school: "It is a law of classification, and not of exclusion, intended and designed to place in one school all the white youth, and in the other all who have any visible taint of African blood."[108] (Almost exactly a year after *Van Camp,* a white heckler taunted Frederick Douglass about the inferiority of blacks and the superiority of whites. Douglass replied: "You evidently think your white skin of great value. I don't dispute it; it is probably the best thing about you."[109])

In some states, a clear movement could be traced away from white-only education, aided, eventually, by timely court intervention. Iowa, which became a state in 1846 – with federal school grants of over 1 million acres of land – set up a common school system explicitly for whites. A second school law in 1848 continued this feature. In 1851, it was repeated once more and a provision was added that "all real and personal property of blacks and mulattos in this State shall be exempt from taxation for school purposes." (North Carolina had passed a similar law eight years earlier in order to clarify the legislative intent of withholding all public education from black children.) Between 1851 and 1857, a severe struggle centered on the rights of Iowa blacks – of whom there were 333 in 1850 and 1,069 in 1860 – in white political circles. As in neighboring Illinois, Republicans in Iowa favored the opening of schools to all.[110] When the state constitutional convention met in 1857, all distinctions of color in the old constitution were abolished. The new constitution, approved by popular referendum, stipulated that the state board of education "shall provide for the education of all the youths of the State, through a system of common schools."

The following year, however, the Iowa legislature backtracked and directed school districts to "provide for the education of the colored youths in separate schools, except in cases where, by the unanimous consent of the persons sending to the school in the sub-district, they may be permitted to attend with the white youths." The state supreme court ruled this law unconstitutional on the ground that the 1857 constitution had given the state board of education rather than the legislature the responsibility for organizing schools. While the Democratic party in 1859 attacked nonsegregated schools, the agitation bore no result. In 1860 and 1862, new school laws passed by the legislature contained no racial distinctions. The 1860 law dropped the 1851 exemption of blacks from paying school taxes. The state supreme court summarized aptly the historical course of Iowa public policy on schools: "First, the total exclusion of colored children from our common schools. . . . Second, the allowance of uncertain, and in practice . . . very limited and inferior common school privileges, dependent on the unanimous consent of the persons sending to the school. Third the allowance of equal common school privileges to all."[111] This pattern can be contrasted with that of Michigan, whose constitution did not require racial separation. Nevertheless, in 1841 Detroit school authorities created a citywide attendance area for black children.[112] The practice lay undisturbed at the end of the Civil War.

Events of the 1850s bore testimony to a growing sense of common plight among free blacks, especially in the North. In their communities the burdens of caste were relieved principally by their own efforts. On the national scene, the decade was a threatening one. It was full of compromises in which the object of negotiations was without representation. In 1850, when the Fugitive Slave Act was passed by Congress, numerous free blacks in northern cities fled to Canada, fearful for their freedom. In 1857, the U.S. Supreme Court was widely interpreted as ruling in *Dred Scott* that a Negro had no rights a white man was "bound to respect." Black leaders were sardonic in their comments on the ruling. Robert Purvis said: "There was nothing new in this decision; it was in perfect keeping with the treatment of the colored people by the American Government from the beginning to this day."[113] William Wells Brown stated that "what Judge Taney had declared officially was only what was said in nearly all the States about the colored men, at the present day."[114]

The end of slavery: the demand for schooling

Eventually, some 200,000 blacks fought in Union ranks – and thus laid the basis for a new America. A pervading self-confidence was increasingly in evidence among northern blacks.

In the South, the war unseated the regime of slavery. No change was so startling as the end of the policy of compulsory ignorance. As soon as

Union armies appeared on southern soil, slaves and their children sought schooling. Slaves in arms received instruction after the day's fighting was done.[115] One of the teachers was Susie King, who as a child had attended a secret school in Savannah. She served the twenty-third U.S. Colored Troops as laundress and nurse during the day and as teacher at night. Another was Charlotte Forten, who left her abolitionist home in Philadelphia to teach the freedmen in Port Royal, South Carolina.

Freedmen were impatient to learn and send their children to school. A meeting of black people in Memphis asked northern groups to send teachers promptly: "We recommend the teachers to bring their tents with them, ready for erection in the field, by the roadside, or in the fort, and not to wait for magnificent houses to be erected in time of war."[116] When the opening of a school for black children was announced in Wilmington, North Carolina, parents wasted no time: "They were to come at 9 o'clock; by 7 the street was blocked, the yard was full. Parents, eager to get 'dese yer four children's name tooken,' came pulling them through the crowd. 'Please, sir, put down desyer.' 'I wants dis gal of mine to jine; and dat yer boy hes got no parents, and I jes done and brot him.'"[117] Many of the teachers were provided by the American Missionary Society, a northern group.

The South became an enormous classroom. In Charlottesville, Virginia, a reporter described the scene:

> And then the whole colored population, of all sexes and ages, is repeating from morning to night, a-b, ab, e-b, eb; i-b, ib; c-a-t, cat; d-o-g, dog; c-u-p, cup; etc. – through all the varieties of the first lessons in orthography. There are some four or five colored schools, and little negro chaps darken every door, with primers in their hands. If we pass a blacksmith's shop, we hear a-b, ab; if we peep into a shoemaker's shop, it is a-b, ab; if we pass by a negro cabin in the suburbs of the town, we hear the sound, a-b, ab; if the cook goes out to suckle her infant, it is a-b, ab.[118]

It was not unique to Charlottesville.

Lewis H. Douglass, the son of Frederick, taught for a time in a freedman's school in Maryland, very near the area where his father grew up. Three of his students, in fact, had been taught by his father once he became literate. Others were children or grandchildren of his father's old associates.

War did not abolish the spirit of proscription in education. In 1864, for example, Congress passed a law apparently granting blacks in the District of Columbia a share of the school fund. The board of commissioners interpreted the measure otherwise. Proceeds of the school tax fund were reserved completely to white schools; white and black children were to share equally only in miscellaneous revenues such as fines, penalties, and forfeitures. The levy court ordered a stop to this procedure. While school authorities complied and divided school taxes equitably, they built new schools during 1864 and 1865 only for white children: none was built for blacks.[119]

The Union government itself became the object of criticism by blacks whose participation in the war emboldened them to speak more openly. In mid-1864, a federal military academy was opened in Philadelphia to train officers to command black troops. No blacks were allowed to enroll, regardless of their previous training or field experience. A mass meeting protested. Especially criticized were the white civilians chosen for the academy, "who are constantly held up to us as making great sacrifices and performing acts of the greatest condescensions in accepting these positions in colored regiments."[120] Blacks could not easily forget that Negro soldiers were paid less than white soldiers for several years and that they were not allowed to command.

On February 9, 1866, Lieutenant Colonel C. T. Trowbridge of the Thirty-third U.S. Colored Troops, made up entirely of ex-slaves, issued General Order Number 1, in the form of a farewell address to the men who had served with him for four years: "The church, the schoolhouse, and the right forever to be free are now secured to you, and every prospect before you is full of hope and encouragement. The nation guarantees to you full protection and justice."[121] Less than five years earlier, all his listeners had been slaves. Now, they were their own men. For the first time in two and a half centuries the American descendants of the West African slaves were free to explore and consolidate their own way of life. Having shot their way to emancipation, they now sought effective mastery of the arts of peace. This meant economic security, education, and full citizenship.

For many generations, most blacks had been denied schooling by the dominant society, by masters in the slave society, or by public authority in the society of free Negroes in the North and South. Those for whom the doors of schools had been open had to rely on the benevolence of private charity or their own intensive efforts. Negroes had to struggle constantly for the right to learn, for the right to be taught in an equal and nonsegregated setting. The conspiracy to keep them in ignorance was pervasive. Most ironic of all, free Negroes were expected to pay taxes for schools they could not attend. Still, they hungered for learning and strove to achieve it in the face of a slavery that survived even in freedom. The claim of whites that Negroes were intellectually incapable of learning was refuted by the desperate attempt of whites to deny them schooling. Whites seemed to fear not that Negroes could not learn but that they would.

2

Separate and unequal: black education, 1865–1950

When the Civil War broke out, public schooling for white children in the South was rudimentary. In no state was there a functioning system of public education. Whatever public schools existed – and they were few – were restricted by law to white children.

In the early postwar years, it was not unusual for a state to create separate school systems on the basis of race to be financed by corresponding separate taxes. Because whites owned immensely more wealth than blacks as a group, black schools financed by black tax revenue alone could only be inadequate. Such an arrangement contravened the theory of public schools established in the North before the Civil War.

Blacks were free, in theory, but the Emancipation Proclamation and victory in the war did not lead to education for Negro children in the South. Negro parents paid taxes in some states to support white education, while their own children were barred from school. They were required in some states to pay double the tax whites paid – to finance separate black schools as well as the schools for whites. But even the double taxes did not guarantee schools for their children.

In the first years after the war, when conservative white governments ruled in the South, a few states enacted limited laws setting up white "common" school systems. In 1866, the Texas legislature set up a school fund to be financed from railroad public land, but its benefits were restricted to white children. The same year Florida created a school fund, but it, too, could not be spent on blacks. Schools for Florida's Negro children were authorized, to be financed by a special tax on blacks, who were thus taxed doubly, as they continued to pay taxes to finance white schools. The next year, the Kentucky legislature required blacks to pay taxes toward the support of white schools, but excluded black children from these schools. Black schools, to be financed by black taxes, were permitted but not compulsory. As a result none was built.[1]

The alternative for southern Negro children was privately sponsored or federally subsidized education.

Schools were established in the South by northern whites for blacks or by blacks for themselves. The Freedmen's Bureau, supported by the federal government, supplemented these efforts. Thus, while the taxes of Negro families in some states went to boost white education, families were compelled to organize private self-help efforts to educate their own children.

"How happy we are you were never slaves," two ex-slaves told their children who were born after the war.[2] To supply their children the once-forbidden education became a sweeping movement. "The movement started with the Negroes themselves," wrote Du Bois, "and they continued to form the dynamic force behind it."[3]

In Gloucester County, Virginia, a freedman who had been a bricklayer, sent for his half brother, William Morris, also a freedman, to open a school. As a slave, Morris had been a butler in the big house and had become literate there. He came and opened the county's first school for black children, housed in a brick shop. For a short time, a second school was opened on land owned by a former free Negro. Still another school was conducted by Frank Page, a freedman who had learned to read a little while serving as a messenger in the Union Army. Announced as a Sunday school "to teach us about the Bible . . . [Page] tried to teach us to read."[4]

Robert G. Fitzgerald, a black graduate of Lincoln University in Pennsylvania, became a teacher of the freedmen in Amelia County, Virginia, some 35 miles from Richmond. His salary was, at times, paid by northern religious organizations; the remainder of school expenses was supplied by the freedmen themselves. As Fitzgerald's granddaughter described it, education gave the ex-slaves "a new image of themselves":

> When he walked along the roads, they'd see him coming and leave their work in the fields to run down and beg him for books. . . . He found out . . . that in spite of the disorganization of their lives, whenever the freedmen made the effort to build a school or house of worship they tended to settle around it and their habits showed immediate improvement. They felt it was something that they *owned* and to which they *belonged*. It made a vast difference in their lives. It would take some of them quite a while to move the awkward distance from saying "Master," to saying "Mister," but it had taken them no time at all to respond with glowing faces to "ladies" and "gentlemen" and "scholars." It gave them a new image of themselves.[5]

Education made freedom real.

During 1867, freedmen in Virginia owned outright 68 schools and supported in part another 155. Three years later, they owned 111 and supported 215. Where outside funds were exhausted and the meager cash resources of the freedmen gone, some freedmen, as in North Carolina, even pledged the crop in the ground to pay school bills.[6]

Intentions aside, the freedmen were unable to create an educational tradition unaided. In 1865, in all Georgia "there were not more than one hundred colored people . . . who were capable of teaching a primary school."[7] As soon as black students in Randolph County, Alabama, schools made the most modest conquest of their blue-backed spellers, they became assistant and, not long after, full-time teachers. A former student recalled compassionately that they "were doing pretty good work . . . the best of them had advanced only about as far as the fourth grade."[8] During mid-1865, an observer in Alabama found a freedmen's school in Montgomery and Mobile but none anywhere else in the state.

Mission schools and the Freedmen's Bureau

The American Missionary Association recruited volunteer teachers to staff freedmen's schools even before the end of the war. Textbooks and instructional materials flowed southward. At war's end, the structure created by the association became the model for many other similar groups. While northern missionary efforts were infused with a deep religious spirit, they were not able to meet the need that existed. These efforts were "concentrated in certain areas – usually larger cities like Raleigh, Atlanta, Nashville, and Washington, or the coastal areas in Virginia, North Carolina, and South Carolina."[9]

The mission schools were far more than simple places for literacy training. Bond characterizes one of the best as providing "a *complete* social and moral, as well as educational, community for the formation of the children, and youth, who attended it."[10] A member of the staff was often a Congregationalist minister.

The Freedmen's Bureau, created by Congress in 1865, helped freedmen and white refugees with immediate necessities such as food, clothing, and shelter. (Land was to be rented to freedmen.) But the law at first made no mention of education. In 1866, the law was amended to include education, and three purposes were cited: (1) to cooperate with groups of citizens who employed teachers and obtained instructional materials by renting or leasing buildings to them, (2) to afford such personnel safe conduct in the operation of schools, and (3) to sell Confederate-owned land for the benefit of freedmen's schools. In 1868, the law was amended again to provide that the educational activities of the bureau would not cease until the states had made adequate provision for educating freedmen at public expense.[11] Most bureau school funds were earmarked for the supply of buildings, but only as a supplement to private endeavor.

Freedmen used the bureau to the utmost. When they could obtain rent-free quarters in a church or elsewhere, bureau rental payments provided operational expenses of the school. Freedmen often made cash contributions as well as contributions in kind by boarding teachers. "In this way, from one-half to two-thirds of the cost was often borne by the freedmen," Parker notes. "It was not uncommon for freedmen with some assistance from the Bureau, to meet the entire expense of the school – to buy a lot, erect the building and pay the teachers. Under these circumstances, the school house would be placed in the hands of trustees chosen from among the group and the building assigned permanently for schools purposes."[12] No precise money equivalent can be assigned to the work and other contributions of freedmen, but the bureau itself spent about $5 million on schools, an indispensable sum. Its availability was one of the most direct results of black participation in the war.

Like the efforts of the missionary societies, the bureau's educational work was concentrated in a few areas. In Texas, for example, bureau schools were mainly around Houston and Galveston. But, the bureau's influence extended beyond the immediate instruction offered. As Woodson points out, in West Virginia this activity acted as an "inspiration which set the whole body of Negroes throughout the state thinking and working to secure for themselves every facility vouchsafed to the most . . . [favored] element of our population."[13]

Still, Rose asserts, "real interest [by northerners] in the work of education flared spectacularly for a few short years following the war, but with the exception of church-supported endeavors, it vanished as abruptly as the most brilliant fireworks display will do."[14]

Although the 1870 census found that the number of Negro children in school had risen over the decade from 33,100 to 180,700, or from 1.9 to 9.9 percent (Table 6), after five years of intense efforts by blacks and their supporters, nine out of ten black children still remained outside any school. Most lived in the South. McPherson writes that "at no time were more than ten percent of the freedmen of school age attending the [religious] societies' schools."[15]

White terrorism against black schools

The white response to schooling for blacks was, with few exceptions, hostile to all schools for Negroes, whether organized by the missionary societies or by the Freedmen's Bureau. In Alabama, a northern teacher could work only under armed guard. In North Carolina, a black teacher in a mission school confided in his diary: "We have been nightly watching for the Ku Klux Klan who desire to pay us a visit."[16] Frederick Douglass, then editor of the *New National Era*, observed that "schoolhouses are burnt, teachers mobbed and murdered, schools broken up."[17] As the national election of 1868 approached, with blacks as a whole eligible for the first time in American history to help elect a president and

Table 6. *School enrollment of Negro children aged 5 to 19 years, 1860–1950*

Year	Number of children	Rate of enrollment per 100 in age group		Number in school	Number not in school
		Negro	White		
1860	1,741,100	1.9	59.6	33,100	1,708,000
1870	1,825,700	9.9	54.4	180,700	1,645,000
1880	2,531,700	33.8	62.0	855,700	1,676,000
1890	2,998,300	32.9	57.9	986,400	2,011,900
1900	3,276,800	31.1	53.6	1,019,100	2,257,700
1910	3,462,200	44.8	61.3	1,551,100	1,911,200
1920	3,586,200	53.5	65.7	1,918,600	1,667,600
1930	3,870,400	60.3	71.2	2,333,800	1,536,600
1940	3,929,800	68.4	75.6	2,687,800	1,242,000
1950	4,114,600	74.8	79.3	3,077,700	1,036,900

Source: Calculated from basic data in U.S. Bureau of the Census, *Historical Statistics of the United States, Colonial Times to 1957* (Washington, D.C.: GPO, 1960), pp. 10–11, 213–214; U.S. Bureau of the Census, *Statistical Abstract of the United States, 1962* (Washington, D.C.: GPO, 1962), p. 26.

Congress, violent whites extended their efforts at repression. Throughout rural Georgia, and even in Savannah, many black schools closed out of fear for the lives of their students and teachers.

During 1870–1871, Wharton reports, a "reign of terror" against black schools controlled eight Mississippi counties: "By the summer of 1871, in a number of counties, not a school remained in operation."[18] In Texas, white teachers in black schools "were criticized, ostracized, and often mistreated."[19]

Almost from the day of its beginning in 1866, the Ku Klux Klan singled out black schools for attack. Mrs. Eliza Lyon, an ex-slave in Demopolis, Alabama, said of her own son, who was a teacher:

> He was just a lad of a boy, and the colored people on the place found that he could write pretty well, and they wanted him to teach them some, and he said he would, and they would pay him and he would teach them, and they went on a month with his school, asking every head four bits a month, and I reckon he had twenty-five scholars, and the white people didn't like it about the colored people learning to read down in that part.[20]

Violence followed. Elsewhere in the state, the Ku Klux Klan regularly burned black schools and ran teachers out of town. In Walton County,

Georgia, klansmen announced they would whip any parent who sent his children to school; they burned the books of a teacher and announced "they would just dare any other nigger to have a book in his house." A Negro leader in Washington County "was accused of being 'too big a man' because he could read and write and had talked of starting a Negro school."[21]

In York County, South Carolina, nearly weekly raids were conducted against Negro cabins, followed by attacks on schools; one school was rebuilt four times. Trelease, the historian of the Klan's career, calls it "a record of sustained brutality which few places in the country ever matched."

Black responses to terrorism were primarily defensive.[22] Repeated attempts were made to gain federal protection and prosecution of the Klan and other sources of violence. Aside from a flurry of legislation and litigation in the early 1870s, governmental concern was at a minimum. Trelease observes that the success of terror undermined the will and capacity of blacks to resist: "Once the federal arrests and prosecutions fell off in 1873, it became ever clearer that terrorism was the surest and quickest road to victory in the South."[23]

Rise of the public schools

The poverty of blacks and the all-too-effective suppression of schools combined to keep education at a minimum in 1865–1870. The continuing private nature of educational efforts, however, was primarily responsible for the superficiality of the effort to provide schools. The Freedmen's Bureau was not intended, nor did it try, to set up a federal system of public schools in the South; it supplemented the private efforts of blacks and of private northern groups. Help from the North based on charity proved invaluable, but failed to meet the challenge in Wendell Phillips's wartime warning: "No nation ever yet educated the mass of its people by the simple instrument of benevolence – never."[24] The educational future of the freedman hinged on the creation of public schools, dependent on the acknowledgment of black citizenship. Even before the Civil War, free Negroes in the North had learned this lesson. The question was: How much progress could be enforced?

A glance at the figures for the census of 1880 suggests the answer (Table 6). Over the decade of the 1870s, the number of Negro children in schools rose by 675,000, more than a fourfold increase.[25]

A fundamental change in southern government and education occurred as a direct consequence of the national congressional elections of 1866. The commanding majority of radical Republicans was pledged to a program of justice to the freedman. Existing southern state governments were dissolved, and the right to vote was conferred upon Negroes. Constitutional conventions held throughout the South in 1867 and 1868 produced basic documents which, among other things, gave the South its first free and universal public educational systems. Du Bois was undoubtedly correct when he observed that "public education for all at public expense, was, in the South, a Negro idea."[26] The extension of democracy thus benefited both oppressed and privileged. In extending rights to Negroes, government, ironically, strengthened the rights and privileges of whites. With ratification of the Fourteenth Amendment in 1868, the Negro's status as a free citizen appeared to be assured; no southern state would dare withhold equal benefits for blacks, or so the law implied.

By 1870, every southern state had created a public school system financed by a state fund.

Negro children flocked to the new public shools. In Mississippi, despite Ku Klux Klan violence directed against tax-supported education of black children, black attendance expanded during 1871–1875. Indeed, blacks attended in large numbers and more regularly than white children. In 1877, about three-quarters of school-age Negro children in Texas were in the public schools. In Virginia during the late 1870s, according to Taylor, "so popular became education among the Negroes that parents who kept their children at home to work were generally branded as unworthy citizens."[27] In Alabama, a nine-year-old field hand and his brother followed a plan of rotation of schooling designed by their mother:

> I took turns with my brother at the plow and in school; one day I plowed and he went to school, the next day he plowed and I went to school; what he learned on his school day he taught me at night and I did the same for him. In this way we each got a month of schooling during the year, and with that one month of schooling we also acquired the habit of studying at home.[28]

By 1880, a third of all black children in the United States were enrolled in public schools.

Inequality in public revenues

A number of states specifically forbade any discrimination in appropriations to black and white public schools. In others, separate and unequal were equated from the beginning. Black citizens were strong enough to enforce equality in some states of the Deep South, paradoxically, but not in border areas. In 1877–1880, per capita expenditures on black and white schools in South Carolina were comparable. In Alabama there was a slight edge in favor of black schools, although this resulted from lower average attendance in black schools. In North Carolina, expenditures were comparable. On the other hand, in Maryland during the

1870s, Negro students received only about one-quarter the amount spent for white children. During the mid-1870s in the District of Columbia, except for the M Street High School, "all the colored schools were undeniably inferior to the white." By the end of the decade, per capita expenditures, which were almost equal in 1875, became markedly unequal. [29]

The last two decades of the nineteenth century were an educational catastrophe for black children and their parents. The number of black children of school age grew by one-quarter, but the proportion attending school fell (Table 6). [30] The black man, deprived of his status as a free citizen, found that in one state after another, his right to vote was denied. Mississippi led the retreat in 1890. Six additional states followed by explicit provision in new state constitutions until 1908. Four states accomplished the same end by more roundabout means. In 1898, the U.S. Supreme Court's upholding of the use of literacy tests for voting in Mississippi acted as a signal for disfranchisement to proceed. Negroes lost the only guarantee they possessed that their children would get an equal and effective claim on the educational resources in their states.

In 1883, black parents brought suit in federal district court, charging that the city of Owensboro, Kentucky, had violated the equal protection requirement of the Fourteenth Amendment by financing schools through two separate taxes. They said that, as a result of the dual financial system, 500 black children were financed by a total tax revenue of $770 and attended school for only three months; 800 white children shared $9,400, and enjoyed a school year of from nine to ten months. The court ruled that "the equal protection of the law guaranteed by this amendment must and can only mean the laws of the state must be equal in their benefit as well as in their burdens, and that less would not be 'the equal protection of the laws.'" This rule did not require exactly equal expenditures between the races; however, the court said, it did "mean the distribution of the benefit upon some fair and equal classification or basis." [31] Three years later, a similar taxing scheme in North Carolina was ruled by the state supreme court to "necessarily discriminate 'in favor of the one and to the prejudice of the other race.'" [32]

The clear implication of both the *Claybrook* and *Puitt* decisions was to strengthen equality of treatment of black and white children. Yet they were used to the opposite end. The decisions required only that no racial distinction enter into allocation of school funds by the state. Nothing was said of other discriminatory techniques, nor were points of distribution of funds other than the topmost state officials mentioned. This left the local level unregulated for discriminatory potential.

States were scrupulous in satisfying the formal requirements of *Claybrook* and *Puitt* and appropriated equal amounts for black and white.

At county levels, where the money was actually allocated to specific schools, the myth of equality broke down. Officials regularly took funds that belonged to black schools and added these to the allocations for white schools. In South Carolina, the result was astonishing. In the late 1870s, equal appropriations were a fact; by 1895, after localization of allocation, per pupil expenditures in white schools were nearly three times those in black schools.[33]

Mississippi, in 1886, set up differential teachers' salaries based on examinations. Black teachers were regularly classified in the lowest group. The practice spread. By 1907, Du Bois said of black teachers' salaries throughout the South that "the salaries are so small that only the poorest local talent can teach."[34] Getting a new school built became a rare achievement. Acquisition of the barest instructional equipment was left to private means. One black teacher, conducting school in Old Poplar's Church, Virginia, explained: "My pupils had to bring pennies until we got a sufficient number to buy even a piece of blackboard. We had no desks or other suitable furniture nor were slates, pencils, or paper furnished, let alone books."[35] Parents in the area collected old rags and exchanged them at the sawmill for lumber. Others gathered a plant whose extract was useful in tanning leather; they exchanged bags of the plant at the general store for nails and windowpanes for the new school. The old school then was closed for two weeks to enable the teacher to help the carpenter construct the building. All this, of course, was within the context of a public school system that seldom delivered capital funds to black schools.

In 1891, the Alabama legislature passed the Apportionment Act, directing the state superintendent to transmit school funds to the townships which were to distribute among the schools "such an amount . . . as they may deem just and equitable." The legislation was legal permission to raid appropriations for black schools. In those townships where Negroes far outnumbered whites – the so-called Black Belt – white schools prospered at the expense of black schools. In fact, the "blacker" the school district, the bigger the raid upon its state apportionment. Essential to the long-run success of the principle of equality was the suppression of effective black protest. Ten years after the Apportionment Act was passed, a state constitutional convention disfranchised Negroes. Bond, the principal authority on these events, writes: "From 1901, with Negroes thoroughly disfranchised, all emphasis was laid on the education of 'white' children in the State. . . . So far as educational campaigns were concerned, Negro children did not exist in the State."[36]

In Texas, the state constitutional requirement of 1869 that free public schools be open to all was enforced fitfully or not at all. In 1876, the legislature created a community system of school finance. A community was an area without definite boundaries, delimited only by the location of school-age children listed as residing in the general area. The operation of schools in a community was purely a matter of local option. Only where Negroes made up a large part of the community was it likely that a local school tax would be levied. Otherwise, only state and county funds were available. When, in, 1884, the state constitution was amended to create a school district system, a number of counties, most with a heavy concentration of blacks, were allowed to continue in the community system. In the older community system a number of blacks had served as trustees; district boards were invariably white. In 1893, joint districts of black and white schools were created, with the trustees of each race to control their respective schools in the district. At the same time, safeguards were written in the law to enforce equal appropriations. In only two years time, a new formula to favor white schools was adopted and trustees were made elective, almost ensuring that only whites would serve. To guarantee this outcome, in 1899 the law was changed to specify that three white trustees were to manage all the schools. Systematic and sweeping discrimination against black schools followed.[37] Three years later, indirect disfranchisement was achieved by a poll tax.

Ironically, at the moment blacks were being denied their proportionate share of school funds, it was widely believed that Negro children were being educated at "the expense of the whites." In fact, as Du Bois wrote in *The Negro Common School* in 1901, "in the years 1870 to 1899 the Negro school systems of the former Slave States have not cost the white taxpayers a cent, except possibly in a few city systems." Table 7 summarizes data gathered and analyzed by Du Bois at the time. It indicates that about one-fifth of the expenses of Negro schools were covered by additional white taxes.

Harlan, a later historian, writes: "If indirect taxes be included, Negro schools under the existing system were receiving little, if any, more than the share of tax funds paid by Negroes."[38] According to Du Bois's careful analysis, in South Carolina, Alabama, Mississippi, and Louisiana Negroes' taxes paid for all their schools as well as part of the cost of white schools.

The very terms of the argument were curious. According to the theory of the public school, the community as a whole bore a responsibility for educating every child. The material inability of some parents to pay the costs of schooling was to be counterbalanced by the community benefit derived from universal education. In the South, the public school was not accepted in this light. In the wake of the Civil War, schools had been provided to Negro children as a grudging concession to political reality. When political reality changed, and Negroes were openly excluded from the rights of citizenship, schools for their children came to be regarded as

Table 7. *Estimated cost and support of Negro schools, 1899* [a]

State	Percent of Negroes aged 5–20 years	Cost of white schools ($)	Cost of Negro schools ($)	Percent of school fund	Contribution of Negroes to schools ($)	Percent of Negroes' contribution
Alabama	46.2	520,000	130,000	20.0	134,334	103
Arkansas	28.1	1,042,459	250,000	19.3	250,000	100
Delaware	18.2	194,300	22,820	10.5	22,826	100
District of Columbia	33.7	728,652	273,186	27.2	204,889	75
Florida	44.1	522,919	133,885	20.4	100,414	75
Georgia	48.3	1,150,612	290,000	20.1	290,000	100
Kentucky	13.1	2,586,032	322,321	11.1	110,000	34
Louisiana	48.6	935,116	200,000	17.6	310,000	155
Maryland	21.1	2,915,464	330,718	10.9	100,000	32
Mississippi	60.0	1,056,186	250,000	19.1	282,229	113
Missouri	5.1	9,128,000	372,000	4.0	275,000	58
North Carolina	34.9	713,143	275,000	27.0	200,000	73
South Carolina	61.1	693,807	203,033	22.6	206,647	101
Tennessee	24.5	2,114,287	400,000	15.9	250,000	63
Texas	21.4	4,136,779	800,000	16.2	640,000	80
Virginia	38.2	1,297,121	350,000	21.2	300,000	86
West Virginia	4.2	1,960,413	72,535	3.5	36,278	50
Total	31.6	31,695,290	4,675,498	12.9	3,712,617	79.4

[a] These figures are careful estimates, but it is not claimed that they are absolutely accurate. The figures for Delaware, Virginia, Kentucky, North Carolina, Georgia, Alabama, and Louisiana are most reliable. Those for District of Columbia, South Carolina, Florida, Mississippi, and Texas are probable. In the cases of Maryland, West Virginia, Tennessee, Arkansas, and Missouri, the data are meager and the figures liable to revision. In all states certain city systems are not included.

Source: W. E. B. Du Bois (ed.), *The Negro Common School* (Atlanta: Atlanta University Press, 1901), p. 87.

expensive indulgences. In neither case, however, were they regarded as a public obligation. To have done so would require acknowledgment that Negroes formed part of the southern community.

Segregation and deprivation: interrelated phenomena

During the period of missionary and Freedmen's Bureau schooling, black and white children attended separate schools. Specific examples of nonsegregated schools in the South are almost nonexistent in the literature. In New Orleans, nonsegregated schools were the rule for a few years during the late 1860s. When the Freedmen's Bureau schools in the District of Columbia opened their doors to all, few whites sent their children. During the 1868–1869 school year, only twenty-seven white children were enrolled along with thousands of black children.

In the constitutional conventions of 1868 and 1869, where freedmen had a chance to speak out, blacks strongly favored desegregated schools. They reflected the broad opinion of ordinary blacks. The essence of black support for desegregation was explained by Bond: "Negroes who supported the movement cared less for the higher principles involved, but were practical enough to see that separate schools meant inferior schools. They wished to use mixed schools as a lever to obtain equality in efficiency."[39] The "higher principles" were enunciated by Douglass in 1872: "We want mixed schools not because our colored schools are inferior to white schools – not because colored instructors are inferior to white instructors, but because we want to do away with a system that exalts one class and debases another."[40]

Black spokesmen worked out a political theory of desegregation. Meeting in the National Civil Rights Convention, in December 1873, they drew up a memorial to Congress, declaring:

> It is an abridgement of the privileges of a citizen to say he shall not, because of his race and color, elect as to the common school he shall attend, subject, of course, to such regulations as are not invidious in their character, and are made to apply alike to all citizens. It is depriving the citizen of his property to say he shall not enjoy, unless under humiliating conditions, the right of ownership, in common, of the public schools, he owning and maintaining them in common, but denied the common use. This, then, is the conclusion: the citizen is entitled to whatever belongs to him, and is not bound to accept an equivalent. It is not an equal protection of the laws to keep a person from the full enjoyment of his property, or to force him to accept what party may regard as an equivalent.[41]

This was an ingenious argument, quite in keeping with the contemporary stress on property that dominated legal thought. Courts, however, placed a much narrower interpretation on what the freedman *owned* and, consequently, on what government *owed* him. [42]

As long as nonsegregated schools – actually or potentially – existed, a state could not retrench selectively. It could when schools were segregated. Segregation had near-fatal consequences, as Franklin explains in "Jim Crow Goes to School":

> While many white Southerners were not averse to slashing educational expenditures across the board, they went as far as possible in cutting expenditures for Negro schools *before* touching the white schools. To be sure, white schools were crippled all over the South, but it was the Negro schools that were all but destroyed at the hands of the enemies of education and of Negroes. [43]

This is a moderate description of what happened.

During the early 1870s, in many black schools the school term was so short and irregular that even children of ordinary intelligence often did not learn to read until the age of twelve or thirteen. And this meager opportunity might require a walk to school of eight miles each way. A walk of five miles in either direction was not unusual. Parents went to some lengths to get their children to school. In Randolph County, Alabama, as one such student described it later:

> When cotton first began to open – early in the fall – it brought a higher price than at any other time of year. At this time the landlord wanted us all to stop school and pick cotton. But mother wanted me to remain in school, so, when the landlord came to the quarters early in the morning to stir up the cotton pickers, she used to outgeneral him by hiding me behind the skillets, ovens, and pots, throwing some rags over me until he was gone. Then she would slip me off to school through the back way. [44]

On Johns Island, off the coast of South Carolina, not even an eight- or ten-mile walk to school guaranteed attendance if economic need took priority. A teacher recalled: "On rainy days when no work could be done in the fields we would have a large attendance. But if by noon the sun came out, the plantation overseer would ride up to school and call for the tenants' children."[45] In other cases, poverty prevented attendance altogether. The son of a freedman in Virginia related: "Although I was only ten when school opened, my father considered me too old to spare time for . . . school."[46]

In Pike County, Mississippi, during the 1890s, from 75 to 100 black children were squeezed into the single-room Cleveland School. "There was no such thing as a certificate of graduation," a former student wrote. "A student went to school as long as he or his parents felt he was receiving any educational information from the particular teacher in question."[47] Around the turn of the century the son of poor farmers in Greenwood County, South Carolina, started attending an ungraded one-room school whose term ran from the end of the cotton harvest in November until February, a maximum of four months. The white school ran for six months. The hurt of conditions in the Upper South was no less. In Durham, North Carolina, a stronghold of the black middle class, separate schools were the rule. Pauli Murray recalled in *Proud Shoes*:

> It was never the hardship which hurt so much as the *contrast* between what we had and what the white children had. . . . Our seedy rundown school told us that if we had any place at all in the scheme of things it was a separate place, marked off, proscribed and unwanted by the white people. . . . We came to know that whatever we had was always inferior. . . . The tide of color beat upon me ceaselessly, relentlessly.[48]

During his own boyhood, recalled Arthur Davis, "in most Southern towns . . . the disparity between the white and Negro schools was so glaring it tended to breed in the sensitive Negro child a definite feeling of bitterness."[49]

Indispensable support for the new regimen of state discrimination and for school segregation came from the U.S. Supreme Court. In 1899, in the *Cumming* case, the Court found no constitutional violation when the Richmond County (Augusta), Georgia, school board closed down the black high school but continued to operate the white one. The Court held:

> While all admit that the benefits and burdens of public taxation must be shared by citizens without discrimination against any class on account of their race, the education of the people in schools maintained by state taxation is a matter belonging to the respective states, and any interference on the part of Federal authority with the management of our schools cannot be justified except in the case of a clear and unmistakable disregard of rights secured by the supreme law of the land. We have here no such case to be determined.[50]

This opinion was written by Justice John M. Harlan. Only three years earlier, he had been the sole dissenter to the Court's decision in *Plessy* v. *Ferguson*, in which he objected to the Court's doctrine that racial separation in public facilities was constitutional so long as the separate facilities were equal. "The Constitution is color blind," Harlan had written in his dissent to *Plessy*. In *Cumming*, however, he was part of a unanimous court that closed its eyes altogether to the burgeoning reality of official inequality in southern education.

Between 1896 and 1899, the U.S. Supreme Court approved the principles of compulsory segregation and the near inviolability of state control of education. Together, these principles created the legal basis for an unrelenting attack upon the educational standards of Negro schooling. Public education for Negro children became an impoverished, rudimentary variant of the kind of schooling judged adequate for white children. Segregation and deprivation fed on each other, but the former was primary.

Racial identity and learning

In the classrooms during the early years after the war, instruction in fundamental skills had been placed within a framework of everyday reality and imbued with a deep respect for the history of black people. This, rather than technical proficiency of teachers, may have been the greatest factor in the success of freedmen's education.

Reading materials supplied by the American Missionary Association during these years, were highly race conscious. "Freedmen's Readers" explained some of the realities of slavery as part of a "radical" view of American life and history.[51] In Alabama, the *Montgomery Advertiser* complained that "some of the school books used by teachers are embellished with all sorts of stories about the cruelties and persecutions of white people toward the blacks, and it will continue to be the case as long as strangers come in and teach them."[52] A New York City publisher, eager to supply whites with textbooks to counter the newer "radical" view, advertised for southern white authors: "Unsectional, Unpartisan, and Unpolitical. . . . Prepared by the most Eminent Southern Scholars and entirely acceptable to Southern Teachers and Parents."[53] It was an ominous omen.

A decade or more later Negro children, labeled inferior and unfit to attend schools with white children, risked self-depreciation at every turn. At stake was their own concept of themselves as black persons. There was no uniform response. In the 1880s, when Du Bois began teaching in a rural Tennessee school, he looked at his students and saw "their faces shading from a pale cream to a deep brown."[54] Whatever the hue of their skin, they faced a common problem.

The youngest of eight children, whose parents were ex-slaves, Benjamin Mays acquired an acute black consciousness in rural South Carolina:

> My heroes were black. . . . Every once in a while, some Negro came along selling pictures of, or pamphlets about, a few Negro leaders. Pictures of Frederick Douglass, Booker T. Washington, and Paul Laurence Dunbar hung on our walls. . . . The Negroes

in the South Carolina Legislature during the Reconstruction and post-Reconstruction years were the men held up to us in high school history classes as being great men.[55]

On the other hand, another young Negro, also the child of slaves, was shocked when he arrived in 1885 at Hampton Institute to hear the old slave songs sung. Although he had been brought up in heavily black Prince Edward County, Virginia, he objected that "we had come to Hampton to learn something better" than Negro songs. After the white president of Hampton, General Samuel Armstrong, explained the songs as part of the young man's legacy, the student admitted to himself: "The truth is it was the first time I had ever given any serious thought to anything distinctively Negro. This also was the first time in my life that I had begun to think that there was anything that the Negro had that was deserving of particular consideration."[56]

Those who escaped the stigma of inferiority were invariably persons of a middle-class background. During the early 1890s in Salisbury, North Carolina, such a child was spared the public schools of that city and attended, instead, Livingstone College, which offered all levels of instruction.[57] He then entered Phillips Exeter Academy and later the University of Pennsylvania. After graduation, he became principal of Smallwood Institute, a new black preparatory school in Clairmount, Virginia. Another kind of refuge was the occasional laboratory school to be found on college campuses. Before World War I, Hampton Institute in Virginia paid all the expenses of the Whittier School, which as a result, was left unregulated by county officials. "Because of this hands-off policy on the part of the county officials," recalled a former student, "we had a good school at Whittier – one which was far better than Syms-Eaton, the local white grammar shcool."[58]

In the District of Columbia where the largest concentration of educated middle-class Negroes in the country lived, the M Street High School, founded in 1870 as a public institution, became one of the finest secondary schools anywhere. Because the school paid federal-level salaries, the most highly qualified black teachers were recruited. In 1899, twenty of the thirty regular teachers had degrees from first-rate northern colleges and universities; five had graduated from Howard, "a far larger proportion of highly trained talent than the white high schools could claim."[59] In the rest of the black school system, much more attention was paid to the most talented students than to the largest number of ordinary students.

In 1910, there were in the entire United States 16,808,272 children aged six to fourteen years. Of these, 2,146,116 (12.8 percent) were Negro and 14,662,156 (87.2 percent) were white; 59.7 percent of the Negro children and 84.7 percent of the white children attended school. However, 93.2 percent of the Negro children lived in the South, and a break-down of school attendance figures by region shows that only 57.9 percent of southern Negro children went to school in 1910 compared with 84.2 percent of Negro children living outside the South. Within the South in that same year, Negro school enrollment varied according to urban or rural residence and according to age. In rural areas, 44.9 percent of children aged six to nine and 65.0 percent of those aged ten to fourteen attended school; in urban areas, the figures were 61.4 and 77.3 percent, respectively. Thus 70.1 percent of urban Negro children went to school in 1910 compared with 55.7 percent of rural Negro children.[60] School en-rollment increased significantly with age and urban residence. Long walk-ing distances, minimal protection from poor weather, and unsanitary and unsafe school structures held down attendance by younger children. In towns and cities, the difference between age groups was considerably smaller than in the countryside, but older children in both areas more frequently were in school. This is perhaps surprising, since more older children – urban as well as rural – worked in the fields; even so, some time was reserved for school attendance.

By 1910, nearly three-fifths of all black 6–14 year olds were enrolled in public schools. Twenty years earlier, it had likely been about two-fifths; forty years earlier it had probably been less than one-fifth. Quantitatively, therefore, progress had been substantial. Yet discerning observers of the time strongly suggested a retrogression after about 1890. In many cases, such a judgment is supported by ample evidence.

During the first two decades of the twentieth century, Negroes were victimized by private and governmental violence. During these years, a black youngster in South Carolina was deeply disturbed by the events: "I lived in constant fear that someday I might be lynched."[61] A young boy who had lived in Arkansas, Tennessee, and Mississippi observed: "I had al-ready grown to feel that there existed men against whom I was power-less, men who could violate my life at will."[62] It was reported in 1923: "In the years from 1900 to 1922 there has been an average of a race riot in the United States every year, half of them in the South and half in the North. . . . In these same years, 1,563 Negroes have been lynched; since the war [i.e., 1918] thirty-four Negroes have been burned alive at the stake."[63] These darkest of all learning experiences were headlined in news-papers as normal facets of the American racial order.

But even the oppressed were stirred by the experience of freedom. Several million ex-slaves still lived in the South in the 1880s and 1890s. By the end of the century, a large first generation of freedmen's sons and daughters had been touched personally by the movement toward free-dom. For years after the Civil War, for example, the freedmen in one Virginia town used to meet under a tree at the old slave market on

Emancipation Day (January 1) and listen to the Emancipation Proclamation read. A grandson recalled: "I can well remember how my grandmother would jump up and down under this tree at such times praying and saying, 'De slavery chains done broke at last. God done set us free!' All the other ex-slaves would join in with tears running down their faces."[64]

Rarely in the history of oppressed people had such concordance reigned between opportunity and achievement. Ex-slaves daily experienced meaningful freedom. Some became rulers, sharing in the business of government. The children had only to heed the evidence of their eyes to know that great events had transpired and that their parents had played a large part in bringing them about. Such a realization undoubtedly deepened the self-confidence of countless black children. It was a common experience during the years 1865–1870 to see the young teaching the elderly or both attending school together. Ida B. Wells of Holly Springs, Mississippi, recalled: "My mother went along to school with us until she learned to read the Bible."[65] In New Orleans, during June 1865, a traveler reported: "The teachers said the cases were quite numerous in which the more intelligent scholars were instructing their parents at home."[66] Another traveler, reporting from Memphis the same month, described the scene in a classroom: "Six years and sixty may be seen, side by side, learning to read from the same chart or book. Perhaps a bright little Negro boy or girl is teaching a white-haired old man, or bent old woman in spectacles, their letters."[67]

The experience of emancipation, tangible and intimate, became a binding force for millions of black people in or of the South. The awareness of this force resolves the wonder of the observer at the extraordinary endurance and survival of the same people. As Bond wrote a generation ago: "It is self-respect that gives to the American Negro that inner security in the face of real or fancied injuries . . . accorded him as a member of a group definitely in its place."[68] This factor is as much racial as it is human. Its value for young and old during times of lynching and disfranchisement was extraordinary.

Descent into inequality, impoverishment, and segregation

The pattern of oppression inevitably affected the schools. "At the beginning of the twentieth century," Bond writes, "the condition of the schools for Negro children in the South was but slightly improved over their condition in 1875."[69] From 1900 on, Negro schools fell farther behind white schools; by 1915 the gap was larger; it reached its greatest extent by 1930. The black-white per student expenditure gap, 50 percent in the seaboard South in 1915, had grown to 300 percent by 1915. During the years 1901–1915, in the same area, "whereas white schools had seats for over 95 percent of the whites of school age, there were seats for barely half of the Negro children."[70] The imbalance in available room fed on itself through the mechanism of state aid. General procedure was for the legislature to appropriate school funds on the basis of the number of school-age children in each school district, as though all were enrolled in school. When these funds arrived in the county, a much higher proportion of black children was not enrolled, in part because of the county's refusal to build sufficient black schools. Thus, part of state aid for black children became a "surplus" available for white children.[71] In predominantly black counties, the "surplus" was extremely large.

Even the encouraging higher enrollment by black children in southern cities was subject to a heavy discount. In 1905, for example, about 9,000 black children of school age lived in Atlanta; their schools, however, had only about 3,000 seats. The black schools were put on split session, reducing the school day for each of 6,000 students by a fifth or more; another 3,000 students were unable to enroll in any school. In rural Greenwood County, South Carolina, a young black who had entered first grade in 1900 recalled that "in the sixteen years since I entered the first grade at the age of six, I had spent only seventy-three months in school – the equivalent of eight nine-month years of schooling."[72] In effect, he had attended school only half time. Yet, the census counted him and the Atlanta children as full-time students and equated their enrollment with that of full-time white students. By 1910, Bullock observes, "the Negro child's portion of the money spent for public education had fallen far below his proportional representation in the population."[73]

The impoverishment of black education in the South was the more bitter for its accompanying disfranchisement. John Hope, black president of Atlanta University, declared in 1905:

> We have had the "Jim Crow" law forced upon us, our public
> schools have become poorer in equipment and teaching force,
> and the salary of teachers has been lowered. . . . Now I believe
> in education, but I also believe in Manhood; and any education
> bought at the price of manhood is worthless and a millstone about
> the neck. I believe in the ballot as a developer of manhood and as
> it procures the right of men.[74]

Hope refused to beg for schools.

The little political power blacks garnered under conditions of general disfranchisement had to be used sparingly, especially for education. In Atlanta, Negro citizens could still vote in elections of slight political importance such as bond referenda. Even minor gains by black schools came through special campaigns. The fledgling Urban League had to carry on such a campaign to have the board of education employ its first two public health nurses for black schools; they were standard in white schools.

In 1908, Negroes in Atlanta tried to defeat a school bond issue that provided no funds for black schools. The issue passed. Six years later, Walter White recalled, the school board abolished the eighth grade in black schools and shifted the savings to the white schools. There was, apparently, no protest. (In 1899, the U.S. Supreme Court had approved a similar action in Augusta, Georgia.) In 1916, the board of education prepared to eliminate the seventh grade of Negro schools in order to save enough money to build a white high school. Blacks were enraged at the pending action. They resented the absence of any black high school in the city. Negroes paid taxes to support white schools, including the planned white high school from which their children would be excluded. This time, an organized protest was mounted, and a local branch of the National Association for the Advancement of Colored People (NAACP) was founded to lead the campaign. The school board rescinded its planned shutdown in black schools.

Emboldened, the local NAACP then informed the board that Negroes would defeat a forthcoming school bond issue designed for the benefit of whites only. A committee visited the school board, but members told the NAACP "with brutal frankness and considerable profanity that none of the bond money was to be spent on Negro schools and that there was nothing colored citizens could do about it."[75] The bond issue *was* defeated. An agreement with the black community followed. In return for support of the bonds, some older black schools would be repaired and the city's first black secondary school would be built. In 1924, the Booker T. Washington High School was completed, with a capacity of 1,000; eleven years later, it enrolled 3,000 students in split sessions. On another occasion, Atlanta authorities promised one-third of the proceeds of a bond issue for black schools in exchange for support in a bond election. After passage of the bond issue, Negro schools received less than 10 percent. Elsewhere in the South, school facilities for blacks other than the barest instruction in conventional elementary grades were rare indeed. In 1911, the entire state of Maryland had a single black public high school in Baltimore. At the time, about 200,000 blacks lived in the state. In 1925, Atlanta's public schools operated forty kindergartens for white children, but none for blacks.

The pattern of inequality and segregation reinforced during Reconstruction was strengthened in the early twentieth century in the South. For example, by 1920, in Mississippi the greatest number of black students – who lived in predominantly black counties – were given barely one-tenth the appropriations spent on white students (Table 8). This was a consequence of the southern system of misappropriating state aid that the legislature had, at least formally, designated for black schools. In the

Table 8. *Per student expenditures in Mississippi, by race, 1920–1921*

Location	Percent Negro population	Expenditure per student		Percent expenditure black of white
		White	Black	
Black counties (19)	78.1	$30.22	$ 3.59	11.9
White counties (12)	18.5	10.49	4.69	46.2
Cities (6)	52.1	50.79	13.32	26.2

Source: Calculated from data in W. E. B. Du Bois, "The Negro Common School, Mississippi," *Crisis* (December 1926).

white counties, ironically, because of the sparsity of black students, no "surplus" existed for the extra benefit of white students.

Black citizens of Mississippi in 1924 addressed a memorial to the state legislature, requesting that all black taxes be earmarked for black schools:

> In view of the very great discrimination in the application of the public school funds contrary to law, and in event such discrimination is to be continued, we would most respectfully ask, in that event, a division on racial lines, of the taxes levied for school purposes, giving to the whites all taxes paid by individual whites, plus their per capita share of school taxes paid by corporations, and let the Negroes receive all taxes paid by them, plus their per capita share of the taxes paid by corporations. [76]

The request was ignored. A year later, black citizens sued in Covington County to break the system of unequal school funds on the basis of race. In *Bryant*, the state supreme court held almost tauntingly:

> It is of course not necessary that every child in the county has the same advantages in the way of education that every child has. . . . The operation and conduct of public schools are practical affairs. You cannot discriminate against people on account of their race or condition, but their rights may depend upon their situation, or they may be classified according to such situation and condition. [77]

In short, the existing system was to be enforced.

In 1925, a group of black citizens asked the Hinds County (Jackson) Board of Education to appropriate money for a Negro school building. The following motion was passed: "The board unanimously voted to allow the Utica Negro School $150 when funds were available from the dog tax."[78]

Because so few people in Mississippi lived in cities, distances to schools were often enormous. In 1924, the state paid more than $1 million for transporting whites; nothing was spent for blacks. A black student described the long walk home in these words: "The same white kids that Momma and other Negro mothers had taken care of – would drive by in the great big shiny yellow and black school bus. And they'd lean out of the windows and shout, 'Let's see you run, nigger!' and the white bus driver could cut at us and make us jump off the road."[79] A daily walk of 12 miles was not unheard of.

The black schools of Mississippi were among the worst in the South. This was not an expression of the state's poverty so much as a result of the extreme local control by whites. Wilson says that during "1890–1910, the county school board was practically absolute in its power to administer the public schools."[80] The statute books were filled with enactments written in the language of equality but designed to maintain inequality. Any locality could vote to impose a tax with which to finance the extension of school beyond the state-financed minimum term of four to six months. But Negroes could not vote; therefore, the short term was the lot of their children's schools. A 1924 law authorized the creation of two agricultural high schools – one white, one black – in each county. Within two years, forty-eight white schools and a single black one had been built. Any group of citizens in a school district could petition the state to consolidate small inadequate schools. The trouble was that the law stipulated "qualified electors" could do this; Negroes in the state had no right to vote.

White control of the schools in heavily black areas was achieved in the face of statutory requirements to the contrary. Du Bois wrote in 1926:

> The law directs that Negro schools should be presided over by Negro Trustees and that the Trustees and County Superintendent shall fix the salaries of teachers but none of the Negro schools have Negro Trustees except rural schools and even there the Negroes are Trustees in name only and the County Superintendent appoints the teachers and fixes the pay. In the towns the Trustees of the schools are white although the law says that all Trustees of schools must be patrons of that school.[81]

Dominant whites operated the public schools as though these were their private property, forcing Negroes at times to resort to private schools as *their* public schools. In Holly Springs, Mississippi, the black public school was conducted in the yard of the jail. While the ancient teacher literally cultivated his garden nearby, "the children spent most of their playtime chatting with the prisoners through the bars of that jail."[82] Rust

College, located in the town, had to offer a full elementary school to meet the educational needs of the black community, but on a tuition basis. Blacks supported the public education of blacks and whites and the education of blacks in some private schools, especially in Negro secondary schools throughout the South, most of which were private ventures that charged tuition.

In a few states, ingenuity was blended with power to produce even more effective deprivation. Such was the case in Oklahoma. There, the state constitution permitted separate schools for blacks and whites; equal accommodations were required but not, in fact, provided. Two types of school organization could be adopted in any county: the district or the separate school. A district system was preferable because it received state aid directly and in addition could levy a district school tax of 15 mills. The separate school system could levy only 1 or 2 mills and received state aid indirectly, through the county superintendent's office. The school law stipulated that the "separate school . . . is hereby declared to be that school in said school district of the race having the fewest number of children in said school district."[83] The district schools were to be those enrolling the racial majority. The county superintendent was also granted the power to designate which was the separate school. Almost without exception, the minority white school where it existed was named the district school; majority black schools were classified as separate schools.

Buildings housing the separate-but-majority schools in Oklahoma were typically in very poor shape. Unlike district schools, the separate schools did not have the authority to issue construction bonds. Negro schools within districts having bonding power – as in cities – received building funds in proportion to their share of current expenditures. But since black schools all over the state received much less money per student than white schools, the poverty of these schools was compounded. In 1923, the Oklahoma Supreme Court rejected a challenge by black parents in Muskogee County. Their school had just been reclassified as a separate school with consequent loss of financial support. The court declared in *State* v. *Albritton*: "The statute [quoted above] does not attempt to deprive colored persons of any rights. It recognizes their right to equal common school advantages."[84]

Students of the problem, struck by the strong relationship between discriminatory allocation of funds and county control of school finance, urged that the connection be broken. In 1926, Bond wrote that "Negro schools in Oklahoma are going to remain below par just as long as the county remains the unit of financial support."[85] Complete state control of finance seemed a way out. Harlan noted that for years the state of Georgia was almost the sole support of schools, and yet discriminatory allocations went on apace. "Simply enlarging the unit of taxation," according to Harlan, "was not a solution of the inequities of southern school finance, even for whites."[86]

By the 1930s, racial discrimination in southern public education had reached its greatest extent. Writing in 1934, Bond maintained that Negro children "now receive a smaller proportion of the public funds in the Southern States than they have at any time in past history." Negro schools, he held, "are financed from the fragments which fall from the budget made up for white children."[87] As a consequence, it was incorrect to speak of a *dual* school system. Davis, writing in the same year, ended his study of East Texas education with this statement: "The Texas educational system has been a dual system in name only; the Texas system is essentially a white system with Negro education incidental to it."[88] Where the disparity in power between black and white was greatest, the dual system became hardly more than an organizational device to transfer funds from blacks to whites within a constitutional framework. Federal policies were coordinated with those of the state. During 1935–1937, for example, two federal agencies – the Public Works Administration and the Works Progress Administration – spent $8 million to build white schools in Mississippi, but only $400,000 on black schools.[89]

Teachers in the South

By the end of the 1920s, nearly 50,000 black teachers worked in the District of Columbia and the seventeen states with mandatory segregation. Aside from ministers, they were the largest professional group in the black community. Du Bois said of them: "I believe in Negro school teachers, I would to God white children as well as colored could have more of them. With proper training they are the finest teachers in the world because they have suffered and endured and nothing human is beneath their sympathy."[90] But public authorities shared no such interest. Nor, indeed, did they see improved preparation of Negro teachers as important. Exceedingly low salaries, scandalously sinking standards of employment, and the lack of positive incentives to acquire further preparation kept the level of instruction low. "Cooks, maids, and yardmen whom white employers wanted to reward for faithful services often found the route to public school teaching made easier by their contacts with influential white people."[91] White employing officials sometimes employed the less-trained applicant if it was a person "who would maintain the point of view of the whites."[92]

In the cities of the South, where teaching positions tended to be better paid than in rural areas, whites often taught in black schools, as they did in Baltimore, for example, until the first decade of the twentieth century, when after a decade-long campaign, they were replaced by black graduates of a one-year program in the city's high and training school. Until 1920, the black schools of Charleston were staffed by white teachers. In 1919, the NAACP had started a campaign, arguing that under the tutelage of white teachers "the children were learning to despise themselves and their race and to regard white folks as their natural masters."[93] After a series of sixteen mass meetings, the collection of over 5,000 signatures, and a series of intricate legislative maneuvers – made difficult by the absence of blacks in the legislature – the city authorities gave in. The next year, Negro principals were hired.

Field supervision of black teachers was rare in the South. "County superintendents," according to Bond, "generally felt no responsibility for the effectiveness of the Negro schools within their areas of control and aside from annual appropriations of small sums paid little or no attention to the Negro schools."[94] In Georgia, Du Bois noted "the absence of any general supervision of colored schools."[95] In Mississippi, he reported, "county superintendents seldom visit Negro schools but lecture to the teachers on certain Saturdays."[96] School officials showed a keen sense of the purpose of education in their instruction to a young black woman who was employed to teach in a Birmingham black school. The school board interviewer told her: "Remember, you did not create the race problem and neither did I. But it is here, and it is here to stay. I want you to go back to Slater School and teach those little Negro boys and girls how to stay in their places and grow up to be good useful citizens."[97] In Mississippi, white teachers could attend teachers colleges part-time the year around, tuition-free. Black teachers might attend six-week "summer normals" for which they paid, in one year, a total tuition of $11,187.50; private foundations paid $3,000; and the state of Mississippi, $1,270.50.[98]

Migration to opportunity

Negro parents in the South sought to maximize educational opportunities within the system of segregation. One way to do this was by migrating to cities, where even black schools generally received less inadequate financial support than in the countryside. The search for work also led to the cities.

A large cityward movement of blacks occurred right after the Civil War. From 1870 to about the end of the century, this movement slowed. In 1900, the percentage of Negroes in some of these cities had even fallen. However, over the forty years after 1880, the number of Negroes living in twenty-five large southern cities rose from 368,000 to 924,000 (Table 9).

Improved schooling did not automatically result from migration. Woofter studied Negro migration within the South during the years 1908–1918. Dividing these years into two equal periods, he found that most counties did increase expenditures for Negro schools as black population rose. During 1908–1913, twelve counties with rising enrollments of black students actually reduced the salaries of black teachers. In 1913–1918

Table 9. *Negro population (in thousands) in forty selected southern and northern cities, 1880, 1920, and 1940*

City	1880	1920	1940
South			
Atlanta	16	63	105
Augusta	10	23	27
Baltimore	54	108	166
Baton Rouge	4	9	12
Charleston	27	32	32
Charlotte	3	15	31
Chattanooga	5	19	36
Columbia	6	15	22
Columbus, Ga.	5	9	17
Dallas	2	24	50
Fort Worth	1	16	25
Houston	6	34	86
Jackson	3	10	24
Jacksonville	4	42	62
Louisville	21	41	47
Macon	7	23	26
Memphis	15	61	121
Mobile	12	24	29
Montgomery	10	20	35
Nashville	16	36	47
New Orleans	58	101	149
Norfolk	10	43	46
Savannah	16	39	43
Shreveport	5	17	36
Washington, D.C.	52	110	187
Total	368	934	1,461
North			
Boston	6	16	24
Buffalo	1	5	18
Chicago	6	109	278
Cincinnati	8	30	56
Cleveland	2	35	85
Columbus, Ohio	3	22	36
Dayton	1	9	20
Detroit	3	41	149
Indianapolis	7	30	51
Kansas City	8	31	42
New York	28	169	504

Table 9. *(cont.)*

City	1880	1920	1940
Philadelphia	32	134	251
Pittsburgh	4	35	62
Saint Louis	22	70	166
San Francisco	2	2	5
Total	133	738	1,747

Source: Richard L. Morrill and O. Fred
Donaldson, "Geographical Perspectives on the
History of Black America," *Economic Geography,*
48 (January 1972), p. 15.

sixteen of the fifty-two counties cut teachers' salaries as the number of black students rose. Of these twenty-eight counties that cut black salaries, twenty-five were predominantly black. Woofter described the process as one of paring black school funds for the benefit of a relatively less sparse white population.[99]

Many blacks moved from the open countryside to villages, especially the larger ones. (A village was defined in 1920 as an occupied place with a population of from 250 to 2,500.)

In the decade of the 1920s many Negroes moved to cities. For the first time in American history, the majority of black school-age children were no longer on farms (Table 10). The number of black school-age children in urban areas increased at a rate six times faster than their number as a whole rose. During the 1930s, Bond observed that "the center of the Negro educational problem, if defined by numbers, should no longer be the rural South, but the urban South."[100] As large numbers of black children completed city elementary schools, pressure for further schooling increased. (In 1930, more than 108,000 Negro children seven to fifteen years of age attended public schools in eight large southern cities.) As usual, when public authorities acceded somewhat to these demands, they did so in a highly discriminatory manner. In the 1928–1929 school year, out of a total of 4,771 accredited high schools in eleven southern states, only 170 or about 6 percent were Negro schools (Table 11). Over the following decade, the total number rose to nearly 6,000, of which 610 or a little over 10 percent were black. In some of these states, the number of black high-school-age youth equaled or exceeded the number of whites.

In 1949, sociologist E. Franklin Frazier wrote that "the mass migration of Negroes to northern cities has enabled a larger proportion of Negro

Table 10. *Urbanization status of Negro children aged 5 to 19 years, 1920*

	1920		1930		Change: 1920–1930	
	No.	%	No.	%	No.	%
Urban	893,378	24.9	1,323,379	34.1	+430,001	+48.1
Rural farm	2,112,918	58.9	1,912,855	49.3	−200,067	− 9.5
Rural nonfarm	580,040	16.2	643,217	16.6	+ 63,177	+10.9
Total	3,586,336	100.0	3,879,451	100.0	+293,111	+ 8.1

Source: Data in Charles E. Hall, *Negroes in the United States, 1920–32* (Washington, D.C.: GPO, 1935), pp. 93–95.

Table 11. *Number of accredited high schools in eleven southern states, by race, 1928–1929 and 1938–1939*

	1928–1929		1938–1939	
State	White schools	Negro schools	White schools	Negro schools
Alabama	315		352	20
Florida	165	9	215	20
Georgia	387[a]	30[a]	448	52
Kentucky	457	16	543	60
Louisiana	353[b]	4[b]	380	35
Mississippi	335		391	15
North Carolina	587	54	715	156
South Carolina	303	3	322	31
Tennessee	353	14	375	57
Texas	944	25	1,273[c]	104[c]
Virginia	402	15	435	60
Total	4,601	170	5,449	610

[a]1931–1932.   [b]1929–1930.   [c]1937–1938.

Source: Commission on Secondary Schools, *Progress and Plans for Negro High Schools Toward Regional Accreditment* (Association of Colleges and Secondary Schools for Negroes, 1945), p. iii.

children to receive a standard American education than at any time in the history of the Negro."[101]

Until the Civil War, the overwhelming majority of black children in the

North attended separate public schools. A review of the experience in three states illuminates the entire northern picture of the development of segregation after the war.

Illinois

At the end of the Civil War, Illinois still operated under a school law that restricted public schools to white children. During the war, the Chicago Board of Education designated certain schools for Negro children, but parents refused to obey the order. The school board relented somewhat and resolved that children who were as little as one-eighth Negro could attend any school.[102] Continued pressure resulted in abolition of Negro schools in 1865. For another five years, the board continued to maintain a black evening school.

In 1869, Negro leaders from all over the state organized a colored convention to demand "equal school privileges."[103] The Illinois Afro-American Citizens Protective Association, representing Negroes in seventy-eight counties, began soon after, among other things, to "secure for colored children equal school accommodations with the white children."[104] State school officials were sometimes sympathetic but by and large ineffectual in changing conditions. Newton Bateman, state superintendent of public instruction, reported at the end of 1868 that "children of color are not included in the numerical basis upon which either their country superintendent or the township trustees apportion the school fund." He noted that the school law made mandatory the refund of school taxes paid by blacks, but "the school taxes paid by persons of color are not generally returned to them." Of black parents, he wrote that "they are trying, by conventions, petitions, and appeals, to reach the ears and hearts of the representatives of the people and the law-making of the State, to see if anything can be done for them."[105] Bateman himself opposed outlawing separate schools; he felt the matter should be left to local option.

In the school law of 1872, the legislature omitted the word "white," but no positive conferral of rights was made. Two years later, in the face of widespread violence against the admission of black children to white schools in Springfield and Jo Daviess County, strong penalties were levied on persons who interfered with the attendance of black children in a public school. The law meant little in southern Illinois. Thirty years after passage a historian reported: "Colored schools exist in many places. Alton has forced its colored people out into schools by themselves."[106] State authorities stood by. The state court of appeals, in 1886, in *People* v. *McFall*, approved of a school board's sending white students to white schools outside their regular area of assignment, although in 1874 the state supreme court in *Chase* v. *Stephenson* had outlawed the building of an all-Negro annex to an elementary school.

In 1908, only 3.6 percent of Chicago's public school enrollment was Negro. About this time no more than three elementary schools were predominantly black. By 1920, following the migration of many Negroes from the South and the institutionalization of residential segregation by the real estate industry, school segregation increased. In that year, ten elementary schools were at least 70 percent black and another dozen ranged from 13 to 70 percent. Wendell Phillips High School became the first predominantly black secondary school in the city. Its itinerary can be traced over a six-year period in *Crisis* magazine:

> 1915: "The Wendell Phillips High School of Chicago is trying to separate white and colored students in social functions."
> 1917: "Colored students of the Wendell Phillips High School in Chicago, Ill., are discriminated against and efforts for their segregation are under way."
> 1920: "The first colored male teacher to be appointed in the Chicago High Schools is Oscar J. Jordan, who will teach fifth year students."
> 1921: "The enrollment of Wendell Phillips High School in Chicago is 75 percent colored and 25 percent white. The Negro enrollment is the largest in the history of the school."

At the beginning of the 1920s, many devices were used to segregate students, despite state law to the contrary. "Several school principals made no secret of their preference for racial segregation," Spear writes, "and employed various subterfuges as possible in a branch school, which . . . kept the proportion of Negroes in the main building below 20 percent while the substandard branch was 90 percent Negro."[107] At the end of the decade, twenty-six schools were at least 85 percent Negro in enrollment; these included Phillips High School and two junior high schools.

The school system regulated the number and location of Negro teachers. Graduation from Chicago Normal College was the standing prerequisite for teaching in the city's schools. In mid-1930 Negroes made up only 6.7 percent of the college's enrollment. A decade later, it was believed in the black community that the college had a Negro quota of 2 percent. In fact, for several years no black applicants were accepted. Once a black teacher's name was placed upon the eligible list, she was not assigned to the first opening: "Applicants whose addresses indicate their race are skipped in filling 'white' positions," Herrick wrote. "A qualified colored applicant may stay on the list for years without being offered a permanent assignment, and she is more likely to do so than is a white applicant."[108] Black teachers were heavily concentrated in the predominantly black schools. In 1930, 308 out of 13,268 teachers were black; 272 of the 308 taught in predominantly black schools. They constituted 33.9 percent of the teaching staff of those schools, but only 2.3 percent of all teachers. Only 36 black teachers taught in nonblack schools.

In schools enrolling about one-third Negro students, typically, no Negro teachers were employed. Herrick reported of these schools: "The principals feel that it is folly to add unnecessarily to the racial friction by putting colored teachers over their white children." Discrimination was practiced extensively against black applicants for substitute teaching positions:

> There are twelve applications from Negroes out of "every three or four" hundred, according to the assistant examiner, but the certificates are never granted to Negroes unless a specific request is made either for one of the individuals or for a Negro teacher. . . . The head of the substitute bureau said that in 1930 she had one hundred and fifty colored substitutes on her list. She marked them colored, as she sends them only to colored schools.[109]

This system of discrimination was made easier by the absence of blacks in the higher reaches of school management. In 1930, only one principal was black. At the end of the decade, total black representation in supervisory positions consisted of one high school principal, one elementary school principal, and a high school dean.

Black children were crowded into predominantly black schools. In 1933, thirty-five elementary schools with classes of fifty and sixty were on double shift; most of them were in the Negro neighborhood on the South Side. Five years later, of fifteen schools still on double shift, thirteen were in black areas of the city. Black groups and civic organizations attacked the practice throughout World War II. In 1944, the campaign reached one of its peaks. The school board announced the end of the double-shift system, but refused to release data on the overcrowding situations in the school.

That year, the board embarked on a program of publicity to counter the criticism. It claimed to have spent $6 million on black schools, but Herrick pointed out that "almost every cent came from Washington."[110] Board literature also tried to show black migrants from Mississippi how much better Chicago schools were than those back home. (To be sure, Wilkerson says, almost as many Mississippi Negroes lived in Chicago as the combined black population of Vicksburg, Meridian, Greenville, and Natchez.[111]) "Pictures of ramshackle one-room Negro schools in Mississippi were placed opposite pictures of Chicago schools, without mentioning that the Chicago buildings shown were jammed with children on double shifts, while in white areas only a very few schools in outlying areas were so crowded."[112]

Within two years after the end of World War II, a change in school board policy seemed imminent. In 1950, a technical committee recommended redistricting some schools "to minimize the extent to which schools have children of only one race group in attendance." Ming observes that the plan, even after it was implemented, "did not eliminate even one such elementary school."[113]

The lack of change in Chicago's schools fed on a state policy which, in some respects, simply ignored constitutional, statutory, and judicial guidelines. Herrick summarizes the statewide situation around midcentury.

> Up until 1947, there was no real challenge to the complete public segregation in schools for all Negro children in the fifteen southern counties in Illinois. The State School Directory for that year listed Negro and white schools separately. Some towns like Edwardsville had four-year white high schools and three-year Negro. In 1947, the Illinois Commission on Human Relations pointed out the six state laws forbidding these practices, and urged the State Superintendent of Public Instruction to withhold state aid from the districts which broke the law. He replied that he had no authority to make such investigation unless the elected state's attorneys in those counties initiated suit against the elected school boards.[114]

The likelihood of states' attorneys undertaking such suits was probably nil. There is no record that any ever occurred.[115]

New York City

In 1880, New York City had 28,000 Negroes, second only to Philadelphia in the North. By 1920, its 169,000 black people gave it the largest Negro population in the country. By 1940, over 500,000 blacks lived in the city, more than in Washington, D.C., Baltimore, and New Orleans combined. Harlem became the best-known black community in the world.

Before World War I, Negro children were not numerous in the city's public schools. In 1908, they made up only 1.2 percent of the city's students. Fewer than 200 black youngsters were enrolled in the high schools. In 1913, Negro children made up 4 percent of the elementary school enrollment. Only seven Negro high school students were graduated. Even in 1924, Kelly Miller wrote: "Until quite recently the fact of a colored student graduating from a high school in the North was so unusual as to demand general notice and flattering comment."[116] A study of Negro high schools in the city concluded that their academic achievement lagged about one-quarter behind that of white students. Black students were more persistent than their white classmates, however, and dropped out less often.[117]

Blascoer found that "as a whole the colored children were making normal progress under normal conditions; that is, in cases where they had attended schools in New York City regularly, their progress was on a par with the white children in the same schools."[118] She stressed the importance of helping the black student to overcome the special problem of racial discrimination.

Between 1910 and 1920, the Negro population of the city increased by two-thirds. Many were newcomers from the South. The principal of PS 89 in Harlem reported that southern children were placed "as far as possible in classes of 25 instead of the usual class of 40–45."[119] This was a school of 2,250 students, more than 2,000 of whom were black. About nine out of ten of its graduates continued on to high school. A district superintendent said that in Districts 15 and 16 "seven out of eight children with a southern school history are overage; three out of eight are more than two years overage. . . . It is nothing unusual to find recent arrivals two, four or more years behind in the scholastic attainments."[120] At PS 119, where southern children attended in numbers, school authorities made curriculum adjustments and introduced prevocational subjects such as "millinery, dressmaking, practical homemaking, industrial art, and cooking."[121] In 1969, children fresh from the South were automatically placed one grade back.

Schools in Harlem were not all black. As of May 1920, five Harlem elementary schools were on double shifts, but there was no correlation between the percentage of black children and the use of the double-shift system. PS 89, which was 93 percent Negro, had 16 double-shift classes; PS 119, 75 percent Negro, had only 8; PS 5, 40 percent Negro, had 24; PS 68, 26 percent Negro, had 7; and PS 90, 13 percent Negro, had 26 double-shift classes.[122] Discrimination was less prevalent than in Chicago because the New York black community was far better organized. National headquarters of the NAACP were located in the city. When authorities of Brooklyn Girls High School informed six Negro seniors they would be unwelcome at the senior prom, one of the six turned out to be the daughter of W. E. B. Du Bois, director of research for NAACP! In a spirited protest, Du Bois met with the superintendent – rather than the principal; the matter was quickly resolved. All seniors would attend the senior prom.[123]

William Pickens, another NAACP official and holder of a doctorate in classical languages, who lived in Harlem, was an active parent. Pickens wrote on many aspects of the national educational scene for the *New York Age*, a Harlem weekly. He admired the interracial cooperation at PS 119 in Harlem. From Augusta, Georgia, he analyzed the efforts of voteless blacks there to negotiate new school facilities. When an official of the city schools proposed to sponsor a lecture series at the YMCA for Negroes only, Pickens warned in a letter: "Let the colored people maintain any 'colored' things and any private institutions which they choose to maintain, but let them never begin to accept anything 'colored' from the City of New York, never and never."[124] He had observed the work of Mrs. Mary McLeod Bethune at her Daytona Normal and Industrial Institute and praised her dedication, but rejected private institutions as a solution to the educational problems of black children generally: "For the only institution that can ever educate the masses is the great university of The Public School."[125]

In response to complaints by black parents about the unsuitability of many textbooks used in the schools, a formal hearing was held by a city commission. Pickens studied the texts used in PS 89 and PS 119. Gordy's *Elementary History of the United States*, he said, was "an effective apology for slavery and for the subsequent treatment of the Negro." He criticized its failure to deal with Frederick Douglass as a black abolitionist and charged that the history of Reconstruction was distorted.[126]

The adequacy of schools for blacks in the city did not become a community issue during the 1920s, although as children and parents streamed in from the South, Harlem's schools became severely overcrowded. Increasingly, black children found themselves in the least adequate buildings. By the early 1930s, observers noted problems of overcrowding, inadequate curriculum, discriminatory reading materials, deliberate segregation, and underrepresentation of blacks in school governance and teaching. In 1935, after a riot in Harlem, Mayor Fiorello LaGuardia appointed Negro sociologist E. Franklin Frazier as head of a committee to investigate conditions in Harlem, and Governor Herbert H. Lehman signed a bill prohibiting educational institutions supported by any public funds from engaging in any discriminatory purposes. By the end of the next year the mayor still refused to release the committee's report on schools, though the general report was out.

Discrimination was rife in the schools of Harlem, according to the suppressed report:

> The Negro in Harlem has made serious complaints against the schools of the community on the grounds that they are old, poorly equipped and overcrowded and constitute fire hazards. . . . The welfare of the children is neglected and racial discrimination is practiced. . . . It seems that many of the white teachers appointed to the schools of Harlem regard the appointment as a sort of punishment. . . . There appears to be a great deal of turnover in white personnel in these schools. . . . The problem of education is the same as all other problems: namely, to make the same educational provisions for the school children of Harlem as are made for children in other parts of the city, and see to it that Negro teachers are admitted to all branches of the teaching staff.[127]

Four months after the inquiry was completed, on September 21, 1935, the *New York Age* reminded Mayor LaGuardia that "since you have taken office you have done much to help solve the problems of the Italian but have forgotten the Negro." One committee suggestion – that a black person be placed on the school board – was criticized by board member James Marshall, who noted a few months later that more than forty "racial" groups lived in the city. It would be impractical, he said, to give each one a representative on the board of education.[128]

The Junior Council of the NAACP led an effort to organize a movement among black parents in Brooklyn to improve schools in the borough. Of 16,000 school-age children in Brooklyn, 6,000 were not in school. Teachers were criticized for failing to understand the special problems of black students. The NAACP recommended that a knowledge of Negro life and history become a prerequisite for teaching and called for organization of parents to combat apathy.

The Committee for Better Schools in Harlem (CBSH), formed in 1936, stimulated many black parents to formulate specific demands on the school system. Large delegations conferred often with school officials. Partly in response to this activity, four new schools were built in Harlem between 1937 and 1941. The CBSH charged that attendance areas were being gerrymandered to segregate white and black children in Harlem. School authorities replied that "elementary and junior high schools must be near the children's residences and in the case of high schools, if zoning were abolished, it would be difficult for the school to contact the parents and the possibility of community cooperation would be eliminated."[129]

Three high schools enrolling large numbers of Harlem youth – Wadleigh, Haaren, and Textile – had opportunities neither for academic nor commercial curricula. The school board's Educational Survey Commission had recommended the building in Harlem of a high school for personal service trades. In 1940, a vocational guidance counselor in a Harlem junior high school charged that specialized trades high schools were rejecting Negro students on the ground that "if we cannot place the boy in the job for which we are to train him, then it is futile to give him the training."[130] Community leaders opposed this policy. The NAACP, Harlem YMCA, and the CBSH met with counselors from Harlem schools, but no change in school policy resulted.

Very few New York City teachers were Negroes. As early as 1924, graduates of Atlanta University, a black school, were declared eligible to teach in the city. By midcentury, however, scattered indications were that black teachers made up about 1.5 percent of all permanently appointed teachers; another 1 percent were said to be substitutes. Half the high schools had no Negro teachers; most Negroes taught at predominantly Negro high schools. At least one teachers' organization, the

Teachers Union, was an energetic exponent of Negro rights in the schools, but was unable to enforce its views in the absence of collective bargaining.

Both in Harlem and Brooklyn, parent groups continued their organizing, but with small results. The focus of their work was highly localized improvements or a change in principals demanded for one or another school. But Negroes remained almost completely outside the circle of citywide power.

New Jersey

In 1881, the state legislature outlawed school segregation. Three years later the state supreme court held that a Negro child had the right to attend the nearest school instead of being assigned to a Negro school. During the next half century or more, both the statute and the decision were violated repeatedly by school boards and the state department of education. Statistics on schools by race were collected and published in state records. The state maintained two vocational schools for Negro students and staffed only by Negro teachers. In challenges to illegal segregation brought by Negro parents before the state commissioner of education, the decision virtually always was rendered on behalf of the segregation. This was true despite overwhelming evidence, conceded by defendant school boards, of conscious intention to segregate.

In 1925, Granger described the situation in the southern part of the state:

> From the university town of Princeton, including the capital city of Trenton, southward to Cape May, every city or town with a considerable Negro population supports the dual educational system, with a building for its white and a building for its Negro pupils of the grammar grades. In the high schools the races are mixed. In no town south of Elizabeth does a colored teacher have a class with white children in it, though wholly colored classes are sometimes found with a white teacher in charge.[131]

Fourteen years later, a commission appointed by the legislature found conditions worse. In the smaller cities and towns with segregated schools also, deterioration of educational conditions had set in.[132]

During the early 1920s, Burlington and Gloucester counties were the only ones in the state to enroll all their black students in all-Negro schools.[133] By 1938, school officials in Mount Holly and Westhampton townships – both in Burlington – not only segregated Negro children to an extreme degree, but "had developed a feeling of racial tension which has spread to relationships between the adult Negro and white residents of the community."[134]

In 1938, 434 Negro teachers were employed in the state; 404 worked in the segregated schools of South Jersey. In six state teachers' colleges, 101 black students were enrolled; this was 3.1 percent of total enrollment. At one of the six, Glassboro State Teachers College, the administration barred Negro students from college dormitories and required them to live off-campus. The president of the college wrote that his administration helped black students "find suitable homes in town among people of their own race where they can live more economically than at the dormitories."[135]

Granger had observed in 1925 that school segregation was restricted largely to the southern part of the state. In northern cities such as Newark and Jersey City, he reported, "white and colored children attend school together from the kindergarten through the high schools, and it seldom occurs to anyone that this is not the most natural thing in the world to do. . . . North Jersey . . . is not interested in . . . [segregated schools]."[136] The state legislative commission of 1939, however, referred to "signs in recent years that many communities in northern New Jersey have either instituted or plan to institute experiments of their own in separate school facilities" and noted that unequal educational facilities were appearing in those communities.[137]

The preceding discussion of schools in Illinois, New York City, and New Jersey makes clear certain leading features of northern schooling for Negro children: (1) northern governmental and school officials were extremely reluctant to grant Negroes their legal rights as recorded in constitutions, laws, and court rulings; (2) in the absence of effective parent action in defense of the rights, Negro children were virtually without other defenders;[138] (3) in creating segregated schools, the initiative usually rested with local school systems, with state governments lending the illegal acts an appearance of legitimacy.

Residential and educational segregation

As blacks moved to the cities, Negro housing became more segregated. In time, the schools followed this pattern.

In 1905, Du Bois described the urban geography of southern residential segregation:

> It is an interesting thing in any southern town to notice where the Negro population lives; sometimes, as in Savannah, the distribution of the population resembles a great O, with the whites in the center and the blacks in the circle around; in Albany, Georgia, the straight central street divided the town almost into a black and white half; in Atlanta we may picture the Negro population as stretched like a great dumbbell across the city, with one great

center in the east and a smaller one in the west, connected by a narrow belt.[139]

The concentration of blacks in certain residential areas was a universal fact of American life, both North and South. In the South, it had no consequences for school; assignment to a school was based on race, not residence. In the North both race and place were considered. During the years 1865–1920, numerous northern courts approved the use of residence as the assignment criterion for white children and race as the assignment criterion for black children. Most whites attended the nearest or a nearby school; blacks attended the Negro school, wherever it was located. Courts almost never conceded that the right to attend a specific school was a principle of law.

From 1910 to 1916, a number of southern and border cities passed ordinances barring Negroes from buying or renting residences in certain areas of the city. All these measures were rendered unconstitutional by ruling of the U.S. Supreme Court in 1917 in *Buchanan* v. *Warley*, a ruling ignored and evaded with impunity. Enactments almost identical with the one struck down in *Buchanan* were placed on the books in various cities, including New Orleans, Indianapolis, Birmingham, Palm Beach (Florida), and Greenville (South Carolina).[140] Nevertheless, the court action spurred a search for alternatives to explicit segregation legislation.

The Chicago Real Estate Board (CREB) led by adopting, in 1917, a policy designed to ensure that Negro residential expansion would occur only a block at a time. Members of CREB were not to sell or rent property to a Negro if he would be the first to enter a hitherto white block. In April 1917, CREB published the report of its committee that prepared the policy. It urged the "block organization of [white] owners," noting that "neighborhood improvement associations may be employed as the nucleus to form such organizations." The need for additional Negro housing was acknowledged, but "in the interest of all," the committee explained, "each block shall be filled solidly and . . . further expansion shall be confined to contiguous blocks, and . . . the present method of obtaining a single building in scattered blocks, be discontinued." Later that year, CREB adopted a resolution "that this Board start a propaganda through its individual members to recommend owners societies in every white block for the purpose of mutual defense."[141]

Race relations in Chicago were aggravated by these and other restrictive measures. In 1919 the infamous Chicago Race Riot was ignited primarily by white aggression. By 1920, according to Spear, "the majority of Chicago's Negroes . . . lived in black enclaves; the 'scattered' portion of the Negro population had almost disappeared. . . . For the most part, the population increase [of Negroes] was reflected less in the expansion of the black belt than in a sharp rise in the density of Negro settlement within the black enclaves."[142]

CREB also helped make use of the restrictive covenant almost universal among white owners of real estate. This was a statement in the property deed that obliged the purchaser not to sell to a Negro or member of other specified minorities. Violations of covenants were enforceable in state courts; the covenants, therefore, took on a public character.

The National Association of Real Estate Boards undertook during the 1920s to install the Chicago system in urban areas throughout the United States. Article 34, Part III, of its Code of Ethics commanded: "A Realtor should never be instrumental in introducing into a neighborhood a character of property or occupancy, members of any race or nationality, or any individuals whose presence will clearly be detrimental to property values in that neighborhood."[143] The effort was sweepingly successful.

It is possible to trace the progress of Negro–native white residential segregation in ten large northern cities from 1910 to 1950. Over the forty-year period, segregation increased in all ten cities. Significantly, most of the increase occurred during the decade of the 1920s; in large measure it was the result of the efforts of the real estate industry.

In 1939, Homer Hoyt wrote that "it is a mere truism to enunciate that colored people tend to live in segregated districts of American cities."[144] He made no distinction between North and South. Unnoticed, in fact, by all but a rare demographer, was the emergence of the urban South as a highly segregated area. Dividing the country into four geographical regions, it can be seen that in 1940 the urban South was more segregated residentially than the Northeast and the West. In 1950, its segregation surpassed the national average. In 1960, the urban South became the most segregated of all. The American city as such had become highly segregated.

Schools in the North adjusted to these demographic changes in fairly uniform ways. Attendance zones were redrawn to separate black from white children. In rapidly changing areas school boards often created optional attendance zones to enable white parents to select schools in accordance with the most recent racial statistics. The grade span of predominantly black schools was sometimes extended to prevent children in these schools from passing on to a nearby advanced white school. At times, Negro students were placed in a separate wing of a school or in an annex or in a separate room, even in the basement. Schools designed for black students were located in the growing number of solidly black residential areas. Blacks were not appointed to school boards and higher managerial posts, thus effectively minimizing protest arising within the school system.[145]

Southern children who came North had much to learn. Maya Angelou, who with her brother had come from Stamps, Arkansas, to Saint Louis, reported that in their new school "we learned to say 'Yes' and 'No' rather than "Yes, ma'am' and 'No, ma'am,'" A generation earlier, another black brother and sister had discussed their parents' instructions: "'Madge,' I asked, 'why shouldn't we call the teacher ma'am? Everyone else does,' 'I don't know exactly,' she replied, 'but I think it's because Mom and Dad don't want us to feel inferior to anyone else.'"[146] Their mother, the daughter of the first black United States Senator from Mississippi during Reconstruction, Senator Hiram R. Revels, feared the taint of color prejudice in nearly all-white Seattle, Washington. No quarter must be given.

Black parents balanced the obvious advantages of urban northern schooling over its southern rural counterpart against widespread difficulties their children experienced in northern schools. Pickens concluded from extensive travels throughout the North: "Where the Negro child is practically alone in a class, he can be 'shut out' by the other pupils and squeezed out by the teachers from all social and other cultural [and] athletic activities. This is done every day."[147] Some Negro students were not called upon by teachers for months.

Inside the nonsegregated schools of the North, black children suffered from many cruelties. Daniel studied conditions in seven northern cities, and wrote: "It is not at all uncommon for a Negro pupil 'belonging' to a mixed school by residence to be asked by a white teacher or pupil: 'Why don't you go to the—school *where you belong*?' The—school is invariably a school attended wholly or almost wholly by Negro pupils, and may be in another part of the city."[148] In one school, Daniel said, black students were allowed in all sports except basketball "because there are too many good basketball players among the colored students." In the mid-1920s, intelligence test scores "became a convenient means of proving the inferiority of Negro mentality and were made the excuse for establishing separate classes." When Negro students felt excluded from school dances, as in some Chicago high schools, they sponsored their own social events. In Syracuse, New York, one who had grown up there said "it was readily apparent to any intelligent youngster that he was living in a society quite as closed as that in Dixie."[149]

Deliberate counseling of black students for careers below their ability was common. In Newark and other places, Pickens reported, "the colored girls have been thus encouraged by some of their teachers: 'What do you want to go through high school for? There is nothing *you* can find to do with a high school education.'" A black professional at the Columbus, Ohio, YWCA wrote: "The boy friends of our 'Y' girls were a special problem, for they saw no reason to remain in school. They knew that, regardless of education, opportunities were closed to them except in the Negro communities of the segregated South."[150]

In 1933, Logan reported:

> In the Boston public school system a few white teachers, who
> hardly act on their own initiative, are becoming increasingly bold-
> er in their efforts to discourage colored students from going to
> the college preparatory high schools and to white colleges. In
> one school, a separate assembly of colored students was ordered
> for the purpose of extolling to them the virtues of manual
> training and of colored schools.[151]

Haley writes:

> In my own two years of interviewing for and writing *The Au-*
> *tobiography of Malcolm X*, I cannot remember Malcolm X ever
> more impassioned than when he recalled his hurt and disillu-
> sionment followed by bitterness after a white eighth grade coun-
> selor told him that, because he was black, he should strive to be a
> carpenter, not a lawyer as Malcolm wanted.[152]

The weight of discrimination was also felt when "realistic" career
choices were made to the violence of one's own deepest strivings. One
young man in Chicago wanted to study liberal arts in high school as
preparation for a college program. Instead:

> The whole argument about *us* being Negroes and all the implica-
> tions of this, and *our* not being able to get jobs and *we* must
> prepare for the future and *we* have to live and *we* should get
> some security and four years of shop would give *us* some basis for
> getting a job if *we* do not go to college and *we* might well not go
> to college because *we* don't have much money – all those argu-
> ments were too much for me. At no point in this debate did
> anyone consider my personal aptitudes.[153]

The writer, it should be noted, was not objecting to the consideration of
group interests so much as an inattention to his own.

Almost a century had passed since the end of the Civil War. The years
document Du Bois's dictum that "probably never in the world have so
many oppressed people tried in every possible way to educate themselves."[154] The ex-slaves had succeeded in creating an educational tradition in the face of extraordinary opposition. Black progress was now
possible by political means, as it had not been under slavery, but political
resistance and vigilantism barred the door of the schoolhouse even more
rigidly for many than slavery had. Segregation, inequality, denial of resources, suppression, intimidation, all conspired to deny education to the
former slaves and the children of slaves.

3

Struggle for public policy: black children since 1950

Midcentury marked a turning point in the history of black America. The movement for equality came under black leadership, embraced unprecedented numbers of Negroes, and became national in scope. A persistent black initiative forced a reformulation of public policies in education.

During the 1930s depression and discrimination had driven Negro living standards to new depths. Inequalities of schooling between black and white children in the South reached their widest extent in almost a century. Segregation spread in southern and northern cities. Yet a countermovement began in the midst of despair. As earlier, political strength was a condition for impetus toward equality. In northern cities, the Negro vote became a counter for political change. New Deal welfare policies relieved significantly extensive unemployment among blacks. In 1936, in a wholesale switch away from the Republican party, Negroes became strong supporters of the Roosevelt administration. The emerging industrial union movement in the Congress of Industrial Organizations enrolled hundreds of thousands of blacks, giving "black and white workers a sense of common interest, of solidarity, that transcended racial lines."[1]

World War II sped the process of transformation. Racial discrimination continued in employment, the armed forces, education, and public accommodations, but black protest was insistent. Membership in the NAACP grew almost ninefold between 1940 and 1946, from 50,556 to nearly 450,000.[2] The group's branches increased threefold to 1,073. Negroes turned to demonstrative actions. The grandest of them was the projected March on Washington, organized in 1941 by A. Philip Randolph, a black labor leader. To head off the protest, President Roosevelt agreed to act against job discrimination and created by executive order the Fair Employment Practices Committee. "The Negro masses," as Dalfiume observes, "simply did not support a strategy of moderating their grievances for the duration of the war." Blacks hastened to point out parallels between Nazi racial doctrines and American racial practices.

In 1944, the U.S. Supreme Court struck down the "white primary" law of Texas, invalidating the single most important means of disfranchising the Negro voter. During the next dozen years, the number of registered

Negro voters in the South rose nearly fivefold, from 250,000 to almost 1.25 million. The Negro vote seemed to be a significant element in the 1948 election of President Truman. A number of state and local measures were enacted on behalf of equal use of public accommodations and fair employment.

Southern schooling had undergone few important changes during the war. In 1946, Du Bois could write:

> The majority of Negro children in the United States, from 6 to 18, do not have the opportunity to learn to read and write. We know this is true in the country districts of Mississippi, Louisiana and a half dozen other southern states. But even in the towns and cities of the South, the Negro schools are so crowded and ill-equipped that no thorough teaching is possible.[3]

Teacher and parent demands for equalization

A new dynamic was introduced into black education when Negro teachers began taking on a new role during the late thirties and wartime. During the war, blacks became more numerous in the ranks of teachers in northern schools. Historically self-restrained from taking public action, even on behalf of their own group interests, they now began to respond publicly. They filed lawsuits demanding salary equalization with white teachers in a test of the doctrine of separate-but-equal. Courts responded almost uniformly in their favor. By 1948, of twenty-seven cases only four were lost. These victories introduced major strains into the structure of southern schools, based as they were on malappropriation of funds for whites that belonged to Negro students. If equal expenditures became a fact, white privilege would exist no longer.

The court victories engendered, in Jones's phrase, a "contagion" among black teachers throughout the South. State authorities moved quickly to create single salary schedules. They provided for state subsidies to those local school districts that pleaded an inability to meet the new requirement, lest impecunious districts be tempted to avoid creating expensive duplicate facilities by ending segregation.[4]

Teacher equalization was often moderated by southern judges. On the one hand, they rejected school board complaints that they could not afford equalization; on the other hand, courts did not grant immediate relief to the teachers, but set up a time schedule over which equalization was to be achieved, thus, some believe, acting to coerce the Negro teachers into softening their demands.

School boards resorted to a "professional rating scale." Salaries were to be set in accordance with the judgment of the subject's supervisors, who presumably would employ defensible professional criteria. Black teachers' salaries most often turned out to be lower than their experience and training warranted. Court challenges to the new system were by and large fruitless. It proved almost impossible for the aggrieved to demonstrate that the assigned salary was set unprofessionally. To fend off suits by black teachers, one school district in Florida provided that any teacher dissatisfied with his or her placement could take the National Teacher Examination and permit the salary to be raised or lowered in accordance with the test score.[5] The test was notorious among black teachers for its uncanny success in yielding low grades to Negro teachers. Consequently, few took up the dare.

The salary gap between black and white teachers narrowed nevertheless. In the dozen years after 1939, the average Negro salary increased from 52.5 percent to 87.2 percent of the average white salary.[6] Black teachers' organizations had developed "a new aggressiveness" that paid off.

Black parents and, in some cases, students, also began to rebel against planned inequality and to demand equalization of facilities and programs. "At that time," NAACP counsel Thurgood Marshall recalled, "the best strategy seemed to be an attack against the segregation system by law suits seeking absolute and complete equalization of curricula, faculty, and physical equipment of the white and Negro schools on the theory that the extreme cost of maintaining two 'equal' school systems would eventually destroy segregation."[7] A number of lawsuits were filed attacking material inequalities and asking for equalization although separate. Some cases were won; their number was not large but their import was. Perhaps 200 cases were filed against southern schools. Neither disfranchisement nor violence could be used to silence protest now. The currents of the time were against both. Southern state governments tried to deflect the movement by a rapid but highly spotty program of improvement of black school facilities.

Increased expenditure on black schools might put off one threat, but it intensified another:

> A modernized physical plant and an increase in the quantity and quality of education mean greater diversity of offerings. Herein lies the danger and real significance of the new legal requirements affecting equality of educational opportunities at the physical and curriculum levels for the social system of the South. New offerings in the schools mean an increase in the number of professionally and technically trained persons at all levels – persons who, once trained, will enter the competitive labor market and thereby earn a greater share of the labor dollar.[8]

Yet the white South of the 1940s and early 1950s was far from ready either to yield its privileges or invest seriously in equalization.

Over the period 1939–1951, in six southern states the black-white gap in current expenditures per pupil narrowed from 57.3 percent to 30.3 percent, although the absolute magnitude of the change was slight. The size of the gap in actual dollars was reduced from $53.85 to $50.12. Discrimination persisted. In seven southern states, by 1951, black children in metropolitan areas received only 76 percent of white allocations; in rural areas, 62 percent. In North Carolina, the figures were 95 and 79 percent; in Mississippi, 51 and 33 percent. Between 1940 and 1952, the value of black school buildings rose, reducing the black-white disparity from four-fifths to slightly more than one-half.[9]

Mississippi, with at least one-tenth of all black children in the South, illustrated some of the dimensions of the challenge of equalization. During the 1953–1954 school year, 95 percent of all the one-teacher schools in the state were black schools. Nearly two-thirds of the state's black children attended schools with three or fewer teachers; only one-sixth of the white children attended such schools. Willie Morris said of the black schools in Yazoo City in 1948: "There were no school buses for Negroes, no indoor plumbing, and no central heating."[10] In Attala County, James Meredith was going to school. "I walked to school over four miles each way, every day for eleven years," he said. "Throughout these years, the white school bus passed us each morning. There was no Negro school bus."[11] By 1952, two years after Meredith graduated from high school, some black students were being bused in Mississippi, but many fewer, proportionately, than whites.[12]

Late in 1953, Mississippi legislators began serious exploration of equalization. In 1954, Walter Sillers, speaker of the state house of representatives, acknowledged that "the cost to equalize will be high because in the past we actually have not maintained a dual system of schools, financially. We have maintained a white system."[13]

Among black leaders there was a deep reluctance to abandon the effort to equalize separate schools. About 1948, recounts the historian Kelly, the matter of strategy was raised by Thurgood Marshall, chief counsel for the NAACP Legal Defense Fund: "At this stage of the game, . . . if the school boards in key southern states had shown a general disposition to accept any kind of gradualist program combining more adequate schools with some primary and secondary desegregation, the Association might well have agreed to cooperate, at least for a time."[14] No such overtures were forthcoming, and so the legal attack turned in a new direction. Segregation, as the source of inequality, was to become the target of a sustained legal campaign.

The legal challenge to segregation

Between 1938 and 1952, the U.S. Supreme Court decided six cases involving inequalities in higher education. These were *Gaines* (1938), *Sipuel* (1948), *Fisher* (1949), *Sweatt* (1950), *McLaurin* (1950), and *Gray* (1952). In each case, provisions for black students were found to be constitutionally objectionable. The Court shuttled between remedies of equalizing separate facilities and outright desegregation. In *McLaurin,* where a Negro was admitted to a previously all-white university, the plaintiff was forced to sit apart, near the door of a lecture room. The court held that this act of segregation of itself impaired McLaurin's equal opportunity to gain an education. This was a virtual declaration that segregation was incompatible with equal treatment. Lawyers for the NAACP Legal Defense Fund seized on the opening. In mid-1950, they began a wholesale attack on segregation as such in elementary and secondary school cases. Until this time, the LDF had argued such cases only on the basis of equalization of separate facilities.

The decision to challenge segregation was historic. In 1934, Horace Mann Bond concluded an important work on the education of black children without proposing that segregation be ended. Indeed, as he recalled later, in 1934 "the institution of racial segregation appeared to be an immutable feature of the American social order."[15] Just sixteen years later, perspectives had altered sharply. A new sense of collective identity among Negroes had emerged from World War II. A readiness and a drive to protest against discrimination emboldened the NAACP to take a more forward position. Black teachers and parents in the South, even the rural South, drew lines with unprecedented daring. In 1954 Lewis found that Negroes as a whole were "developing a new sense of personal dignity and group pride . . . more akin to the pride of an integrating cultural minority than to pride as such."[16] The managers of the segregated southern system were growing less secure in their conviction that segregation was the surest protection for their privileges.

The new legal strategy required for success close support by black communities. The earlier strategy of challenging unequal facilities in higher education drew very little community support. Few Negroes had been personally involved and, therefore, the effort seemed somewhat abstract. In the late 1940s, when the LDF and the NAACP turned to the common schools, community interest rose.

In Summerton, South Carolina, black parents in 1949 petitioned the school board to relieve severe overcrowding in the black high school. When no action resulted, an NAACP lawyer drew up a formal petition that was signed by 107 parents and children. After a period of inaction, in 1950 a formal lawsuit was entered, requesting not equal facilities but the end of segregated schools altogether. A year later, black high school students in Farmville, Virginia, carried on a strike against deplorable conditions at the school. At first the Negro Parent-Teacher Association supported demands for a new, although separate, high school. After an NAACP lawyer suggested the attack be on separation as such, parents agreed. The school board was petitioned to stop segregating. It refused. In May 1951, parents entered a lawsuit challenging segregation.

In Topeka, Kansas, black plaintiffs acknowledged material equality of black and white schools, but challenged segregation. And in Wilmington, Delaware, a state court granted parents' request that their children be admitted to a superior white school until both schools were equalized.[17] In Washington, D.C., parents challenged the principle of segregation. All five cases were heard together by the U.S. Supreme Court in 1952–1955. They are known as the *School Segregation* cases.

The NAACP Legal Defense Fund, whose staff Marshall headed, represented the plaintiffs. Robert Carter, an LDF lawyer who handled the Topeka case and now a federal judge in New York, told the Court in 1952: "It is the gravamen of our complaint . . . that . . . we have been deprived of the equal protection of the laws where the statute requires appellants to attend public elementary schools on a segregated basis, because the act of segregation in and of itself denies them equal educational opportunities which the Fourteenth Amendment secures."[18]

When counsel for the defendants demonstrated that various southern states were narrowing the racial gap in per student expenditures, LDF attorneys denied equality would ever be gained by this route. Thus, Spottswood Robinson explained that "even though Virginia could spend $26 millions – an enormous sum by Virginia standards – all that we succeed in doing is moving from a present 61 cents to 79 cents per Negro student for each dollar that is invested in buildings and sites for white students."[19]

In the 1953 hearings, the NAACP submitted a long historical brief designed to show the role of segregated education in creating an official caste system in the United States:

> Controlling economic and political interests in the South were convinced that the Negro's subjugation was essential to their survival, and the Court in *Plessy* v. *Ferguson* had ruled that such subjugation through public authority was sanctioned by the Constitution. . . . Without the sanction of *Plessy* v. *Ferguson*, archaic and provincial notions of racial superiority could not have injured and disfigured an entire region for so long a time.[20]

The rights of the aggrieved children "to learn and grow" and "to be treated as entire citizens of the society into which they have been born" were at stake. In the oral argument, LDF attorney James Nabrit inquired "whether under our Constitution the federal government is authorized to classify Negroes in the District of Columbia as untouchables for the purpose of educating them for living in a democracy."[21]

On May 17, 1954, the Court handed down a unanimous opinion in *Brown* v. *Board of Education of Topeka* (347 U.S. 483). The central contention of the plaintiffs was upheld: "In the field of public education the doctrine of 'separate but equal' has no place. Separate educational facilities are inherently unequal. . . . We hold that the plaintiffs and others similarly situated . . . are, by reason of the segregation complained of, deprived of equal protection of the laws guaranteed by the Fourteenth Amendment."

The court witheld any immediate orders regarding implementation. It announced that it would hold hearings later in the year before deciding upon specific measures of relief.

The *Brown* decision was hailed as initiating a new era in American history. Du Bois wrote: "I have seen the Impossible happen. It did happen on May 17, 1954."[22] Much remained to be done against discrimination in travel, public accommodations, health, and elsewhere. Yet *Brown* was hailed as a "great victory," by black leaders and the black press, although Muse notes: "There was no dancing in the streets. The significance was not quickly grasped by the Negro masses."[23]

As he had done so often in his long life, Du Bois summed up both sides of the black equation of anticipation and fear. In an address delivered in February 1955, he spoke of *Brown*'s possible long-run effect on American democracy. The decision confronted "Negroes with a cruel dilemma."[24] On the one hand, "they want their children educated. That is a must, else they continue in semislavery." On the other hand, "with successfully mixed schools they know what their children must suffer for years from southern white teachers, from white hoodlums who sit beside them and under school authorities from janitors to superintendents who hate and despise them. They know, dear God, how they know." He predicted that most of the best black teachers would lose their jobs "because they will not and cannot teach what many white folks will want taught."[25]

A large cultural price for the end of segregation would have to be paid by blacks. Du Bois wrote: "They must eventually surrender race solidarity and the idea of American Negro culture to the concept of world humanity, above race and nation. This is the price of liberty. This is the cost of oppression."[26]

"Eventually" was a long way off. Du Bois was by no means urging an end to a study of black history and culture. He wrote: "Much teaching of Negro history will leave the [desegregated] school and with it that brave story of Negro resistance. This teaching will be taught more largely in the

home or in the church where, under current Christian custom, segregation by race and class will remain until the last possible moment."[27]
(Seven years earlier in the *Chicago Defender,* Du Bois had predicted that
within another generation every American college and university would
offer a standard course in Negro culture.)

In April 1955, the Supreme Court conducted a five-day hearing on the
implementation of *Brown.* Nearly a year had elapsed since the decision.
The Court had collected numerous suggestions from plaintiffs, defendants, and other interested parties, including attorneys general from each
of the southern states.

The temper of the hearing was curious. Counsel for the plaintiffs was
full of foreboding; the opposition was deferential but defiant. One issue
was paramount: would the Court set a deadline for desegregation? Without a definite date, no specific commitment to action would follow.

Counsel for Clarendon County, South Carolina, warned: "I think if you
ordered the trustees tomorrow to comply or else, that that would destroy
the public school system of South Carolina." In Virginia, warned another
lawyer, "an integrated system of public schools would require more than a
court decree. It would require an evolutionary change in the attitude of
people in Virginia, both Negro and white." The attorney general of Texas
told the Court: "Texas loves its Negro people." His colleague added that
"Texas enjoys harmonious relationships and has made excellent progress
in economic, educational, and social advancement." Counsel for the District of Columbia informed the justices that "we have always had a school
system which largely, though in two halves, was perfectly equal side by
side." In reply to charges the South created and enforced a caste system,
a North Carolina attorney explained: "Race consciousness is not race
prejudice. It is not race hatred. It is not intolerance. It is a deeply ingrained
awareness of a birthright held in trust for posterity."[28]

These protestations of good faith and high moral ground, mixed with
practical reminders of the power dominance of whites in the South, were
expected by the LDF legal staff. What was disturbing was the possibility
that the Court would be impressed by such arguments. In that case, the
Court would effectively negate *Brown* by depending on the good faith of
local authorities, who in matters tinged by race, had historically demonstrated bad faith. *Brown* would, then, remain a vague declaration of
general rights which no specific child could claim as a basis for action. An
order that proclaimed gradualism as an operative principle would necessarily confer constitutional rights on some and withhold them from most
others.

This problem had been anticipated even before the *Brown* proceedings
started. In April 1952, Howard University held a national conference on
"The Courts and Racial Integration in Education," attended by most, if

not all, the LDF attorneys who later argued the *Brown* case before the Supreme Court. At the conference, James M. Nabrit, Jr., stressed that "the Constitution gives the Negro the fundamental right to enjoy *now* all benefits offered by the state, without any limitations based on race."[29] Before the Court, during the first round of hearings late in 1952, the same point was made more than once. Jack Greenberg, an LDF attorney, held "that if constitutional rights are being denied our respondents, they are entitled to those rights as quickly as those rights can be made available." During the 1953 hearings, Thurgood Marshall told the Court that desegregation could be accomplished within a year: "If they don't have staff enough to do these administrative things, the sovereign states can hire more people to do it."

During the 1955 hearings, Marshall spoke extensively on the issue. He warned against allowing the pace of desegregation to be left up to the states, Should this happen, Marshall pointed, out, "then the Negro in this country would be in a horrible shape. He, as a matter of fact, would be as bad, if not worse off than under the 'separate but equal' doctrine for this reason." District court judges would tend to accept school board pleas for more time, and the right to a desegregated education would be nullified. "This is a national Constitution," said Marshall. "There is no place for local option in our Constitution." Various justices continued to speak of the difficulties and complexities of desegregation. To this, Marshall replied, exasperated: "This Court is not dealing with the complexities, this Court is dealing with whether or not race can be used [in school assignments]."

Most of all, the plaintiffs wanted a definite court order installing desegregation in the litigated districts by September 1955. Marshall stated: "If we cannot get that, then we say that the least that would do us any good at all would be a decree which included four items: (1) That this Court make the clearest declaration that not only those statutes but others are in violation of the Fourteenth Amendment. We think it is necessary for that to be put in the decree. (2) That they start immediately to desegregate. (3) File reports. (4) That it must end at a certain day." Justice Frankfurter objected that the Court had to take into account "certain unalterable facts of life that cannot be changed even by this Court"; he referred to administrative problems. Marshall replied that gradual desegregation could never be effective. Further, he expressed shock "at arguments of the impotency of our government to enforce its Constitution." Without a decree that included a time limit, he concluded, "there will be no protection whatsoever for the decision of this Court rendered on May 17."

On the last day of the final hearing, in April 1955, Marshall repeated the plaintiffs' view, adding a charge of racism, although the target of the charge was not clear. "This time limit becomes a part of the effectiveness . . . of the May 17 decision," he told the Court. "But," he continued, "I don't believe any argument has ever been made to this Court to postpone the enforcement of a constitutional right." He then added: "The argument is never made until Negroes are involved."[30] Essentially, only Negroes were being asked to forgo their rights.

The position of the national administration on a deadline was expressed in testimony by Solicitor General Simon E. Sobeloff. He opposed placing any general deadline at all in the final decree. On the other hand, he advocated instructing the district judges to inform school districts they must produce a plan within ninety days; extension could be given if necessary. "The thing ought not to be left hanging in the air indefinitely."[31]

Seven weeks later the Supreme Court decided *Brown II* (349 U.S. 294). The cases were remanded to the respective U.S. District Courts to fashion specific decrees. "At stake," wrote the Court, "is the personal interest of the plaintiffs in admission to public schools as soon as practicable on a nondiscriminatory basis." Defendants, the Court held, will be required to "make a prompt and reasonable start toward full compliance." The district courts were to facilitate the admission of the plaintiffs "to public schools on a racially nondiscriminatory basis with all deliberate speed." The Supreme Court thus failed to set either a general deadline, as plaintiffs' lawyers had urged, or even a flexible deadline for the guidance of district judges.

In the retrospective opinion of at least one LDF lawyer, Robert L. Carter, *Brown II* was "a grave mistake." The clear implication of the deliberate speed formula "was movement toward compliance on terms that the white South could accept." In agreeing to less than immediate enforcement of every child's constitutional right, Carter wrote, "the Warren Court sacrificed individual and immediate vindication of the newly discovered right to desegregated education."[32] Justice Hugo Black said much the same thing some years later. *Brown II* weakened *Brown I* in several respects; it strengthened it in none.

First years of Brown

Scores of black parents responded to *Brown* by drawing up petitions and filing lawsuits to permit their children to enter hitherto white schools. In almost every case, the efforts were repulsed by a broad range of techniques. Black parents in Orangeburg, South Carolina, petitioned the school board in July 1955, to reorganize the schools on a nondiscriminatory basis. The fifty-seven signers were immediately subjected to severe economic pressure, including discharge from jobs and cutting off of credit. Blacks retaliated during the fall and winter with a concerted boycott of white businesses. Black families suffered greatly during the action, but it was ineffective; no change in schools followed. Throughout the South similar tactics greeted entry petitions. During the 1955–1956 school year, many black communities in the Deep South struck back with ineffective boycotts. During the spring of 1955, petitions of black parents in Virginia were rejected by school boards in Newport News, Norfolk, Alexandria, Charlottesville, Arlington County, and Isle of Wight County. In Yazoo City, Mississippi, the NAACP in 1955 petitioned for desegregated schools; fifty-three Negroes had signed. The usual firings occurred; sharecroppers were evicted; grocers refused to sell food to signers. Within several weeks, all signers had withdrawn their names. Parents in Savannah, Georgia, petitioned during 1956, but in vain.

Black parents turned to individual litigation to pry the doors open, just as many had before *Brown*. Neither Congress nor the president offered a helping hand. Since the cost of carrying a single lawsuit to the highest level averaged around $15,000, no ordinary black parent could afford such recourse.[33] Unless a collective means of raising funds were found, resort to the court was a theoretical possibility only. More often than not, federal judges ruled against black parents. Two full years after *Brown II*, not one black child was attending a white school in Alabama, Florida, Georgia, Louisiana, Mississippi, North Carolina, South Carolina, or Virginia. And in 1957 more black children attended all-Negro schools than a year before.

Attempts were made to lighten the financial burden on black parents. In Congress, bills were introduced in 1957 and 1960 including a provision that the Department of Justice could represent the complaining parents. In both cases, the provision was dropped. Southern senators and representatives blocked all efforts to enlist Congress and the executive branch in the school desegregation fight.

Federal court rulings on behalf of desegregation were flouted without penalty in several instances. In 1956, a federal court ordered the school board of Mansfield, Texas, to open the town's white high school to black students. (They were being bused 40 miles daily to a black school in Fort Worth.) White mobs demonstrated and threatened violence against any Negro registrants. Governor Allen Shivers urged the board to turn away the black children; this was done. In a second case that week a federal court ordered two black students admitted to Texarkana Junior College. Violence encouraged by the college president stopped the order from being put into effect. This ended the matter. The following year, federal troops were finally called out by President Eisenhower when Arkansas Governor Orval Faubus interfered with the court-ordered entry of nine Negro students into a Little Rock high school. Peltason summarizes the experience of six years:

Between 1954 and 1960 there were at least twelve incidents in which rioters, sometimes with the tacit encouragement of state and local officials, tried to thwart the execution of a federal court order. Except in Clinton, Hoxie, Nashville, Little Rock, and New Orleans, federal executive authorities refused to intervene, and they did so in these [five] instances only after local officials begged for help.[34]

This quasi abdication of executive responsibility raised a question about the nature of the constitutional right to a desegregated education: was it a right or an opinion?

Southern state legislatures enacted an extraordinary array of laws to further hobble desegregation (Table 12). These included measures to drive the NAACP out of the states, permit schools to be closed if ordered desegregated by courts, repeal compulsory attendance laws to permit white children to absent themselves from segregated schools, help finance private segregated schools, and cut off state aid to desegregated schools. Most effective of all such legislation were the pupil placement laws.

The percentage of black students attending desegregated schools rose extremely slowly. But it did rise. In most cases, this increase was not the result of long-term erosion of segregationist sentiment. It was a planned affair. In 1956 William T. Joyner, North Carolina attorney and vice-chairman of a state committee on strategy to avoid desegregation, recommended what became the legal basis of tokenism:

> I think that some mixing is inevitable and must occur. . . . One of the nightmares which besets me on a restless night is that I am in a federal court attempting to defend a school board in its rejection of a transfer requested by a Negro student, when a showing is made that nowhere in all the state of North Carolina has a single Negro ever been admitted to any one of the more than 2,000 schools attended by white students.[35]

Joyner urged that for tactical reasons a few Negro children should be admitted to white schools. This advice was followed. In 1957, six black children in Greensboro were enrolled in two schools, five in Charlotte, and one in Winston-Salem. That made four schools that were now counted as "desegregated" – and less likely to be cited by a court as segregated.

The precise mechanism of tokenism was the pupil placement law whose purpose "was to make it necessary to bring individual suits in each school district so that no single decision ordering desegregation could be effective against the whole state school system."[36] Without mentioning race, these laws forced individual black children who wished to attend white schools to traverse an obstacle course strewn with application forms, tests, and appeals. Extremely few Negro children completed the journey. Essentially, pupil placement laws permitted children to be assigned to their traditional school initially. In the South, this meant, in effect, assignment by race. The U.S. Commission on Civil Rights in a 1962 staff report called the pupil placement laws "the principal obstacle to desegregation in the South."[37] State and lower federal courts regularly approved the laws. When black parents appealed to courts against the manifest intention of placement authorities to maintain segregation, judges directed them first to exhaust all state administrative remedies. Often, this was enough to discourage any further appeals. Carter observes:

> For eight years after its [1955] implementation decision, the [U.S. Supreme] Court refused to review any case in which questions were raised concerning the validity of pupil placement regulations or the appropriateness of applying the doctrine of exhaustion of administrative remedies to frustrate suits seeking to vindicate the right to a desegregated education.[38]

Only in 1963, in the *McNeese* case, did the U.S. Supreme Court rule that the doctrine need not stand in the way of appeal to federal courts.

After a decade of *Brown*, 90.7 percent of the South's black children still attended all-black schools, 400,000 more than in 1956. Nearly 333,000 black children attended school with white children. Some 3,000 school districts in the South included both black and white children; another 6,000 did not. This meant that on an average about 315 Negro students per school *district* attended a desegregated school. Of course, this figure is purely schematic. Actually, in 1963–1964, 89.2 percent of all black children in desegregated schools in the South lived in the border states. That same year, only 34,110 (1.2 percent) of the nonborder South's 2,894,563 black children attended desegregated schools.

Quality segregated education?

The longer desegregation was staved off, the longer the historical system of black disadvantage endured. When *Brown I* was announced, the inferiority of black schooling in the South was still pronounced. Nothing in *Brown* changed that. Indeed, the U.S. Supreme Court dealt with the inequality of tangible resources by declaring that "separate educational facilities are inherently unequal." Commenting on this, a student of Mississippi schools writes: "The word inherently is almost meaningless in light of the manifest inequality that existed in the racially separate schools of Mississippi" in 1954.[39]

Table 12. *Major legislation against school desegregation in seventeen southern and border states and the District of Columbia*

	Ala.	Ark.	Del.	D.C.[b]	Fla.	Ga.	Ky.
Legislation[a]	X	X			X	X	
Anti-NAACP/barratry	X	X			X	X	
Closure of schools permitted							
Compulsory attendance	X	X			X	X	
amended or repealed					X	X	
Emergency powers to officials							
Freedom of choice—	X	X			X	X	
Segregated/Desegregated			X	X			X
Human rights commissions	X	X			X	X	
Interposition/protest	X	X			X	X	
Legal defense authorized							
Limitations of federal powers proposed	X	X			X	X	
Private schools	X				X	X	
Authorized/encouraged	X	X				X	
property sold/leased to	X	X			X	X	
Pupil assignment							
Racial designations	X						
removed					X		
required	X	X	X		X	X	X
Scholarships out-of-state	X				X		
Segregation by sex	X	[c]			X	X	
Segregation committees	X	X				X	
Sovereignty commissions							
State constitutional provision for public schools removed	X						
Teachers	X				X		
tenure/removal	X	X				X	
protected in private schools							
Tuition grants to schools/students	X	X				X	
Withheld aid to desegregated schools	X	X				X	

[a]The table indicates types of legislation passed, not the number. One bill often included several features; several bills might duplicate each other. Several laws included have been held unconstitutional or been repealed.

[b]D.C. Board of Commissioners.

[c]Appointed without legislation.

Source: Reed Sarratt, *The Ordeal of Desegregation: The First Decade* (New York: Harper & Row, 1966).

In the ten years after 1954, southern school authorities succeeded in retaining segregation, despite *Brown*. And as in the past, segregation continued to function as a means of channeling resources unequally. In the 1960–1961 school year, Arkansas was spending on each black pupil only 77 percent of what it spent on each white pupil. This covered only current expenditures. Of 102 black high schools in the state, only 16 were accorded the same accreditation rating received by the white high schools in the same communities.[40]

Mississippi, while still totally segregated in 1962, saw a great disparity in local moneys that were added to state aid. According to the state superintendent of public instruction, local moneys per black student were only 27 percent of those per white student. It was reported that in 1957 current expenditures per Negro pupil were 86 percent of those per white pupil in Alabama, Arkansas, Florida, Georgia, Mississippi, and South Carolina. More localized inequalities persisted in other states. In Guilford County, North Carolina, the eight predominantly white high schools were accredited; none of the three black ones was. The Baltimore school superintendent stated in 1959 that "in general, our colored schools were not as good as our white schools before 1954 and the differences have not been completely eradicated in five years."[41] Eight black students in Sevier County, Tennessee, were bused 50 miles daily to attend a black high school in Knox County. In 1959, "there was not a single accredited Negro high school in Savannah."[42] In Havana, Arkansas, black high school students in mid-1964 were bused for a round trip of 120 miles to attend a black high school; in Yancey County, North Carolina, black high school students took an 80-mile round trip daily to Asheville.

Officials in a number of southern states spoke extensively of a school-building program for Negro schools. Published data were those issued by school authorities. Apparently no independent audit or check could be made of actual expenditures. Involved, also, was a strong public relations interest by state leaders in demonstrating a genuine concern for high-quality black schools, even though this concern had been a constitutional requirement since 1896.

In the South as a whole, after *Brown*, expenditures on building black schools undoubtedly increased sharply. Yet as journalist Weldon James reported: "Despite the superiority of Negro percentage increases, actual total values reported for 1955–56 and 1956–57 showed that white plant value totals remained greatly superior."[43] In Mississippi, the number of one-room schools was reduced. In 1951, there were 1,409; in 1965, there were only 13. From 1955 to 1970, about half of the allocations by the Mississippi State Educational Finance Commission were designated for black schools. (About half the school children in the state were black.) In Woodville, when a new high school for blacks opened in 1960 to the general admiration of the black community, a young black student reflected:

> As most of them, students, teachers, and principals alike, were bragging about how good the white folks were to give us such a big beautiful school, I was thinking of how dumb we were to accept it. I knew that the only reason the white folks were being so nice was that they were protecting their own schools. Our shiny new school would never be equal to any school of theirs. All we had was a shiny new empty building where they always had the best teachers, more state money, and better equipment. [44]

When this school was built, no Negro children attended school with whites in the entire state.

In many southern states, material inequality continued under segregation or token desegregation, while states spent tax moneys to fight desegregation and finance private white segregated schools. In Virginia, during 1961–1962, public funds amounting to $2,060,859 in tuition grants were transferred to white children who wished to avoid attending a desegregated school. In 1963–1964, Louisiana granted a total of $3,500,000. The transfer of public school property to private schools was authorized by law in seven states and tuition grants in eight states. Segregation was financed by public funds, thereby compelling "the Negro taxpayer to pay for insulting himself."[45]

Unequal achievement

Before 1954, the myth of equal-though-separate was believed by few persons familiar with the facts of southern education. Yet direct evidence of comparative achievement disparities by race was not available. One reason for this is the earlier deliberate failure to gather statistics on Negro learning. In the public schools of the District of Columbia, for example, before 1954 achievement tests were given to white but not Negro children.

Texas, the largest southern state, was not untypical. In 1953–1954, the state's association of school administrators surveyed the quality of Texas education. Based on a study of 80 percent of the state's school children, the academic achievement of white pupils was ranked "very satisfactory"; that of Negro pupils was classed as "unsatisfactory." Governor Allen Shivers said "we still have a long way to go in obtaining separate but equal schools." In 1956, while three out of five white fourth-graders in Dallas were at or above grade level in reading achievement – the pivot of school success – only one of eight Negro children was so classified. In Houston during 1961 white first-graders averaged grade *B*; Negro first-graders averaged *C*. Three years later, 40 percent of the students in Houston's all-Negro Texas Southern University were taking, the school's dean of arts and sciences said, courses to supply them with knowledge they should have learned in high school.[46] An investigator for the U.S. Commission on Civil Rights recalled, in 1964, that eight years earlier the average Negro eighth-grader in Houston had lagged behind the average white eighth-grader nearly a year and a half in spelling and three and a third years in reading (paragraph meaning). He did not report later data.[47]

During the 1956–1957 school year, the Educational Testing Service studied academic achievement of Atlanta children. Among fourth-graders, half the Negroes but only one-tenth the whites were two or more grades below the national median on reading achievement; nor was the situation essentially unlike this in Georgia as a whole.[48] In 1959, as noted above, Baltimore school superintendent John Fischer acknowledged that "our colored schools were not as good as our white schools before 1954." In 1956, eighth-graders in Dade County (Miami) took an arthmetic achievement test. On the average, white children scored above the national norm; Negro children were two years below the norm. District of Columbia Negro sixth-graders, in a series of achievement tests given during September 1955 to June 1956, lagged consistently behind white children in, among others, arithmetic (six months) and paragraph meaning (one and one-fifth years). In Louisville, Negro sixth-graders lagged one and one-half years behind white sixth-graders.[49]

In Tennessee, the usual pattern held. Negro sixth-graders in Nashville were more than two years behind white children. Knoxville superintendent Thomas N. Johnson reported that Negro children were almost one and one-half years behind white children.[50] In Memphis, Negro eighth-graders lagged two years and two months behind whites in achievement. A study for the U.S. Commission on Civil Rights commented that the state's educators frequently complained that Negro students lagged, on the average, from one and one-half to two grade levels.[51]

The conclusion reached in 1962 by a similar study covering Virginia could apply more or less to the other southern states: "Negro education in Negro schools is not equal to the education provided whites, either in tangible aspects or, more importantly, in intangibles. Officially. very little is being done to improve the quality of this education. At present the educational opportunity of white and Negro children in the state is not [even] comparable."[52]

During the years 1954–1964, southern educators in desegregated schools responded to achievement differentials by initiating or expanding ability grouping and tracking systems. This was the case in the District of Columbia, Saint Louis, Baltimore, and Wilmington, Delaware.[53] When the tracking plan was first introduced for District of Columbia tenth-graders in 1956, the 1,118 white and 2,822 black children were distributed as follows:[54]

College preparatory course
315 (86.7 percent) of whites
50 (13.7 percent) of blacks
Terminal course
685 (30.7 percent) of whites
1,453 (69.3 percent) of blacks
Basic course
158 (10.7 percent) of whites
1,319 (89.3 percent) of blacks

The college preparatory track was virtually all white; the basic track was overwhelmingly black. Little was tried to narrow the achievement gap, and less was accomplished. Before desegregation, the offering of special classes, including provisions for "slow learners," was common in the white schools of the District of Columbia, "but the Negro side of the school system had relatively few because of the lack of funds allocated for the purpose." School authorities claimed that tracking was a means of improving student performance by moving to higher tracks. Seven years after initiation of tracking, 96.9 percent of junior high school students in the District of Columbia were still in the track they had occupied two years earlier.[55]

The movement in the South
In 1956, the Alabama legislature outlawed the NAACP; for the next eight years the legal fight against the law raged. One week after the law was passed, black citizens in Birmingham formed the Alabama Christian Movement for Human Rights. Its primary value was defensive. In 1957, Rev. Fred L. Shuttlesworth attempted to enroll his children in all-white Phillips High School:

> A mob of people armed with chains, brass knuckles, pipes and knives set upon us. . . . Mrs. Shuttlesworth was stabbed in the hip, Ruby Fredericks, our second daughter, had her foot hurt in a car door by one of the men and I was beaten with a chain and brass knuckles, knocked several times to the ground, had most of the skin scrubbed off my face and ears, and was kicked in my face and side as members of the mob really set out to kill me.[56]

The experience was repeated often throughout the South. In rural Alamance County, North Carolina, where no schools were desegregated, Negro mothers were asked how they would react to conflict over desegregation. Responses were more frankly militant to black questioners than to white. These mothers, a scholar concluded, projected "a new image of the Negro, one that permits him to see himself as an equal . . . to those in white society."[57]

The glacial pace of southern desegregation from 1955 to 1960 or so engendered deep disappointment among older blacks. Among Negro youth, disillusionment with the courts led many to seek more direct and effective approaches. In February 1960, four students from North Carolina Agricultural and Technical College for Negroes in Greensboro took it in their minds to sit at the lunch counter of a white store and wait to be served. Within the next few days, thousands of students in the South repeated this nonviolent form of protest. Even when attacked by white mobs and police, the protesters did not strike back. This public defiance promised much because it meant that the powerless need not remain weak. It highlighted as nothing before the potential of nonviolent protest. Two months after the first sit-in, Dr. Martin Luther King's Southern Christian Leadership Conference sponsored a national meeting of sit-in leaders. Out of the meeting came the Student Nonviolent Coordinating Committee (SNCC). College and high school students became the prime movers of new currents of energy in the South.

The focus of work now was voting rights. Immense efforts were invested in voter registration campaigns during 1961–1965. In Mississippi, black student leader Robert Moses explained SNCC's decision to depend on youth:

> In general, anybody who had a specific economic tie-in with the white community could not be counted on when the pressure got hot. Therefore, our feeling was that the only way to run this campaign was to begin to build a group of young people who would not be responsible economically to any sector of the white community and who would be able to act as free agents.[58]

Student workers were beaten and jailed, but usually bounced right back.

In Americus, Georgia, "as elsewhere, the demonstrators were almost entirely high school students." A number served up to 46 days in jail in one stretch for registration activity. In Chapel Hill, North Carolina, in an early action during 1963 "almost all of them [were] Negro young people." From 1960 forward in the same city it was "the high school students from the Negro community [who] revolted first." In south Florida black communities, it was reported by a student worker:

> We were able to get the principals of all the [black] schools in these areas to send memorandums to the parents, make daily announcements about the location of the [registration] books in the community, and also instruct the leaders of the student organizations to help in the distribution of leaflets, canvassing, and

office work. About 50 of each student body participated in one way or another.[59]

Student school transportation routes became ideal avenues of information in the black communities: "In Southwest Georgia, an elaborate grapevine for announcing meetings, news, and the like was set up on the school buses that went to all the reaches of the counties."

At least as often, black principals did all they could to prevent political activity by black students. In 1961, students at Burglund High School in Macomb, Mississippi, sat in at the Woolworth's store. The principal excluded two of them from registration for the next school year. In protest, 128 students walked out. They were offered the chance to return if they signed a pledge to abstain from further civil rights work. Some 80 refused to do so; it was reported that they were encouraged by their parents. SNCC opened Nonviolent High School in Macomb to accommodate the nonsigners: "We carried on our classes for a week or two weeks, until finally we got word from Campbell College in Jackson that they would accept them all."[60] In Lanier High School in Jackson, when black students spent the lunch hour in the schoolyard, singing freedom songs, and refused to return after the bell sounded, the principal called police: "When the cops came, they brought the dogs. The students refused to go back. . . . Mothers who lived near the school . . . joined the students in fighting off the dogs."[61]

In Canton, some student canvassers were unable to go back to school because they lacked school clothes. Since many parents had been fired from jobs because of their children's activity, they were too poor to afford any new clothes.

Despite the violence and the jailing, voter-registration work was showing important results. Between 1962 and 1964, black registration in eleven southern states grew from 1,476,000 to 2,146,200 or by nearly one-half. This equaled the growth of registration in the preceding decade.[62] While, of course, it was adult Negroes who became voters, the young were the cajolers and organizers. One black college rights worker reflected in 1964: "When I listened to the older Negroes sing, I knew that it was the idea of heaven that kept them going. To them heaven would end their troubles. But listening to the teenagers, I got an entirely different feeling. They felt that the power to change things was in themselves."[63] In fact, however, the spirit of the young was increasingly shared by the old.

Around 1960, young blacks in the South turned away from the courtroom and toward electoral activity and large-scale nonviolent demonstration. One assumption of their work was that they could count on the federal government for protection, if not encouragement. They soon learned otherwise. Both Republican and Democratic federal administrations failed to enforce the *Brown* decision. Yet by 1963, mass pressures from the South, supplemented by movements in the North, gathered national force. For the first time since Reconstruction, a coordinated civil rights legislative approach was undertaken.

Segregation in the North, 1950–1963

Black children in the North attended systematically inferior and segregated schools. In 1952, Bond estimated that about a fourth of black school children in northern elementary schools and about half in high school were "physically integrated." Five years earlier, Reddick, writing of the North as a whole, had estimated that "of all school-going Negroes in this area, one-fourth of them attend schools thoroughly mixed, another two-fourths . . . attend schools as distinctly separate as in the South."[64] The school boards were even more segregated. Bond reported in 1952 that he knew of only six Negro members of school boards in the North and West.[65]

School segregation grew during the 1950s. Official explanations usually described the development as a response to residential segregation. Yet numerous evidences of deliberate segregation existed. In Detroit, a school board member testified to the practice of altering school boundaries as the racial composition of the attendance area changed; in this way, black and white children were strictly separated. In Philadelphia, the fact of increasing segregation was clear, although its genesis was not obvious. Between 1956 and 1963, the percentage of black children in heavily black (80 percent or more) schools rose from 72 percent to 85 percent. In New York City, between 1955 and 1965, the number of black and Puerto Rican segregated schools rose from 52 to 201. By 1960, the city's private schools enrolled over a third of all white elementary school children but only a twelfth of all nonwhite pupils.[66]

The academic inferiority of black schooling in the North was documented by studies in various cities. In Philadelphia, schools were divided into Group A (70 percent or more white) and Group B (70 percent or more Negro). With reference to a reading test, 92 percent of Group A but only 30 percent of Group B children performed at or above the median grade level (sixth grade).[67] During the 1961–1962 school year, all high school students in Saint Louis were distributed among three tracks according to achievement, with Track I the highest achievement group. In the all-Negro or predominantly Negro high schools, 16 percent of the students were in Track I, 53 percent in Track II, and 31 percent in Track III. In the white high schools the respective percentages were 40, 55, and 5.[68]

In Oak Park, Michigan, white fourth-graders given a series of achievement tests scored up to a year over grade level; Negro fourth-graders scored from six months to a year below grade level.[69]

In Berkeley, California, the predominantly Negro Burbank Junior High School demonstrated a sharp inferiority in learning achievement. In 1963, for example, median percentile scores for eighth-graders in Burbank were: reading, 16; writing, 19; arithmetic, 17. For all eighth-grade students in Berkeley the scores were: reading, 88; writing, 89; arithmetic, 90.[70] In October 1963, sixth-graders in fourteen Berkeley elementary schools took various achievement tests. Students in the four most heavily Negro schools (61.8 to 96.8 percent Negro) scored 1.3 grades below level; students in the most heavily white schools (98.3 to 99.5 percent white) scored 1.5 grades above level. In nearby Oakland, Negro elementary school students scored about half the achievement level of white students in reading and mathematics.[71]

In Portland, Oregon, Negro children consistently learned less than white children. An official committee observed that "the results of the educational process are poor in schools which are predominantly Negro."[72]

In Bridgeport, Connecticut, reading achievement scores of Negro and Puerto Rican pupils in Grades 6 to 8 lagged nearly a full year behind grade level and more than a year behind the mean scores of children in white schools.[73]

In New York City, Negro and Puerto Rican children were behind mainland whites in reading achievement. What is worse, between 1955 and 1962 the gap widened (Table 13). In nearly all-Negro Central Harlem, 30 percent of the third-graders and 81 percent of the sixth-graders were below grade level in reading comprehension. In the third grade, Central Harlem students lagged a year behind the achievement of New York City pupils; in the eighth grade, the lag lengthened to two and a half years.[74]

In Chicago, Negro children achieved less even when matched by socioeconomic status with white children. Sixth-grade Negro students were from one to two full grade levels behind in "word knowledge." A tutoring organization reported of two large Chicago high schools, one all-Negro and the other predominantly Negro: "At Du Sable . . . 82.5 per cent of the September, 1963, entering class read below grade level. More than two-thirds of the entering students at Hyde Park High School are enrolled in remedial classes due to reading and math deficiencies."[75] In an all-Negro upper-grade center (seventh and eighth grades) near these two high schools, the June 1963 graduating class was at a median reading level of only fifth grade.[76] In Boston, Negro second-graders fell nearly half a year behind in reading; sixth-graders were almost a full year behind.[77]

The *Brown I* decision made no specific reference to schools in the North. Yet the separation and the deprivation of northern black education were evident to many observers.

In a number of northern cities protests and boycotts against segregation in the schools began in the months and years after *Brown.*

Table 13. *Reading achievement of black and Puerto Rican children and of white children, New York City, 1955 and 1962*

	1955			1962		
School grade	Black and Puerto Rican children [a]	White children [b]	Lag	Black and Puerto Rican children	White children	Lag
3	2.5 [c]	3.7	1.2	2.9	4.4	1.5
6	4.7	6.9	2.2	4.8	7.9	3.1
8	6.0	8.4	2.4	6.1	9.6	3.5

[a] Children in schools with 90 percent Negro and Puerto Rican students.
[b] Children in schools with 90 percent white students.
[c] Grade year level.

Source: Calculated from data in *A Study of the Problems of Integration in New York City Public Schools Since 1955* (New York: Urban League of Greater New York, September 1963), p. 9.

Less than a month after *Brown I* was decided, the Intergroup Committee on New York's Public Schools, an interracial group, called for an investigation of the schools. Psychologist Kenneth B. Clark, president of the group, charged that inferior education in the elementary schools ensured that black children "cannot compete with other children in high schools."[78] Other civic organizations joined in the pressure, and within months thoroughly documented studies of the extent of segregation and inadequate education were completed. In 1955, Rev. Milton A. Galamison, a black minister from Brooklyn, led a number of campaigns by black parents against gerrymandering for segregation. The parents objected to sending their children to overcrowded schools while nearby white schools had empty seats. (This was a widespread practice in urban centers, North and South.[79]) Success came in the form of a busing program. A thousand or more children attended previously white schools. Parents were circumvented in the next several years by school board construction policies, which far overbalanced any such small move toward desegregation. Between 1957 and 1959, of thirty-three new schools built, nine were all white in enrollment and ten all black. In 1958, a small group of black parents in Harlem withdrew their children from what they regarded as inferior schools and created their own freedom school. The use of the school strike as a protest technique was unprecedented in New York City.

By 1960, the slow pace of progress and the failure of older civil rights groups in the city to mount effective campaigns led Rev. Galamison to create the Parents Workshop for Equality. One of his first proposals was for a citywide boycott of schools against segregation. The action failed to materialize, but the school board was shocked into granting a modest open enrollment program. It allowed limited numbers of black and Puerto Rican children to attend schools outside black areas. Many administrators were extremely hostile to open enrollment and actively interfered with the optimum operation of the plan:

> Every imaginable obstacle was put in the path of the mother who wished to transfer her child. The home school principal warned and threatened her with dire consequences to her child; she was not given the list of receiving schools more than twenty-four hours before she had to choose one; no information about them was made available; the schools offered were many miles away; the buses were late and slow; the receiving school was ill-prepared and the children met with hostility from both teachers and the receiving community.[80]

Rogers states that open enrollment and related programs "were subverted in their implementation by the professional staff." Aaron Brown, a black member of the school board during these years, agrees.[81]

Between 1960 and 1964, blacks in New York City built a strong movement for integration; support in the Puerto Rican community grew, and considerable numbers of whites joined in. Nevertheless, few concrete advances were won. The peak of protest was attained in 1963–1965 in the form of several school boycotts. In February 1964, nearly 500,000 students stayed away from school; the following month, more than 350,000 repeated the action on behalf of integration. In the second action Malcolm X joined the line of march. Antiintegration sentiment became more open; indeed, an antidesegregation boycott occurred in the city in September 1964. When the school board still refused to take any effective action, another boycott was called. This time, the target was "600" schools, which enrolled so-called problem children. The boycott extended over some weeks, but proved fruitless.

In Chicago a large-scale movement of blacks against pervasive school segregation began around 1960.[82] In 1965–1966, 90 percent of black elementary school students attended schools that were 90 to 100 percent black.[83] (Corresponding percentages in Detroit, Indianapolis, and Newark were 72.3, 70.5, and 51.3.) The U.S. Commission on Civil Rights staff in 1963 commented that "the tenacity with which Chicago confined its Negro pupils to neighborhood schools, and refused to rezone attendance areas on the fringes of the concentrated Negro residential areas or to relax its no-transfer-from-zone-of-residence rules is well known."[84] Double shifts, whose demise had been announced by the school board in 1948, continued to be assigned disproportionately to black children.[85]

Mobile classrooms were employed to keep Negro children in over-crowded schools from being transferred to underutilized classrooms in white schools. Liberally assigned to black schools, few mobile classrooms were used in white schools. Blacks were almost totally excluded from apprenticeship programs in the labor-sponsored Washburne Trade School. [86]

Blacks in Chicago organized on a citywide basis before developing campaigns around conditions in single schools (as had been the case in New York City). In 1962 an effective coalition of black and white groups, the Coordinating Council of Community Organizations (CCCO), was formed. Under its guidance, schools became the principal focus of the civil rights movement in Chicago. On October 25, 1963, a CCCO call for a boycott of schools met with an overwhelming response when 224,000 children stayed out, almost all the black children in the schools. Continued school board reluctance to discuss demands for desegregation brought on a second boycott on February 25, 1964; 172,000 students participated, a decline in participation principally caused by the relative defection of middle-class blacks. Opposition to the second boycott came especially from the Democratic party, the metropolitan press, the NAACP, and the Urban League, which refused to support the action. Lower-class blacks apparently held firm.

Few concrete results within the schools could be traced to the boycotts. The general civil rights activities in Chicago, which gained statewide publicity, influenced events in the state at large. The Armstrong Bill, requiring school districts to revise attendance boundary lines to reduce segregation, defeated twice before, passed in 1963. Two years later, it became the prototype for the Massachusetts Racial Imbalance Law.

In Boston, the direct action movement began in 1962 and centered on the issue of jobs for Negroes. After six months, it broadened to include school desegregation. When school authorities refused any concession whatever, leaders prepared what would be the first large-city school boycott – in Boston it was called Stay-Out for Freedom. On June 18, 1963, some 3,000 students did, indeed, stay out. They attended well-planned freedom schools, where black leader Noel Day explained, they received what "was lacking in the public schools – that is: education that was relevant to the needs of the children, treated them with dignity, involved their interests, and challenged their capabilities." The stay-out was repeated on February 26, 1964; some 10,000 students participated this time.

In Cleveland, on April 20, 1964, more than 75,000 students boycotted. Nearly 20,000 children boycotted in Gary, Indiana. In Chester, Pennsylvania, police used extraordinary violence to put down prolonged demonstrations on behalf of desegregation during March and April 1964. A series of boycotts or demonstrations on behalf of desegregation occurred in New York state – in Mount Vernon, Buffalo, Amityville, Albany, Utica, and Newburgh.[87]

The Civil Rights Bill

Early in June 1963, President Kennedy told a West Coast audience: "We must recognize that segregation in education – and I mean de facto segregation in the North as well as the proclaimed segregation in the South – brings with it serious handicaps to a large population."

In a matter of days, several alternative bills were introduced into Congress, each vying to become the civil rights act. Had it not been for extraordinary political activity of Negroes in various parts of the country, the stage of national legislation would not have been attained.

On June 19, 1963, President Kennedy sent to Congress HR 7152, the administration civil rights bill. On July 2, 1964, President Johnson signed it into law. From the viewpoint of achieving equal educational opportunities, the Civil Rights Act of 1964 skirted the main problems and evaded especially the task of integrating urban schools.

Proponents of school integration might, for all practical purposes, not have existed; Congress felt, or at least responded to, no such influence. The organized civil rights groups demoted school integration to a secondary position; the political forces were only too glad to cooperate.

The original administration bill had provided:

1. The U.S. Commissioner of Education was directed to conduct a national survey of the denial of equal educational opportunities because of race, color, religion, or national origin in public schools at all levels.
2. In cases where local school boards requested it, the commissioner was to provide technical assistance to help put into effect desegregation plans or to deal with problems arising from "racial imbalance." (This last term refers to school segregation arising out of residential segregation.)
3. The commissioner could grant funds to colleges to set up special workshops for teachers and others who had to deal with desegregation and racial imbalance problems.
4. The commissioner could grant funds directly to school boards, upon application, to help them deal with desegregation and racial imbalance.
5. The attorney general could file class or individual suits on behalf of persons who were being deprived of equal protection of the law by a school board refusing to carry out desegregation. This section made no mention of "racial imbalance."
6. No federal funds could go to state programs that were being administered so as to deny any person benefits because of race, color, religion, or national origin.

The bill would set up procedures to deal with problems of previously segregated Negro children whose academic achievement was sharply lower than that of the favored white children. Teachers would be brought together to study the best techniques and methods. Several provisions gave the initiative to the school board, not the government. Nothing in the original bill directed or even empowered the government to order a local school board to desegregate or to rectify a racial imbalance. School boards were not directed to desegregate or to rectify racial imbalance. The status quo persisted. The bill contained nothing to suggest that intervention by the attorney general in civil rights cases, which had been sparing, would now become more meaningful on school matters. The financial approach in the bill left much to be desired. No money was to be supplied to educate children, especially the children who had been deprived of an equal education.

The educational provisions of HR 7152 were not expected to draw much party opposition. Senate minority leader Everett M. Dirksen had conferred with President Kennedy on the bill and met with representatives of the Department of Justice, Ted Sorenson – President Kennedy's close adviser – and Senators Mike Mansfield and Hubert Humphrey, the Senate majority leader and his assistant. Senator Dirksen recalled later that "for myself I could accept all except title II, dealing with [public] accommodations and facilities." Administration supporters and the minority leader thus endorsed the school provisions.

In the Senate Judiciary Commiteee northerners outnumbered southerners eleven to four, but Senator Sam J. Ervin of North Carolina took the offensive on school matters without being joined in debate by any of the northern senators. Ervin protested that the bill supported the "racially imbalanced school theory," which, he said, "contemplates that school children are to be denied the right to attend public schools in their own neighborhood and transported vast distances in buses to public schools in other communities, if such action is necessary to mix the schools in other communities racially."[88] Senator Ervin implied that the bill gave the federal government power to initiate such moves. This was not the fact.

> *Senator Ervin*: Is it your position that the powers conferred upon the Attorney General to bring about school desegregation cases include the power to bring school desegregation cases to achieve desegregation in what may be called imbalanced schools?

> *Attorney General Kennedy*: No; I do not think we have that authority.

Senator Ervin pursued the matter at a later session:

> *Senator Ervin*: And when the school board says to a child, "You cannot attend your neighborhood school because we are going to

put you in a bus and transport you to schools in other communities in order that those schools may have the right proportion of students of your race," I say they are violating the interpretation placed upon the 14th Amendment in the *Brown* case. They are denying those children the right to attend their neighborhood schools because of their race.

Attorney General Kennedy: I think that if that is the only factor that is present, Senator, I would agree with you.

Attorney General Kennedy seemed to mean that if pupils were shifted simply to change racial ratios, this went beyond a proper interpretation of desegregation.

The Senate committee's hearings were inconclusive. But they did highlight the main object of attack by segregationists – the racial imbalance idea.

In the first phase of the House hearings, two Republican Congressmen – Representatives William E. Miller of New York and William C. Cramer of Florida – renewed the attack on "racial imbalance." Attorney General Kennedy denied that achieving racial balance was an administration objective.

In the Senate hearings, Mr. Kennedy had informed Senator Ervin that federal government officials were being sought out frequently by local school officials for informal advice on desegregation. Because the problem was spreading, a more formal procedure was needed.

Secretary Celebrezze, a former mayor of Cleveland, in his testimony was no mere theorist. "Basically," he told the House committee, "racial imbalance in any community comes because of school district lines."[89] Officials could draw lines and in the drawing manage to separate pupils by race. "Would federal funds be cut off to a school board that created racial imbalance?" Representative Cramer asked. "If," answered Secretary Celebrezze, "we come to the conclusion after due investigation, after due hearings, that they are using [attendance] district boundaries as a device to promote segregation, and we have the law or the authority, which we probably don't have now, then we would have a right to cut off funds." Racial imbalance was not the same as segregation, several Congressmen argued; imbalance resulted from residential patterns, segregation from deliberate legal action. Chairman Emanuel Celler suggested to Secretary Celebrezze:

> *Mr. Celler*: Some criteria might be added to this bill that would not only help you in your determination as to whether or not there was discrimination, or whether or not racial imbalance is the discrimination referred to in Title VI [dealing with cutoff of federal funds]. It would also be a governing force, a restraint upon a Secretary of Health, Education and Welfare to prevent him

from acting capriciously and arbitrarily. Now we have often put these standards in bills of this character. You would not object to that, would you?

Mr. Celebrezze: I would not object, but I would object in making it mandatory.

Mr. Celler: Certainly we would not want to put such a bridle on you to make it impossible for you to act.

Clearly in the offing was some kind of amendment to define racial balance.

When hearings resumed, Representative Cramer brought up racial balance once more. Chairman Celler stated to him: "You may quarrel with it, but I think it is essential to have that language." Unexpected criticism came from two quarters. Witness Joseph Rauh of Americans for Democratic Action said he was "somewhat surprised by the phrase. I am not certain what it adds to the word 'desegregation'. . . . I am just not clear what racial imbalance is." Sidney Zagri, legislative counsel for the Teamsters Union, said: "If racial imbalance refers to an imbalance created by segregated neighborhoods then I suggest that the way to proceed with that problem is to provide for legislation to desegregate housing." (Seven weeks before, officials of six New Jersey Teamster locals in Passaic, Bergen, and Hudson counties pioneered in demonstrating union support for integrationists' demands for racial balance in the schools of Englewood, New Jersey.)

When public hearings ended in August, the school provisions of HR 7152 were unscathed except for the racial balance matter and the new power of the attorney general to file suits on behalf of desegregation. By October the subcommittee released a substitute for HR 7152 that dropped all references to racial imbalance.

Representative William M. McCulloch of Ohio, ranking Republican on the full committee and subcommittee, later explained his own opposition: "The committee failed to extend this assistance to problems frequently referred to as 'racial imbalance,' as no adequate definition of this concept was put forward. The committee also felt that this could lead to the forcible disruption of neighborhood patterns, might entail inordinate financial and human cost and create more friction than it could possibly resolve." Internal evidence also suggests that chairman Celler did not oppose the change.

No public hearings were held on the subcommittee substitute, but Attorney General Kennedy testified in executive session (later released for publication), addressing himself to the omission of racial balance:

It is not clear from the bill in its present form that the Commissioner [of Education] may offer assistance to local agencies seeking to deal with the variety of special educational problems which arise as a result of the often divergent educational backgrounds and experiences of pupils attending integrated schools.

For example, a prior lack of availability of equal educational opportunities to Negroes will sometimes create curricular, grading, classroom, and other difficulties in racially integrated schools serving children of varied scholastic backgrounds. Such problems exist wholly apart from whether such schools were ever previously segregated or whether, if they were, desegregation is pursuant to court order or a juridically approved plan.

Thus, it would be helpful if the bill would make it clear that assistance may be given with respect to such problems.

The attorney general was seeking to put meat on the bones of equal educational opportunity. Without the phrase about racial balance, such efforts might be ineligible for federal aid.

Before any action could be taken, a substitute for the bill was prepared by some Judiciary Committee members in the closest consultation, apparently, with the Department of Justice. According to Representative William T. Cahill of New Jersey, "Robert Kennedy and the gentleman from Indiana, Charlie Halleck, deserve[d] the major portion of the credit" for the bill.

The substitute omitted any reference to racial balance and narrowed the grounds upon which the federal government could cut off funds to localities. It dropped all reference to "insurance, guaranty, or otherwise" from the original HR 7152 language, permitting a cutoff in any federal financial aid concerning a "grant, contract, loan, insurance, guaranty, or otherwise." This exclusion effectively shielded all housing and other construction programs benefiting from federal mortgage insurance or guarantee. Although federal insurance and guarantee programs had little application to educational facilities, federal grants were made through the U.S. Office of Education to colleges for agriculture and mechanical arts, cooperative vocational education, school construction and survey, maintenance and operation of schools, library services, defense educational activities, and training in the teaching of foreign language. Finally, the new substitute bill dropped authorization for the attorney general to enter an ongoing desegregation case, restricting him to initiation of cases.

In parliamentary maneuvering the first substitute recommended earlier by the subcommittee was voted down. Representative Celler then offered the new substitute, ruling that neither debate nor amendments nor questions would be permitted. In a roll call vote, the motion passed and was then reported to the House for adoption.

The newest version of HR 7152 represented a weakening of the original bill's educational provisions. Omission of racial balance indicated a high degree of agreement between the administration and prominent Republicans. The original bill had virtually no fair employment provision worth the name. But in the much improved subcommittee substitute and in the bill as it reached the floor of the House, all employees of a state or a local government were excluded, including teachers and related personnel.

Representative Celler's analysis of the bill said: "There can be no longer any doubt whatsoever that the right to be free from racial discrimination in public education is a real and present right protected by the Constitution of the United States."[90] Nevertheless, this right did not include racial balance. "There is no authorization for either the Attorney General or the Commissioner of Education to work toward achieving racial balance in given schools. Such matters, like appointment of teachers and all other internal and administrative matters, are entirely in the hands of the local [school] boards. This bill does not change that situation."[91]

Representative John V. Lindsay of New York City, who favored the bill, emphasized: "This legislation . . . does not . . . force acceptance of people in schools, jobs, housing or accommodations because they are Negro. It does not impose quotas or any special privileges of seniority or acceptance. There is nothing whatever in this bill about racial balance." Representative Watson of South Carolina was unmoved. "I understand from the press reports that it is a matter of the forced mixing in the school, perhaps trying to bring in the racial balance system which is foreign to education." Representative McCulloch rose to say: "Again, I wish to make it unmistakably clear that the legislation now before the Committee has no effect and can have no effect on racial imbalance, as that term is known."[92]

Representative Roberts of Alabama attacked the power of the attorney general to file suits on behalf of desegregation, predicting that the commissioner of education would use his power to set standards for federal aid in such a way as "to promote race mixing and to relieve 'racial imbalance.'"[93] He asked: "And what about a county in Idaho which has no Negroes? Should not we gather up some colored families with little colored children and send them to Idaho?" Representative Roberts was unaware that three months earlier Fred T. Haley, industrialist and president of the school board of Tacoma, Washington – if not Idaho – had told a meeting of the city's teachers: "Indeed, were not six percent of Tacoma's school children Negro, we should seek to import that useful handful to help us bring the pressing realization of a world grown suddenly small [where the white is in the minority] to our young, before they grow up to face that shattering but palpable fact."[94]

On February 6, the fifth day of debate, Representative Cramer rose to offer an amendment. To the section of the bill already defining desegregation as "the assignment of students to public schools and within such

schools without regard to their race, color, religion, or national origin,"
Mr. Cramer moved to add:

> But desegregation shall not mean the assignment of students to
> public schools in order to overcome racial imbalance. . . . The
> purpose is to prevent any semblance of congressional acceptance
> or approval of the concept of "de facto" segregation or to include
> in the definition of "desegregation" any balancing of school at-
> tendance by moving students across school district lines to level
> off percentages where one race outweighs another.[95]

Representative Celler, floor manager of the bill, announced that "the
amendment offered by the gentleman from Florida is acceptable." The
Cramer amendment was incorporated into the bill without any recorded
vote, and no representative spoke against it. It is nearly impossible to
resist the surmise that the handling of the amendment had been arranged
beforehand. The House passed HR 7152 with the Cramer amendment
intact 290 to 130, with 11 members not voting. (On the floor of the House,
the committee's bill was amended to add safeguards against arbitrary
action by an official in any effort to cut off federal funds because of discrimination.)

The original administration bill failed to order the speeding up of school
desegregation. At best, it aimed only to repair some of the damage caused
Negro children by generations of school segregation, North and South.
But the House refused to allow even this. So-called de facto segregation,
characteristic of cities everywhere in the United States, was systematically excluded from the House bill. By all odds the most powerful provision of the House bill – Title VI, barring the discriminatory use of certain
federal funds – hardly created a stir during the floor debate. Yet, as
Orfield notes, "Title VI gave the government a tool to change the central
public institutions of the southern caste system."[96] Inclusion of it was a
tribute to the doggedness of black Representative Adam Clayton Powell
of Harlem, who never tired of pushing for such a measure during the
1950s.

The administration first agreed to drop the words "racial balance."
With acceptance of the Cramer amendment went the possibility of doing
anything about segregation related to residence. During Senate debate
later on, Senator John Sparkman of Alabama asserted of the Cramer
amendment: "The administration did not ask for that provision." It is
equally clear that the administration did not resist it, either. A very broad
coalition of representatives rallied behind the amendment. Neither party,
section, nor ideological lines divided the coalition. Northerners and
southerners, Republicans and Democrats, Fair Dealers and otherwise,
were united.

Ordinarily, the bill would have been referred to the Senate Judiciary

Committee for hearings. To avoid subjecting the bill to Mississippi's Senator James O. Eastland, committee chairman, the bill's managers preferred to send it directly to the floor of the Senate. A southern filibuster began, to be ended by a cloture vote three months later.

A strategic aim of the southerners was to perpetuate the outdated idea that Negroes were segregated residentially only in the North. So successful were they that northern senators were placed on the defensive throughout the quarter year of filibuster.

Take, for example, the Cramer amendment. This proviso was never referred to by the name of its sponsor. The myth was created that the House amendment had been introduced by a northerner to protect his section's ghettos from desegregation through racial balancing. Senator Ervin created the myth: "When the bill was before the House, the advocates of the bill amended it so as to specify that the bill should not require the implementation of the racially imbalanced school theory. . . . They did so in order to pacify parents in northern cities when de facto segregation exists as a result of residential patterns."[97] Representative Cramer was from Florida. The census of 1960 had found that "Florida and Texas . . . were more urbanized than . . . Ohio, Michigan, and Pennsylvania."[98] Cities like Miami and Houston were even more segregated residentially than Chicago and New York. The Cramer Amendment was thus as much a southern as a northern device. (Also, Senator Ervin notwithstanding, Representative Cramer was not an advocate of HR 7152; he was one of its strongest critics in committee and on the floor of the House.)

Sometimes, differing and inaccurate versions of the myth were given by the same person. On one occasion Senator Sparkman stated: "Actually the amendment was written into the bill on the floor of the House. It was offered by none other than . . . Congressman Celler. . . . Mr. Celler said at the time that he was induced to do it because of the many protests that had arisen." The accuracy of the first sentence is supported by the documentary record. But the second sentence is contradicted by the same record. Representative Cramer had introduced the amendment and Representative Celler immediately accepted it, without calling for a vote. As for the third sentence, the official edition of the *Congressional Record* contains no such statement by Representative Celler. It is, of course, possible that he made the statement elsewhere.

The budding myth was better served by an indefiniteness of sponsorship and an inscrutability of motive. No northern senator rose to inquire what effect the Cramer Amendment would have on, say, Birmingham and Montgomery, both in Senator Sparkman's state and both highly segregated.

Northern defensiveness expressed itself in other ways: busing, for example. Senator Russell Long of Louisiana declared about New York

City that "an attempt is being made to transport white children from one community 50 miles, if need be, so as to obtain 50 percent racial mixture, and to transport colored children 50 miles in another direction, so as to bring the races together."[99] Senator Long was joined by numerous southern colleagues in similar charges. The practice of busing students to rectify racial imbalance was branded as unjust to children and irrelevant to educational goals. Senator Long's remark about New York City was extremely wide of the mark. No children were transported anywhere near 50 miles. A number of Puerto Rican and Negro children were transported, at school board expense, for various purposes including racial balance. In September 1964, some few non-Puerto Rican white children were bused, but for short trips averaging about fifteen or so minutes. Nor did a "50 percent racial mixture" requirement or goal exist in New York. This figure referred to a request by State Educational Commissioner James E. Allen, Jr., to all the state's school boards to report the racial composition of schools; he had noted in the letter directing the survey that *for purposes of the survey only* he would consider any school racially imbalanced that had over 50 percent Negroes enrolled.[100]

No northern senator took the floor to document the extensive ongoing southern practice of compulsory busing for racial segregation. Busing had long been a prime technique of enforcing segregation in the schools of South Carolina. As the state's senior senator, Olin D. Johnston, reported: "In South Carolina, all pupils, white and colored, are transported by buses from their homes to their schools."[101] "Their" schools were, of course, racially determined. In New Orleans, "buses were [being] used primarily to maintain racial segregation."[102]

The single forthright northern statement in defense of busing to achieve integration was made by Senator Jacob Javits of New York.

> *Senator Talmadge*: Does the Senator favor compulsory transfer of children to achieve an appropriate racial balance?
>
> *Senator Javits*: The Senator from New York said he would favor some limited amount of transportation and assignments, in aid of the so-called Princeton Plan.
>
> *Senator Talmadge*: Is that compulsory or noncompulsory?
>
> *Senator Javits*: It is no more and no less compulsory than the law requiring children to attend school at a central district, where a bus picks them up or where parents can transport them. If the parents keep them home, they are violating our laws by preventing the children from going to school. So if the Princeton Plan is compulsory, it is no more and no less compulsory than school attendance and fixing a place of attendance at a certain point in

accordance with the needs of the children. I see nothing wrong or abusive in that.[103]

The Princeton Plan is a technique of desegregating two nearby schools by placing the lower grades in one school and the upper grades in the other. A single enlarged attendance district is created for both schools; all children in the district attend the school in which their grade is located. Another name of this technique is "pairing."

Still another aspect of northern defensiveness was the reluctance to acknowledge the presence of segregation in the North. Senator Allen J. Ellender of Louisiana seemed to specialize in twitting the northerners on this: "The North has been just as effective in promoting segregation as the South. The only difference is that southern segregation has been open and above board. It has been honest, while in the North it has been swept under the rug."[104] Somewhat later on, Senators Ellender and Javits touched on the matter:

> *Senator Ellender*: And I might further say that segregation is segregation, whether de facto or de jure.

> *Senator Javits*: Nothing could be further from the fact.[105]

When Senator Paul H. Douglas attacked the slow pace of southern school segregation, he was answered with a counterattack on northern segregation. Northern segregation patterns, Senator Douglas declared, "are brought about, not by law, but by choice, with some degree of pressure from the whites, it is true." Was there not an element of hypocrisy in the northerners' complaint against southern segregation? "When the charge of hypocrisy is made," stated Senator Douglas, "it is true only to a relatively small degree."

Senator Javits denied the very existence of de facto segregation: "The newspapers . . . speak of something called 'de facto segregation in New York.' That is a complete misrepresentation under the law because there is no segregation in law in New York."[106] In New York's public schools, he claimed, there was not a single all-Negro school; in only 9 percent – or, he stated at another time, 19 percent – of the schools could racial imbalance be said to exist. Nor could the city's parochial school system be called segregated; while all the students in it were of one faith, there were Negro as well as white Catholics. What was happening in southern schools could in no meaningful sense be equated with racial imbalance in New York City. Javits described what he regarded as the fundamental difference between the two processes:

> In the South – where the social order is segregation and where there is constant opposition to desegregation of the public schools, and where that development is proceeding at a snail's

pace under court order, as compared with . . . New York, where the whole climate and the people are in favor of correcting racial imbalance in schools and in housing patterns which underlie the imbalance in the schools.[107]

The existence of school segregation in New York City was, in fact, thoroughly documented. On May 12, 1964, the official state Allen Report called for "the earliest possible elimination of *de facto* school segregation in New York City." The Allen Report described as segregated any school enrolling more than 90 percent Negro and Puerto Rican students or more than 90 percent white students. This was the same definition used a decade before by the Public Education Association study of the city's school segregation. After evaluating all the desegregation steps taken during 1954–1964, the Allen Report declared:

> We must conclude that nothing undertaken by the New York City board of education since 1954, and nothing proposed since 1963, has contributed or will contribute in any meaningful degree to desegregating the public schools of the city. Each past effort, each current plan, and each projected proposal is either not aimed at reducing segregation or is developed in too limited a fashion to stimulate even slight progress toward desegregation.[108]

Senator Javits had cited the absence of all-Negro schools. It is more significant to speak, as the Allen Report does, in terms of a 90 percent Negro and Puerto Rican school. Under that measure, nearly one-quarter of the city's elementary schools were Negro-segregated. Six months before issuance of the Allen Report, the Urban League of Greater New York reported that nearly 200 elementary schools enrolled 80 percent or more Negro and Puerto Rican students.[109] Contrary to Senator Javits's statement, the Urban League study showed that 235 elementary schools and 55 junior high schools were imbalanced according to State Commissioner Allen's provisional measure of 50 percent Negro and Puerto Rican. By any known measure, the schools of New York City were more segregated than ten or five years earlier.

Segregation in parochial and private schools has been little studied. Fewer than 10 percent of the city's parochial and private school students are Negroes, the Allen report said. As a whole these schools are far more segregated than the public schools.[110] Nationally, the private school movement was beginning to stir on the matter of segregation.[111]

Northern defensiveness reached a peak when Senator Javits conceded erroneously: "It is a fact that in the South, residential patterns differ from the way they apparently have developed in a city like New York."[112] The passion to see a difference where none existed was in the largest measure due to a lack of knowledge. But it also derived from a psychological need to perpetuate the traditional distinctions between North and South. This way, the "northern" position could benefit from moral superiority. If, however, the "South" is disappearing, so, in all logic, must the "North." Senator Wayne Morse stated one aspect of the case with his usual directness: "I ask Senators to name a state – any state – and I will declare that in that state there is a substantial body of public opinion opposed to delivering the Constitution to the Negroes of America."[113]

The lack of ghettos in the South, held Senator Richard Russell, is "particularly true in the small communities."

> *Senator Russell*: The Senator from Alabama well knows that particularly in the rural communities and the small towns, the two races–
>
> *Senator Sparkman*: Live in the same general neighborhood.
>
> *Senator Russell*: In the same general neighborhood.[114]

Senators Russell, Sparkman, and Johnston, separately or together, contended that (1) most southern Negroes live in the countryside and (2) no residential segregation exists in smaller cities and the countryside. Neither contention can be supported by current information. Nor does history lend any support.

In 1940, about half of all southern Negroes lived on farms; in 1950, about one-third; in 1960, less than one-sixth. Between 1950 and 1960 alone, the number fell from 3.1 million to 1.5 million. During the same decade, the number of Negroes living in small and large southern cities rose from 7.2 million to 10.0 million. Much of the latter growth reflected a migration of rural Negroes to cities of less than 50,000 population. The movement of Negroes into southern small cities was, on such a scale, unprecedented. The Taeubers, studying the period 1940–1960, found that both large and small southern cities had high – and rising – rates of residential segregation.[115]

Once cloture was assured, the bill's managers sped up their work. A quartet of ranking senators – Dirksen, Kuchel, Mansfield, and Humphrey – altered the House version of HR 7152. The resulting substitute bill further weakened efforts toward school integration. It passed virtually without change from the floor.

Most important was another obstacle laid in the way of remedying racial imbalance. The House version had forbidden the commissioner of education to grant funds to help solve problems arising out of racial imbalance. During Senate floor debate, however, Senator Dirksen had wondered whether the attorney general could not do what the commissioner of education was forbidden to do. He pointed to a part of the House bill that empowered the attorney general to file suit to "materially further the public policy of the United States favoring the orderly achievement of desegregation in public education." If the attorney general was thus armed with a broad declaration of public policy favoring desegregation, might not a court grant his request for ordering racial balance?

The possibility was foreclosed by two sections of the quartet's new substitute bill. The words "public policy of the United States favoring" were omitted. Further, a new restrictive clause was added:

> Nothing herein shall empower any official or court of the United States to issue any order seeking to achieve a racial balance in any school by requiring the transportation of pupils or students from one school to another or one school district to another in order to achieve such racial balance, or otherwise enlarge the existing power of the court to insure compliance with constitutional standards.

Senator Leverett Saltonstall summed up its intent: "The whole purpose of the substitute amendment is to see that the courts will not be given by this law any more power on the question of busing and the question of racial imbalance than they have at the present time."[116] The evidence is strong that the managers of the substitute bill intended far more than that. They permitted the legislating of residential segregation and the neighborhood school into the Civil Rights Act.

In 1963, U.S. District Judge Beamer ruled in the Gary, Indiana, case, *Bell* v. *School City of Gary*, that a school board has no constitutional obligation to desegregate schools if it was not responsible for creating the existing racial imbalance. The decision was upheld by an appeals court; the U.S. Supreme Court refused to grant a review. Judge Beamer held that "requiring certain students to leave their neighborhood and friends and be transferred to another school miles away, while other students, similarly situated, remained in the neighborhood school, simply for the purpose of balancing the races in the various schools would in my opinion be indeed a violation of the equal protection clause of the Fourteenth Amendment." The mere fact of separation laid no constitutional obligation on a school board. "Racial balance in our public schools," the court ruled, "is not constitutionally mandated."[117] The *Bell* doctrine rested on a 1955 decision in South Carolina, *Briggs* v. *Elliott*. There the court decided: "The Constitution . . . does not require integration. It merely forbids discrimination. It does not forbid such segregation as occurs as the result of voluntary action."[118] Apparently, in the absence of an explicit statute or policy requiring segregation, a school board did not need to move a finger to remedy the segregation that seemed to be the purely fortuitous result of housing segregation. Despite extensive evidence that northern school boards were often active participants in creating "fortuitous" segregation, the *Briggs* and *Bell* doctrines became for some years the reigning judicial interpretation.

On the floor of the Senate, Senator Humphrey told his colleagues how he and Senators Dirksen, Kuchel, and Mansfield had written the new section: "As to racial balancing, Judge Beamer's opinion in the Gary case is significant in this connection. In discussing this case, as we [four] did many times, it was decided to write the thrust of the court's opinion into the proposed substitute." The neighborhood school system, Senator Humphrey noted, was proper as long as it remained bona fide, that is, not designed to enforce segregation. Were a school board so to misuse the neighborhood school system, he continued, the attorney general could intervene "for the purpose of preventing denial of equal protection of the laws."[119] (This last ground was part of the Fourteenth Amendment and existed independently of the Civil Rights Bill.)

Yet Judge Beamer had regarded as unconstitutional even a racial balance plan that was voluntarily adopted by a school board. The Dirksen-Kuchel-Mansfield-Humphrey substitute bill prohibited any federal court from using the soon-to-be-passed Civil Rights Act to achieve the same result. Thus, the substitute bill ruled out any federal means whatever to desegregate schools in most racially imbalanced urban centers.

Another new clause in the bill read: "Nothing in the title shall prohibit classification and assignment [of students] for reasons other than race, color, religion, or national origin." This denied once more that racial balance could be even one of many reasons for shifting students. It may well be described as a nondesegregation clause. One cannot very well diminish racial segregation without taking race into account.

Unlike the House, the Senate excluded from coverage all employees of a state or subdivision. Thereby all public school teachers were denied federal protection of their employment. The Senate went further and explicitly also exempted "an educational institution with respect to the employment of individuals to perform work connected with the educational activities of such institutions." Neither clause was debated.

The original Civil Rights Bill, introduced in June 1963, contained nothing about racial discrimination in apprenticeship. Subcommittee Number 5 had inserted such a provision in its short-lived substitute. The full House Judiciary Committee retained this feature, as did the House itself when it approved HR 7152. In the Senate, however, the Dirksen-Kuchel-Mansfield-Humphrey substitute embraced, in addition, the craft union position. An amendment was inserted – and adopted without floor debate – that forbade federal action to compel what the U.S. Department of Labor had proposed in vain a year before. The main effect of this action was to keep the skilled trades as white as ever. Public schools that made tax-supported facilities available to racially restricted apprenticeship classes were thus given – if they sought it – another reason to continue subsidizing segregation. (Contrarily, another part of the bill authorized a cutoff of federal funds to any state that used the funds in a racially discriminatory way.)

The Senate substitute contained a number of other less significant, if not unimportant, changes. The pettiest was a bar on allowances for dependents of teachers who attended workshops financed by the Office of Education to learn how better to meet the problems of desegregation. The other changes dealt with suits to enforce desegregation to be filed by the attorney general and the matter of cutoff of federal funds.

The bill now stipulated that the attorney general must believe the case meritorious before proceeding to sue a school board. Before filing any suit, the attorney general was required to notify the school board in question about the complaint and give it an undefined "reasonable time to adjust the conditions alleged in the complaint." Another change gave the attorney general the right to file suit on behalf of a person whose personal safety would be jeopardized if he filed it. (Omitted was a House stipulation that the attorney general could sue a board upon the board's failure to achieve desegregation; the reason for this change is somewhat unclear, given the rest of the bill.)

Agencies were directed to issue rules interpreting the application of cutoff of federal funds. Findings of an investigation were required to be made part of a written record. And any termination of federal aid, ordered after a due investigation, could affect only the specific aid program investigated.

On June 19, 1964, the Senate passed the substitute bill. It was sent to conference, where it was adopted without change. On July 2, 1964, President Johnson signed it.

The Civil Rights Act of 1964 contained eleven titles:

> Title I. Strengthened the federal role in prevention of racial discrimination in voting.
> Title II. Outlawed racial discrimination in public accommodations in interstate commerce.
> Title III. Gave the U.S. Attorney General the right to sue to desegregate public facilities. ˙
> Title IV. Empowered the U.S. Commissioner of Education to help school districts to desegregate and the Attorney General to institute lawsuits to force desegregation of schools or colleges.
> Title V. Enlarged the powers of the U.S. Commission on Civil Rights to conduct inquiries.
> Title VI. Forbade the racially discriminatory use of federal funds in any federally assisted program.

Title VII. Created the Equal Employment Opportunity Commission to outlaw job discrimination because of race, color, religion, sex, or national origin.

Title VIII. Directed the U.S. Department of Commerce to supply the Commission on Civil Rights with current statistics on registration and voting.

Title IX. Regulated the authority of the Attorney General in prosecuting certain cases involving equal protection of the laws.

Title X. Created the Community Relations Service to help resolve community disputes based on race, color, or national origin.

Title XI. Made a series of miscellaneous provisions.

For the first time in American history, Congress had debated problems of school segregation and discrimination and emerged with a powerful commitment to end both. Title VI pledged the power of the purse to the purpose of equal educational opportunity. TItle IV placed the legal resources of the federal government in the service of the same purpose. Under the combined force of both titles, the pace of desegregation in the South was bound to accelerate.

Yet the act was not self-executing. The course of congressional debate showed the hesitation, doubt, and confusion that pervaded the ranks even of supporters of the measure. The seeds of future trouble were there – the fear of racial balance, the issue of busing, once used to enforce segregation and now dreaded as a tool to enforce desegregation.

The pace of desegregation

During the years 1965–1969, black children and adults participated in an extraordinary number of demonstrative actions on behalf of desegregation. Table 14 lists only some of these; undoubtedly, many more occurred. In the South, blacks were always the organizing and sole participating parties. In the North, blacks led actions that were often interracial. The actions were local, but their collective impact was significant. With passage of the Voting Rights Act in 1965, growing black electoral strength in the South added further stimulus to local desegregation. Numerous black parents gained for the first time an overall understanding of the fate of black education in the local school system. More were emboldened to demand remedial action and to leave less in the hands of school staff and school board. By the mid-1960s, schools complained less frequently about the apathy of the black parents.

Negro parents who had attended desegregated schools preferred their own children to do the same. In one local community after another, blacks expressed a dominant opinion in favor of desegregation. National public opinion polls showed solid black support for desegregation. Negroes had

Table 14. *Organized local desegregation actions, 1965–1969*

Place	Form of action
Atlantic City, N.J.	Picketing of school board
Austin, Tex.	Demonstration
Benton Harbor, Mich.	NAACP helps defeat bond issue
Bogalusa, La.	School boycott
Boston, Mass.	Sit-in at school
Bridgeport, Conn.	Demonstration
Buffalo, N.Y.	Demonstration
Charlotte, N.C.	Demonstration
Chicago, Ill.	School boycott
Cordele, Ga.	Demonstration by students
Crawfordville, Ga.	Demonstration
Darby, Pa.	Picketing of school
Detroit, Mich.	School boycott
District of Columbia	School boycott
Englewood, N.J.	Unauthorized group registration at white school, parent demonstrations
Evanston, Ill.	NAACP threat to help defeat bond issue
Fayette, Miss.	Boycott of stores
Fulton County, Ga.	Boycott
Gainesville, Fla.	Boycott
Gary, Ind.	School boycott
Grenada, Miss.	Demonstration, school boycott
Hillsborough, N.C.	Boycott
Houston, Tex.	School boycott
Huntsville, Tex.	Demonstration
Jacksonville, Fla.	Picketing of school board, school boycott
Laverne, Ala.	School boycott
Lexington, Ky.	Demonstration
Lincolnton, Ga.	School boycott
Lorman, Miss.	Demonstration by students
Maywood, Ill.	Demonstration
Memphis, Tenn.	Boycott and demonstrations
Menlo Park, Cal.	Picketing of school
Milwaukee, Wis.	School boycott, picketing of construction site, picket line
Natchez, Miss.	Boycott of stores, citywide school boycott
New York, N.Y.	School boycott
Niagara Falls, N.Y.	Boycott
Oakland, Cal.	School boycott
Peoria, Ill.	Sit-in at school board office
Philadelphia, Pa.	Picketing of school
Phoenix-South Holland, Ill.	School boycott
Pittsburgh, Pa.	Picketing of school board

Table 14. *(cont.)*

Place	Form of action
Port Gibson, Miss.	Boycott of stores
Providence, R.I.	Demonstration
Riverside, Cal.	School boycott
Rochester, N.Y.	Boycott and demonstrations
Saint Paul, Minn.	Picketing of school board
Seattle, Wash.	School boycott
Springfield, Mass.	Sit-in at school board office
Swan Quarter, N.C.	Boycott
Sylvester, Ga.	Demonstration
Teaneck, N.J.	School board elections
Tipton County, Tenn.	Demonstration
Toledo, Ohio	Boycott of school
Trenton, N.J.	Demonstration on behalf of Chester movement for integration
Tuscaloosa, Ala.	School boycott
Wadesboro, N.C.	School boycott
Washington, Ga.	Demonstration
Waycross, Ga.	Boycott
West Palm Beach, Fla.	Demonstration
Woodville, Miss.	Demonstration

Source: Meyer Weinberg, *Desegregation Research: An Appraisal*, 2nd ed. (Bloomington, Ind.: Phi Delta Kappa, 1970), pp. 334–336. This listing is based on reports in *Integrated Education*, 1965–1969.

far less attachment than whites to the concept of the neighborhood school because in so many cases that school was a poor one. A sharp difference existed between black and white opinion, although during the sixties white opinion became more affirmative about desegregation.

The Civil Rights Act brought a great deal more desegregation in its first four years than *Brown* had produced in the preceding fourteen (Table 15). Nevertheless, the burden for desegregation still did not lie where *Brown II* lodged it – on the school board. Individual parents still needed to initiate legal action.

During 1964–1969, when two federal agencies – the Department of Health, Education, and Welfare (HEW) and the Department of Justice – were in charge of desegregation, Justice Department lawyers filed a decreasing number of desegregation suits and stayed away almost entirely from enforcement in large southern and border cities. Under Title IV of the Civil Rights Act, the attorney general did file some cases.

Table 15. *Percentage of Negro students attending desegregated schools in seven southern states, 1963–1964 and 1968–1969*

State	1963–1964	1968–1969
Alabama	0.007	7.4
Georgia	0.052	14.2
Louisiana	0.602	8.8
Mississippi	0.000	7.1
North Carolina	0.537	27.8
South Carolina	0.003	14.9
Virginia	1.630	25.7

Source: U.S. Commission on Civil Rights, *Federal Enforcement of School Desegregation* (Washington, D.C.: The Commission, September 11, 1969), p. 31.

Early in 1965, HEW had issued a set of desegregation guidelines explaining the precise implementation procedures for Title VI, vague in many critical respects, but far more detailed than the text of *Brown II*. Southern congressmen kept up an unrelenting battle, using budget and political threats, to attempt a watering down of the guidelines. While the administration held fast at first, by mid-1966, pressures from North and South mounted. Severe weakening of administrative enforcement became evident during 1967 and 1968.

HEW exercised no effective supervision over court-ordered desegregation. In 130 southern school districts enrolling some 3 million children, federal aid was approved perfunctorily by HEW without investigation. The number of HEW personnel working on desegregation dropped from 75 in 1965 to 34 in 1969. The potential enforcement effect of Title VI of the Civil Rights Act was voluntarily relinquished by the federal government.

Within the administration in general, civil rights seemed to be a major programmatic concern. In February 1965, President Johnson created the President's Council on Equal Opportunity with Vice-President Humphrey as chairman. Its assignment was to invigorate and coordinate civil rights enforcement in all federal agencies. Apparently, the council's work was satisfactory. Suddenly, however, in September 1965, the council was abolished by presidential order: "Mr. Humphrey was called to the White House and told about the impending order which was already approved."[120] In succeeding years, HEW developed "the most effective Title VI operation of any Government agency." Early in 1969, the ranking civil rights executive in HEW wrote to a representative of the incoming Nixon administration: "The other Departments and Agencies [must] cease shirking their responsibility to enforce civil rights laws and executive orders. . . . With the exception of litigation initiated or joined by the Department of Justice, there has been virtually no enforcement of civil rights provisions by any other [agency] of Government."[121] A general lassitude of civil rights enforcement existed by the beginning of 1969.

During the first Nixon administration, 1969–1972, these negative trends in the executive and legislative branches accelerated. Nevertheless, desegregation in the schools prospered. The federal courts had resumed a leadership role.

Desegregation had been unable to proceed while the burden of desegregation rested on parents rather than school boards. After *Brown II*, individual litigants were required to undertake lawsuits to admit their children. The southern pupil placement laws were succeeded during the late 1950s and early 1960s by "free-choice" desegregation plans, which were regularly accepted by federal courts and HEW. If space were available in a school a student selected, he could attend, regardless of race. If no space were available, the student would be reassigned to the school he was then attending. School authorities often declared a white school "overcrowded." Intimidation of black children was common.

Then, in 1966 and 1967, in the *Jefferson County* case, the U.S. Court of Appeals for the Fifth Circuit held that school "boards and officials . . . have the affirmative duty under the Fourteenth Amendment to bring about an integrated, unitary school system in which there are no Negro schools and no white schools – just schools." The court explicitly reversed its earlier acceptance of the doctrine in *Briggs* v. *Elliott* that a school board need only offer Negro children a chance to desegregate but not do anything more if segregation persisted. The court held: "Freedom of choice is not a goal in itself. It is a means to an end. A school child has no inalienable right to choose his school." This pointed in the direction of a pragmatic test – freedom of choice is acceptable of it helps achieve a larger end – desegregation.

In 1968, a unanimous U.S. Supreme Court went further. In *Green*, repeating its injunction that the time for "deliberate speed" had run out, the Court held that "the burden on a school board today is to come forward with a [desegregation] plan that promises realistically to work, and promises realistically to work *now*." School boards must produce plans that promise "meaningful and immediate progress toward disestablishing state-imposed segregation." The Court referred explicitly to "the affirmative duty to take whatever steps might be necessary to convert to a unitary system in which racial discrimination would be eliminated root and branch." In the first years after *Brown II*, acknowledged the Court, the emphasis was "on obtaining for those Negro children courageous enough to break with tradition a place in the 'white' schools." Now, however, the time had come to "convert promptly to a system without a 'white' school and a 'Negro' school, but just schools."[122]

The next year, the Supreme Court ruled in *Alexander* that "continued operation of segregated schools under a standard of allowing 'all deliberate speed' for desegregation is no longer constitutionally permissible." The Mississippi school districts involved were directed to operate "now and hereafter only unitary schools."[123] The decision was handed down on October 29, 1969; nine days later, the Fifth Circuit ordered school districts to desegregate no later than December 31, 1969. At the time *Alexander* was decided, nearly nine out of ten black children in the state attended all-black schools. With implementation of *Alexander* in 1970, the proportion plummeted to one out of ten.

A landmark case, *Swann*, decided by the Supreme Court in 1971, rivaled *Brown* itself in importance in one respect. For the first time, the Supreme Court dealt with the implications of residential segregation for school desegregation. Nearly twenty years earlier, during a strategy conference among plaintiffs' counsel in the *Brown* litigation, Robert C. Weaver had warned that "as long as we do not do anything about residential segregation, we are something like the Australian who was given a new boomerang and . . . spent the rest of his life throwing the old one away."[124] *Brown II* did not take residential segregation into account. In fact, the Supreme Court in *Brown II* advised district courts that they might consider problems arising from "revision of school districts and attendance areas into compact units to achieve a system of determining admission to the public schools on a nonracial basis." Clearly, given segregated housing, the more compact the school attendance area, the greater the racial concentration in that school. *Brown I* and *II* were thus compatible with growing segregation of schools whose geographical attendance areas separated the races.

In *Swann*, the Court observed that since 1954 the achievement of desegregation "had been rendered more difficult by changes . . . in the structure and patterns of communities, the growth of student population, movement of families, and other changes, some of which had marked impact on school planning, sometimes neutralizing or negating remedial action before it was fully implemented." A more direct reference to residential segregation came further on: "People gravitate toward school facilities, just as schools are located in response to the needs of the people. The location of schools may thus influence the patterns of residential development of a metropolitan area and have important impact on composition of inner city neighborhoods." The building of schools in segregated areas, continued the Court, "may well promote segregated residential patterns which, when combined with 'neighborhood zoning,' further lock the school system into the mold of separation of the races."[125]

In the Charlotte-Mecklenburg school district, children of different races were concentrated in various parts of the district. To insist on compact attendance areas would guarantee segregated schools. Therefore, concluded the Court, it is permissible to have attendance areas that "are neither compact nor contiguous; indeed, they may be on opposite ends of the city." In a school district marked by past discrimination, an effective remedy for segregation might well "be administratively awkward, inconvenient and even bizarre in some situations and may impose burdens on some." As for mandatory transportation to effect a necessary desegregation plan, the Court stressed that assignment to the nearest school would not dismantle the dual system, given residential patterns. As a result, "desegregation plans cannot be limited to the walk-in school."

Table 16. *Negro pupils attending public elementary and secondary schools, 1968, 1970, 1972*

Area[a]	Total pupils	Negro pupils	Negro pupils in 0–49.9% minority schools		Negro pupils in 80–100% minority schools		Negro pupils in 100% minority schools	
			No.	%	No.	%	No.	%
Continental U.S.								
1968	43,353,568	6,282,173	1,467,291	23.4	4,274,462	68.0	2,493,398	39.7
1970	44,910,403	6,712,789	2,225,277	33.1	3,314,629	49.4	942,801	14.0
1972	44,646,625	6,796,238	2,465,377	36.3	3,072,581	45.2	759,758	11.2
North and West (32 states)								
1968	28,579,766	2,703,056	746,030	27.6	1,550,440	57.4	332,408	12.3
1970	30,131,132	3,188,231	880,279	27.6	1,805,382	56.6	373,030	11.7
1972	29,916,241	3,250,806	919,393	28.3	1,818,782	55.9	355,148	10.9
South (11 states)								
1968	11,043,485	2,942,960	540,697	18.4	2,317,850	78.8	2,000,486	68.0
1970	11,054,403	2,883,891	1,161,027	40.3	1,112,792	38.6	415,190	14.4
1972	10,987,680	2,894,603	1,339,140	46.3	864,564	29.9	250,860	8.7
Border (6 states) and D.C.								
1968	3,730,317	636,157	180,569	28.4	406,171	63.8	160,505	25.2
1970	3,724,867	640,667	183,956	28.7	396,455	61.9	154,581	24.1
1972	3,742,703	650,828	206,844	31.8	389,235	59.8	153,749	23.6

[a]Districts with fewer than 300 students are not included; no figures for Hawaii are available.

Source: Public release by U.S. Department of Health, Education, and Welfare, Office for Civil Rights, January 14, 1971; unpublished compilation by OCR, "Fall, 1972, Racial and Ethnic Enrollment in Public Elementary and Secondary Schools."

Together, *Green, Alexander,* and *Swann* enabled desegregation in the South to become a practical reality rather than an abstract constitutional right. In 1956–1957, 96.1 percent of black students in the seventeen southern and border states plus the District of Columbia attended all-black schools; in 1968–1969, the figure had become 56.3 percent; and in 1970–1971, 19.0 percent. Table 16 shows the sharp changes that occurred between 1968 and 1970. By the latter year, North and South were about equally desegregated. The South had more black children in majority-white schools; it also had more than the North in all-black schools.

Southern segregation was changing. Yet as Bennett wrote in 1971: "The black victims of the southern system are being forced to bear the cost of changing the system."[126] The cost was most palpable in the form of personal intimidation of black students, reduced financial support of mainly black schools, segregation by classroom inside perfunctorily desegregated schools, and discharge of black school personnel.

Black principals were discharged or demoted in large numbers (Table 17).[127] Black teachers lost their jobs, especially in rural areas where teachers might need to work with large numbers of white children (Table 18). Black students often suffered insult and violence in desegregated schools; still, by and large they supported efforts to make desegregation work.[128]

Desegregation came nearly overnight in Mississippi, seemingly precluding continuation of the traditional practice of shortchanging black students for the benefit of whites. Yet as recently as 1962, school districts spent four times more local funds on each white student than on each black student, and in 1967–1968, in sixty-eight of seventy-two school districts, more was spent on each white than on each black student.[129]

Table 17. *Changes in reported number of black and white principals between 1968 and 1970*

State	Number of school districts reporting, 1968 and 1970	Number of black principals			Number of white principals		
		1968	1970	Change	1968	1970	Change
Florida	49	211	154	−57	1,026	1,082	+56
Georgia	123	342	276	−66	894	969	+75
Louisiana	49	366	298	−68	741	781	+40
Mississippi	74	199	158	−41	332	288	−44
Total	295	1.118	886	−232	2,993	3,120	+127

Source: U.S. Court of Appeals for the Fifth Circuit No. 30,338, *U.S.* v. *State of Georgia, Brief Amicus Curiae for the National Education Association,* March 8, 1971, p. 39.

Table 18. *Reporting districts where ratio of black to white teachers declined, 1968–1970 and 1969–1970*

	Number of districts reporting 1968–1970	Number decreasing 1968–1970	Percent decreasing 1968–1970	Number of districts reporting 1969–1970	Number decreasing 1969–1970	Percent decreasing 1969–1970
Alabama	72	56	78	64	38	59
Florida	55	39	71	53	36	68
Georgia	143	108	74	128	86	67
Louisiana	55	34	62	59	44	75
Mississippi	92	52	57	98	52	53
Total	417	289	69	402	256	64

Source: U.S. Court of Appeals for the Fifth Circuit No. 30,338, *U.S.* v. *State of Georgia, Brief Amicus Curiae for the National Education Association*, March 8, 1971, p. 19.

New techniques were employed. When schools in a heavily black district were desegregated and white children were enrolled in private schools, school tax rates were cut. In many such places, black students continued to attend the old black school while the former white school was boarded up.

White civic and school officials employed a broad repertoire of evasions of constitutional obligations. During a six-month period during 1970–1971, nearly 2,000 separate complaints about failures to permit legally ordered desegregation to proceed were reported to federal authorities (Table 19). Twice during 1970 the National Education Association sent experienced observers into Louisiana and Mississippi to study desegregation.[130] "What is happening . . . is not *integration*; rather it is *disintegration* – the near-total disintegration of black authority in every area of the system of public education," their report concluded. Yet "for black citizens, and their white supporters, to concede defeat would be to collaborate in that defeat." Further discouragement came from observing the operations of the Emergency School Assistance Program (ESAP). Many boards of education in the South who were operating their schools in flagrant violation of the statute's provisions received federal funds.[131]

Desegregation itself was socially defined in the South as blacks entering white schools; whites were never assigned to black schools. Implicit was the evaluation of white as superior. Typically, when desegregation was effected, the black school was closed and its students entered the white school bereft of any evidences of status and position in student affairs. Federal courts and administrative officials regularly accepted such desegregation.

Table 19. *Instances of noncompliance and interference with desegregation,*
August 15, 1970 to February 15, 1971

Complaint or activity	Number of incidents reported
Noncompliance	
Segregated classes	107
Segregated busing	113
Segregated extracurricular activities	94
Lack of desegregation	37
Teacher firings, demotions, contract violations	419
Transfer of public school property to private academies	48
Attendance zone violations (inter- intradistrict transfers)	145
Discriminatory practices in schools	267
Violations of HEW-ESAP[a] guidelines	148
Total	1,378
Interference	
Sit-ins	29
Boycotts	121
Threats	82
Violence – school	105
Violence – community	59
Tensions	205
Total	601

[a] Emergency School Assistance Program.

Source: U.S. Department of Justice, Community Relations Service, *Activities Relating to the Desegregation of Public Schools: August 15, 1970–February 15, 1971* (Washington, D.C.: GPO, 1972), p. 9.

In 1968, black people in rural Swan Quarter, Hyde County, North Carolina, suddenly rebelled against a school board desegregation plan, approved by HEW, that would close down two black elementary schools and absorb their students in a single white school.[132] Black parents called for a plan to retain all three schools but send white children to the black schools as well as blacks to the white school. When the school board refused, parents conducted a year-long boycott. Mr. and Mrs. Chanlain Hardy – he a field hand and she a domestic – said: "Our whole lives were tied up in the [black] school. We did without to help the school. Everybody gave what they could spare in support of our school, and now they want to close them down."[133] The movement held firm despite tear gas attacks on protesters and the punitive reduction of welfare checks by the amount of student allowances for families whose children were boycotting. According to leaders, a basic issue was the failure of the school board to consult with the black community before deciding upon a plan. They stressed support for desegregation, but only if the burdens were equitably shared.

A share in the power to decide, equality of sacrifice, and mutual respect were at the heart of the Swan Quarter movement. They were also, in fact, the prime elements of currents of black thinking throughout the South. Swan Quarter symbolized a fundamental attack on three facets of the system of white supremacy. That system never brooked community decision making by any but whites. The idea of equality of sacrifice assumed an equality of status incompatible with white supremacy. The call for mutual respect was less resisted than uncomprehended by dominant whites. Hyde County was mostly black, as was its school district. Yet all five members of the school board were white. Such disproportion was at the very center of the problem of black education in the South. In other parts of the South, the disproportion overwhelmed black people.[134] Unexpectedly, however, in places like Mississippi, the traditional structure of power was challenged frontally (Table 20).

When, in 1970, Mississippi schools were comprehensively desegregated and white students were assigned to predominantly black schools, some white parents sent their children to private white schools; some did not. Munford found that the degree of "white flight" was unrelated to any "tipping point" of an individual school. White flight was slight in some predominantly black schools.[135] Closely interrelated were white flight and the blackness of a school district, not of a single school. In general, according to Munford, the blacker the district, the greater the white flight.

It was not control of a school but political control of the community as a whole that concerned white citizens. In majority-white school districts, the system of white supremacy would not be seriously bent by classroom desegregation. In twelve such districts studied, the percent of white flight ranged from 6 to 41. In fifteen majority-black districts, however, the range was from 22 to 100 percent.

Whites suspected that the activity of black and civil rights groups was designed for larger political ends. Perhaps, observed Munford, this surmise was quite correct: "All the districts with the worst white flight (and largest black population) had black elected officials in 1970." Whites fled a view of the future they could hardly grasp. "Whites hated and feared domination by the long-subservient black majority."

Both in Swan Quarter, North Carolina, and in Mississippi the struggle for equal educational opportunity pointed up the political nature of the challenge. The tendency of the southern desegregation movement was

Table 20. *Groups working for desegregation in Mississippi school districts*

Group	Number of school superintendents who identified group as present in district
Civil rights groups	
National Association for the Advancement of Colored People	54
North Mississippi Legal Defense Fund	20
The Delta Ministry	12
Southern Christian Leadership Conference	6
National Education Association	5
Congress of Racial Equality	4
Student Nonviolent Coordinating Committee	2
Urban League	1
School-related groups	
Concerned Negro parents	41
Local Negro Parent-Teacher Associations	40
Concerned White parents	23
Local white Parent-Teacher Associations	22
Local Mississippi Teachers Association (Negro)	17
Local Mississippi Education Association (white)	12
Biracial group of concerned parents	9
Community groups	
Informal citizens group (Negro)	50
Informal citizens group (white)	31
City councils	14
Informal citizens group (biracial)	13
County supervisors	8
Black coalition or caucus	2

Source: James M. Palmer, *Mississippi School Districts: Factors in the Disestablishment of Dual Systems* (State College: Mississippi State University, August 1971), p. 54.

increasingly toward effective community control, whether or not under exclusively black direction. Mississippi showed this most clearly. During 1968–1969, a close student of the southern scene reported he had found "no full-fledged community control movement."[136] The community control component in southern desegregation was still barely recognizable.

The North since 1964

After 1964, organized black community action on schools in the North continued to revolve around the goal of desegregation, but decreasingly so. In Chicago, Dr. Martin Luther King presided over the high point of desegregation struggles. When the movement inspired by his leadership failed to win substantive concessions in schools, housing, and employment, Dr. King left the city late in 1966. A year later, Chicago's black citizens supported the goal of desegregation more firmly than the year before. In New York City, repeated failure by the city school board to carry through on its promises to desegregate produced a growing disillusionment in black circles. Significant numbers of leaders turned toward an exclusive concern with controlling the local schools, whatever their racial complexion. Unlike the South where control and desegregation were double objectives, in many northern communities – New York City, Detroit, and several other places – the isolation of one from the other helped neither.[137] The dominant white community opposed both.

Historically, the emerging community control movement was another effort by Negro Americans to achieve effective control over the education of their young. Under slavery and half freedom, this right existed hardly at all. Desegregation was a parallel expression of the same effort.

A generation earlier, Horace Mann Bond had predicted that the new black-segregated schools then being built in northern cities would fail to educate their students within twenty years or so. During the 1960s the sweeping failure of urban schools became commonplace. Segregation, as in the South, prepared the way for wholesale deprivation of minority and poor children. By whatever measure, predominantly black schools in the North were failures. The difficulty was not color as such. Even in the poorest northern black school, for example, about a fifth or a quarter of the children learned to read at or above grade level. The problem was not whether any learning could occur in an all-black school. Rather, it was that for the great majority of children enrolled in such schools, failure was the norm. In 1970, seven out of ten black children in the North attended schools in which the enrollment was 80 to 100 percent Negro. In the South, the proportion in similar schools was nearer to six out of ten (Table 16). In the last third of the twentieth century, the school experience of black children had lost any geographical peculiarity. Deprivation was the common experience throughout the country.

If geography lost its relevance, history did not. The traditional relative deprivation of black and poor children was documented almost wherever specific schools for black and white were compared empirically in the same communities. Federal programs designed specifically to supplement local school district expenditures for educating poor children were transformed illegally by the districts into substitutes for local spending.

The local funds thus released were then added to already disporportion-ately high expenditures on educationally privileged children.[138] While such diversion of funds was a clear violation of the law, state education agencies failed systematically to audit expenditures, as required by law, and to supervise projects.[139] Ironically, federal funds widened the very gap they were presumably designed to narrow. This misuse of federal funds retarded the readiness of local communities to educate all their children.

Older-fashioned material deprivation continued. In the South, it was regularly reported that before white children entered a formerly all-black school much cleaning and repairing occurred. In the North, this stimulus was absent as desegregation remained minimal. The maldistribution of experienced teachers, building resources, and instructional programs, combined with sinking academic achievement levels, spelled deprivation for many thousands of black students.[140]

The law and the judiciary

Neither *Brown* nor the Civil Rights Act of 1964 dealt with urban-style segregation. A common defense of northern school boards when charged with segregation during the 1950s and early 1960s was to point to residential segregation as the real culprit. Yet as one legal expert contended in 1965: "In every case of racially imbalanced schools sufficient responsibility can be ascribed to government to satisfy the requirement that stems from the equal protection clause's proscription of unequal treatment by government."[141] No grand legal principle to this effect could have been proclaimed by any high court. Yet pragmatically, just such a structure of legal reasoning came into being by the opening of the 1970s. It took two main avenues: (1) state actions against so-called de facto segre-gation and (2) federal lower court actions against deliberate efforts to sustain de facto segregation.

During the decade after 1962, several northern states adopted legisla-tive, judicial, or administrative standards that permitted or required the disestablishment of segregation, whatever its origin. The novelty lay in creating a positive obligation for school boards to desegregate, regardless of how the segregation originated. This was held by the supreme courts of California, Illinois, Massachusetts, Pennsylvania, and Washington. By administrative action, New York adopted the same policy. A number of other states adopted regulations that fell short of binding requirements.

In the federal courts, plaintiffs had the difficult assignment of proving conscious intent by school boards. Because the segregative techniques were often seemingly neutral, proving intent was not feasible. Over time, the matter of intent receded, to be replaced by a simple test of whether school board measures to segregate were adopted in the face of clear alternatives. Northern urban cases began to make headway through the federal courts. Examples of old-fashioned deliberate, de jure segregation were not uncommon in these proceedings. Desegregation orders were entered and implemented in a number of cities, among them Pontiac, Michigan; New Rochelle, New York; South Holland, Illinois; San Francisco, California; Indianapolis, Indiana; Kokomo, Indiana; Pasadena, California; Denver, Colorado; Benton Harbor, Michigan; Reno, Nevada; Oxnard, California; Kalamazoo, Michigan; and Minneapolis, Minnesota.

Federal administrative action against northern segregation flared momentarily in 1965 when HEW froze federal aid to Chicago schools. The complainants, a coalition of civil rights groups in Chicago, had accused the board of de jure segregation. The freeze was ended after a few days when Chicago's Mayor Richard J. Daley asked President Johnson to reverse the action. This was done. One day before the freeze was cancelled, U. S. Commissioner of Education Francis Keppel announced: "In the case of Chicago, complaints other than de facto segregation have been made, and it is in regard to some of these that new commitments of funds are being deferred at this time."[142] (Authority to move against de jure segregation rested with the Fourteenth Amendment as enunciated in *Brown*.) Presidential intervention in the matter was widely interpreted as a corrective of the Office of Education's stretching of the doctrine of de facto segregation. In fact, the initial complaint was one of deliberate segregation, and presumably the office was dealing with it in those terms. The defect in the Chicago episode was not so much constitutional as political.

Political intervention against desegregation moves was hardly unknown before Chicago. Congressmen often took such steps. Senator John Stennis intervened successfully on behalf of the Columbus, Mississippi, school board, while Representative George Mahon, chairman of the House Appropriations Committee, gained delays for the Lubbock, Texas, board of education. The Chicago intervention was more fateful because its national impact was strongly negative. It damaged morale within the civil rights enforcement unit of the Office of Education. Enforcement actions slowed across the country.[143] While an unknown number of northern school systems were contacted by HEW in the years after 1967, only a handful of such cases reached public notice. There was little reason to believe that much was accomplished.

With the change of political administration in 1969, the severely weakened administrative enforcement of civil rights underwent further deterioration. In 1969 and 1970, for the first time, federal legal resources were placed at the disposal of parties fighting desegregation. The intent of Congress in passing the Civil Rights Act of 1964 was to lend aid to private persons who lacked the resources to protect their children's constitutional rights. The Department of Justice frequently could be found on the side trying to slow down the implementation of those very rights. Presidential leadership was exerted so as to impair the momentum of the general movement toward effective desegregation. All the hesitations and doubts reflected in the 1963–1964 congressional debates on the Civil Rights Act surfaced. Northern and southern congressmen united behind a program of constriction and scare.

Curiously, it was in such a context that the country achieved record levels of desegregation. In 1968, two-thirds of black children in eleven southern states were in all-black schools; in 1970, about one-sixth; and in 1971–1972, about one-eleventh. A far smaller proportion of children attended segregated schools in the South than had done so in 1954.[144] Very likely this was also so in the North compared with 1954. On the other hand, in the years after 1960, segregation rose to new heights in most northern cities. In those northern cities that were ordered to desegregate, however, segregation rates fell very sharply.

The passage of the Civil Rights Act of 1964 resulted in significant increases in desegregation, but not until the end of the decade did the South turn the corner. New interpretations by the Supreme Court were basic to this progress. Administrative enforcement of legislation and court orders ranged from tepid to cool. One reason for the rising tide of antiintegration sentiment among whites was the very success of desegregation. As court-ordered measures proved workable and after an early period of difficulties tolerable if not acceptable among whites, the prospect of further desegregation grew.

The exact form assumed by antidesegregation opposition changed with the times. Around 1971, it revolved around the issue of busing because the Supreme Court's *Swann* decision of that year gave constitutional approval to busing as one device to attain desegregation and because the decision seemed to open the way to effective desegregation of cities, both North and South. The resulting national uproar about busing obscured a significant fact: at the time *Swann* was handed down, considerably fewer than a majority of America's 49,883,000 school children were walking to school. A study by the U.S. Department of Transportation showed that in 1971 only 42.1 percent of children walked or bicycled to school; the rest used school bus (38.2 percent), public transportation (3.0 percent), private automobile (16.3 percent), or other means (0.4 percent).[145] Motor transportation had a better safety record than walking; still, agitation against busing mounted. Busing became the focal point of opposition to desegregation.

Largely in response to the atmosphere engendered by the civil rights movement, researchers and writers on problems of minority children found much larger audiences than before. Unfortunately, the new efforts gave birth to an interpretive framework that rapidly became an orthodoxy. This view insisted that the failures of schools were caused by faults of the children and their parents. Primary emphasis was upon the individual deficiencies of minority and poor children, presumably stemming from their parents' modest socioeconomic status. The Coleman Report, which in 1966 became the favorite text of this new variety of social determinism, declared that school resources between black and white schools were highly comparable, that learning differences among children within a school were greater than those between schools, and that the principal factor in explaining differences in academic achievement consisted in the social class composition of student bodies. Little attention was given in the Coleman Report to the possible role of schools in engendering and perpetuating educational inequalities.

The Coleman Report bore numerous progeny. Seldom has a single piece of social science research been so often reanalyzed. It was not surprising, however, that since the repeaters asked no basically new questions of the data, they got essentially the same answers. This was proclaimed as independent confirmation of the original research. A decade after the Coleman data were gathered, they had not been replaced or supplemented by research of a comparable scope that attempted to discover the role of the school. Psychologist Kenneth B. Clark was the foremost spokesman for the contrary viewpoint that stressed the positive educative potential of schools. He contended that the schools as a whole accepted the norm of massive nonachievement for minority children. The doctrine of social determinism he rejected as incompatible with the basic learning potential of nearly all children. Social scientists paid little heed to Clark's argument and continued to employ the model of the Coleman Report. Exceedingly few studies were made to test Clark's view.

Ironically, this was not a new experience for Clark. When he supplied the U.S. Supreme Court with the essential social science evidence for the *Brown* decision in 1954, he was criticized by a number of social scientists who denied the solidity of the research. During the succeeding two decades, however, when numerous opportunities for research into desegregation arose, these same critics failed to undertake the research whose absence they had earlier lamented. In both cases, Clark was in closer touch with the empirical realities of race and schools.

Constituting a movement whose moral grandeur cast a light far beyond their own ranks, blacks raised anew many questions of the public good. In education, the idea of the public school was tested once more. It had foundered on the rock of race more than a century earlier. Blacks now challenged the capacity of the political system to summon a new sense of common purpose. But the greatest mark of the historic moment was that the initiative rested, in part at least, in the hands of black Americans. It was inconceivable that *this* could be undone by mere national fatigue or even fear. Before the Civil War, Douglass defined equality as that condition in which color of skin conferred neither privilege to whites nor disadvantage to blacks. The American public schools were far from this. A century after emancipation, the schools for blacks were unemancipated still – often separate, unequal, dehumanized. The miracle was that the belief in learning among blacks had not been contained or suppressed. Each time hope was crushed, by the courts or the legislature or the educational establishment, it rose again. Occasionally, as in *Brown* or the Civil Rights Act, public institutions supported this hope, encouraging expectation that, even when unfulfilled, nurtured new demands for equal and unsegregated education. Those who deplored low academic achievement among black children seldom acknowledged that, given the circumstances of overwhelming educational oppression, it was miraculous that any survived.

4

Mexican-American children: the neighbors within

The experience of Mexican-American children in the schools, like that of blacks, has been one of discrimination and exclusion. The first public schools in the Americas had developed in Central America and Mexico. In the Spanish Conquest of the sixteenth century one of the first Indian institutions to suffer extinction was the public school. The second conquest, by Americans in the nineteenth century, continued the subjection. Both sets of conquerors regarded the Mexican people as useful labor and little more. Public education all but disappeared from Mexican soil for nearly four centuries. Cultural dominance was a more difficult conquest: edicts and displays of force are often futile against the intimate everyday renewals of a traditional way of life. The Anglo approach to cultural autonomy of the conquered, however, was less outright suppression than cultural hegemony. Participation in political and economic life took place on Anglo terms. The schools followed suit. When it proved impossible to continue withholding instruction from the descendants of the conquered, the schools grudgingly offered them the merest taste of education. The lessons of subordination formed the most vital part of the curriculum. The schools renewed the conquest every semester.

For several centuries before the Spanish Conquest of 1519, Indians had built extensive formal public school systems. Best known were those established by the Aztecs. Aztec society rested on a power hierarchy of warrior nobility, priest, and merchant, and a large commoner class of free peasants. Public schools were open to all members of the kinship group or *calpulli*. Outside the kinship group were the serfs and slaves who formed a majority of the population; for most of these, schooling was prohibited.[1]

At birth, the Aztec child was marked for a designated life task: if a girl, a loom was placed in her hands; if a noble's son, an implement of the craft. About the age of ten or twelve – but sometimes earlier – the sons of merchants, craftsmen, and commoners began to attend a house of youth (*telpochcalli*) to receive instruction in the practical art of war and the equally practical realm of religion. Sons of the nobility attended a seminary (*calmecac*) where they received "instruction that prepared them to be priests, public officials, and military leaders." Teachers, drawn from the priesthood, concentrated on inducting the future ruling class into the rites of power.[2]

Among the Maya Indians, Zapotecs, Toltecs, and others, similar educational structures existed. Maya children, at the age of seven or eight, attended temple schools taught by priests. About the age of twelve, boys entered boarding schools *(internados)*, where they studied military subjects. Sons of nobles and middle-class persons attended separate *internados*. Apparently, commoners did not attend any school. Still, Keen reports the contention of a late nineteenth-century Spanish writer, Francisco Pi y Margall, that "education had made the Aztecs a cultured people; even their plebians were better instructed than the coarse, ignorant Spanish soldiers."[3]

During Spanish rule in Mexico, from 1519 to 1821, the conquerors suppressed the Indians' educational institutions as instruments of native power. Popular education – such as it was – was private, Catholic, and Spanish. Only a tiny group of upper-class Indians benefited. Of the 5 million people in Mexico at the end of the colonial period, only 0.5 percent was literate.

In California, at the northern rim of the Spanish empire in America, Indians were often skilled craftsmen. Instruction for literacy was minimal, but occasionally, a stunning exception could be found. In 1540, missionaries in New Spain founded Santa Cruz de Tlaltelolco Academy. A number of Indian graduates of this school stayed on as teachers or became teachers in the humanities at monasteries. "In this way," observes a writer, "some Indians became teachers of their conquerors, who did not feel humiliated to receive training from those who had reached so high a position."[4]

The Spanish Crown tried through the school to abolish use of Indian languages. In 1793, King Carlos IV decreed that schools in the American empire should replace Indian languages with Castilian. Two years later, the head of each mission in California – which in 1800 numbered eighteen and enrolled some 15,000 Indians – was directed to start a school to "teach the Indians to speak, read, and write Spanish, to the absolute exclusion of the native language."[5] The padres saw the native people as simple children who constituted the only available labor supply. Literacy was an impossible luxury, and the missions failed to implement the royal order. Missionaries shared the widespread belief among Europeans in the Spanish American domains that the native people could best dignify their existence by docility and intellectual innocence.

In 1821, Mexico won its independence from Spain. In the Constitution of 1824, the Mexican Congress received the power to control education. Nevertheless, no public elementary schools were established. School laws remained mere declarations of intention. In 1842, a law proclaimed compulsory education for children aged seven to fifteen years; it never was implemented. During the decade 1825–1835, missions in California took more seriously their educational function: Indian and mestizo children attended schools with the white colonists. In these years missions were secularized, thus ending even the most modest evidences of schooling. Near the end of the 1840s, the only schools in California were two part-time institutions in Monterey and San Jose.

Increasing numbers of white United States citizens emigrated to California. During the mid-1840s, these immigrants set up voluntary schools for their children. Indians in the vicinity were not allowed to attend these or any other schools. As Childers explains, "unless they could show some Spanish or Mexican blood relationship, they scarcely existed legally."[6]

At the end of the second military conquest of Mexico in 1846–1848, Mexicans who chose to remain in the new American territories were guaranteed the rights of citizens.[7] Perhaps as many as 200,000 Mexican-Americans lived in the Southwest by 1900.[8] A tiny Mexican-American upper class shared power where the ruling Anglos could not avoid it, but most Mexican-Americans occupied low ranks within their own cultural group, and all were subordinated to the Anglo. In Anglo society, the Mexican-American was significant principally as cheap, exploitable labor.

Education mirrored these social facts. In New Mexico, at first the most populous of the new territories, Anglo authorities were in no hurry to create public schools for the Spanish-speaking majority. As early as 1855, a school law provided a tax for building schools. The measure was rejected almost unanimously in a referendum (5,016 to 37).[9] In 1860, another school law was passed, but failed to provide funds. Not until 1871 was the first public school organized in New Mexico. Five years later, 133 schools enrolled 5,625 pupils, or an average of 42 per school. In 111 of these schools (83 percent) classes were conducted wholly in Spanish; in 10 schools, wholly in English; and in 12 schools (9 percent), in both English and Spanish. Congress was petitioned repeatedly to grant funds to provide an adequate number of schools; it refused. In 1898, fifty years after conquest, Congress did make a small land grant to help finance higher education, including normal schools.

The territory's first full-scale school law was passed in 1891; it provided for a compulsory seven-month school year, but no school tax. Schools funds were to come from "licenses and fines, chiefly those from the gambling and liquor industries,"[10] niggardly support undoubtedly related to the fact that the most who could benefit were Spanish-speaking children. Small, poor Hispano villages in the state could not afford to supplement the tiny state appropriation and had no schools at all. Further, an administrative ruling that English was to be the sole language of instruction led to protests and an attempt to place Spanish-speaking teachers in non-English-speaking communities. By 1908, the territory's 41,000 elementary school students were almost evenly distributed among English- and Spanish-language schools.

Scarce territorial funds were diverted from the common schools to higher education and, therefore, to the use of Anglos. Early in the life of territorial New Mexico – it became a state in 1912 – the majority of the people were Spanish-speaking and controlled the territorial legislature. Anglos reserved control over the executive, administrative, and judicial branches and, therefore, over contacts with Congress and the president. Land grants obtained from Congress in 1890 financed the nine-year-old University of New Mexico and other colleges, designed primarily for the Anglo-American population. Elementary school for the mass of the Spanish-American people suffered in consequence. In 1903, not even half New Mexico's school-age population attended school; the average school year was four and a half months. Pressure from the Hispanos resulted in the founding during 1909 of New Mexico Highlands University in Las Vegas to train Hispanos to become rural teachers. It moderated only in part the complaint that state funds went disproportionately to Anglo higher education. In 1901, J. Francisco Chaves, the territory's chief school officer, predicted that with continuation of the practice "we shall more than ever witness the humiliating spectacle of that which is now partially apparent – taxpayers of New Mexico supplying funds devoted largely to the higher training of youth from Texas, Mexico, and Arizona, even from California and Missouri, while their own children are yet poorly served in the lower grade schools and wholly unable to qualify for admission to the higher institutions."[11]

In 1912, when New Mexico became a state, it received federal land grants of 8,711,324 acres for common school purposes. It was allowed to use 5 percent of the net proceeds for school purposes.[12] No other state received as large a federal school grant. (All of it, of course, was part of the booty of the Mexican-American War of 1846–1848.) The new state constitution, Article X, Section 10, provided:

> Children of Spanish descent in the state of New Mexico shall never be denied the right and privilege of admission and atten-
> dance in the public schools or other public educational institu-
> tions of the State, and they shall never be classed in separate
> schools, but shall forever enjoy perfect equality with other chil-
> dren in all public schools and educational institutions of the
> State.

Article VIII required that teachers be equally proficient in both Spanish and English. At El Rito, a normal school was established to train teachers in Spanish. Yet only English could be used in the classroom. Another indication of state policy was the unbroken failure of authorities to enforce

Article VIII. An inevitable consequence was widespread failure of Hispano children in the task of mastering a curriculum couched in an alien
language.

Similar patterns of educational deprivation existed in Texas. Under
Spanish rule, there was no public education, and Mexican rule (1821–
1836) was little different. The Texas Declaration of Independence, March
2, 1836, cited the lack of schools as a principal grievance against Mexico:
"It has failed to establish any public system of education. . . . It is an
axiom of political science, that unless a people are educated and enlightened, it is idle to expect the continuance of civil liberty, or the
capacity for self-government." Independence did not bring public education. Instead, the new Anglo leaders of Texas became preoccupied with
economic changes, importing Negro slaves to work the cotton plantations,
using Mexican laborers in the range-cattle industry.

Public and private schools: separate and unequal

Before the Civil War, several tentative steps toward a statewide
system of public schools were taken by the legislature. In 1839–1840,
sales of 4.2 million acres of public lands allotted to the 238 counties of the
republic were intended to create a county school fund (only the interest
earned on the fund could be spent). Article X, Section 2, of the 1845 Texas
Constitution reserved one-tenth of all public revenues to a "perpetual"
school fund. A year after the Civil War, a school fund was created for
white schools only. Under the full pressure of blacks during Reconstruction, Texas was finally compelled to create a statewide system of schools,
and in 1873, the legislature reserved one-half of all unappropriated public
land to a state system of schools, though the land, unfortunately, was sold
at low prices, reducing school revenues. Local taxpayers – as in New
Mexico – did not see any point in taxing their own property to support the
education of other people's children, especially if these were blacks or
tejanos. By the 1880s, a statewide network of schools was finally attained,[13] but if *tejano* children attended before 1900 the information is
lost.

Along the Mexican border, wealthier *tejanos* sent their children to
private Spanish-language schools. The dame school, a Spanish-language
parlor school operated by women who were graduates of normal schools
in Mexico, stressed Mexican culture and excelled the usual public school
facilities available to Mexican-American children. Other private schools
were begun by American Protestant missionaries as early as 1852 in
Brownsville. Nearly half were boarding schools for an international clien-
tele, some with bilingual instruction. Numerous youngsters from Mexico
attended, some walking across the border every school day.

Public schools for Mexican-American children became available slowly
and usually on a segregated basis. In 1891, twenty years after the opening

of public schools in Corpus Christi, the first Mexican-American children were admitted, but only to a separate school. Eleven years later the Seguin school district opened a segregated school for "Mexicans."[14] In San Antonio, the Navarro School was opened in 1898 to "Mexicans,"[15] with classes conducted in English. In 1915, the school's administration reduced the curriculum to essentials to allow for concentration on English.

Austin's school board as early as 1916 referred in its minutes to a school for Mexicans. In 1919, a single teacher in McAllen had 190 Mexican-American pupils in a separate school. That same year, write Rangel and Alcala, "after several citizens in the Pharr district objected to the presence of Mexican-American students in the district's brick school building, the Phaar Board accepted a proposal to transfer these students to a nearby Mexican church."[16] In Uvalde in 1911, a school for Anglo children was open a month longer than a school for Negroes and Mexican-Americans.

By 1920, a pattern had emerged for Texas as a whole: separate schooling in greatly inferior facilities for Mexican-American students; deliberate refusal to make educational use of the child's cultural heritage, especially the Spanish language; and a shorter school year.

In the southern part of California, control of the great cattle ranches rested in the hands of the Californios, the descendants of Spanish and Mexican recipients of land grants. Anglo businessmen bought cattle, lent money, and sold goods to the Californios. It was in part on the basis of this "cash nexus" that a certain Yankee tolerance for Californio culture existed.[17] In 1855, although state school authorities required that English be the sole language of instruction, the schools of Santa Barbara – then a predominantly Californio town – managed to ignore the order. Los Angeles – also a Californio town – followed the English-only rule. During the 1860s and 1870s, according to Forbes, a number of bilingual and bicultural schools in the Los Angeles area existed under Californio control.[18]

After a flood of Anglo immigration during the last quarter of the nineteenth century, the Mexican-American population, including Californios, fell from one-quarter of the population in 1880 to one-tenth a decade later. During the first decade of the twentieth century, the number of Mexican-born residents in the state rose from 8,000 to 34,000; in 1920, the figure was not far from 90,000. Between 1920 and 1940, the Mexican-American population rose to 2.5 million. But the patterns of Mexican-American schooling varied little, if at all, from those before World War I.

In 1928, when Manuel conducted the first study of the education of Mexican-American children in Texas, they represented 13 percent of the school population (Negroes were 16.8 percent). He reported that at least

40 percent were not attending any school.[19] Nearly half were in the first grade and only one twenty-fifth in high school. Their classrooms were far more crowded than classrooms attended by Anglo children; their school year was shorter, sometimes only half as long; they were often segregated, and where this was the case, physical facilities were seriously inferior. Teachers in Mexican-American schools frequently received the same salary as those in Anglo schools, but they taught many more children and per pupil teaching costs were lower. Manuel reported: "Not infrequently the Mexican school is regarded as a training school from which the most capable teachers may be drawn to other schools."

In at least seventeen school districts, no school at all was provided for Mexican-American children.[20] One county superintendent in western Texas told Manuel: "I have recently learned that there are Mexicans in two or three districts who really wanted to send their children to school, but the 'whites' scare them out of it. They tell them if they send their children to school, they will be out of a job. Of course, in order to hold their jobs they will not send them to school." Another superintendent explained that Mexican-American children must be given only a minimal education:

> Most of our Mexicans are of the lower class. They transplant
> onions, harvest them, etc. The less they know about everything
> else, the better contented they are. You have doubtless heard
> that ignorance is bliss; it seems that it is so when one has to
> transplant onions. . . . If a man has very much sense or education
> either, he is not going to stick to this kind of work. So you see it is
> up to the white population to keep the Mexican on his knees in an
> onion patch. . . . This does not mix well with education.

The prevailing Anglo view was well represented by the secretary of a chamber of commerce of whom Manuel wrote: "To him the education of these children is a *charity*, not a civil duty."

Academic retardation and deprivation

In the Southwest patterns of discrimination, segregation, and financial deprivation dominated the education of Mexican-American children throughout the second and third quarters of the century as it had the first quarter. The consequences were, predictably, underachievement and alienation.

Deprivation and failure were built into the Texas public school system. One of the most effective devices was the practice of automatically retaining Mexican-American children in first grade for two or even three years. Children were so assigned on the basis of ethnicity, not ability. In these classes, typically, neither specially trained teachers nor innovative instructional techniques were used because of the severe financial shortchanging of such schools. In a Mexican-American school in San Antonio, three first-grade classes were on half session and some of these children worked on ranches in the spring. The principal reported that "many of the boys look forward to the fourth grade and fourteenth birthday when they will be free from school duties."[21] Around 1920, some 11,000 Mexican-American children in San Antonio were enrolled in the city's elementary schools; only 250 attended high schools. In El Paso, Mexican-American students made up half the enrollment in elementary schools; they constituted less than one-fourth of all high school students. Elsewhere, as in the Sonora district, Mexican-American children were not permitted to register in the high school at all. In the Bishop district, they were excluded from the district high school but were allowed to register in the high school of another district. Nonenforcement of compulsory attendance laws was deliberate. Anglo farmers in Nueces County outside Corpus Christi simply did "not want the Mexicans to receive much education."[22] Many of these same farmers sat on school boards, where they could put their educational philosophy into effect. As an instrument of exploitation, the schools often seemed to be hardly more than an extension of the cotton field or the fruit-packing shed.

In the company town of Sugar Land (run by the Imperial Sugar Refinery and the Marshall Canning Company), of the great bulk of Mexican-American students who were "poured" into the first grade, only a few "grains" spilled over into the eighth grade. In 1936–1937, 55.6 percent of the students were in the first grade, fewer than 1 percent were in eighth grade; in 1939–1940, the percentages were 59.5 and 1.9.[23] This large-scale retardation could not be attributed to excessive mobility of families, for the labor force of Sugar Land was fixed and not migratory.

Retardation of Mexican-American children was widely acknowledged to be a fault of the school. In 1920 Stowell reported:

> Public school authorities have been frank to place part of the blame . . . upon a course of study conceived for use with American [sic] boys and girls and upon methods designed for use with pupils who come from a different environment and who already understand the English language. . . . The Mexican pupil is not only expected to learn all that an English-speaking pupil learns but to learn it in a language which he does not understand.[24]

In fourteen San Antonio schools studied during 1925, intelligence quotient scores were found to be strongly related to language. When Spanish-language tests were administered to Mexican-American children, nearly 70 percent scored higher than they had on an English-language test. Over a five-year period, 85 percent of the children in one of the all-Mexican-American schools had failed the first grade. As Paar observed, it was "a tremendous waste of teaching. Evidently the method of teaching Mexicans must be at fault."[25]

When students in another Mexican-American school in San Antonio during 1923–1924 took intelligence tests, children in the first two grades scored zeroes. "And yet," wrote Harris, "these children were neither all morons nor imbeciles. The tests were entirely out of these children's experiences and language difficulties made the tests entirely unreliable in classifying the pupils into groups. . . . If any conclusion at all can be drawn . . . it is that Mexican children respond satisfactorily to whatever comes within the range of their previous experiences."[26] Such views were unrepresentative, unfortunately, even among educators. The school's role was frankly assimilative, and children had to learn to manage within those limits. What a few educators saw as a defect, most regarded as a virtue.

Mexican-American children paid a high price for learning this negative lesson. One youngster in Nueces County, Texas, lamented:

> I was the only Mexican in my high school, and well liked by the Americans. I used to go to picnics with them and drink water out of the same cups and pitchers. Then we came to the Alamo in our study of history, and then it was 'gringo' and 'greaser.' They expelled me from the baseball nine and would not sit with me anymore, and told me to drink out of my own cup.[27]

"Some Americans don't like to talk to me," another child said. "I sat by one in [the] high school auditorium and he moved away. Oh my God, it made me feel ashamed. I felt like walking out of school."[28] In Del Rio, a resident recalled, Mexican-American students "were discouraged from continuing their high school education by physical beatings."[29]

Parsons sat in on numerous classes in Castroville, California, and compiled an extensive log of teacher practices that illustrated the everyday reality of ethnic cleavage. Anglo "helpers" were used by teachers; no Mexican-American children were ever so used. Often and systematically teachers ignored Mexican-American children's hands in favor of calling on Anglos. Often, while Mexican-American children were reciting, teachers interrupted them to listen to an Anglo child. Teachers related informally with Anglo children, inquiring about family affairs and the like; with Mexican-American children they were very strict. Teachers went out of their way to praise and encourage Anglo children, while just as regularly criticizing Mexican-American children. Frequently, teachers explained to Parsons that preferential treatment for Anglo children was necessary because they were going to grow up to lead Castroville and they might as well get used to it early.[30]

Self-devaluation, shame and feelings of inferiority often resulted from this regimen of inequality. Mexican-American students in Grant High School in Houston, Texas, felt this perhaps as much as in Castroville. At Grant, one student told Mary Ellen Goodman: "It feels bad when people don't talk to you. . . . They are better off financially. Our parents have the dirty jobs. I feel as if I am in a foreign country.[31] A principal response by Mexican-American students was to organize exclusive social groupings.

At a high school in Lubbock, Texas, known by Anglo tradition as the Home of the Westerners, young Mexican-American students who wanted to organize a Chicano club were told by the principal: "You cannot be an organized Westerner and an organized Chicano at the same time, so you better choose between the two."[32] The five local high schools employed only eleven Mexican-Americans, eight of whom were janitors; two were teachers, and they taught at the high school with the largest enrollment of Mexican-Americans. An alumnus of Lubbock High said he "was *todo escamado* [scared stiff] when I was called upon to give an oral report. My English was terrible and the students laughed at me because I didn't know the words and those words I did know I could not pronounce!"[33]

The schools of the Southwest were decreasingly effective in educating Mexican-American children in the liberal arts and skills of modern life. They succeeded beyond measure, however, in instructing the same children to play a subordinate role in the dominant Anglo society. Parsons studied the schooling of Mexican-Americans in Castroville, California, "the world's artichoke center." Ethnic cleavage he found to be almost complete. Except for one teacher in the town, "not a single Anglo had ever been inside a Mexican home."

In Castroville Mexican-Americans made up 57 percent of school enrollment; the principal and teachers – all Anglo – overestimated the percentage. Most teachers were also convinced Mexican-American children are less intelligent than Anglo children. Parsons checked IQ scores and found little difference in the mean scores of Anglos and Mexican-Americans (Table 21).

Ability grouping was practiced to an extreme degree with the high-ability classes almost entirely Anglo. A teacher explained to Parsons that such classes are kept as "small as possible because we feel that the brighter pupils deserve a chance to get as much as they can out of school without being held back by the kids who are dull or just lazy or don't care."[34]

Mexican-American children who might aspire to careers other than those of their fathers were often explicitly discouraged by school personnel. A student who later became a teacher and a state senator told his principal that he wanted to transfer to a better school in the Anglo part of San Antonio. The principal replied: "Well, no use your going to the North Side schools. You're not going to compete on the North Side. If you stay

Table 21. *Mean IQ scores of Anglo
and Mexican-American
schoolchildren in Castroville,
California*

Grade	Anglo	Mexican-American
3	97	91
4	110	92
5	111	104
6	111	99
7	104	97
8	97	95

Source: Data from Theodore W. Parsons,
Jr., "Ethnic Cleavage in a California
School" (doctoral dissertation, Stanford
University, 1965).

over here with your people, you may end up being a leader. If you go over there, they are going to minimize your potential and you are going to be competing with white students. . . . Rather than to have you mongrelize and water down the races, you ought to stay on your part of town."[35] Another young man, who later became one of Mexico's outstanding educators, attended school for a time in Eagle Pass. When the Mexican heritage was demeaned in class, he told the teacher: "We had a printing press before you did."[36]

The consequences of this persistent discrimination were what one might expect. A recent survey by the U.S. Commission on Civil Rights found that student-holding rates, reading achievement, and extracurricular activity were all less for Mexican-Americans than for Anglos.[37] The data on student-holding rates in Texas and California are given in Table 22. In the Southwest as a whole, reading achievement as measured by the percentage of students reading at or above grade level, showed an increasing gap between Anglos and Mexican-Americans. In the fourth grade, 74.7 percent of Anglos and 48.7 percent of Mexican-Americans read at grade level. In the eighth grade the percentages were 71.8 and 35.8; in the twelfth grade, 66.3 and 37.4. In none of the five states in the region were fewer than 44 percent of the Mexican-American students reading below grade level. Academic retardation was acute. In Texas, 22 percent of Mexican-American children, but only 7 percent of Anglo children, repeated the first grade; in California, the corresponding percentages were 10 and 6. In extracurricular activities, Mexican-American students were underrepresented regardless of the ethnic composition of the school's enrollment. "The ultimate test of a school system's effectiveness

Table 22. *Proportion of Anglo and Mexican-American children remaining in school and entering college in Texas and California, 1969*

Grade	Anglo		Mexican-American	
	California	Texas	California	Texas
1	100.0	100.0	100.0	100.0
8	100.0	100.0	93.8	86.1
12	85.7	85.1	63.8	52.7
Enter college	46.9	53.0	28.2	16.2

Source: Data from U.S. Commission on Civil Rights, *Mexican-American Education Study*, Vol. II (Washington, D.C.: GPO, 1971–1972), pp. 14, 17.

is the performance of its students," wrote the commission. "Under that test, our schools are failing."

In 1971, the U.S. Bureau of the Census provided a systematic collection of population statistics relating to Mexican-Americans.[38] Mexican-Americans numbered 5,254,000; 86.6 percent of them lived in the five southwestern states of Arizona, California, Colorado, New Mexico, and Texas. It was a young population: the median age was 18.6 years compared with 28.0 years for the population of the entire country; 77.0 percent had children under the age of 18, compared with the nationwide average of 55.2 percent. It was a poor population: more than two-thirds (68.7 percent) of the 1.1 million families earned less than $10,000 a year for full-time, year-round work, compared with 48.2 percent of the total population. The Mexican-American income position was probably bleaker than these figures suggest, for two reasons: (1) many were less than full-time, year-round workers and (2) average family income had to finance larger families. (Table 23 shows the occupational position of Mexican-Americans.) Fewer than one in twelve of employed Mexican-Americans were farm workers. Parity between Mexican-Americans and all employed persons was nearest realization among blue-collar workers, especially among craftsmen. Continued concentration at less skilled, lower-paying occupations resulted in sharply lower family incomes. In 1971, median family income for Mexican-Americans lagged 37.4 percent behind median family income overall.

In general, compared with the total adult American population, nearly six times more Mexican-Americans completed fewer than five years of elementary school (Table 24) and less than half as many Mexican-Americans completed four years of high school or more. For those aged fifty and over, who were born in 1917 or before, neither in Mexico nor in the United States had much public education been available during these

Table 23. *Percentage of total population and Mexican-American population of men aged 16 years and over engaged in various occupations, March 1972*

Occupation	Total population	Mexican-American
White-collar workers	41.5	17.5
Professional and technical	14.1	4.8
Managers, administrators, except farm	13.2	5.6
Sales workers	6.3	2.6
Clerical workers	6.9	4.5
Blue-collar workers	46.6	62.5
Craftsmen and kindred	20.7	20.9
Operatives, including transportation	18.7	27.2
Laborers, except farm	7.2	14.3
Farm workers	4.6	8.3
Farmers and farm managers	3.0	7.9
Farm laborers and foremen	1.6	0.4
Service workers	9.2	11.7
Total number employed	49,401,000	1,088,000

Source: U.S. Bureau of the Census, *Selected Characteristics of Persons and Families of Mexican, Puerto Rican, and Other Spanish Origin: March 1972* (Washington, D.C.: GPO, July 1972), p. 7.

years. Mexican-Americans aged twenty-five to twenty-nine, on the other hand, born during 1943–1947, had still been effectively excluded from adequate schooling, especially from high schools.

Dropout rates among Mexican-American high school students approached 100 percent until about 1950.[39] At that time, in Texas, school administrators estimated that about one-fifth of all migrant children never entered school at all, despite compulsory attendance laws. Continued immigration from Mexico, both legal and illegal, often inflated the number of uneducated. Most of the *braceros* who came to the United States in the 1940s and 1950s were young adults. Given the virtual absence of adult education provisions for this population, all but a few remained uneducated. Their children were not much better off.

Cultural suppression through language

By midcentury, one of the oldest practices of the school in the Southwest was to campaign against the Spanish language, a form of "cultural exclusion" that isolated Mexican-Americans. At best, schools ignored the language; at worst, students were punished, even humiliated

Table 24. *Percentage of total adult population and Mexican-American adult population completing less than five years of school or four years of high school or more, March 1972*

Age (years)	Total population	Mexican-American	Ratio: Mexican-American to total
Completed less than five years of school			
25–29	0.8	7.3	9.1:1
30–34	1.4	12.6	9.0:1
35–44	2.5	21.0	8.4:1
45–54	3.4	33.1	9.7:1
55–64	5.6	47.9	8.6:1
65 and over	12.2	74.8	6.1:1
Total	4.6	26.7	5.8:1
Completed four years of high school or more			
25–29	79.8	42.9	1:1.9
30–34	73.9	40.1	1:1.8
35–44	66.8	28.0	1:2.4
45–54	59.8	14.2	1:4.2
55–64	46.7	8.8	1:5.3
65 and over	32.0	0.6	1:5.3
Total	58.2	25.8	1:2.3

Source: U.S. Bureau of the Census, *Selected Characteristics of Persons and Families of Mexican, Puerto Rican, and Other Spanish Origin: March 1972* (Washington, D.C.: GPO, July 1972), p. 5.

publicly, for using it on school grounds. During the years 1957–1961, Madsen found in Hidalgo County, Texas, that "a virtual crusade is going on . . . to encourage the exclusive use of English."[40] Teachers visited homes of their students, trying to persuade parents of the importance of using English. A parent described one teacher's visit: "She burst in here like a rooster without even waiting for an invitation. This is my home and I will decide what is done here. And she tried to tell me not to speak the language of my forefathers. She does not understand nor does she want to." Such efforts to replace Spanish with English proved counterproductive.

The language policy of most schools in the Southwest, according to the U.S. Commission on Civil Rights, has consisted primarily of ignoring Spanish. One-third of the schools actively discouraged the use of Spanish in classrooms; in Texas, the proportion was two-thirds. The commission also found that, except in Texas, about two-thirds of Mexican-American first-graders spoke English as well as their Anglo peers. The percentage of

Table 25. *Percentage of Mexican-American first-graders who do not speak English as well as their Anglo peers, by composition of school and socioeconomic status*

Composition of school (percent Mexican-American)	Socioeconomic status			
	High	Middle	Low	Total
0– 24.9	19.4	32.4	41.0	28.4
25– 49.9	34.4	38.0	50.2	40.7
50– 74.9	26.4	36.9	51.0	42.8
75–100.0	28.3	46.0	70.0	62.3

Source: U.S. Commission on Civil Rights, *Mexican-American Education Study*, Vol. III (Washington, D.C.: GPO, 1971–1972), p. 49.

Mexican-American first-graders who did not speak English as well as their Anglo counterparts was 47 for the entire Southwest; for Arizona, the percentage was 30; for California, 36; for Colorado, 27; for New Mexico, 36; and for Texas, 62.[41] English-speaking competence varied significantly by socioeconomic status and ethnic composition of the school (Table 25).

Since for an appreciable number of children the Spanish language is either primary or secondary, the commission sought data on the prevalence of special instruction in language. Extremely little of significance was found. Fewer than 3 percent of all Mexican-American students in the Southwest were affected by bilingual instruction: "With the exception of a few districts in Texas, almost all bilingual education today is offered in small, scattered pilot programs."[42] Another 5.5 percent were affected by programs teaching English as a second language, aimed not at biculturalism but at enabling non-English-speakers "to become assimilated into the dominant culture." Remedial reading instruction in English touched only slightly more than another tenth of all Mexican-American students. The commission found that the schools paid little attention to the representation of minorities in the curriculum: "Only 4.3 percent of the elementary and 7.3 percent of the secondary schools surveyed . . . include a course in Mexican-American history in the curricula."

Carter's description of a crucial social role of the southwestern school – "Mexican-American children learn their future subordinate role in society by practicing it at school – is enhanced by widespread teacher belief in the cultural (and even biological) incapacity of Mexican-American children to learn. Carter distinguishes between different varieties of institutional success: "The fact that the school failed to Americanize or to raise the group status of so many Mexican-Americans was evidence of its success. Local society functioned well with an easily controlled, politically impotent and subordinate ethnic caste."[43]

The United States is one of the few countries in the world where bilingualism is a "problem." As Andersson and Boyer explain: "The problem arises only when a population through emigration or conquest becomes a part of a community where another language is spoken and this language is imposed on them through the school system or by other authorities." It is not the mere plurality of languages but its social and historical context that creates the problem. Basing their judgment on a review of evidence, Andersson and Boyer predict:

> If the Spanish-speaking children of our Southwest were given all
> of their schooling through both Spanish and English, there is a
> strong likelihood that not only would their so-called handicap
> . . . disappear, but *they would have a decided advantage over
> their English-speaking schoolmates, at least in elementary school,*
> because of the excellence of the Spanish writing system. There
> are no "reading problems," as we know them, among school
> children in Spanish-speaking countries. [44]

Yet in Los Angeles, for example, the correlation of low reading achievement and Mexican-American ethnic group "approaches a near-certain prediction."[45]

Growth of segregated and inferior education

Not only cultural exclusion through rejection of a language and culture but segregation was institutionalized in southwestern schools during the 1920s. Texas school boards created in Mexican-American sections neighborhood schools which then became Mexican-American schools. Between 1922–1923 and 1931–1932, the number of such schools doubled from twenty to forty in the state. A decade later, such separate schools were maintained in 122 districts within 59 Texas counties.[46] Mexican-American children were often required to register at "their" school even though they lived nearer an "Anglo" school. Thus, the neighborhood school principle of assignment by propinquity, which was denied black children, was also denied Mexican-American children. Anglo children, on the other hand, were not limited by the neighborhood – or even the county – school principle. In Brooks County, for example, while Mexican-American children attended the common school of the county, Anglo children who were residents of the same county attended school in a separate independent district.[47] In Nueces County, Anglo children were bused to the city school building; Mexican-American students were relegated to the rural school. When Anglo children found themselves living nearer a Mexican-American school, they could readily transfer to an Anglo school. Taylor found that in two Anglo schools, separate classrooms were maintained for Mexican-American children.[48]

Occasionally, when the number of Mexican-American children in a city expanded rapidly, a new school district was created to siphon them off from Anglo schools. This happened in 1929; authorities in the Del Rio district organized the San Felipe district for Mexican-American children in the same city.[49]

One study of Texas found that segregation in the upper grades led to low enrollment in high school. In five cities the following percentages of Mexican-American students were attending high school: Weslaco, 1 percent; Mission, 4 percent; El Paso, 6 percent; Brownsville, 30 percent; and Laredo, 50 percent.[50] McAllen and Harlingen resembled the first three cities; Eagle Pass and Rio Grande City, the last two. Little is known of the quality of the high schools serving Mexican-American children. However, in Rio Grande City and Zapata, local taxpayers contributed nothing to the operation of the schools; in Laredo and Eagle Pass, local school taxes were exceeded by the state contribution. One superintendent explained frankly that "Mexicans in this district draw about $6,000 state aid, and we spend on them about $2,000. This is true everywhere in Texas. We also have an $18,000 property tax and all that goes on the white school."[51] Segregation was the means by which a system of privilege could be administered readily.

An Anglo member of the Corpus Christi school board said: "The Mexican is not the equal of me. He may be smarter and all right in business, but I don't want to discuss school affairs with a Mexican on the same board with me."[52] A school official told Taylor: "Some Mexicans tried to send their children [in the bus to the town school] and complained to the trustees. Some white man, either his landlord or the landlord's agent, told the Mexicans to shut up."

Segregation of Mexican-American children was widespread in California, too. In 1928, when 65,572, just under one-tenth of all students, attended public and private schools in the state, the enrollment of sixty-four schools in eight counties was 90 to 100 percent Mexican-American. San Bernardino County had 16 such schools; Orange, 14; Los Angeles, 10; Imperial, 8; Kern, 8; Ventura, 4; Riverside, 2; and Santa Barbara, 2.[53] An advisory committee reported to Governor C. C. Young that these schools were not separate schools. Independent data suggest otherwise, at least in some of the cases. One source holds, for example, that the schools of Ventura County were segregated until World War II.[54]

Orange County, by the school year 1933–1934, had fifteen all-Mexican-American schools, enrolling 2,727 students.[55] Another 1,310 students attended schools with Anglos. The Mexican-American school buildings were distinctly inferior to those of the Anglos. In a comparison of facilities, with a maximum score of 1,000 as measured by the standard Strayer-Engelhardt Score Card, the average score of ten Mexican-American schools was 593, with a range of 390–819; for Anglo schools, the average score was 714, with a range of 589–782. Mexican-American parents pressed for better school facilities for their children. About 1,000 of the families – perhaps between a quarter and a third of the total – owned enough property to pay property taxes. Roughly the same proportions of Mexican-Americans attended Mexican-American and Anglo schools. Throughout the Southwest, and not in California alone, middle-class Mexican-American children were often permitted to enroll in an Anglo school.[56]

In Brawley, the principal city in the Imperial Valley, 200 miles north of Mexico, the Miguel Hidalgo School, a 95 percent Mexican-American school, enrolled about 1,500 students in the early 1930s. Fourteen of its classes were on double session, and in some of the classrooms there were as many as 86 children at a time. Because of the large number of children engaged in field jobs, enrollment rose and fell with the crop season. Holliday reported in 1935: "Every three years teachers are changed in the Brawley Elementary System due to the Tenure Law. The best teachers from the Mexican school are 'promoted' to the American schools in order to provide experienced teachers there. As a result the teachers [in the Mexican school] are inexperienced as a group . . . Excellent work usually means a change."[57] More than a decade later, Penrod wrote that the Hidalgo School in Brawley was "the one to which all Latins must go if they cannot pass the English-language examination which would permit them entrance into one of the other schools."[58] Negro and Portuguese children were also assigned to Hidalgo.

Penrod described several pervasive practices of exclusion in southern California:

> In some instances school buses carrying Mexican children passed by one or more schoolhouses designated for "Anglo" use only in order to deposit Mexican children from any section of town in a school set aside for the use of all Mexican residents of that community regardless of their proximity to other school facilities. Where "Anglo" and Mexican schools were situated on the same property, adjoining playgrounds were marked off so that one group would not trespass on the other's assigned area. . . . At times group protests were launched in which Mexican-American residents demanded clarification of policy, especially in districts where "Anglos" obtained transfers with no difficulty.[59]

Some of these practices were duplicated throughout the Southwest.

San Bernardino, a citrus center, operated a segregated school system after 1926. Earlier, 60 percent of one elementary school consisted of Mexican-American children. When the building became crowded, a second school was built three blocks away. It was to be an all-Mexican-American school.[60] The erection of the school coincided with an increased influx of Mexican immigrant families. Mexican-American children were assigned to the segregated school rather than to an Anglo one depending on their "prosperity, cleanliness, the aggressiveness of parents, and the quota of Mexican-Americans already in the mixed schools." Over the heads of the few Mexican-American children in Anglo schools lay "the disciplinary threat of being sent to the Mexican school for 'failure to adjust.'"[61]

In 1936, the school board reinforced segregation by building a junior high school – the city's second – deep in the West Side, where Mexican-Americans lived. Feeder arrangements guaranteed the perpetuation of segregated attendance patterns: "The small alumni of the 'mixed' school are permitted to attend the 'mixed' junior high school on the other side of town; but the alumni of the 'Mexican' elementary school go on to the 'Mexican' junior high, there to complete the major part of their schooling under segregated conditions."[62] Since there was no segregated high school, Mexican-American graduates of the segregated junior high finally entered a nonsegregated school at that point.

The personal cruelties inherent in official segregation were felt in many ways. In one part of Los Angeles County, Mexican-American and Anglo children attended the same school but were graduated on different nights. A new refrigerator was authorized, but when it was delivered, it was taken to the Anglo school. The Anglo school in turn handed down its old one to the Mexican-American school. Some Mexican-American parents in Chino enrolled their children in Anglo schools, despite obstacles. In the mid-1940s Lehman wrote: "Many of the parents attended the segregated school and they recall the struggle they had trying to overcome their inferiority complex and their language handicap when they were promoted to junior high school."[63] Teachers at the Chino school firmly implemented the view that "the degree of social adjustment . . . [Mexican-American students] attain is dependent upon the degree to which they speak, think, dress, and act like other Americans."[64] In Bakersfield, an observer said, "such remarks as 'well, you can't expect much from that class, it's full of Mexicans!' or 'You can't teach these Mexicans anything!' are frequently heard when teachers talk shop."[65]

During the 1930s, in San Dimas, a Los Angeles County community where the Ku Klux Klan was a significant force, the elementary school was segregated by classroom; Anglo and Mexican-American children attended the same school, but used different classrooms. Although Mexican-American children in seventh and eighth grades were not subject to the rule – perhaps because they were so few in number – they were forced to use facilities and equipment of lower grades. In San Fernando Valley schools, Mexican-American students who applied for work permits received them readily, especially during the walnut season. In the county as a whole, the necessarily irregular school attendance of children of farm laborers was reinforced by a requirement of the Los Angeles County Department of Charities. According to Scott, this agency "adopted the policy of always sending the families out with the men when work was available at a distance, fearing that if left alone, the Mexican male would be too likely to form other family attachments. Thus, the children would be taken out of school each time the father obtained employment, even temporary, in another area."[66] Whatever the motivation, the policy affected children adversely.

The poverty of Mexican-Americans in Los Angeles City seriously affected school attendance. Before the depth of the Depression of the 1930s was reached, Mexican-American children seemed widely distributed throughout the school system, although the highest proportion of Mexican-American students attended the high school in the Negro community of Watts.

During the 1930s, about 500,000 persons were deported to Mexico from the United States. The Depression reduced the need for a super-surplus of agricultural laborers and strained local relief budgets in southwestern towns and cities. Welfare officials used welfare payments as a means of coercing Mexicans and Mexican-Americans alike to be "repatriated." Half of those deported were, in fact, American citizens. Many were children. The older ones especially had "acquired 'American' ways, made 'American' friends; many protest[ed] against returning to Mexico."[67] Other adults were told that if they refused repatriation they could not receive any more welfare and their file would be closed with the notation "failed to cooperate." Even in much smaller Mexican-American settlements, such as in Detroit, similar events occurred. A special Mexican Bureau was created in the Detroit Department of Public Welfare: "Any Mexican asking for aid was first turned over to the Mexican Bureau to discuss repatriation."[68]

Repatriation signified a profound rejection by dominant American society, thus strengthening the reluctance to acquire a citizenship that permitted its beneficiaries to be forcibly exiled. Many of the *repatriados* were sent on their way in retaliation for striking against low wages and intolerable working conditions. Traditional American labor unions refused to permit them to join and withheld support from any strikes by Mexican-Americans. Repatriation had, however, an unanticipated stabilizing effect on Mexican-American communities, relieving the pressure of a constantly augmented labor force. As residential stability grew, Mexican-Americans took increasing advantage of schooling opportunities in cities, but the bitterness engendered by repatriation caused many to reject the values of the dominant society.

World War II stirred a new civic and ethnic consciousness among

Mexican-Americans. Mexican-American youth entered the armed forces and other Mexican-Americans assumed new economic roles in defense industries.

The schools, however, seemed to emerge from the war years unscathed by any new spirit. Even in an urbanized area such as Dallas, it was estimated that some 10,000 children of elementary school age were not enrolled in any school. Most were Mexican-Americans.[69] Segregation continued in force almost everywhere. This is a small sample of school segregation in wartime Texas: Alice, Bluntzer, Brady, Cameron, Geronimo, Lolita, Melvin, Midland, Ozona, Pearland, Robstown, San Marcos, and Sugar Land. In a few predominantly Mexican-American communities in Texas, like Laredo and Brownsville, some measure of political representation was attained in city hall and school board, but in the large cities, including San Antonio, no Mexican-American sat on the board.[70] After the war, Mexican-American veterans became the most dynamic force for change in their communities. In Texas they organized the American GI Forum; in the twenty-five years after its formation the forum filed more than 200 legal actions against segregated, inferior schools. In towns and cities, veterans led the way in breaking through imposed housing and other restrictions.[71] While the veterans' movement had a strong middle-class tinge, its concerns reached beyond individual advancement. In Chino, California, the return home of Mexican-American veterans touched off a new interest in voter registration. The new voters helped elect a Mexican-American city councilman.[72] Without a broad political base, the veterans' movement in the Southwest could not challenge segregation in any effective way.

In Raymondville, Texas, Mrs. Santos V. Lozano wrote:

> For more than 15 years, only our Latin American children
> have gone to school only half days; in other words, they have been
> getting only half a year of school. Year after year, we have ap-
> pealed to the school board to see if something could be done about
> this problem, but we have been told that "there are too many
> Latin American children," that they are far more than the Anglo
> Americans, and they "didn't know what to do about it."[73]

Mrs. Lozano observed that resort to the ballot box was a way out. She reported that for the first time in the history of Raymondville two Mexican-Americans had run for trustees of the schools. Both lost, but the campaign produced a record turnout.

In California, traditional segregation persisted into the postwar years. As of 1946, according to Penrod, Mexican-American children attended twenty-eight compulsorily segregated schools in Los Angeles and one in San Diego.[74] During the late 1940s, when an Anglo housing development

in eastern Los Angeles was built, Mexican-American children were removed from the nearby school, thus leaving it for the exclusive use of the
Anglo children. Although the Mexican-American children lived across the
street from the now-exclusive school, they were forced to attend a school
several blocks away. A sustained campaign by parents resulted in reversing
the action by the early 1950s. Mexican-American students in Brawley in
Imperial County continued to be assigned to Hidalgo School if they could
not pass a test in English. School board gerrymandering in southern
California was severe. "Boundaries were even so designed that they ran
down the center of a street without including the dwellings on either side
in order to connect two settlements of Mexicans and place them in the
same school."[75]

In Texas, a 1948 survey of 799 school systems reported that over one-
sixth of these systems practiced some degree of segregation.[76] Julian
Suarez, a well-to-do father of school children in Poteet, Texas, complained in an affidavit:

> In the public schools our children of Mexican descent are segre-
> gated . . . up to and including the fourth grade. Up to two years
> ago they were segregated only up to and including the second
> grade. In the first grade our Mexican children are attending in
> two shifts; some go in the morning and some in the afternoon,
> for lack of space. There is room for them in the first grade in the
> Anglo-American school, but authorities will not accept our
> children there.[77]

The inferiority of segregated schools was documented throughout the
postwar years. Three out of four Mexican-American students in Texas
during 1943–1944 were failing to make a year's progress during the
academic year. Financial disparity between Anglo and Mexican-American
schools did not diminish. School facilities were almost uniformly inferior.
In 1949, Gilbert reported that "in most cases . . . the Spanish-speaking
pupils are denied the benefits of certain welfare programs and certain
student or school activities that are found in the Anglo schools."[78] Gilbert
stressed that the discrimination occurred in the face of equal per pupil
state appropriations and higher-than-average assessed valuation per student in counties with large numbers of Mexican-American students.
Teachers in Mexican-American schools often received about $500 less
than teachers in Anglo schools.

Separate schools for Mexican-Americans had been built in Austin in
1916, 1924, and 1935. In 1949, Mexican-American first-graders in one
school were separated from their Anglo classmates. Two other schools
shared a joint attendance area: Zavala School, all Mexican-American; and
Metz, 80 percent Anglo. "Many Anglo children attending Metz live closer

to Zavala school," Cromack found, "and must cross a busy thoroughfare to attend Metz school."[79] Academically, Mexican-American students in Austin lagged seriously. In 1947–1948, they constituted nearly three-fourths of all elementary students, one-fifth of junior high students, and only one-thirteenth of senior high students. Mexican-American students made up from one-sixth to one-fifth of the city's enrollment during 1943–1947, but only one-sixtieth of all graduates.

In Edcouch-Elsa, Texas, three segregated schools served that citrus and vegetable center. Elsa Elementary and North Edcouch Elementary were all Mexican-American while South Edcouch was all Anglo. Pupil-teacher ratios at the first two were 38:1 and 28:1 to 51:1 and at the third 33:1. Calderon, who taught in the city, reported that "Spanish-speaking children were compelled to spend two years in the first grade without regard to the ability of the student."[80] School buildings were greatly inferior for Mexican-Americans, down even to the merest detail. In South Edcouch, for example, the school lavatories had a wall separating each pair. In North Edcouch, there were outside lavatories and no separating wall between each pair. Classroom lights were shielded in South Edcouch; a bare light bulb hung from the ceiling in North Edcouch. Children in Anglo schools received instruction in musical instruments; the others did not. On the school bus, the Mexican-American children sat in the rear.

The correlation between segregation and proportion of Mexican-Americans in the community was practically zero. In Waco, Texas, for example, Mexican-American students constituted only 9.2 percent of enrollment. Nevertheless, sixteen elementary schools were 90 percent or more Anglo and another five from 60 to 89 percent Anglo. One school – Jefferson – was 90.8 percent Mexican-American. Through a free-choice transfer system, the enrollment of Anglo children in Jefferson was lower than the number of such children who lived in the school's attendance area.[81] As elsewhere in the state, Mexican-American children were automatically retarded for a year and their high school enrollment was hardly more than a tenth of their enrollment in elementary school. As of 1957, Ramirez reported the absence of special education classes at the three schools with the highest enrollment of Mexican-Americans.

Inequality in financial resources

Discrimination against Mexican-Americans in the schools included denial of equality in allocation and distribution of financial resources.

During the 1920s, as the Mexican-American population of Texas grew rapidly, state school appropriations also rose. Differential attendance rates of Anglos and Mexican-Americans had permitted these school funds to be skimmed in the interest of Anglo children. Legally, provision of schooling to all children was an obligation, not a charitable act, and indeed, Texas school districts were scrupulous in counting every last child in their jurisdiction for purposes of receiving state aid, apportioned according to the number of school-age children in the district. If none of the Mexican-American children in seventeen districts went to any school, state funds collected in their name were transferred to the benefit of Anglo children. Local school officials neglected to appoint attendance officers and thus, in effect, guaranteed "surplus" funds for Anglo children. In some cases, all schooling was denied Mexican-Americans. In his annual report for the school year 1928–1929, the state superintendent of public instruction acknowledged the notoriety of skimming, but challenged the practice only with a rhetorical question: "Shall the state continue to distribute money to districts reporting a large number of scholastics [?] who do not attend school and are not really wanted since there are practically no efforts being made in such districts to enforce the compulsory attendance law? . . . [Some] sections of the state really encourage a small enrollment."[82] The state did nothing to change this practice.

When some of the Mexican-American children attended school, the costs of educating them were kept low by inferior facilities; part of the state aid then was malappropriated for Anglo children. This system of official deprivation had been perfected throughout the South for discriminating against black children. A special irony lay in the fact that the state school fund used to discriminate against Mexican-American children in Texas was based largely on land taken from Mexico in 1836.

The 1968–1972 inquiry of the U.S. Commission on Civil Rights into discriminatory patterns of public finance concentrated on Texas because that state had the bulk of the region's predominantly Mexican-American school districts and schools. In addition, the intricacy of California expenditure reporting procedures precluded the discovery of per pupil spending out of nonfederal funds. Unfortunately, given the data available, the commission could not ascertain whether financial disparities existed between Anglo and Mexican-American schools within the same districts. Between districts, however, it was found that "children in predominantly Chicano districts receive about three-fifths the financial support provided to their counterparts in Anglo districts."[83] The central mechanism for this discrimination was the system of state aid to schools. For some years the state had provided about half of local school expenses through its Minimum Foundation Program. Most of the remainder came from locally levied property taxes. All but 10 percent of the state funds was used for salaries of professionals, principally teachers. The less qualified the teacher, the lower the state allotment. "Teachers in districts with the heaviest Chicano concentration," the commission found, "are nearly twice as likely to hold no college degree at all as those in primarily Anglo districts,"[84] Predominantly Mexican-American districts had difficulty attracting sufficient teachers and thus forfeited available state aid; affluent Anglo districts experienced no such difficulty. In Bexar County, a poor "Chicano district, with five times less property value than the Anglo district, received less state aid per pupil than its wealthier Anglo neighbor."[85]

Local property taxes were computed, presumably, so as to match tax rate with ability to pay. The actual effect was the opposite. Property owned in predominantly Mexican-American districts was assessed at a higher ratio to its actual value than was property in predominantly Anglo districts. Local school funds were – owing to Mexican-American poverty – necessarily restricted. Because school construction in Texas was financed wholly out of local funds, based on bonds limited to no more than one-tenth of a district's assessed valuation, new building in Mexican-American districts suffered.

In summary, the commission found the school finance program of Texas discriminatory in that it (1) implicitly assumed that Mexican-American children required no more than Anglo children; (2) guaranteed, nevertheless, that Anglo children would receive significantly more from the state; and (3) forced heavy dependence on local property taxes that were incapable of supporting equal, let alone equitable, expenditures. These patterns were of ancient vintage.

Ambivalence of the courts on discrimination and segregation

Unlike European and other immigrants in the United States, Mexican immigrants in Texas had to resort to legal action to establish the right of their children to attend public schools. The school board of Coryell County refused in 1921 to permit an eight-year-old child, Pete Peralez, to attend school on the ground that "neither he nor his parents are citizens of the United States, both parents and child being born in Mexico, and never having applied for naturalization papers."[86] When parents appealed to the state superintendent, he, in turn, asked the state attorney general for an advisory opinion. The state attorney general pointed out that the state's school law required that "every child in this state, of scholastic age, shall be permitted to attend the public free schools of the district or independent district in which it resides at the time it applies for admission." He advised that Coryell County be overruled.

The authority of local school boards to segregate black students was a matter of explicit state law in Texas. No such authority was specified for Mexican-American children. By ruling of the state department of education, however, county school trustees were accorded considerable power to classify schools: "The county trustees have authority to classify schools in the county on the basis of conditions and needs regardless of the wishes of the residents of the school district. Classification of schools in a county is a matter left to the discretion of the county board of trustees."[87] Numerous boards of trustees interpreted this general authorization as permission to segregate Mexican-American children.

In 1928, this point became a legal issue. The Charlotte schools in Atascosa County defended their practice of segregating Mexican-American students in a separate building. A parent, Felipe Vela, had been turned away when he tried to register his daughter Amada in the "American" school. The school board denied it based the action on ethnic grounds, asserting it had depended on educational considerations such as grouping children of irregular attendance and language difficulties. Upon an appeal by the father to the state superintendent of public instruction, S. M. N. Marrs, the local board was directed to admit the girl because she was a good student and could keep up with American students.[88] In the appeal, both parties agreed that segregation could not rest on an ethnic ("racial") ground. Upon further appeal by the school district, the Marrs ruling was approved by the state board of education.

In 1929, Mexican-Americans in Texas formed the League of United Latin American Citizens (LULAC), their first national ethnic-protest organization. Point 24 of its statement of aims and purpose asserted: "We shall oppose any tendency to separate our children in the schools of this country."[89] The next year, LULAC challenged segregation in Del Rio Independent School District, where Mexican-American children were compelled to attend a separate school for the first three grades. LULAC won a local court injunction against the practice, but this was appealed by the school board. In *Salvatierra*, the higher court struck down the earlier decision and dissolved the injunction on the ground that there was no demonstrated intent to segregate because of race. It reasoned that:

> An unlawful discrimination will be effectuated if the rules for the separation are arbitrary and are applied indiscriminately to all Mexican pupils in those grades without apparent regard to their individual aptitudes or attainments, while relieving children of other white races from the operation of the rule, even though some of them, as for instance those who tardily enter the terms, may be subject to the classification given the Mexican children.[90]

Following the reasoning of *Vela*, the court approved segregation for educational reasons but not on the ground of race. The court's distinction was highly academic and without any consequence for children. Race continued to be used as the basis for school segregation. The state failed completely to reexamine the schools in the light of *Salvatierra*. The next year, in 1931, LULAC created an education committee and settled down for a long campaign.

In *Salvatierra,* Mexican-Americans had gained acknowledgment as members of the "white race." Rangel and Alcala explain the strategy of seeking to be declared Caucasians as flowing from the then reigning *Plessy* v. *Ferguson* doctrine. In the absence of a state law requiring segregation of Mexican-Americans, they claimed equal treatment with all other "whites." The crucial point was to leave little leeway to be treated as blacks under both state law and U.S. Supreme Court ruling.

California, like Texas, had no statute requiring segregation of Mexican-American students. The same end was accomplished there by official administrative action. As of 1930, the California school law stated that "trustees shall have the power to establish separate schools for Indian children and for children of Mongolian descent." In January of that year, a ruling by State Attorney General U. S. Webb provided a legal basis for segregating Mexican-American students. He wrote: "It is well known that the greater portion of the population of Mexico are Indians, and when such Indians migrate to the United States they are subject to the laws applicable generally to other Indians."[91] The Mexican-American was "white" in Texas but "Indian" in California.

When the California school law was amended in 1935, care was taken not to disturb the newfound Indianism of Mexican-Americans. The revised provision read:

> The governing board of the school district shall have power to
> establish separate schools for Indian children, excepting children
> of Indians who are wards of the United States government and
> children of all other Indians who are descendants of the original
> American Indians of the United States, and for children of
> Chinese, Japanese, or Mongolian parentage.[92]

The wording left a loophole for continuing to segregate those "Indians" from Mexico formerly know as "Mexicans." Mexican-American parents in California were left with the slightest of legal goals – eventual classification as Caucasians, although in Texas this was already a reality without beneficial consequences. The provision in the school law was not repealed until 1947.

When, in 1943, a Mexican-American couple in Fullerton successfully challenged the legality of a restrictive covenant against "Mexican" occupation of a house, Judge Albert Ross declared the occupants to be members of the Caucasian race and their exclusion a violation of the Fifth and Fourteenth amendments.[93] The decision "set off a chain of reaction against infringement of the rights" of Mexican-Americans.[94]

A logical next step was to confront segregation in the schools. Mexican-American parents sued four school districts in Orange County,

California, to admit their children into Anglo schools and to declare illegal any segregation of Mexican-American children. U.S. District Judge Paul J. McCormick ruled in *Mendez* that the system of segregation was unconstitutional.

Judge McCormick held that separate-but-equal facilities for Mexican-American children did not amount to equal protection of the law. He stipulated: "A paramount requisite in the American system of public education is social equality. It must be open to all children by unified school association regardless of lineage." Evidence, according to the court, had established the retarding effect of segregation on the learning of English, the fostering of antagonism among children of different groups, and the suggestion of "inferiority among them where none exists." Separate classrooms for language problems were permissible, but only when the criteria for placement include "credible examination by the appropriate school authority of each child." Judge McCormick's ruling was upheld on appeal by all seven judges of the U.S. Court of Appeals for the Ninth Circuit. One of the seven, Judge Denman, suggested the school authorities reponsible for the segregation should have been tried for a felony. In effect, *Mendez* directly contradicted the 1930 ruling by State Attorney General Webb.[95]

Rangel and Alcala argue that *Mendez* did not outlaw school segregation as such for being a violation of the Fourteenth Amendment. They suggest that the decision failed to preclude the passage by the legislature of a law to segregate Mexican-American children.[96] Whatever the precise interpretation, Mexican-American parents did not wait. They filed a number of successful lawsuits asking for an application of *Mendez*. In Modeno, such a suit was followed by the election of a Mexican-American to the school board. In anticipation of more litigation, numerous other school boards "voluntarily" desegregated.

Mendez soon became involved in Texas school decisions. During 1946, L. A. Woods, Texas state superintendent of public instruction, informed the superintendent of Pleasanton public schools by letter that "the Latin-American children have as much right under the law to nice rooms, good equipment, textbooks, and an uncrowded situation as the Anglo Americans." He warned against separating Mexican-American children beyond the second grade for language purposes.[97] This was not far from *Mendez*. In 1947, the state attorney general was queried whether the Cuero Independent School District could erect a separate school for Mexican-American students through the first three grades if placement of students were based on individual testing. The attorney general said yes, holding that "the legislature has expressly provided for segregation and special treatment of certain classes of pupils termed 'exceptional students.'" Apparently, this was the first time Mexican-American students with language problems were equated with mentally handicapped and others usually subsumed under the label "exceptional." He added, however, that under *Salvatierra* and *Mendez* placement must be on an individual, not racial, basis.[98]

The following year, Mexican-American parents in Bastrop, Caldwell, and Travis counties brought a class action in federal district court to abolish separate schools for their children. In *Delgado*, the court declared the practice to be in violation of the Fourteenth Amendment. Separation was specifically approved for a single year in first grade; thereafter, only following the administration of "scientific and standardized tests, equally given and applied to all pupils."[99] September 1949 was set as the deadline for any required construction to facilitate consolidation of hitherto segregated schools. The court dropped the state board of education as a party to suit. On the other hand, the state superintendent of public instruction was specifically named in the judgment: "The defendant, L. A. Woods, as State Superintendent of Public Instruction, is hereby permanently restrained and enjoined from in any manner, directly or indirectly, participating in the custom, usage or practice of segregating pupils of Mexican or other Latin American descent in separate schools or classes." Superintendent Woods moved quickly to implement the injunction. In July 1948, he issued a set of regulations emphasizing, among other things, that segregation by race or descent had never been legal in Texas and had so been held by state courts and, in *Delgado*, by a federal court. Upon investigation, Woods found the Del Rio Independent School District to be violating *Delgado*. In February 1949, he made the official finding and in April affirmed it on rehearing.

> I hereby confirm my previous ruling of withdrawing the accreditation from the Del Rio Independent School District, removing them from the accredited list of schools, and do here hereby declare it to be an illegally operated school to which teachers who are the holders of valid teachers' certificates, issued through this office, are not eligible to teach without having their teachers' certificates cancelled, after the beginning of the scholastic year of 1949–1950, which begins on September 1, 1949. The removal of Del Rio School from [the] accredited list is still effective as of February 12, 1949.[100]

Just three months later, in July 1949, the state board of education revoked the Woods decision. Woods himself soon departed from office as a result of reorganization undoubtedly hastened by his prompt effort to enforce *Delgado*.

Within nine months of taking office, Woods's successor, State Education Commissioner James W. Edgar, received complaints of violation of

Delgado from at least twenty-two cities. The cases dragged on without consequential result. Segregated schools in Hondo and Pecos were found by Edgar not to be in violation of *Delgado*. In Driscoll, most Mexican-American children still spent three years in the first grade.[101] In Kyle, Seguin, and Lockhart, violations continued.[102] The main burden of *Delgado* was systematically rejected by school districts, with the cooperation of state authorities. Twice in eighteen years, the Del Rio district had been ordered to stop segregating Mexican-American children: in *Salvatierra* (1930) and in *Delgado* (1948). (In 1971, in *United States* v. *Texas*, a federal court again condemned segregation in the district.)

Issuance of the *Brown* decision by the U.S. Supreme Court had, at first, only a slight effect on segregation of black students. It affected Mexican-Americans even less. Under *Plessy*, Mexican-Americans had sought the legal status of Caucasian in order to claim equal school rights. In the first decade or so after *Brown*, school authorities started to use them as sham Caucasians. When desegregation of black schools became unavoidable, federal courts in Texas accepted plans that brought together black and Mexican-American students. Thus, Anglo students continued to attend separate schools, only now with the approval of federal courts. In Salinas's phrase, Mexican-Americans were "being *used* as whites and not *treated* as whites" in order to avoid Anglo desegregation.[103]

In the classrooms as in the courts, the same fundamental two-sidedness was apparent. Speaking especially of schools in Texas, Garcia stated that "the Mexican-American child today is still being treated like a 'colonial child' instead of . . . an American citizen."[104] A school counselor in Los Angeles, Perez, said: "While their kids are in school, they are told they are Americans and yet they are treated as Mexicans."[105] The tension between both poles was apparent in part even among Mexican-Americans themselves. At issue was the ethnic identity of Mexican-Americans. In legal terms, the question became: Do Mexican-Americans constitute an identifiable minority group? If so, they could gain the protection of the Fourteenth Amendment and *Brown* on their own terms.

Before 1954, state courts in Texas repeatedly rejected claims of separate minority status for Mexican-Americans. California courts – both state and federal – did recognize the claim. Two weeks before the U.S. Supreme Court decided *Brown*, it ruled in *Hernandez* v. *Texas* that systematic exclusion of Mexican-Americans from jury duty violated the equal protection clause of the Fourteenth Amendment. Nearly a decade earlier, Texas courts had twice refused to reach a similar conclusion on jury selection. In *Sanchez*, a state court noted that equal protection had been applied by the Supreme Court only to races, not nationalities. In *Salazar*, another court ruled: "The complaint is made of discrimination against nationality, not race. The Mexican people are of the same race as the grand jurors. We see no question presented for our discussion under the 14th Amendment to the Constitution of the United States." By 1954, *Hernandez* superseded this doctrine. Yet given the unbroken record of Texan inaction in the face of school rulings critical of segregation, Mexican-Americans made no attempt to apply *Hernandez* to Texas school affairs.

Rise of protest, demands, and demonstrations

The decade following *Brown* ended with passage of the Civil Rights Act of 1964. To some degree, Mexican-Americans formed part of the civil rights movement that brought the legislation into being. The development of union organization among Mexican-American farm laborers under the leadership of Cesar Chavez during the latter half of the 1960s greatly encouraged civic expression by Mexican-Americans. Ethnic assertiveness leaped forward under the impetus of the youthful Chicano movement, and renewed attempts were made through legal channels to achieve minority status.

Improvement of schools was a leading object of community political organization by Mexican-Americans. Between 1930 and 1960, a number of lawsuits had been sponsored by these groups, especially in Texas but also in California. During the early 1960s, Mexican-Americans made tentative efforts to join their cause with that of the general civil rights movement. In the summer of 1963, the United Civil Rights Committee in Los Angeles was formed. When Mexican-Americans tried to join, they were spurned. In August, a conference was held in the city on the educational problems of Mexican-American children; many of the panelists were Mexican-American teachers from the city's schools. Among the demands of the conference were calls for culture-free IQ tests, smaller classes and more individual instruction, a stress on Mexican-American contributions to American life and history, and a contention that instruction in English as a second language should not foreclose instruction in Spanish. When, later in the month, a citywide civil rights demonstration took place at city hall, the Mexican-American community was represented in the leadership.

Here and there over the Southwest, Mexican-American educators started to play a heightened role in their community's school concerns. But their participation tended to be cast in a mold of professionalism. The urgency of the need for reforms barely filtered through.

In 1968, the urgency exploded into public view when Mexican-American students took matters into their own hands. Showing their impatience with conversational modes of educational change, they conducted school boycotts or "blowouts." In Texas alone, over a two-year period, demonstrations occurred in Uvalde, Crystal City, Edcouch-Elsa,

Kingsville, Alpine, San Antonio, Sierra Blanca, Lubbock, Abilene, and San Marcos.[106] In Denver, Chicago, and Albuquerque, students organized public protests. But the earliest and largest of the actions occurred in Los Angeles. In March 1968, some 12,000 students in five predominantly Mexican-American high schools called a boycott.

Demands numbered thirty-six, covering a very broad range of subjects. In one degree or another, these became the standard demands of the Chicano student demonstrations:[107]

1. Predominantly Mexican-American schools should have Mexican-American administrators.
2. Nonacademic assemblies should not interfere with the institutional program.
3. Bilingual personnel should be encouraged to join the staff at all levels.
4. In predominantly Mexican-American schools bilingual and bicultural education should be compulsory for Mexican-American – but optional for other – students.
5. New high schools should be built immediately and the community permitted to name them.
6. Buildings that are not earthquake-proof should be rehabilitated.
7. Student menus in the cafeterias should be "Mexican-oriented."
8. Class size should not exceed twenty students per teacher.
9. Students must not be asked to perform janitorial services.
10. Staff should learn about the school's culture and community.
11. All corporal punishment should be abolished.
12. Number of counselors should be increased and more Mexican-American counselors sought.
13. Number of classes should be increased both in required and elective courses.
14. Neither student nor teacher should suffer for having spoken out in favor of improved education.
15. Students should be able to circulate whatever literature they want.
16. Excessive failure grades in East Los Angeles schools call for an evaluation of the grading system.
17. Dress and grooming standards should be set jointly by parents, students, and teachers.
18. Homogeneous grouping of students should be abolished.
19. Textbooks should be used that portray truthfully the life and history of Mexican-Americans.
20. IQ tests should contain a community component while students from "communities with different knowledge source material" should be allowed a 10 percent leeway in scoring.

21. All libraries in East Los Angeles High schools stocked with Spanish-language materials should be expanded.
22. Students with nonacademic majors should be encouraged to take academic courses.
23. Teachers of non-English-speaking students should be competent in Spanish.
24. All high school campuses should be open.
25. Prejudiced teachers or administrators should be removed.
26. "A concerted, concentrated reading program" should be initiated in all classrooms, not just in remedial classes.
27. Restrooms should be kept open during the school day.
28. ROTC should be eliminated.
29. Student body offices should be open to all students, and high academic average should not be a prerequisite.
30. Rules governing suspension should be regularized after consultation between community, administrators, and teachers.
31. Swimming pools should be provided for high schools in East Los Angeles.
32. Community parents should be employed as teachers aides.
33. Teachers should be protected from dismissal or transfer for political or philosophical disagreement with administrators.
34. The shortage of Mexican-American teachers, especially males, and administrators should be remedied.
35. In-service training should be provided to teachers on the "problems and values of the Greater East Los Angeles community."
36. The industrial arts program should be revitalized.

Except for cultural demands, the students' priorities aimed at providing students in East Los Angeles high schools with conditions thought to be standard in other high schools. Few were in any sense revolutionary. Their conventionality was startling. Those strategists who designed the demands did not wish, apparently, to tarry over complicated and unprecedented measures. They simply sought acknowledgment that Mexican-Americans had, on the one hand, distinctive needs, and on the other, needs in common with all other students. Similarity of needs suggested equality of treatment. The sight of thousands of young Mexican-Americans demanding participation in decision making even in limited areas of school governance disturbed school authorities.

The thirty-six demands had been formulated during six months of community meetings before presentation during the boycott.[108] After agreeing to negotiate, the school board granted amnesty to all participants, but the Los Angeles County grand jury returned criminal indictments against thirteen leaders of the boycott, charging them with conspiracy to commit a disturbance and fourteen additional counts. Eleven of the thirteen were members of the Brown Berets, militant exponents of Chicano consciousness, or the United Mexican-American Students, a college group. Maximum penalty on the charges was forty-five years in the penitentiary. Bail for each of the thirteen was set at $12,500. After a demonstration of some 2,000 marchers, bail was lowered to $1,000 and then to $250. A week later some Mexican-Americans who were in Washington, D.C. as part of the Poor People's Campaign demonstrated before the offices of the U.S. Department of Justice. They asked authorities to help free the thirteen on the ground that the Treaty of Guadalupe Hidalgo of 1848 guaranteed "a bilingual education and an education respectful to our culture and history."[109] In time, the defendants were found not guilty. After a prolonged campaign in the Mexican-American community, the school board reinstated a teacher who was one of the thirteen.

Resistance to Chicano school demands was often exceedingly severe. In Uvalde, Texas Rangers were called out when a boycott started in 1970. Uriegas describes other consequences: "Teenage boycotters lost after-school jobs, and all male boycotters over the age of 18 were reclassified by the local draft board. . . . Parents of boycotters also lost jobs or were subjected to daily pressure from their Anglo employers to return their children to school. . . . School board President Dishman took to the editorial columns of the local newspaper with the charge that the boycott was communist inspired."[110] During the boycott, mothers cooked hot meals with food donated by merchants. A mother of nine children who opposed the action was won over when her two eldest told her: "We are willing to pay the price, Mama. We know we will never make it in school, but we want to give our brothers and sisters a chance." Student demonstrations became communitywide actions.

When city and school authorities refused to compromise or even bargain, Mexican-Americans sometimes organized politically to replace them. In Crystal City, Texas, for example, not until 1946 did the first Mexican-American youngster attend high school.[111] Under the leadership of La Raza Unida, a newly organized political party, Mexican-Americans won control of the city hall and board of education. The superintendent was discharged and soon found another position in nearby Lockhart. When Mexican-Americans there learned of his background, they demanded he be discharged; he was.[112] In San Marcos, Mexican-American students conducted boycotts in 1971 and 1972. Soon after the second boycott ended without result, school board elections were held. Two Mexican-Americans won seats on the seven-member board, and a third lost by only fourteen votes. Political power as an instrument of educational equality was being tested, but the scope of the testing was narrow and limited. Protest had not yet begun to bear fruit.

Administrative action on discrimination

Title VI of the Civil Rights Act of 1964 had outlawed the discriminatory use of federal funds on the grounds of national origin as well as race and color. Still, the potential of the provisions was not employed for some years. Gerry writes that "between 1954–1970 neither the courts nor the Executive Branch seriously attacked either the segregation of Mexican-American . . . children or the invidious discriminatory practices utilized by school districts in the operation of educational programs within schools."[113] Late in 1969, the Office for Civil Rights for HEW began systematic exploration of discrimination against "national origin minority group children."

In 1970, U.S. District Judge Woodrow Seals ruled in *Cisneros* that Mexican-Americans constituted an "identifiable ethnic minority with a past pattern of discrimination" in Corpus Christi, Texas.[114] After another set of hearings on a detailed desegregation plan, the decision was upheld on appeal by the U.S. Court of Appeals for the Fifth Circuit. On the same day, the appeals court also decided the Austin, Texas, case in *United States* v. *Texas Education Agency,* repeating its findings of an ethnic minority. With respect to *Brown's* finding of the harm caused to children by segregation, the appeals court commented: "We see no reason to believe that ethnic segregation is any less detrimental than racial segregation." Before 1954, the court said, the Austin school "used dual-overlapping attendance zones, student assignment policies, and site selection" to segregate Mexican-American children. When Anglos, blacks, and Mexican-Americans made up "a tri-ethnic" school system, the desegregation plan could not deprive any of the parties "of the benefits of equal educational opportunity." Specifically forbidden was a plan that placed only blacks and Mexican-Americans in the same school. School authorities were directed to seek to employ more Mexican-American teachers.[115]

While judicial doctrines were being brought abreast the hopes of Mexican-Americans, progress in the schools lagged. A former regional officer of the Office for Civil Rights testified in 1970 that in the Southwest many schools "still segregate Mexican-Americans in separate classes . . . and segregate Mexican-Americans and Negroes in the same separate classes."[116] When Vela visited the Austin, Texas, school district, he recounted:

> I shall never forget the response . . . when I asked the lady in
> charge of testing for the district, whether the fact that the
> Mexican-American schools in Austin had the lowest test scores
> was due to a language barrier. Her response was "No, it's inherent." I responded that I was a Mexican-American. In a rather

surprised voice, she answered: "Well, you're just an exception to the rule, it's still inherent."[117]

These attitudes were beyond the reach of an ordinary desegregation plan.

So educationally debilitated had many school districts become after generations of segregation, that the educational implications of a court order for desegregation were not readily sensed. Courts were at times pressed to direct the preparation of rather detailed educational guidelines. In the case involving San Felipe – Del Rio, Texas, for example, U.S. District Judge William Wayne Justice required the submission of an educational plan including "bilingual and bicultural programs, faculty recruitment and training and curriculum design and content." Nearly four months later, in December 1971, Judge Justice approved a comprehensive plan with the following elements:[118]

1. Professional staff treatment and assignment
2. Curriculum design and content and instructional methodology
3. Student assignment and classroom organization
4. Staff development
5. Parent and community involvement
6. Special education
7. Noninstructional support
8. Funding and timing
9. Evaluation of comprehensive plan

Suggestions were also made for seeking federal and other funding.

Federal administrative action started in 1970. Under authority of Title VI of the Civil Rights Act, the Office for Civil Rights issued a memorandum relating to discrimination because of national origin.[119] School districts were assigned the affirmative obligation to provide special instruction whenever "inability to speak and understand the English language excludes national origin – minority group children from effective participation in the educational program offered by a school district." After two years of enforcement, the Office for Civil Rights reported it had negotiated plans for a dozen Texas school districts found to be out of compliance with the 1970 memorandum. Another twenty-eight districts were under investigation.[120] The total impact of these early efforts was modest. The Office for Civil Rights frequently recommended that local school districts undertake bilingual programs. Because, however, the districts almost always regarded these measures as "extra," they sought outside funds rather than provide support in their regular budget. When federal funding for bilingual education fell far short of requests, little changed in the classrooms.

Various states revised long-standing policies or initiated new ones. The constitution of New Mexico required that teachers be able to teach bilingually. Obviously ignored, the provision was useless. In 1968, in response to a challenge by Hispanos, the state's attorney general ruled that the constitutional requirement was optional. Three years later, the official reversed the earlier ruling and declared the provision mandatory, urging the legislature to require teacher-training institutions in the state to train a sufficient number of bilingual teachers.[121] Massachusetts in 1971 became the first state to require by statute that school districts enrolling more than twenty pupils of non-English-speaking background must provide bilingual instruction.[122] The actual number of children in the United States receiving a bilingual education grew only slightly over the levels found by the U.S. Commission on Civil Rights in 1969 and 1970. This threw a cloud over claims of significant progress for Mexican-American children. Rangel and Alcala write that desegregation "without accompanying compensatory programs . . . does not provide equal opportunities because Chicanos have special educational needs impairing their ability to succeed in the English-language environment of public schools."[123]

During 1968–1972, the U.S. Commission on Civil Rights conducted the most detailed survey yet made of Mexican-American education.[124] The *Mexican-American Education Study* made a special analysis of schooling in the Southwest.

Seven out of ten Spanish-surnamed students in the United States were attending school in the Southwest. Of these 1,397,586 children, 46.3 percent were in California, 36.1 percent in Texas, 7.4 percent in New Mexico, and 5.1 percent each in Arizona and Colorado. In Texas, about two-thirds of Mexican-American students attended school in or near twenty-seven counties along the Mexican border. In the Southwest as a whole, most Mexican-American students attended urban schools. In Arizona, 19.2 percent were in the Tucson school district; in California, 20.2 percent were in Los Angeles; in Colorado, 26.1 percent were in Denver and 13.5 percent in Pueblo; in New Mexico, 27.3 percent were in Albuquerque; and in Texas, 9.1 percent were in San Antonio, 6.7 percent in El Paso, and 6.3 percent in Houston. Ethnic isolation was most pronounced in Texas, where four out of ten were in schools 80 percent or more Mexican-American; in California, only one of ten were in such schools. Ethnic isolation of Anglo students was also especially severe in Texas: three-quarters attended schools 90 percent or more Anglo, while only 7 percent of the state's Mexican-American students attended Anglo schools.[125] The side-by-side coexistence of predominantly Anglo and Mexican-American school districts, even in general areas of Mexican-American predominance, was "not unusual," the U.S. Commission on Civil Rights said.[126]

Mexican-American school board members were generally few in number, except in New Mexico where they held some 40 percent of the posts, the same proportion as Mexican-American students. Virtually all the remaining board members were in predominantly Mexican-American school districts in South Texas. Among all professional school personnel, Mexican-Americans were under-represented in southwestern schools: they constituted only 10.4 percent of superintendents, 7.1 percent of central staff members, 5.4 percent of counselors, 4.0 percent of teachers, 3.6 percent of librarians, and 3.0 percent of principals.[127]

The findings of the Commission on Civil Rights demonstrate the essential continuity of Mexican-American education in the United States: (1) a high degree of segregation, (2) an extremely low academic achievement, (3) a predominance of exclusionary practices by schools, and (4) a discriminatory use of public finance. The pattern is similar to that imposed upon black children, who were also regarded by the dominant white society as inferior. Denial of an equal education was a powerful instrument of continued oppression. Those who were not permitted to learn were deemed incapable of learning and could, logically therefore, be confined to a lower status in the society.

5

Indian-American children

The white design against Indian education was, like that of whites against blacks and Mexican-Americans, all-embracing and consistently oppressive.

The white conquest that was powerful enough to wrest some 2 billion acres of land from the Indians[1] was followed by repeated and continued efforts to bring about the disintegration of Indian society and culture. Formal education to the conquerors seemed useful to hasten this disintegration. The Indians accepted the education of their conquerors only when it did not compromise their own self-respect and ethnic identity. When, as in the case of the Cherokee and sister tribes, Indians were able to retain both, their educational achievements outstripped those of the conquerors themselves.

When armed resistance became impossible, and cultural engulfment seemed all but irresistible, Indians somehow maintained the core of their identity. "The institutions that serve Indians," said William Penseno, Ponca, vice president of the National Indian Youth Council, "were created by man, and the Indians were created by God. Surely the institutions are more amenable to change than the people."[2] For the first time in American history, the Indian people organized to change the educational institutions of the country.

During their many centuries in North America, the Indians built tribal societies and traditional ways of life out of a wilderness. Tribal education prepared children for a meaningful, competent life. Its principal social values, cooperation and collective organization, encompassed and made possible both individual variation and tribal solidarity. In the collective, cooperative, noncompetitive Indian society, the family, and through it the tribe, became the primary social organization of Indian societies. Education was a basic social necessity.

North American Indian education was highly formal in its goals and informal in its means. So far as is known, formal schools like those the Aztecs developed did not appear among North American Indians. Pettitt says:

The result was not merely to focus community attention on the child, but also to make the child's education a constant challenge to the elders to review, analyze, dramatize, and defend their cultural heritage. Their own beliefs, understanding, and faith, their personal integration in the culture, and their collective unity, all were promoted by the necessity of assuming the role of educators of their children.[3]

Education occurred in a context of seeming indulgence. Corporal punishment of children was almost unknown. The threat of bodily pain stirred little fear among people who stressed the need to withstand pain and suffering without complaint, but also, children were often viewed as bearing an intimate relation with the supernatural; to punish the child would be to flout the gods. Yet actual misbehavior did not go unpunished. The disciplinarian was typically the brother or the mother. Uncles often served also as teachers, an allocation of responsibility that was an extension of the basic social relation of brother and sister. Critical in disciplining children, or avoiding the need for it, was an ever-present evil spirit who could swoop down on the misbehaving.

Pettitt writes of "primitive pedagogy," implying the presence of a conscious, designed series of instructional strategies. Praise of desired learning by public ceremonial means was a tribal strategy to stimulate learning. Ridicule might follow praise, but never indiscriminately or universally. Ridicule was "generally reserved as the prerogative of specific individuals whose identity is determined by kinship, by occupancy of societal or public office, or by some other publicly recognized criterion."[4] Sheer imitation of adults, without social supervision, occurred in the realm of play, not education.

The conferral of personal names was another instructional strategy. Through names, young children learned an approved personal identity. Their names could change as they registered significant achievements. The child's name was not a label, but public notice that the tribe had won another defender of its way of life. During the 1860s and 1870s, a Sioux remembered with pain: "I had to bear the humiliating name 'Hadakah,' meaning 'the pitiful last,' until I should earn a more dignified and appropriate name."[5]

Education made extensive use of religion. The search for a guardian spirit aimed to produce "an independent, self-confident, and self-reliant personality, buoyed up by an inner conviction of his ability to meet any and all situations."[6] Special functionaries, shamans, and priests, to intercede with the supernatural acquired specialized knowledge through long periods of study.

Oral literature authenticated the cultural life of the tribe. A Sioux explained:

> Almost every evening a myth, or a true story of some deed in the past, was narrated by one of the parents or grandparents, while the boy listened with parted lips and glistening eyes. On the following evening, he was usually required to repeat it. . . .
> The household became his audience, by which he was alternately criticized and applauded. This sort of teaching at once enlightens the boy's mind and stimulates his ambition. His conception of his own future career becomes a vivid and irreversible force.[7]

Lessons in history were recited by the tribal historian whose "documents" consisted of bundles of variously colored sticks, one bundle with the number of his own years, another composed of sticks representing the important events of history, each marked with the number of years since the event.

Indian intellectual life extended far beyond the sphere of traditional education.[8] In response to the universal challenge of sickness, Indians developed a large body of effective medical knowledge. Herbal remedies for internal disorders were used not only by their Indian discoverers, but by whites on the frontier. The medicine man was a physician and priest, as well as a tribal leader.

Traditional education did not disappear with the arrival of white men in America. Examples of its persistence are legion.

During the colonial period, when whites sought to separate the Indian from his land, education for Indians, usually coupled with Christianization as a goal, was skimped by the English colonists. Around 1650, for example, some 20,000 Indians lived in New England. The merest handful was ever educated in a white school, although the children of some Indian servants in New England homes learned rudiments of literacy from their masters or in dame schools. The Indian children and women sold into slavery after the colonists' bitter war against the Pequot Indians in 1637, according to Allen, did receive instruction.[9]

Isolated missionaries here and there undertook the schooling of Indians. Eleazar Wheelock in New Hampshire seems to have taught some forty or fifty male Indians between 1754 and 1768. John Eliot, working in the Massachusetts Bay Colony, reported in 1674 that he had taught nine Indians to read and seventy-two to write English. The Moravians conducted missions among Indians in Georgia, Pennsylvania, New York, and Connecticut. They were unique among the missionaries because they encouraged Indian children to retain their native language.

Indians, even those who completed a round of schooling in English, found little to admire in white ways. Whether schooled in England or the colonies, most Indians returned to a way of life that had served their needs for many centuries.

Education as a tool of pacification

Indian education first entered the arena of American public policy not as an act of benevolence but as an instrument of military strategy. In 1775, when the Revolutionary War against England broke out, the Continental Congress donated $500 to Dartmouth College for the education of Indian youth, "a purely military measure," Layman notes, "designed to conciliate the northern tribes and to prevent attacks upon the outlying settlements of New Hampshire."[10] Even the American Revolution was in part an effort by colonists to open the Indian lands of the Ohio Valley to white appropriation, a move England resisted for its own imperial reasons. Ironically, in 1775, Americans made the first federal expenditure on Indian education in an effort to pacify New England Indians and thus help ensure the conquest of Indian land to the west.

After the end of the Revolutionary War in 1783, white settlers poured into the Ohio Valley, accompanied if not preceded by American soldiers.

In 1790, white settlers in the Ohio Valley signed the secret Kaskaskia Treaty with the Creeks, with "the first provision for contributions by the United States for organized education."[11] Few other treaties contained provisions for educational annuities. If Indians wanted educational facilities, they had to use part of the land annuities paid for cession of their land for this purpose. In 1802, Congress, faced with the application of Ohio for statehood, enacted a law authorizing a maximum expenditure for Indian education of $15,000 per year. Education was increasingly viewed as a means of pacifying the natives.

After the close of the War of 1812 and the tribal wars to defend their land in the South, Indians were encouraged by financial incentive to leave their land and go west of the Mississippi to make way for slave-cultivated cotton expansion. In 1819, Congress passed the Indian Civilization Act, providing, among other things, for an annual educational expenditure of $10,000. By such means Indians might learn to become farmers – a farm needs much less land than a hunting ground – and master "the habits and arts of civilization." Secretary of War John C. Calhoun viewed the schools as auxiliary to the government policy of removal. "Indian schools in which the desirability of such an emigration could be inculcated in the youth of the tribes," he wrote, "would be of inestimable value in effecting the plans of the government."[12] For the Indians to build schools east of the Mississippi was unacceptable to the government, which wanted them out of the valuable cotton lands.

When, by 1830, little movement westward by Indians had occurred, the federal government undertook to negotiate "a series of forced and fradulent treaties."[13] Within a decade, some 125,000 Indians were forced to leave the lands they had held under prior assurance in earlier treaties of permanent possession. Provisions for cession of land were written into the treaties, and in return some of the proceeds from the sale of this land were handed over to the Indians to finance schools. These moneys came in the form of school annuities or a school fund against which orders could be drawn. In 1834, $31,500 per year was being spent on education under provisions of fourteen different treaties.

None of the Indian schools was operated by the federal government. Instead, from 1819 on, federal contracts were signed with church missionary societies to conduct these schools. Yet the Indians supplied most of the funds for their own education. During 1845–1855, a total of $2,154,267.75 was spent on education of the Indian. The source of this money was as follows: Indian treaty funds, $824,160.61 (38.2 percent); funds of Indian nations, $400,000 (18.6 percent); private societies, $830,000 (38.5 percent); and the Federal Civilization Fund, $102,107.14 (4.7 percent). Congress refused to supplement its $10,000 annual school disbursement, even when Indian tribes requested it.[14]

Modest numbers of children attended these schools (Table 26). In 1824, about 500 Indian children were reportedly enrolled; by 1842, 2,132; in 1848, somewhat above 2,800 students. These figures are undoubtedly incomplete.

The "Civilized Tribes" and white education

The response of the tribes to the white approach to their education included eagerness for education but without loss of cultural heritage.

Schooling was most successful among the southern Indians, the so-called Five Civilized Tribes (Cherokee, Creek, Chickasaw, Choctaw, and Seminole), who, at the end of the Revolution, were settled on the lands between Tennessee and Mississippi. They were, as a group, distinguished from most other tribes by the relative ease with which they modified various aspects of traditional Indian culture.

In 1763 a group of Cherokee invited Moravian missionaries to open a school, but nothing resulted. Two years later, a delegation traveled to London to request schools, but warned also against white settler expansion onto their lands. The trip was in vain. A few Cherokee youths attended white schools in the colonies. As late as 1817, only a single school existed for all the southern Indians.[15] When Congress set up the Civilization Fund in 1819, missionaries responded with alacrity. They hurried to those Indians most likely to welcome them. By 1820, many Cherokee parents were taking an active part in their children's education. They attended the schools' yearly examinations and sent back sons and

Table 26. *Attendance in federal Indian schools in the United States,
1825–1886*

Year	Number of schools	Number of pupils	Year	Number of schools	Number of pupils
1819, 1824[a]			1861	162	5,950
1825	38	1,159	1862	75	2,776
1826	40	1,248	1863	89	2,643
1827	40	1,291	1864	47	1,458
1828	40	1,291	1865	48	2,165
1829	45	1,460	1866	69	2,872
1830	52	1,601	1867	90	4,041
1831	43	1,215	1868[d]	109	4,633
1832	51	1,979	1869[e]	20	1,200
1833[b]	58	1,835	1870	60	3,095
1834			1871	256	5,981
1835	29		1872	260	6,180
1836	52	1,381	1873	285	9,026
1837			1874	345	10,958
1838	46	1,425	1875	329	10,501
1839	44	2,104	1876	344	11,328
1840	29	975	1877	330	11,515
1841	35		1878	366	12,222
1842	52	2,132	1879	354	13,443
1843			1880	393	13,338
1844	45	2,644	1881	383	14,292
1845	58	2,508	1882	391	14,394
1846			1883[f]	284	15,118
1847			1884	433	19,593
1848	103	3,682	1885[g]	261	9,314
1849–1860	[c]	[c]	1886	531	21,231

[a] First actions taken by Congress for Indian instruction were in 1819 and 1824; no statistics
are available for these years.
[b] $500 appropriated for erection of shops.
[c] Statistics imperfect or missing.
[d] New York schools not reported.
[e] New York schools and schools for Five Civilized Tribes not reported.
[f] Religious societies and government; no reports from Creek day schools, owing to
disturbances in the nation.
[g] No report of Five Civilized Tribes.

Source: Alice C. Fletcher, *Indian Education and Civilization* (Washington, D.C.: GPO,
1888), p. 197. (U.S. Congress, 48th, 2nd session, Senate, Executive Document No. 95, Serial
Set No. 2264.)

daughters who ran away from classes. But missionary teachers put many a young Cherokee to flight by inept efforts to teach in a foreign tongue. This was a familiar scene:

> The teachers, being without knowledge of the Indian languages and, with rare exception, devoid of any wish to learn them, taught only in English pupils who rarely knew any English at all. Under such conditions reading became a matter of memory without meaning; writing, of copying without comprehension; and arithmetic, an exercise in misunderstanding. Small wonder that the "scholars" were addicted to running away from school.[16]

This kind of thing soon gave way as a result of an extraordinary Cherokee achievement.

In 1822, Sequoyah invented a Cherokee syllabary, permitting the language to be written. It was embraced by Cherokees with the greatest enthusiasm. Sequoyah visited one village after another, leaving in his wake a corps of literate Indians. Schools in Cherokee territory became bilingual. Books were published in Cherokee. In 1828, the Cherokee Nation began publication of the bilingual *Cherokee Phoenix*, a weekly newspaper which the Indians themselves edited, printed, and published. The paper became the nation's voice in the fight to avoid removal westward from Georgia.

In 1827, Cherokees adopted a republican constitution that declared: "Religion, morality, and knowledge being necessary to good government, the preservation of liberty, and the happiness of mankind, schools and the means of education shall forever be encouraged in this nation."[17] At the time, their schools were financed in part by a school fund held in trust by the federal government. The money came from the sale of a 12-square-mile piece of Cherokee land as provided in a treaty of 1819.[18] Each year the fund yielded $50,000 for schools. When federal authorities pressed southern Indians to move west and Cherokees continued to resist, federal negotiators succeeded in corrupting a small group of Cherokee chiefs. President Jackson misrepresented the action as the authentic voice of the Cherokee Nation. The 1835 Treaty of New Echota, as it was known, increased the Cherokee school fund to $200,000 a year. It laid the basis for a system of high schools. Two years before the treaty, missionaries on the spot estimated that three-fifths of the Cherokees were literate in their own language and one-fifth in English. In 1841, the Cherokee National Council created a national system divided into eight school districts and eleven schools. A school superintendent was chosen; he appointed a board of directors for each of the schools. By 1843, a total of 500 students were in school. Six years later, the number tripled. The Cherokee National Council was aware of the need for improving classroom instruction, and in 1850 teachers and school directors formed the Educational Association of the Cherokee Nation.

"By 1852," writes Layman, "the Cherokee Nation had a better common school system than either Arkansas or Missouri," the two neighboring states.[19]

The Choctaws were more dependent on the missionaries, who were invited in 1817 to operate schools. Missionaries invented a form of written Choctaw, using the Roman alphabet. By 1830, eleven schools enrolled 260 children and employed twenty-nine teachers. Some 250 adult Choctaws were literate in their own language. When Choctaws were forced westward, the Choctaw Nation built new schools and contributed to the support of the mission schools. In 1842, a national school system was organized. A board of trustees controlled the tribal schools, but not the mission schools. In each district the chiefs appointed a board member who was responsible for establishing day schools in the district; he also appointed teachers. The board signed contracts with missionary societies to operate boarding schools.[20]

Choctaw parents seemed eager for their children to learn English, and the schools were conducted in that language; but in Sabbath schools, "it was the custom for entire families to camp near the church or school house on Saturday and Sunday and receive instructions in arithmetic, reading, and writing, in the Choctaw language."[21] During 1837 alone, missionary societies published 30,500 copies of tracts in the Choctaw language. Between 1830 and 1860, enrollment of children in schools rose from 260 to 900; 500 of these were in day schools, the remainder in boarding schools.[22] After 1853, all schools in the Choctaw Nation were under public control. That year, a superintendent was appointed to administer all the schools.

The Chickasaws lagged in schooling. By the mid-nineteenth century they succeeded in stabilizing a comprehensive school system. Between 1837 and 1844, there were no schools for Chickasaw children. In 1849, six day schools were operating, each autonomously governed by a board of trustees who selected sites. By 1851, 180 Chickasaw children were in schools. Chickasaw schools practiced a public examination near the close of each school year. Friends, parents, and others were invited to the examinations, which were preceded by a barbecue. The chiefs and great men of the tribe addressed the children after the tests were over.[23] The Chickasaw legislature made an annual appropriation of some $2,000 to buy clothing for school children. Each child received $12; the superintendent was directed to keep a strict accounting of clothing expenditures to ensure that the children were benefited.

Each of the five southern tribes practiced slaveholding of Negroes, and many free Negroes lived among the tribes, which permitted escaped slaves to settle on their lands. Indeed, this was one reason white Georgians demanded that the Cherokees be forced to leave.

Among the Seminoles, blacks were the equals of the Indians and served as counselors to the chiefs. It may be supposed that among the Seminoles, and very likely among the Cherokees and Creeks too, some blacks had access to schools. The Chickasaws and Choctaws were less hospitable. In 1853, the Choctaw National Council forbade any children of slaves to attend tribal schools.[24] Missionaries of an abolitionist persuasion were excluded from Choctaw lands. Most slaveholders among the Choctaws were half-breeds.

At the outbreak of the Civil War, the great majority of all Indians in schools were among the southern tribes. In the North and the West, another "few hundred" students could be counted. Almost all the teachers were missionaries who sought to "civilize" and to Christianize the Indian. Indians, for the most part, rejected this invitation to self-hatred; they welcomed missionaries as teachers, not as preachers. Among the Creeks, all Christian religious instruction was forbidden. Where superior force and trickery combined to deprive Indians of their homelands, as in the South, they did not become demoralized. Instead, they resisted by developing creatively new institutions and practices, such as a written language and schooling, both major achievements on any scale of values.

Federal control of Indian education: Civil War to 1920

In one critical respect the new Indian schooling differed from its pre-Civil War counterpart: control of education was completely in the hands of federal authorities. Whenever elements of Indian control persisted after 1865, they were weakened and finally eliminated. Schooling came to be viewed by most Indians as a conqueror's device.

Before the Civil War, reservation life had been comparatively unregulated by federal authorities. Reservations of the southern tribes were autonomous, self-ruling communities. After the war, when Indian-owned land was seized – often in direct violation of treaties – to become farms, livestock ranges, metal and coal mines, irrigation streams, and railroad beds, more reservations became totally administered communities. In 1887, passage of the General Allotment Act resulted in the conversion of much of each reservation into individually owned plots of land; this was, in part, an effort to destroy the material base of tribal unity. It also permitted the sudden availability of so-called surplus lands for sale to whites without consultation with Indians. To the reservations came an increasing number of "white superintendents, farm agents, teachers, inspectors, and missionaries . . . [who] to a large extent succeeded in destroying Indian culture."[25] By century's end, President Theodore Roosevelt exulted that the allotment law "is a mighty pulverizing engine to break up the tribal mass."[26]

It was in a context of wars of conquest, extermination, starvation, and cultural pulverization that education was to play its role. Brigadier General James H. Carleton, who led a war of destruction against the Navajo during the Civil War, spoke of them as "wolves" and called for "domestication" of their children. "The education of these children is the fundamental idea," Carleton wrote, "on which must rest all our hopes of making the Navajo a civilized and a Christian people."[27]

Navajo: a pledge on education

The Navajos, the largest of all Indian tribes, had been assigned to a reservation soon after conclusion of the war against Mexico. They resisted the assignment for years. In 1868, after a five-year exile, the Navajos agreed to a treaty. Two articles dealt with education.[28] Article 3 stipulated that the United States would "cause to be built . . . a schoolhouse and chapel, so soon as a sufficient number of children can be induced to attend school." In Section 6, the Navajos agreed "to compel their children . . . between the ages of six and sixteen years, to attend school." The United States agreed that "for every thirty children between said ages who can be induced or compelled to attend school a house shall be provided, and a teacher competent to teach the elementary branches of an English education shall be furnished." Federal authorities, according to Woerner, "grievously failed to honor" the treaty.[29] Many more families wanted their children to attend than the number for whom places were available. Nearly a quarter of a century after the treaty was signed, a grand total of 75 students attended the single school on the reservation. At this time, 1892, the tribe numbered 16,000. Attendance thus represented less than 0.5 percent of the population; eleven years later the proportion had risen to 3.0 percent.

In the years following the treaty, Navajos addressed themselves not to education but to livelihood. For centuries, the Navajos had been "self-supporting corngrowers, sheepherders, and weavers."[30] When they returned from their five years of exile and imprisonment in 1868, they were impoverished. Between that date and 1880, they succeeded in persuading Congress to double the size of their reservation. Sheepherding became a prime industry, helping the Navajos to regain their economic independence. Federal authorities continued to seek educational programs that would constitute "a concentrated attack on tribal ways."[31] The programs, Woerner concludes, were "futile."[32] Had federal officials made schools available, even for mistaken programs, they would have been more successful. But the chronic shortage of schools for Navajos continued. So sweeping was the need that a special congressional appropriation of

$250,000 in 1912 solved little. In 1918, some 81 percent of school-age Navajo children were unable to attend school; two years later, the figure was 72 percent. In 1924, the situation was unchanged (Table 27).

The exceedingly slow pace of progress was exemplified by the government boarding school at Fort Defiance. There, in 1915, after thirty years of existence, the school finally graduated its first class from the eighth grade. Many of the graduates were seventeen or eighteen years of age. A teacher explained:

> They had started their school life with no knowledge of the English language, and all the way through their eight years they had devoted but half the day to the traditional school subjects, the other half being set aside for industrial training; so it was no wonder that they were somewhat older than white pupils graduating from the same grade.[33]

Table 27. *Growth of Navajo education, 1865–1955*

		Children aged 6–18 years			
Year	Total Navajo population	Total number	Number in school	Percent out of school	Percent in school
1868	9,000	3,015	0	100	0
1878	11,850	3,970	0	100	0
1888	18,000	6,030	35	99	0.05
1898	20,500	6,867	185	97	3
1908	22,600	7,571	770	90	10
1918	29,959	10,036	1,881	81	19
1928	40,000	13,400	5,000	68	37
1930	41,786	13,998	5,719	59	41
1935	45,000	15,075	6,681	56	44
1940	48,722	16,322	6,164	62	38
1945	57,722	19,337	6,543	66	34
1946	59,522	19,940	8,142	59	41
1947	61,051	20,452	9,239	55	45
1948	63,025	21,113	9,584	55	45
1949	65,000	21,775	11,099	49	51
1950	69,167	23,170	12,751	45	55
1953	74,567	24,980	16,143	35	65
1954	78,000	26,130	23,671	9	91
1955	80,000	26,800	24,560	8	92

Source: William H. Kelly, *A Study of Southern Arizona School-Age Indian Children 1966–1967* (Tucson: Bureau of Ethnic Research, University of Arizona, 1967), p. 61.

Hopi: the "Hostiles" and the "Friendlies"

No Indian tribe was monolithic in its attitude toward white-sponsored schools. Among the Hopis, the split was profound and enduring.[34]

Oraibi, Arizona, the Hopi capital and the oldest continuously inhabited town in North America, was split into two opposed camps as early as the 1890s. The "Friendlies" tended to be more accepting of white ways, including schools; the "Hostiles" especially resented the schools and refused to send their children. At one time, the Hostiles imprisoned the village chief and held him until he was released by federal forces. After many years, the split led to the end of common celebration of religious rites.

It was not unusual for federal troops to surround a Hostile community, force the children into wagons, and carry them off to distant boarding schools. Navajo policemen came looking for hidden students. Alerted in time, grandmothers would take up to a dozen little girls off on a hurried picnic. When children were caught and sent to a nearby day school, they often ran back home at recess. "One principal, in desperation, got himself a .22 rifle with blank bullets. When he shot at the boys they stopped running."[35] In 1906, both factions in Oraibi came to blows, and the Hostiles were ejected forcibly from their homes. Seventy-five Hostile men were arrested and sentenced to ninety days at hard labor until they agreed to send their children to school. (A number who still refused were sent to prison for a year.)

While the men were serving their ninety days, they worked near the boarding school where their own children were in attendance. One former student recalled the scene as their fathers, hobbled with ball and chain, were marched by the school: "An officer with a stick would see to it that they did not stop to talk to their little girls. After that, each morning we ran out to see if our fathers went by. We would cry if we saw them and cry if we didn't."[36] After the first year or two, the children of Hostiles were permitted to spend summer at home, but when they failed to return to school in the fall, soldiers rounded them up and kept them at the school year-round.

Whether students were from Friendly or Hostile families, the Hopi schools seemed alien. One boy who started school received, for some unexplained reason, the new name of "Max." The next year, in another school, he was renamed "Don." On Memorial Day, the school celebrated: "We stuck little flags in our caps, took bunches of flowers, and marched out to the graves of two soldiers who had come out here to fight the Hopi and had died."[37]

Speaking Hopi in school was forbidden, "but on the way home, to show their contempt for the rules they delighted in calling out names in the Hopi way."[38] When children were transported to boarding schools, the first response was fear. One little girl recalled those early nights: "Evenings we would gather in a corner and cry softly so the matron would not hear and scold or spank us. I would try to be comforter, but in a little while I would be crying too."[39] The rigor of institutional life repelled them: "Seems like that was the first English we learned, 'Get in line, get in line,' all the time we had to get in line."[40] At the Phoenix Indian School, which offered upper grades to Hopi and other children, the regimen was military: "We marched to the dining room three times a day to band music. We arose to a bell. . . . Everything was done on schedule."[41] Many children attempted escapes. One family from Camp Verde was said to have had a child on the road at any given time, either escaping or being returned from an escape. Punishment for attempting an escape included (for girls) the cutting of grass with scissors while wearing a sign, "I ran away," or (for boys) a term in a campus jail or being dressed in girl's clothes.

Hopi children away at boarding schools were often used as cheap labor in nearby or distant occupations, especially during summers. Students at the Sherman Indian School in Riverside, California, were sent to the Imperial Valley or San Bernardino to pick cantaloupes or work on a dairy farm.

Having mastered the white man's school lessons was no guarantee that the student thereby absorbed his way of thinking. After a successful round in Keams Canyon primary school, one Hopi lad recalled:

> I had learned many English words and could recite part of the Ten Commandments. I know how to sleep on a bed, pray to Jesus, comb my hair, eat with a knife and fork, and use a toilet. I had learned that the world is round instead of flat, that it is indecent to go naked in the presence of girls, and to eat the testes of sheep and goats.[42]

He added, pointedly, "I had also learned that a person thinks with his head instead of his heart."

Several years later, after completing the course at the Sherman school, the same young man reflected:

> I could talk like a gentleman, read, write, and cipher. I could name all the states in the Union with their capitals, repeat the names of the books in the Bible, quote a hundred verses of Scripture, sing more than two dozen Christian hymns and patriotic songs, debate, shout football yells, swing my partners in square dances, bake bread, sew well enough to make a pair of

trousers, and tell "dirty" Dutchman stories by the hour. It was important that I had learned how to get along with white men and earn money by helping them. But . . . I had a Hopi Spirit Guide whom I must follow if I wished to live. I wanted to become a real Hopi again.[43]

At the age of thirty, he became the Sun Chief of Oraibi.

But some were weaned from tribal ways. Helen Sekaquaptewa came from a family of Hostiles. As a child of five she was forced into a school which, contrary to all warnings, she admired: "It was pleasant and warm inside. I liked to wear the clothes they gave us at school."[44] She spent much of the following thirteen years in boarding schools, where she was a bright student. She and a girl friend would pretend they were "two eastern society women."[45] At the age of twenty she returned home, but realized: "I didn't feel at ease in the home of my parents now."[46] When she married she raised her children in the Mormon faith.

Polingaysi Qoyawayma, also of a Hostile family, had from an early age "a desire to share the good things of the white way of living."[47] She, too, graduated from Sherman Institute and returned to Oraibi, more to test her own feelings than out of an intention to remain. When her parents hesitatingly invited her to share her old quarters, she berated them: "Why haven't you bought white men's beds to sleep on? . . . When I was a little girl I did not mind sleeping on the floor and eating from a single bowl into which everyone dipped. But I am used to another way of living now, and I do not intend to do these things."[48]

She left after deciding to become a teacher. Her first job was at the school in Hotevilla she had attended as a small child. There she became a highly successful teacher of young Hopi children. Her goal, her "one consuming desire" was "to achieve a good life, independent of both white people and her own Hopi people, but esteemed by both."[49] This was not a practical goal in the 1890s.

Many others stood fast. When Helen Sekaquaptewa's elderly father counseled his grandsons, he told them: "You of the younger generation, stand for what is right. Go to school and be diligent, don't play around, but learn the white man's language and his ways so you can come back and help your people and fight the palrama [white man] in his own way."[50] He was the eternal Hostile.

By 1920 or thereabouts, the Hopi people, like the Navajos, were only minimally involved in the schools. The government's zeal in forcing white education upon Indians was not matched by an eagerness to meet even the limited concession of Indians that they would accept such schooling. The growing tendency of Navajos and Hopis to accept schooling rose from pragmatic considerations, not from a conviction of the superiority of white ways.

Sioux: broken government promises

Mission schools among the Sioux had existed as early as 1837. The Indians, who learned to their sorrow of the white man's rapacity, could hardly believe the missionaries when they professed merely a wish to teach their young. "Was it possible" the Wahpeton Sioux of Lac-qui-parle asked a celebrated missionary, Stephen Riggs, "that white men and women would come here and teach year after year, and not expect, in some way and at some time, to get money out of them?" Not only did Riggs and his colleagues do so, but Riggs himself gained a profound knowledge of the Sioux language as he undertook to compile a Sioux-English dictionary. He explained:

> To learn an unwritten language, and to reduce it to a form that can be seen as well as heard, is confessedly a work of no small magnitude. Hitherto it has seemed to exist only in sound. But it has been, all through the past ages, worked out and up by the forges of human hearts. It has been made to express the lightest thoughts as well as the heart throbs of men and women and children in their generations.[51]

Riggs's respect for the fullness of Indian language stood in sharp contrast to prevailing misconceptions that Indian languages were "devoid of terms for anything other than the most ordinary material objects."[52]

During the 1850s and 1860s, numerous attacks were leveled against the Sioux to clear them out of the way of white farmers, miners, railroad builders, and ranchers in Iowa, Minnesota, Nebraska, Dakota, and later, Wyoming. White arms were superior, and except for extraordinary though momentary reverses such as the Sioux defeat of Custer in 1876, the Sioux were forced back. In the 1868 treaty recording a vast cession of land to the federal government, the standard education clauses were included.[53] Provision was made for the building, at federal expense, of a schoolhouse "so soon as a sufficient number of children can be induced by the agent to attend school." As in the case of the treaty with the Navajos, signed the same year, the United States government violated the educational – as well as other – provisions of the Sioux agreement. Five years after the treaty, the government had failed to construct a single boarding school.[54] Between 1872 and 1892, the Sioux near Flandreau, South Dakota, depended on a mission school. The first year the school opened, an observer recalled: "The pupils wore blankets and no hats. Often the whole family came to school and the work was carried on anywhere they wished to go."[55] In 1892 the government built a school. Five years later, it was overcrowded. Many students were refused admission.

The early 1890s became a time for school building in Sioux country. By 1892, more than twenty federal boarding schools had been built. Parents avoided at least one, at Fort Peck. In 1886, "the police went to work according to instructions and after some parents were denied rations, and others were jailed, fifty children were received at the agency school."[56] These techniques were by no means uncommon. The school appears to have been unstable in other respects. From 1885 to 1900, it had eleven different principals.

Charles Eastman, born a Sioux with the name Ohiyesa ("the winner"), was graduated as a physician from Boston University in 1890 and accepted a position as government physician at Pine Ridge reservation in South Dakota. There he was "much struck with the loss of manliness and independence in these, the first 'reservation Indians' I had ever known."[57] These seemingly apathetic Sioux in 1890 and 1891 were swept by the Ghost Dance religion, based on a prophecy that the Indians were about to rout the whites and return to their lands. Fearful of the consequences, federal authorities were uncertain how real the threat was. At Pine Ridge "the large boarding school had locked its doors and succeeded in holding its hundreds of Indian children, partly for their own sakes, and partly as hostages for the good behavior of their fathers."[58] Indian police were sent to arrest Sitting Bull – the most honored of all Sioux leaders – in the mistaken belief that he was leading the Ghost Dance movement. He was killed by the police. Federal troops panicked afterward and massacred about 300 Indian women, children, and some men at Wounded Knee. This was the last military encounter between white and Indian during an extraordinarily bloody century.

Eastman had followed his remark about reservation Indians with the well-meant sentiment that "I longed above all things to help them regain their self-respect." The remark suggests that the Sioux were completely demoralized, which was far from the case. They had suffered a military defeat. They had lost much of their land through unequal treaties and conversion of the reservation to private property. They had lost the buffalo. But they endured.

After destruction of the buffalo herds, federal authorities hoped to turn the Sioux toward farming pursuits and gave the Sioux some head of cattle to raise. The Sioux, who viewed men – even white men – as part of the nature they knew so well, saw nothing un-Sioux in turning this part of nature to their own account. The Sioux became excellent stockmen. Cattle companies tended to overrun Indian-operated land and disperse Indian cattle. Still the years 1900–1920 were a period of comparative prosperity. The provision of schooling opportunities lagged, even during these years.

Northern Plains and Pacific Coast tribes: more broken promises
In 1855, federal representatives signed Lame Bull's Treaty with the Blackfeet Indians, pledging $15,000 yearly to educate children and

instruct adults in "agricultural and mechanical pursuits."[59] From 1864 to 1872, the reports of Indian agents on the reservation mentioned education only once "and then only to express an opinion against education for the savages."[60] The first school was opened only seventeen years after the treaty. In 1878, no more than twenty children attended school for more than a month, although the total number eligible was 1,200.[61] Two children learned to read and write that year, leading Chief White Calf to say the school "amounted to nothing." From 1879 to 1889, from one-twelfth to one-fifth of the eligible children enrolled in the boarding school; of these, an average of one to three in four attended. About 75 percent of all eligible children were enrolled in the Willow Creek boarding school during the 1890s; average attendance ran around 82 percent. Until Willow Creek was built in 1892, a chronic shortage of space existed. Three years earlier, thirty-two students were stuffed into a room designed for half that number. When facilities became available, parents sent their children in large numbers. In 1905, a public school was started in nearby Browning, Montana, but it was designed for the use of children of the white Indian agent and town businessmen. When a school district was organized in 1919, apparently some Indians were allowed to attend.

The Flathead Indians had been promised schools in an 1855 treaty. The first one was built around 1900. It was never large enough to meet the demand. Berven explains: "Year after year the annual reports of the school superintendent and the agent mention government promises to construct a large government boarding school on the reservation. . . . The promises never materialized."[62] Indians sought to enroll their children despite the prevailing efforts to suppress any traces of Indian culture in the classroom. The wife of an agency physician recalled of the years around 1900: "Some children hardly dared speak at all because they knew very little English and were afraid to say anything in Indian for fear of being punished."[63] When the earliest public schools were built on the reservation, like the Montana school, they were probably designed for white children of the Indian agent's family and those of white townspeople.

In 1854 and 1855, Indians and federal authorities signed two treaties – Medicine Creek and Point Elliott – containing promises to establish schools on the Pacific Coast. The promises were not kept. The U.S. Court of Claims, after examining voluminous evidence covering the latter half of the nineteenth century, wrote of the former treaty:

> Nonobservance is completely established. . . . The failure of the Government to observe these obligations, except in a most feeble way, is marked and irrefutable. . . . There is no reliable evidence that an agricultural and industrial school was established until fifty years after the treaties were made. . . . Official reports

confirm the fact that educational facilities were lamentably inadequate for the Indians and never available to all of them. The
record is positive and extensive as to these facts.[64]

Indian parents in Washington were eager for their children to enroll in
what schools there were. Over the fifty-year period, 1875–1925, attendance at government Indian schools in Washington was consistently
strong (Table 28).[65]

The average overall attendance of about 75 percent was high, even
compared with non-Indian rates of attendance.

Among the Nez Percé, whose children attended a mission school in the
late 1830s, a historian reports that "many of the parents were careful
about going away [on a hunt] and taking their children with them, because it took them out of school and they got behind the other children in
learning to read." During the late 1880s "Indians named 'Queets' who
lived near the Quinaielt Reservation were so anxious to have their children educated in their own village that they went into the forest and
hewed out the lumber for a school. . . . The government furnished such
items as doors, windows, lock, nails, and furniture."[66] In 1900, "one
Indian family, on hearing that the [Colville Boarding School]. . . . was
going to open, brought their children 125 miles and camped near the
school until it opened."[67]

In California, the concept of educating Indians was unacceptable to the
white population. During the first years after American acquisition of

Table 28. *Attendance in government Indian
schools in Washington state, 1875–1925*

Period	Percent of students attending
1875–1876 to 1879–1880	78.2
1880–1881 to 1884–1885	78.5
1885–1886 to 1889–1890	82.9
1890–1891 to 1894–1895	77.5
1895–1896 to 1899–1900	72.2
1900–1901 to 1904–1905	72.9
1905–1906 to 1908–1909	69.2
1910–1911 to 1914–1915	79.2
1915–1916 to 1919–1920	64.0
1920–1921 to 1924–1925	73.3

Source: Data from James Lynn Pester, "The History of
Indian Education in the state of Washington." (master's
thesis, University of Washington, 1951), pp. 106, 113,
121, 131, 144, 151, 160, 171, 176, 183, 191.

California, writes Cook, "all Indians were [considered by whites as] vermin, to be treated as such."[68] Whites murdered Indians without suffering prosecution. Immediately after admission of California as a state, in 1850, federal agents arrived to negotiate treaties of cession with Indian tribes. Eighteen treaties were negotiated during the next two years. Each one ceded vast tracts of land, specified reservation areas, and established various federal obligations to the Indians, including the standard promise of education. One such document stated:

> The United States will . . . employ and settle among said tribes
> . . . one principal schoolteacher, and as many assistant teachers
> as the President may deem proper to instruct said tribes in reading, writing, etc., and in the domestic arts, upon the manual
> labor system; all the above-named . . . teachers to be maintained
> and paid by the United States for the period [of] five years, and
> as long thereafter as the President shall deem advisable. The
> United States will also erect suitable schoolhouses . . . and dwellings, for the accommodation of the school teachers.[69]

These provisions never were put into effect.

In fact, the treaties themselves were repudiated in toto by the U.S. Senate in a secret vote in 1852, primarily in response to pressure from white Californians who were horrified to contemplate the possibility that valuable farmlands and gold deposits might be enclosed within reservations. The Indians' lands were seized without compensation. Many Indians became peons and low-paid farm laborers. Others were captured and sold as slaves. Indian children were often kidnapped and sold outright into slavery. Others became forced laborers through use of the 1850 indenture law.[70] The number of Indians fell by more than 80 percent between 1845 and 1880; many were victims of war, homicide, disease of European origin, and starvation.

Without treaties, school opportunities were nonexistent. When, in 1854, a petition was received by Congress to establish a government school for Indians in California, the House Committee on Indian Affairs rejected the request with what is perhaps the shortest congressional document on the Indian. The complete report stated: "That they have considered the memorial, and recommend that the prayer of the petitioner be not granted."[71] Some thirty years later, federal policy changed. A few schools were established. In 1886, there were four Indian schools in the entire state, with 353 out of 1,140 eligible children attending. For another 69 eligible children on two reservations, no school was available.[72] So bitter were the life experiences of Indians that many distrusted the schools. At Round Lake, for example, the school building was burned down by Indians in 1883, 1912, and 1914.

Public schools in California were almost a closed preserve to Indian children. Where they could gain admittance, in most cases it was only into a segregated school. In the school laws passed during 1863–1864, Indians – as well as blacks and "Mongolians" – were excluded from white schools, but school districts were permitted to establish a separate school for the excluded children upon the receipt of a petition from at least ten parents. In 1866, the law was eased, permitting "half-breed Indian children and Indian children who live with white families or under the guardianship of white persons" to enter the white school.[73] Indian children could be admitted to the white school provided that a majority of white parents did not object. During 1869–1873, it apparently was impossible for an Indian child to attend a white school in California. During 1873–1880, on the other hand, legislation restored the possibility of attending school. For whatever reasons, between 1880 and 1902 the school law omitted all restrictions on Indian attendance. In 1902 and once more in 1909, the legislature again permitted the building of separate schools; once such a school was built in the district, Indian children could not attend any other public school.

It is not known how many Indian children attended public schools under any of these laws. Probably almost none did. In 1910, a group of Indians near Colusa pressed successfully for the creation of an all-Indian public school district. Between 1913 and 1915, Indians in the Lake Mendocino area organized to demand either a separate public school or admittance of their children to the white school. They were aided in these campaigns by the Indian Board of Cooperation, a private group headed by the Methodist minister, Reverend F. G. Collett.

In 1917, a group of Indians in Lake County challenged the traditional exclusion of Indians from the polls. In the *Anderson* case the state supreme court upheld their contention. Indians from Mendocino, Lake, and Sonoma counties organized the Society of North California Indians and the Mission Indian Federation. By 1920, Forbes observes, "the Indians of the Far West were beginning to experiment with new forms of concerted action ranging from petitions, to law suits, to organizing in order to make their desires known. A new era had not yet dawned, but its birth could be anticipated."[74]

Southern tribes: federal versus tribal control of education

During the Civil War, the southern tribes aligned, in general, with the Confederacy, but each tribe was split into opposing sides on the issues of the war. Schools closed all over Indian territory as the federal government withheld school funds during the war. In 1866, treaties ended Indian participation in the war. Each tribe or nation made its own settlement.

The Cherokee Nation ceded an 800,000-acre tract of land in Kansas to the federal government, which was to sell it and use 35 percent of the proceeds as a school fund. This was done. Between 1868 and 1880, the number of students in Cherokee schools rose from 1,454 to 5,304.[75] A decade later, the Cherokee Nation was spending more than $80,000 annually for schools. New facilities were built: "Many of the school houses were frame buildings, well equipped with modern facilities for ventilating, lighting and heating, though the rude log cabin structure was still to be seen." While the Cherokees were very proud of their educational achievement, even by the late 1890s, they had not succeeded in involving many back country full-bloods in the schools.[76]

At the height of its development, Cherokee schooling suffered a death blow. In 1893, Congress created the Davis Commission to negotiate the extinction of independent Indian nations in Oklahoma Territory. This was to be accomplished by complete conversion of tribal lands into private property. With the approaching end of tribal government, tribal schools would also disappear. Cherokees objected that the new policy was a frontal violation of the Treaty of 1828's guarantee of autonomy. In 1906, the federal government took over the tribal schools, ending the most sustained and successful experience of community control of schools in the country's history.[77]

Among the Choctaws, tribal schools did not recover from the Civil War until 1867, when they reopened. Two years later, 1,764 students attended eighty-four day schools. Two-thirds of the teachers were Choctaws, who were themselves educated in tribal schools or in schools located in the "states."[78] In 1884, attendance was made compulsory and fines levied for absence. The Choctaw National Council supplied free textbooks to all students; deaf children were sent to a special facility in Illinois, and blind children received special training. In the fall of 1892, three new boarding schools were opened with principals who were Choctaws, one a black man. Choctaw boarding schools, as a rule, "maintained scholastic standards that would be a credit to any school system."[79] The day schools were of lesser quality. Teachers published for a time the *Choctaw-School Journal*.

Finances for the schools came entirely from Indian funds. A major source was the money owed the Choctaw Nation in exchange for extensive land cessions made to the federal government in earlier years, money invested by the U.S. Treasury in the name of the Choctaws. Royalties from minerals and leasing charges for land rented to non-Choctaws were another source. Toward the end of the nineteenth century, writes Debo, "the Choctaw Nation had a much higher proportion of educated people than any of the neighboring states."[80]

Choctaw education aimed at a broader preparation than the usual vocational schooling prescribed for Indians by federal educators. When, in 1899, the federal government absorbed the Choctaw schools, the new superintendent, according to Debo, "condemned the emphasis on cultural subjects as unsound and unsuited to the people, and attempted by stressing vocational training to change at once the whole purpose of Choctaw education."[81]

Chickasaw education was somewhat less developed, but no less determined, than Cherokee and Choctaw education. After the Civil War, schools multiplied. English remained more or less the language of instruction. In 1898, the Chickasaw Council started supplying textbooks to students. In one respect, the Chickasaw schools seemed to be unusually successful: "Most . . . were built in the full-blood communities with native teachers and trustees."[82] Chickasaw could be heard in the schools alongside the English-language teaching.

The Chickasaw Nation resisted the federal takeover as long as possible. Between 1899 and 1901, a bitter argument went on with federal officials, with Chickasaws demanding that the government pay coal and asbestos royalties due them; the government insisted that Chickasaw control of the schools first be relinquished. A temporary compromise was reached in 1901, but the federal government took full control five years later when the Chickasaw Nation was declared nonexistent.

Ex-slaves among the southern tribes were, for the most part, adopted as members of the tribe and given equal – though separate – school facilities. Under governmental pressure, they also received some land rights, though usually not to tribal land as such. The Cherokees treated the freedmen most considerately; the Chickasaws refused to adopt them and withheld school rights for more than fifteen years after the Civil War. As late as 1894, the Choctaw Colored Citizens Association was protesting publicly about unequal school opportunities.

Alaska: savages by court decree[83]

From 1867, when the United States purchased Alaska from Russia, to 1884, the only schools in the territory were operated by missions. In 1884, Congress passed the Organic Law for Alaska and directed the secretary of the interior to provide schools "for the education of the children of school age in the Territory of Alaska, without reference to race."[84] Fifteen years later, Congress repeated the stipulation in an appropriations act. Nevertheless, in 1902 school boards in Juneau and Ketchikan turned Indian and Eskimo students away.[85] Three years later,

Congress reversed its policy and created a dual school system for Alaska. Incorporated towns could organize a school district if no fewer than twenty white children resided there. Section 7 of the law covered schools for white children and "civilized" children of "mixed blood." Others could go to separate schools:

> The schools specified and provided for in this Act shall be devoted to the education of white children and children of mixed blood who lead a civilized life. The education of the Eskimos and Indians in the district of Alaska shall remain under the direction and control of the Secretary of the Interior, and schools for and among the Eskimos and Indians of Alaska shall be provided for by an annual appropriation, and the Eskimo and Indian children of Alaska shall have the same right to be admitted to any Indian boarding school as the Indian children in the States or Territories of the United States.[86]

In 1906, the school board of Sitka – then capital of Alaska – issued an order excluding from the local schools the children of three mixed-blood families on the ground that the children were not living a civilized life. The order was upheld in court.

"The Indian in his native state," the court declared in *Davis* v. *Sitka School Board*, "has everywhere been found to be savage, an uncivilized being, when measured by the white man's standard."[87] Persons of mixed blood who live among Indians have generally been regarded as Indians. Congress must have had this in mind, according to the court, as well as "the fact, upon which the rule is based, that where mixed bloods live among and associate with the uncivilized they become subject to and influenced by their environment as naturally as water seeks its level." By civilized persons, the court held, Congress meant those who had "put off the rude customs, modes of life, and associations, and taken up their abode and life free from an environment which retarded their development in lines of progressive living, systematic labor, individual ownership and accumulation of property, intellectual activity, and well-defined and respected domestic and social relations."

Still, the court felt duty-bound to set down its own concept of civilization:

> In the case at bar I am of the opinion that the test to be applied should be as to whether or not the persons in question have turned aside from old associations, former habits of life, and easier modes of existence; in other words, have exchanged the old barbaric, uncivilized environment for one changed, new and so different as to indicate an advanced and improved condition of

mind, which desires and reaches out for something altogether distinct from and unlike the old life.

This definition was then applied to the children of the three families.

The first plaintiff claimed he was civilized for he (1) was a Presbyterian; (2) spoke, read, and wrote English; and (3) owned a business which he operated "according to civilized methods." He lived in his own house within the Indian village just outside the limits of Sitka. The court commented: "Civilization . . . includes . . . more than a prosperous business, a trade, a house, white man's clothes, and membership in a church." Of the children of a second plaintiff the court observed that while his family lived in a separate house within the Indian village, "certain it is that the children are unrestrained, and live the life of their native associates, rather than a civilized life." As for a third plaintiff, the court conceded: "It appears that the pots and pans and kettles and frying pans are not left upon the floor, after the native fashion, but are hung up, and that curtains drape the windows of their house. This indicates progress; but does it satisfy the test [of civilization]?"

Residence was the ultimate basis of the court's ruling. If the children in question had lived in the town of Sitka and played with "civilized" children, the court might have ruled otherwise. But living among barbarians meant playing with the children of barbarians.

In 1913, the *Crawford* case was decided in Oregon. William Crawford, a Klamath half-blood, had a land allotment on the Klamath Indian Reservation, but chose not to live there. As the court noted: "The petitioner, his wife, and his children have voluntarily adopted the customs, usages, and habits of civilized life." Between 1910 and 1912, the Crawford children attended the Klamath County public schools. In September 1912, however, they were excluded. The school board had set up separate schools for white children and for Indian children, including half-bloods. Crawford sued to get his children into the white school and lost in the lower court. The Supreme Court of Oregon granted Crawford's request for a writ of mandamus on the school board. "These children," the court held, "are half white, and their rights are the same as they would be if they were wholly white."[88] The principle of separate schools was thus accepted by the court. Unlike the Sitka case, racial considerations were foremost. On the other hand, by 1927 federal authorities were challenging the action of the Sitka school board in excluding an Indian student solely on the ground of race.

The position of the half-blood had eased by 1929, at least in Ketchikan, where a new case arose involving half-bloods. As the court reported in *Jones* v. *Ellis:* "The general right of children of mixed blood to attend the city schools has been virtually conceded in the argument in this case, and that such is the general practice is shown by the pleadings." The school board had excluded Irene Jones, a half-blood, from the white school; she had been assigned to an Indian school on the ground that the sixth grade in the first school was crowded: "Being a child of mixed blood, she could attend the school for Indian children . . . and . . . in view of the overcrowded condition, it was the reasonable thing to exclude her because she could attend this other school."

The court rejected this reasoning. First, "conceding the right of Irene Jones to attend the [white] territorial schools, however, it cannot be contended that she should be deprived of this right by reason of the fact that she had a right also to attend the Indian school."[89] Second, no evidence was produced to demonstrate overcrowding, nor was it shown that other means had been exhausted of relieving overcrowding. Indeed, the school enrolled four out-of-district children who would have to make way for the resident Irene Jones. The court interpreted the federal statutes as not requiring racial segregation in Alaskan schools.

The educational cleavage between Indian and settler reflected political and religious factors as well as racist theory. In 1869, two years after Alaska was purchased from Russia, the Sitka city government started a school for children of settlers. Within four years it closed for lack of funds.[90] During the first generation of American rule this was the pattern of education for the settlers. Much more attention was paid to the schooling of Indians and Eskimos by religious missionaries whose first interest was proselytization. A religious combine, headed by the Presbyterian leader, Sheldon Jackson, gained federal subsidies for mission schools at a time when local schools for settlers received no public moneys.[91] Settler resentment at religious power ran high. Federal subsidies stopped in 1893, but the white settler schools were no better off as a result.

In 1900, the congressional Alaska Civil Code provided that towns could retain half of local taxes collected and use the funds for settler schools. These schools were locally controlled and were not even coordinated on an Alaska-wide scale. This isolation strengthened the feeling of separateness from the natives in mission and in federal government schools. After 1918, settler schools were financed by the territorial government, relieving town-dwellers of their local school tax burden. Schools for Indians, always financed by the federal government, were minimal; during the 1920s, for example, there was not a single high school for natives in Alaska.[92]

Reservation education: repression and contempt

By around 1920, the system of Indian education was based on the destruction of tribal economy and society, the civic powerlessness of Indian people, and a federal school bureaucracy marked by a strong sense of cultural superiority. The geographical isolation of the reservations facilitated control by the dominant society. In towns bordering the reservation, local whites formed alliances with federal reservation personnel; together, they shared a community of contempt for the Indians. In sparsely settled territories and states, the cash flow of federal annuities and reservation payrolls created a considerable local stake in the reservation regime. Indians were a significant market for white-produced goods and services. Local business interests were salient politically on the statewide scene, and thus in Congress and the national administration.

The reservation system constantly recreated the "Indian problem." It kept Indian people together and resulted in the perpetuation of traditional cultural elements. In two states with large Indian populations, school attendance for children aged seven to thirteen rose sharply between 1910 and 1920: in New Mexico the attendance rate doubled from 31.5 percent in 1910 to 66.6 percent in 1920; in South Dakota, the rate rose from 64.9 to 79.1 percent.[93] In Arizona, with more than 10,000 school-age Indian children in 1915, just about half attended school. Barely a third of the Navajo children were in school.[94] At the end of the first fifty years of reservation history (1868–1918), about one-fifth of school-age Navajo children were in school.

This mixed picture of attraction and repulsion can be explained by two practicalities. On one hand, Indians were increasingly forced to seek some adaptation to the ways of the dominant society; on the other hand, they sought to protect their children from the harshness of government schooling.

Forcing Indian children into schools by arrest and kidnapping was a customary practice. Another technique, suggested by U.S. Secretary of the Interior W. M. Teller in 1884, was described in Rule No. 1 of *Rules for the Conduct of Indian Boarding Schools:* "Agents are expected to keep the schools filled with Indian pupils, first by persuasion; if this fails, then by withholding rations or annuities or by such other means as may reach the desired end."[95] The technique of withholding rations was widely used. An elderly Blackfeet Indian recalls that "a family's ration of food was cut off if anyone in the family was caught singing Indian songs or doing Indian hand craft."[96] In 1893, Congress specifically granted the secretary of the interior the power to cut off rations in order to force parents to send their children to school; two years later the law was amended to require parental permission if a child were being sent to a boarding school located off the reservation.[97] Congress repealed the section permitting cutoff of rations. In 1913 Congress again specified that rations could be held back in order to compel parents to send their children to a school. The law applied specifically to Osage Indians.[98] In 1927, the Indian agent of the Seminole Reservation in Florida reported that "the Indian Town Camp which I was preparing to move here refused to come . . . and I promptly cut off their ration supply. At the end of three weeks of starvation they moved here and placed their children in school."[99] Fifteen years later a leading authority on Indian law said "It is no longer the practice to withhold annuities to compel attendance."[100] There is some doubt that the practice did stop.

Denial of the rights of Indian parents

Federal authorities often failed to accord Indian parents ordinary common law rights over their own children.

In 1883, an Indian mother in Sitka, Alaska, agreed to send her eight-year-old son to a private mission school for five years. When she sought to withdraw him after three years, school authorities refused and called the agreement a binding contract. Can-ah-couqua, the mother, applied to the U.S. District Court for a writ of habeas corpus. The judge refused on the ground that it would not be in the best interest of the child to be returned to its mother. He found:

> It is the experience of those who have been engaged in these Indian schools that, to make them effectual as disseminators of civilization, Indian children should, at a tender and impressionable age, be entirely withdrawn from the camp, and placed under the control of the schools. . . . The Jurisdiction asserted in equity to remove an infant from the custody of its parent, or to withhold that custody after it has been surrendered, and a desire is expressed to again assume it, is admitted to be of great delicacy, and attended with embarrassment and responsibility. But when sound morals, the good order and protection of civilized society unmistakably demand it, the court has no alternative.[101]

Cohen comments that this ruling stood in contrast with accepted procedures in custody cases involving white parents and children.[102]

Lelah-puc-ka-chee, a young woman of the Sac-Fox tribe, was being kept in an off-reservation Indian school near Tama, Iowa, despite her wish to leave. Earlier, when she had first insisted she be released, and was supported in her demand by her parents, the Indian agent had asked a court to appoint him as her guardian. The court complied with the request. This action was struck down by a U.S. District Court in Cedar Rapids, which acknowledged the duty of the agent to ensure attendance at the school but held that the duty "does not include the power to compel . . . attendance by force, contrary to the wishes of their parents."[103] The court reminded the agent of the 1894 law requiring parental consent before a child could be placed in an off-reservation school. The judge's understanding of Indian parental fears was unusual:

> The school and attendance thereat should not be made a matter
> to be feared, but on the contrary, the Indians should be led to
> understand that this school is an institution of their own reserva-
> tion, and that attendance thereat and success therein will benefit
> their children as Indians, and that it is not the purpose to wean
> the children from the tribe, and convert them into mere hangers-
> on of the whites.[104]

Little heed was paid to this advice by reservation officials. Seeking new
devices to get around the 1894 law and the *Lelah* ruling, they hit upon the
idea of using the state courts.

Malin, the Indian agent for the Sac-Fox reservation, went before a state
court and asked to be named guardian so that he could ensure the school
attendance of fifteen to twenty Indian children. His request was granted.
When the children were sent to a federal school near Toledo, Iowa, two
escaped to their home where their mother, with the aid of an Indian
named Peters, transported the children to a hiding place. Because Peters
had driven the wagon, he was arrested and charged with the crime of
"enticing away a child of fifteen years." Upon directed verdict, the jury
found him not guilty. He sued Malin for damages and was awarded
$10.[105] The case landed in federal court on a technical point regarding the
damage suit. This gave the court an opportunity to present the view that
because Indians were not subject to state laws, resort to the state courts
had been out of order.

In each of the three cases, authorities overrode the elementary legal
right of parents. Among the Cherokees, on the other hand, where the
effective control of schools lay with the Indians, compulsory attendance
never became forced attendance, nor was there an opportunity for ne-
glecting parental rights.

The "white man's road"

By 1920, Indian education rested on a firm official conviction that
Anglo-Saxon Christian ways were far superior to those of any Indian
culture. Richard Henry Pratt, founder of Carlisle Indian School (1879–
1918), wrote: "I do not believe that amongst his people an Indian can be
made to feel all the advantages of a civilized life, nor the manhood of
supporting himself and of standing out alone and battling for life as an
American citizen."[106] Pratt could not have understood the Hopi who
reported that "my father, grandfather, and two great-uncles urged me to
forget about school and become a man."[107] That anyone should prefer to
support *himself* and stand *alone* seemed to Pratt self-evident.

Suppression of Indian languages was a postulate of federal Indian education. This had not always been the case. In 1828, when the federal
government was eager for the Cherokees to consent to move west beyond

the Mississippi, a clause was placed in the treaty providing that the United States would pay "one thousand dollars towards the purchase of a Printing Press and Types to aid the Cherokees in the progress of education, and to benefit and enlighten them as a people, *in their own, and our language.*"[108]

After the Civil War, when victorious federal troops were the real negotiators, treaties stipulated "an English education," as in the Navajo treaty of 1868.

In 1880, the commissioner of Indian affairs amended the regulations governing federal schools: "All instruction must be in English, except insofar as the native languages of the pupils shall be a necessary medium for conveying the knowledge of English, and the conversation of and communication between the pupils and with the teacher must be, as far as practicable, in English."[109] Seven years later, instruction and use of textbooks in native languages were forbidden by the commissioner.

Indian children were notoriously slow learners of the English language. An experienced teacher noted that the slowness of the children at Fort Yuma, California, was in part an act of resistance: "It was not altogether that English was difficult for them to learn, but they had been taught from earliest childhood to despise their conquerors, their language, dress, customs – in fact, everything that pertained to them."[110] All the more did the schools see this attitude as one to be modified or even reversed. In many federal boarding schools, Indian children "were taught to despise every custom of their forefathers, including religion, language, song, dress, ideas, and methods of living."[111] These lessons were learned more readily than instruction in reading, perhaps because they were taught with greater conviction. Younger Indian children, especially, were almost defenseless before such education. Forbes points out that "even when 'turned off' by the schools, [they] were under great psychological pressure to conform to the dominant society."[112]

Until the Civil War, when Indian schools were operated principally by missionaries – publicly or privately financed – the goal was to Christianize and civilize the Indians. The sure sign of the former was conversion; of the latter, work at a manual occupation. Neither goal was effectively reached.

After the Civil War, especially when the federal government took a larger hand in educational affairs, occupational education became almost the exclusive concern. Indian children who graduated from a distant boarding school and returned home faced the problem of matching their new skills to reservation needs. Most often, the match was nonexistent. Students were frequently trained for jobs off the reservation, but discrimination made these jobs unavailable. Back, then, they went to the reservation. The schools had not prepared youngsters for reservation life; what was there to prepare *for*? Thus, it was charged that educated Indians "returned to the blanket" instead of using their schooling. Both among the Papagos and the Navajos a significant number of returned graduates did make a good adjustment on or off the reservation, but success was defined to mean that it was the greater as the child became less an Indian. A Hopi woman recalled: "Most of my chums gave up and went back to their Hopi ways when they returned home from school."[113]

Numerous Indian parents acknowledged the need for their children to learn new ways. One of the first Indians to become a physician, a Wahpeton Sioux, recalled his father's telling him that "one would be like a hobbled pony without learning to live like those among whom we must live."[114] A teacher, defending Indian students against the derision in the "back to the blanket" charge, stressed "the great sacrifice of the parents who love their children just as white parents do, yet give them up to be trained to disregard age-old traditions of the Indian, and follow the 'White Man's Road.' "[115] Many times the returnees suffered taunts from their more traditional peers. As Hagan writes: "The Sac and Fox people still prized most prowess in war. Educated Indian youths found themselves scorned or ridiculed as always."[116]

The Indian agent and school patronage

The moral atmosphere of the reservation was shaped initially by war and conquest. Administration of reservations constituted part of a general system of political patronage and corruption, operated at the expense of the Indians.

The reservation was ruled autocratically by the Indian agent, supported by a growing army of federal functionaries, along with the help of small numbers of Indians. The rapid turnover of Indian agents reflected the patronage needs of the political party in power rather than reservation needs. Between 1878 and 1898, the Sacaton Agency (Puma) had eleven different agents. Frequently, unless school superintendents and principals had established independent political connections, they left along with the departing agent. On an Oregon reservation during 1901–1904, a principal repeatedly put on "shows" for the white townspeople. One of the teachers explained that "her anxiety to please the people of the neighboring town was at least partially due to her desire to retain the political influence which had often been a support to her in time of disagreement with the agent."[117]

The teaching staff in Indian schools was, in general, exceedingly unsatisfactory. Political appointees were selected first. Because of the assimilative character of the schooling, teachers were not appraised in terms of their success or failure in taking the Indian culture into account in their classwork. The very opposite was the case. By and large, teachers and supervisors in the system accepted and implemented the goals of the system. On the tiny isolated Chippewa Grand Portage Reservation near Duluth, Minnesota, in 1919 "it was practically impossible to get teachers to come and stay any length of time and most of the appointments were clerks or temporary teachers."[118] Five years earlier, the school employed a housekeeper who also taught domestic science and did some sewing for Indian women. At the very end of the 1890s, some teachers were selected by civil service examinations, but no noticeable change resulted.

Beginning in 1915, teachers in the Indian Service were to be held accountable for the academic success of their students. Teachers who failed more than 30 percent of their students were to be discharged. "To guard against unmerited promotion," Pester writes, "the schools were to give examinations to their pupils, which were uniform to the whole service."[119] Whether such a program was actually enforced is not known. Numerous Indian parents continued to complain that their children were simply passed along without learning. In 1916, just a year later, the Indian Service published a standard curriculum for all Indian schools that was strongly vocational. Less and less was heard of academic achievement.

Equal citizens and civic action

After 1920, a number of Indian communities started to engage in concerted political and legal activity on behalf of tribal rights and education. With passage by Congress of the Citizenship Act of 1924, the last Indians were finally proclaimed equal citizens of the United States and the state in which they resided. Where Indians had the right to vote – and most did – they began exercising it more frequently. An increased self-confidence led them, in two instances, to challenge the federal government for violating treaties.

In the first case, filed in 1923 by the Sioux Tribe, the U.S. Court of Claims was asked to declare the U.S. Government in violation of the Sioux treaty of 1868 and to assign damages of some $18 million. Specifically at issue was Article VII of the treaty in which the government had undertaken to provide a school and a teacher for every thirty students who could be "induced" to attend. During the years between 1871 and 1889, it was alleged, such facilities had not been supplied. The court noted that "the plaintiffs cite the record as one consistently overwhelming in establishing not only the willingness of the parents to compel their children to attend school, but also their persistent complaints over the absence of schoolhouses, and their protests against the failure of the Government to observe Article VII."[120] Judge Booth did not directly reject the contention but argued extensively that until about 1881 the Sioux refused to remain within the limits of the reservation; the Oglala Sioux did not settle down until 1878, a decade after the treaty was signed. Thus, regular school facilities could not be made available to all. During this early period, the court held, the government had "furnished school facilities in excess of the demand for them from the Indians themselves." No such definitive statement was made concerning the latter part of the period.

The Sioux plaintiffs argued that under Article XVI of the treaty of 1868, an off-reservation "unceded territory" of somewhat indefinite boundary was recognized. Sioux were to retain hunting rights and the government pledged to exclude whites from that land. When the Sioux during the 1870s exercised these hunting rights they were within the then treaty rights. It was improper for the government to contend that the treaty obligation for building schools and providing teachers was not binding in face of the mobility of the Sioux.

The court rejected the idea of paying money damages on the ground that there existed no reasonable way of calculating them. Plaintiffs had estimated current per student costs and applied them to the years in question. The court objected that there was no student census for those years so that the plaintiffs were operating in the dark. In reply, the Sioux cited Article X of the treaty, under which the Indian agent of the reservation was directed to take a census. That he failed to do so was not the fault of the plaintiffs. The court agreed the government should not be allowed to profit from its failure to obey the treaty in this respect. Nevertheless, concluded the court, "the measuring of damages, making restitution for an alleged loss in money, is one which in itself resists calculation."[121]

The Sioux had filed the original petition of complaint with the court in 1923. It lay there unmolested for the next eleven years. In 1934 it was amended. Two years later, the decision was handed down. It had taken, in all, thirteen years for the Sioux to receive a negative reply.

In 1926, another petition was lodged with the U.S. Court of Claims by the Duwamish and other tribes in Washington state.[122] They charged the federal government with having violated pledges in two treaties of 1855 – Point Elliott and Medicine Creek – to create schools immediately after signature. The government's failure was glaring. Yet the court held no damages could be paid inasmuch as the claim was merely a moral claim and not one based on statutory obligation.[123]

The *Sioux* and *Duwamish* cases are significant because (1) they sought to use judicial process on behalf of treaty enforcement, (2) in neither case did the court reject the basic substantive argument of plaintiffs, and (3) the ambling pace of the court in arriving at opinions suggested that, given the Indian's lack of political power, he could expect little basic change from the federal courts. It was on the state level that more progress was achieved.

Entry into the public schools

The first public schools on or near reservations were usually designed for children of white reservation functionaries. Before 1890, no federal financing was available even for these schools. In 1890, however, the commissioner of Indian affairs offered to pay any public school $10 per quarter for each Indian child enrolled. In explanation, he wrote that "the public schools are the most effective means of Americanizing our foreign population."[124]

Until 1924, in California Indian children could be excluded from a public school only if a separate school were also available for them and for Oriental children. In addition, however, the school law stated: "In School districts . . . where the United States government has established an Indian school, or in an area not to exceed three miles from the said Indian school, the Indian children of the district, or districts, eligible for attendance upon such Indian school, may not be admitted to the district school."[125] An Indian parent from Inyo County, whose child was eligible for attendance at a nearby reservation school, chose instead one of the county's public schools. The child was refused entrance solely on the ground of race. Because the state had not made a practice of building "minority schools as alternatives" to the public school, the reservation school served as the minority school. It was this feature of the law that was challenged before the state supreme court in the *Piper* case.

The court agreed with the plaintiffs. "The education of the children of the state," it held, "is an obligation which the state took over to itself by the adoption of the [state] constitution." This obligation could not be discharged in a nonstate institution: "To argue that petitioner is eligible to attend a school which may perchance exist in the district but over which the state has no control is to beg the question. However efficiently or inefficiently such a school may be conducted would be no concern of the state." Nor was the court impressed by the school district's complaint that the cost of building of an Indian public school would be prohibitive: "This is a consequence for which the courts are not responsible." The defendant was advised to go to the legislature for financial help. In 1907, the North Carolina State Supreme Court had ruled that Indian children had no right to attend a public school where a reservation school was available. Judge Connor dissented in *State* v. *Wolf,* presaging the line of reasoning followed in *Piper* by the California court. Indians in Oklahoma won the unreserved legal right to attend public schools by virtue of the *Sunrise* case in 1918.[126]

Initial Indian entry into the public school did not bring with it equal participation in the governance of public education. Forbes notes that many small Indian public school districts were formed in California and

Nevada during the 1920s and 1930s, but although "the bulk of these districts were potentially controlled by Indians . . . many were, in fact, controlled behind the scenes by the . . . [Bureau of Indian Affairs], by white missionaries, or by white superintendents."[127] This was the rule very nearly everywhere Indians attended public schools.

A prime motivation of Indians' interest in public schooling was the hope that if their children could share the same facilities used by the more privileged white children, greater achievement would result. Public schools became increasingly interested in Indian enrollment as federal tuition money became available.

Sometimes, the experiment of public education failed. On the Turtle Mountain Reservation in North Dakota, for example, schooling had caught on early in the tribes' relations with whites. During the 1830s and 1840s, Father George Antoine Belcourt used to follow the Indians who went on a buffalo hunt in order that their children should not miss out on schooling. When, several decades later, the Sisters of Mercy founded a school in Yankton, the Indians – mostly Chippewas and Metis (French–Indian) – paid tuition with furs and hides. In 1916, the four government day schools on the reservation were made into public schools. The federal government paid the school district tuition based on the actual days of attendance of each Indian pupil. Just seven years later, the number of schools increased to seven. Nearly 80 percent of the eligible children attended. For some reason, the public schools started to deteriorate toward the end of the decade. In 1928, most school-age children were out of school. The next year, the federal government withdrew the Indian children from the public schools. Two years later a large consolidated school was built.[128] The example of Turtle Mountain was not typical.

Upon the forced dissolution of tribal schools of the five Indian nations in 1906, Oklahoma became the state with the largest enrollment of Indian children in public schools. By 1918, a state court had directed a school district in Comanche County to enroll Indian children whether or not federal school facilities were available. The school districts were loath to make very strong efforts to enforce school attendance upon Indian children. The less that aid was used for Indian children, the more was available for white children in the same school district. After World War I, according to Drain, the school law of Oklahoma "provided that no aid shall be extended to any district in which Indian children are enrolled if the State compulsory [attendance] law is not enforced alike for Indians and whites, or where Indian children are not accorded the same privileges, opportunities and attention as the white children."[129] Virtually no independent check was made on such claims by school districts since the attendance figures were reported by classroom teachers and "certified" by school district clerks.

The Johnson-O'Malley Act: diversion of federal funds to whites

A basic legal framework for relations between public schools and the federal government was created by the Johnson-O'Malley Act of 1934. It authorized the secretary of the interior to contract for the education of Indians with states or territories and – after an amendment two years later – their subdivisions, as well as "any State University, college or school, or with any appropriate State or private corporation, agency, or institution." The law authorized the secretary to establish minimum standards of service "that are not less than the highest maintained by the States or Territories with which . . . contracts . . . are executed."

In time, federal policies on this subject were codified and recorded as Title 25 of the Code of Federal Regulations. The purpose of the Johnson-O'Malley Act (hereafter JOM) was specified:

> 33.4 (b) The Program will be administered to accommodate unmet financial needs of school districts related to the presence of large blocks of nontaxable Indian-owned property in the district and relatively large numbers of Indian children which create situations which local funds are inadequate to meet. This Federal assistance program shall be based on the need of the district for supplemental funds to maintain an adequate school after evidence of reasonable tax effort and receipt of all other aids to the district without reflection on the status of Indian children.

Another important policy was established:

> 33.5 (d) States entering into a contract under the provisions of this part shall agree that schools receiving Indian children, including those coming from Indian reservations, shall receive all aid from the State, and other proper sources other than this contract which other similar schools of the State are entitled to receive. In no instance shall there be discrimination by the State or subdivision thereof against Indians or in the support of schools receiving such Indians, and such schools shall receive State and other non-Indian Bureau funds or aid to which schools are entitled.

Other provisions required equality of facilities, instructional personnel, and equipment and materials.

Federal funds were to flow to public schools provided they supplied to Indian children the best education available in the state. Local school districts were to tax reasonably so that an adequate education could be offered both Indian and non-Indian children. The federal funds were not to take the place of, but merely to supplement, local funds. States were not to use federal funds as a substitute for local funds. It would not be acceptable for a school district to reduce its own expenditures by the amount of federal funds. Should this be done, Congress would be in the position of permitting schools to spend less local money on Indian than on non-Indian children.

Yet this is more or less what happened within a year after passage of JOM. In 1935, the Oklahoma legislature enacted a law creating a fund on which poor school districts could draw in order to offer a program of minimum acceptable quality. Few districts with Indian children could use the fund because the state law deducted federal aid from any amount due under the law. As a result, many very poor districts would receive nothing from the state fund. In those cases, the goal of JOM would be clearly aborted; no poor district would offer Indian children *supplemental* services if it was receiving no supplemental funds. After objections by the federal Office of Indian Affairs, a compromise was reached which still violated the spirit of the law. Before grants were calculated from the new state fund, only half of all federal funds would be deducted. Thus, half of the federal funds under JOM would be available for supplemental education for Indian children.[130] In effect, therefore, an administrative agency of the federal government had agreed that half of a state's JOM grant could be spent on non-Indian children, or to lower the local tax rate, or for whatever purpose was chosen by local authorities.

The use of JOM funds for non-Indian children and purposes soon became the prevailing practice in public schools. At first, this was a response in part to the desperate plight of many local school districts during the Great Depression of the 1930s. All over the country, school districts were unable to pay teachers, and educational programs were being cut severely. JOM money appeared as a godsend to such local schools. They treated it as general aid to education – which it was not, according to Congress. As a consequence, Indian children profited minimally from a piece of "special" legislation. After the financial crisis of Depression years, school districts continued to merge JOM funds into general school funds and thus more or less frustrate the legislation.

Very occasionally in the first thirty years after passage of JOM complaints were raised against this practice. After the mid-1960s, however, the picture began to change. In June 1966, a meeting of the Governors' Interstate Indian Council made up of Indian appointees of each governor, called for remedial action because "a number of States reduce State funds paid to local school districts when that district receives or is eligible for funds from the Johnson-O'Malley Program."[131] During 1967–1968, a number of Indian leaders testified on educational problems before a U.S. Senate subcommittee. Domingo Montoya, chairman of the All-Indian Pueblo Council in Albuquerque, stated: "From what I see in the schools when I visit them I wonder if any of the Johnson-O'Malley money ever reaches our children."[132] He urged that JOM contracts be made with Indian tribes rather than with states or school districts. A statement from the Lummi Reservation in Washington state read that "the Johnson-O'Malley Fund loses its identity once it gets into the Ferndale School District."[133]

At the same time, a more detailed inquiry into the education of Indians in New Mexico was being conducted. Smith found a sweeping failure by public schools to pinpoint JOM funds for Indians only. For 1967, according to budget intention, over $50,000 was set aside for special books on Indian subjects. "Many of the classrooms visited," Smith reported, "had no such books."[134] And further: "In a number of schools, supplies were provided for all students, Indian and non-Indian alike, from Johnson-O'Malley funds. One superintendent said that Johnson-O'Malley funds were considered as part of the system's general operational funds, and were used accordingly." As for the law's criteria that the level of services financed by JOM funds must be equal to the highest standards in the state, Smith emphasized: "very few [school districts] meet these criteria."

Federal regulations required that JOM funds could go to a school district only if the district was making a reasonable local tax effort and could not find the needed funds elsewhere. During 1969–1970, the U.S. Comptroller General investigated charges that JOM funds were, in large measure, being used to replace local school funds and thus permit the lowering of taxes on local property. The JOM record of three states – Arizona, New Mexico, and South Dakota – was studied in detail; during 1967–1969, these states received two-thirds of all JOM funds.

In Arizona, the comptroller general found the state and counties were systematically using JOM funds as a substitute for local funds, a violation of federal regulations. In 1966–1967, more than $1.5 million in JOM funds was used in Arizona. Thirty-one of the recipient districts had lower-than-average tax rates. If these districts had increased their tax rate only to the average statewide rate, the federal payment could have been reduced by $363,000. As it was, the lesser amount was saved by local taxpayers rather than by the federal government. And the result was a failure to offer Indian students supplementary services.

In New Mexico, representatives of the comptroller general visited an unnamed school district – one that received nearly 30 percent of the state's JOM funds:

> We were told that the JOM funds had been commingled with other school funds and deposited into the regular school operating fund and the State textbook fund. The district was not required by the State to account for, or to report on the use made

of, the funds or to demonstrate that the services provided were
required to meet the unique needs of eligible Indian students
that could not be met by local, State, or other Federal resources.[135]

Similarly, in South Dakota it proved impossible to find any documentary
evidence that the Bureau of Indian Affairs had required JOM recipient
districts to demonstrate that they were making a reasonable tax effort.

Navajo experience with JOM had proved disappointing to the tribe.
One problem, of the type just reviewed, affected Navajos especially because they were concentrated in Arizona and New Mexico. Another problem was the unrepresentativeness of public schools attended by Indian
children. Peterson Zah, the head of the Navajo Legal Services Project,
testified:

> On the Navajo Reservation . . . the Window Rock School Dis-
> trict and the Granado School District both within the Arizona
> public school system, districts with 99 percent Indian enroll-
> ment, cannot institute Navajo cultural enrichment programs
> under state standards. The Window Rock district has only two
> Indian members on the five-man school board. The Granado
> District has no Indians on the five-man school board.[136]

The lack of representation allowed the purposes of the legislation to be
"perverted."

Zah also brought forward a charge that had not been discussed earlier.
Congressional expectations that the public school would welcome Navajo
children, he held, had been disappointed. The states of New Mexico and
Arizona, Zah declared, "consciously and artfully succeed each year in
keeping significant numbers of Indian children out of their school systems." This was accomplished in two ways: (1) by refusing to bus children
to public schools, and (2) by failing to build schools nearer the homes of
reservation children. In New Mexico, he noted, state aid per student was
$400. Because 11,000 Indian children in the state could find no place in the
public schools, the state saved some $4.4 million. These children at-
tended federally supported reservation schools. More than that, Zah
added, sending Indian children to reservation schools reduced welfare expenditures: "The BIA [Bureau of Indian Affairs] pays for the food and
shelter for students in its schools, thereby relieving the state [from]
having to pay for these needs of Indian students on welfare."[137]

Separate and unequal

The NAACP Legal Defense Fund and the Harvard Center for
Law and Education prepared a study of federal aid to Indian education,

by far the most comprehensive and realistic yet made. Indian interviewers talked with 445 Indian parents and officials in sixty school districts in eight states.

On the matter of equality of Indian schooling the Legal Defense Fund study reported:

> In large districts where Indian enrollment is concentrated in certain schools close to the reservation, there is typically a vast difference in the quality of education, the condition of the school, and the provision of books and supplies offered in these schools from those offered in the predominantly non-Indian schools. The differences are so obvious as to lead to the inescapable conclusion that Indians are not receiving an equal share of anything.[138]

After examining the concrete operations of JOM, the report emphasized the absence of any degree of parental control over the children's education:

> In Wakpala, S.D., the superintendent has repeatedly told the people not to make any trouble, or their school will be closed and their children transferred to boarding schools. . . . The Governor of the Acoma Pueblo in New Mexico told our interviewer that the superintendent of the Grants School District swore at him and told him to leave his office when the Governor tried to get information about Federal programs.

In every significant respect the Legal Defense Fund reported verified previous critical findings about the JOM program.

A generation of JOM showed that the Bureau of Indian Affairs had "abandoned Indian children to the states." In turn, the state education departments abandoned the children to the school districts. There, they were treated in accordance with historical patterns of discrimination and deprivation. Neither bureau nor state department nor school board was held responsible for enforcing the JOM law. Accountable to itself alone, the local school district turned away Indian parents' efforts to gain information about, let alone a degree of control over, expenditures presumably designated by Congress for their own children. So long had the Bureau of Indian Affairs operated JOM by acquiescence and the state by self-accountability, that when the Navajo tribe in 1972 insisted upon an explanation for extraordinary differences between JOM grants – ranging from $9 to $486 per student – neither the bureau nor the New Mexico State Education Department was able to reply.[139] Indian experience with JOM was repeated in its essentials in other federal programs designed in part for Indian children: (1) Title I of the Elementary and Secondary Education Act, (2) Public Law 815, and (3) Public Law 874.

Passage of the Johnson-O'Malley Act was an aspect of a federal government movement that had focused on enrolling Indian children in public schools (see Tables 29 and 30). Once accomplished, however, the transfer was followed by a federal retreat from responsibility. After the public schools took over on the Blackfeet Reservation "instead of maintaining a vigilance to assure the Blackfeet of the first class education that was necessary to raise them above their environment," Howard notes, "the Bureau retrenched to a minor support role and gave up its leadership."[140] A generation later, Blackfeet Chief Earl Old Person, told a congressional committee:

> On our reservation, we are short at least twelve classrooms. As a result, students from the first through the third grades are only getting half an education as they only go to school half a day in order to make room for other students of the same age. We have had to discontinue the only kindergarten on the reservation for lack of space.[141]

Many Indians had thought a transition to public schools would automatically mean an improvement of physical facilities.

Elsewhere, exclusion of native students from public schools continued. In Alaska, Indians and Eskimos during the 1930s were still channeled into federal schools by the Bureau of Indian Affairs and kept out of the predominantly white public schools run by the territorial government. Children of mixed blood, however, were admitted to the territorial schools upon the insistence of their parents, one of whom was "white." In 1939, it was reported that "full-blood Natives are discouraged by the Territory from attending its schools."[142] As late as 1945, the schools of Nome were segregated. Joseph Senungetuk, an Eskimo, recalled:

> During 1950–59, as a student in the Nome public schools, I was beaten by half-breed boys for being an Eskimo, and personally witnessed the discrimination against the King Island Eskimo children. The white students generally kept to themselves, as though to make believe we didn't exist. The Native children gathered in their own village groups. The latest village group now being taunted by both white students and Natives of other villages is the Saint Lawrence Islander.[143]

Upon achievement of statehood, Alaska's public schools were opened to all.

Navajo and Cherokee: aspiration and deprivation

The experience of two tribes – the Navajos and Cherokees – exemplifies many of the problems of Indian education. In both tribes,

Table 29. *Number and percentage distribution of Indian children aged 6–18, reported in annual school census by type of school and by state of reporting agency, school year 1967–1968* [a]

State	Number of children	Federal schools No.	Federal schools %	Public schools No.	Public schools %	Mission and private schools No.	Mission and private schools %	Total all schools No.	Total all schools %	Not enrolled No.	Not enrolled %	Information not available[c] No.	Information not available[c] %
Alaska	19,792	7,094	35.8	11,534	58.3	842	4.2	19,470	98.4	72	0.4	250	1.3
Arizona	39,368	16,616	42.2	16,804	42.7	2,544	6.5	35,964	91.4	2,923[b]	7.4	481	1.2
Colorado	670	19	2.8	595	88.8	17	2.5	631	94.2	39	5.8		
Florida	391	109	27.9	255	65.2	6	1.5	370	94.6	21	5.4		
Iowa	194	64	33.0	126	64.9	2	1.0	192	99.0	2	1.0		
Kansas	1,010	14	1.4	979	96.9	4	0.4	997	98.7	13	1.3		
Mississippi	1,312	1,160	88.4	126	9.6	4	0.3	1,290	98.3	22	1.7		
Montana	9,590	867	9.0	7,511	78.3	779	8.1	9,157	95.5	216	2.2	217	2.3
Nevada	1,669	1,215	72.8	343	20.5	86	5.2	1,644	98.5	25	1.5		
New Mexico	29,244	8,835	30.2	16,627	56.8	1,847	6.3	27,309	93.4	59	3.9		
North Carolina	1,524	950	62.3	494	32.4	21	1.4	1,465	96.1	1,664[b]	5.7	271	0.9
North Dakota	8,502	3,273	38.5	3,293	38.7	798	9.4	7,364	86.6	257	3.0	881	10.4
Oklahoma	23,316	990	4.2	21,282	91.3	22	0.1	22,294	95.6	683	2.9	339	1.4
South Dakota	11,712	4,397	37.5	5,167	44.1	1,380	11.8	10,944	93.4	402	3.4	366	3.1
Utah	2,359	1,058	44.8	1,125	57.7	38	1.6	2,221	94.2	134	5.7	4	0.2
Wyoming	1,435	64	4.4	1,100	76.6	154	10.7	1,318	91.8	84	5.8	33	2.3

[a] Data are for children for whom the Bureau of Indian Affairs has educational responsibility as enumerated by BIA agencies in annual census of Indian children. These data do not include Indian children for whom the BIA does not have direct responsibility in those states.

[b] Mostly Navajo children living in isolated rural areas.

[c] Indian mobility accounts for most children in this category.

Source: Estelle Fuchs and Robert J. Havighurst, *To Live on this Earth: American Indian Education* (Garden City, N.Y.: Doubleday, 1972), pp. 342–343.

Table 30. *American Indian students and
teachers in public schools, fall 1970*

State	Number of students	Number of teachers
Alabama	39	2
Alaska	10,070	40
Arizona	19,541	57
Arkansas	497	11
California	16,854	271
Colorado	1,218	31
Connecticut	415	4
Delaware	76	1
District of Columbia	7	1
Florida	1,394	13
Georgia	406	6
Idaho	2,192	7
Illinois	2,520	33
Indiana	677	14
Iowa	526	5
Kansas	1,468	29
Kentucky	48	5
Louisiana	250	34
Maine	564	2
Maryland	373	15
Massachusetts	504	9
Michigan	4,375	63
Minnesota	7,172	55
Mississippi	103	0
Missouri	1,372	58
Montana	8,474	37
Nebraska	2,150	10
Nevada	2,839	12
New Hampshire	68	0
New Jersey	471	12
New Mexico	19,216	90
New York	5,669	69
North Carolina	14,168	438
North Dakota	1,133	7
Ohio	1,115	13
Oklahoma	28,918	600
Oregon	3,727	42
Pennsylvania	511	12
Rhode Island	160	2
South Carolina	295	4
South Dakota	7,536	9
Tennessee	305	1
Texas	3,589	131

Table 30. *(cont.)*

State	Number of students	Number of teachers
Utah	4,733	5
Vermont	12	0
Virginia	975	20
Washington	10,577	72
West Virginia	88	3
Wisconsin	6,937	44
Wyoming	916	2
Total	197,243	2,401

Source: U.S. Department of Health, Education, and Welfare, Office for Civil Rights, *Directory of Public Elementary and Secondary Schools in Selected Districts, Enrollment and Staff by Racial/Ethnic Group, Fall 1970* (Washington, D.C.: GPO, 1972), pp. vii–xiii.

aspirations for education deepened after the turn of the century despite frustrations at cultural loss and at low school expectations for their children. The Navajo school problem was the most formidable educational challenge to federal authorities. In many ways, it exemplified the principal problems of government schooling of Indians. By 1928, two-thirds of school-age Navajo children did not attend school. This failed to change greatly during the next twenty years. At no time during this period did as many as half attend. As in the years after the Treaty of 1868, federal authorities were reluctant to meet the Navajo demand for schools. To do so, it was held, would require an extensive system of new roads and buses. The physical isolation of Navajo dwellings from one another was notorious. Meanwhile, with so little schooling available, people of the tribe were failing spectacularly in achieving basic English literacy. A study of selective service records for 1943 through 1946 revealed that nearly nine out of ten Navajo men aged eighteen to thirty-eight were illiterate. The minority of Navajo children in school, reported Sanchez, who studied the reservation during 1945–1946, was enrolled in "makeshift schools which are materially and administratively unsound, inadequate, and uneconomical."[144] Many so-called day schools were operated as though they were dormitory schools. Many students slept overnight in emergency quarters. The school at Hunter's Point, near Window Rock, was such an institution: "It is a two-teacher school. . . . Out of 55 children enrolled there last year, six or eight came on a day basis. The rest lived at the school in a makeshift, loghouse dormitory built by the

Navajos. The patrons also helped to pay for the assistants needed to care for the children."[145] With such minimal federal expenditures in mind, it must have struck administrators that conversion to a full-scale public school system would entail great increases in federal money outlay.

The Depression of the 1930s was not nearly so disastrous to Navajos as to the Sioux and many non-Indians. A basic reason was the greater self-sufficiency among the Navajos. In 1937, according to Hulsizer, the Navajos were 90 percent self-supporting, principally by raising and selling sheep and corn.[146] During World War II, the traditional pursuit of sheep raising became less significant, and children were increasingly released from economic duties. The movement of Navajo men into the armed forces produced an interest in gaining new skills through schooling. Both processes added a strong stimulus to the demand for Navajo schools. As Underhill put it: "The Navajos were ready for school. But the schools were not ready for them."[147] An extraordinary Navajo push for schools finally produced results. Between 1945 and 1955 the number of school-age children on the reservation increased by over 156 percent. By 1955, the degree of Navajo school attendance was fully comparable with that of the national population.

The content of this schooling was another matter. Although the schools were located directly on a reservation inhabited by a tribe of whom more than 95 percent were full-bloods, Navajo language was positively discouraged in the schools. On the one hand, recalls a Navajo woman, "English was not spoken in any Navajo hogan, and during their summer vacation, the children forgot much of what they had learned at school." Yet once back in the boarding school in Toadlena, "extra duty was given those caught speaking Navajo."[148] Thirty-five years later, Navajo children were still being penalized for using their own language in school.[149]

A sometimes crushing burden was laid upon Navajo children by the schools' negative evaluation of their language and even their striving. The first Navajo to become a physician, Taylor McKenzie, told a gathering of his personal struggle:

> I was told that, because I am a Navajo, I would not be successful in reaching my goal. I fought for my goal, to prove among other things, to myself especially, that there was nothing inherently detrimental in being a Navajo that would obstruct my progress. When finally, I made the grade, I looked back in retrospect and determined that the Navajo is a human being and that he is intelligent. I breathed a sigh of relief.[150]

A bright, striving Navajo boy contradicted the stereotype to whom the reservation schools assigned endless work of a simple occupational sort.

By the late 1960s, the future of the Navajo tribe, including its children, had come to rest on the viability of the reservation way of life. Historically, the view of the dominant society had most often been: disperse the Indians and with the subsequent disappearance of the reservation, individual Indians will adapt to majority ways. The schools, both government and public, based their teachings on the same supposition. But the Navajos had not dispersed. Their numbers doubled between 1870 and 1898, 1898 and 1932, 1932 and 1958. By 1990, the projected population is expected to be 240,000, double that of 1968. In 1968, four out of five Navajos were below age thirty-four, so that the potential for further population growth is great. To support this expanding population in the post-World War II years, the Navajos earned considerable income from royalties on uranium, gas, coal, and oil worked on the reservation by outsiders.

The Navajo tribal council spent these funds for community wide projects such as emergency relief, baby layettes and clothing for schoolchildren, college scholarships and loans, revolving credit fund, and roads. In addition, some of the funds were invested in tribal industrial projects, including forest products, industry, and motels.

The present role of the Navajos in the larger economy has its close counterpart in the field of education and has been described accurately by Aberle: "At present Navajos are not being integrated as a tribe into the larger society, but being squeezed dry by it, and . . . they are being neither integrated nor assimilated into the larger society as individuals but pushed into its lower echelons on most unfavorable terms."[151]

With the destruction of the Cherokee Nation, its reservation, and its schools in 1906, one could have expected the end of traditional Cherokee ways. Many became assimilated into white society; still, in the 1960s, there were more Cherokee-speaking Indians in eastern Oklahoma than in 1900. It was unusual to find a child who did not understand Cherokee; two-thirds spoke it, and a number were bilingual. Those Cherokees familiar with Sequoyah learned it after their thirtieth year or so. On the other hand, during the mid-1960s one source reported that "the average Cherokee cabin is likely to be as devoid of a single scrap of Sequoyah as it is of a copy of Catullus."[152] Among the Eastern Cherokees, in North Carolina, an elective course in Sequoyah was being offered, at least during 1940, in a reservation school.[153]

The loss of tribal schools spelled the end of the widespread bilingual literacy that had distinguished Cherokees in the nineteenth century. In the public schools of northeastern Oklahoma the Cherokee children were served poorly. During the thirty-five years or so after 1932, the percentage of Cherokees who could read English well increased only from 38 to 58. The median school grade completed among Cherokees over eighteen years of age rose from third grade in 1933 to fifth grade in 1952 to second half of the fifth grade in 1963.[154] "Should a Cherokee move to one of the cities of Oklahoma," writes Wax, "he would encounter a population whose median level of school completion was six or more years beyond his own."[155]

A project during the late 1960s in which Cherokee matrons were the field researchers studied the public schools attended by their children. Cherokee parents were found to be, not apathetic but "strongly concerned about the schools and their offspring." They were surprisingly well-informed about the schools. In the classrooms, typically, one found "a small aggregate of English-speaking pupils in continual discourse with teachers, while about them was a silent group of Cherokee."[156] Many of the white teachers were born and raised in the area and so were not unfamiliar with Cherokee ways.

The project found that Cherokee parents maintained a "phenomenally" high level of educational aspirations for their children.[157]

Andrew Dreadfulwater, chairman of the Original Cherokee Community Organization, recalled his own difficulties in public school: "I couldn't see how a gingerbread could get [out] of an oven and run, see."[158] He explained how the Cherokee child, completely unregimented at home, was subjected in public school to an unremitting schedule: "You get to the point where you have to do this at 9 o'clock, you do this at 10, and you do this at 12, and you go back and do the same thing day in and day out. I think it's kind of boring to Indian children." Mrs. Lucille Proctor, a Cherokee, had personally visited 160 Cherokee families to discuss school problems. She reported: "I have found that many [children] have been promoted from grade to grade even though they didn't earn their grade, and when they reached high school it was difficult for them to do high school work." The reports of parents convinced her that "the teachers dislike the Cherokee children and mistreat them."[159]

The effect of termination of federal support

During the early 1950s, federal authorities momentarily attempted to shed their historical responsibility for support of the Indians. Some sixty reservations were "terminated." This meant that no services to Indians were any longer to come from the federal government. Tribal lands could be sold as private property. Reservations were converted into mere civil subdivisions of the states in which they were located. So eager was the Bureau of Indian Affairs to accomplish these ends that it arranged for the suspension of special services for Indians in California in anticipation of termination legislation. Even though such legislation was never passed, the suspension of services continued in force. Thus, California, which had been the first state to sign an agreement under the Johnson-O'Malley Act of 1934, lost all JOM funds in 1958. They were not reinstated until 1970, and then only in small measure.

The Klamath and Menominee tribes experienced complete termination. Both had voted to accept the measure in the mistaken belief that they would then possess sufficient resources to make it alone. In each case, education suffered for the change.

In 1961, the Klamath Reservation in Oregon was terminated. Some seven years later Wilford C. Wasson, a Coos Indian and a member of the Counseling Center at the University of Oregon, found in a study of schooling that the dropout rate had risen to 90 percent. Before termination, about three-fifths of Klamath Indian students had graduated from the reservation high school. "This high Indian dropout rate," wrote Wasson, "is blamed on the parents and homelife by the school and on the prejudice of teachers and school administrators by the parents." His own judgment was that "to a great extent the parents are right and the schools are prejudiced." Wasson also criticized disciplinary practices of the school: "The usual punishment for nonconformity is to send the child home for a week. For most students this is equivalent to sending him home for a year because he isn't allowed to make up any of the work or exams he has missed. If he protests . . . he is making trouble and is sent home for another week."[160]

Termination came to the Menominees in 1961. Economically, this was a disaster. Whatever elements of self-support the Menominees had tended to slip away. By 1970, four out of five welfare recipients in Menominee County were Indian children. Difficult as the home situation was, the schools made matters worse. Teachers and administrators were uninterested at best and vicious at worst. When parents approached a superintendent of Bohemian ancestry with a request that the schools teach more about the Indian heritage, he refused, noting that he had had no "Bohemian identity" courses while a student.[161] Menominee parents were highly critical of inattention to Indian culture, the low quality of teaching, and excessive physical discipline. In 1969, out of seven teachers in Neopit, only one had an academic degree. Parents protested against their children being promoted despite their failure to learn much. During 1969, Indians formed the Menominee County Parents and Students for Better Education. Three issues were paramount: they demanded that the school board adopt an Educational Bill of Rights; they called for an end to certain disciplinary procedures; and they advocated electoral reapportionment so that Menominees could elect some members of the school board. Although Indians made up 30 percent of the school district enrollment, the school board was all white. After the demands were rejected, the protest movement subsided. A year or so later, new stirrings were evident among parents and students.

Tribal language and self-determination

The schooling of Indian children continued to be culturally deficient. In 1972, a Senate committee inquired of the Bureau of Indian

Affairs whether the schools in tribes not terminated were paying attention to the problem of teaching Indian heritage. The bureau replied that "all of the Areas which operate Federal schools provide orientation programs to acquaint 'the teacher with the history and traditions of the people she serves.' These brief programs vary in quality and at best are inadequate."[162] The bureau had at least improved its candor if not its capacity to educate Indian children. The same year, the field staff of the National Study of American Indian Education reported on the basis of very extensive interviews that "though many teachers voiced support for a policy of 'cultural pluralism' and wanted a course in Indian history and culture, few if any understood the native culture or the idea of 'cultural education.' "[163]

The degree to which traditional culture still held sway among Indians can be tested, in part, by the frequency of use of native language. Among Navajos, for example, it is almost universal, even among children. About two-thirds of Cherokee youth, as noted above, can speak Cherokee. Nearly all understand it. On the other hand, Pulitzer Prize novelist N. Scott Momaday, himself a Kiowa, says "few young Kiowans . . . are learning to speak Kiowa." In Iowa, "the Mesquakies have all but lost their language now, except for the older ones." At the Cheyenne River Reservation, in South Dakota, fewer than half the Sioux children can speak Lakota. On the Blackfeet Reservation few parents speak an Indian language. In Chicago, almost all Indian youngsters interviewed in a study "said they did not know their tribal language, and did not hear it at home." The last member of the tiny Ohlone tribe in California who could speak his language died in 1917.[164]

Loss of tribal language was closely connected with the group's contact with white education. The Navajos and the full-blood or rural Cherokees with least contact have held on to their language. In a few melancholy cases, where schools finally came around to permit the native language to be spoken in school, few knew the language well enough to do so.

Important as the matter of tribal language was, by the 1970s it had become a secondary educational question. Indian identity was now seen as hinging on self-determination of Indian life. Control of the reservations, including the schools, became the overarching issue. Growing numbers of urban Indians concerned themselves with the same issue. At the heart of self-determination was self-government. "The Indians' right of self-government," according to Cohen, "is a right which has been consistently ignored by treaty-makers and legislators, and very widely disregarded by administrative officials."[165]

Whatever powers Indians received were trivial and tangential. The basic colonial relationship endured. Education as a principal means of colonization remained firmly under governmental control. The goal of cultural obliteration was pursued consistently. In 1934, Congress provided for formal tribal self-government through tribal elections; the measure is known as the Indian Reorganization Act. Under the law, as Forbes indicates, "no power at the national or regional levels was actually transferred to democratically-chosen Indian boards."[166] Control of Indian education shifted increasingly from federal to state auspices, but the colonial spirit was undiminished. In 1961, California created a State Advisory Commission on Indian Affairs without any Indian members.

Even the elected tribal council lacked autonomy. Rupert Costo, Cahuilla, president of the American Indian Historical Society, charged:

> There is strong evidence that the tribal governing bodies are the creatures of the Bureau [of Indian Affairs], and do not dare to run counter to the policies and instructions of the Bureau – or they will soon be disposed of. . . . In Fort Hall, Pine Ridge, Rosebud, and many other areas of the Plains, the tribal governments are usually puppets of the Bureau.[167]

At the Blackfeet Reservation, the bureau's superintendent or his staff attended all tribal council meetings; "tribal council members are seldom, if ever, allowed to attend the superintendent's staff meetings."[168]

Demands for Indian control of schools were most often presented as the only effective road to maintenance of Indian identity. The cultural approach, warned August Little Soldier, tribal chairman of the three affiliated tribes at Fort Berthold Reservation, "does *not* mean that one teaches the Indian how to become a white man, then teach him a trade. The cultural approach means that he is taught how to use his values (he becomes even more Indian) in taking advantage of vocational or liberal educational opportunities and becoming self-supporting. . . . He is even more Indian than ever because he has learned how to *use* his values in a new setting."[169] A certain impatience was voiced about white-sponsored "demonstration" and "pilot projects" in the community control of Indian schools. Sam Deloria, Standing Rock Sioux, director of the planning office of the Oglala Sioux tribe, declared: "If it is not the right of the Indian people to run their own schools, then we should evidently line up like applicants to save the children, waiting for an Indian expert to adopt us so that we may go through the motions of being involved."[170] Indian youth, he insisted, could prepare for meaningful adaptation to the contemporary world only under the tutelage of community-controlled schools. "Obviously," Deloria explained, "only Indians can regain their own pride – can you imagine an Indian saying 'thanks to that white man, I now have my pride, without him I would still be somewhat lacking in self-respect.'" Nor should Indians be allowed to experiment only along certain approved lines: "Indian communities should have the opportunity to run the best or the worst, the most bizarre, the most imaginative, or most orthodox school systems in the country."

During the early 1970s, much rhetoric was heard concerning Indian parents' participation in school affairs. In 1972, the Bureau of Indian Affairs reported that 152 parent councils existed at various schools in accordance with the requirement of the Elementary and Secondary Education Act. No evaluation of the councils had been made.[171] The councils were advisory on specific projects and had nothing to do with the school as a whole. During 1970, President Nixon announced an intention to hand over responsibility for many Indian activities to the Indians. Nearly two years later, Navajo tribal chairman Peter McDonald wrote that the pledge had "not been effectively implemented because some of the key top level Washington staff personnel appear to have other ideas."[172]

The principal currents of change in Indian education originated among the Indian people themselves. Among the Saint Regis Mohawks, New York, a prolonged boycott resulted in the placement of two Indians on the district school board. Agreement was reached on offering Mohawk as well as Spanish, French, and Russian.[173] Among the White Mountain Apaches in Arizona, an intratribal struggle arose over widespread dissatisfaction with a tribal-council-appointed school board. Mixed into the conflict were issues such as the lack of Indian cultural content in courses and a low-quality educational program. Late in 1970, a thousand Apaches attended a protest pow wow sponsored by the National Indian Youth Council. Growing numbers of lawsuits were being entered on behalf of Indian parents demanding equal educational opportunities for their children.[174] In 1971 a Native American Legal Rights Fund was organized to prosecute such cases.

One traditional American means of protest – electoral activity – was little utilized by Indians. On a national scale, their small number precluded any meaningful campaign, though local and statewide campaigns were sometimes successful. At times, the margin of Indian votes in western states determined elections.[175] Indian candidates running in mixed areas stood small chance of winning, no matter how qualified for the position. In 1969, a Pawnee Indian holding a master's degree – representing considerably more education than his white opponent – ran for the school board in Pawnee, Oklahoma. The town newspaper supported the white, who won easily.[176]

Academic underachievement

Indian parents over the years reserved their severest criticism for the failure of schools to help their children achieve academically. In a study commissioned by the Bureau of Indian Affairs and completed in 1969, it was reported that teachers in government boarding schools regarded academic achievement as relatively unimportant. Only a tenth of them ranked it as an important goal in their teaching.[177] Theories were developed to explain away school responsibility for low achievement. Thus, the commissioner of Indian affairs referred to "sociocultural factors" that explained the scholastic difficulty of Indian students in college.[178] A number of Indian students have never experienced any special difficulty in college, and yet were not any the less "sociocultural" Indians. This mode of analysis was repeated in another form by the executive committee of the Oglala Sioux tribe, which endorsed the minimalistic statement that "efforts at Pine Ridge Agency to improve the quality of education for Indian children have not been totally ineffective, considering the social and economic status of many of the parents of our students."[179] The parents, after all, were Oglala Sioux and were poor. It is doubtful that the executive committee communicated to members of the tribe at large its conviction that the failure of their children to achieve in schools was not principally due to shortcomings of the schools but to themselves.

From time to time, the Bureau of Indian Affairs issued statements relating to its own responsibility in the area of academic achievement. In 1963 it set a goal of closing the educational gap between Indian and non-Indian students by 1970. As time wore on, and the gap persisted, the bureau pushed the end date farther forward. By 1971, the end date had become 1976. In 1972, the goals were as follows: "(1) 90 percent of all Indian youth graduate from high school, (2) by 1976 the achievement level of Indian students at least equal that for non-Indian youth, (3) 50 percent of the graduates enter college, and (4) the remaining 50 percent be either employed or enrolled in technical training."[180] It proved impossible, in any case, to judge whether the bureau was moving toward these goals because the agency failed to collect systematic achievement test data.

In 1971–1972, the comptroller general of the United States examined critically the bureau's educational goals and its efforts to attain them. He sought especially to discover why so little progress had been made toward eliminating the Indian–non-Indian achievement gap. Two basic reasons were cited: (1) the bureau had not adequately communicated its goal to area offices and schools, and (2) no specific plan existed to reach the goal. The comptroller general reported to Congress:

> Officials at BIA's central office and at the three area offices and
> twelve schools visited agreed that the education programs were
> not designed to reach the goal of raising the achievement level up
> to the national average by 1976. In fact, officials at five schools
> and at one area office told us that they were not even aware of this

goal. Officials at the seven other schools and two area offices told us that they had heard of the goal. They said, however, that they had not made a specific effort to design their programs to reach this goal because they had not been officially notified of it and had not received any guidelines or instructions from the central office concerning it.[181]

After nine years of announcements, it turned out there was really nothing to announce.

6

Puerto Rican children

In all its history, Puerto Rico has never been a modern independent nation. Under Spanish rule from 1493 to 1898, a distinct Puerto Rican nationality emerged only early in the nineteenth century. During the last half of the century, nationalism and the independence movement flourished in some middle-class circles. An abortive uprising at Lares in 1868 marked the furthest extent of the revolutionary movement. When the United States acquired Puerto Rico thirty years later, "the majority of the population – the peasants and workers – of course remained on the periphery, accepting the change of sovereignty with the same fatalism with which they accepted hookworm, hurricanes, and tuberculosis."[1]

Between Spanish and North American rule, the average Puerto Rican found little to choose. American economic domination was so complete that any alternative seemed chimerical. In cultural life, Americanization of education retarded the rise of Puerto Rican consciousness. Not only their language, but their traditions and history as well suffered in the day-to-day curriculum of the school. Puerto Rico was a colony in every sense – economic, political, and cultural. As late as 1943, Governor Tugwell referred publicly to himself as "a colonial governor."[2]

Puerto Rican anthropologist Ricardo Alegria, head of the Institute of Puerto Rican Culture, warned that the "two cultures could live together and interchange ideas, but only if those cultures are both in an equal status."[3] He cautioned against the adoption of a foreign, rootless culture. Maldonado-Denis declared that the Puerto Rican public schools served "the United States goal of spiritual domination."[4]

Indian people had been the first to settle the island world of the Caribbean. On the island later known as Puerto Rico the Taino tribe predominated, with its society of classes: the *caciques*, or chiefs, the *nitaynos*, or lower aristocracy, and the *nabories*, the common folk. No slave class is known to have existed in the Taino tribe.

Religion played a central role in their lives; accordingly, priests had a special importance. They were medicine men and masters of a rich pharmacopaeia of herbs. The cacique bore a high responsibility of teaching his children the history of the village.[5] Written communication was restricted

to a pictographic script, and the history of the tribal village was perpetuated orally.

Possibly during the twelfth or thirteenth century, the Caribbean islands were invaded by the Carib Indians from the coast of the southern
mainland. The Caribs conquered wherever they went. In Puerto Rico
they left a military heritage that was used, although ineffectually, by the
Taino people when confronted with the Spanish invasions after 1493.

Gold was what the Spanish sought. Indians were enslaved and forced to
seek gold for their masters. So many died so quickly that by 1510, only
seventeen years after the Spanish had come to the island, Indian slaves for
the mines were being imported from the mainland.

In 1510–1511, Indian leaders quietly gathered their forces to mount a
full-scale revolt against the Spanish, but superior Spanish arms resulted in
total defeat. Within another quarter century or so, few Indians could be
found anywhere on the islands. Spanish laws passed to protect or benefit
Indians were ignored by owners of Indian slaves. Thus, a law of 1513 that
required owners of forty or more Indian slaves to teach them to read and
write was ignored.[6] The destruction of the Indians of the islands was
capped by a myth that they had somehow been especially vicious people.

Blacks entered Puerto Rican history near the beginning of the sixteenth
century as slaves from Africa, but slavery was abolished in 1873, and a
fairly large group of free blacks lived on the island. The interior remained
inhabited by descendants of the Spanish and Indians.

Puerto Rico was ruled by a tiny group of aristocrats. Education, such as
it was, was designed for children of the privileged class. Preparation for
the priesthood took place in monasteries. From time to time, royal governors issued orders requiring some kind of educational facility in each
district, and in 1781, the king of Spain directed those parents able to pay
to send their children to a school. Little resulted from this. By 1797,
seven out of ten Puerto Ricans were illiterate.

Pressure from middle-class parents resulted after 1820 in the creation
of secondary and professional schools designed for their children. After
about 1850, state-built schools were opened to some poor children without payment of fees. So eager were the parents of these children that they
swamped the schools. The result was not the expansion of schools but the
control of attendance of poor children. One reported that each San Juan
teacher was authorized to admit thirty poor children: "Twenty poor
children were allotted to each first class school, fifteen to a second class
school, and eleven to a third class school."[7]

These schools were financed by tuition and funds from island authorities. Extremely few children from the countryside ever saw the inside of any school through the nineteenth century.

In 1897, Spain agreed to grant Puerto Rico a degree of self-rule, but the

Spanish-American War came soon after and with the peace treaty "the island of Puerto Rico, with nearly one million inhabitants, was ceded to the United States, given away like a box of cigars or a piece of furniture."[8]

During 1898–1901, when American military authorities ruled the island, an official census showed that only one out of every twelve school-age children (five to seventeen years old) was in school.[9] Statistics gathered by the Spanish two years before revealed illiteracy to be at 82 percent. Testimony submitted to the Carroll inquiry by U.S. Consul General Hanna in November, 1898, reported:

> Even the uneducated men and women of the island come to us and beg us to use our influence with the United States to establish the American school system throughout this country for the education of their children. The education of the poorer class has been sadly neglected. The child of the poor man has had no opportunity to procure an education.[10]

When Dr. Henry K. Carroll, who presided over the survey, asked an island official whether there were separate schools for blacks and white children, the answer was no. "Do parents raise objection to this?" Carroll asked. Again, the reply was no. He dropped this line of questioning. Racial separation was one of the features of American schooling not exported to Puerto Rico.

Carroll predicted that "both Spanish and English may be used side by side for years to come," yet in his recommendations on education, he stressed that the schools should be conducted in the English language only.

American colony: educational neglect

From 1898 on, Puerto Rico became a complete American colony. The people of the island were regarded more or less as residuals of American military-economic concerns.

Education in Puerto Rico followed the prevailing world colonial patterns. Typically, the colonizing government exercised a positive disinterest in educating the native people.

The American government exhorted Puerto Ricans to educate themselves, but refused unconditionally to contribute any of its own funds for that purpose. American Brigadier General George W. Davis advised Washington: "If the island is to have an efficient school system it must be implanted. It does not possess the elements for creating one, and it has not the resources to meet the expense."[11] The advice was rejected. Neither did Puerto Rico receive any school lands, the traditional American means of encouraging popular education. During the years 1901–

1920, school expenditures on the island totaled nearly $31 million. Puerto Ricans supplied all of this sum.[12]

The human cost of such expenditures was exceedingly high, given the extreme poverty of the islanders. Puerto Ricans strained to educate their children. In most isolated rural villages, where public funds were unavailable, people did as best as they could. One elderly woman recalled:

> In my youth we had schools – the teachers were people who could read and write a little bit, and they taught the others. The parents paid the teachers 75 cents a month for each child. I didn't go to school for very long myself; like the others, I used to take lunch to the teacher. One day a child would bring corn griddle cakes and milk. Another day, they would take yucca and sweet potato with codfish in oil, or boiled corn – new corn –*sancochoa* [boiled in salt], as they call it in the country, and the teacher would eat it with a bottle of coffee.[13]

So spare were schooling opportunities in the rural area in 1899, that in San José, a coffee-growing district, only 1.5 percent (92 of 6,161) of children under ten years of age were in school.[14]

During the first thirty years of American rule, Puerto Ricans came to carry an extraordinary burden for schooling. In 1920, the United States had 31.7 children aged six to fourteen for every 100 of its people; Puerto Rico had 43.3. Eight years later, education expenditures of the insular government took up nearly 40 percent of total insular operating expenses. In 1898, under the Spanish, only 4.5 percent of expenses had gone for schools.

Despite these heroic efforts, schooling opportunities were minimal. Rural schools extended only for the first three grades and were almost universally on double sessions. During 1918–1920, the percentage of rural schools under this arrangement ranged from 87 to 90. In effect, these children received, at best, the equivalent of one and a half years of schooling. For most, this was the total of their education. The financial burden was simply too heavy. As a result, while the number of children in school rose, and school buildings multiplied, the amount of money spent on each child *fell* in relation to American standards. In 1901, per pupil costs in Puerto Rico were 64.1 percent of those in the United States; by 1918 the figure dropped to 31.3 percent.[15]

In urban areas, schools were more plentiful and adequate. During 1920, 56.4 percent of rural school-age children, but about 60 percent of urban children, attended school. Urban schools were graded through the eighth grade. Full-fledged graduates, however, were few in number. Of every 1,000 urban first-graders who started school in 1911, only 200 remained in eighth grade. Of 1,000 who began in 1920, 393 remained in eighth grade. Clark compared the elementary school dropout rates for rural and urban children during the years 1917–1923 and found that 0.4 percent of the former and 54.3 percent of the latter reached seventh grade.[16]

Secondary schools remained, as they had been under the Spanish regime, a preserve for children from wealthier families. Between 1919 and 1937, the proportion of all public school students who were enrolled in high schools rose only from 2 to 5 percent.[17] So thorough had the winnowing process been in the common schools that Clark formulated a statistical law: "A sample . . . which includes none below eighth grade graduates . . . represents the children of the middle and upper classes."[18] It was from these circles that the American occupation drew technical and professional personnel to staff administrative and business positions on the island. The strongest pro-American sentiments were found among them.

In the absence of United States aid, schools derived all their support from island sources. Insular expenditures in 1927–1928 made up 81.6 percent and municipal funds 18.4 percent of school expenditures. The primary source of municipal – but not of insular – revenues was a property tax. Extreme differences in insular expenditure per student existed between localities. Clark explains this outcome in terms of "the rules in effect governing the use of Insular money [which] prevent its distribution in a manner to equalize fully or even approximately, school opportunities for the entire population."[19] Analyzing school expenditures in two groups of municipalities of varying economic circumstances, he found that expense per pupil enrolled was $30.94 in seven wealthy municipalities compared with $18.00 in seven poor municipalities; expense per child aged eight to fourteen years was $31.67 in the wealthy and $14.32 in the poor municipalities.

The poor were especially penalized by the property tax because of its tendency to raise rents and the price of food. Schools suffered financially as a result of the outright refusal of some large American corporations to pay the assessed taxes. These firms, reputed to have strong political connections in the United States, were able to turn away tax collectors with impunity.[20]

English only

While the occupying power manifested small concern over the quantity and quality of schooling in Puerto Rico, its educational policy was based on the goal of Americanization. English was to be the language of classroom instruction.

An exaggerated sense of American patriotism quickly spread throughout the schools. "In 1900," observes Osuna, "the average Puerto Rican child knew more about Washington, Lincoln and Betsy Ross and the American flag than the average child in the United States."[21] American-appointed commissioners of education proudly reported to Washington their success at instilling a sense of American patriotism. "In almost every city of the Island, and at many rural schools," wrote an early commissioner, "the children . . . saluted the flag at the opening of the school day. . . . The pupils then sang 'America,' 'Hail Columbia,' 'Star Spangled Banner,' and other 'patriotic songs.'"[22] Commissioner Juan B. Huyke, the first such official of Puerto Rican birth, was no less a patriot than his predecessors. In 1921, he informed school personnel that the schools "must implant the spirit of America within the hearts of our children." For parents' meetings, Huyke suggested the following theme: "American Patriotism: wear the flag in your heart as well as in your buttonhole."[23] The Americanized schools excluded any treatment of historical Puerto Rican culture. An upper-class student noted that in 1917, upon entering the third year of a high school organized by cultural nationalists, he took his first course in Puerto Rican history.

American authorities hoped to graft the English language onto the Puerto Rican school system. Since only a few Puerto Rican teachers were prepared to teach the new language, American instructors were imported. They were viewed by many Puerto Rican teachers as spoilsmen. The Diffies in 1931 characterized the effort as extremely wasteful: "Why spend millions of dollars to teach English to people who were 80 percent illiterate, in preference to teaching them their own language? . . . There were almost 300,000 children for whom there are no school facilities."[24] The Americans' insistence on the use of English in institutions tended to crowd out other educational problems.

As early as 1907, about four-fifths of all classes were reportedly conducted in English; in the remaining fifth English was studied as a separate subject. In 1910, Commissioner Edwin G. Dexter reported to Washington that "89.5 percent of all graded schools were taught wholly in English, . . . compared with 66.7 percent the preceding year."[25] Graded schools were located only in urban areas and were not numerous. The use of English in rural schools was relatively rare. During 1909–1910, 124 rural teachers were granted their request to teach English only in their classes.

Puerto Rican opposition to the English-only policy was persistent. Among the leaders in the movement were teachers' groups. In 1913 and 1915 attempts were made in the House of Delegates to require that Spanish only be used through the eighth grade. Island authorities stopped the measures from passage. In 1915, students at Central High School in San Juan, the capital, circulated petitions on behalf of the measure. The student leader, Francisco Grovas, was expelled; a strike followed, and an islandwide protest movement resulted, leading to the creation of an alternative high school that stressed the cultural interests of Puerto Rico.[26]

Under Commissioner Huyke, bulletins to teachers on behalf of English-only became frequent. In September 1922, he directed that "teachers in all grades above the fourth will use English as [the] medium of instruction in all subjects except physiology in the fifth grade and the Spanish language itself." Two months later, he urged teachers to "make it a point to stimulate the study of Shakespeare's language by every conceivable device." In 1923, Huyke forbade the publication of school newspapers if these were printed in Spanish only; at least half the contents, he ruled, must be in the English language.[27]

During the mid-1920s, the teaching of both Spanish and English occupied nearly half the average school day.[28] How confused the Puerto Rican child became depended on the state of the language question. One Puerto Rican recalled: "I went through elementary, high school, and normal school during . . . the period during which English was the medium of instruction at all levels. . . . I did not know a word of English, and my teacher did not know a word of Spanish. I did not know where one word ended and the other began."[29]

From 1900 to 1905, a strict English-only policy was proclaimed. Spanish continued to be used in almost all elementary schools; high schools were conducted in English. During the regime of Commissioner Dexter, schools were instructed to teach children English even before they knew Spanish.[30] This extreme approach was moderated considerably later on. Between 1916 and 1934, Grades 1 through 4 were conducted in Spanish and the upper grades and high schools in English. Because of the immense dropout rate, very few children received meaningful instruction in English. Spanish-only was extended to all elementary grades during the years 1934–1937. At the same time, English was taught as a special subject, by trained teachers and for double class periods.

During the 1930s, language became more than ever a political issue. In that decade the tide of independence sentiment seemed about to swamp the occupying power. Student-initiated proindependence demonstrations became common. They were repeatedly suppressed by education and police authorities.

The Roosevelt administration was deeply disturbed at the outbursts for independence. It tightened up the language issue. Appointment of a commissioner of education was delayed for fear that too independent-minded a candidate might inadvertently gain office. In 1937, President Roosevelt appointed Jose M. Gallardo commissioner and outlined in a letter the contours of a renewed Americanization program:

> It is an indispensable part of American policy that this coming generation of American citizens in Puerto Rico grow up with

complete facility in the English tongue. It is the language of our Nation. . . . Puerto Rico is a densely populated Island. Many of its sons and daughters will desire to seek economic opportunity on the mainland or perhaps in other countries of this hemisphere. They will be greatly handicapped if they have not mastered English. . . . English is the official language of our country.[31]

Commissioner Gallardo announced new procedures, but after five years, nothing had changed. Elementary instruction was being given in Spanish; secondary, in English. Gallardo started a purge of the teaching staff: "He began slowly to eliminate those teachers in the public schools and the university who had been outspoken in their *independista* sentiments or who had been critical of any program to stress the teaching of English."[32]

Achievement and economic mobility

Puerto Rican educators preferred to contend with more substantive educational issues. In 1925, they had been greatly encouraged by the results of islandwide achievement testing. Children in Grades 2 through 12 took Spanish-language editions of the Stanford Achievement tests. Sussman summarizes the results:

> In . . . language and arithmetic . . . they were close to, and sometimes above, the U.S. Continental norms. In arithmetic computation and reasoning the children in the first four grades surpassed the continental children even on tests administered in English. They also did better in the early grades on the Pintner non-language mental ability tests. U.S. children overtook and slightly surpassed the Puerto Rican pupils at grades 7, 8, and 9.[33]

Where the socioeconomic contrast between Puerto Rican and mainland children was greatest – in the early elementary grades – the Puerto Rican children showed their largest achievement advantage. The opposite was the case for children in secondary schools.

Success brought little reward beyond more overcrowding and shortages. Table 31 shows the growth of elementary school enrollment during the years 1910–1940. Enrollment as a whole increased by one and one-half times; the number of sixth-graders increased tenfold.[34] Much of the improvement bypassed the rural schools. During the 1930–1931 school year, for example, one-third of all students in urban schools were first- and second-graders; in rural schools, they constituted virtually twice that proportion.[35] Most ominous was the persistent inability of the schools to enroll even half of all school-age children (Table 32). The greater part of out-of-school children lived in the rural areas.

In the mid-1930s, Rosario wrote that "there is no more monotonous and

Table 31. *Attendance in Puerto Rican elementary schools, 1910–1940*

Year	Grade 1	Grade 2	Grade 3	Grade 4	Grade 5	Grade 6	Total	Percent in Grade 1	Percent in Grade 6
1910	48,031	21,079	12,518	5,919	3,066	1,889	92,502	51.9	2.0
1920	73,173	31,549	27,491	21,018	8,890	5,323	167,444	43.7	3.2
1930	63,794	45,189	39,732	25,061	16,263	11,038	201,077	31.7	5.5
1940	62,395	54,246	47,425	31,001	25,020	19,936	240,023	26.0	8.3
Change, 1910– 1940 (%)	20.9	157.3	278.9	423.8	716.0	955.4	159.5		

Source: Data from Oscar Emilio Porrata, "Retardation in the Elementary Urban Schools of Porto Rico" (master's thesis, University of Chicago, 1934), p. 4.

Table 32. *School enrollment and total school-age population in Puerto Rico, 1900–1940*

Year	Number of school-age children	Number of children in public school	Percent of children in public school
1900	320,770	26,204	8.2
1910	357,918	93,640	26.2
1920	428,556	176,096	41.1
1930	530,955	219,591	41.4
1940	589,898	282,825	47.9

Source: Data from Juan Jose Osuna, *A History of Education in Puerto Rico* (Rio Piedras, P.R.: Editorial de la Universidad de Puerto Rico, 1949), p. 626.

dreary existence than that of the *jibaro* [country] children."[36] Some fourteen years later, Osuna wrote flatly that "the child of the *average* family is permanently hungry and undernourished."[37] An approximate measure of the effect of these conditions on the health of young Puerto Ricans was the 78 percent selective service rejection rate of Puerto Rican men from the island. (On the mainland, rates ranged from 15 to 40 percent.)[38]

The proliferation of New Deal relief agencies on the mainland brought token aid to island schools. In the 1937–1938 school year, Puerto Ricans spent more than $19.4 million on education. All federal sources contributed some 2 to 4 percent of Puerto Rican expenditures. Most of the mainland money was used for school buildings. A United States government-sponsored study in 1939 declared: "If a reasonable goal in education, such as is required in a democracy, is to be realized in Puerto Rico, the amount of money expended for education must be increased to perhaps three or four times the amount that is now spent. This cannot be done without very large Federal grants-in-aid."[39] Such grants were never forthcoming, nor was there ever any kind of continuing educational grant.

During World War II, educational conditions deteriorated. The proportion of school-age children in school fell. Inequalities within the school system did not diminish. In 1942, Tugwell said that "we still allow certain privileged areas to receive large proportions of municipal monies for school services, while other areas have scarcely any income at all. This situation can only be met by the establishment of an equalization school fund which will give the child in the mountains the same advantages as the child in the rich sugar areas."[40] No such fund was created.

After the war, fundamental economic changes in Puerto Rico deeply affected education. Essentially, insular authorities decided upon a sweeping program of industrialization to be accomplished primarily by mainland firms to be attracted by the enticements of cheap labor, exemption from

Table 33. *School enrollment and total population aged 6 to 12 years in Puerto Rico, 1940–1959*

Year	Number of children aged 6–12 years	Number of children in school	Percent of children in school
1940	348,661	242,085	69.4
1945	389,079	283,491	72.9
1950	423,789	355,403	83.9
1955	433,078	434,220	100.0
1959	461,500	427,953	92.7

Source: Luis Nieves Falcon, *Recruitment to Higher Education in Puerto Rico, 1940–1960* (Rio Piedros: Editorial Universitaria Universidad de Puerto Rico, 1965) p. 209.

federal income taxes, and the cost-free provision of port and other service facilities. The island economy responded, and industrial employment rose.

For the first time in its history, Puerto Rican society came to have a relatively large middle class composed of native businessmen, representatives of United States firms, local bureaucrats employed by the insular government, and professionals. In the rural areas, little changed. The gap between city and countryside simply widened.

Elementary schools expanded greatly (Table 33). Over the twenty-year period, elementary school enrollment increased nearly two and one-half times faster than the number of elementary-school-age children. High school enrollment rose more than *twenty* times faster than the number of high-school-age children.[41] These were unmistakable signs of substantial progress.

At the same time, old inequalities persisted and even intensified. The schooling gap between city and countryside widened. The booming middle class occupied an increasingly privileged sector of the educational structure. And sheer financial inability to provide full-time instruction in all schools dominated the educational scene.

In 1961, more than three out of five elementary pupils attended school for only three hours a day. The proportion was considerably lower in secondary schools. In rural schools by 1967 somewhat fewer than half the students were still on short-time schedule. The proportion of rural children in the school population declined only relative to the rise in urban population. At the end of the 1960s, as many as 40 percent of students were dropping out before reaching the sixth grade. By the 1960s, Nieves Falcon said, "the rural schools had become the 'poor relations' in the system, underprivileged and neglected. . . . This depressed situation of the rural schools had been perpetuated by prevailing practices and the absence of an official conscience towards them."[42] The declining importance of farm exports meant that the government felt less obliged than ever to undertake programs to improve rural schools.

During the post-World War II years, the island's middle classes created avenues by which their children might more readily enter the University of Puerto Rico and, thus, careers of high status and rewards. Wherever possible, they turned public facilities to their advantage. In 1964, three out of four graduates of San Juan public high schools drawing on upper income families passed entrance examinations to the university. This was a very high level of academic achievement. When the University of Puerto Rico opened laboratory elementary and secondary schools for the children of its faculty, government officials "used their political influence to find places for their children."[43] None attended these exclusive schools except children of faculty and bureaucrats.

In Puerto Rico as a whole, about one-tenth of all students attended private schools; but in the urbanized San Juan metropolitan area, about one-third of all secondary school students were in private schools. An analysis of seniors in private and public high schools showed that while fewer than one-fifth of the latter came from the top two socioeconomic strata, more than half the former did. Important cultural consequences resulted because the private schools – Catholic or even non-church-related – used English as the first language of instruction. Children of highest ranking business executives and others were thus prepared to attend colleges on the mainland. Most went to the University of Puerto Rico instead.[44]

Nieves Falcon contends that the great expansion of education after the 1940s lowered the quality of public schooling and reduced the degree to which the poor had access to higher education. Elementary school enrollment increased, while the percentage of students dropping out after sixth grade rose between 1940–1941 and 1953–1954.[45] Before 1940, public schools had offered higher quality education than private schools. After that, according to Nieves Falcon, as the children of the wealthy were siphoned off to private schools, grading standards became lax and quality fell. The influx of economically poor students coincided with a deterioration in quality. Because of the growing number of poorly prepared students, the enrollment at the University of Puerto Rico became increasingly unrepresentative of the island's society.

The mainland: language barrier

The profound poverty of Puerto Rico prepared the way for many thousands of islanders to migrate to the mainland. When economic distress reached the lowest depths on the island, as it did during the latter 1930s, an unusually large number of professionals and semiprofessionals migrated. Ordinarily, Puerto Rican migrants were drawn from the poorest sectors of the island's urban centers.

During the 1940s and 1950s, average annual net migration from Puerto Rico increased sharply. Suddenly, the schools of New York City were filled with children fresh from the island. In October 1949, nearly 29,000 Puerto Rican students were in the schools; four years later, they numbered about 54,000. In 1956, one-eighth of the city's enrollment was Puerto Rican; nine years later, one-fifth.[46] In specific school districts, the ethnic composition changed rapidly.

These students and their teachers were almost complete strangers. During the 1946–1947 school year, nearly three-quarters of the Puerto Rican children entering New York City schools did not speak English.[47] Far more of the teachers could not speak Spanish.

Very few children in the elementary schools of Puerto Rico were taught much English. Most dropped out before completing school at a time when nearly all elementary classroom instruction was given in Spanish. In the rural areas, which began to send many migrants in the early 1950s, English was almost unknown to most students. No wonder that their English reading ability lagged far behind national test norms. Yet the lag need not have remained. A mainland study examined two schools with a large number of Puerto Rican students. One was found to be much more successful than the other in teaching reading. Morrison explained: "The difference is the fact that the first school had been working consistently for a period of years to improve its teaching of English and . . . had made substantial advances in every phase of the program; the second school had drifted on the easy assumption that it was doing a good job."[48] Throughout the school system the principal burden of change was laid upon the student rather than the school.

Over the years, the city schools used the device of C classes for non-English students as well as an informal buddy system. The C classes enrolled a maximum of fifteen children to enable the teacher to give each one individual attention. In 1949, however, a committee appointed by the mayor examined C classes in practice and reported that "there were very few . . . with fifteen pupils or less, while those having thirty-six pupils or more were numerous."[49]

Puerto Rican children who spoke English were often used as substitute staff. Around 1950 in Brooklyn, this was the scene in PS 16:

> To compensate for the fact [Puerto Rican] Coordinator . . . . does not speak Spanish and the few teachers who have studied Spanish can scarcely make themselves understood to the Puerto Rican children, a squad of bilingual fifth and sixth graders have been organized to serve as go-betweens between Spanish-speaking parents and children, and the English-speaking

staff. These children help in the office in matters of registration, transfers, translating forms and letters. They interpret messages of the Administration over the public address system and in Assemblies and help the Parents' Association distribute clothing to the needy children.[50]

Bilinguality was thus accepted where it facilitated the housekeeping functions of the school. In the classroom, the policy was English-only.

The schools converted what was essentially a language problem into a learning barrier. The first Puerto Rican member of the House of Representatives said of his New York City school days in the 1940s: "I know . . . how amazed all the teachers were at the remarkable improvement of my intelligence quotient as I went from one grade to the other. . . . I did not have the heart to tell them that all that happened was that I learned to speak English."[51] A study of 116 Puerto Rican tenth-graders, classmates at the High School of Commerce, showed unmistakably that IQ rose along with the length of attendance in the city's schools (Table 34).[52]

The teaching force in New York City included almost no persons of Puerto Rican origin. Many trained teacher-aspirants were turned away by the board of examiners on grounds other than teaching competence. During the 1930s through the 1950s, the board regularly failed qualified applicants who had an accent.[53] In 1948, after numerous calls for help, the board created a temporary position, the substitute auxiliary teacher (SAT). These were Spanish-speaking teachers, most of them from Puerto Rico, and all possessed of a single characteristic that prevented them from

Table 34. *Relation of IQ of Puerto Rican tenth-graders in New York City to knowledge of English language (indicated by length of attendance in mainland schools)*

Numbers of years in mainland schools	Number of pupils tested	Average IQ
1–2	29	72
2–3	33	73
5–6	28	82
7–8	16	87
9–10	10	93

Source: Data from J. Cayce Morrison, *The Puerto Rican Study, 1953–1957* (New York: Board of Education, 1958), p. 84.

attaining permanent status – they spoke English with an accent. In 1949, ten SATs were appointed to work with parents, a ratio of 1 SAT for every 2,870 Puerto Rican students. In 1953, when the number of Puerto Rican children had nearly doubled, the number of SATs was doubled.

Certain other special-function positions were created, without any broad effect. In 1950, six teachers in the junior high schools of the city were named Puerto Rican coordinators to help teach English. The fact that most of them understood no Spanish interfered with their work. Four years later, their number was increased to eighteen.[54]

Beginning in 1963, Spanish-speaking auxiliary teachers became fully licensed, that is, appointed to tenured positions. Their number remained very small. In 1967, 125 served in the entire school system. For many regularly tenured teachers the prospect of teaching an onrush of Puerto Rican children was met "not only with adamance, but more markedly with fear, trepidation and feelings of inadequacy."[55] Such teachers felt abandoned by the central school administration and school board. (The first Puerto Rican was appointed to the school board in 1967.) Teaching in Puerto Rican – as in black – schools meant unfavorable working conditions. Split sessions for Puerto Ricans were common during the 1950s and 1960s. In 1956 alone, fifty-four classes in PS 191 were on split session, and no specialized personnel was available in the school to help Puerto Rican children, who constituted about three-fifths of the enrollment of the West Side Manhattan school district.[56] During 1953 and 1954, in a virtually all-Puerto Rican high school, six principals held office.[57]

In 1951, PS 108 was opened in East Harlem and soon became a severely crowded predominantly Puerto Rican school. Of forty-six teachers there, exactly half had less than three years of experience. Another twelve were substitutes. Dworkis said of the school's first two years: "By 1953 the first and second grades were on split schedule; lunch had to be served in three shifts; and classroom space was so limited that the introductory classes for Puerto Ricans had to be held in a converted stock room."[58] Yet despite these conditions, the school was respected by children and parents alike and suffered from little vandalism.

Messer holds that in the absence of substantive solutions, the system retreated into public relations. As early as 1951, she wrote, "a qualified status quo . . . replaced dynamic evolution in the development of a program for Puerto Rican children"; a film was made of an exemplary school and shown frequently. During the following decade, Messer continues, "publicity-minded Discovery Day celebrations and requisitions for textbooks that incorporate the contributions of migrants to American life . . . cannot remedy the more troubled areas of the [educational] program for Puerto Rican students."[59]

The failure of the schools fell upon the students. In 1958, a large-scale inquiry reported: "Much of the currently large backlog of retarded language learners . . . is chargeable to lack of adequate tools for assessing the abilities of non-English speaking pupils."[60] Individual teachers decided which level of language competence required what treatment. Because teachers typically did not know Spanish, they communicated it imperfectly. "Orientation" classes became, in many cases, receptacles for students whose language problems were simply beyond the competence of any staff member. Sometimes non-Puerto Rican children with behavior problems were placed in the classes. At William Morris High School in the Bronx, in 1960, thirty-one Puerto Rican boys were enrolled in sub-level English classes. Yet all had attended "transition" classes in their earlier academic careers: sixteen for three years; four each for four, five, and six years; three for seven years.[61] No conclusive evidence was found that the transition classes had benefited these students in any substantial way.

During 1953–1957, a school board staff committee carried out the privately funded Puerto Rican Study on the plight of the Puerto Rican child. Perhaps most important of the steps recommended were the call for a "uniform policy for the reception, screening, placement, and periodic assessment of non-English-speaking pupils" – and for special instructional materials. No heed was paid the study, although repeated references were made to it.[62]

The study in 1957 stressed the need for adequate diagnostic tests to facilitate proper placement of non-English-speaking students; yet no adequate test was developed. A rating scale required teachers to judge the degree of language retardation. Over the following years many teachers complained of the inadequacy of the scale. In 1969, a dozen years after completion of the study, an evaluation team criticized the rating scale in these words: "The question of what a non-native speaking child is is also a problem. For some it is anyone whose last name sounds Spanish. For others it is any pupil who is rated D, E, or F . . . and for still others it is any pupil who is rated other than A on the scale."[63] (A is described as "speaks English, for his age-level, like a native – with no foreign accent or hesitancy due to interference of a foreign language." F means "speaks no English.")

By hinging the Puerto Rican child's educational progress onto a language problem and then failing consistently to take meaningful measures to solve that problem, the school system in effect abandoned the average Puerto Rican student. Levels of academic achievement were exceedingly low. As their numbers grew, the scope of frustration widened. Teachers were frequently, perhaps even typically, viewed by the children as antagonists. Repeatedly, children complained of inconsiderate teachers.

In a Bronx high school, Willis studied the lack of academic achievement by two sets of Puerto Rican children. One group, composed of twenty dropouts, was exceedingly critical of former teachers. But so were twenty other students still attending the school. They reported that their teachers considered as stupid any student who could not speak English. Another said some teachers became angry at students who had trouble with English. One student, on the other hand, praised his teachers. Willis reported that "six students said that some teachers pronounced their names 'funny.' Nine students said that they had had teachers who never learned their names. Five students said that they had had teachers who never learned to distinguish them from some other boy in the class."[64] Few of the teachers in the school, Willis felt, accorded their Puerto Rican students respect and recognition.

Students complained of the insensitivity of teachers. In JHS 65 in Manhattan, an investigator reported that "fifteen of the eighteen Puerto Rican pupils indicated that they would be happier in school if the teachers were kinder."[65] Two years later, another study of the school was made. This researcher wrote that Puerto Rican students "liked those teachers who understood them, never screamed and didn't pick on them unless they deserved it."[66]

As the Puerto Rican child failed to receive effective instruction in English, he sought for ways to endure in the classroom. One young man said: "As time went on, I would always take notes and kept a very neat book and pretended to know what was going on in class, making believe I understand what the teacher was talking about. . . . The fact that I had not learned anything didn't mean too much to the teacher; she passed me anyway because I was sweet and cooperative."[67]

In junior high school, he added, the possibility of learning was greater – each student had a number of teachers rather than only one as in elementary school. Doris Rodriguez accused teachers of extreme discrimination: "When we ask a question, they call us 'dumb' or 'stupid' and they don't answer us. When they address themselves to the white kids, they address them differently. . . . To the white kids, they say, 'Oh, you didn't understand it,' but to us, 'I don't know what is the matter with you, are you dumb?'"[68] A young lady, asked what she had done in school inasmuch as she could barely read, replied: "I used to do other things. Maybe I asked to get a pass to go to the bathroom and stay there a half hour."

The inability of teachers to converse in Spanish created another learning barrier. Puerto Rican students became accustomed to loneliness in the classroom. The non-English-speaking student was isolated: "You feel like you do not even belong there. You wonder what you are doing there. . . . It is frightening and . . . really boring." In an elementary school, a Puerto Rican girl said she could not speak with her teacher: "All she talked to me in was English. I used to sometimes stare at her and try to understand what she was trying to tell me, and the thing was that I got help from other students in the class who spoke Spanish. They used to translate what she used to say to me, and this is how I started."[69] Later, in an English class at the High School of Art and Design, the same young woman found herself the only Puerto Rican in the room. "I would sit there. . . . She [the teacher] would have a discussion with the rest of the students where I just couldn't come in. . . . I felt isolated from the rest of the students." The impatience of a teacher with the halting English of students greatly disturbed them. A graduate student recalled this experience at Morris High School in the Bronx and asked that any teacher "at least grant us the courtesy of giving us the patience until we get what he is trying to teach."

Academic achievement: New York City

Quantitative data on academic achievement, other than for single schools, were not publicly available until the early 1950s; on a systemwide basis, not until 1966.

As was true of IQ scores, achievement scores rose with length of residence in New York City. In the early 1950s, Puerto Rican tenth-graders were given English-reading tests; their scores and the scores of mainland-born non-Puerto Ricans are shown in Table 35.

While prevailing stereotypes relegated all Puerto Rican children to the bottom of the academic heap, a number achieved at satisfactory levels. When the 1954 achievement scores of eighth-, ninth-, and tenth-grade children were consolidated, some Puerto Rican children surpassed the average scores of non-Puerto Rican children (Table 36). The longer children attended mainland schools, the higher the scores. Nevertheless, over one out of eight of the island-born, island-schooled youngsters exceeded the reading achievement of mainland-born and educated non-Puerto Ricans.[70]

In 1958, Padilla reported that in New York City, "the school does not teach what [Puerto Rican] parents traditionally have accepted as education, namely the three R's."[71] Three years later, only one-tenth of Puerto Rican third-graders in a Manhattan school were found to be reading at grade level or above. Among eighth-graders, only one-eighth were at grade level or above; for nearly two-thirds there was more than a three-year lag.[72]

In 1966, the enrollment of twenty-five elementary and three junior high schools was over 70 percent Puerto Rican. In none of the twenty-eight schools did students score at or above the norm in reading. Second-graders were 0.8 grade behind the norm; fifth-graders, 1.6 grades behind; sixth-graders, 1.4 grades behind; and both seventh- and ninth-graders, 2.3 years behind.[73] For Puerto Rican children alone, the lag was probably even greater. Three years later, a citywide analysis of reading scores in predominantly Puerto Rican schools showed that 70 percent of

Table 35. *Scores of tenth-grade Puerto Rican and non-Puerto Rican children on English-reading test*

Population category	National norm	Average score	Lag
A. Island-born, island-schooled	10.6	4.9	5.7
B. Island-born, mainland-schooled	10.6	7.1	3.5
C. Mainland-born of Puerto Rican parents	10.6	8.0	2.6
D. Mainland-born of non-Puerto Rican parents	10.6	8.6	2.0

Source: Data from J. Cayce Morrison, *The Puerto Rican Study, 1953–1957* (New York: Board of Education, 1958), p. 75.

Table 36. *Percentage of eighth-, ninth-, and tenth-grade Puerto Rican children in each population category whose achievement scores surpassed those of non-Puerto Rican children*

Area of competence	Population category [a]		
	A	B	C
Ability to understand spoken English	9	26	42
Ability to read English	13	30	32
Ability to do arithmetical computations	20	27	37
Nonverbal intellectual ability	12	31	44

[a] A, island-born and island-schooled; B, island-born and mainland-schooled; C, mainland-born of Puerto Rican parents.

Source: Data from J. Cayce Morrison, *The Puerto Rican Study, 1953–1957* (New York: Board of Education, 1958), p. 128.

second-graders, 82 percent of fifth-graders, and 81 percent of eighth-graders read below grade norms.[74] Retardation on such a large scale was reminiscent of the condition of education back on the island.

This was especially the case with respect to dropouts. Vazquez described the implications of the 1966–1969 data:

> In 1966, 10,142 Puerto Rican students entered the 10th grade in New York City. Two years later, there were only 4,393 in the 12th grade – a dropout rate of 56 percent. . . . Of the 4,393 Puerto Ricans who did reach the 12th grade in May, 1969, only 1,628 were eligible to receive academic diplomas. . . . [If we add

dropouts in the seventh and eighth grades], the . . . figures
might rise to eighty percent or possibly as high as eighty-five
percent. [75]

This high dropout rate far exceeded that of black and other mainland
students.

More startling, it apparently surpassed even the dropout rate in Puerto
Rico itself. In 1969–1970, 37.2 percent of students in Puerto Rico who
began school in 1958–1959 completed high school. [76] While Puerto Rico
spent $342 per pupil in 1970–1971, New York City expended about four
times as much. A sizable part of these funds consisted of federal moneys
designed to help educationally disadvantaged students, of whom Puerto
Rican children in the city constituted a large proportion. On the island, no
such funds were available. Yet quantitatively, Puerto Rican youth fared
no worse on the island than in New York City. Quality comparisons
between schools in Puerto Rico and schools in New York City attended by
Puerto Ricans are extremely difficult to make.

Education for Puerto Rican children in New York City was not merely
truncated in duration; it took on a distinctive character as well. A study of
JHS 52 in the Melrose area of the South Bronx reported laconically in
1958: "Since the Puerto Rican pupils cannot profit from the orthodox
curriculums of the school, modifications have been necessary. Throughout the child's stay in school stress is placed on language, arts, health,
nutrition, safety and consumer education." [77] Well-behaved Puerto Rican
children who attained a passing grade of at least sixty-five were placed on
the school honor roll. In non-Puerto Rican schools the standards were, of
course, much higher. Even when a substitute auxiliary teacher was available for Spanish-speaking children, she had very little time to spend with
them. In 1948, the ranking historian of Puerto Rican education, Juan José
Osuna, visited twenty New York City schools and urged that Puerto Rican
children be given at least two hours daily special instruction in English. [78]
Eight years later, at PS 16 in Brooklyn, Puerto Rican children were
receiving special instruction for one to two hours *weekly*. [79]

Teachers formulated a special educational theory for Puerto Rican children. It made academic achievement secondary to the acquisition of
mainland culture. A great deal of time was spent in direct instruction on
grooming, personal demeanor, and practical life skills. Bucchioni has
called this "education for failure." He explained:

> The teacher, in light of the general academic failure of Puerto
> Rican pupils, in reality attempts to appease and condition them
> to the point of resignation to their life situation. The teacher's
> objective then becomes that of sending her pupils into the world,
> resigned and adjusted, but also with the belief that if they but

work hard enough, they will be able to improve their life chances.[80]

Bucchioni's evaluation echoed a widespread belief among Puerto Rican parents and community leaders.

Parental concern

On the island, especially in rural areas, parents took a deeply personal interest in the schools. An auxiliary teacher, born in Puerto Rico, explained that "on the island the parents are used to do things for the school – repair jobs, building a fence, painting, bringing presents to the teachers. Why do they do this? Out of a spirit of service, they want to do something for the school and for the teachers of their children."[81] A Puerto Rican mother in New York City distinguished between the island and the city:

> Our activity as parents . . . is radically different in New York
> from our experience in Puerto Rico. There we had trust in the
> schools and a feeling that the teacher knew what was best for our
> children, and had their interest at heart. The common practice
> has always been for the Puerto Rican mother to say to her chil-
> dren: "Obey your teacher, in school she is your mother, so obey
> her as you do me."[82]

It took Puerto Rican parents some time to realize that such trust might be misplaced in a school system that systematically failed their children. Back on the island, after all, shortage of funds was the primary educational problem; surely, parents thought this could not also be a problem in New York City.

The relative lack of Puerto Rican parental involvement in school affairs was in part cultural, rather than the consequence of apathy. On the West Side of Manhattan, for example, enrollment in the twelve schools of District 8 went from 18.5 percent Puerto Rican in 1946 to 61.8 percent Puerto Rican ten years later. Yet even in 1952, when 43.8 percent of the enrollment was Puerto Rican, the executive boards of the PTAs in the area contained not a single Puerto Rican parent. Only after a concerted community campaign by groups including the Riverside Neighborhood Assembly did the situation change. In 1956, two PTA presidents and numerous executive board members were Puerto Rican.[83]

Resistance to the introduction of Puerto Rican cultural and related matters was strong. In February 1953, in a predominantly Puerto Rican area, plans were tentatively made to invite Puerto Rican Governor Luis Muñoz-Marín as a speaker. Local School Board No. 8 adopted this mo-tion: "The entire School Board is strenuously opposed to having the Gov-ernor invited as it is feared that it will encourage more of his constitutents to flood our already overcrowded area."[84] In 1952, a conscientious teacher attended a summer workshop at New York University on Puerto Rican culture. In the fall, she wrote: "My efforts and enthusiasm were squelched by the PTA who resented anything being done for Puerto Rican pupils, such as notes in Spanish, films, songs and dances, which was not done for children of other nationalities."[85]

The deepest parent dissatisfaction was with the failure of the schools to teach their children. In a church near PS 168, Manhattan, the minister late in the 1950s "listened long hours to complaints by parents who felt that their children were being cheated of a proper education."[86] The Puerto Rican Study recommended in 1958 that the schools work closely with Puerto Rican parents. Little, in fact, was done. Padilla in 1958 attributed the inaction to the schools: "Actually, given the kinds of relationships that exist between the school personnel and parents and the attitudes displayed by many teachers and principals toward the neighborhood and its people, one could not expect the development of a vigorous and active parents' organization."[87]

Schooling came to be viewed increasingly by parents as a means by which the larger community deliberately ensured the perpetuation of Puerto Rican economic failure. One mother declared: "What they teach our children is exactly what they want our children to learn and how they want our children to turn out. So that later in life these children cannot grow up and take their rightful position as leaders or directors within that system and become their bosses" (see Table 37).[88] This stark diagnosis accounted amply for the historical pattern of educational failure.

Growing realization of the failure of the schools to educate their children led parents to more public protests. It also led to closer cooperation with groups of black parents whose children suffered the same fate. In 1964, Puerto Ricans joined a citywide school boycott in opposition to segregated, inferior schools. Sexton observes: "When East Harlem turned out for the integration boycott it was the first time in the community's history, or the city's, that Puerto Ricans joined with Negroes in protest and pursuit of a common goal."[89] Some positive changes occurred in predominantly Puerto Rican schools and these aroused further citizen action.

The new spirit of protest was made more effective by changes on the political scene. The rise of the national civil rights movement emboldened local groups everywhere. But the impact was slow to take effect among Puerto Ricans. Until the mid-1960s, Puerto Ricans did not vote frequently, although in Puerto Rico itself voters turned out at an 80 percent rate. New York state law imposed a literacy test upon would-be voters. In 1957, for example, only 85,000 out of a potential 266,000 Puerto Ricans in New York registered to vote. Eight years later, however, a provision of the federal Voting Rights Act in effect outlawed literacy requirements.

Table 37. *Percentage of total population and Puerto Rican population of men aged 16 years and over engaged in various occupations, March 1973*

Occupation	Total population	Puerto Rican
White-collar workers	40.2	22.6
Professional and technical	13.6	4.7
Managers, administrators, except farm	13.6	5.8
Sales workers	6.2	2.2
Clerical workers	6.8	9.9
Blue-collar workers	46.9	56.2
Craftsmen and kindred	20.9	13.5
Operatives, including transportation	18.9	33.9
Laborers, except farm	7.1	8.8
Farm workers	4.6	1.1
Farmers and farm managers	3.0	0.0
Farm laborers and foremen	1.6	1.1
Service workers	8.2	20.1
Total number employed	50,890,000	274,000

Source: U.S. Bureau of the Census, *Persons of Spanish Origin in the United States, March 1973* (Washington, D.C.: GPO, May 1974), p. 5.

Registrants had only to demonstrate that they had at least a sixth-grade education, in Puerto Rico or elsewhere, and thus satisfy any literacy requirement. Expanded Puerto Rican voting resulted. This pried open a slight avenue, at least, to citywide power and an adequate school system. Wherever Puerto Rican children were in school, their parents took a far more active role.

Puerto Rican education outside New York
An estimate made in 1968 held that nearly 400,000 Puerto Rican children attended schools in the entire country. It would seem that about 160,000 Puerto Rican children attended school outside New York City.

Margolis, for a 1968 survey, visited sixteen schools in Bridgeport, Chicago, Philadelphia, Newark, Hoboken, and Paterson, as well as New York City. He found an unrelieved picture of poor education and guidance: "I did not find a single Puerto Rican school counsellor in all the cities I visited. The high school counsellors I did find – some white, some black – were without exception uninformed, unsympathetic and unintelligent in their dealings with Puerto Rican children."[90] Dropouts were extremely high in city after city. Margolis inquired about Puerto Ricans who had graduated from high school and were attending college: "No school system I visited has bothered to count, but in some high schools they answer not by numbers but by names. So few Puerto Ricans are going to college that a principal can usually count them on one hand."[91] In Newark, Puerto Rican girls who had majored in secretarial studies were unable to fill out a job application form.

The Connecticut State Advisory Committee to the U.S. Commission on Civil Rights conducted hearings in 1971 on the Puerto Rican communities in Bridgeport and New Haven. A student in Bridgeport testified: "I feel that the teachers don't care about the students. . . . A Spanish speaking student comes into the room. Immediately that person is considered dumb without even being given a chance."[92] In Bridgeport, where Puerto Ricans made up 22 percent of elementary school and 13 percent of high school enrollment, only 10 out of 1,180 teachers were Puerto Ricans. In New Haven, the number was 15 out of 1,260.

In Massachusetts, some 2,500 Puerto Rican school-age children were not attending school in 1970. Dropout rates in Boston and Springfield were high. Out of 4,729 teachers in Boston, only 5 were Puerto Rican. "The present bilingual programs in Chicago," according to one source in 1970, "are five miniature programs only servicing 541 students."[93] Puerto Rican and Mexican-American public school students numbered over 50,000 in that city.

All in all, Puerto Rican children suffered the same schooling wherever they lived.

Puerto Ricans and immigrants: a comparison of bootstraps

Puerto Ricans were frequently compared with earlier immigrants from Europe. Concentrated in a city of immigrants, it was often supposed that they would sooner or later emulate the careers of their predecessors. Thus, it was expected that Puerto Ricans would rise economically and socially, would educate their children through the ample opportunities on the mainland, and would more or less become integrated into the larger American society. Failure to attain these ends was allegedly because they somehow lacked the required drive, ability, or cultural background.

The Russian Jews were the group most often made the standard of comparison. They, too, had arrived poor, speaking an unfamiliar language, and had been relegated to a ghetto. Yet unlike the Puerto Ricans, the Jews had succeeded in every sense, not least of all, educationally. One question frequently asked about the Puerto Ricans – Why can't they do the same? – was often followed by another one – Why can't they wait until they do?

To equate the Puerto Ricans and the Russian Jews, however, is to do violence to the traditions and integrity of both groups.

In one respect at least, Jews differed from all other immigrants: they fled a country but not a fatherland. Becoming Americanized did not mean that they must first be de-Russified. Whenever the shadow of Imperial Russia crossed the immigrant Jew's mind, it set off a curse on his lips. From the 1870s forward, Jews in Russia had suffered periodic attacks blessed if not organized by the government. Their youth were excluded from full educational opportunities, especially in the universities. In the closely knit local Jewish communities, Yiddish, not Russian, was the treasured language. They learned Russian only as an economic necessity. Bilingualism was a centuries-old pattern of Jewish life. Neither in their religious schools nor in everyday social relations did Russian play a part. When Jewish children in New York schools were taught in English only, they did not in the least feel deprived. So long as Yiddish could be used at home and in the community, it was well enough. Thus, when a future philosopher recalled his earliest days in New York City as a Jewish immigrant in 1892, he wrote without rancor that "my school attendance during the first year meant nothing to me except as an opportunity to hear English spoken."[94]

The acquisition of English was eased somewhat by private Jewish community organizations. In 1890, the De Hirsch Fund created the Educational Alliance. Among its most valuable projects were the special small classes in which newly arrived Jewish children were taught English. "As soon as a child learned enough English, and an opening for him was found," wrote Berrol, "he was entered in public school."[95] These classes became models for the later C classes in public schools. Most non-English-speaking children were placed in first grade, whatever their age. In New York City, this practice was stopped in 1903. Throughout the country it was still a widespread practice in 1920.[96]

Jewish children flocked to the schools. In 1891, only 1,000 of the 60,000 or so Jewish children living on the East Side were not enrolled in school. On the Lower East Side, school absenteeism was a minimal 8 percent. By 1905, some thirty-two schools in the area were at least 90 percent Jewish in enrollment. In such schools, there was an effort by authorities to employ Jewish teachers and principals wherever possible. Thus, in 1914, according to Berrol, "the personnel of P.S. 120 on Rivington Street in the very heart of the Jewish ghetto . . . was headed by a Jewish principal and assistant principal and had twenty-five Jewish teachers out of a staff of 68 while P.S. 2 on Henry Street had seventeen Jewish teachers out of a total of 57."[97]

Jewish children made good progress through the schools. In 1908, for example, 7.3 percent of all native-born white school children in New York City attended high school; for foreign-born Jewish children the figure was 2.9 percent. (In Chicago, the corresponding figures were 8.9 and 5.8 percent.) High school attendance was the route to college, and by the beginning of the century a majority of students at the city's public colleges were Russian Jews. As a result, observes Berrol, "although the greatest number of Jewish staff members were not to appear in the public schools until the late 1920s, even by 1914, enough were present among the faculty to challenge the previous Irish preponderance."[98]

Yet Jews who aspired to be teachers had to contend with discrimination. In 1920, Thompson reported that "children of Russian [Jewish] parentage, educated in the public schools and in American colleges, frequently fail to pass tests for teaching positions in New York [City] because of their inability to pronounce correctly such words as 'English,' 'finger,' 'younger,' 'singing,' 'anchor.' " Nevertheless, as early as 1908, 6 percent of the city's teachers were Jews.

New York schools were determined to "make Americans" of all immigrants, Russian Jews included. In 1918, the city's superintendent of schools defined Americanization as "an appreciation of the institutions of this country and absolute forgetfulness of all obligations or connections with other countries because of descent or birth."[99] Jews, as noted above, were not burdened by a sense of obligation to Russia and were eager to take on American ways. School staff welcomed the resultant adaptability. Scrappy evidence suggests that non-Jewish teachers were, on the whole, quite friendly to the newcomers.[100]

Jewish children continued to lag behind others, despite all advances. Their dropout rate exceeded that of native-born white children. Thus, in 1908, 82 percent of all native-born white high-school-age children in New York City were in high school, but the percentage for foreign-born Jewish children was only 3.1. (In Chicago the figures were 10.2 and 3.9 percent.) Numerous Jewish youngsters joined the ranks of the unskilled and the semieducated.

Two general factors, however, worked in favor of Jewish schooling. One was political, the other socioeconomic, in character. Before World War I, Jews became voters in large numbers in New York City. McSeveny reports that "East European Jewish newcomers did vote in numbers large enough to influence politics, particularly in their area of concentration, the Lower East Side."[101] Both Tammany Hall and the Socialist party competed for the Jewish vote. It may be surmised that the appointment of Jewish teachers and principals was in part a response to such political factors. In addition, the Russian Jews arrived during a time of great economic expansion. From 1880 to 1910, the labor force grew from 17 million to 37 million. With education, the second generation rose to upper occupational groups. This trend was true of many immigrants besides Jews. The close association of education and higher income was furthered by the concentration of Jews in cities where greater educational opportunities existed.[102]

Russian Jewish children made a fairly successful adjustment to the schools, as judged by contemporary standards. Their tradition of bilingualism facilitated acquisition of a new language; their unattachment to Russian culture enabled them all the more to adopt a new way of life. More or less welcomed into the school system, Jewish children on the Lower East Side gave their schools a distinct ethnic character. Anti-Jewish discrimination in the schools continued in the name of nondialect speech. However, political power, based on electoral activity rather than economic wealth, was translated into employment of Jewish personnel in the schools. By the late 1920s, large numbers of Jews were becoming teachers. Soon thereafter they rose into higher levels of the bureaucracy.

In 1908, 105,308 foreign-born Jewish school children made up 18 percent of total enrollment in New York City.[103] In 1965, 211,706 Puerto Rican children constituted 19.8 percent of enrollment. In terms of relative student progress, Puerto Rican children lagged far behind other students. Every important compilation of academic achievement scores showed Puerto Rican students seriously behind. Over the years, few indices of achievement took a turn for the better. In 1963, fewer than 2 percent of the city's high school graduates receiving academic diplomas were Puerto Ricans. By 1970–1971, this number had risen, but Puerto Rican dropout rates were still severe. Both black and Puerto Rican students suffered about a 65 percent dropout rate between tenth and twelfth grades. The corresponding rate for mainland whites was 35 percent.[104]

Fundamental to poor achievement was the continued incapacity of the school system to meet the language problem. According to board of education data, in 1970–1971 some 95,000 Spanish-speaking students in the city schools had moderate to severe language problems. Only about 1,900 of these students were enrolled in the three bilingual schools then in operation. A 1970 study by the Puerto Rican Forum of twenty-two elementary schools enrolling large numbers of non-English-speaking students found only two schools offering as much as thirty minutes a day in special language instruction.[105]

How could this failure compare with the success in teaching English to Jewish immigrant children? Yiddish was a *private* language that Jews did not desire to have incorporated within the classroom. Consequently, teachers did not come to view Yiddish as a competitor language. In addition, the presence of Yiddish-speaking teachers was helpful to Jewish students. One former student said, "I myself, when I started kindergarten, did not speak a word of English. I just spoke Jewish. When I started elementary school, the fact that there were teachers that understood Yiddish was a tremendous crutch. . . . It was a help to me and my parents, who came to school to find out my progress, to speak to someone who spoke the same language as we did."[106] At no time did the private or extracurricular use of Yiddish threaten the official monolingual and assimilationist policy of the school system.

Table 38. *Spanish-surnamed professionals in New York City public schools, 1970*

Position	Total number	Number with Spanish surname	Percent with Spanish surname
Principals	932	8	0.9
Assistant principals	2,256	10	0.4
Teachers	60,228	805	1.3
Other instructional staff	4,340	173	4.0
Full-time central staff	4,482	117	2.6
Total	72,238	1,113	1.5

Source: U.S. Commission on Civil Rights, *Hearing Held in New York, February 14–15, 1972* (Washington, D.C.: GPO, 1973), p. 267.

The Spanish of Puerto Ricans, on the other hand, had a *public* character. Until 1959, classroom use of Spanish was forbidden. The Puerto Rican Study at no point proposed a bilingual policy; it viewed the language problem as one of teaching English, but it remained ineffectual in not proposing ways to teach. Teachers in predominantly Spanish-speaking schools felt overwhelmed and thus threatened by Spanish. Few acquired a conversational acquaintance with the language, although more gained a bookish knowledge of it.

School authorities exhibited a positive disinterest in providing Spanish-speaking children with Spanish-speaking teachers. As late as 1970, an extremely small number of professionals in the schools were Spanish-surnamed (Table 38). Proportionately, Jewish teachers before World War I outnumbered Puerto Rican teachers in 1970 by more than four times.

Through the 1950s, the school board refused to permit applicants with a Spanish accent to become fully accredited teachers. During the 1960s, as a result of a change in policy, some such teachers became fully licensed. In the teaching force as a whole, Puerto Rican teachers were an exceedingly tiny group. Not that potential candidates were altogether lacking. King recalled his recruitment of candidates in the unlikeliest places: "What we did was try to raid the factories [in New York City] where a great number of . . . Puerto Ricans who had served in the schools as teachers in Puerto Rico were now serving as people who would be putting handles on pocket-books or some equally challenging professional job in a factory."[107] These underemployed professionals were university graduates and credentialed to teach in Puerto Rican schools.

Both the Russian Jews and the Puerto Ricans came to the United States in search of a more adequate and secure livelihood. But the former integrated much more rapidly than the latter. For one thing, Puerto Ricans were viewed as colonials whose proper place was at the bottom of the American social order. The bulk of them arrived during the post-World War II economic boom, but lack of education severely limited their ability to share in its benefits. Before World War I, immigrants who did not complete elementary school found a productive career nevertheless. After World War II, such opportunities contracted.

Politically, also, the Puerto Ricans were much less able than the Russian Jews to summon up their electoral power; the literacy requirement saw to this. Economically, Puerto Ricans were closed off from an autonomous role by lack of capital and the relative decline of small business opportunities over the years. Occupationally, Puerto Ricans were left with a disproportionately large share of the lowest paying jobs, such as those in service industries. But most basic to the contrast was the differential role of the schools.

The public schools failed to "work" for the Puerto Ricans anywhere near as effectively as they had for many immigrant groups. Numerous Puerto Ricans believed school authorities were determined not to educate their children. Repeatedly and almost unanimously, Puerto Rican students testified to the animus shown them by teachers and other school staff. The exclusion of Puerto Ricans from classroom duties and from the school board itself underscored the feeling.

Only under the most sustained community pressure was any quarter given. Only after two federal courts strongly criticized the historical absence of black and Puerto Rican principals did the school system start to relent on its policy.[108] It undertook a more energetic affirmative program of recruitment of Puerto Rican and black supervisory personnel.

During the Civil War, abolitionist Wendell Phillips said: "The government that makes all its mistakes on one side must have a constitutional bias in that direction."[109] With reference to the education of Puerto Rican children, the New York City school board evidenced a strong constitutional bias, for it rarely blundered into affording the children an equal educational opportunity.

The first sizable number of Puerto Ricans who moved to the mainland, soon after World War I, met with no unusual difficulties. During the 1940s and early 1950s, Puerto Rican organizations in New York City centered on activities related more to the island than to the city. Only several hours' flying time separated the migrants from their old homes. Yet the Puerto Rican identity of migrants was sorely tried. In schools and employment, Spanish became a handicap, and the language tended to serve increasingly as a private means of communication. Denigration of the culture of the Puerto Rican child at school was an ever-present reality. "Day after day," a young Puerto Rican in New York City testified, "children go home humiliated, flustered with discouragement and feeling totally useless."[110]

In time, many Puerto Rican children adopted elements of this negative image of themselves. During the mid-1950s in New York City, Padilla reported the youngsters did not seek to learn Spanish. In school, "they learn to pronounce English with 'the New York accent' that is so desirable to them and to their parents." New York-born Puerto Rican children, Padilla noted, regarded themselves as New Yorkers rather than orienting themselves toward Puerto Rico.[111]

In 1969, Buitrago Hermanet compared the ethnic identification of Puerto Rican children in Springfield, Massachusetts, and in Puerto Rico. She found that "Puerto Rican seventh graders living in the United States have a greater ethnic identification as Puerto Ricans than Puerto Rican seventh graders living on the Island."[112] More important, however, the researcher also found that both on the mainland and the island, Puerto Rican children were adopting North American ways of life. The migration, Buitrago Hermanet holds, "complicated but [it] did not create the relationship between Puerto Rico and the United States, and the basic problems of identity are related to this relationship."

On the mainland, cultural tendencies were in flux. Amid the Americanizing forces of public schools, Puerto Rican youth in colleges adopted a stronger nationalist position. Special programs in Puerto Rican studies were begun after intense pressures by these students. In New York City, Babin observes, such studies were expanding at a time when they were being neglected on the island.[113] After a joint Puerto Rican–black student sit-in at the City College of New York, authorities granted a demand that prospective teachers in the city colleges be required to take courses in Spanish.[114] At the same time, Puerto Ricans were becoming more integrated into the political structure of the mainland as they sought with some success to join ethnic cohesion to political power.

For the mainland-born, the center of Puerto Rican gravity was increasingly found on the mainland rather than in Puerto Rico. This was not so much a repudiation of the past as an affirmation of the future. With not far from half the Puerto Ricans on the mainland living outside New York City, their cause started taking on a nationwide character. Their stake in the American public schools grew accordingly.

Part II
Higher education

7

Guarded preserve: black students in higher education

American higher education traditionally enforced the prevailing concepts of educability. Before the Civil War, free Negroes were excluded almost as completely as were slaves from higher institutions. During the century after the Civil War when blacks succeeded in creating college opportunities for thousands of their youth, two principal obstacles prevented the fullest growth: (1) the positive disinclination of white-controlled institutions, North and South, to share their resources with minority youth; and (2) the unrelenting preoccupation of public policy, on all governmental levels, to restrict educational opportunities to the children of dominant social groups. Racial and ethnic exclusion was even more sweeping and effective among colleges and universities than among common schools. The greater intellectualism of the former did not moderate the operation of exclusionary trends.

Some 500 colleges probably existed in 1870. Another 700 or so had already failed by 1865. Yet, virtually no black person ever saw the inside of any of them. As of 1825 the black scholar-theologian Alexander Crummell revealed: "I know of no Academy or College which would open its doors to a negro. . . . An eminent friend of mine, the noble, fervent, gentlemanly Rev. Theodore S. Wright, then a Presbyterian licentiate, was taking private lessons in theology, at Princeton; and for this offense was kicked out of one of its halls."[1] In 1838, the abolitionist jurist William Jay wrote that not as many as a dozen blacks had attended northern colleges during the preceding three decades. Woodson raised the possible maximum to fifteen students before 1840. Between 1834 and 1841, at least five references in the *Liberator* made clear the deliberate exclusion of almost all blacks from nothern colleges.[2] In 1853, Watkins, a black writer, reported no change.[3]

In 1856, Wesleyan University in Connecticut practiced exclusion as a general policy. When, in 1845, Brown University excluded a black student, authorities explained that if he were admitted "southern patronage would be withdrawn." Union College had refused entrance more than once. In 1838 Dartmouth admitted a bright young black, Thomas Paul of Boston; but afterward Paul was not permitted to join the college debating society because of his color. Even when black students attended northern colleges, often they felt tolerated rather than welcomed. The *Liberator*, which had reported all these trends, wrote in 1834 that "a mere nominal admission into these seminaries is of little value to a colored person, while his fellow students do not regard him as an equal, and his instructors countenance them in this injustice."[4] Charlotte Forten, daughter of the well-known black abolitionist family in Philadelphia, who attended a normal school in Salem, Massachusetts, wrote in her diary in 1855: "I have met girls in the school room . . . they have been thoroughly kind and cordial to me . . . perhaps the next day met them in the street . . . they feared to recognize me; these I can but regard now with scorn and contempt. Once I liked them, believing them incapable of such meanness."[5]

In October 1840, the *Liberator* reported, Amherst allowed a black young man to register and attend classes. Six months later, when an antislavery group asked to meet at the college, they were turned away. A mob of white Amherst students disrupted the subsequent session at a public hall. Admission of a black student did not guarantee commitment to equality.

Colleges often bowed before the anti-Negro prejudice of their white students. In 1846, for example, two Liberians sought entrance to the Pittsfield Medical School, a *Liberator* story reported. The faculty laid the matter before the student body. When a single southern student voted in the negative, rejection followed. Two years later, President Everett of Harvard warned white students there that he would refuse to abide by their decision to exclude a black applicant, even if all the whites left.[6] But Everett was a rare college official, even of Harvard.

In 1850, for example, the Harvard Medical School admitted three black students. Two were sponsored by the American Colonization Society, which planned to send them to Africa upon completion of their studies. The third was the black leader from Pittsburgh, Martin R. Delany, who came with high recommendations from white physicians in his area. (Delany had been rejected by three medical schools, including that of the University of Pennsylvania.)[7] At Harvard, Delany hoped to follow the prescribed program of two semesters of instruction before the examination for the degree. By December 1850, many white fellow students started a movement to exclude the three black classmates. Out of a total of 108 students, 60 signed a petition of exclusion; nearly 50 students opposed the proposal. Proponents of exclusion expressed a fear that their medical degree would be cheapened if it were gained in the company of black students; they objected to social intercourse with the latter and feared that the initial admission of several black students would lead ultimately to a flood of them.

At first, the faculty rejected the petition. In less than two weeks, they were converted. Together, teachers and petitioners convinced Dean Oliver Wendell Holmes to notify the black students that they could complete the first semester of work but then they had to leave, without an opportunity to take a degree. "Being denied a chance for that precious degree," Ullman writes, "was the worst blow Delany had ever suffered." It was a blow administered by native northerners; only 4 students of 116 in the class resided in slave states. Indeed, more than 100 of Delany's erstwhile classmates were New Englanders. Exceedingly few blacks succeeded in gaining a medical education elsewhere. In 1849, Bowdoin Medical College graduated two black students; Yale Medical School admitted one black in 1855. The *Liberator* kept its readers informed of this progress.

Oberlin College constituted the greatest exception. Founded in 1833, it began accepting black students two years later. During the 1840s and 1850s, blacks made up from 4 to 5 percent of total enrollment.[8] In 1853, Horace Mann became president of Antioch College, a school that regularly admitted some blacks. The May 28, 1858, issue of the *Liberator* reported that Mann had refused to accept a $6,000 contribution offered on condition that Antioch reject the application of a black woman.

Until the Civil War, black participation in higher education was almost imperceptible. Its scale can be judged by contrasting relative graduation statistics. By 1865 or so, American colleges had graduated a total of from fifteen to twenty-eight black students. In the school year 1869–1870 alone, they conferred 9,372 degrees upon virtually all-white student enrollments.

Emancipation of the slaves created, for the first time, the conditions for the higher education of blacks.

The characteristic features of American higher education during the years 1865–1900, when black higher education took form, were these:

> 1. Small size. In 1869–1870, the average American college
> enrolled 93 students and employed 10 teachers; by 1899–1900,
> the figures were 243 and 24.
> 2. Private auspices. All but a few colleges were denominational,
> with the college president typically a clergyman.
> 3. Conglomerate enrollment. To ensure a supply of students,
> colleges as a matter of general practice organized preparatory
> departments which enrolled young students. "In 1870," reports
> Rudolph, "there were only five states in the country where none
> of the colleges was doing preparatory work."[9]
> As late as 1896, of a large sample of college freshmen, fully 40
> percent came from preparatory departments of colleges. Six

years later more than one-quarter of all students enrolled in American colleges were in precollegiate preparatory departments.

4. Instability and persistence. Four-fifths of all colleges organized outside New England prior to 1865 failed. A number of small colleges persisted despite little justification save local refusal to give up.

5. Color line. Southern colleges, virtually without exception, barred black students from attending. Selected northern colleges explicitly excluded blacks. In the country as a whole, black teachers were employed only in black schools.

6. Variable quality. "By the end of the nineteenth century," according to Rudolph, "it could be said that among the purposes of the American college was the purpose not to take learning very seriously." In 1911, an official of the U.S. Office of Education – himself a former president of a state university – attempted an evaluation of 344 colleges from the viewpoint of how well they prepared their graduates for further study. After visiting many campuses and inspecting academic records covering the previous five years, he ranked only one-sixth of the colleges in the top one of four classes; their credits could be accepted without question. In any event, however, the report was suppressed by both presidents Taft and Wilson.

The characteristic American college during the generation after 1865 was a small, mediocre, private institution, whose durability was both doubtful and puzzling, which only moderately saw its purpose as the promotion of scholarship, which enrolled collegiate and often whatever other students it could corral, and which, in great measure, hewed to the color line.

Private and public colleges in the South

Public responsibility for black higher education was not acknowledged by southern white governments. Church societies in the North played a dominant role in providing facilities and personnel. The American Missionary Association (AMA) was foremost in this work. The men who were sent down south by AMA to do college work had been excellently educated in the best colleges of New England. They were well acquainted with the general structure of American higher education. And from modest beginnings they intended to create a series of colleges incorporating the most worthwhile aspects of existing institutions.

Their greatest contribution was to place before the nation the goal of colleges open to all youth. As Horace Mann Bond stresses, the missionaries expected to teach the poor, both black and white. The charters of the institutions they organized either specifically forbade any racial distinctions or were silent on the issue. That the schools ultimately became *Negro* colleges was a matter of external political pressure, not original design.[10] As the Reconstruction fever cooled, southern white authorities outlawed interracial attendance. In other cases financial pressure was exerted to force still-idealistic colleges to prohibit whites from attendance. Unable simply to abolish common schools for black children, southern states felt compelled to provide teacher-training institutions to supply the common schools. Such public institutions were almost always by law made into one-race schools. For many years, these segregated normal schools were the sum and substance of public higher education for Negroes.

The campaign to separate and subordinate blacks and to convert democratic colleges into Negro colleges was all too successful. By deliberately withholding secondary schools and even elementary schools, the southern states burdened the existing black educational institutions with concerns that all but bowed them down to the ground. By 1902 somewhat more than one-quarter of all American "college" students were in fact enrolled in precollegiate programs. In 1900, about nine-tenths of all students in the Negro institutions were precollegiates.[11] The difference is largely accounted for by the dearth of public high schools for Negroes. In 1896, over two out of five white college freshmen received their collegiate preparation in public high schools.[12] The corresponding figure for black college freshmen was nearly zero. Atlanta, for example, did not receive its first public high school for Negroes until 1924. Not having sufficient high-schoolers to enter collegiate work, the Negro colleges were forced to enroll elementary school students in order to feed their secondary department. When Kelly Miller began teaching at Howard University in 1890, he recalled, "a student entering above the first year preparatory was considered a marvel."[13]

In the academic year 1899–1900, only fifty-eight of the ninety-nine Negro colleges had any collegiate students. Those enrolled in mission colleges received the most thorough training. Teachers in such colleges "made no concession to inferiority, assumed or real; the number of students allowed to enter upon or complete the college course was rigidly restricted. . . . They did not . . . patronize the men and women they taught, but treated them as human beings."[14] Yet not all received such devoted attention. Du Bois in 1910 described what he regarded as eleven first-grade Negro colleges. Each enrolled at least twenty collegiate students and required fourteen or more units of high school work for entrance. Without exception, all were private mission colleges. Together, the eleven colleges enrolled fewer than 700 students.[15]

From the beginning, whites constituted the faculty and administration of the mission colleges. White-initiated, white-financed, and white-led, the colleges resisted early movements to place blacks on the faculty. In

1894–1895, only 4 percent of the faculty of the five AMA colleges were black; twenty years later the figure rose to 28 percent.[16] Colleges under the control of Negro churches, and thereby more dependent on southern black rather than northern white financing, tended to have many more black teachers. Rejection of white paternalism was the major impetus behind the movements for employment of more blacks. At the same time, southern government circles were pleased with the reduction of interracial contact. Black leaders such as Du Bois warned in 1920: "We do not believe in the exclusion of white teachers from all Negro colleges. . . . We need and need desperately to keep clear and fair every point of human contact between the races; and the school is by far the best remaining medium."[17] Many more qualified black instructors were available by 1910 than could find places in black colleges. They were, of course, uniformly excluded from employment in northern colleges as well as in southern white institutions.

Until the eve of World War I, black higher education was inevitably private education.

Atlanta University, an AMA college chartered in 1867, became "the first educational institution of higher learning in Georgia to open its doors to all people, regardless of race, color, or creed." Because of the dearth of common schools in the city, the elementary enrollment of the university averaged some 60 percent over the years 1869–1894. The first dozen college students enrolled in 1872; half of these graduated four years later with bachelor's degrees. Under the influence of radical reconstruction, the state legislature agreed in 1874 to make an annual appropriation of $8,000 to Atlanta University; this entitled the state to appoint a board of visitors to exercise a degree of regulation over this private institution. Ex-Governor Joseph E. Brown, named chairman of the board, announced before his first visit: "I know the Negroes. Some of these pupils were probably my slaves. I know that they can acquire the rudiments of an education, but they cannot go beyond. They are an inferior race, and for that reason, we had a right to hold them as slaves, and I mean to attend these examinations to prove we were right." After the visit, however, Brown declared: "I was all wrong. I am converted."[18]

In time the board of visitors used the state appropriation as leverage for changes in Atlanta University. Certain books in the library were objected to as being antisouthern; repeated criticisms were made of a small number of white children attending classes; and exception was taken to the "social equality" shown between white teachers and black students. In 1887, the legislature ended the $8,000 payments.

Atlanta University remained under attack for its refusal to follow the color line. Still, most black teachers employed in the Atlanta schools were graduates of the university, an indirect confirmation of the superiority of the institution. By 1912, the university's collegiate department accepted only graduates of four-year high schools. Academic success did not lead to support from public or philanthropic funding agencies. After 1900, as Bond observes, "gifts to Negro liberal arts colleges declined to a starvation level and the endowments of the industrial schools mounted."[19]

Around the turn of the century, industrial education was presented as a substitute for liberal arts and professional education for blacks. It was sustained by the social reality of exclusion from meaningful citizenship and careers. In the name of practicality, as defined by dominant white society, young blacks were to be trained to occupy fixed "places" at the bottom of southern society. Southern white power and northern white philanthropy fixed on industrial education as a double solution to civic and economic problems. It was expected that a modest trade would pacify any black civic disquietude as well as guarantee a continuing docile labor supply. Many black educators viewed industrial education as another fact of black existence with which one would have to live. White acclaim and funds flowed to black institutions. Hampton Institute and Tuskegee Institute were prime beneficiaries. Even then, philanthropic aid was a trickle in contrast to the flow of funds to white higher education in the North and South. In an effort to attract northern funds, many black colleges added trade courses to their liberal arts offering. From time to time, students rebelled at the consequent downgrading of the curriculum.[20]

At the 1913 dedication of a new building in Nashville, part of the state normal school for Negroes, the president of the state board of education said:

> I had just as well be plain about it and say to you Negroes here
> that the whole thing is meant for you to keep out of politics. . . .
> Your way to preferment is over the sometimes hard but
> entirely safe road of industry and economy. Here in this school
> you have every chance to become a wage earner that will bring
> you always a comfortable living.[21]

Booker T. Washington, principal of Tuskegee, who represented the view that blacks should concentrate on practical industrial training in the black communities of the country, was criticized bitterly by a minority of black educators. In the last five years of his life, however, Washington moderated his hitherto almost exclusive emphasis upon industrial education. In 1910, he proposed that somewhere in the South there be created "at least one large, thoroughly equipped university where the cultural needs of the Negro people could be studied and where such of them as desire to be teachers, doctors or ministers of the gospel could be thoroughly equipped for their work."[22]

Enrollment of black students in college-level courses, even after a half

century, remained very low. Black higher education was simply too impoverished to make further headway. As in the case of the common
schools, public support was indispensable.

Public higher education in the South was one of the numerous innovations of Reconstruction. The means was the Morrill Land Grant Act of
1862. In that year Congress awarded to each state land grants of 30,000
acres for each senator and representative in Congress as of the 1860 census. Funds derived from land sales were to finance the higher education
of students seeking instruction in agriculture and mechanical arts. The
law's sponsor pointed out twenty-six years later that the funds were also
designed to aid "those who might prefer to adhere to the classics."[23]

Even while the Civil War raged, three slave states implemented the
law by founding land grant colleges (Kentucky, Maryland, and Missouri).
At war's end, three more were preparing to open such institutions (Mississippi, North Carolina, and Texas). Still more were delayed by events of
the war. Consequently, late in 1865 a bill was introduced into Congress
to extend deadlines. It was apparent, also, that Morrill colleges in former
slave states were being reserved for white students only. In January 1866,
the House Agriculture Committee sponsored an amendment to the 1862
law: "That in extending the provisions of this act to the States lately in
rebellion, it shall be on the express condition that no person shall be
excluded on account of race or color from the benefits of the school or
educational funds arising from the lands thus donated."[24] Debate on the
floor of the House criticized the provision as "premature," and in the
March 1866 committee report no mention was made of race or color. The
Congress that took such action – or inaction – was purely northern in
membership, since the body had refused in December 1865 to seat any
southern members who had been elected earlier that year. And yet the
same Congress in March 1866 passed the Civil Rights Act forbidding state
discrimination against citizens on account of race or color.

Southern state governments ignored the Civil Rights Act and proceeded to set up white colleges. Only in four states was Morrill money
also spent on black colleges. Mississipi, in 1871, made an appropriation to
Alcorn Agricultural and Mechanical College. The following year, Virginia
State College at Petersburg was created. In 1873, Arkansas founded Arkansas Agricultural, Mechanical, and Normal College (Arkansas AM&N).
While the legislation creating AM&N omitted any mention of race – given
the Reconstruction political situation in Arkansas – it assured the exclusive Negro character of the school by putting it in Pine Bluff, the heart of
blacks in the state. A year earlier, when the University of Arkansas had
opened, a black person applied for entrance. The president ordered him
admitted but directed that he spend the day in a nearby outhouse. After
that, blacks turned toward AM&N.[25]

The Georgia legislature had played light with the Morrill Act. Section II of a 1874 law stipulated that the $8,000 annual payment to Atlanta University "shall be in lieu of any claim of the colored population of the State upon the proceeds of the Agricultural Land Scrip, donated by the Congress of the United States." Yet the actual appropriation was charged against general state funds rather than the account received from the federal land grant. As a result, the state of Georgia felt free to use the payment as it wished without fear of any federal consequence. The payment was discontinued, as noted above, when university authorities refused to stop the attendance of some white students in the otherwise all-black school.

Exceedingly small amounts of money per student were available for black students; yet all black persons formed part of the population base of the formula for calculating Morrill benefits. Obviously, once again black citizens simply helped finance the higher education of white Southerners.

In 1864, radical Republican leader Representative Thaddeus Stevens had said of the Morrill Law: "It was intended to be national and to establish a national system of education, bestowing national property for that purpose."[26] In practice, authorities in thirteen ex-slave states, including Georgia, withheld land grant funds from black higher education. Four others made little more than a token response. Continued agitation at this injustice led to the second Morrill Act in 1890. State governments were offered substantially increased land grant benefits for racially dual college systems provided the funds were "equitably divided." Congress thus gave official sanction to separate-but-equal higher education, the first explicit federal approval of segregated education. The new law also required "full and detailed annual reports" by college presidents. Power to cut off federal grants for failure to comply with the law was lodged with the secretary of the interior.

The incentive was effective. Each of the fourteen former slave states without a black land grant college promptly established one, and thereupon became eligible for greatly expanded grants. Gates estimates that annual funds under the 1890 measure were "greater than all A and M institutions were expending on agricultural education in 1890 and greater than the total income all the institutions had received from the endowment derived from proceeds of the grants of 1862."[27] These were the funds to be "equitably divided" among black and white colleges.

Southern state governments, then, proceeded systematically to misappropriate the share of Morrill funds that belonged to black colleges. While states were obligated to share the costs of black land grant colleges, they frequently failed to do so.[28] In Georgia, the state in 1881–1882 appropriated some $14,000 for white colleges and $8,000 for a black one. By 1913–1914, the figure for white public colleges had risen to $539,000; the black college appropriation was unchanged.[29] States also rigidly controlled the curricula of the new colleges. Most of these black land grant colleges had been private institutions. When they attempted to adopt liberal arts programs, despite criticism state authorities vetoed the efforts. Liberal arts colleges were maintained as trade schools.[30] Black educators were urged to set out in more innovative directions toward vocational education.

The relative impoverishment of black land grant colleges was extraordinary, even in the light of traditional southern practices. After a decade of the second Morrill Act, expenditures on white land grant colleges exceeded those for black ones by a ratio of approximately 26:1. A quarter century after 1890, the institutions were, in Davis's phrase, hardly more than "land grant high schools."[31] By 1916, not a single college-level course was taught in the black land grant colleges.[32] The secretary of the interior apparently took no action to enforce the statutory requirement that Morrill funds be "equitably divided."

Houston wrote in 1935 that "from the time that President Hayes recalled the Federal troops from South Carolina [1877] there have been no known Negroes in state universities in the deep South."[33] For a number of years, Berea College in Kentucky was a rare example of interracial southern higher schooling. Its charter of 1855 provided that "this college shall be under an influence strictly Christian, and as such opposed to sectarianism, slaveholding, caste and every other wrong institution."[34] In 1904, the state legislature enacted the Day Law, which outlawed any interracial schooling, levied money fines on students and teachers, and forbade the construction of any branch building less than 25 miles distant from the original structure. Four years later, a challenge of the constitutionality of the measure was rejected by the U.S. Supreme Court in *Berea College* v. *Kentucky*. A state had the right to compel a corporation to amend its charter, according to the Court, thus avoiding the constitutional question.[35]

Black youth – most of them sons and grandsons of former slaves and some former slaves themselves – attended college in increasing numbers before 1900. A survey made in 1900 by Du Bois found a total of 2,330 Negro graduates (Table 39).[36] Astonishingly, as of 1890, the college-going rate of black youth exceeded that of native white youth born of foreign parents and closely approached that of native white youth of native white parents. Of youths aged fifteen to nineteen years, the percentages attending college were 20.44 for native whites born of native white parents, 18.76 for blacks, and 14.74 for native whites born of foreign parents. Of youths aged twenty and over, the corresponding percentages were 1.78, 1.21, and 0.93.[37] The relative significance of the rates for Negroes must be modified somewhat because of the greater importance of precollegiate programs in Negro colleges.

Table 39. *Negro college graduates prior to 1900*

Period of graduation	Graduates of Negro college	Graduates of northern college	Total	Percent Negro college
Before 1876	137	75	212	64.6
1876–1880	143	22	165	86.7
1880–1885	250	31	281	89.0
1885–1890	413	43	456	90.6
1890–1895	465	66	531	87.6
1895–1899	471	88	559	84.3
Unknown	58	64	122	47.5
Total	1,937	389	2,326	83.4

Source: Data from W. E. B. Du Bois (ed.), *The College-Bred Negro* (Atlanta: Atlanta University Press, 1900), p. 42.

Private and public colleges in the North

Until 1900, one-sixth of all black graduates in the United States held degrees from northern colleges. Since 1826, the annual average of such graduates slightly exceeded five; between 1876 and 1900 the average was barely thirteen per year.

Oberlin College alone accounted for one-third of these graduates.[38] During the post-Civil War generation, Negro enrollment at Oberlin constituted about 5 or 6 percent of all students. Some attended the preparatory department. According to the archivist of the college, during the years 1865–1939, "black students were treated differently from white students at Oberlin College." During the 1880s, the color line made an abrupt appearance there. A professor objected to the practice of black and white students sharing common rooms and called for an end to it. A committee of six Negro students protested to the president, but segregated rooming was introduced nonetheless. Negro girls were forced to eat at separate dining tables, but this restriction was lifted after protest. By 1910, black students were forced to form their own literary society after exclusion from three men's societies on campus. When black Oberlin varsity athletes were placed in segregated housing quarters when playing other colleges, administrators refused to challenge the practice. "By 1913," writes Bigglestone, "it was tradition that no more than two Negro girls were taken at any one time into the college's residence halls."

Although the growth of racial segregation at Oberlin was an open secret in black communities, black parents continued to send their children because the institution's academic work seemed untouched by any racial considerations.[39] One Negro alumna of the class of 1884 recalled a curious episode from her student days:

One day Matthew Arnold, the English writer, visited our class and Professor Frost asked me both to read the Greek and then to translate. After leaving the class, Mr. Arnold referred to the young lady who had read the passage of Greek so well. Thinking it would interest the Englishman, Professor Frost told him I was of African descent. Thereupon Mr. Arnold expressed the greatest surprise imaginable, because, he said, he thought the tongue of the African was so thick he could not be taught to pronounce Greek correctly. [40]

Northern colleges and universities in general did not welcome Negro students. In 1900, Amherst College president, George Harris, replied to an inquiry from W. E. B. Du Bois: "Where shall they obtain a liberal education? With few exceptions, I think it should be in Southern colleges. The color line is so sharply drawn in Northern colleges (unfortunately) that a Negro is at a great disadvantage, not in studies, but socially."[41]

An official of Vassar College wrote Du Bois: "There is no rule . . . that would forbid our admitting a colored girl, but the conditions of life here are such that we should hesitate for the sake of the candidate to admit her and in fact should strongly advise her for her own sake not to come." From faraway South Dakota State College it was reported, Du Bois said, that "the attitude towards Negro students is not favorable with the student body."

The pattern of racial discrimination was widespread among the foremost American colleges and universities. According to Du Bois in 1913, northern colleges had for a decade been discouraging Negro attendance. At Cornell University, he reported, blacks were in the process of being excluded from dormitories. Columbia University and the University of Chicago were accused of devising various means to minimize the number of Negro students in their summer sessions. When, in 1900, Yale University was asked to fill out a questionnaire on Negro graduates it referred the inquirer, Du Bois, to the institution's Negro janitor. After several requests, the information was supplied by academic authorities. Princeton excluded Negroes until after World War II. A leading professor at Princeton was reported by Du Bois to have lectured in 1915 that "98 percent of the [Negro] race were sexually immoral; that even educated Negroes were only 'grown up children' and that neither Negroes nor women ought to vote." Unknown to Du Bois, a favorite Harvard history professor of his and one of his closest advisers years before, Albert Bushnell Hart, had confided to the Harvard president that "I have been convinced for years . . . that the Negro race, as a race, is inferior to the white." In 1921, a black newspaper criticized a public lecture by another Harvard professor who held that some races were innately inferior. Harvard reportedly graduated some forty black students between 1884 and 1922. During the 1890s, most Negro students found a place in social activities with white fellow students. While Harvard admitted blacks, President Eliot early in the twentieth century expressed private reservations about the desirability of social contacts between black and white students. In 1915, Harvard established segregated freshman dormitories.

Rutgers admitted its third Negro student in 1915, 149 years after founding. This student, Paul Robeson, was an unbelievable combination of intellectual brilliance, musical talent, and athletic prowess, unmatched by any of his classmates.[42]

Veysey's characterization of American higher education around 1900 is documented repeatedly: "a parade of Anglo-Saxon names and pale, freshly scrubbed faces."[43] That year, 2.5 percent of the enrollment at the University of Kansas was black. From 1873 to 1909, sixty graduates were black, fewer than two a year. In Iowa, from 1880 to 1909, eleven different colleges graduated a total of thirty-four Negro students, or an annual average of slightly over one for the entire group of colleges. Indiana colleges over the period 1861–1900 graduated one Negro for every three years.[44] Black representation in northern public and private colleges was thus minuscule. It approached significance only in contrast with the lack of black students in southern white colleges. Few colleges publicly announced quotas, but their existence was well known to blacks. Even northern institutions that had accepted Negro students for decades followed restrictive policies. When, in 1927, the newly appointed president of Oberlin College was asked whether greater numbers of black students would be welcomed, his response was: "Definitely no."[45]

Catholic colleges were notoriously exclusionary. Despite repeated protests, the Catholic University of America refused from 1922 to 1936 to accept any black students. In 1926, the only Catholic colleges enrolling Negro students were Fordham University and the University of Detroit. A study published in 1948 reported a total of seventeen Negro students enrolled in ten Catholic colleges. Roche found that "at least 22 Catholic colleges and universities totally excluded Negroes," and another seven partly excluded Negroes. In 1931, Holy Cross, Notre Dame, and Worcester refused to admit blacks.[46]

Possibly the most ingenious exclusion was exercised by Ohio University in Athens, Ohio. Prior to 1923, a relative handful of southern black students had enrolled in the school. That year, however, the board of trustees adopted a resolution: "Students who are not permitted to attend their state universities in their home states will not be permitted to matriculate at Ohio University."[47] Since blacks were the only persons excluded from white state universities in the South, the resolution effectively excluded them as well from Ohio University – all without any mention of race.

The numbers of black students enrolled in northern colleges and universities grew each year. In 1924, there were 1,400; in 1928, 2,225; in 1931, 2,500; and in 1932, 2,538.[48]

By and large, public colleges in the North after World War I were open to Negro students who applied. Occasional exceptions, however, existed. A study conducted in 1941 discovered such a state college in the mountain West.[49] In 1930, the municipal University of Dayton explained its exclusionary policy: "We do not admit Negroes into our day classes because of the considerable number of students we have from the Southern States. However, they are admitted into the Law Classes and the Evening College Classes which are almost wholly composed of Dayton people."[50] Skidmore College, a private college, on the other hand, accepted Negroes only as day students – daily commuters between the college and their homes.

Black enrollment was highly concentrated. In 1928, 1,182 of the 2,225 Negro college students in the North attended just ten institutions:[51]

Ohio State University	250	State University of Iowa	98
University of Kansas	145	University of Illinois	92
Temple University	138	Northwestern University	77
New York University	131	Columbia University	73
University of Pittsburgh	114	Oberlin College	64

Ohio State maintained its high position in the following decade.

Some limited movement of black students occurred between the North and South. In 1938–1939, one-seventh of the black students in a selected group of northern universities were from the South; the rest were residents of the home state of the institution they attended. Indeed, the southward flow of black students exceeded the northward movement. During 1938–1939, Negro colleges in Kansas, Ohio, and Pennsylvania enrolled 218 southern black students. Almost four times as many (946) northern black students from these same states attended black colleges in the South. The North was a net exporter of black college students.[52]

Evaluation of exclusionary and enrollment practices

In 1947, a government document appeared that reflected, in part, the thirst of Negroes for equality of opportunity. The President's Commission on Higher Education set off a national debate on issues that heretofore had been restricted to the pages of black journals and newspapers. The commission pointed to "the single, most outstanding factor in the whole situation" as the existence of as many intellectually gifted young people outside the colleges as students who attended the colleges. Singled out for attack were "the prevalence of quota systems and policies of exclusion." For minority students enrolled in colleges, "the frustrations of social discrimination in the dormitories, in honorary societies, in fraternities and sororities, on athletic teams, and at social functions – strike at [their] personal dignity."[53]

Everywhere segregation existed, in the North and in the South, black facilities were shortchanged. There could be "no fundamental correction of the total condition until segregation legislation is repealed." The virtual exclusion of Negro students from medical schools was extensively documented and criticized. In 1946, when Howard and Meharry graduated 134 Negro physicians, all the remaining medical schools in the United States together produced only 20. The professional medical and dental societies were allocated "a substantial part of the blame" for the exclusionary practices.

A significant minority of commission members – the first signatory was Arthur H. Compton, Nobel laureate in physics and chancellor of Washington University in Saint Louis – dissented from the recommendation to end segregation. They wrote: "We are concerned that as rapidly as possible conditions should be improved, inequalities removed, and greater opportunity provided for all our people. But we believe that efforts toward these ends must, in the South, be made within the established patterns of social relationships, which require separate educational institutions for whites and Negroes."[54] During the following months, the higher education community debated other aspects of the commission report.

Early in 1948, the Association of American Colleges held its annual meeting, on the theme "Colleges for Freedom." Under the chairmanship of Syracuse University chancellor, William P. Tolley, a report on minority groups in the colleges was submitted to the meeting. It acknowledged that "many colleges discriminate against minority racial and religious groups." Yet the report failed to call for any legal action: "We are . . . opposed to any infringement of the freedom of the independent college."[55] The most stringent safeguard against discrimination proposed by the Tolley committee was the setting up of an AAC national commission to hear and investigate complaints. By a vote of 220 to 91 the annual meeting then approved a resolution that "the problem of discrimination should be solved by education and voluntary action and not by coercive legislation."[56]

Howard University president, Mordecai Johnson, termed the Tolley report "an act of benevolent condescension." His criticism of its identification of law with coercion was answered by President Daniel L. Marsh of Boston University, who contended that "there is no greater tyranny than that of a minority group in the saddle." Although delegates opposed affirmative legal action against discrimination, they voted 261 to 40 to recommend and work for the repeal of laws requiring the exclusion of any student on the ground of race, color, or creed. No study has been made of the record of AAC in following up this resolution.

The actual condition of racial discrimination in northern colleges was made an object of official study apparently in only a single state, New York, in the school year 1946–1947. In New York City, 5.0 percent of Negroes aged eighteen to twenty-one, compared with 40.7 percent of all youths in that age group, attended college. In Upstate New York, the percentages were 1.8 and 21.6; statewide, they were 4.2 and 32.1. (The national college-going rate was 16 percent.) Out of 206 private colleges in the state, 7 acknowledged using racial criteria for admission. Of 71 state colleges, 28 had no Negro students, and for the larger group as a whole, black enrollment averaged 1.2 percent. The most common aid in discriminating against Negro applicants was the requirement that a photograph be submitted with the application. In 1946, this requirement was widespread in New York State. Of 39 high schools in the state that enrolled some Negro students, the principals of 16 schools reported having encountered some discrimination in enrolling their black graduates in college.[57]

Private black colleges: North and South

By the eve of World War I, black America had established a tradition of higher education. The private black college was the principal avenue of its achievement. Nearly 4,000 Negroes had graduated by that time, about one-sixth of them women. Fully 70 percent of the entire group completed their courses during 1890–1909. The most important source of Negro graduates were eight Negro colleges, six located in the South and two in the North. These schools accounted for 1,977 graduates in the period 1890–1909:[58]

Lincoln University (Pa.)	617	Howard University (D.C.)	182
Biddle University (N.C.)	275		
Fisk University (Tenn.)	245	Atlanta University (Ga.)	163
Shaw University (N.C.)	218	Bennett College (N.C.)	139
		Wilberforce University (Ohio)	138

Negro emigration from the South created a more favorable bargaining position for those who remained. During the 1920s, southern governments were readier to grant educational concessions. The expansion of elementary and secondary schooling for blacks created a growing reservoir for Negro higher education, especially in the South. Participation in the armament economy of World War I as well as in actual warfare helped destroy the village parochialism of southern blacks and to raise their aspirations. In the North, the Negro migrants and their children increasingly utilized educational opportunities, including those existing in public colleges and universities. A greater racial solidarity expressed itself in organizational form by the creation of the National Association for the

Advancement of Colored People. Especially through its organ, the *Crisis*, edited by Du Bois, the NAACP was a vital force in teaching blacks the necessity of higher education. As Negroes came to participate more widely in the urban industrial order, a middle class emerged that was especially receptive to the rewards of a college education.

The traditional black college had existed as a middle-class island amid a great sea of black misery. The black campus and the black community had existed apart. In 1935, the historian Woodson wrote: "We would close up seventy-five percent of the so-called Negro colleges and universities and the race would be better off. There would be less miseducation of the youth." He was criticizing what he felt was the failure of black institutions to teach Negro youth about black history and culture.[59] He felt the black colleges were concerned with making white men and women out of black youth. A generation later, defenders of autonomous black colleges identified black colleges with blackness.

By the 1970s, the line between black college and black community had grown far less distinct. The black college had little future without the black community, for as more black youths gained their college educations in public institutions, the greater possibility arose of a black voice in the determination of policy for those predominantly white institutions. This was the solid political ground upon which sentiment for desegregation rested. It also constituted the basis in some states for a continuation of the traditional politics of limited concession within a context of segregation.

Among the earliest Negro college graduates after the Civil War had been many ex-slaves. "I was born a slave," one said. "I learned the alphabet in 1868 near Nashville, Tennessee, and graduated from college in 1878." Another was a slave until eleven and entered college in 1875. Another was thirteen before being freed and had only about nine months of schooling before reaching the age of twenty-one.[60] Johnson characterized this first generation of black college graduates as seeking social emancipation through higher education.[61] They grew up in poor homes of little educational background, yet sought passionately to achieve schooling. By the 1920s, black college students, although far poorer than their white counterparts, were a somewhat privileged group of Negroes. Nearly half of Fisk University's entering freshmen during 1926–1928 came from families whose principal parental occupations were business and the professions; the parents of another quarter of the students earned a livelihood as domestic servants and unskilled laborers.[62] "For many years," Du Bois remarked in 1927, "the Hampton students have been a selected group, coming, in large part, from the best homes of black Virginia."[63] Late in the 1930s, a sample of twenty-five Negro colleges found that "while professional workers constitute only 1.5 percent of the male

Negro gainful workers in the United States, they constitute 19 percent of the fathers of Negro college seniors. . . . Unskilled laborers constitute 31.7 percent of the male workers but constitute only 10.2 percent of the fathers of college seniors."[64] Increasing numbers of southern black college students were sons and daughters of the black urban middle class.

Quality of education

The traditional Negro colleges underwent profound changes in the 1920s. From 1914 to 1931, enrollment in the black colleges grew by 181 percent; enrollment in collegiate-level courses grew by nearly 1,700 percent. The portion of total enrollment represented by collegiate enrollment rose from 13.6 percent to 60 percent. The number of Negro institutions offering college work grew from 33 to 106. By 1931–1932, more than 22,000 Negro students were taking collegiate courses.

Of the 110 black colleges in 1914–1915, two-thirds had no endowment funds; the endowment of the remaining institutions totalled $8.4 million. Eleven years later total endowment of 99 institutions had risen to $20.3 million; more than 70 percent of this represented the endowment of Hampton Institute and Tuskegee Institute, which had attracted comparatively large gifts from foundations and individuals on the basis of their industrial noncollegiate curricula. By 1931–1932, endowment had risen to $31.5 million, but 75 colleges had either a negligible endowment or none at all. The income of black colleges was small and did not grow proportionately with enrollments, especially in private colleges.[65]

By the close of the 1920s, 170 accredited public high schools for Negroes existed in nine southern states. Six times as many were unaccredited. In 1933, Caliver noted that two-thirds of the accredited schools had gained new status only during the preceding five or six years.[66] Most of the rural South was bereft of secondary school facilities for Negro youngsters. Sometimes, a single school served a county extending hundreds of square miles.[67] The least inadequate Negro high schools were in the cities. As early as 1916, Pickens observed that while the best of such schools were in Cincinnati, Washington, and Saint Louis, the percent of black children enrolled was lower than in the relatively nonsegregated schools of Boston, Cleveland, and New York.[68] Miller, on the contrary, insisted that the separate urban schools enrolled more black students.[69] Du Bois joined him in this judgment.[70] No direct resolution of the debate is possible. During the late 1930s, a national study found that students in Negro colleges who had been graduated from northern high schools were clearly superior on various tests of scholastic ability.[71] Since, however, Negro students who entered college were exceptional, one cannot judge the quality of their high schools by these students' own academic success.

With the rise of Negro high schools, black colleges could concentrate more on collegiate work. Toward the end of the 1920s, for the first time more than half the students in these colleges were enrolled in college work.

Enrollment in black colleges rose significantly in the 1950s and 1960s (Table 40). Surprisingly, the black colleges by 1967–1968 enrolled barely half of all Negro college students.[72]

Increased expenditures for public black colleges only slightly reduced the differentials between black and white institutions. In 1955, the ratio of whites to blacks in the South was 4:1. Yet at the same time, the following white/black ratios existed for important indicators of educational quality:[73]

Number of higher institutions 6:1	Library expenditures 11:1
Degrees conferred 8:1	Current income 11:1
Enrollment 9:1	Library volumes 18:1
Value of buildings and grounds 10:1	Preparation of faculty 16:1

During the next fifteen years or so, the gap was narrowed significantly. In 110 black colleges, per student outlay grew by 137 percent between 1962–1963 and 1968–1969; the corresponding figure for all four-year public colleges was 16 percent. Other indices were less favorable. From 1959 to 1969, the endowment of black colleges fell from three-fifths to only one-half that of white colleges. Over a similar period, the share of federal support in current income fell for black public colleges but rose for all public colleges.[74]

A fairly direct comparison of black and white colleges in the South was undertaken by Bowles and Costa. Colleges were matched in a rough fashion and evaluated by conventional measures of educational quality. The findings included the following:

Table 40. *Enrollment in four-year Negro colleges, 1953–1968*

Year	Private colleges (51)	Public colleges (35)	Total (86)	Percent public
1953–1954	25,569	37,764	63,333	59.6
1957–1958	29,495	44,237	73,732	60.0
1961–1962	34,830	58,105	92,935	62.5
1965–1966	44,105	75,593	119,698	63.2
1967–1968	48,541	85,382	133,923	63.8

Source: Data from Frank Bowles and Frank A. Costa, *A Profile of Negro Higher Education* (New York: McGraw-Hill, 1971), p. 83.

> With the exception of mean endowment, the historically Negro private colleges, as a group, have relatively lower status than do the historically white colleges on all the measures of educational availability or attainment. . . . The top Negro colleges have significantly higher status than do the majority of white colleges on all measures. . . . The lowest among the Negro colleges have about the same relative status as do the bottom white colleges on all the measures . . . except the value of buildings, grounds, and equipment. . . . Many of the observed differences between historically Negro colleges and historically white colleges are more a function of size and financial support than they are a function of race.[75]

No blanket evaluation fitted the entire group of black or white colleges, a fact of variability that contradicted the often-repeated, though ill-informed, declaration that black colleges as a group were at the bottom of the academic heap.

Curiously, perhaps, virtually no studies were on record testing the relative efficacy of comparable white and black colleges in academic achievement. Scores of studies, on the other hand, reported the average academic ability of entering classes in black and white colleges. In 1970, three researchers of the Educational Testing Service compared students at seven predominantly black and seven predominantly white colleges. They studied the degree to which each group of schools fostered the kind of achievement measured by the Graduate Record Examination Area Tests. These are standard tests, widely used in American higher education. The researchers found "no evidence for believing that one group of colleges is any more or less effective than the other in improving the academic achievement of students who have similar aptitude test scores at the time of entrance to college."[76] One could also point to the seeming lack of any productive learning environment at this or that small rural state college.[77]

Most Negro colleges were ill-prepared to raise their standards. In 1884, when a young Negro graduate of Oberlin College accepted her first teaching position at Wilberforce University, she said, "I taught everything from French and mineralogy in the college department to reading and writing in the preparatory department."[78] In the typical small American college, such a span of duties was far from unusual. In black colleges, with even smaller collegiate enrollments, teachers made do as best they could. Advanced training proceeded slowly among Negro college teachers. After the Reconstruction years, white higher education in the South, including graduate study, was forbidden to the Negro student. Not that the Negro teacher had much time for study. His teaching load was exceedingly high;

he had no graduate assistants to aid him; and without protection of tenure, his personal status was insecure.

Library facilities of Negro colleges were extremely scanty. Laboratory equipment for teaching biology, according to a survey in 1926, was "seriously deficient."[79] In physics and chemistry it was even worse.

During the mid-1920s, a detailed study of Negro higher education was conducted by the U.S. Office of Education. Some of its findings illustrated starkly the plight of the average black college. Arkansas AM&N College, the state's sole public facility for blacks, was located in "an unsightly neighborhood of Pine Bluff surrounded by railroad yards, and its buildings are in a run-down condition and wholly inadequate for its needs."[80] The Negro land grant college in Maryland, Princess Ann Academy – a two-year-old junior college – had issued no catalogue; information about its academic program was inadequate; it had no library. Southern University, Baton Rouge, Louisiana, had a library of "a few hundred volumes."[81] Of Morris College in Sumter, South Carolina, federal authorities reported, "for all practical purposes the institution has virtually no library."[82] At Lincoln University in Missouri, there was no instruction in agriculture or mechanical arts despite the fact that the school was the state's Negro land grant college.[83]

Accreditation: exclusionary practices

During the first twenty-five years of this century, formal accreditation of colleges by states and regional associations became more or less standard practice. Accreditation was a primary prerequisite for foundation funding and for state recognition before public funding could take effect. It was necessary if holders of undergraduate degrees were to gain admittance to graduate schools without penalty. Accreditation was also a status symbol.

As a rule, southern state governments and accrediting associations excluded black institutions from their attention. Few or no attempts were made to encourage black colleges to seek accreditation; one reason was the necessary expenditure of public funds if such a goal were pursued. However, state accreditation was frequently given to Negro normal schools, which provided necessary teachers for Negro common schools. Teachers prepared in such institutions were not accredited as teachers for white schools.

In 1922, a Negro educator in Texas wrote the state department of education about accrediting his college. He described "the strange reply that the department had not considered the probability of applying standards to Negro schools or colleges."[84] The Georgia State Department of Education acknowledged in the mid-1920s that "while the standards of the Southern Association of Colleges and Secondary schools are rigidly adhered to in accrediting white universities and colleges . . . it does not strictly enforce these requirements in granting recognition to Negro higher educational institutions."[85] Kentucky was sweepingly unconcerned with standards of Negro higher education:

> The State department of education does not have a definite stan-
> dard basis for the accrediting of Negro higher educational institu-
> tions, maintains no regular list of approved Negro colleges, and
> conducts no examination of them. While the State grants
> teachers' certificates to graduates of one of the colleges surveyed,
> a rating of its teacher-training work is not made through an actual
> appraisal or inspection.[86]

Tennessee maintained a list of approved teacher-training courses at Negro colleges, but failed to concern itself with work done in the remainder of the college.[87]

The medical schools of Howard University and Meharry College trained all but a few of the black physicians in the country. In 1912, Howard was admitted as a regular member of the Association of Medical Colleges. Graduates of Howard and Meharry who took examinations for state licenses performed comparatively well. Hazen wrote in 1933: "Until a few years ago [test results] showed an average of 15 to 20 percent failures from the graduates of the two schools; . . . [now reports of state medical examiners show] percentages of passing grades equal to all save a very few of the white schools."[88]

In 1913, Du Bois reported that except for graduates of Howard, recipients of bachelor's degrees from Negro colleges "must do one or some-times two years of undergraduate or special studies" before receiving advanced degrees from front-rank northern universities.[89] A decade later, this was not true of a fair-sized group of black colleges. Drake said of his four years at Hampton Institute, which he entered in 1927:

> Hampton was in transition from trade school to college in those
> days, but between New England-type schoolmarms and a couple
> of brilliant black professors I received a good liberal education
> plus training to teach high school. I also absorbed the "service to
> the race" values and learned to appreciate Negro history, music,
> and folklore. It never occurred to me that what I was getting was
> inferior.[90]

Numerous parallel testimonials emanated from Fisk, Atlanta, Morehouse, Talladega, and other colleges.

When heads of these colleges sought accreditation, they were ignored. In 1928, the Association of Colleges for Negro Youth – founded in 1913 – requested a meeting on accreditation with the Southern Association of

Colleges and Secondary Schools. The letter lay unanswered for a year. In 1929, the Southern Association received a grant from the General Board of Education to conduct a preliminary evaluation of Negro colleges. The resulting report listed only 9 out of about 150 institutions as possibilities for full approval. These were Fisk, Morehouse, Johnson C. Smith, Shaw, Spelman, Talladega, Virginia State, Virginia Union, and Winston-Salem Teachers.[91] Ordinarily, the next step would have been to make final selections, declare them accredited, and admit them to membership. Instead, in 1930, the Southern Association took an action without parallel in any other region of the country. It refused to *accredit* the colleges because this would have opened its membership rolls to the colleges. Instead, it declared seven colleges *approved;* membership was therefore denied. Also unique were the two classes of approval. Only one college – Fisk – was ranked *A*. Six others were ranked *B:* Morehouse, Johnson C. Smith, Spelman, Talladega, Virginia State, and Virginia Union. Heretofore, colleges had been accredited or not accredited. The creation of the lesser category, "approved," strongly implied "that standards were being watered down when applied to the Negro schools."[92] For the next quarter century, black administrators continued to seek equal treatment and full membership. Full membership was achieved only in 1957 and equal treatment four years later.

By the eve of World War II, only eighteen Negro four-year colleges were accredited by one or another regional accrediting association; sixteen were private, eleven public. Nine states lacked a public Negro college that was accredited by the regional association; in five other states, neither private nor public colleges were accredited. The American Association of Teacher Colleges accredited only three public and no private Negro colleges.[93] The Association of American Universities accredited only two black private colleges so their graduates could enter any graduate school without the necessity of passing entrance examinations.

The South's public black colleges continued to suffer from their historical underfinancing. Most state legislatures preferred to maintain both the isolation and the relative inferiority of these colleges. In accordance with tradition, white legislatures voted occasional improvements. In nearly every case, these simply awarded to a black college what every white college in the state had taken for granted for many years. In North Carolina, Florida, and Mississippi, legislatures appropriated "catch-up" funds to black colleges. Between 1967 and 1971, $2.3 million was spent this way in the first state; in 1968, $600,000 was appropriated to Mississippi Valley State College for library and faculty development; and Florida Agricultural and Mechanical University (FAMU) received special funds for compensatory programs.[94] The "catch-up" funds could be viewed as fragmentary restitution for generations of systematic misappropriations. In no real sense could they enable the overcoming of relative disadvantage between black and white institutions. Any strategy for public black colleges had to come to terms with this fundamental fact.

Black faculty at white institutions

The maintenance of all-white faculties was a virtually immutable policy of northern colleges and universities. During the 1920s, Harvard and Chicago employed only one black scientist each in a nontenured position.[95] Yet many qualified Negro scholars were available. Du Bois wrote in 1934: "Not one of the twelve colored Ph.D's of last year, trained by highest American and European standards, is going to get a job in any white university."[96] As far back as 1876, when advanced degrees in physics were extremely rare in the United States, a black man, Edward A. Bouchet, had received a Ph.D. degree in that field from Yale. He had no alternative but to teach in a black institution and closed his career as the principal of black Lincoln High School in Gallopolis, Ohio. By 1936, a sizable group of black Ph.D.s was available for employment, but fully 80 percent of them taught in just three black institutions: Atlanta, Fisk, and Howard. During the decade beginning with 1937, 279 black students received Ph.D. degrees. In 1940–1941, a national survey found no Negroes holding tenured positions in any American university.

In 1940, only two or three black persons were employed in northern institutions of higher education. At least two of these worked in laboratories and performed no teaching duties. During the years 1940–1945, two foundations concerned themselves with the problem of encouraging universities to employ more Negro staff members. In 1940, the Rosenwald Fund made the first comprehensive survey of black faculty. It discovered only two black staff members, yet claimed most of the credit for stimulating the employment of fourteen additional faculty by 1945.[97]

During World War II, the Rosenwald Fund subsidized the employment of two additional black scholars. Salaries were paid for anthropologist Allison Davis at the University of Chicago and artist Hale Woodruff at New York University. In 1945, the General Education Board followed suit by creating, at New York University, a three-year visiting professorship in Negro culture and education. Sociologist Ira de A. Reid of Atlanta University was assigned the position. When the Rosenwald Fund made a second survey, in mid-1946, the number of black faculty had risen to seventy-five (Table 41).[98]

By 1958, according to Moss, about 200 Negroes taught in white higher institutions. Almost a fifth of this number (39) was employed in New York State alone. Moss estimated that the 200 constituted 10 percent of all black college teachers in the United States.[99] For New York State, be-

Table 41. *Negro faculty at selected white institutions, 1945–1947,*
1967–1968

	1945–1947 [a]	1967–1968 [b]
Number of institutions contacted	600	179 [c]
Number replying	179	138
Percent response	29.8	77.1
Number of respondents supplying complete information	178	130
Number of respondents reporting Negro faculty members	42	79
Percent reporting Negro faculty members employed	23.6	60.7
Total number of Negro faculty members reported	75	785
Total number of all faculty at institutions supplying information for the survey (approximate)	40,000	60,000
Percent of Negroes on the faculties of all institutions supplying information for the survey	0.002	0.013
Estimated number of Negroes in the U.S. having completed five or more years of college	3,550 [d]	194,000 [e]

[a] Survey conducted by the Rosenwald Fund.
[b] Survey conducted by the Southern Education Reporting Service.
[c] The institutions represented by this number are the same ones which replied to the 1945–1947 survey.
[d] Estimated by Fred G. Wale of the Rosenwald Fund in 1947.
[e] Estimated by U.S. Bureau of the Census, March 1966.

Source: A. Gilbert Belles, "Negroes Are Few on College Faculties," *Southern Education Report*, 4 (July-August 1968), p. 23.

tween 1949 and 1956, only four additional black teachers were added in two more institutions. By 1960, according to Moss, 5,910 black college teachers (3 percent of the total) were employed in the entire country. He estimated that 18 percent of these, or about 1,065, worked in colleges and universities outside the South.[100] In 1967, the Southern Education Reporting Service surveyed all 179 colleges that had responded to the Rosenwald survey of 1946 (Table 41). Employment had increased tenfold – from 75 to 785 or from 0.002 to 0.013 percent over twenty-two years.

The failure to employ Negro faculty was not the result of a shortage of qualified candidates. Wale, the director of education of the Rosenwald Fund, wrote in 1947 of the average college administrator: "Consciously or unconsciously, he has never seriously considered a Negro as eligible for a faculty."[101] Even at universities where the social sciences were most renowned, exclusion of black faculty was quite conscious. Bond wrote:

"As late as 1946, according to Dr. Robert Maynard Hutchins, the University of Chicago opposed the appointing of Negroes to the faculty, and . . . William F. Ogburn, a respected sociologist protested that all of the white graduate students would withdraw if the Negroes were appointed."[102] An eminent white member of the sociology department recommended to Professor Ogburn, who headed the department, that he employ Dr. E. Franklin Frazier, the best-known black sociologist in the country and president of the American Sociological Society in 1948. Professor Ogburn replied that this would not be possible because the wives of the white professors would object.[103]

Despite Ogburn's claims, experience at the University of Chicago suggested that graduate students were no obstacle to the employment of black scholars. Williams said of Professor Allison Davis's appointment in the school of education at the university in 1941: "Davis was readily accepted by his white students. It was his white colleagues on the faculty who proved to be a problem. Some of them shunned him, even walking out of the faculty club when he entered."[104] In 1948, Marcuse polled department heads at Cornell University on their attitudes toward employing Negroes. More than seven out of ten stated they would have no hesitation in hiring a qualified black faculty member in their departments. An even greater percentage thought their colleagues and students would approve. Yet no Negroes were employed at Cornell.[105] In 1972, a study by Rafky of 554 black professors in colleges outside the South reported persistence of unfavorable conditions: "Black professors complain of social slights and rebuffs, presumably due to prejudice, by their white colleagues; . . . 90 percent [of the black professors] believe that schools outside the South exclude black faculty from the pool of qualified applicants and more than one-quarter agree that blacks must be better qualified than whites to be hired or to receive tenure."[106] Considerable informal evidence supported these views.

A federal program to remedy the relative lack of minority – and women – faculty members took shape by the close of the 1960s. Legal authority for the program was based on Federal Executive Order 11246, which forbade any contractor with the federal government to discriminate on account of race, color, nationality, or sex. Contractors were directed to formulate a plan for affirmative action to overcome existing disparities. Many colleges and universities, in part dependent on federal contracts, sought to fulfill the requirement.

Columbia University, one of the prime contractors in higher education, was probably typical of many other institutions. In 1972, 11.7 percent of its faculty consisted of minority persons. In the various schools that make up the university, the percentages of minority-group faculty were as follows:[107]

Law school   0.0   Journalism school   6.7
Library service   0.0   Architecture school   10.0
Business school   1.1   Health sciences division   12.9
Arts school   6.2   Social work school   18.2
Arts and sciences
    departments   6.6

Salary groups at Columbia varied directly with percentage minority (Table 42). Under federal pressure, more and more colleges pledged to pursue goals of faculty employment on a nondiscriminatory basis.[108]

Black graduate study and research

Black efforts to attain an undergraduate education achieved considerable results. The road to graduate education, however, was rocky, full of detours, all but impassable. By impoverishing the public black colleges, southern state legislatures guarded against any development of graduate study. Public funds were used in an exceedingly discriminatory way. In 1930, state-financed white institutions in the South enrolled more than 11,000 white students in graduate and professional study. At the same time, not even one Negro in the South was receiving state-supported graduate or professional training.

Once in a college or university, Negroes were discouraged from enrolling in certain courses. In the *Crisis*, Miller reported from the University of Kansas that "the Dean of Engineering School regularly calls in all colored engineering students and advises them to get out of his school."[109] At New York University, Negro women students were not permitted to enroll in the physical training course. Butler University allowed only ten new black students a year to enter its College of Liberal

Table 42. *Relation of salary to proportion of minority-group faculty members at Columbia University, 1972*

Classification	Average salary ($)	Minority as percent of full-time faculty
Professorial-research	14,090	16.0
Professorial-staff	12,280	27.3
Specialist-managers	11,160	35.1
Semiprofessionals	9,890	38.3
Technicians	8,540	44.6

Source: Data from *Columbia University Affirmative Action Program, April 10, 1972.*

Arts and Sciences while no limits were placed on black enrollment in the College of Religion. Temple University was said to have excluded Negro students from "certain courses."[110]

Exclusion was common in fields that would lead to graduate professional work. This was particularly true in the study of medicine. During the 1920s when instructional strategies shifted away from the classroom and toward more practical work in clinics and hospitals, medical institutions objected to black students in such medical roles and the university involved did not object. Consequently, wrote Johnson in 1938: "Negro students have found increasing difficulty in getting the necessary clinical experience needed for graduation, especially in obstetrics and gynecology."[111] Earlier in the decade, Hazen observed that the 100 Negro medical graduates from Howard and Meharry could intern only in ten hospitals – all of which had limited facilities. The reluctance of community hospitals to accept black medical students may have been the reason why Negro students were permitted to attend the University of Kansas Medical School for only two years. As early as World War I, black students at McGill University in Canada had protested the announced exclusion of Negro students from its medical school "on the excuse that their presence is objected to by the Maternity Hospital solely on account of their color." For a number of years, Negroes were excluded from the colleges of medicine and engineering at the University of Cincinnati. In 1932, that university admitted a Negro woman student to the medical school. In 1928, the medical school of Northwestern University began a policy of exclusion of black students.[112]

Quota systems were widely applied to Negroes. In 1923, the Colgate-Rochester Divinity School in Rochester, New York, had a quota of two Negro students per year. Butler University had an annual quota of ten.[113] Black students preparing to teach were frequently, with the acquiescence of the college, denied the opportunity to do their practice teaching in the neighboring public school system. Even the rare black apprentice teacher from Hamline University was rejected by the Saint Paul public schools. The public high schools of Philadelphia regularly rejected black practice teachers from the University of Pennsylvania. Black practice teachers were permitted in the Oberlin elementary schools, but Oberlin High School regularly barred black apprentices from Oberlin College, although Negro students enrolled in the institution's music conservatory were accepted, an exception made because "music practice teaching was done by two students and one of the two was always white."[114]

Blacks continued to be completely excluded from the graduate schools of southern universities. Those who sought advanced training were obliged to go north. During the late 1930s, more than half of such students enrolled in northern institutions attended Teachers College of Columbia

University and the University of Chicago. A large proportion were specializing in the field of education; fewer in the social sciences. Northern black students who attended southern colleges, on the other hand, were either undergraduates or, in a very few cases, students in one of the two medical schools in Nashville and Washington, D.C. At the end of the 1930s, about one-twelfth of the enrollment of southern black colleges consisted of northern students.[115]

By 1946, black medical school graduates throughout the country were still unable to intern at university-connected hospitals. At the University of Chicago, the chapter of the Congress of Racial Equality waged a long campaign against the exclusion of black interns. In addition, CORE charged that few Negroes were admitted as patients to university hospitals. Discriminatory medical internships were a standard practice of American universities, except at Howard and Meharry. As the civil rights movement developed, universities – and medical schools – became more sensitive about their traditional exclusionary practices, often citing "excellence" as the criterion.

Discrimination against Negroes in professional health studies was extreme in New York State. Even in New York City, fewer than fifty Negroes were graduated from medical schools between 1920 and 1945. Throughout the state in the fall of 1946, Negro students constituted the following percentages of enrollment in each type of school: dental, 0.6; nursing, 1.3; medical, 0.7. One nursing school said that "before Negro students [who applied] could be admitted, the school would need to consult cooperating institutions."[116]

The new exclusion was caused in part by the distressingly small reservoir of potential black medical students produced by urban high schools and in part by the refusal of medical schools to undertake special academic and financial aid measures for black and other minority applicants.[117]

Research was not a characteristic activity of the average Negro college; nor was it of the average white college. In the white land grant colleges, training of technical and scientific personnel was a principal program. In their black counterparts, research was virtually unknown.

Federal research funds were invariably directed away from the black land grant colleges. In 1887, for example, Congress passed the Hatch-George Act, appropriating funds to establish a scientific experiment station at each land grant college. The legislation provided that the money "shall be divided between such institutions as the legislature of such State shall direct." Without exception, each southern state chose white institutions. The same thing happened with the McIntyre-Stennis forestry research law under which funds were allocated by each governor.[118] These inequities were added to the more fundamental one of severe shortchanging of black land grant colleges in basic financing. In 1933, according to

Davis, long-time president of West Virginia State College, "the Association of Land-Grant Colleges and Universities has been importuned to throw its great power behind the work of land-grant colleges for Negroes, but as yet has not done so."[119] At the time, black land grant colleges were excluded from membership in the association – a policy that did not change for twenty-one years.[120]

Black scholarship operated under extraordinary burdens. Perhaps the heaviest was the refusal of white society to acknowledge blacks as autonomous researchers, capable as any other of investigating significant intellectual problems. In 1925, Sumner stressed that the aspiring black scholar was faced by "the dire necessity of establishing contact with a white scholar or influential white citizen. Through such contacts the intellectual Negro in several striking instances has been enabled to have vouchsafed for him some security in his academic environment and to gain recognition for his works. Without establishing contact with a white scholar, he has very little hope of recognition for his work."[121] In few areas of the South were Negroes permitted to use research facilities and reference collections and then only under "humiliating terms."[122] In the North opportunities in scientific research were not significantly better. Du Bois, in 1939, listed nine northern colleges and universities in which he reported blacks had not a fair chance to work at their research specialty: Boston University, Bowdoin College, Brown University, University of Cincinnati, De Pauw College, Harvard University, University of Chicago, Williams College, and Yale University. He also held that certain northern universities were guilty of discrimination when it came to awarding the Ph.D. degree to blacks.

National scholarly organizations cooperated in retarding black scholarship. In passive ways, scholarly journals and meetings simply omitted to report on subjects on which Negro scholars worked. More actively, some groups excluded blacks from membership. This was the case, for example, with Phi Delta Kappa, the professional fraternity for graduate study in education, an exclusion which affected many since this was the graduate field in which Negroes tended to concentrate. Also, the American Association of University Professors segregated black members. At the organization's 1939 convention, the chapter from Howard University was told its delegates might attend meetings in New Orleans "but of course they could not be guests at the hotel and would have to enter through the back door."[123] Back home in Washington, D.C., some of the same Howard professors were regularly excluded from formal affairs of Phi Beta Kappa, despite the fact that they had won membership in first-rate universities in New England. This sort of treatment had a long pedigree in the city. In 1915, the Harvard Club of the nation's capital invited recent Harvard graduates to join the group. A new history Ph.D. from Harvard, Carter G. Woodson, filled out the membership application and returned it. After a time, it was returned with an explanation that since he was a Negro he could not join.[124]

Yet as black undergraduate enrollments grew, pressure for graduate and professional facilities rose. By the opening of the 1930s, three private Negro colleges offered graduate instruction – Howard, Atlanta, and Fisk. The first was best-endowed, primarily because of relatively large federal contributions, and became the preeminent black graduate school. In view of the growing demand, however, not one or even three graduate centers could begin to meet the need. Public facilities were the obvious answer, just as they had been for white graduate and professional students. Yet whatever graduate facilities existed in connection with black public colleges were more or less a sham.

During the mid-1930s, to fend off black demands for entrance into the University of Arkansas, the state supervisor of colored schools offered purportedly graduate courses at Arkansas AM&N College at Pine Bluff. The credits were not transferable to the state university; later, in fact, the credits were attributed to AM&N. At the same time, blacks in Texas were still waiting for the state to redeem its pledge, included in the state constitution of 1876, to establish a university for Negroes "when practicable." Seventy years later, the pledge was being mocked. In Missouri, a 1921 state law created the Board of Curators for Lincoln University. The act directed the board to "afford the Negro people of the state opportunity for training up to the standard furnished at the state University of Missouri whenever necessary and practicable in their opinion." But the board never even established specific goals of equality, let alone plans for achieving them.[125]

Opposition of the state governments to black graduate education was the most basic factor. Secondary, although not unimportant, was the traditional belief among southern whites that the provision of advanced training for Negroes was not a public responsibility. It could be left to private philanthropy and the resources of black people. The Rosenwald Fund, for example, stressed black initiative with funds for building local schools, to be supplemented by its own contribution. In effect, therefore, the state was relieved of that part of the responsibility.[126] Graduate training in Atlanta University and Fisk University would have been inconceivable without philanthropic aid. Neither governmental nor philanthropic aid was available to expand graduate instruction for blacks. In 1931, when the National Advisory Committee on Education completed its report to the president, a minority report written by the heads of three black colleges – John W. Davis of West Virginia Collegiate Institute, Mordecai

Johnson of Howard University, and R. R. Moton of Tuskegee Institute – stressed the utter insufficiency of educational facilities for Negroes, including professional education, and called for direct federal grants to the states for the sole purpose of Negro education.[127] There was little realistic possibility of such grants.

Relief from the courts

Black aspirants to graduate schools turned in the early 1930s to the courts for relief. The central core of these legal efforts was to force the creation of equal, if separate, graduate facilities. Applications to enter southern state-financed graduate schools were based on the contention that equal opportunities were not available in existing black colleges. In time, a more basic goal was set: to make maintenance of two equal higher education systems so expensive as to force desegregation out of a desire to economize.

In 1933, a Negro sued to enter the school of pharmacy of the University of North Carolina. He lost the case on a technicality: he could not produce a certified record of his undergraduate record because the president of the college refused to submit one. Two years later, Donald Murray, who had graduated from Amherst College, applied to the law school of the University of Maryland. The board of regents rejected Murray's application and advised him to apply for an out-of-state scholarship grant that was soon to be made available to any Negro citizen of Maryland. Murray went to a state court and contended that his exclusion violated the equal protection clause of the Fourteenth Amendment. He was upheld and the university admitted him; meanwhile, it appealed the case. The appeals court upheld the decision.[128]

This unprecedented decision placed a black man in a state-supported professional school. News of it was featured prominently in the Negro press. For fear, however, that the celebration exceeded the achievement, caution was voiced by Charles H. Houston, chief lawyer for the NAACP. "Shout if you want," he advised, "but don't shout too soon."[129] As for the value of the *Murray* decision as a precedent, Houston predicted that "the other southern state universities are not going to confess error just because Murray obtained a favorable decision in Maryland." Houston's skepticism was merited, as events soon demonstrated.

A few days after the *Murray* decision was rendered, a similar lawsuit was filed in Missouri by Lloyd Gaines. He hoped to enter the law school of the University of Missouri. Higher educational opportunities for Negroes in Missouri had been extremely slim. Lincoln University, in Jefferson City, bore small resemblance to the state university despite the 1921 law that lodged with the board of curators of Lincoln the option of creating academic programs that would equal the level of those offered at the

University of Missouri. In fact, the 1921 law had also appropriated to the account of Lincoln University $500,000 "from any unappropriated portion of the general school funds." A lawsuit challenging the appropriation was filed and upheld by a state court, in *Lincoln University* v. *Hockman.* The appropriation was voided on the ground that Lincoln could not draw on public school funds since it was a separate state teacher-training unit and not part either of the state university or the public school system. During the 1920s and 1930s, Lincoln was operated with the barest minimum of funds.

In 1936, Gaines's suit was lost in a lower state court when the judge ruled that the plaintiff could either (1) petition Lincoln University to establish law courses or (2) apply for an out-of-state scholarship. The ruling was upheld by the state supreme court in 1937 in *Gaines* v. *Canada et al.* In the fall of 1938, the U.S. Supreme Court heard an appeal and handed down its decision near the end of the year. The majority opinion upheld Gaines's claims and stressed that "the basic consideration is . . . what opportunities Missouri . . . furnishes to white students and denies to Negroes solely on the ground of color." Rejected was the provision for out-of-state tuition:

> The white resident is afforded legal education within the State; the Negro resident having the same qualifications is refused it there and must go outside the State to obtain it. That is a denial of the equality of legal right. . . . The obligation of the State to give the protection of equal laws can be performed only where its laws operate, that is, within its own jurisdiction. It is there that the equality of legal right must be maintained. . . . No state can be excused from performance by what another state may do or fail to do.[130]

The case was sent back to the Missouri State Supreme Court for rehearing. Gaines disappeared before the date of the new hearing, so the case faded away.

The Missouri legislature, seeking ways to sidestep the *Gaines* decision, set out to continue its all-white policy for the state university by enabling Lincoln University to create parallel-quality courses.

The Taylor Act was passed in 1939 and accomplished two things: (1) the board of curators of Lincoln was directed (until then it had had the option) to set up parallel-quality programs; and (2) the sum of $200,000 was appropriated for the sole purpose of organizing new departments or schools within Lincoln. Legislators – all white – hoped that constitutionally defensible alternatives existed to the admission of black applicants to the state university.

Almost overnight, Taylor funds were used to open a law school of

Lincoln University in Saint Louis. On the day it opened, twenty-nine students registered. They were met by black pickets who asked the students not to register. The pickets, members of the Colored Clerks Circle of Saint Louis, carried signs reading: "I Have Self-Respect: How About You?" and "Don't Be a Traitor to Your Race: Stay Away from This School."[131] By fall 1943, no students were registered. Two years later, a visitor found seven students being taught by three full-time teachers. The school was accredited, and its library contained 31,000 volumes.[132] The same visitor also found a tiny school of journalism, established as a result of the 1941 *Bluford* case in which a black journalist had sought entrance to the University of Missouri school of journalism. He observed a single instructor teaching a single student in a classroom designed for forty or fifty students.

The *Gaines* decision embodied the equal-though-separate doctrine. It enjoined equal treatment of black and white, permissibly through separate facilities of equal quality, or alternatively by common facilities. *Gaines* rejected not segregation but separation involving different quality educational opportunities. Without exception, the southern states succeeded in avoiding both terms of the judicial equation. Separate facilities were not equalized; common facilities were not created. Instead, the illusion of equal quality was projected by a measurable, if only minimally significant, narrowing of the gap between black and white graduate schooling. Common facilities were created only on a microscopic scale. All these measures were welcomed on the psychological rule that even the tiniest draft of water slakes more than the largest mirage.[133]

Four principal devices were used by southern states to minimize the desegregative import of *Gaines*:[134] (1) out-of-state scholarships for black students, (2) regional arrangements, (3) increased aid to black colleges, and (4) one-by-one court-ordered admission of students to white institutions.

Out-of-state scholarships were available to Negroes who wished to take graduate or professional courses not offered by the state Negro colleges but available at the state university. NAACP counsel Houston attacked the scholarships as another discriminatory device. He pointed to Missouri, which spent nearly $1,000 per white student enrolled in the University of Missouri "while it banishes its Negro students with a pittance never over two hundred dollars per student."[135] In addition, Houston pointed out, there was an element of risk by the Negro student who selected an out-of-state university because it was not known how much a specific institution spent per student. On the other hand, "there is no uncertainty . . . about the per capita expenditure on the education of white students in the home state university."

Regional arrangements were presumably established in order to make up for the uneven distribution of graduate opportunities. A student who wanted to enroll in a program that was not offered in his own state could apply for financial help from a regional association of southern states. More than two-thirds of the beneficiaries were white students. Meharry Medical College became the medical school to which all black applicants for a medical education were sent. Benjamin Mays, president of Morehouse, charged that the regional arrangement "not only perpetuates and extends segregation but it perpetuates inequality."[136] In fact, the regional arrangement widened the gap between black and white advanced schools in the South. As Jones explains:

> Since the contractual powers of the Board of Control were limited, by terms of the compact, to institutions of the region, and inasmuch as Negroes were barred from all schools of the region offering work at certain professional graduate and technological levels, the net effect of the Board's contractual arrangements has been that of extending the opportunities of whites for training in these areas while adding nothing to those of Negroes.[137]

While selected individual black students benefited, as a group they continued to suffer relative disadvantage.

State aid to black colleges increased during the *Gaines* years. The content of some aid was purely psychological. As Jones put it, Negro colleges were renamed universities, principals became presidents, and the word *Negro* was omitted from the new name. Greater financial means were also made available. Over a fifteen-year period, the black-white gap diminished among the land grant colleges of eleven southeastern states (Table 43). But nothing was done about reducing the accumulated discrepancy between black and white colleges.

The governor of Delaware frightened the state legislature into a fit of seeming generosity when in 1953 he recommended that all-black Delaware State College be discontinued and the state university opened to all

Table 43. *Per student expenditures in white and Negro land grant colleges in eleven southeastern states, 1932–1948*

Type of college	1932–1933	1938–1939	1947–1948
White land grant colleges	$301.71	$285.53	$391.41
Negro land grant colleges	$170.16	$178.59	$353.79
Percent Negro of white	56.4	62.5	90.4

Source: Data from James A. Colston, "State Financial Support of Higher Education in Georgia" (doctoral dissertation, New York University, 1958), p. 118.

students. During the next five years Delaware State received legislative appropriations of $3.5 million, far more than the amount received during the preceding six decades.[138]

Much of the new expenditure was wasted because of the haste with which southern state governments established a record of action, regardless of long-term planning considerations. Graduate schools appeared at Negro colleges that only the day before, so to speak, lacked chalk and erasers. Between 1942 and 1950, Jones notes, graduate and/or professional facilities were created on black college campuses in Alabama, Florida, Louisiana, Missouri, North Carolina, South Carolina, Tennessee, and Virginia.[139] The Kentucky legislature acted to avoid the operation of a federal court order permitting blacks to attend the University of Kentucky where parallel courses were unavailable in black colleges. It appropriated $45,000 to establish a graduate school at all-black Kentucky State College. The Kentucky Negro Educational Association objected to the effort to set up a complete graduate school without adequate funding: "The administration at Kentucky State College . . . has been barely able to obtain the minimum requirement as an 'A' rated school offering the Bachelors Degree."[140] In Texas, a black university arose from a lawsuit filed in 1946 by Heman W. Sweatt. He had sued for entrance into the law school of the University of Texas. The state agreed to offer a law course equal to that offered by the state university, but it would be taught in the state's black land grant institution, Prairie View College. Sweatt turned aside this kind of solution, insisting that segregated education was inherently inferior and that the proper remedy was to open the state university to all. A shadow of a dual law school was created, but no students appeared. A state court directed Sweatt to apply at the new school. An appeals court, quoting heavily from *Plessy* v. *Ferguson*, upheld the lower court. The U.S. Supreme Court agreed to hear a further appeal; arguments were heard early in 1950. While refusing to accept Sweatt's argument against segregation as such, the Supreme Court reversed the Texas courts in *Sweatt* v. *Painter*. It stressed the actual inequality of the two law schools: "In terms of number of the faculty, variety of courses and opportunity for specialization, size of the student body, scope of the library, availability of law review and similar activities, the University of Texas Law school is superior." It was also superior, added the Court, because of its national reputation, the position and influence of its alumni, and the greater likelihood that many persons who attend will later hold decision-making responsibilities.[141] Texas Southern University, created as a ploy in 1947, became the Negro university with a law school attached.

Throughout the South, the new graduate and professional programs and schools were meager. For the most part the minimal character of the offerings expressed a conscious desire of state authorities to do the least necessary. The relative backwardness of graduate education in the region was another limiting factor. In 1948, Bond recalled:

> It was an illuminating experience, several years back, to a number of officials in Negro colleges, to be called in conference with the Deans of Southern Graduate Schools. To some of us, as we heard the offerings described in the white graduate schools, it soon became painfully evident that in the creation of Negro graduate schools on a shoestring there was not as great an intent to discriminate as some of us had thought; for some of these honest gentlemen planned only to reproduce in Negro colleges what their own institutions provided.[142]

Bond, as well as a number of black college officials, had received his own graduate education in a leading graduate school of the country and thus viewed the best the South had to offer in a large frame.

A limited number of black graduate students attended previously all-white graduate schools. White universities followed the legal strategy of forcing each black applicant to fight a long legal battle to gain the right to attend. Each such victory was an important individual event, but the resulting general pattern was no more than the sparest tokenism. The successful use of one-by-one admission of blacks into graduate schools provided a model for creating tokenism in the southern common schools during the late 1950s and early 1960s.

The most protracted case of one-by-one entry involved an effort by Virgil Hawkins to enroll in the law school of the University of Florida. Litigation extended over nine years, from 1949 to 1958. Along the way he was subjected to intense intimidation. "When I first filed this suit," Hawkins told an interviewer, "I was working with a Negro life insurance company as district manager in Gainesville [where the University of Florida is located]. I was asked to withdraw the suit and when I didn't do so I was fired." He was pressed to enroll instead at all-black Florida Agricultural and Mechanical University. "Florida A and M has a makeshift law school which was put up for me to go to," he said. "At one time it had seven full-time professors with only three students."[143] In 1955, after the state supreme court ruled he could not be excluded from the University of Florida because of race, a lower state court ordered that a public opinion survey be made on the issue. Results showed that if desegregation were permitted dire consequences would follow. More than half the alumni asserted they would cut off any financial contributions to the university; two out of five parents of students would withdraw or transfer them; and three out of five parents of white high school graduates declared they would not permit their children to go to a de-segregated public university. In the end, Hawkins was not permitted to enroll because he was judged unqualified.

Between 1949 and 1954, eighteen southern and border graduate schools opened their doors to black students. It was done grudgingly and on the most minimal basis. As a graduate dean explained: "We refused admission of Negroes to all departments until required to do so by court order."[144] Most of the eighteen graduate schools first admitted one or two students. The new black graduate students were very highly concentrated in the field of education. In the state university enrolling the largest number of Negroes, fully nine out of ten were in education. Negro graduate students were more numerous in summer sessions where, again, most were in education. Much of what was represented as the opening of southern graduate schools turned out to be an increase of black enrollment in graduate departments of education. Black students in graduate departments of natural sciences, social sciences, or humanities were exceedingly rare.

Segregation in student services

Room and board

Typically, white colleges segregated black students in housing quarters. A study by the U.S. Office of Education characterized the situation in the North during the late 1920s in these words: "There are . . . certain dormitories in which Negroes may not live. In some institutions no Negroes lived on the campus; in other cases, certain dormitories were open to a limited number of Negro students while in others none were admitted. . . . The dormitories are generally closed to them."[145] In 1931, a number of public and private colleges refused to permit Negro students to live in their dormitories:[146] Bryn Mawr College, Bucknell University, Colorado College, Dickinson College, Indiana University, Kansas State College, Knox College, Macalester College, Ohio University, State University of Iowa, Sterling College, Temple University, University of Arizona, University of Cincinnati, University of Kansas, University of Michigan, University of Minnesota, University of Oregon, University of Pennsylvania, University of Southern California, Villanova University, Washington and Jefferson College, Whittier College, and Wittenberg College. Negro students protested often against this practice, individually and collectively. Sometimes, policies were changed as a result. In 1917, the *Columbia University Bulletin of Information* said: "Since no special arrangements are made for colored students, such students in case they are unable to make arrangements with friends, are advised to write for information regarding room and board to the Residence Bureau, Teachers College, Columbia University." Since this appeared to notify black students not to expect places in university dormitories, the NAACP protested. The next year, the offending sentence was omitted.[147] Six years later, the university was shaken when a black law student received a death threat from the Ku Klux Klan. This had been preceded by the formation of a committee of white students who asked that the black be barred from the dormitories. The administration rejected the demand. In 1932, many Negro students in Teachers College, Columbia, lived in university dormitories without incident.[148]

Some colleges discriminated against black students on the ground of sex. At the University of Chicago, Ohio State University, and the University of Michigan, Negro men but not Negro women were allowed to live in dormitories. When Benjamin E. Mays arrived at the University of Chicago, a poor South Carolinian by birth but also an honor graduate of Bates College in Maine, he was shocked to discover segregated housing by race and sex: "At the university, Negro women could not occupy the dormitories," he said. "Negro men could live at Goodspeed Hall, but only because Goodspeed was the dormitory reserved for graduate students in the Divinity School."[149] At Ohio State University, black women students were regularly excluded from college dormitories as well as other campus facilities. When the practice was challenged in a lawsuit, a state court upheld it on the ground that the activities were social privileges rather than educational necessities.[150]

At the University of Michigan when the new Moser-Jordan Dormitory opened in 1930, Negro women were excluded from it and assigned to a separate dormitory. After a year of sustained protest, the university allowed two black women to live in "regular" dormitories, while a matron was assigned to the black women's dormitory. At Oberlin College, a de facto housing quota existed for black women students: "As late as 1940 dormitory directors were objecting if asked to take more than two black girls per dormitory or if required to have them for two or three successive years." In an apparently unique case, when black women (and men) were excluded from dormitories at the State University of Iowa, the Iowa Federation of Colored Women's Clubs purchased a home to serve as a women's dormitory.[151]

Racial segregation in student housing at Harvard began in 1915. All white freshmen were required to live in the freshman dormitory; black freshmen were housed separately. Although the rule was breached slightly during World War I, in 1922 the college administration notified two black freshmen, William J. Knox, Jr., and Cecil Blue, that they must leave the freshman dormitory. Knox, who came from New Bedford, told a black newspaper: "My friends and I have found that activities of Southern students and alumni had considerable to do with the barring of myself and other colored men." A petition of protest was signed by numerous prominent Harvard alumni and presented to President A. Lawrence Lowell.

"If Harvard were faced by the alternative of either admitting Negroes to the freshmen halls where white students are compelled to go or of excluding Negroes altogether," wrote Lowell to the alumni, "it might be compelled like other colleges, to adopt the other alternative." In a later letter, Lowell dwelt again on compulsion: "Men from the South and Southwest come to us in considerable numbers, and cannot be compelled to room or eat with colored people. We owe to the colored man the best possible opportunities for education, but we do not owe to him inclusion in a compulsory social system with other people when it is not mutually agreeable." Commenting on sentiments such as these, the editor of the *New York Age*, a black newspaper, declared: "If this matter had transpired at Yale University where there has always been some degree of prejudice against the Negro or at any other large university in the country it would have been bad enough; but for it to have transpired at Harvard is discouraging beyond expression."[152]

The petition rested in administrative offices. The issue erupted several months later. In December 1922, Roscoe Conkling Bruce, a Harvard honor graduate of the class of 1902, applied for regular freshman accommodations on behalf of his son, then attending Phillips Exeter preparatory school. When the application arrived at the registrar's desk, he sent it on to President Lowell with the notation: "Roscoe Conkling Bruce is a *colored man*." Lowell rejected the application, explaining to Bruce that to admit a Negro to the freshman halls would be to "compel men of different races to reside together."

Bruce replied that it ill became "a great mother of culture avoidably to accentuate the consciousness of racial differences among Americans. . . . The distribution of human excellence in . . . every . . . race begins at zero and ends at infinity. . . . Even courts of law deal with men upon their ascertained merits as individuals. Shall a world-famed nursery of the humanities be less humane?" In January 1923, Lowell attended the Harvard Club in New York City, where he defended his views.

After Lowell once more wrote Bruce, Bruce replied:

> If the principle which you are applying to the present case of rooming in the same building is conceded, the day may come when it will be applied to the class, the classroom, the campus, the university itself. Of course I protest. . . . Granted that the wind just now is blowing in the direction of reaction, does it . . . behoove a great and responsible center of enlightenment to be caught, like some paltry straw, in the gust? The way to lead is not to follow.

Numerous dignitaries, including Lowell's predecessor, Charles W. Eliot, attacked the restrictive policy. In March 1923, in an action interpreted as a reversal of Lowell's policy, the Harvard Corporation resolved that "as to the capacity of the Freshmen Halls all the members of the Freshmen Class shall reside in the Freshmen Halls." Oddly enough, however, the resolution also provided that "men of the white and colored races shall not be compelled to live and eat together, nor shall any man be excluded by reason of his color." Adoption of the resolution ended public discussion of the issue. It did not change anything else at Harvard. For the next thirty years or more, black freshmen continued to be excluded from the regular freshman halls. If they wished to live on campus, they were compelled to live in Dana Palmer House or Warren House.[153]

When a student was excluded from a dormitory he had to find another place to eat. The U.S. Office of Education study of the late 1930s reported:

> On some campuses the public eating places were open to all students alike; on other campuses only certain places were open; on one campus separate booths or tables were set aside for Negro students. . . . In some instances there were almost no public eating places in the city to which the Negro students were admitted. . . . In one instance an official apologized for segregated eating places on the campus by saying that the institution would lose its out-of-state white students if the Negro students were not given separate booths.[154]

Especially galling was the exclusion of black students from restaurants in the community. This was the case in Columbus, Ohio, adjacent to the campus of Ohio State University. In Ann Arbor, Michigan, an activist student wrote: "Negro students are thrown out of restaurants in the town without the slightest move on the part of the University [of Michigan] administration to use its immense influence in favor of the rights of citizen-students paying tuition in this state-provided school."[155]

After World War II, discriminatory student housing lingered on. The old outright exclusion of black women was rescinded almost universally, but indirect segregation continued. Comer said that, at Indiana University, "the dormitories had been racially integrated a few years before, but it was still the custom to put blacks together in an otherwise integrated dormitory." At Rutgers University, "black students were automatically roomed with black students." In the immediate postwar period, CORE discovered that the University of Chicago, "through its membership in several 'neighborhood improvement associations,' actually contributed money to evict Negroes who had moved into apartments covered by restrictive covenants." In 1962, CORE took up another campaign at the

University, "charging the University with maintaining a discriminatory off-campus housing list and barring Negroes from apartment buildings it owned." After a time, the practice was ended. Into the 1960s, Northwestern University, however, recognized the right of white women students or their parents to object to their placement in a dormitory room which would be shared by a black woman student.[156]

Financial aid and employment

Whether the evidence from only two colleges was typical is difficult to say. At the University of Michigan, during 1939–1940, the 100 Negro students made up about 1 percent of total enrollment. Interviews with a number of them discovered that "employment such as assistant instructors, scholarship fellows, library assistants, store clerks, etc. in most schools are almost entirely reserved for whites."[157] At the State University of Iowa, a black student was told at the University Employment Bureau that Negroes had no chance to get jobs at the University Hospital. The head librarian told her that if she applied for a job in the library she would be treated the same as if she were a foreign student. Eleven of eighteen Negro students who worked off-campus at Iowa did porter work.[158]

The postwar expansion of higher education undoubtedly drew more than ever upon poor and minority students. But the greater gains accrued to the benefit of nonpoor and majority students, especially in the late 1960s.[159] In 1947, the President's Commission on Higher Education had pointed with alarm to the large number of intellectually gifted but poor and minority youth unable to attend college. A quarter of a century later, such young people were in college, but many were shunted into community colleges. In 1973, a panel of the College Entrance Examination Board observed that "male black students at the top achievement level are nearly three times as likely to attend a two-year college as a male white student at the same achievement level."[160]

Black students at all levels of higher education experienced very difficult financial pressures. A black alumnus said his first semester at Harvard was "a nightmare. With every dime I owned riding on my performance, and with future income already mortgaged by a large loan, I found my grades to be half D's and half F's at midterm."[161] He finally graduated with honors. A counselor of black students at Duquesne University described the intense pressures of economic need: "Always hungry, always poorly clothed, never financially solvent, always inadequate, are not conditions conducive to learning and growing academically."[162]

The black student came to bear the label "risk." As an administrative officer at Princeton explained the fate of such a student: "The financial packaging he receives reflects this risk since there is less in outright grant for scholarship and more aid in the form of loan and work-study to justify a calculated possible failure before the end of a four-year period."[163] Federal appropriations for student aid became a significant factor in the late 1960s; by 1970–1971, they reached $3 billion. These funds were of critical importance to numerous individual students, but of small benefit to many poor and minority students. As Milner notes: "A surprising portion of student aid tends to go to the middle class rather than the lower class."[164]

To black college students in the North, the presence of a nearby black community was a matter of the highest importance. There could be found housing quarters, meals, leads on possible student employment, and relaxation. Soon after John Hope, from Augusta, Georgia, entered Brown University in 1890, his life "became closely interwoven with the life of the colored community of Providence."[165] One of his favorite enjoyments was attendance at meetings of the Black Civil War Veterans. When Du Bois attended Harvard, his social life centered on the black community. Still, the college had small direct impact on black communities. Few black youngsters became students. This was true even in the case of schools located in cities of large black population. At the University of Pennsylvania, for example, the first Negro graduate is said to have entered in 1879, and both his parents were English-born; yet Philadelphia had the largest black population of any northern city, exceeded in the South only by New Orleans, Baltimore, and Washington, D.C.[166] Before the Civil War, an extensive network of private common schools for blacks had existed. The university failed to draw on the graduates of these schools. Nor did the colleges employ many blacks even in subordinate jobs. In 1935, when nearly 500,000 Negroes lived in New York City, none was employed as a teacher or a clerk in the City College of New York. There, an undergraduate group, the Summer Forum, campaigned for increased black employment. At Hunter and Brooklyn colleges, also municipal institutions, local chapters of the National Student League conducted campaigns.

Extracurricular activities

During the 1920s, intercollegiate athletics became a large-scale business enterprise. The practice, in regard to race, varied from year to year and campus to campus. Before World War I, the presence of a black player on a football team was highly novel. Numerous colleges refused to play against such teams. Yet in 1912, Purdue University failed in an effort to have the State University of Iowa bench a black footballer before a game, and the University of Nebraska resisted efforts by the University of Kansas to force the withdrawal of a black player from the former's football team. When the Missouri Valley Conference apparently joined the pressure, Nebraska resigned from the conference.[167] On the other hand,

Rutgers University benched Paul Robeson, its preeminent star, in 1916 because of demands by Washington and Lee College.[168] Three years later, when the U.S. Naval Academy objected to a Negro athlete on a University of Pennsylvania team, his teammates voted not to play without him, but Penn's athletic manager refused to permit the cancellation. By the 1930s, participation of black athletes in Big Ten football games was common, though it remained customary to bow to requests from opposing teams to bench Negroes upon demand.[169]

With rare exceptions, Negro players were excluded from intercollegiate basketball.[170] Davis, while a student in the 1920s at Kansas State College, described the response of some fellow black students when he told them he was going to attend a basketball game: "Why pay, they say, five dollars each semester to see games played in which Negro lads are barred from competing? We have men capable of playing upon some of the athletic teams if they were only given a chance to make good."[171] Both the University of Chicago and the University of Illinois excluded blacks from basketball teams, said the *Crisis* of February 1937.

Race relations in intercollegiate athletics were dominated by the intercollegiate athletic conference. In 1940 Mackey found that "there are agreements among college coaches of various sports not to use Negro athletes." Exclusion from basketball as a matter of conference policy was reported by every college that belonged to a conference. (A total of 126 colleges was contacted.) Two sports – track and boxing – were comparatively open to black athletes in conference competiton. Just about every other sport was closed. Conference discrimination against black athletes was greatest in the Midwest, especially in states bordering the South.[172]

Negroes at the State University of Iowa were barred from intramural basketball and wrestling. Some white students had threatened to abstain from sports should blacks be permitted to participate. Jenkins reports:

> The Head of the [Physical Education] Department explained
> that the purpose of the intramurals is to secure as widespread
> participation in the competition of the various sports as possible.
> If large numbers refuse to compete, this objective could not be
> attained. The University officials interviewed stated that they
> had no objection to the participation of Negro players and felt it
> unfortunate that conditions should be as they are.[173]

Black women at Iowa were permitted to participate in all intramural sports, including basketball.

Swimming was surrounded by a near-taboo against Negro women. At the University of Kansas both black women and men were excluded from the pool; they were excused from attendance on days when swimming was to be part of physical education sessions. Negro women at the University of Cincinnati were barred from swimming classes but were permitted to enroll in segregated, after-hours classes. The deepest-felt grievance of black women at the State University of Iowa was their exclusion from daytime swimming classes and their relegation to separate evening sessions. Some white women students, however, seemed not at all troubled by the prospect of an interracial swim; they often joined in at the nighttime swim sessions presumably established for blacks alone. University authorities refused persistently to permit the black women the same arrangement accorded black men – the opportunity to swim with their white peers.[174]

The advent of the civil rights movement in the 1950s swept away from northern institutions the web of restriction on the participation of black athletes in various sports. In the South, white schools began to permit black players to join teams. In 1963, the University of Texas lifted a prohibition against blacks playing on university teams. College barriers fell as professional sports teams opened up. On many college campuses, a considerable number of black students were financed by athletic scholarships, a device used by many more white than black athletes. The overall organization of college sports hinged in large part on these financial considerations. Black athletes were least advantaged in this area.

At Michigan State University, a highly sports-minded institution, black athletes were pressured by athletics counselors to specialize in physical education courses and earn a degree in that field (HPER). The special counselors, charged black athletes, were exclusively concerned with maintaining an athlete's eligibility for Big Ten competition rather than general university eligibility. One athlete said: "I wanted to be a history major. I ended up in HPER and will graduate in it now because I've got so many credits in it."[175] Black athletes graduated at only slightly more than half the rate of white athletes. Practice time infringed heavily on study time.

Black athletes suffered various forms of discrimination. Certain positions, especially quarterback on the football team and pitcher on the baseball team, were not open to blacks. It was assumed that Negro players lacked either the leadership quality or the intelligence to quarterback or pitch for a team. Coaches during the early 1960s had explicitly forbidden blacks to date white women students. Late in the decade, athletes reported that the prohibitory attitude was still in effect, but not explicitly stated.

In 1968, Michigan State's black athletes boycotted team activities, citing these grievances:[176]

1. MSU is not hiring enough Negro coaches.
2. MSU is discouraging black students from participating in certain sports, especially baseball.

3. MSU does not employ enough blacks in jobs in Jenison field-house, the intramural building, the picket office, and the ice arena.
4. There are no black trainers or doctors to treat all athletes.
5. The athletic counselor is "under undue pressure" assisting all athletes and should have a black assistant.
6. Academic counseling is designed to place blacks in courses where they will maintain eligibility. They are forced to take nonacademic courses rather than academic courses that will enable them to graduate in four years.
7. MSU has never elected a Negro cheerleader.

Two years later, at MSU, one of the eight assistant football coaches was black, one of three assistant basketball coaches, one of three assistant track coaches, and one of four trainers. Two blacks were cheerleaders, and more blacks were employed in athletic facilities. The grievances on academic matters were apparently not remedied.

In 1972, black athletes in the Big Ten Conference of universities organized a protest to the conference, embodying grievances common to all ten campuses. "Big Ten intercollegiate athletics," charged the complainants, "has failed to provide the majority of black athletes with even an education." Universities in the conference, it was held, failed to employ qualified blacks:

> The Big Ten universities currently employ forty officials in football and thirty-six officials in basketball. Of these, only two – one in football and one in basketball are black, yet black athletes constitute from thirty to sixty percent of the players in these sports. . . . In eight Big Ten schools, only one black was found in an assistant director role. No other blacks were found in any other administrative or managerial position.[177]

Black athletes' protests in many universities brought prompt retaliation by university authorities, especially in the shape of cancellation of athletic scholarships.

"The attitude of the Northern institution toward the Negro student," wrote Du Bois in 1926, "is one which varies from tolerance to active hostility."[178] This was descriptive of the area of social activities on the campus. Administrators tended toward greater defensiveness in discussing this area and resorted frequently to doctrines of institutional neutrality. President John E. McGilvrey of Normal College in Kent, Ohio – the predecessor of Kent State University – probably was highly representative of university administrators when he explained in 1927:

> Colored students . . . are welcomed to all official social functions of the college, such as the President's reception, the faculty re-

ception to the students and the college receptions at the close of the year. Beyond this the college would not wish or undertake to dictate to either white or colored students in *student* social activities. . . . We would not like to require either group to admit the other to their respective social functions, dances, etc., for no benefit would likely result.[179]

In another institution, "the Dean of Men . . . stated that colored students are welcome to the university and to all that it offers, but that they must not expect the University to solve the race problem."[180]

Yet characteristically, northern colleges gave active support to the continuation of anti-Negro student policies. Positive statements and actions by administrative officers and functionaries most often perpetuated dominant campus sentiments and practices. Through the interplay of attitude and authority, the black student was constantly reminded – if he could ever forget – that he was "something of an 'outsider' on the northern college campus."[181]

At times, black students found color prejudice pursuing them into the most arcane precincts. Thus, in an intercollegiate fruit-judging contest sponsored by a state horticultural society, William Cain, a Negro, belonged to the team from Iowa State College, Ames. The fruit-judgers from the University of Missouri withdrew in protest. Thereupon, Iowa defeated the University of Nebraska team.[182]

At the University of Chicago, Negroes were not permitted to enter the Reynolds Club, the university's center for organized student activities, until 1924. A decade or so later, Negro students at the University of Illinois were excluded from the student union building. At Northwestern University, a black student was refused admission to the university bathing beach. Negro students at the University of Kansas were barred from all official student social events such as parties, proms, and dances. At Oberlin during the 1930s, black students could not participate in dramatic presentations "except for roles where they played the maid or the butler." Instances were numerous where black students had bought tickets for a campus social event or simply sought entry as a matter of right, and had been excluded. In one case, white students who objected to having several Negro students at the junior prom got the dean of men to persuade the students that they ought not to attend.[183]

In 1949, Langston Hughes put the problem before Jess B. Simple: Should your nephew Delbert go to a black or a white college for his medical education? Simple advised:

> If you get to be a doctor, you are going to doctor *me*. I am black. Now, how can you doctor me if you don't know me? . . . No, I will tell Delbert not to go to no white school and be snubbed when he asks a girl for a dance, and be barred out of the hotels

where his football team stays – no matter how smart he gets in the head. Fact is, I cares more about Delbert's heart, anyhow, than I do his head.[184]

The advent of more Negro students modified the traditional isolation they suffered on white campuses. But Simple was probably not greatly encouraged.

During the early 1950s at Indiana University, a black alumnus recalled: "One of the things wrong at Indiana was that, officially, all activities were open to all students. Some of us felt in our hearts that we were sometimes just being tolerated, but that couldn't be proved. . . . The uncalled for, ludicrous and senseless acts of racism are the memories that gnaw at my gut."[185] A decade later, many black students at Indiana reported to a researcher that "Indiana University's official policy on services and facilities differed from its practice." Others said they felt isolated from general campus life.[186] While old exclusions had disappeared (housing, especially), a general sense of exclusion remained. The situation on campus appeared to be that blacks were strangers to whites. In fact, the reverse was nearer the truth.

In 1970, Bennett studied early interracial experiences of black and white residents in thirteen dormitories of Indiana University. He located 94 blacks and 432 whites whose homes were in Marion County (Indianapolis), Indiana. He concentrated on two-block areas. Blacks, Bennett found, were much more likely to have interracial experiences because their housing and elementary schooling had been considerably less homogeneous than those of white dormitory-mates. Blacks reported more interracial friendships than whites.[187] In short, black students were more experienced than whites in living in a nonsegregated environment. Yet most investigative efforts explored adjustment problems of black rather than white students on campus.

Old-fashioned discrimination did not altogether disappear. Exclusion of blacks from fraternities was practiced into the 1960s, for example, at the University of Illinois and Rutgers University. The same was true at the University of Texas until 1967.[188]

During the early years of initial desegregation in southern white universities, black students had experiences quite similar to those in the North. During 1960, 110 Negro students in a total of twenty-three predominantly white institutions were interviewed. Students from one group of these schools reported "not only did they attend formal meetings, lectures, and special events, but they . . . also took an active part in informal and social affairs." Further probing, however, yielded the following report:

> As to more subtle matters, the Negro students interviewed in
> most instances believed that they were not accepted on their

individual merit either by the administration or the general student body. The reports of many of the students on the classroom attitude of the instructors and the majority-group students indicate that the Negro student at a predominantly white college continues to feel that he is thought of as different, or as an outsider.[189]

The first two black students enrolled at the University of Georgia suffered virtual exclusion from all but classroom activities. A reporter wrote: "As Hamilton [Holmes] began his final ten-week quarter at Georgia, he had never eaten in a university dining hall, studied in the library, used the gymnasium, or entered the snack bar. He had no white friends outside the classroom. No white student had ever visited him, and he had never visited one of them."[190] At the University of Arkansas law school, on the other hand, white students took the initiative in arranging for the removal of a wooden railing built to contain a black student in the classroom.[191]

In Tennessee, from 1963 to 1965, 929 black undergraduates entered seven formerly white state institutions; 306 graduate students attended five previously all-white graduate schools.[192] Nearly nine out of ten black graduate students were only part-time students; more than six out of ten were working for graduate degrees in education. The undergraduates had a most restricted existence; none was allowed in fraternities or sororities and very few were allowed to live in dormitories. Only about one-third participated in any extracurricular activities.[193] In response to a query whether they felt they were accepted by white students, 84 percent replied affirmatively; of these, 53.6 percent said they were not excluded from normal extracurricular activities such as clubs and fraternities, but the remaining 46.4 percent indicated a negative or undecided attitude. A sizable minority of black graduate students (28 percent) pointed out teachers' negative attitudes toward them.

By 1972, neither in the North nor the South were interracial campuses according black students many opportunities for equality of treatment in the area of social activities. In a study of four Upstate New York colleges, where black enrollment averaged 2 percent, similar conditions existed as did contemporaneously at four Tennessee institutions: University of the South, University of Tennessee at Knoxville, University of Tennessee at Chattanooga, and Vanderbilt University. At the Chattanooga campus, Ernest Varner, president of the Black Student Association, summarized the lack of social relations between black and white students: "The only way we meet is in class or in the streets." Informal social relations were at the barest minimum. The situation seemed no different at the University of the South, where 0.4 percent of the students were black, than at the University of Tennessee at Chattanooga, where the figure was 7.9 percent.[194]

Black student organizations

Before the 1960s, fraternities and sororities were the primary form of black student organization on predominantly white campuses. They were the only socially acceptable form of black collective identity on these campuses and a refuge from extensive white discrimination. On small campuses, where only single or pairs of black students found themselves, too few for a fraternity, a severe personal crisis might ensue. Ballard recalls how he and "another black had the misfortune to become the first of our race to enter Kenyon College. . . . Social life revolved around the fraternities, from which we Blacks were automatically excluded. . . . The only surcease from this eight-semester social ordeal for the three of us who remained came when the Black community in a nearby town provided us with Black warmth, food, and emotional support."[195] According to Comer, at Indiana University during the early 1950s: "Most black students spoke to each other as we crossed the campus, even to those who were strangers. We needed group support. When somebody didn't speak or preferred 'not to identify,' he was a marked man, scorned for trying to be white."[196] A decade later, an alumnus of Washington University in Saint Louis, described a very different practice: "I can recall numerous instances in the early 60's when I would encounter other black students on the paths of Washington University and many would either look the other way or hold their heads down and not speak." At Harvard, until the mid-1960s, "there was . . . a *dispersal* of the small number of Negro students throughout the nooks and crannies of Harvard College." Another source, however, referring to blacks who graduated from Harvard during the same years, has written that "many of them are highly critical and more than a little bitter about the racism they encountered."[197]

Black students often sought to lose themselves. In interracial gatherings of college students in the Boston area, for example, "they did not dare to be noisy, to play the music of their choice, or to appear in any way not to share the same styles and appreciation of arts enjoyed by white students." Socially, black students closely approximated the social position of their white peers. During 1961–1966, blacks in private New England colleges "represented largely the managerial and professional segments of the black population." A relative failure to participate in the civil rights movement was another aspect of Negro students' efforts to moderate their black identity. "From the 1962–63 school year to the present," Clark wrote in 1966, "there has not been one Negro active in the Columbia. [University] chapter of CORE for more than a week." All in all, black students in the private schools incorporated within themselves the characteristic features of these schools; they were colorless, competent, and quietistic. Even when blacks organized into a Negro Students Association, as they did at San Francisco State College before 1965, their motivation was social. Often, wherever black students were among the first on campus, they tended to interpret their difficulties as "specific and individual" rather than as reflecting any shortcomings of the university.[198]

Desegregation in higher education after Brown II

Brown II was handed down in May 1955. During the next year and a half it formed the basis for allowing Negroes to attend four heretofore all-white postsecondary schools in Texas: North Texas State College, Texas Western College, Texarkana Junior College, and Lamar College of Technology. In 1955, a federal district court in North Carolina ruled that *Brown* applied to colleges as well as primary schools; the following year, the U.S. Supreme Court affirmed the decision. In 1956 the state higher educational institutions of Tennessee were held to be in violation of *Brown* and were ordered to desegregate. Through one ruse or another, states such as North Carolina and Tennessee were able to avoid desegregation of their higher educational system.[199]

Except for occasional spectacular attempts by isolated individuals to enroll in a Deep South university, the issue of applying *Brown* to public higher education disappeared from public view. Segregated public higher education became a privileged enclave, beyond the effective reach of constitutional doctrine. Passage of the 1964 Civil Rights Act created a new basis for action against segregated schools. This measure brought a significant increase in desegregation of the common schools as school districts sought to avoid a cutoff of federal funds. The same technique was not used in higher education.

In 1968, however, U.S. District Judge Frank Gray, Jr., found the State of Tennessee to be operating a racially discriminatory system of public higher education. He ordered the drawing-up of a statewide desegregation plan.[200] The Gray ruling rekindled interest in the issue. The director of the Office for Civil Rights (OCR), Mrs. Ruby Martin, explored ways of applying the Civil Rights Act to segregated university systems. Institutions of higher education that segregated black students were notified that they were endangering federal grants. Political pressure was felt immediately by enforcement officials. As one of them wrote: "Fred LaRue, a White House Assistant from Mississippi, paid a visit to express his – or rather Senator John Stennis's – concern over the issue of desegregating college dormitories in Mississippi, a request recently made by our Atlanta Office."[201] From January 1969 to February 1970, OCR notified ten states that they were operating segregated systems of higher education: Louisiana, Mississippi, Oklahoma, North Carolina, Florida, Arkansas, Pennsylvania, Georgia, Maryland, and Virginia. In these states most blacks were attending only a few colleges; whites were concentrated at the others. Each state was called upon to prepare a statewide desegregation plan.

Louisiana

Southern University was created as a Negro state normal school in 1880. Two years later it was reorganized. A state constitutional amendment set a $10,000 per year ceiling on state appropriations. Only in 1919 was it removed. In 1923–1924, Southern graduated its first two collegiate-level students. In 1956, when Negro students began applying for entrance into Louisiana State University in New Orleans (LSU-NO), the state legislature established a branch of Southern in the city (SUNO). As the chairman of the state senate committee on higher education later explained: "SUNO was started and operated in New Orleans as a means of preventing in a quiet manner the attendance of Negroes at LSU-NO."[202] This purpose was well understood in the black community. H. Rap Brown, graduate of SUNO and militant black leader, reflected: "I lived near Louisiana State University and I could see this big fine school with modern buildings and it was for whites. Then there was Southern University, which was about to fall in and that was for the niggers. And when I compared the two, the message that the white man was trying to get across was obvious."[203] By every standard measure of educational quality, Southern University was profoundly inferior to the state university, as it was designed to be.

By 1970, Southern enrolled 8,237 black students, making it the largest center of black collegiate enrollment in the United States. Within the black community especially, however, there was deep dissatisfaction with SUNO. SUNO students, in a demonstrative action during 1969 against the inadequacies of their school, marched over to LSU-NO and demanded the right to register there. This symbolic ceremony, participated in by from 200 to 600 SUNO students, was only one aspect of the bitter feelings about the use of police force to put down SUNO student protests. Several days after the demonstration, the NAACP advocated a merger of SUNO and LSU-NO "with certain provisions such as equal consideration for the retention of administrators and faculty." A month later, the Urban League of Greater New Orleans released a statement, declaring: "Southern University New Orleans is a damn lousy school. . . . Rather than to continue to play games and attempt to fool people, SUNO should be merged with LSU-NO . . . and hopefully make it possible for everybody to get a decent education in a 20th century university, versus a 19th century glorified high school." Black leaders called on federal authorities to enforce the Civil Rights Act against state authorities.[204]

In the fall of 1969, the OCR, then headed by Leon Panetta, agreed to seek action by a meeting in Baton Rouge with state officials, including the governor. The meeting consisted of fencing and feinting and little more.

After it ended, the principal spokesman of the state, Theo Cangelosi, invited Panetta and others to his home for a reception. At the affair, Panetta recalled:

> When the conversation turned back to higher education desegregation, Cangelosi revealed the hand that was being played.
> "Leon, we've got you over a barrel and you know it. . . . If you keep pushing, we'll submit a [desegregation] plan that will provide for the closing of Southern . . . and you'll have the blacks all over you. . . . Yep, it'll desegregate all right, but you and I know it would never happen." I smiled politely, not really knowing what to say in response. "So the key is don't push too hard," Cangelosi closed.[205]

Several months later, in February 1970, Panetta was forced to resign. After his departure, the prospects of desegregation in Louisiana faded away. The Nixon administration dropped the entire effort in the other nine states as well.

In 1971, Southern was shaken by new student protests against the school's inadequate educational programs, dictatorial administrative methods, and lack of effective faculty and student government. The movement continued well into 1972. The main campus at Baton Rouge was closed, then reopened. In November, SUNO was occupied by police, who had been invited by the college administration. At Baton Rouge there were forebodings of an armed attack: "On the morning of the ninth [of November] over 1,500 students, faculty, parents, and Black members of the State legislature formed a human ring around the building."[206] One week later, police shot and killed two Southern students. An official state inquiry into the deaths concluded: "Leonard Brown and Denver Smith were shot as they were running away. . . . They were not under arrest and were not resisting arrest and were not armed. . . . There was no justification in law enforcement for their being shot."[207] Other investigations reached similar conclusions.

On the day of the Southern killings, November 16, 1972, a federal district court in Washington, D.C., ruled in *Adams* v. *Richardson* that the U.S. Department of Health, Education, and Welfare must resume its college desegregation program. In Louisiana, black support for joining SUNO and LSU-NO remained high. Among students, more opposition was heard. A group of SUNO students stated that "while it is true that a merger would bring on five times as much physical plant for SUNO students, it would also subject us to five times the bureaucracy, five times as much racism, and five times as much irrelevancy." The state NAACP renewed its support for merging "racially indentifiable colleges and universities within close proximity." It called also for parity of racial representation on all higher educational governing bodies and protection for the rights of black administrators, teachers, and students in any merger.[208]

State authorities rejected any plan for desegregating the black colleges, for that would require assignment of some white students from LSU-NO to SUNO. Governor Edwin W. Edwards told an interviewer frankly:

> Let me just put it on the table and say something that I know is going to get me in trouble. The only justification for Southern and Grambling is to have an all-black institution. If the HEW and the federal courts insist that we make a chocolate milk faculty out of LSU and Southern and Grambling and [Louisiana Tech at] Ruston, then there's no longer justification for maintaining both institutions.[209]

State policy remained unchanged since the views put forward by Cangelosi four years earlier. The state was willing to countenance low quality colleges for blacks. Should it be pressed to lighten the dark and darken the light at each college, the state preferred to eliminate the black colleges altogether. Such a move would mean common facilities for all public college students in the state, but the state counted on black opposition to the closing of Southern and Grambling.

Florida

Florida Agricultural and Mechanical University was created in 1887 as a state normal school for Negroes and underwent several name changes. From 1921 to 1926, it awarded a total of thirty-nine bachelor's degrees. A federal survey in 1928 concluded that "the institution has good opportunity of developing into an excellent State college for Negroes." In the following years, the state legislature was far more concerned with keeping the college Negro than improving it. A law school had been organized in 1949 at FAMU in order to keep Negroes out of the law school at the University of Florida. Between 1953 and 1966, the FAMU law school graduated fifty students; the state's other three law schools produced another one Negro student during the same years. In 1966, the FAMU law school was closed. Four years later, the law school of the University of Florida enrolled only 6 blacks out of a total of 889 students.[210]

FAMU, as a virtually all-black institution, served primarily youths of poor families (Table 44). The problem of improving the quality of education at FAMU became entangled with the racial character of the institute. Because FAMU was only 3 miles away from nearly all-white Florida State University, in Tallahassee, the issue of a merger came up often. The chairman of the state board of regents reportedly held "that until secondary education for Negroes in Florida improved to a point where all high school graduates had comparable ability to pass entrance tests at state

Table 44. *Family income class of students at Florida Agricultural and Mechanical University and at all other state universities*

Family income class ($)	Percent of FAMU students in income class	Percent of students in all other state universities in income class
Under 4,999	59.8	14.8
5,000–9,999	30.7	41.5
10,000–19,999	9.5	43.7
20,000 and over	9.9	7.9

Source: Data from Douglas M. Windham, *Education, Equality, and Income Redistribution: A Study of Public Higher Education* (Lexington, Mass.: Heath Lexington Books, 1970), pp. 46–47.

universities, it was important to have A&M." In 1969, the new president of FAMU, Benjamin Perry, agreed, explaining that the university should remain separate "as long as the attitude [of the general community] is one of toleration rather than acceptance of blacks, as long as the attitude is tokenism rather than quality, as long as there's still a gap in the educational preparation of a discernible segment of the population."[211]

Academic achievement scores of Florida elementary and high school students did not evidence any general upward movement. The state legislature added to the problem of FAMU by persisting in a pattern of discriminatory financing of state universities. In 1971 FAMU charged that while it accounted for 6.2 percent of the state's public university enrollment, it received only 3.1 percent of appropriations. In addition, legislative bodies attempted to prevent any state university from easing admission standards to permit more Negro students to enroll. In order to make FAMU more attractive to black students, the state legislature financed a greatly strengthened pharmacy program. Its graduates had a virtual passport to small entrepreneurship. Throughout Florida, the pharmacist is one of the state's most ubiquitous businessmen. Other new programs were announced.[212] The net effect of the improvements was to strengthen the existing appeal of FAMU for blacks rather than to exercise a new attraction to whites. This was reminiscent of developments during the *Gaines* era.

Arkansas

In January 1969, OCR notified the state of Arkansas that it must desegregate public higher education. Black students were concentrated, as they had been since the 1870s, in the state's sole public black college – Arkansas AM&N. The school's president, Lawrence Davis, did not oppose merger in one form or another. OCR had discussed redistributing various curricula among the state's colleges and universities. Davis noted, however:

> Even considering the example of economy HEW pointed up as possible as a result of cooperation between AM and N College and one other institution, since no mention was made [by OCR] of any desirability of giving AM and N exclusive responsibility in any education area nor of transferring or reducing the curricula of any other institution, there is no reliable guarantee that white students would attend AM and N College in larger numbers. On first glance, it appears that the only thing assured is that integration would be fostered at the expense of AM and N College and that its academic status would be gradually diminished and finally phased out.[213]

The latter remark referred to a further OCR suggestion that AM&N specialize in technical programs and that its education programs be transferred to a predominantly white institution.

The head of OCR reported on a conference with president Davis:

> Most of the technical programs were two-year programs, while those in education ran four years. Were we trying to turn the black college into a two-year school? "Why emasculate our college in favor of another?" he asked, and the way he put it, we should have talked first of exchanging four-year curricular for other four-year programs.[214]

This confession confirmed the fears of many blacks that even friendly federal moves were not thoroughly thought out.

Unlike Louisiana and Florida, where dominant state powers opposed a black-white college merger, in Arkansas the legislature moved quickly toward a merger. In 1971, a bill was hurried into law (Act 512) that prescribed general conditions for a merger. The actual merger was soon directed by state officials. A state hearing was held to consider objections. Black leaders who testified were critical, not of the proposed merger, but of the fact that the previous year's legislation had been drawn up without black counsel. The state NAACP called for a university system in which all units – to include every institution, and not only AM&N – would play an equal part. An AM&N faculty member, Dr. Albert Baxter, told the hearing: "I support integration and change but I oppose change when only black people are being changed."[215]

As merger talk proceeded, various black community forces adopted their own positions. Leading a large delegation of AM&N students to the state capital, Tomie McCall, president of the student body, addressed the

House and Senate separately. He warned against repeating the inequities of much of "so-called integration" in the public schools where black students were mistreated, black teachers fired, and black administrators shifted to lesser positions. He told the legislators: "If there is going to be integration, let there be integration. If there is going to be a merger, let there be a merger, but not an absorption or a takeover."[216] Earlier, leading black lawyer John W. Walker insisted that merger involved an exchange of powers. If one party dictated the terms and reserved all effective powers, that was absorption, not merger. When state university officials failed to move, Walker filed suit, claiming the forthcoming absorption denied equal protection to black students, faculty, and staff. He asked, among other things, for a plan to "excise all vestiges of segregation from within the named colleges and their auxiliary institutions . . . substantial inclusion of black administrators and faculty members into each state institution of higher learning . . . [and a] unitary, nonracial salary schedule for all state universities."[217] Six weeks later, AM&N became a unit of the University of Arkansas.

Pennsylvania

In 1969, Pennsylvania became the only northern state cited by OCR as maintaining a segregated system of state higher education. In September 1968, "among 50,387 undergraduates at Pennsylvania's thirteen predominantly white state colleges . . . only 371 – or 0.71 percent – were Negro."[218] On the other hand, the enrollment of Cheyney State College was 85 percent Negro. Such a scale of disproportion closely resembled, if it did not in cases exceed, the situation in some southern states. The concentration of black students was the key.

From 1837 to 1914, the present Cheyney existed as the Institute for Colored Youth. In 1914 it became the Cheyney Training School for Teachers; in 1932, a state college. From 1914 onward, the school received state teacher-training funds. All its students were black and they found employment only in black common schools. In 1920, Cheyney asked the state superintendent of public instruction to issue teaching certificates to Cheyney graduates. "We shall be willing to issue special certificates to the graduates of your institution," replied the superintendent, "authorizing them to teach in schools in the State which are maintained for colored children."[219] After protests, it was agreed to grant certificates without restriction of race. Nevertheless, Cheyney's graduates continued to teach black children only.

The school's board of managers well knew the racial realities of Pennsylvania. Under the Normal School Act of 1854, the state had been divided into thirteen districts, a school to be located in each one. In 1913, the last of the thirteen – West Chester Normal – was purchased by the state. It was located only 8 miles from Cheyney. In 1914, the state asked the legislature to permit Cheyney to become a fourteenth teachers' college; the request was granted. Why two teachers' colleges were needed in such proximity was not explained. A likely explanation lay in a minute of a meeting of the Cheyney Board of Managers for November 19, 1918: "There is no normal school in Pennsylvania where Negroes are really welcomed and there is danger that our state may fall behind if something cannot be done to change the situation."[220] State authorities had created one normal school where Negroes *were* welcomed and at the same time preserved the predominantly white character of the other colleges.

For years, Cheyney represented the almost exclusive chance for a black student to achieve a state-supported higher education. In 1940, a survey of forty-seven colleges in the state found that only seventy-five Negro students were attending a higher institution other than Cheyney or private Lincoln University.[221] Even fewer than this small number attended public colleges outside Cheyney. The thirteen state colleges, which in 1968 enrolled so very few Negro students, were the renamed old state teachers' colleges authorized under the 1854 law.

The prospect of desegregation of higher education did not engage the public concern of black communities in the state. In 1969, the Pennsylvania Department of Education established a desegregation goal for thirteen state colleges; its goal for 1975 was set at 10 percent black enrollment. Black enrollment in 1968 was 0.71 percent; in 1971, it rose to 2.8 percent.[222]

Other states

Historical patterns of discrimination had everywhere created racially distinguishable colleges of greatly differing quality. The movement to desegregate these structures arose in a number of states.

In Alabama, a three-judge federal court directed the desegregation of forty-four state-operated community colleges and trade schools. Each school was to assure that Negroes held at least 25 percent of all teaching and staff positions. Desegregation moves in Georgia arose from two sources: the OCR and federal courts. In response to the former, the state university system in 1973 prepared a seven-year plan at the end of which the numerical enrollment gap between black and white would have grown from 91,873 in 1972 to 102,143 in 1979. The percentage of black students, however, was scheduled to rise from 5.9 to 12.6. Three historically black colleges – Fort Valley, Savannah, and Albany – were to be retained. A federal court in 1973, however, directed the state board of regents to desegregate Fort Valley because it was academically inferior to other state colleges. The suit had been brought by white residents of Fort Valley, Georgia, and two white faculty members, who charged that "the college was a 'diploma mill' maintained by the regents to keep academically poor blacks out of white colleges." Dr. Benjamin Mays, president emeritus of Morehouse College, commented publicly: "They state bluntly and plainly that Fort Valley is not good enough for white students to enroll there. Of course, this may be true, certainly when compared with Georgia Tech and the University of Georgia. It has to be true since all black-supported institutions have been shortchanged from the beginning." He opposed desegregation, however, if it meant raising standards at the expense of black representation.[223]

In Tennessee, the federal court's 1968 requirement of desegregated state higher education had not been implemented five years later. The immediate issue of the suit involved two state institutions in Nashville: predominantly black Tennessee State University and predominantly white University of Tennessee at Nashville. The state seemed intent on strengthening UT-N until it completely overshadowed TSU; the former was started in 1947; the latter, in 1912. Repeated moves strengthened UT-N, even though the state was obliged by OCR in 1969 to develop a statewide desegregation plan. A public statement of TSU faculty noted that West Virginia, Missouri, and Kentucky had desegregated their black public colleges "by upgrading those institutions, rather than bringing in a mainly white school for white students who don't want to integrate."[224] The chancellor of UT-N described TSU as a "dying institution" and accused its students of wanting to retain TSU as a black school.[225] This was contradicted by an earlier public statement by the TSU Student Council and Faculty Senate: "It is our wish to be the state university in Nashville, to which all interested persons might go for their educational needs. It is not our desire to limit our services to black citizens, as some may suppose."[226] The state continued proposing to retain both TSU and UT-N.

In Texas, the issue arose of merging predominantly black Texas Southern University with the predominantly white University of Houston. A quarter century after TSU opened, Heman Sweatt, the black plaintiff whose case led to the creation of the college, was severely critical of a merger:

> I don't want to see it absorbed by people who don't understand
> black students or their needs. . . . [During the 1940's I spent
> four years on my case] because I believed in integration. . . .
> But I don't believe in it today, not in the prostituted form
> we've had. Not when it's based on us giving up everything
> so that black institutions can be absorbed and controlled by
> people who don't understand what they are all about.[227]

Within a year, students at the law school of TSU boycotted the school, protesting "insufficient facilities." The dean supported their action. A teacher said TSU students saw the law school of nearby University of Houston as a desirable standard. The entire plant of TSU reflected a similar inadequacy.

Black colleges throughout Texas continued to exhibit the traditional gap. A newspaper reporter visited black Prairie View A&M College, a unit of predominantly white Texas A&M, 60 miles away. The contrast, he found, permeated even small aspects of campus life: "I noticed the non-existence of televisions in the lobbies of the student union and the dormitories. Whereas at Texas A. and M. and the U. H., color TV's are taken for granted."[228]

Desegregation of black colleges

At the July 1973 national convention of the NAACP, a bitter debate revolved around a resolution on desegregation in higher education. Originally, the resolution stressed the value of maintaining predominantly black colleges for black pride. On the floor, the resolution was changed. As Executive Secretary Roy Wilkins described it:

> The delegates passed a resolution which was very clear in calling for the joining of white and black state-supported colleges. The resolution carefully refrained from commenting on the black private college situation. Public desegregation is the objective. The NAACP delegates quite correctly give priority to state-supported schools, for these represent public policy.[229]

It was the first time NAACP had grasped the issue of higher education so frontally.

For several months before the NAACP convention, an intense discussion on the issue had ensued in many black communities. In April 1973, at a National Black College Conference in Greensboro, North Carolina, attended by 320 students from more than sixty-five schools, three reasons were cited for the movement to merge black colleges into white institutions:[230]

> 1. Black campuses have become centers of militant political action and thus "a clear and present danger to the tranquility of the American status quo."
> 2. New industries in the South need stable race relations in order to assure smooth and profitable operations.
> 3. Southern legislators would like to take over new black college facilities for the use of white students.

This mode of analysis was carried further by McWorter, who contended that propertied sectors of the black population were linked, in a dependent relationship, with one or another ruling group of whites. With specific reference to Southern University, he held that the black middle class in Louisiana saw its political and economic interest in maintaining the existing situation at Southern. Not even discussing desegregation, by omission he regarded it as a secondary question. Instead, he endorsed the goal of Students United, a student group at Southern, "to transform the present educational system so that it will aid in the building of a more humane society."[231]

Another critical voice against desegregation of black colleges was the National Association for Equal Opportunities in Higher Education, consisting of presidents of black colleges. It favored desegregation of predominantly white colleges. When, early in 1973, a federal court issued a final order on desegregating state colleges in ten states, the NAEOHE objected to "predominantly black colleges . . . being viewed as segregated and discriminatory on the basis of race." It was the white colleges that needed desegregation. "The problems of blacks in access to higher education are related to discriminatory patterns in majority white institutions, not majority black institutions."[232] An official of the group asked: "When has any predominantly black college been found guilty of practicing a biased admissions or hiring policy?"

Control of and rebellion among black students

Traditionally, students in black colleges had been subjected to a severe regimen and close scrutiny of personal conduct. Both were aspects of white control of their institutions. Located, as so many black colleges were, in a predominantly white countryside or town, their students were under an eternal watch. Being on one's best behavior was interpreted by black college administrators as meaning self-subjection to quasi-military regulation. Political orthodoxy was not less highly valued by dominant white society. An alumnus of Morehouse College said only a course or two in philosophy were offered around World War I because "if students were exposed to the creative process which causes them to raise profound questions about meanings and to seek answers, they may go on to raise questions about the structure of the institution which made it possible for them to get their college education. . . . The total issue involving the segregated schools in our society would have to be dealt with."[233] Davis observed: "Every effort is made to teach servility and pacificism."[234]

At Tuskegee, not untypically, "the faculty looked down on the students as ignorant sharecroppers." At Fisk, during the 1920s, Du Bois, a famed alumnus, charged, "the [white] president and most of the white teachers have no confidence in their students, no respect or hope for the Negro race and are treating the students with suspicion and governing them by fear."[235]

Despite efforts at pacification, the 1920s were years of rebellion by black students. Among the campuses affected – some more than once or even twice – were Livingstone College, Hampton Institute, Fisk University, Howard University, Lincoln University, Shaw University, Johnson C. Smith University, Kittrell College, Saint Augustine's College, Knoxville College, and Wilberforce University.[236] Here and there, students called for increased academic requirements. Many protests were couched in terms of greater student rights in college governance or the end of specific galling personal regulations, in the context of the customary authoritarianism of the black campus and despite the steady gaze of white society. Even on campuses, however, where student docility and quietism were hallmarks, the 1920s saw changes. At Hampton, once regarded in such lights, student strikes announced a new day. Yet as a whole the campus encounters were preliminary and tentative. On virtually all campuses, the old order persisted.

At Lincoln University in Pennsylvania, the young poet Langston Hughes was shaken by the contrast of an all-white administration and faculty and an all-black student body. "Between faculty and students," he wrote, "there were practically no social or comradely relations of any kind." The college board of trustees had repeatedly rejected efforts to place any blacks in their midst or on the faculty. Hughes conducted a public opinion survey among his classmates and discovered there was general acceptance of an exclusively white faculty: "The reasons given were various: That Lincoln was supported by 'white' philanthropy, therefore whites should run the college; that favoritism and unfairness would result on the part of Negro teachers toward the students; that there were not enough Negro teachers available; and that things were all right as they were, so why change?" Hughes was shocked and said the results demonstrated an "open belief [by students] in their own inferiority."[237]

In 1932, Hughes, having graduated from Lincoln and now a well-known literary figure, made a lecture tour of some fifty black colleges and high schools. "To set foot on dozens of Negro campuses," he wrote, "is like going back to mid-Victorian England, or Massachusetts in the days of the witch-burning Puritans." Playing cards, dancing, and smoking were forbidden. Tuskegee maintained "a library that censors all books on race problems and economics to see that no volumes 'too radical' get to the students." Academic freedom had only a slight existence: "Freedom of expression for teachers in most Negro schools . . . is more or less unknown." Hughes saw only one way out: "I see no hope for a new spirit today in the majority of the Negro schools of the South unless the students themselves put it there." He regarded acquiescence to the color line as the root cause of campus quietism. Many of the colleges, he complained, "are doing their best to produce spineless Uncle Toms, uninformed, and full of mental and moral evasions."[238]

Until the 1930s, representatives of the NAACP were unwelcome on black campuses. Colleges headed by white presidents were especially reluctant to permit them. Pickens, a long-time field agent of the national NAACP, noted in 1937 that "the 'bravest' colored schools . . . proved to be the private colleges headed by all-Negro faculties, where the president was of good courage." As for colleges headed by reluctant whites, Pickens wrote acerbically: "The white head of a Negro public school [i.e., college] in the South does not try to influence the speech of a stranger; he prevents it. He invites only those who can compress the most words into the fewest ideas."[239] (Pickens's latter comment undoubtedly applied to numerous white colleges as well.)

Ultimate reform required an independent capacity to finance the black colleges and a protective frame of political control around them. Lacking both, the rebels could only hope to modify slightly the white dominion over the black colleges. As education improved at some of the colleges, the impetus for broader protests was stemmed.

The new spirit of independence and criticism was short-lived. During the 1960s, however, black college students trod where their predecessors dared not: they attacked the basic institutions of racial segregation off the campus. They boldly left "the compound."[240] In the process, they completely altered the shape and pace of the national civil rights movement and began a process of changing the character of black higher education in the South.

The entire region was swept by black student protest. In 1960, students from North Carolina A&T College sat in at a Woolworth's store in Greensboro. Within days, a movement sprang up. Within 90 miles of Greensboro were ten black colleges, a tenth of the total in the South. All became part of the protest. At Shaw University, a student leader recalled the first sit-in: "We began to think about it, and the more we thought the more we saw ourselves in relation to it." At Alabama State University, another student described a similar process: "When we discovered that the kids in Greensboro had made a move, we felt we were obligated to show our hand. So a few of us got together and decided we would try to organize a little student movement."[241]

About one out of four black college students in the South participated in the sit-in movement during 1960–1961. Graduates of black colleges in the class of 1964 were found by Fichter to be "almost seven times (33 percent) as likely as white students (5 percent) to report that they had participated in campus movements for civil rights for minorities."[242]

Activism was greatest among students on private college campuses whose families were comparatively middle class in status.[243] Yet the movement was neither composed nor led by social elites. And over the decade of the 1960s, both public and private colleges played equally indispensable roles. The very breadth of the movement tended to cloak important characteristics of individual colleges.

North Carolina A&T, for example, was very much a poor man's college. Since it was public, one might expect the hand of the state government to lay heavily over its affairs. However, the college had established a certain independence. As early as 1937, A&T students had boycotted the town movie house for excising scenes using Negro actors; in 1955, they had booed Governor Hodges three times when he used the word *nigra*. Unlike the situation at other black colleges, some eighty student organizations were nearly completely controlled by students. Tuskegee Institute, which had begun under the most modest circumstances, by the 1960s had become a predominantly middle-class school. "Students at Tuskegee Institute," according to a student leader Ernest Stephens, "are told that they must learn to project the Tuskegee image – a very dignified, refined type thing." A Tuskegee alumna commented sardonically that "the middle-class group in Tuskegee has a very, very paternalistic attitude toward the non-middle-class group who work in their homes. The whole thing is a parody of white society." Yet under the press of events, Tuskegee became the scene of a spirited student protest movement.[244]

At Howard University, the birthplace of the legal assault on school segregation during the 1950s, students took little part in the burgeoning civil rights movement during the early 1960s. One observer said, because they were "middle class in origin, steeped in Greek organizational protest," he thought that "a paternalistic administration contributed to this atmosphere by strictly regulating campus groups, while denying Howard students the rights which many white institutions had recognized for decades."[245] In 1966 and 1967, the movement for black power took strong hold at Howard.

The student movement against segregation met with rising success in the fields of voting and public accommodations; yet a plateau was quickly reached, and by 1966 a certain pessimism developed. On numerous campuses, student protest was becalmed as students turned back to their books. Another contingent of students, however, developed new directions of protest. While the group bore the label of black power, it showed a growing disillusionment with nonviolent protest and a rejection of cooperation with whites; it stressed group pride and cohesion. Black studies programs were a consequence. So was the end of hopes of cooperation, minimal in any case.

Historically, violence had been directed against, not from, the black college. Southern police authorities had traditionally considered the black campus their special precinct. Police had almost a free hand in disciplining Negro students. Nothing resembling respect for the sanctity of this campus ever developed in the South. During the great upheavals of the early 1960s, official violence against students increased. In 1960, when students at black South Carolina State College at Orangeburg demonstrated in support of the Greensboro sit-ins: "In 40-degree weather, firemen and police turned high-powered hoses on marching students, sending several who had been hit squarely to the hospital. The 350 students, still wet, were then herded into an open stockade."[246] The campus of FAMU was ringed by state police by order of Governor Collins, to stop students from demonstrating downtown.

In 1966, Sammy Younge, Jr., an active student at Tuskegee, was killed by a white townsman. Nobody was punished for that. Two years later, police in Orangeburg, South Carolina, killed three South Carolina State College students; twenty-seven other students had been wounded, all but two or three shot from the rear or side. In 1970, two black students at Jackson State College in Mississippi were killed by bullets of law officers. (One of the dead was a high school senior visiting Jackson.) Some dozen more students were wounded.[247] In 1972, two black students were killed by police without cause at Southern University in Baton Rouge, Louisiana.

Such events were completely outside the experience of white colleges in the South or the North. When, after the mid-1960s, black activist students increasingly forswore nonviolence, students nevertheless did not arm themselves; it was unarmed students who were killed, usually while in flight from police. Large-scale shows of armed force became more frequent on and around black campuses.

Black student distrust of white governmental authority deepened. Often the officials who defended police actions against students were the same persons who met delegations of black students on issues of college merger and college budgets. The resulting suspicion strengthened among black students a closer identification with black colleges. Some leaders interpreted the black college as a colonial outpost in an armed territory.[248]

Blacks on white campuses

The consciousness of being black on white campuses was heightened by exclusions and deprivations. Redding's father instructed him gravely on the eve of his departure for Brown University: "Son, remember you're a Negro. You'll have to do twice as much better than your classmates. Before you act, think how what you do may reflect on other Negroes. Those white people will be judging the race by you. Don't let the race down, son."[249] It was a heavy burden. Miller resented the monolithic approach of white students to blacks: "They can never refer to you in the singular. You are always addressed as one of 'you fellows.' "[250]

Both for reasons of fellowship and self-defense, Negro college students organized collectively where numbers made it possible. To be sure, they first sought to join existing social organizations but these were almost invariably defined as "white." In 1906, black students at Cornell University formed the first Negro fraternity, Alpha Phi Alpha. Black students seized on this kind of organization, almost despite their small numbers. In 1929, for example, when fewer than fifty black students attended Indiana University, three different national Negro Greek-letter groups existed on campus. In 1914, eleven Negro students at the University of Michigan began a chapter of Kappa Alpha Nu fraternity. When black students at the University of Pennsylvania were barred in 1920 from joining the "white" fraternities, they organized the Daniel Hale Williams Surgical and Oral Society to honor the Negro inventor of open-heart surgery. A chapter of Kappa Alpha Psi began in 1914 at the State University of Iowa and in 1933 still had only nine members. Another group on the same campus, organized in 1922, had fifteen members by 1933.[251]

Negro Greek-letter societies were generally excluded from all-campus interfraternity councils and thus occupied a marginal status. This was the case, for example, at the University of Michigan and the University of Chicago. In 1937, the matter came to a head on the latter campus in the form of a clash between liberal tendencies among white students working against continued exclusion and fear that admission of a black group would lead to social equality. Specifically, the issue became: Would the black group insist on attending the interfraternity ball? One informant reported that admission would follow a written pledge by the fraternity not to exercise "its rights and privileges to attend the ball." A survey of 354 colleges in 1941 discovered more instances of anti-Negro discrimination in the area of fraternities and sororities than in any other aspect of campus life.[252]

Interracial student action organizations were virtually unknown. At the University of Michigan the Negro-Caucasian Club was such a group. It existed under especially narrow terms: it was to be recognized for one year only, and the name of the university was not to be used in the club's activities.

Most black students in northern colleges pursued goals comparable to those of their white peers. As residents of the state in which the school was located, they enrolled as a matter of right and not to "make a point." There is little evidence that the discrimination they experienced was unexpected. They learned that it was an unavoidable part of the cost of gaining an education. As one Negro woman student put it: "I would be a fool to let these immature white students ruin my chance for a college education. I must go on."[253] A young man transferred to Bowdoin after a semester at a black college where he had been sent by his parents. While he had enjoyed the immersion in black life, he chose his new school to learn another view of life. In his junior year at Bowdoin, he admitted having acquired a "white perspective" and was melancholy for feeling out of sorts in black company back home. Yet he saw the Bowdoin experience as valuable because "the doors that will be closed to us later on have been opened for four years."[254] Another black graduate, this time of the University of Michigan, summarized his experience in bitter terms: "The Negro student," he concluded, "in attending a white school may expect to find the denial of unlimited opportunity, the occurrence of racial embarrassments, and the concrete proof that American democracy is the white man's democracy. . . ."[255]

Nevertheless, between 1965 and 1968, the black presence on northern university campuses was altered significantly. In New York City, whose municipal colleges enrolled fewer than 2 percent Negro students, a maneuver by black members of the state legislature brought about specially financed programs during 1964–1965. Under the College Discovery and SEEK programs, black and Puerto Rican students were accepted for matriculation who ordinarily would have been rejected because of poor high school records. By 1968, some 1,500 SEEK students were enrolled in the municipal senior colleges. Many other colleges followed suit in one way or another. By fall 1968, "almost half of the nation's colleges and universities were making some effort to recruit and/or to provide special services for students from disadvantaged backgrounds."[256] These efforts increased sharply the number of black students on college campuses.

The ideology of black nationalism stirred the collective apathy of black students, and by 1968 some sixty-five Afro-American college groups existed in the country. Stressing black control, the groups led large-scale protest actions. Ballard has listed fifteen demands that appeared on one campus after another:[257]

> 1. That there be a department of black studies, with the faculty and chairman elected by the students and black faculty (in some cases) of the college
> 2. That a special quota for black students be established by the university which, at a minimum, would equal the percentage of blacks in the population at large
> 3. That special dormitory facilities be established for black students
> 4. That a cultural center for black students be created
> 5. That the administration grant a specific number of full, associate, and assistant professorial lines to the department or school of black studies
> 6. That the curriculum developed by black faculty and students be approved by the college
> 7. That special funds be allocated for academic assistance of black students

8. That no black student be expelled for academic reasons for a period of two years

9. That the chairman of the department of black studies report directly to the president of the university

10. That the racial criteria for faculty recruitment be waived in the case of black faculty members

11. That black students involved in this action receive amnesty from criminal and academic sanction

12. That black students receive passing grades if they were involved in this political action

13. That black students be permitted to receive credit for work done in the community

14. That black faculty and students have veto power over the hiring of any black faculty and administrators in the college

15. That black counselors be hired who can relate to the real needs of black students

While no national coordinating body prepared uniform demands, the similarity was striking.

Basically, the black students' demands attempted to reverse the exclusionary and discriminatory results of previous years. The numerical demands, for example, were simply expected to undo the negative quotas of the past. (A negative quota is a ratio of 100:0.) The curriculum demands did not aim to supplant any existing offering, but to ensure the installation of new courses. In 1947, Du Bois had predicted that "the time will come when a course in American Negro culture will be a central study of students of sociology, not only in Negro colleges but in white colleges and universities of the world."[258] Black students were hastening the day.

The newest black student, who came from the poorest sectors of northern society, registered the clearest victory in the contests of 1968–1969. Demand No. 2 guaranteed him a place where, given the normal processes, he might have waited for a decade. Demand 7 alerted colleges to the special educational needs of the new collegians. These were real gains. Responses to demands 1, 5, 6, 9, 10, 13, and 14 were very uneven. In 1971, Miller estimated that "there are at least 200 Afro-American Studies programs and probably as many as 400 other institutions which offer courses in Afro-American Studies." At the same time, he noted, "many programs had either been phased out or had their activities severely curtailed."[259] Because of inadequate funding and planning, the greatest bulk of black studies courses consisted of undergraduate-level work. Extremely little graduate research was done in the field. As a result, the long-term need for training teaching and research specialists remained largely unmet.

The events of 1968–1969 were historic in a basic sense: they established the permanent claim of black students to a place of their own making on the university campus. A twenty-year-old black sophomore at Berkeley said after the strike on that campus that "I got more out of participating in the strike than I've gotten out of my last sixteen years of life. I think I lived more in those eight weeks than I have for a long time. . . . I had to become more aware of what I was capable of doing."[260] Another lesson was discussed widely: the university was seen as a skilled manipulator of black issues. "American institutions of higher learning," Clark declared, "are racially contaminated, and, therefore, cannot be effective and healthy educational institutions." Yet universities knew where to concede and where to hold the line:

> If a university administration can restore harmony and the image of innovation by a no-strings-attached financial grant to a separate black studies program that may cover a few salaries or subsidize a gas station, it need not move to transform itself into a genuinely non-racial institution dedicated to developing human beings and to helping them develop effective strategies for fundamental social change.[261]

It was this kind of transformation that black power was still unable to bring about.

Black enrollment, 1960–1970

Four-year colleges
During the 1950s and early 1960s, the country's colleges and universities moved slightly away from exclusionary practices. In the South, the legal process resulted in a few black students being admitted. In the North, the same result was reached by the beginnings of black pressure. Whatever the region, black enrollment was essentially similar. In 1954, about 45,000 Negro students attended traditionally white institutions outside the South, a level of black enrollment not reached in southern white colleges until 1967. Assuming the existence of some 1,000 colleges in the North and about 600 in the South, average Negro enrollment was 45 per northern institution in 1954 and 75 per southern institution in 1967.

During the later 1960s, gross enrollment figures for blacks rose, but in the average traditionally white college, North or South, it remained small. In 1969, according to Egerton, less than 2 percent of the enrollment of eighty state universities and land grant colleges was Negro. Table 45 shows black undergraduate enrollment in twenty-eight state universities as of 1970. Omitting the eight senior units of the City University of New York, black enrollment in fifteen northern universities averaged just over 3 percent; it was 2 percent for the thirteen southern universities. The extraordinary importance of CUNY is obvious. Its enrollment was

Table 45. *Enrollment of black undergraduate students in selected southern and northern state universities, 1970* [a]

Institution	Total enrollment	Black enrollment	Black as percent of total enrollment
South			
University of Alabama	10,055	232	2.3
University of Florida	16,075	236	1.5
University of Georgia	13,440	123	0.9
University of Kentucky	13,210	136	1.0
Louisiana State University	13,553	387	2.9
University of Maryland	25,037	862	3.4
Mississippi State University	7,115	178	2.5
University of North Carolina	11,688	240	2.1
University of Oklahoma	13,913	391	2.8
University of South Carolina	10,671	280	2.6
University of Tennessee	17,174	325	1.9
University of Texas	31,114	256	0.8
University of Virginia	6,504	117	1.8
Total	189,549	3,763	2.0
Average	14,581	289	2.0
North			
University of California (L.A.)	16,620	635	3.8
University of Colorado	14,971	293	2.0
University of Illinois	23,367	944	4.0
University of Indiana	20,689	738	3.6
University of Iowa	12,614	151	1.2
University of Kansas	14,358	349	2.4
University of Massachusetts	15,733	629	4.0
University of Michigan	19,071	732	3.8
University of Missouri	15,780	356	2.3
Rutgers University	9,445	680	7.2
City University of New York (8)	58,286	6,383	11.0
Ohio State University	32,691	917	2.8
University of Oregon	10,274	165	1.6
Pennsylvania State University	20,585	618	3.0
University of Washington	20,220	524	2.6
University of Wisconsin	22,424	657	2.9
Total	327,128	14,771	4.5
Average	20,446	923	4.5
Total minus CUNY	268,842	8,388	3.1
Average minus CUNY	17,923	559	3.1

[a] Figures are for the main campus where more than one facility exists. CUNY is an exception because of its unusual importance.

Source: Basic data in U.S. Department of Health, Education, and Welfare, Office of Civil Rights, *Racial Ethnic Enrollment Data from Institutions of Higher Education, Fall 1970* (Washington, D.C.: GPO, 1972).

17.8 percent of the total enrollment of the twenty-eight institutions surveyed; yet its black enrollment accounted for 43.2 percent of black enrollment for the fifteen northern universities.

In the 1960s, the rate of college going as a whole expanded; however, b!ack youth lost in position relative to whites (Table 46). For Negro graduates, the gap was probably greater than shown in the table, since rates for other components of "nonwhite" were most likely higher, on balance, than those for blacks.

According to a careful estimate by Egerton, black college enrollment rose from 4.6 percent in 1964 to 4.7 percent in 1969. Berls reported that from 1965 to 1967 the enrollment of Negro college students dropped from 5.8 to 5.2 percent of total enrollment. Corresponding estimates for 1972 ranged from 6 to over 9 percent. The generally higher level of these later estimates suggests that a definite rise in black enrollment occurred around the turn into the 1970s. Even more likely, however, a large part – perhaps even most – of the increase occurred not in the four-year colleges and universities but in the community colleges, discussed below.[262]

During most of the 1960s, colleges and universities recruited selectively, searching for highly talented black students. Between 1961 and 1973, black enrollment at Harvard increased about tenfold, from 100 to 1,000; the admissions office noted in 1973 that "between 75–80 percent of the black students admitted to Harvard in recent years could not be categorized as disadvantaged." Scholastic Aptitude Test scores of Harvard blacks in the classes of 1973–1976 averaged over 600.[263] This level far

Table 46. *Percent of high school graduates entering college, 1963–1968* [a]

Year	Nonwhite	White	Gap
1963	38.1	45.6	7.5
1964	38.7	49.2	10.5
1965	43.4	51.7	8.3
1966	31.6 [b]	51.7	20.1
1967	41.9	53.1	11.2
1968	46.2	56.6	10.4

[a] All figures have been rounded.
[b] This appears to be a misprint; perhaps number should be 41.6 instead of 31.6.

Source: Panel on Financing Low Income and Minority Students in Higher Education, *Toward Equal Opportunity for Higher Education* (New York: College Entrance Examination Board, 1973), p. 21.

exceeded that of collegiate blacks in general as well as the averages of many white selective colleges and institutions. An intense competition arose among traditionally white institutions to attract relatively few black students. As time wore on, the stakes rose. In the early 1970s, a newspaper reported: "Maine's Bowdoin College, actively recruiting black students, flies seniors from Washington's Cardozo and Eastern High School to Maine for the weekend on an all-expenses-paid trip to look the campus over."[264] A study of 159 colleges in 1968 found that 75 had no special programs for "high-risk" students with substandard academic preparation. Of the 84 with some kind of program or special effort, "no more than six or eight are working with students who are unquestionably high risks. . . . Those [students] whose past performance has been blunted by discrimination and poverty represent a risk that very few colleges are willing to take."[265]

Community colleges

By 1973, four out of ten black college students in the United States attended community colleges, outnumbering students in traditionally black colleges (25 percent) and black students in traditionally white four-year colleges (35 percent). Enrollment in community colleges overall rose from 564,071 in 1960 to 1,810,964 a decade later.[266] Two-thirds of the enrollment existed in only six states: California, Florida, Illinois, Michigan, New York, and Texas. One-third of the national total was accounted for by California alone.

A certain mystery surrounded community college enrollment statistics. Goodrich and colleagues surveyed community colleges that reported a full-time minority enrollment of 120,468. However, "when asked to specify the academic level of these full-time students, the responding institutions were able to account for only 68,536 full-time minority students."[267] This margin of possible error was extraordinary, even for the field of enrollment statistics.

By the mid-1960s, the stream of blacks toward community colleges was well under way. In the Far West in 1965, 49 percent of all white undergraduates attended community colleges; 71 percent of black undergraduates attended such colleges. The graduation record of community college students was only half that of senior college students of comparable ability. In the absence of any change in this record, increasing black enrollment threatened to dampen, if not diminish, the rate of graduation among blacks. On the one hand, community colleges were for many black youth a sole opportunity. On the other, the opportunity was limited. During the late 1960s, Knoell studied the enrollment of blacks in the community colleges of Dallas, Fort Worth, Philadelphia, Saint Louis, and San Francisco. She concluded that "were it not for these colleges, the college-attendance rates for black students would be shockingly low. The problem . . . appears not to be one of recruitment, but of insuring successful performance after admission."[268]

During the 1960s, the community colleges operated with a concept of the community that largely ignored minority youth. When some numbers of blacks began to enroll, little that was creative was done to meet their specific educational needs. In the mid-1960s, an inquiry in California found an almost total lack of remedial programs. An official study of the Educational Opportunity Program in California community colleges, completed in 1970, found the program successful on all three levels of the state's higher education system, although relatively little detail came from the community colleges. The director of the study, Professor Harry Kitano, reported that "most of our interviewers who went to the community colleges . . . were shocked by such things as racist remarks made by staff and teachers."[269] Black and other minority students suffered an exceedingly heavy attrition rate in community colleges. Goodrich reports they experienced a drop between freshman and sophomore years of about two-thirds, more than double the rate for all community college students. Clearly, efforts to bring equal opportunity to blacks in higher education would require effective remediation for past educational deprivation. The appearance of equality is no substitute for the reality. Further, community college programs would require monitoring to ensure that a new separate and unequal educational system – a new teaching system – is not established in the name of opportunity.

Present gains, future hopes

By 1970, more than 350,000 black young people were enrolled full-time in colleges and universities (Table 47). A century earlier their forbears had been hounded and pursued out of learned institutions as unfit. After a short-lived attempt at nondiscriminatory higher education, young blacks had been relegated to segregated and grossly inferior facilities. Not only in the South, but even in the North they met rejection and, at best, were tolerated.

A powerful structure of deprivation was constructed by government and the learned professions. Against this formidable opposition, blacks endured where they could and progressed where they dared. More than in the area of the common schools, blacks in higher education depended on their own efforts. By the 1970s, higher education as a whole was finally within the grasp as well as the reach of young blacks. But new obstacles of differential educational quality based on economic discrimination took on a new strength. The future of blacks in higher education, nevertheless, seemed more enduring than ever, for it was increasingly based on a self-aware student population. Ultimately, the fate of black higher education seemed more closely linked than ever with the future of the black community.

Table 47. Enrollment of students in full-time undergraduate, graduate, and professional schools, by ethnic group, fall 1970

Type of school	Black		Spanish surname		American Indian		Oriental		Nonminority		Total
	No.	%	No.	%	No.	%	No.	%	No.	%	
Undergraduate	344,819	6.9	102,788	2.1	26,914	0.5	51,705	1.0	4,439,542	89.4	4,965,768
Graduate[a]	16,334	4.2	4,830	1.2	1,290	0.3	7,579	1.9	362,329	92.3	392,362
Medicine	1,752	4.1	340	0.8	43	0.1	768	1.8	39,598	93.2	42,501
Dentistry	570	3.8	100	0.7	17	0.1	242	1.6	14,053	93.8	14,982
Law	2,454	3.9	686	1.1	192	0.3	277	0.4	58,550	94.2	62,159
Total	365,929	6.7	108,744	2.0	28,456	0.5	60,571	1.1	4,914,072	89.7	5,477,772

[a] The category "graduate" includes enrollment in professional schools except medical, dental, and law schools.

Source: Basic data in U.S. Department of Health, Education, and Welfare, Office for Civil Rights, Racial and Ethnic Enrollment Data from Institutions of Higher Education, Fall 1970 (Washington, D.C.: GPO), pp. 116, 177, 185, 190, 200.

8

Higher education for other minorities

The higher education of Mexican-Americans, Indian-Americans, and Puerto Ricans paralleled the experience of black Americans. Unlike blacks, however, these groups had no Reconstruction during which – ever so fleetingly – they exercised genuine political power. Consequently, governmental redress was minimal. By failing to fulfill the obligations to supply common schools and by excluding minority children from secondary schools, communities kept the potential supply of minority college students at a negligible level for many years. Blacks were left with segregated higher institutions, but the other three minorities lacked even these. In time, extremely small numbers were admitted to higher institutions, but on the campuses they suffered much of the exclusion and discrimination familiar in black higher education.

Indian-Americans

Between 1769 and 1973, Dartmouth College enrolled 187 Indians and graduated 25, or 1 every eight years. During the college's first century, a single Indian was graduated. Yet the charter of Dartmouth included among its purposes "the education and Christianizing of Indians, Utes and others." Harvard College, in its charter of 1650, referred to the "education of the English and Indian youth of this country in knowledge" as its purpose. The following year, the college applied for a grant from the Society for Propagation of the Gospel in New England to erect a building in which Indians would be educated. The grant was made and the Indian College was built in 1656. Four years later no Indian had registered. During the remainder of the century, apparently only four Indians attended Harvard. Until the end of the colonial period, a single additional Indian entered the college. In 1698, the Indian College was torn down and the bricks used to construct a new building. In exchange for the bricks, Harvard promised that future Indian students "should enjoy their Studies rent free in said building." This provision became a dead letter.[1]

The College of William and Mary, the principal institution of higher education in the Southern colonies, did not include Indian education in its charter of 1691. Soon thereafter, however, it became profitable to do so. In the estate of Robert Boyle, the English physicist, funds were set aside for the education of Indian children. The president of William and Mary, Dr. James Blair, eagerly pursued the allotment of £14 per Indian child. Indeed, the college was afflicted by a shortage of children. Layman describes a letter of November 17, 1711, to the Council of Trade in London from Governor Alexander Spottswood stating that it was the custom of the college's governors to purchase children of tribes captured in war to make sure that William and Mary could continue to have the benefit of Boyle's donation.[2] Until the American Revolution, names of Indian students continued to appear occasionally on the rolls of William and Mary. According to Ortiz, Princeton University "has not had more than two Indian students at a given time in almost two hundred years."[3]

During the nineteenth century, Indians only rarely enrolled in colleges. Between 1876 and 1890, Charles Eastman, a Wahpeton Sioux, attended four different colleges: Beloit, Knox, Dartmouth, and Boston University. He received a medical degree from the last named institution. Eastman was a most untypical Indian in that he was eager to assimilate: "This was my ambition," he wrote, "that the Sioux should accept civilization before it was too late."[4] Between 1900 and 1950, extremely few additional examples of Indian collegians came to note. A study of persons born on the Flathead Reservation in Montana between 1905 and 1935 found that by 1955 twenty-one had graduated from college; another eighty-eight had some college.[5] During the late 1950s, a study of the Blackfeet Reservation noted the large number of failures among those who entered college with deficient high school preparation. In 1960–1961, fifty-three Blackfeet young people were enrolled in higher education.[6] Apparently, very few graduated. According to Fuchs and Havighurst, in 1957 about 2,000 Indians were attending some kind of postsecondary institution. This figure included vocational training institutes as well as conventional colleges. By 1970, these scholars estimated, the figure had risen to 10,000.[7]

An official federal study in 1970, however, discovered the more accurate figure to be almost triple the Fuchs-Havighurst number. Without taking into account enrollment in Alaska and Hawaii, a total of 28,456 were engaged in full-time undergraduate, graduate, and professional study. Of these, 5,678 were in California, 3,679 in Oklahoma, 1,926 in Texas, 1,378 in New York, 1,274 in Illinois, 1,047 in Pennsylvania, 1,011 in Washington, and 12,463 in other states.[8] The recency of Indian attendance is underscored by the fact that this 1970 compilation is the sole benchmark for later comparisons.

Indian students sometimes attended the highest quality public institution in the state in accordance with some parity measure. Thus, nearly one-fifth of all Indian college students in Arizona attended the University of Arizona. In Washington, nearly one-sixth attended the University of Washington. In Oklahoma, however, fewer than one-twentieth attended the University of Oklahoma; and in Texas barely one-twentieth attended the University of Texas. In Illinois, only one-fourteenth attended the University of Illinois. In each of these states, Indian students were overrepresented at the lesser quality public and private institutions.

During the fall of 1970, California higher institutions enrolled 5,362 Indian undergraduate students – one-fifth of the national total. Of these, 94 percent (5,021 students) attended public institutions: 352 (7.0 percent) were enrolled in the state university; 1,316 (26.2 percent), in state colleges; and 3,353 (66.8 percent), in community colleges.[9] Dropout rates were known to be high, but few precise statistics were available. Indian students were concentrated in community colleges whose ability to generate students who would ultimately earn bachelor's degrees was far inferior to that of four-year colleges. The dropout rate for community colleges was considerably higher than for the other institutions, especially for minority youth.

Indian students were strangers on college campuses. More alien even were their cultures. As early as 1937, the University of Oklahoma, located in a major center of Indian life, refused to establish a program of Indian studies.[10] Pembroke State University, in North Carolina, had been an all-Indian college between 1945 and 1955; after that it was opened to students of all races. But Indian culture apparently never played a primary role in the educational life of the institution during any of its history.[11]

In all but a few cases, during the 1960s American colleges threw open their doors, but little else, to Indian students. At the University of Alaska a representative of the Native Student Committee of Education told a congressional committee that "the greater majority of the Alaskans . . . are psychologically and socially almost totally unprepared to meet and cope with the westernized university situation."[12] He attributed the unreadiness to the failure of the schools controlled by the Bureau of Indian Affairs to bring "the level of native education up to par with that being received by the students in public schools."

Almost everywhere Indian students found themselves a tiny minority, nearly bereft of any special help. Frequently, they were subjected to personal indignities. After demands by the Indian students, counseling assistance was offered to meet their distinctive needs. Academic success often eluded Indian students. At Black Hills State College in South Dakota, to which Indian students came from seven nearby reservations, the dropout rate was said to be 80 percent in 1964. Despite the location of the college, Indian students constituted only 3.8 percent of its enrollment in 1970. Organized campaigns by Indian students on numerous campuses resulted in the offering of programs or courses in Indian studies. These were an effort to meet problems of cultural identity, academic progress, and self-defense against discrimination. An evaluation of the programs was not easily reached. As Buffalohead noted, however: "In many ways . . . the mood, the temper, and the intellectual ferment among Indian students is more encouraging and significant than the programs themselves."[13]

Mexican-Americans

The collegiate history of Mexican-Americans had barely begun by World War I. All but excluded from the common schools of Texas, where most lived, they produced few students for the colleges in the state. Over a quarter century, Mexican-American enrollment in the University of Texas never rose above 1.3 percent of the total enrollment (Table 48).[14] Even this compilation may be too optimistic. In 1930, while the above data reported that 1.6 percent of total "white" collegiate enrollment in Texas was made up of Mexican-Americans, another source stated that it was about 0.5 percent.[15] The registration figures for the University of Texas in the mid-1930s vary from twenty or thirty to Table 48's estimate of three or four times that number.[16]

During the years 1928–1945, 271 Mexican-Americans graduated from the University of Texas; this number represented 1.1 percent of all degrees awarded in these years. Most of these Mexican-American university students were, according to Renner, "descendants of 'old Spanish and Mexican families' and long-term political refugees" from Mexico. He also assumes that their socioeconomic status and graduation rate were higher than those of their Anglo classmates.[17] Obviously, it was a thin top layer of

Table 48. *Enrollment of Mexican-Americans in University of Texas, 1920–1945*

Year	Total enrollment	Enrollment of Mexican-Americans	
		No.	%
1920	4,071	26	0.6
1930	6,041	73	1.2
1940	10,316	110	1.1
1945	9,191	114	1.2

Source: Data from Ruth Ann Douglas Fogartie, "Spanish-Name People in Texas with Special Emphasis on Those Who are Students in Texas Colleges and Universities" (master's thesis, University of Texas, 1948), p. 62.

Mexican-American society that supplied the bulk of college students through World War II.

After the war, the GI Bill of Rights enabled some poorer youth to enter college. But the numbers remained modest. In the decade 1946–1955 the number of Mexican-American graduates from the University of Texas slightly more than doubled from the period 1928–1945; it rose from 271 to 574. Over the longer period the proportion of Mexican-Americans receiving degrees to all recipients of degrees rose only from 1.1 percent to 1.8 percent.

In other states of the Southwest, Mexican-American youth entered colleges in larger numbers. By 1958, California enrolled nearly 36,000 college freshmen of Mexican-American origin, several thousand more than in Texas. In the Southwest as a whole in 1958, Mexican-Americans made up 5.7 percent of all college freshmen.[18] The gap between freshman entry and graduation widened as enrollment increased.

By 1971, Mexican-American students made up one-tenth of total college enrollment in the five states of the Southwest (Table 49).[19] The absence of data on graduation rates made it more difficult to weigh the significance of rising enrollments. At that, the 10.2 percent enrollment rate could be compared with the fact that Mexican-Americans constituted 17 percent of college-age youth in the region in 1970.

Mexican-American students were considerably overrepresented in community colleges and underrepresented in public four-year institutions (Table 50). While nearly equal proportions of all college students in the

Table 49. *Enrollment of Mexican-Americans in colleges in the Southwest, 1971*

State	Total enrollment	Enrollment of Mexican-Americans	
		No.	%
Arizona	79,000	6,000	7.6
California	839,000	78,000	9.3
Colorado	87,000	5,000	5.7
New Mexico	36,000	8,000	22.2
Texas	374,000	48,000	12.8
Total	1,415,000	145,000	10.2

Source: Data from Richard I. Ferrin, Richard W. Jonson, and Cesar M. Trimble, *Access to College for Mexican-Americans in the Southwest* (New York: College Entrance Examination Board, July 1972), p. 19.

Southwest attended community colleges and public four-year colleges (43.6 and 46.0 percent), the disproportion was enormous in the case of Mexican-American students (61.1 and 28.5 percent).

The new Mexican-American collegian urgently required financial aid. The poorer he was, however, the less aid he received and the harder he was required to work for it. Ferrin and colleagues discovered that the average Mexican-American college student at various types of colleges received aid in 1970–1971 as shown in Table 51. The student at the public four-year college – almost certainly better-off than the community college student – received more in outright grants than the latter student did in all forms of aid. The latter student also was required to work in exchange for aid more than twice as often as students in senior institutions. (The same pattern was true of black and Anglo students.)

Table 50. *Enrollment of Mexican-Americans in community colleges, public four-year colleges, and private colleges, in the Southwest, 1971*

College type	Total enrollment	Enrollment of Mexican-Americans	
		No.	%
Community	617,000	88,000	14.3
Public four-year	651,000	41,000	6.3
Private	147,000	15,000	10.2
Total	1,415,000	144,000	10.2

Source: Data from Richard I. Ferrin, Richard W. Jonson, and Cesar M. Trimble, *Access to College for Mexican-Americans in the Southwest* (New York: College Entrance Examination Board, July 1972), p. 19.

Table 51. *Financial aid to Mexican-Americans in community colleges, public four-year colleges, and private colleges in the Southwest, 1970–1971*

College type	Grants		Loans		Jobs		Total ($)
	$	%	$	%	$	%	
Community	55	32.7	40	23.8	73	43.5	168
Public four-year	176	33.4	233	44.2	118	22.4	527
Private	449	52.7	286	33.6	117	13.7	852

Source: Data from Richard I. Ferrin, Richard W. Jonson, and Cesar M. Trimble, *Access to College for Mexican-Americans in the Southwest* (New York: College Entrance Examination Board, July 1972), p. 30.

Prior to World War II, the sparsity of Mexican-American students on college campuses underscored their extreme minority status in the Southwest. Both in the classroom and in student activities, they were treated, at best, with condescension.

During the early 1940s, for example, teachers at the University of New Mexico created "a dual system of marking" according to which Mexican-American students were not expected or required to match Anglo levels of achievement. In social affairs they were permitted to attend only a single dance a year and were totally excluded from fraternities and sororities. Twenty-five years later, Mexican-American students were finally admitted into these organizations.[20]

By the late 1960s, four-year colleges in the Southwest still had token enrollments of Mexican-Americans. Mexican-Americans in Los Angeles sent few of their children to the universities of the area. In 1968, 2.3 percent of the undergraduate enrollment at UCLA consisted of Mexican-Americans. A year earlier, San Fernando Valley State College enrolled only seven Mexican-American students. At the University of Texas in 1967, they made up 3 percent of enrollment, hardly a major departure from the historical situation there.[21]

On the eve of the 1970s, Mexican-American college students had come to be the cutting edge of the Chicano movement. A major goal of the movement was to effect a sharp increase in college-trained Mexican-Americans who would help unify Chicano communities in behalf of programs of common benefit. Where feasible, the students established working relationships with black and other minority students seeking greater access to higher education. In most cases, however, Mexican-Americans organized separate campaigns. The focal point of their work was the creation of Mexican-American studies programs and departments. They pressed institutions to offer special aid and facilities to entrants who had gained only poor academic preparation in the region's secondary schools.

One of the most spectacular successes occurred at California State University at Northridge (formerly San Fernando Valley State College). There, in 1969, a Chicano studies department began at a time when only thirty Mexican-American students were in attendance. Four years later, as Acuna writes:

> We have twenty fulltime faculty positions, offer over eighty sec-
> tions on the Chicano, and carry over six thousand semester
> hours. We have 1,400 Chicano students at CSUN on financial
> aid. . . .Close to fifty percent of our students come to us with a
> "D" average from high school. However, although the attrition
> rate among Anglos [at CSUN] in the first two years, matriculat-
> ing with above "E" average, is 65 percent, our attrition rate is

only 38 percent. What we have proven is that if Chicanos are motivated and receive financial support, they will make it.[22]

While lesser successes occurred elsewhere, only organized and continued Chicano pressure brought any success at all.

A special problem on numerous California campuses involved competition between organized Chicano and black student organizations. According to Vaca, "as Negroes have come to dominate the Educational Opportunities Program for minorities at the University of California at Berkeley, the recruiting of Mexican-American students has dropped almost forty percent."[23] In 1969, a closed statewide meeting of EOP representatives was held in Santa Barbara. The Chicanos walked out of the meeting when black delegates refused to support the following resolution: "Each institution of higher education must reflect in its student body representation of Chicanos proportional to the Chicano population of its immediate service area or to the Chicano population statewide, whichever is higher."[24] Fundamental to the conflict was the sparse supply of funds which became even more strained as time went on. While the Kitano report had found the EOP to be on the whole successful academically, adequate financing did not follow.[25]

Employment discrimination against Mexican-American scholars was frank if not refreshing. One well-trained historian, the possessor of a doctorate in his field, applied for a position in a California state college. After criticizing the source of the degree (the University of Southern California), the departmental chairman turned him away: "[He] capped his refusal to hire me by saying, 'We already have a Mexican.' Another strong factor, he said, was that since my parents were Mexican it was doubtful that I could be objective in teaching Latin American history."[26] Soon thereafter, a Texan was hired for the position.

Employment of Mexican-American faculty increased as Chicano studies grew. Otherwise, few more than ever taught in other academic departments. Servin wrote in 1970 that "there are only a few more Mexican-descended college history instructors today than there were in the thirties."[27] As of 1973, it was estimated that only eighty Chicanos were full-fledged scientists. (These were defined as holders of a doctorate and engaged in research.) To help expand this group, a new organization was formed that year – the Society for the Advancement of Chicanos and Native Americans in Science. Its statement of policy declared that "interaction between society and science is essential. No modern society can function without meaningful dialogue between the society and its scientific community. The involvement of the Native American and Chicano communities in scientific education, research, and administration has been meager."[28] Within existing scholarly and professional organizations,

Mexican-Americans formed separate caucuses to put forward Chicano viewpoints.

Puerto Ricans

Before the 1960s, Puerto Ricans rarely attended mainland colleges. A certain number of upper-class island families sent their sons to the mainland for a higher education. Few who lived in New York City could afford the luxury. A greater barrier than economics was the failure of the city's public schools to prepare youth for further education.

In 1958, barely half the Puerto Rican students in secondary education attended academic high schools. After nine years of special efforts in the Puerto Rican community, the figure rose in 1967 to almost 70 percent. This was a significant improvement. The number of Puerto Rican students enrolled in academic high schools rose from 8,852 to 29,908 during these years.[29] Many, however, dropped out before graduation, and other students scored low academic averages. In the 1968 freshman class enrolled in all parts of the City University of New York (CUNY), only 897, or 5 percent of the total, were of Puerto Rican origin.[30] Most of this group had gained entrance as special students in the compensatory SEEK program.

In 1969, however, Puerto Rican and black students in CUNY undertook a campaign to force university authorities to effect a large increase in minority enrollment. During the spring, students occupied part of the City College of New York. After negotiations, agreement was reached to establish a School of Urban and Third World Studies. It was also agreed that by fall 1970 half the freshman class would be recruited from predominantly minority high schools, without regard to traditional academic grade averages. Instead of this procedure, a system was installed in 1970 – under the name "open admissions" – which dropped the preferential feature and guaranteed a place in CUNY to every graduate of a city high school.[31]

A sharp increase in the enrollment of Puerto Rican freshmen resulted (Table 52). Although the 1971 figures represented only one-twelfth of CUNY enrollment, it was enormous compared with earlier experience.

Yet Puerto Rican students tended – along with black students – to be concentrated in the community colleges rather than the senior colleges of CUNY. In some of the latter, Puerto Ricans made up a tiny part of enrollment. During 1971, they represented only 2.9 percent of the Brooklyn College student body; in Queens College, 2.1 percent. On the other hand, the following year City College of New York was said to enroll 800 Puerto Rican students, more than any senior college outside Puerto Rico.[32] In the community colleges attrition rates exceeded one-third. Over half the open admissions freshmen stood in need of intensive help in reading and writing, but many failed to receive sufficient aid to survive.

Central to the installation of open admissions in CUNY was the notably close cooperation between Puerto Rican and black students. Strategy and tactics were formulated in close concert. Public statements were invariably made in the name of black and Puerto Rican students. Here and there in CUNY, faculty members from both groups worked with the students.

Outside New York City, the bulk of Puerto Rican college students were enrolled in community colleges. In Chicago, for example, Puerto Rican enrollment in the municipal community colleges probably equaled such enrollment in the remainder of public higher education in the state of Illinois.

By the early 1970s, Indian-American, Mexican-American, and Puerto Rican youth could look forward to increased access to the nation's colleges. The gates had been pressed open by forces outside these institutions. Indeed, the colleges ended their policies of exclusion and indifference only by labeling the newer students as "special." Consequently, their education waited upon the availability of externally supplied financial aid. Customary curricula and traditional discriminatory practices, such as exclusion of minority faculty, continued almost without pause. Minority students found themselves increasingly concentrated in institutions of lesser quality, a situation that cast a shadow over undoubtedly increasing enrollments. This was a feature of American higher education as a whole during the years following World War II and affected many white students as well.[33]

Table 52. *Enrollment of Puerto Rican freshmen in City University of New York, 1968–1971*

Year	Number of Puerto Rican freshmen	Percent Puerto Rican of total freshmen
1968	897	5.0
1969	1,195	5.9
1970	3,018	8.5
1971	3,372	8.6

Source: Data from David Rosen, Seth Bunner, and Steve Fowler, *Open Admissions: The Promise and the Lie of Open Access to American Higher Education* (Lincoln: Nebraska Curriculum Development Center, University of Nebraska, 1973), p. 85.

Part III
Conclusions

9

To educate all the children of all the people

The American public school is a product of the nineteenth century. Inevitably, it came to bear the mark of the times. The impact of economic and legal institutions upon race was of fundamental importance.

History and law

In the course of the century, the American economy underwent two concurrent developments: (1) a transition from production for subsistence to production for sale, and (2) a shift from ownership and control by persons directly engaged in production to the effective operation of business by large-scale owners of capital. Basic to both was the growing availability of supplies of labor and private land. Immigrants – both voluntary and forced – provided cheap labor. From the Indian and from other countries were wrested great areas of land, quickly converted into private property. Black slave labor predated the nineteenth century inasmuch as the plantation economies were from the outset highly commercialized arrangements. But the slave economy reached its high point on the eve of the Civil War.

The minority people were an incident to the economic development of nineteenth-century America. To provide them with civic services such as education was regarded as a misuse of scarce resources. Exclusion from communal educational service laid no moral opprobrium upon the excluders. Their action was innocence itself. In a highly commercialized society, a basic moral rule was: "business is business." The immorality of slavery evaporated amid such strategems. Schools were all too ready to adopt the same reasoning. They often explicated their interest in training minority children to fulfill subordinate life roles.

Little protection of minorities came from the law. The very idea of individual legal protection was, to be sure, fairly novel. But American law during the century was dynamic. It is difficult to imagine the country's economic development without the creative help of the changing law. The corporate form of business, for example, was not an American creation. But modern corporate law is one of the unsung products of America. Such creativity and flexibility were not in evidence, however, when racial issues were in the fore. This was true even when the same legal principle could have been applied in both areas.

Consider, for example, the issue of citizenship. The federal courts proved most flexible when the concept was applied to economic matters, but resisted such pliability with reference to Negroes.

In 1809, the U.S. Supreme Court decided the *Devaux* case. Georgia had collected a state tax levied upon the Savannah branch of the Bank of the United States, a federally chartered corporation. The bank sued in federal court to recover payment. Georgia denied the existence of a federal issue; Section 2, Article III of the Federal Constitution extended the jurisdiction of federal courts to cases "between citizens of different states." Corporations, insisted Georgia, were not citizens and thus could not have access to federal courts. The court agreed.

"That invisible, intangible, and artificial being, that mere legal entity, a corporation aggregate," declared Chief Justice John Marshall, "is certainly not a citizen." He held that only real persons could be citizens. The officers of the corporation, being real persons, could sue and be sued in federal courts. But the corporation itself could not enter federal legal procedures. *Devaux* also prescribed that a firm's owners could sue or be sued in federal courts provided they lived in a state other than that of the contending side. Presumably, this diversity in state residence created a diversity of state citizenship that extended beyond the courts of a single state. Under this condition, recourse to a federal court was permissible. The *Devaux* court was unable to conceive of a totally abstract person – a corporation – possessing full legal rights.

Thirty-five years later, however, the Supreme Court reversed *Devaux* in *Louisville, Cincinnati, and Charleston Railroad Company* v. *Letson.* Corporations as such were recognized as citizens of a state, possessing full capacity to use the courts. An artificial person thus became real before the law. What had happened between 1809 and 1844?

By 1844 America was a commercialized society. It had become usual for men to conceive of themselves as producers and sellers for impersonal ends. Almost half the total labor force worked for wages or salary and thus were sellers of their own labor power. Forced labor was bought and sold on the market. In agriculture, world markets claimed major portions of the cotton and other raw materials output of the country. Factory production in the textile industry and transportation advances were hurtling America toward economic dominance. By midcentury, American per capita output still lagged behind that of England, but was ahead of France. No institution was more significant in that growth than the business corporation. And none was more demanding on the originality and creativity of Americans. The modern business corporation was one of the country's greatest contributions to the world economy. With commercialization and industrialization growing apace, legal thought turned to practical business problems. The expansion of corporations forced the courts to review older doctrines and face up to altogether new problems.

Flexibility and adaptation were not, however, in evidence when the courts confronted black rights. During the same interval of years, citizenship became an issue among Negroes. In 1834, Prudence Crandell had been compelled to close her school for Negro girls. A state law forbade any noncitizen of Connecticut from attending a school in the state, thus excluding blacks from out-of-state. Miss Crandell's attorney contended that "if allegiance is due from our colored population, its correlative is due from the government, viz. protection and equal laws." He asked "if a man of color in New York or Pennsylvania should sue a white citizen of Connecticut in their Federal Court, would it be a good plea in abatement that one of the parties is a man of color?"[1] The state court avoided deciding that question.

The issue endured, even so. In 1849, William Wells Brown, escaped slave and author, wrote Wendell Phillips: "This is emphatically an age of discoveries; but I will venture the assertion, that none but an American slaveholder could have discovered that a man born in a country was not a citizen of it."[2] Watkins, a black leader from Boston, told an emancipation meeting in 1853 that he called into question "the validity of the process by which I am made a pilgrim and a stranger; the *modus operandi* by which I am made an alien in the land of my birth."[3] Four years later, the Supreme Court directly rejected the contention that a black person could be a citizen of this country. In *Dred Scott*, the court withheld from living, breathing human beings a right it had conferred on artificial persons just thirteen years earlier.

After the Civil War, legislation passed on behalf of Negroes ironically met a similar fate. The Fourteenth Amendment, designed to confer citizenship upon Negroes, was converted by courts into a protective shield against state regulation of corporate activity. Legislation like the Civil Rights Act of 1875 explicitly enacted to protect blacks was often ruled unconstitutional or construed so narrowly as to lose effectiveness. In few, if any, other areas of judicial activity was the approach of courts so legalistic and rigid. Even when, after decades of agitation, a point was finally yielded, few practical consequences for Negroes flowed at first because of the terms of the ruling. The nonconsequences of *Brown*, for example, left little to celebrate except an abstract victory. Repeatedly, vague principles were adopted "on principle" by unprincipled school boards. Actual enforcement of these hard-won court victories was often left to the victim of the injuries complained of.

Economically powerless minorities waited in vain for positive court responses. Only when the minorities developed significant political power and forced a change upon basic American public opinion did the courts begin to adapt ancient doctrines to new circumstances, though the impetus to develop such power no doubt was influenced by the expectations fostered by *Brown*. Self-organization of the minorities, the mainspring of these events, was often forgotten, while credit was accorded the judiciary for generating new directions in constitutional law. By the last quarter of the twentieth century, the condition of minority constitutional rights was precarious. Legal rights unsecured by economic power have always had an especially difficult existence in the United States. As recognition of this fact led minorities into the political arena with ever greater energy, public institutions such as the schools came under the closest scrutiny.

Racism and class

American educational history was deeply influenced by racism, another heritage of the nineteenth century. Racism is the doctrine of racial or ethnic superiority, including the justification of differential rewards based on the presumed differences. Racism without privilege would be mere individual prejudice. The social impact of racism derives from its role as a policy, not as an individual attitude. Racism is thus always collective and thereby institutional. From their outset the public schools have been racist in spirit and structure. Deprivation has been the lot of minority (and poor) children by direct exclusion but also indirectly by impersonal and systematic procedures. By refusing to build sufficient elementary schools for Mexican-American children in 1900, the territorial government ensured that almost none of these children would ever progress to the state university. This guaranteed the character of the University of New Mexico as an Anglo institution and made it superfluous to exclude minorities by stipulation.

In 1903, Du Bois wrote that "the problem of the twentieth century is the problem of the color line." A half century later, he reformulated this thought. Racism, he now held, was not an isolated factor, born out of race hatred alone. Rather, it interacted with general systems of exploitation and oppression, especially those based on economic interest and social privilege. Racism remained a real factor, but it was both obscured and implemented by larger forces.[4]

Du Bois's newer insight is insufficiently understood today. In contemporary discussions of racism, the topic is treated as though it were a subdivision of individual psychology, and without inquiring about its genesis. Du Bois's approach would be to search out those community conflicts that "count," to define the salient social groups whose interests are involved in the conflicts, and to discover how the issue of race is used by these interests to attain those goals that "count." A conflict over segregated schools might turn out to have relatively little to do with race but relatively much to do with real estate groups who wish to maintain existing patterns of residence and levels of real estate values and with a construction industry that wants to build new schools even though vacant classrooms abound but are "closed" to black students.[5]

Black communities themselves exemplified the interaction of race and class. In the midst of the Depression of the 1930s, the president of Wilberforce University accused many black college graduates of gross rapacity: "The idea of exploitation of their people is almost as great among the young educated Negroes as among the whites, and too many young Negro college graduates look upon the mass of Negroes as their prey for exploitation."[6] In the course of the 1960s, economic developments favored the upper levels of black communities; the gap between top and bottom widened.[7] Evidences of absolute downward movement could be found in New York City where, during 1963–1964, one out of ten black men had less schooling than their fathers.[8] Another one-third of black men in the city had no more education than their fathers had achieved.

Class factors probably played a role in every significant movement concerning schools in black communities. Where segregation had most severely handicapped black children, in the poorest areas of the South, devotion to desegregation was strongest, though not exclusive. Middle-class forces were less mindful of desegregation and stressed the employment of black leaders in schools. In Atlanta, during the early 1970s, an agreement was reached by which a minimum of desegregation would be accepted in exchange for expanded black employment of upper school staff personnel, starting with the superintendency. Enthusiasm for the agreement was strongest among middle-class circles and weakest among the poor in Atlanta.[9] The latter, more dependent on actual school changes than the former, tended to stress the absence of commitment on system-wide benefits.

Class factors played a similar role in the history of other minorities. Throughout the Southwest propertied Mexican-Americans frequently were exempted from many of the grosser indignities and deprivations. Their children attended predominantly Anglo schools and colleges. In Puerto Rico, similarly situated groups became "Americanized," acquired a familiarity with the English language, adopted the more conventional aspects of American patriotism, and entered – or aspired to enter – the service of American private or governmental enterprise on the island. Most Puerto Ricans, living in isolated circumstances of rural poverty, did not soon experience the immediate cultural consequence or the economic benefits of the American occupation. Community life of Indian-Americans was probably the least differentiated of all four minorities. The margin of privilege was so narrow for them and the sweep of poverty so nearly complete that deprivation became the overwhelming norm. Nowhere was this so clear as in the area of schooling.

Ethnic persistence

The four minorities saw no contradiction between schooling and the maintenance of their ethnic autonomy. They sought, in varied ways and with differing degrees of success, to provide an education for their children. Few Americans were firmer believers in the importance of schooling. When exclusion from public facilities was total, the most meager private resources were used to finance schooling. Where exclusion was by law, campaigns were conducted to change the law. Separate schools were accepted if the alternative was none at all. Sooner or later, however, a campaign was undertaken to create common schools for all children. Minorities acted out citizen roles even as they lacked legal confirmation of such status. They organized petition campaigns, conducted boycotts, and initiated lawsuits.

The racism of dominant white society was separatist in ideology. In all but the rarest cases, it was whites who initiated and enforced the separation of minority children from their own. Black preferences were usually in favor of equal participation in a common facility. Blacks rarely had the luxury of a choice. Even the best white friends of the Negro found it difficult to grasp the daily penalties he suffered because of his color. White abolitionists saw the black man's principal problem as slavery, but black abolitionists – all free Negroes – who no longer suffered personally from slavery placed the ending of racial discrimination at the top of their agenda. Nevertheless, men like Garrison thought that the end of slavery would remove the main support of racial discrimination. This reasoning seemed weak to many black leaders who had felt the fury of northern racism even in the absence of slavery.

To blacks, the concept of northern Negro communities as *colonies* seemed to get at the heart of their plight. During the generation or so before the Civil War, colonization usually referred to the movement, principally by whites, to encourage American blacks to emigrate to Africa. Monetary incentives as well as education were offered to draw them out of the country. In this sense, colonization was a kind of benevolent banishment. Near the surface of colonizationist thought lay the judgment that blacks had no future in America. In Negro circles, colonization seemed an apt description of internal banishment as well. In 1835, abolitionist Child criticized the policy of a school for the blind which refused to admit black children; the school had set up a small hut in the backyard in which, Child charged, the black children "are to be colonized."[10] He called the hut "a Liberia." When, in 1862, black leader John Rock declared that "we are colonized in Boston," the context of his remark was an explanation of how economic opportunities were denied blacks in Massachusetts despite their formal right to vote and to ride in nonsegregated public conveyances.

The first significant numbers of black students entered public schools after the Civil War. There they pursued the same curricula available elsewhere. No distinctive black education was available either in the private or the public schools. The communal element in black education consisted not so much in this or that aspect of instruction as in the determination to gain a just share of the community's educational resources. Nothing buoyed that spirit as much as the Civil War. This conflict was the greatest shared experience of Afro-American history. Without it, the slave songs would have been merely dolorous reminders of a hard past. With it, the songs are constant reminders of the capacity of the Negro people to participate in their own emancipation. In other lands, such a profound, pervasive movement customarily formed the core of nationalistic memories. Here, it played a similar role, only within a biracial framework.

Until the past decade or so, black culture failed to become an integral part of schools attended by Negro children. Whether in North or South, instruction depended almost wholly on efforts by individual teachers. Traditional black colleges failed to deal with Afro-American culture in a central way, wishing to establish further their similarity to white colleges. Apparently, it was not until 1936 that a traditional black college first required students to take a course in black studies.[11] In the North, public schools shied away from the field. Permission to teach about black life was granted as a concession. Thus, the legislature of Illinois amended the state school code in 1931 as follows: "History of the Negro race may be taught in all public schools." Thirty years later, the law remained unchanged. During the early post-World War II years, several northern states began to require fairer treatment of blacks and other minorities in textbooks. The enactments were not enforced. As a consequence, the unprecedentedly large public school enrollments after 1945 depended on textbooks that ranged from racist to condescending in their discussion of the Negro.

The public schools were systematically inhospitable to Spanish-speaking minorities as well. In the Southwest, the very presence – let alone the culture – of Mexican-Americans in the schools was resented. Yet the Spanish language continued as a vigorous element of community life. Its persistence was attacked by school officials, who transformed a language difference into a learning handicap.

Neither Puerto Ricans nor Mexican-Americans could turn to the Roman Catholic parochial school as a protector of their language and culture. Both in Puerto Rico and Mexico the Church was an upper-class institution with little regard for either the social or cultural interests of the people. Parochial schools tended to serve a narrow circle of children. In the United States, too, the Catholic Church organized few schools for Puerto Ricans and Mexican-Americans. Polish immigrants in Buffalo or Chicago sent their children to Polish-language church schools; yet no such option ordinarily existed for the Spanish-speaking minorities.

For these groups especially, traditional culture was nurtured in the family and the home. Their ethnic awareness depended, too, on a proliferation of hometown clubs organized in the new land. The outright rejection by the schools of the Spanish language did little to shake the devotion of the people. Middle-class elements in the Spanish-speaking communities were readier than others to forsake the traditions.

Only during the 1960s did the schools begin an accommodation to Afro-American and Spanish-speaking cultures. In both cases, sharp community conflict preceded even those modest moves. The public schools resisted significantly modifying their standard of cultural assimilation.

Even these stirrings of change, however, failed to disturb the denigrative impact of the schools upon Indian-American children. The schools, both federal and local, thoroughly excluded Indian content from the curriculum. Even where many thousand Indian children attended schools in a relatively compact area – as on the Navajo Reservation – only a tiny proportion of the teachers were themselves Indian, and the curriculum was culturally estranged from the students.

The rebirth of ethnic consciousness among the four minorities during the 1960s was epochal in one special respect. In each case, demands were made that the public schools take on responsibility for ethnic education. This was another evidence of growing self-confidence by the groups. Ethnic autonomy lost some of its private character and became more a public fact.

Community and schools

In a geographical sense, American public education has been state controlled and locally administered. This feature resulted in localism becoming the mechanism for directly misappropriating funds designed for the benefit of Negro, Mexican-American, and Indian children. State governments were conscious partners in this educational plunder of the minorities. State governments in the North as well as the South refused to exercise educational superintendence over their public schools. Again and again they turned aside complaints by minority parents. In states containing large cities, state educational agencies abdicated regulatory functions in such cities. As a result, racial discrimination and deprivation in large cities were countenanced and encouraged.

State and local governments fostered a distorted sense of the public interest wherever ethnic and economic differences separated children in the same school systems. Failure to challenge the existence of clear inequalities allowed them to be accepted as legitimate. The object for parents then became how they could maintain their advantage or lose their disadvantage. Parents whose children received a discriminatorily higher allotment became wedded to the unequal system. Their primary concern was that their children continue to receive a larger share. Parents of the deprived children worked to obtain for them an education somehow equal to that enjoyed by the privileged children. The system of unequal expenditures thus bred among parents a mentality of "more than" and "as much as." As a result, there was little room for considering whether the system achieved a good education for either group of children. The continuation of the system inevitably crowded out considerations of improving the education of all. With the pressure of the system oriented away from improvement, it came to be regarded as a positive virtue if the system simply maintained the existing level of quality. A vested interest has been described as an institutionalized right to something for nothing. This applied to the public schools even when the "something" was not much.

Attempts by minority communities to control the schools their children attended rarely succeeded. Too often, this goal was pursued by use of private schools. The utter poverty of the group usually doomed the effort or condemned the children to a second-rate education. In one case, however, outright community control on an ethnic basis was highly successful; the schools set up by the five southern tribes, preeminently the Cherokees, attained a level of quality which at times surpassed that of public school systems in neighboring states. Very special circumstances made this possible.

During the 1820s and 1830s, the federal government chose to buy the Cherokee lands east of the Mississippi. In return for the lands, the Cherokees received money, among other things, to be used to set up bilingual schools. While force and fraud finally pushed the Indian into the desolate plains across the Mississippi, schools were built under the agreed-upon arrangement. Forty years later, the situation had changed. When federal authorities in 1868 dictated peace treaties to the Navajo and Sioux Indians, no provision was made for Indian-controlled schools or for bilingual instruction. Indeed, no actual schools were provided for a number of years. The Indian-controlled Cherokee schools operated in all for some eighty years. They were closed down and placed under state authority in 1906, the year when, by act of Congress, the Cherokee Nation ceased to exist. Community control of schools had been possible because a minority possessed actual sovereignty over a definite territory. Once that sovereignty was destroyed, the basis for an independent Cherokee culture was gravely weakened. The language and customs of the Cherokees lost their protective framework. Thirty years later, the University of Oklahoma refused to teach any courses in Indian culture.

Black and Mexican-American communities never exercised territorial sovereignty within the borders of the United States. A small number of all-black towns that did arise in Oklahoma and elsewhere were exceedingly poor and could not support an adequate school system. In Texas, separate school districts for Mexican-Americans were organized, but this was a means of cutting off minority children from the benefits of the schools the Anglos had built in adjacent districts.

During the 1960s, a movement for community control arose in New York City and a few other urban centers. Its appeal had two factors: (1) it expressed the historical demand of minority parents to control the education of their children, and (2) it expressed profound dissatisfaction of minority parents with the low quality of education provided by urban school systems. On one hand, the movement was a declaration of self-confidence by black and Puerto Rican parents in their ability to act on behalf of their children. On the other, it was an announcement of political import – if mostly for future realization – about the disillusionment of minority parents with the established institutions of school governance. Teachers' unions, administrators' organizations, and political parties combined to oppose calls for community controls. It was not, however, the localism but the transfer of power involved in community control that aroused the greatest opposition. Since power was not concentrated in the communities themselves, the problem of controlling citywide centers of power swiftly became a critical concern of minority communities. The pace of political organization quickened accordingly, especially where cooperation developed between two or more minorities.

School staffs

Historically, school staffs enforced the system of exclusion and discrimination. Zealous white teachers and principals frequently initiated exclusory actions. Occasionally, white voices were raised in defense of black children's education. In 1856, for example, at a convention of the New York state teachers' organization, Susan B. Anthony, the feminist leader and a teacher in Rochester, strongly condemned the exclusion of Negro children from many schools in the state. When delegates failed to take up the challenge, Miss Anthony pledged to raise the issue again the next year.[12] This she did. Four separate resolutions were presented. One read: "Resolved, that the exclusion of colored children from our public schools, academies, colleges and universities, is the result of a wicked prejudice against color." Another resolved that "*all* proscription from educational advantages and honors, on account of color, is in perfect harmony with the infamous decision of Judge Taney [in the *Dred Scott* case], that 'black men have no rights which white men are bound to respect.'" While the majority of a committee approved the resolutions, the convention adopted the minority report which stated limply that "the colored children of the state should enjoy equal advantages of education with the whites."[13]

Equivocation marked the outer bound of professional willingness to defend equal educational opportunities. After the Civil War and the subsequent rise of national professional organizations, the situation did not change in its essentials for nearly a century. University schools of education, intimately interlocked with local school systems, also failed to oppose racially discriminatory features of the schools. Both the National Education Association and the American Federation of Teachers organized separate locals for black teachers. The AFT abolished such locals in 1956, the NEA more than a decade later.[14]

National teachers' organizations cooperated in legislative and fund-raising efforts on behalf of general civil rights goals during the 1960s. In few local areas, however, could the groups be found actively cooperating with minority group movements for desegregation. In cities like Chicago, the teachers' union followed the lead offered by a school board and superintendent who were notorious for their opposition to desegregation. In New York City, the teachers' union became the leading defender of the racial status quo. From time to time, it actively manipulated racial issues for partisan purposes. The rising militancy of teachers' groups was limited to the benefit of the material interests of their members. Local teachers' organizations have proved no more sensitive to the needs of minority children than organized administrators, teachers colleges, and state and local school officials.

Black teachers' and administrators' organizations were in an equivocal position. They were primarily concerned with their own material well-being. Yet they found themselves, willy-nilly, in the public arena as the spokesmen for black educational interests. Since they lacked a significant power base of their own and in fact were at the mercy of white political authorities, they hesitated to risk dismissal. At the level of the individual school, however, Negro teachers and principals were often bolder. More informal avenues of influence enabled them to press for additional funds or personnel. Examples were not lacking, to be sure, of near-complete acquiescence to the barest budgets. Yet black teachers' organizations in the South laid the basis for fundamental educational change when they took to the courts in the late 1930s and early 1940s.

Noneducational movement

The history of American education includes a history of affirmative efforts not to educate. During much of Mexican and Puerto Rican history, the lower classes – including Indians and blacks – were excluded from educational facilities. Upper-class representatives were frank to argue – when they bothered to at all – that only a select few deserved an education. Nor can it be said that any mass protests arose at such exclusion through much of the nineteenth century. In the United States, similar aristocratic views dogged the supporters of public schooling.

Compulsory ignorance, however, was a distinctive American policy of noneducation. It was based on a positive fear by the southern ruling classes that blacks were all too educable. The policy of forbidding the education of slaves or free Negroes was an affirmation of the ability of blacks to learn rather than of the conviction argued by many theologians, scientists, and educators that blacks could not learn. The laws were also a peculiar acknowledgment of the attractions of freedom.

In the pre-Civil War North, most black children were either excluded altogether from school or segregated. In certain areas, they attended schools in common with white children. Objections to nonsegregated education were often couched in unembarrassed racist terms. Yet the very success of nonsegregated schools encouraged the thought that common schools for all would benefit the entire community.

The Boston school committee, seeking to establish a psychological theory to justify its persistent policy of segregation, in 1846, at a time when most towns in Massachusetts had desegregated their schools, insisted that black children could not benefit from a common education. It contended that black students were competent in instructional matters dependent on memory but would fall behind in the use of "the faculties of invention, compassion, and reasoning."[15] The absence of similar complaints in other towns where schools were not segregated suggested a factual weakness of the argument. Nor did Boston authorities point to any specific schools. At this time, all but a few Negro children in Boston were assigned to one school. For two years, black parents had conducted a running battle with the principal of the Smith School. In 1844, after a careful, exhaustive study, they had concluded the principal believed in the inferiority of his pupils. "If a man conscientiously imbibes a belief that a race of persons, with whom he is thrown in contact, are an inferior class," the parents declared, "will he not begin imperceptibly to himself, to treat them as such?"[16] It could well have been the discredited principal of the Smith School who provided the school committee with the psychological theory of inferiority two years later.

A general racism infected the North before the Civil War. Even Horace Mann shared the belief in inborn inferiority of blacks. But it must be emphasized that the broader educational segregation and deprivation of minority children were based on power and status arguments. Unlike the Bostonians, most partisans of segregation defended its attractions without trying to justify exclusion of black children on intellectual grounds. Blacks were to be discriminated against simply because they did not share in the power arrangements. But they had no power, after all, because they were

black. The advent of intelligence tests early in the twentieth century
provided a new basis for an intellectual defense of exclusion or invidious
distinctions. By the close of World War I, leading psychologists had constructed theories of intellectual worth that equated minority status with
low academic ability. The public schools obliged by adopting the same
line of reasoning. It was accomplished effortlessly because it was conso-
nant with the general exclusionary trends developed over the previous
decades. Having lived so long by the practice of inequality, the schools
easily slipped into accepting the pseudoscientific theory of inferior intellectual ability.

When academic sensibilities began to prohibit linking low ability with
race – as was the case during the 1940s and 1950s – social class became the
culprit. Not since John Calvin had so many plain human beings been
consigned to the nether regions. Predestination by social class became the
new orthodoxy. In the 1960s, a stage was reached when a psychologist
appropriated the reasoning if not the words of the Boston school committee of a century earlier. Jensen held black children to be less capable than
white children in abstract or conceptual thinking but equal or superior in
learning dependent on memory. He attributed an intelligence quotient
lag of blacks overwhelmingly to genetic inheritance rather than environ-
mental discrimination.[17] Investigators were unable to produce experimental data or direct empirical evidence from school settings in which
academic performance of black and white children as such could be distinguished by strict racial criteria. Instead, analogies were offered with
test differences between individual white children. Ability differences
between individuals within a single race were asserted without evidence
to explain differences of a similar magnitude between races.

Much of the force of public debate about racial differentials in intelligence derived from a fundamental confusion. Involved were two separate
questions, neither capable of immediate scientific demonstration. The
first issue concerned the practical social capacity of large groups of people
("races") to conduct civilized life including specific careers, problematic
life situations, in family and community, in the creation of artistic products, and other practical challenges. To find any race inferior in this
sense would require evidence of incapacity that persisted *even when the
opportunity had been made available.* No such evidence was brought
forward that held for blacks *but not for members of any other race.* The
second issue involved a judgment whether any racial differences in intellectual ability would persist in the absence of all social discrimination.
Having mistakenly thought they settled the first issue, it was further
assumed by many that the second was thereby also resolved. To "settle"
the second question would require an absolute equality of social conditions. Nobody seriously claimed this already obtained. Nor were any of
the adherents of the inherently inferior school of thought perceptibly

active in community movements to equalize conditions. Guesses about the eventual outcome ranged widely. Anthropologist Washburn, for example, thought it just as likely that blacks would perform in a superior way under equal conditions.[18]

The debate evaded educational issues. Both sides tended to accept declarations that lacked the most elementary documentation. For example, Jensen had written that compensatory education was tried and found wanting. The only controversy involved the explanation of the failure. In fact, however, the practice of compensatory education was exceedingly defective in most basic respects. Much of the money designed for such use was misappropriated for ineligible middle-class children. Neither federal nor state governments supervised expenditures. Exceedingly unimaginative instructional approaches were employed, thus repeating the failures of noncompensatory education. Racial isolation was the context of most compensatory efforts.

The debate was interminable because of the confusion of historical questions with questions of the future. Gross unrealism led many participants in the debate to treat premises as facts. Schools were thus relieved of a share of the responsibility for educational failure. Two foundations of public noneducation were race and social class, the former immutable by virtue of biology, the second irremediable in the absence of major social changes. This ideology, couched in the language of science, dominated educational practice. A search for highly talented minority and poor white youth, sporadic and ill-financed as it was, implied that these young people were merely "exceptional." For the great mass of the remaining children, a norm of nonachievement was tolerated.

Historically, the significance of race in education has been underestimated. More recently, many analysts of right and left persuasions have interpreted minority children as essentially poor children, defining their plight as economic rather than racial. Another view is that the four minorities discussed in this book are not unlike all other minority children so that their problems are those of any ethnic group. Both these views evade the dominant role of race in American education.

Race continues to be one of the most basic political issues in American life. Governmental authorities and educators may indeed wish to avoid direct consideration of this fact and continue to speak of education as a nonpolitical area. One is reminded of the Wendell Phillips–Horace Mann debate. When Phillips accused Mann of ignoring racial discrimination in the Boston schools, he also observed that Mann concerned himself with technical educational innovations. Immersion in the pedagogical dimension of education was a tested means of avoiding political conflict. But, Phillips charged, Mann was not so much avoiding conflict as refusing to declare his own contribution to that conflict.

In pre-Civil War America, educational philosophizing did not reach the issue of race as such; race was not considered a problem but a condition of life. American educators persisted in this analysis for nearly a century more. Except for black educators and social critics, and the rarest white educator, race was immune from discussion as a problem. Even a philosopher such as John Dewey, who made democracy in education a central point of his analysis, apparently never wrote an article dealing with race in education. A social scientist such as Thorstein Veblen, who spared little in American society, also seems never to have discussed race as an issue. Race was admitted into the select circle of scientific problems only when the impingement of minority peoples in practical affairs stirred new political discontents. Only a century after the Civil War were racial and ethnic concerns finally permitted to assume the status of "problems." The political element was still dominant, but it was a new politics. For the first time in American history, through a more democratic politics than ever before, American education was forced to contemplate the requirements of a system to educate all the children of all the people.

The study of history perfects the art of looking forward, not backward. In the perspective of several centuries, the future cannot but be influenced by a novel feature: millions of minority parents and children are self-aware of their rights and increasingly skilled in contending for those rights. The schools cannot long resist such a momentous fact.

Notes

Notes

Introduction: race in American education

1 See Thorstein Veblen, *The Place of Science in Modern Civilization and Other Essays* (New York: Viking, 1942), pp. 1–31. The title essay was written in 1906.

2 Thomas F. Pettigrew and Kurt W. Back, "Sociology in the Desegregation Process: Its Use and Disuse," in Paul F. Lazarsfeld, William H. Sewell, and Harold L. Wilensky (eds.), *The Use of Sociology* (New York: Basic Books, 1967), p. 706.

3 *Ibid.*, p. 707.

4 *Ibid.*, p. 711.

5 See Martin Luther King, "The Role of the Behavioral Scientists in the Civil Rights Movement," *American Psychologist* (March 1968).

6 Herbert Blumer, *Symbolic Interactionism: Perspective and Method* (Englewood Cliffs, N.J.: Prentice-Hall, 1969), p. 22.

7 *Ibid.*, p. 33.

8 *Ibid.*, p. 51.

9 See Ellwood P. Cubberley, *Public Education in the United States: A Study and Interpretation of American Educational History*, rev. ed. (Boston: Houghton Mifflin, 1934), pp. 485–486, 663, 669, 745.

10 Both leading authorities on higher education totally ignore the subject of college discrimination against black students. John S. Brubacher and Willis Rudy, *Higher Education in Transition: A History of American Colleges and Universities, 1636–1968*, rev. ed. (New York: Harper & Row, 1968); Frederick Rudolph, *The American College and University* (New York: Knopf, 1962).

11 In 1958, Louis R. Harlan, in his excellent *Separate and Unequal: Public School Campaigns and Racism in the Southern Seaboard States, 1901–1915*, acknowledged the contribution of Bond. Few others have followed in his footsteps.

12 Martha E. Layman, "A History of Indian Education in the United States" (doctoral dissertation, University of Minnesota, 1942).

13 See Roger Daniels, *Concentration Camps, U.S.A.: Japanese Americans and World War II* (New York: Holt, 1972); William D. Zeller, *An Educational Drama: The Educational Program Provided the Japanese-Americans during the Relocation Period, 1942–1945* (New York: American Press, 1969); and *Chinese-Americans: School and Community Problems* (Chicago: Integrated Education Associates, 1972).

14 See Roger E. Wyman, "Wisconsin Ethnic Groups and the Election of 1890," *Wisconsin Magazine of History*, 51 (summer 1968), pp. 269–293.

Chapter 1. The system of compulsory ignorance: black children to 1865

1 Alexander Crummell, *The Attitude of the American Mind Toward the Negro Intellect*, The American Negro Academy Occasional Papers, No. 3 (Washington, D.C.: The Academy, 1898), p. 9.

2 The term was apparently first used by James Simpson of the Society of Friends in England. In 1865, after visiting Richmond, Virginia, he described the lack of learning shown by slave children as they attended their first schools: "Their ignorance has, in fact, been compulsory." See extracts from Simpson's report to the Friends in *Liberator*, August 11, 1865. Some forty years later, W. E. B. Du Bois also used a similar term, apparently independently.

3 Basil Davidson (in collaboration with F. K. Bush and the advice of J. F. Ade Ajayi), *The Growth of African Civilization: A History of West Africa, 1000–1800*, 2nd ed. (London: Longmans, 1967), p. 164.

4 Akin L. Mabogunje, "Urbanization and Change," *in* John N. Paden and Edward W. Soja (eds.), *The African Experience*, Vol. I, *Essays* (Evanston, Ill.: Northwestern University Press, 1970), p. 338.

5 In 1830, there were 2,009,043 slaves and 797,167 Negro children under the age of ten years in the United States. The latter figure included a relatively small number of free Negro children.

6 Elizabeth Donnan (ed.), *Documents Illustrative of the History of the Slave Trade to America*, Vol. II (New York: Octagon, 1969, reprinted), p. 584.

7 *Ibid.*, pp. 220, 327, 590.

8 H. Easton, *A Treatise on the Intellectual Character and Civil and Political Condition of the Colored People of the United States; and the Prejudice Exercised Towards Them . . .* (Boston: Knapp, 1837), p. 51.

9 John Spencer Bassett, *Slavery in the State of North Carolina* (Baltimore: Johns Hopkins Press, 1899), pp. 66–67.

10 Frank J. Klingberg, *The Appraisal of the Negro in Colonial South Carolina: A Study in Americanization* (Washington, D.C.: Associated Publishers, 1941), p. 105.

11 *Ibid.*, p. 69.

12 Charles S. Sydnor, *Slavery in Mississippi* (New York: Appleton, 1933), p. 253.

13 Carter G. Woodson, *The Education of the Negro Prior to 1861*, 2nd ed. (Washington, D.C.: Associated Publishers, 1919), p. 161.

14 James Benson Sellers, *Slavery in Alabama* (University: University of Alabama Press, 1950), p. 117.

15 Harrison Anthony Traxler, *Slavery in Missouri, 1804–1865* (Baltimore: Johns Hopkins Press, 1914), p.83.

16 Carter G. Woodson, *The African Background Outlined: Or Handbook for the Study of the Negro* (New York: Negro Universities Press, 1968, reprinted), p. 319.

17 Susie King Taylor, *Reminiscences of My Life in Camp with the 33rd United States Colored Troops Late 1st S.C. Volunteers* (New York: Arno Press, 1968, reprinted), p. 5.

18 Letter from Birney, *Liberator*, October 4, 1834.

19 *Liberator*, February 8, 1839.

20 Quoted in J. Winston Coleman, Jr., *Slavery Times in Kentucky* (Chapel Hill: University of North Carolina Press, 1940), pp. 78–79.

21 *Liberator*, January 16, 1836.

22 Woodson, *African Background*, p. 342; *North Star*, December 5, 1850; quoted in Philip S. Foner (ed.), *The Life and Writings of Frederick Douglass*, Vol. II, *Pre-Civil War Decade: 1850–1860* (New York: International, 1950), p. 136.

23 Helen Catterall (ed.), *Judicial Cases Concerning American Slavery and the Negro*, Vol. I (Washington, D.C.: Carnegie Institution, 1936), p. 105.

24 John Hope Franklin, *The Free Negro in North Carolina, 1790–1860* (New York: Russell & Russell, 1969, reprinted), p. 169; John H. Russell, *The Free Negro in Virginia, 1619–1865* (Baltimore: Johns Hopkins Press, 1913), p. 145.

25 U.S. Commissioner of Education, *Special Report of the Commissioner of Educa-*

tion on the *Improvement of Public Schools in the District of Columbia, 1871,* Part II, *Legal Status of the Colored Population in Respect to Schools and Education in the Different States* (Washington, D.C.: GPO, 1871), p. 395.

26 Ellen M. O'Conner (ed.), *Myrtilla Miner: A Memoir* (Boston: Houghton Mifflin, 1885), p. 17.

27 *Ibid.,* p. 24.

28 Petition 12130, March 16, 1838; quoted in James Hugo Johnston, *Race Relations in Virginia and Miscegenation in the South, 1776–1860* (Amherst: University of Massachusetts Press, 1970), p. 51.

29 Luther Porter Jackson, *Free Negro Labor and Property Holding in Virginia, 1830–1860* (New York: Atheneum, 1969, reprinted), p. 20. A similar law was passed in North Carolina; see U.S. Commissioner of Education, *Legal Status of the Colored Population,* p. 368.

30 Woodson, *Education of the Negro Prior to 1861,* p. 182.

31 U.S. Commissioner of Education, *History of Schools for the Colored Population in the District of Columbia* (Washington, D.C.: GPO, 1871), p. 218.

32 Franklin, *Free Negro in North Carolina,* pp. 211, 224.

33 *Ibid.,* p. 98.

34 Woodson, *Education of the Negro Prior to 1861,* p. 167. See also Sydnor, *Slavery in Mississippi,* p. 53.

35 U.S. Commissioner of Education, *Legal Status of the Colored Population.* For complete section of the treaty, see Hunter Miller (ed.), *Treaties and Other International Acts of the United States of America,* Vol. II (Washington, D.C.: GPO, 1931), p. 501.

36 Lafayette M. Hershaw, *The Status of the Free Negro Prior to 1860,* Papers of the American Negro Academy (Washington, D.C.: The Academy, 1916), p. 43.

37 This aspect is not treated in William W. Freehling, "The Founding Fathers and Slavery," *American Historical Review,* 77 (February 1972), pp. 89–91, where an increase in number and percentage of free Negroes is discussed without reference to the growing difficulties they experienced in the Upper South.

38 Sellers, *Slavery in Alabama,* p. 393. On free Negro illiteracy in Virginia, see Russell, *Free Negro in Virginia,* p. 145.

39 Woodson, *Education of the Negro Prior to 1861,* p. 228.

40 Edward Raymond Turner, *The Negro in Pennsylvania: Slavery, Servitude, Freedom, 1639–1861* (New York: Negro Universities Press, 1969, reprinted), p. 133. See also H. C. Wright to William Lloyd Garrison, September 16, 1842, *Liberator,* September 23, 1842.

41 *Liberator,* July 13, 1833.

42 Robert Purvis, "Appeal of Forty Thousand Citizens Threatened with Disfranchisement, to the People of Pennsylvania," *Liberator,* April 13, 1838.

43 *Liberator,* December 5, 1845.

44 Leonard L. Richards, *"Gentlemen of Property and Standing": Anti-Abolition Mobs in Jacksonian America* (New York: Oxford University Press, 1970), p. 40.

45 *Liberator,* August 26, 1859.

46 Frank U. Quillin, *The Color Line in Ohio: A History of Race Prejudice in a Typical Northern State* (Ann Arbor: Wahr, 1913), p. 33.

47 *Liberator,* August 4, 1843.

48 See Ray Allen Billington (ed.), *A Free Negro in the Slave Era: The Journal of Charlotte L. Forten* (New York: Collier, 1961), *passim.*

49 *Liberator,* October 18, 1839; *Liberator,* January 11, 1856; and Howard H. Bell, *A Survey of the Negro Convention Movement, 1830–1861* (New York: Arno Press, 1969, reprinted), p. 262.

50 Numerous extracts from black newspapers and periodicals are reproduced in

Martin E. Dann (ed.), *The Black Press, 1827–1890: The Quest for National Identity* (New York: Putnam, 1971).

51 Emma V. Browne to William Lloyd Garrison, April 1, 1858, *Liberator*, April 16, 1858.

52 *Freedom's Journal*, June 1, 1827; quoted in Dann (ed.), *The Black Press*, pp. 293–294.

53 Charles T. Hickock, *The Negro in Ohio, 1802–1870* (Cleveland: Williams, 1896), p. 90.

54 See *Liberator*, October 3 and 10, 1835.

55 *Liberator*, April 7, 1854. See also Nell in *Liberator*, February 16, 1855.

56 Bell, *Survey of the Negro Convention Movement*, pp. 58–59.

57 *Liberator*, March 2, 1849.

58 *Liberator*, December 16, 1853.

59 Josephine Brown to Samuel J. May, April 27, 1954; quoted in Carter G. Woodson (ed.), *The Mind of the Negro as Reflected in Letters Written During the Crisis 1800–1860* (Washington, D.C.: Association for the Study of Negro Life and History, 1926), p. 364.

60 Quoted in Robert H. Bremner, *Children and Youth in America: A Documentary History*, Vol. I, *1600–1865* (Cambridge, Mass.: Harvard University Press, 1970), p. 445. See also Easton, *A Treatise*, p. 41.

61 *Liberator*, October 6, 1848.

62 Arthur W. White, "Mid-Nineteenth Century Movements for Desegregated Schools in Six Northern Communities," *Integrated Education*, 10 (November–December 1972), pp. 37, 41.

63 *Liberator*, August 13, 1858.

64 *Liberator*, March 18, 1842.

65 *Liberator*, March 15, 1844.

66 White, "Mid-Nineteenth Century Movements," p. 39.

67 The entire report is reprinted in *Liberator*, August 2, 1844.

68 See William Howe to George T. Downing, February 10, 1857, *Liberator*, February 27, 1857; various letters, *Liberator*, April 17, 1857; and quarterly report by Charles W. Slack, chairman of Everett School, *Liberator*, December 13, 1861.

69 Martin R. Delany, *The Condition, Elevation, Emigration, and Destiny of the Colored People of the United States Politically Considered* (Philadelphia: privately printed, 1852), p. 195.

70 *Liberator*, May 21, 1852.

71 The complete address is printed in *Liberator*, August 15, 1862.

72 *Liberator*, June 16, 1863.

73 *Liberator*, August 22, 1862.

74 Reprinted from the *New York Tribune* in *Liberator*, November 19, 1858.

75 *Liberator*, February 23, 1844.

76 Crummell, *Attitude of the American Mind Toward the Negro Intellect*, p. 12.

77 *Liberator*, July 13, 1860.

78 *Liberator*, February 14, 1862.

79 *Liberator*, August 15, 1862.

80 *New Orleans Tribune*, February 1865; quoted in James M. McPherson (ed.), *The Negro's Civil War: How American Negroes Felt and Acted During the War for the Union* (New York: Vintage, 1967), p. 17.

81 *Liberator*, May 14, 1852. The letter is dated December 21, 1851. For a criticism of Mann's views by a meeting of black citizens, see *Liberator*, October 22, 1852.

82 The debate between Phillips and Mann can be found in *Liberator*, March 25, April 8, April 15, April 29, May 6, May 13, and May 20, 1853.

83 *Liberator,* December 24, 1847, editorial signed "P." See also article signed "W. P." in *Liberator,* February 11, 1848.

84 *Liberator,* August 21, 1846.

85 See, for example, *Liberator,* April 17, 1857.

86 Fletcher Harper Swift, *Federal and State Policies in Public School Finance in the United States* (Boston: Ginn, 1931), pp. 67–68: "The funds of Federal origin were wheel, ballast, and lever of the states' systems of free schools." See also Swift, *A History of Public Permanent Common-School Funds in the United States, 1795–1905* (New York: Holt, 1911).

87 Calculated from data in Paul W. Gates, *History of Public Land Law Development* (Washington, D.C.: GPO, November 1968), p. 804.

88 *Liberator,* April 6, 1838.

89 *Lewis v. Henley et al.,* 2 Ind. 335 (1850).

90 *Liberator,* November 21, 1845.

91 *Liberator,* May 3, 1834.

92 *Liberator,* October 27, 1848.

93 *Liberator,* May 21, 1841.

94 Gilbert T. Stephenson, *Race Distinctions in American Law* (New York: Appleton, 1910), p. 184.

95 Hickock, *Negro in Ohio,* p. 81.

96 N. Dwight Harris, *The History of Negro Servitude in Illinois and of the Slavery Agitation in That State* (Chicago: McClurg, 1904), p. 230.

97 *Ibid.* On the other hand, the legislature was quite definite when, in 1826, it had exempted masters of black apprentices from the traditional responsibility of teaching them to read and write; see Harris, p. 229.

98 Bremner, *Children and Youth in America,* p. 438.

99 *Josiah Hughes v. Samuel Jackson,* 12 Md. 450 (1858).

100 *Needles et al. v. Martin,* 33 Md. 609 (1871). See also *Chandler v. Ferris,* 1 Harrington 454 (1834).

101 *Chalmers v. Stewart,* 11 Ohio 386 (1842).

102 *Lewis v. Henley et al.,* 2 Ind. 334–335 (1850).

103 *Roberts v. The City of Boston,* 5 Cushing 209 (1850).

104 *Liberator,* October 7 and November 10, 1854. In 1899, William Monroe Trotter, a black leader in Boston, married Geraldine Louise Pindell, niece of William Pindell; see Stephen R. Fox, *The Guardian of Boston, William Monroe Trotter* (New York: Atheneum, 1970), pp. 22–23.

105 *Liberator,* February 23, 1855.

106 *Jeffries v. Ankeny et al.,* 11 Ohio 372 (1842).

107 *Thacker v. Hawk et al.,* 11 Ohio 38 (1842).

108 *Van Camp v. Board of Education of Logan,* 9 Ohio St. 415 (1859).

109 *Liberator,* November 9, 1860.

110 Eric Foner, *Free Soil, Free Labor, Free Men: The Ideology of the Republican Party Before the Civil War* (New York: Oxford University Press, 1970), pp. 286–287.

111 *Clark v. The Board of Directors,* 24 Iowa 272–273 (1868). This decision contains an excellent historical review of state legislation and policy. Apparently, school segregation in Dubuque remained undisturbed during the Civil War; see Jacque Voegeli, *Free but Not Equal: The Midwest and the Negro During the Civil War* (Chicago: University of Chicago Press, 1967), p. 172.

112 *People ex rel. Joseph Workman v. Board of Education of Detroit,* 18 Mich. 419 (1869).

113 *Liberator,* April 10, 1857.

114 *Liberator,* August 7, 1857.

115 Reports on wartime developments in black schooling can be found in the sources in the preceding notes as well as in Billington, *A Free Negro in the Slave Era*, and Bell Irvin Wiley, *Southern Negroes, 1861–1865*, 2nd ed. (New York: Rinehart, 1953).

116 *Liberator*, January 29, 1864.

117 U.S. Commissioner of Education, *Legal Status of the Colored Population*, p. 368.

118 *Liberator*, October 20, 1865.

119 U.S. Commissioner of Education, *History of Schools for the Colored Population in the District of Columbia*, pp. 268–269.

120 *Liberator*, August 5, 1864.

121 Quoted in Susie King Taylor, *Reminiscences of My Life in Camp*, p. 49.

Chapter 2. Separate and unequal: black education, 1865–1950

1 U.S. Commissioner of Education, *Legal Status of the Colored Population*, p. 347.

2 Rackham Holt, *Mary McLeod Bethune: A Biography* (Garden City, N.Y.: Doubleday, 1964), p. 7. Mary was the fifteenth of seventeen children; her older sisters and brothers had been slaves.

3 W. E. B. Du Bois, "Reconstruction and Its Benefits," *American Historical Review* (1909–1910), p. 782.

4 Thomas Calhoun Walker, *The Honey-Pod Tree: The Life Story of Thomas Calhoun Walker* (New York: Day, 1958), pp. 17–19.

5 Pauli Murray, *Proud Shoes: The Story of an American Family* (New York: Harper & Row, 1956), p. 179.

6 U.S Commissioner of Education, *Legal Status of the Colored Population*, pp. 368–369.

7 Richard R. Wright, *A Brief Historical Sketch of Negro Education in Georgia* (Savannah: Robinson, 1894), p. 31.

8 William H. Holtzclaw, *The Black Man's Burden* (New York: Neale, 1915), p. 14.

9 Marjorie Holloman Parker, "The Educational Activities of the Freedmen's Bureau" (doctoral dissertation, University of Chicago, 1951), p. 202.

10 Horace Mann Bond, *Black American Scholars: A Study of Their Beginnings* (Detroit: Balamp, 1972), p. 40.

11 Parker, "Educational Activities of the Freedmen's Bureau," pp. 41–44.

12 *Ibid.*, p. 93.

13 Carter G. Woodson, *Early Negro Education in West Virginia* (Institute: West Virginia Collegiate Institute, 1921), p. 8.

14 Willie Lee Rose, "'Iconoclasm Has Had Its Day': Abolitionists and Freedom in South Carolina," in Martin Duberman (ed.), *The Anti-slavery Vanguard: New Essays on the Abolitionists* (Princeton: Princeton University Press, 1965), p. 204.

15 James M. McPherson, *The Struggle for Equality: Abolitionists and the Negro in the Civil War and Reconstruction* (Princeton: Princeton University Press, 1964), p. 399.

16 Murray, *Proud Shoes*, p. 221.

17 *New National Era*, April 6, 1871; quoted in Foner (ed.), *Life and Writings of Frederick Douglass*, Vol. IV, pp. 242–243.

18 Vernon L. Wharton, *The Negro in Mississippi, 1865–1890* (New York: Harper Torchbook, 1965), p. 245.

19 Lawrence D. Rice, *The Negro in Texas, 1874–1900* (Baton Rouge: Louisiana State University Press, 1971), p. 211.

20 U.S. Congress, *Joint Select Committee to Inquire into the Conditions of Affairs in the Late Insurrectionary States, Testimony* [Ala.] (Washington, D.C.: GPO, 1872), pp. 1268–1269.

21 See Allen W. Trelease, *White Terror: The Ku Klux Klan Conspiracy and Southern Reconstruction* (New York: Harper & Row, 1971), pp. 84, 86, 122, 261, 265, 305–306, 320–321, 365.

22 See Herbert Shapiro, "Afro-American Responses to Race Violence During Reconstruction," *Science and Society*, 36 (Summer 1972), pp. 158–170.

23 Trelease, *White Terror*, p. 420.

24 *Liberator*, February 17, 1865.

25 Du Bois wrote: "The Negro school system established by the Negro reconstruction governments reached its culmination in the decade, 1870–1880"; "The Economic Revolution in the South," *in* Booker T. Washington and W. E. B. Du Bois, *The Negro in the South* (Philadelphia: Jacobs, 1907), p. 103.

26 W. E. B. Du Bois, *Black Reconstruction in America* (New York: Russell & Russell, 1962, reprinted), p. 638.

27 Alretheus Ambush Taylor, *The Negro in the Reconstruction of Virginia* (Washington, D.C.: Association for the Study of Negro Life and History, 1926), p. 157.

28 Holtzclaw, *Black Man's Burden*, pp. 30–31.

29 W. E. B. Du Bois (ed.) *The Negro Common School* (Atlanta: Atlanta University Press, 1901), p. 49.

30 Enrollment rates for white children also fell during the same period. The primary reason was the lower rate of attendance of foreign-born whites and their children. Many immigrants entered the United States during these years.

31 *Claybrook* v. *Owensboro*, 16 Fed. R. 302 (1883).

32 *Puitt* v. *Commissioners*, 94 N.C. 519 (1886).

33 George Brown Tindall, *South Carolina Negroes, 1877–1900* (Columbia: University of South Carolina Press, 1914), p. 216.

34 Du Bois, "Economic Revolution in the South," p. 103.

35 Walker, *Honey-Pod Tree*, p. 45.

36 Horace Mann Bond, *Social and Economic Influences on the Public Education of Negroes in Alabama, 1865–1930* (Washington, D.C.: Associated Publishers, 1939), p. 192.

37 William R. Davis, *The Development and Present Status of Negro Education in East Texas* (New York: Teachers College Columbia University, 1934), p. 38.

38 Louis R. Harlan, *Separate and Unequal: Public School Campaigns and Racism in the Southern Seaboard States 1901–1915* (Chapel Hill: University of North Carolina Press, 1958), p. 19.

39 Horace Mann Bond, *Education of the Negro in the American Social Order* (New York: Octagon, 1966, reprinted), p. 56.

40 *New National Era*, May 2, 1872; quoted in Foner (ed.), *Life and Writings of Frederick Douglass*, Vol. IV, p. 346.

41 Herbert Aptheker (ed.), *A Documentary History of the Negro People in the United States* (New York: Citadel, 1951), pp. 639–640.

42 See *Civil Rights Cases*, 109 U.S. 3 (1883), in which the U.S. Supreme Court struck down the Civil Rights Act of 1875. The statute did not contain any reference to separate schools, although an early draft outlawed school segregation.

43 John Hope Franklin, "Jim Crow Goes to School," *South Atlantic Quarterly* (spring 1959), p. 234–5.

44 Holtzclaw, *Black Man's Burden*, p. 30.

45 Septima Poinsetta Clark with Le Gette Blythe, *Echo in My Soul* (New York: Dutton, 1962), p. 36.

46 Walker, *Honey-Pod Tree*, p. 18.

47 Jesse O. Thomas, *My Story in Black and White: The Autobiography of Jesse O. Thomas* (New York: Exposition, 1967), p. 13.

48 Murray, *Proud Shoes*, pp. 269–270.

49 Arthur P. Davis, "I Go to Whittier School," *Phylon*, 21 (1960), p. 156.

50 *Cumming* v. *County Board of Education*, 175 U.S. 545 (1899).

51 Walter L. Fleming, *The Sequel of Appomattox* (New Haven: Yale University Press, 1920), p. 218.

52 *Montgomery Advertiser*, July 24, 1867; quoted in Walter L. Fleming (ed.), *Documentary History of Reconstruction* (Gloucester, Mass.: Peter Smith, 1960, reprinted), p. 181.

53 E. Merton Coulter, *The South During Reconstruction, 1865–1877* (Baton Rouge: Louisiana State University Press, 1947), p. 329.

54 W. E. B. Du Bois, "A Negro Schoolmaster in the New South," *Atlantic Monthly*, 83 (January 1899), p. 101.

55 Benjamin E. Mays, *Born to Rebel: An Autobiography* (New York: Scribner, 1971), p. 2.

56 Robert Russa Moton, *Finding a Way Out: An Autobiography* (College Park: McGrath, 1969, reprinted), p. 59, 61.

57 John C. Dancy, *Sand Against the Wind: The Memoirs of John C. Dancy* (Detroit: Wayne State University Press, 1966), p. 72.

58 Davis, "I Go to Whittier School," p. 155.

59 Constance McL. Green, *The Secret City: A History of Race Relations in the Nation's Capital* (Princeton: Princeton University Press, 1967), pp. 137, 245.

60 This summary of 1910 data is based upon an analysis of census materials by the present writer.

61 Mays, *Born to Rebel*, p. 49.

62 Richard Wright, *Black Boy* (New York: Harper & Row, 1945), p. 65.

63 W. E. B. Du Bois, "The Hosts of Black Labor," *Nation*, 116 (May 9, 1923), p. 541.

64 Walker, *Honey-Pod Tree*, p. 318.

65 Alfreda M. Duster (ed.), *Crusade for Justice: The Autobiography of Ida B. Wells* (Chicago: University of Chicago Press, 1970), p. 9.

66 Whitelaw Reid, *After the War: A Southern Tour: May 1, 1865 to May 1, 1866* (New York: Moore, 1866), p. 253.

67 J. T. Trowbridge, *The South* (Hartford, Conn.: Stebbins, 1866), pp. 337–338.

68 Horace Mann Bond, "Self-Respect as a Factor in Racial Advancement," *Annals*, 140 (1928), p. 23.

69 Bond, *Education of the Negro in the American Social Order*, p. 115.

70 Harlan, *Separate and Unequal*, pp. 14, 259, 131, 166.

71 The mechanism, without discussion of racial factors, is analyzed in Swift, *Federal and State Policies in Public School Finance*, p. 213.

72 Mays, *Born to Rebel*, p. 40.

73 Henry Allen Bullock, *A History of Negro Education in the South: From 1619 to the Present* (Cambridge, Mass.: Harvard University Press, 1967), p. 179.

74 John Hope, "Negro Suffrage in the States Whose Constitutions Have Not Been Specifically Revised," in *The Negro and the Elective Franchise*, American Negro Academy Occasional Paper No. 11 (Washington, D.C.: The Academy, 1905), pp. 59–60.

75 Walter White, *A Man Called White: The Autobiography of Walter White* (New York: Viking, 1948), p. 32.

76 W. E. B. Du Bois, "The Negro Common School, Mississippi," *Crisis* (December 1926), p. 102.

77 *Bryant et al.* v. *Barnes, Tax Collector*, 106 So. 116 (1925).

78 Charles H. Wilson, Sr., *Education for Negroes in Mississippi Since 1910* (Boston: Meador, 1947), p. 40.

79 Charles Evers, *Evers* (New York: World, 1971), p. 44.

80 Wilson, *Education for Negroes in Mississippi Since 1910*, p. 45.

81 Du Bois, "Negro Common School, Mississippi," pp. 92, 95.

82 Anna Arnold Hedgman, *The Trumpet Sounds: A Memoir of Negro Leadership* (New York: Holt, 1964), p. 22.

83 Quoted in *Jumper v. Lyles*, 77 Okla. 57 (1919).

84 *State* v. *Albritton*, 98 Okla. 160 (1923).

85 Horace Mann Bond, "The Negro Common School in Oklahoma," *Crisis* (July 1928), p. 245.

86 Harlan, *Separate and Unequal*, p. 210.

87 Bond, *Education of the Negro in the American Social Order*, pp. 171, 244.

88 Davis, *Development and Present Status of Negro Education in East Texas*, p. 137.

89 Wilson, *Education for Negroes in Mississippi Since 1910*, p. 55. See also article by N. P. Brown, *New York Age*, February 22, 1936.

90 W. E. B. Du Bois, "The Tragedy of 'Jim Crow,'" *Crisis* (August 1923), p. 172.

91 Bullock, *History of Negro Education in the South*, p. 183.

92 Carter G. Woodson, *The Rural Negro* (Washington, D.C.: Association for the Study of Negro Life and History, 1930), p. 189.

93 "Colored Teachers in Charleston Schools," *Crisis* (June 1921) p. 58.

94 Bond, *Social and Economic Influences on the Public Education of Negroes in Alabama, 1861–1930*, p. 270.

95 W. E. B. Du Bois, "The Negro Common School in Georgia," *Crisis* (September 1926), p. 143.

96 Du Bois, "Negro Common School, Mississippi," p. 94.

97 Ellen Tarry, *The Third Door: The Autobiography of an American Woman* (New York: Guild Press, 1966), p. 79.

98 Du Bois, "Negro Common School, Mississippi," p. 95.

99 Thomas Jackson Woofter, Jr., *Negro Migration* (New York: Gray, 1920), pp. 165–166.

100 Bond, *Education of the Negro in the American Social Order*, p. 202.

101 E. Franklin Frazier, *The Negro in the United States* (New York: Macmillan, 1949), p. 417.

102 Mary J. Herrick, *The Chicago Schools: A Social and Political History* (Beverly Hills, Cal.: Sage, 1971), p. 53. See also St. Clair Drake and Horace R. Cayton, *Black Metropolis: A Study of Negro Life in a Northern City*, Vol. I (New York: Harper & Row, 1962), p. 44.

103 Drake and Cayton, *Black Metropolis*, Vol. I, p. 44.

104 Rayford Logan, *The Negro in American Life and Thought: The Nadir, 1877–1901* (New York: Dial, 1954), pp. 234–235.

105 U.S. Commissioner of Education, *Legal Status of the Colored Population*, p. 343.

106 Harris, *History of Negro Servitude in Illinois*, p. 242.

107 Allen H. Spear, *Black Chicago: The Making of a Negro Ghetto, 1890–1920* (Chicago: University of Chicago Press, 1967), p. 205.

108 Mary J. Herrick, "Negro Employees of the Chicago Board of Education," (master's thesis, University of Chicago, 1931), pp. 12–13.

109 *Ibid.*, pp. 19, 34.

110 Herrick, *Chicago Schools*, p. 270.

111 Doxey A. Wilkerson, *Special Problems of Negro Education* (Washington, D.C.: GPO, 1939), p. 154.

112 Herrick, *Chicago Schools*, p. 270.

113 William R. Ming, "The Elimination of Segregation in the Public Schools of the North and West," *Journal of Negro Education* (summer 1952), p. 268. Compare, however, Herrick, *Chicago Schools*, p. 285.

114 Herrick, *Chicago Schools* (MS copy); see *Integrated Education*, 9 (September-October 1971), p. 58.

115 On possible enforcement during 1949 in East Saint Louis, see Pauli Murray (ed.), *States' Laws on Race and Color* (Women's Division of Christian Service, Methodist Church, 1951), p. 130.

116 Kelly Miller, *The Everlasting Stain* (Washington, D.C.: Associated Publishers, 1924), p. 174.

117 Marion Jacob Mayo, "The Mental Capacity of the American Negro" *Archives of Psychology*, 28 (November 1913), pp. 21, 25, 45.

118 Frances Blascoer, *Colored School Children in New York* (New York: Public Education Association of the City of New York, 1915), pp. 11, 16–17.

119 *New York Age*, January 17, 1920.

120 *New York Age*, March 12, 1921.

121 *New York Age*, January 10, 1920.

122 *New York Age*, March 21, 1921.

123 *New York Age*, May 1, 1920.

124 *New York Age*, June 11, 1921.

125 *New York Age*, November 19, 1921.

126 *New York Age*, March 4, 1922.

127 Quoted in Celia Lewis Zitron, *The New York City Teachers Union 1916–1964* (New York: Humanities Press, 1968), pp. 86–87.

128 *New York Age*, March 14, 1935.

129 *New York Age*, June 20, 1936. See also Kelly Miller, "Is the Color Line Crumbling?" *Opportunity* (September 1929), p. 285: "The Negroes in Harlem are as completely penned in to residential boundaries as if the outlines had been plotted on a paper by a political geographer."

130 Quoted in Zitron, *New York City Teachers Union 1916–1964*, p. 90.

131 Lester B. Granger, "Race Relations and the School System: A Study of Negro High School Attendance in New Jersey," *Opportunity* (November 1925), p. 327.

132 New Jersey State Temporary Commission on the Condition of the Urban Colored Population, *Report . . . to the Legislature of the State of New Jersey . . . 1939* (Trenton: The Legislature, 1939), pp. 39–40.

133 See Table 27, "Colored Day Schools," New Jersey Board of Education, *Annual Report . . . for the Year Ending June 30, 1920* (Trenton: State of New Jersey, 1921), p. 315.

134 New Jersey State Temporary Commission on the Condition of the Urban Colored Population, *Report . . .*, p. 40.

135 *Ibid.*

136 Granger, "Race Relations and the School System," p. 327.

137 New Jersey State Temporary Commission on the Condition of the Urban Colored Population, *Report . . .*, p. 41.

138 See August Meier and Elliott Rudwick, "Negro Boycotts of Jim Crow Schools in the North, 1897–1925," *Integrated Education*, 5 (August-September 1967), pp. 57–68. Cities studied in this article are Alton, Illinois; East Orange, New Jersey; and Springfield and Dayton, Ohio.

139 W. E. B. Du Bois, "The Negro South and North," *Bibliotheca Sacra*, 62 (July 1905), pp. 504–505.

140 Thomas J. Woofter (ed.), *Negro Problems in Cities* (Garden City, N.Y.: Doubleday, 1928), p. 70; Jack Greenberg, *Race Relations and American Law* (New York:

Columbia University Press, 1959), p. 278; *The State* (Columbia, S.C.), January 16, 1963.

141 Rose Helper, "The Racial Practices of Real Estate Institutions in Selected Areas of Chicago," (doctoral dissertation, University of Chicago, 1958), pp. 2, 587, 588.

142 Spear, *Black Chicago,* pp. 201, 216, 142, 146.

143 Helper, "Racial Practices of Real Estate Institutions in Selected Areas of Chicago," p. 520.

144 Homer Hoyt, *The Structure and Growth of Residential Neighborhoods in American Cities* (Washington, D.C.: GPO, 1939), p. 62.

145 See Bond, *Education of the Negro in the American Social Order,* pp. 374–382; Bond, "The Present Status of Racial Integration in the United States, with Especial Reference to Education," *Journal of Negro Education* (summer 1952), p. 244; L. D. Reddick, "The Education of Negroes in States Where Separate Schools are Not Legal," *Journal of Negro Education* (summer 1947), p. 209; V. V. and Eleanor O. Oak, "The Illegal Status of Separate Education in New Jersey," *School and Society,* May 21, 1938; New Jersey State Temporary Commission on the Condition of the Urban Colored Population, *Report . . . ,* pp. 38–45; and Robin M. Williams, Jr., and Margaret W. Ryan (eds.), *Schools in Transition: Community Experiences in Desegregation* (Chapel Hill: University of North Carolina Press, 1954), p. 50.

146 Horace R. Cayton, *Long Old Road* (Seattle: University of Washington Press, 1964), p. 13.

147 William Pickens, "Colored Student Discouraged in Mixed Schools," *New York Age,* February 18, 1922.

148 Quoted in Woofter (ed.), *Negro Problems in Cities,* p. 182.

149 George S. Schuyler, *Black and Conservative: The Autobiography of George S. Schuyler* (New Rochelle, N.Y.: Arlington House, 1966), p. 29.

150 Hedgman, *The Trumpet Sounds,* p. 31.

151 Rayford W. Logan, "Educational Segregation in the North," *Journal of Negro Education* (January 1933), p. 65.

152 Alex Haley, foreword to Marcus A. Foster, *Making Schools Work* (Philadelphia: Westminster, 1971).

153 James Forman, *The Making of Black Revolutionaries: A Personal Account* (New York: Macmillan, 1972), p. 31.

154 Du Bois, "The United States and the Negro," *Freedomways* (1971), p. 16.

Chapter 3. Struggle for public policy: black children since 1950

1 August Meier and Elliott Rudwick, *From Plantation to Ghetto,* rev. ed. (New York: Hill & Wang, 1970), p. 242. See also W. E. B. Du Bois, "Race Relations in the United States, 1917–1947," *Phylon,* 9 (1948), p. 236.

2 Richard M. Dalfiume, "The 'Forgotten Years' of the Negro Revolution," *Journal of American History,* 55 (June 1968), pp. 99–100. See also Neil A. Wynn, "The Impact of the Second World War on the American Negro," *Journal of Contemporary History,* 6 (1971), pp. 42–53.

3 W. E. B. Du Bois, "Education," *Chicago Defender,* October 19, 1946.

4 Butler A. Jones, "Law and Social Change: A Study of the Impact of New Legal Requirements Affecting Equality of Educational Opportunities for Negroes upon Certain Customary Official Behavior in the South, 1938–1953" (doctoral dissertation, New York University, 1955), p. 350.

5 *Ibid.,* pp. 334–350. See also *Turner* v. *Keefe,* 50 F. Supp. 647 (1943).

6 Ernst W. Swanson and John A. Griffin (eds.), *Public Education in the South, Today and Tomorrow: A Statistical Survey* (Chapel Hill: University of North Carolina Press, 1955), p. 59.

7 Thurgood Marshall, "An Evaluation of Recent Efforts to Achieve Racial Integration in Education Through Resort to the Courts," *Journal of Negro Education*, 21 (1952), p. 318.

8 Jones, "Law and Social Change," p. 492.

9 For expenditures, see Swanson and Griffin, *Public Education in the South*, pp. 66–69; for value of buildings, see Truman M. Pierce and others, *White and Negro Schools in the South: An Analysis of Biracial Education* (Englewood Cliffs, N.J.: Prentice-Hall, 1955), p. 164.

10 Willie Morris, *Yazoo: Integration in a Deep-Southern Town* (New York: Harper & Row, 1971), p. 17.

11 James Meredith, *Three Years in Mississippi* (Bloomington: University of Indiana Press, 1966), pp. 60–61.

12 Edgar L. Jones, "Transportation: From Bare Feet to White Bucks," *in* Patrick McCauley and Edward D. Ball (eds.), *Southern Schools: Progress and Problems* (Nashville: Southern Education Reporting Service, 1959), p. 57.

13 *Jackson Daily News*, March 10, 1954; quoted in James M. Palmer, *Mississippi School Districts: Factors in the Disestablishment of Dual Systems* (State College: Mississippi State University, 1971), p. 25.

14 Alfred H. Kelly, "The School Desegregation Case," *in* John A. Garraty (ed.), *Quarrels That Have Shaped the Constitution* (New York: Harper & Row, 1964), p. 257.

15 Bond, *Education of the Negro in the American Social Order*, p. x.

16 Hylan Lewis, "Innovations and Trends in the Contemporary Southern Negro Community," *Journal of Social Issues*, 10 (1954), p. 26.

17 See Benjamin Muse, *Ten Years of Prelude: The Story of Integration Since the Supreme Court's 1954 Decision* (New York: Viking, 1964), pp. 8–10.

18 Leon Friedman (ed.), *Argument: The Oral Argument Before the Supreme Court in Brown v. Board of Education of Topeka, 1952–55* (New York: Chelsea House, 1969), p. 12.

19 *Ibid.*, p. 104.

20 NAACP, *Brief for Appellant in Nos. 1, 2 and 4 for Respondents in No. 10 on Reargument, Supreme Court of the United States*, October term, 1953, pp. 61, 191.

21 Friedman, *Argument*, p. 280.

22 W. E. B. Du Bois, "We Rejoice and Tell the World. . . . But We Must Go Further," *National Guardian*, May 31, 1954.

23 Muse, *Ten Years of Prelude*, p. 19.

24 W. E. B. Du Bois, "Two Hundred Years of Segregated Schools," *in* Philip S. Foner (ed.), *W. E. B. Du Bois Speaks: Speeches and Addresses, 1920–1963* (New York: Pathfinder Press, 1970), p. 283.

25 *Ibid.* For earlier expressions by Du Bois of one or another side of the same dilemma, see "The Tragedy of 'Jim Crow,'" *Crisis* (August 1923), pp. 170–171; "Does the Negro Need Separate Schools?" *Journal of Negro Education* (July 1935), p. 335; "Education," *Chicago Defender*, October 19, 1946.

26 Du Bois, "Two Hundred Years of Segregated Schools," p. 283.

27 *Ibid.*, pp. 283–284.

28 See Friedman, *Argument*, pp. 382, 423, 428, 460, 495, 502, for these quotations.

29 James M. Nabrit, Jr., "An Appraisal of Court Action as a Means of Achieving Racial [Integration] in Education," *Journal of Negro Education*, 21 (1952), p. 428.

30 See Friedman, *Argument*, pp. 167, 234, 400–403, 439, 524–525 for quotations. See also Loren Miller, *The Petitioners: The Story of the Supreme Court of the United States and the Negro* (New York: Pantheon, 1966), p. 351; Lewis M. Steel, "Nine Men in Black Who Think White," *New York Times Magazine*, October 13, 1968, p. 112; and Howard Moore, Jr., "*Brown v. Board of Education:* The Court's Relation-

ship to Black Liberation," *in* Robert Lefcourt (ed.), *Law Against the People: Essays to Demystify Law, Order, and the Courts* (New York: Random House, 1971), p. 57.

31 Friedman, *Argument*, p. 513.

32 Robert L. Carter, "The Warren Court and Desegregation," *Michigan Law Review*, 67 (1968–1969), p. 243.

33 Jack W. Peltason, *Fifty-Eight Lonely Men: Southern Federal Judges and School Desegregation* (New York: Harcourt, 1961), p. 100. For rulings see also Reed Sarratt, *The Ordeal of Desegregation: The First Decade* (New York: Harper & Row, 1966), p. 220.

34 Peltason, *Fifty-Eight Lonely Men*, p. 51.

35 See Sarratt, *Ordeal of Desegregation*, p. 187.

36 *Ibid.*, p. 31.

37 U.S. Commission on Civil Rights, *Civil Rights U.S.A.: Public Schools, Southern States, 1962* (Washington, D.C.: GPO, 1962), p. 4.

38 Carter, "The Warren Court and Desegregation," p. 244.

39 Palmer, *Mississippi School Districts*, p. 22.

40 Arkansas Advisory Committee to the U.S. Commission on Civil Rights, *Public Education in Arkansas, 1963: Still Separate and Still Unequal* (Washington, D.C.: GPO, September 1963), pp. 10, 13.

41 *Southern School News* (January 1965), p. 9; (July 1959), p. 5; (February 1963), p. 7.

42 U.S. Commission on Civil Rights, *1964 Staff Report on Public Schools* (Washington, D.C.: GPO, 1964), p. 47; and *Civil Rights, U.S.A.: Public Schools, Southern States, 1962*, pp. 97–98.

43 Weldon James, "Buildings and Equipment: Too Many Pupils, Too Few Dollars," *in* McCauley and Ball, *Southern Schools: Progress and Problems*, p. 54.

44 Anne Moody, *Coming of Age in Mississippi* (New York: Dial, 1968), p. 187.

45 Robert G. Armstrong, "A Reply to Herbert Wechsler's Holmes Lecture 'Towards Neutral Principles of Constitutional Law,'" *Phylon*, 21 (fall 1960), p. 224.

46 For quotations, see *Southern School News* (October 1954, November 1956, February 1961, April 1964).

47 Harry K. Wright *in* U.S. Commission on Civil Rights, *Civil Rights U.S.A.: Public Schools, Southern States, 1963, Texas* (Washington, D.C., GPO, 1964), p. 36.

48 *Southern School News* (September 1957), p. 16. See also Bernice Cooper, "An Analysis of the Reading Achievement of White and Negro Pupils in Certain Public Schools of Georgia," *School Review* (winter 1964).

49 For quotations and data cited, see *Southern School News* (July, September, November 1956, July 1959).

50 *Southern School News* (December 1956, September 1960).

51 U.S. Commission on Civil Rights, *Hearings Held in Memphis, Tennessee, June 25–26, 1962* (Washington, D.C.: GPO, 1962), p. 170; Lawrence W. Knowles, *in* U.S. Commission on Civil Rights, *Civil Rights U.S.A.: Public Schools, Southern States, 1962* (Washington, D.C.: GPO, 1962), p. 113.

52 Edward A. Mearns, Jr., *in ibid.*, p. 212.

53 See Sarratt, *Ordeal of Desegregation*, pp. 110–111; Richard M. Morehead, "Special Services: Lunchrooms, Libraries and Learning," *in* McCauley and Ball, *Southern Schools: Progress and Problems*, p. 72; Muse, *Ten Years of Prelude*, p. 36.

54 Jeanne Rogers, "Nation's Showcase?" p. 159, *in* Don Shoemaker (ed.), *With All Deliberate Speed: Segregation-Desegregation in Southern Schools* (New York: Harper & Row, 1957).

55 Elias Blake, Jr., "The Track System in Washington, D.C.," *Integrated Education* 3 (April-May 1965), p. 31. See also Carl F. Hansen, "A Defense of the Track System," *Integrated Education*, 2 (June-July 1964), pp. 48–49.

56 Fred L. Shuttlesworth, "Birmingham Revisited," *Ebony* (August 1971), p. 114.

57 Dorothy E. Pitman, "Reactions of Desegregation: A Study of Negro Mothers" (doctoral dissertation, University of North Carolina, 1959), p. 199.

58 Robert Moses, "Mississippi: 1961–1962," *Liberation*, 14 (January 1970), pp. 14–15.

59 Pat Watters and Reese Cleghorn, *Climbing Jacob's Ladder: The Arrival of Negroes in Southern Politics* (New York: Harcourt, 1967), p. 194. For data and quotations cited, see Forman, *The Making of Black Revolutionaries*, pp. 338–339, and John Ehle, *The Free Men* (New York: Harper & Row, 1965), pp. 34, 48.

60 Moses, "Mississippi: 1961–1962," p. 14.

61 Moody, *Coming of Age in Mississippi*, p. 245.

62 See data in Watters and Cleghorn, *Climbing Jacob's Ladder*, p. 27.

63 Moody, *Coming of Age in Mississippi*, p. 336.

64 Reddick, "Education of Negroes in States Where Separate Schools Are Not Legal," p. 296.

65 Bond, "Present Status of Racial Integration in the United States," p. 244.

66 Eleanor B. Sheldon, James R. Hudson, and Raymond A. Glazier, *Administrative Implications of Integration Plans for Schools: Open Enrollment in New York City* (New York: Russell Sage Foundation, 1963), p. 10. For data on Detroit, see Remus G. Robinson, *in* U.S. Commission on Civil Rights, *Hearings Held in Detroit, Michigan* (Washington, D.C.: GPO, 1961), pp. 181–184. See also U.S. Commission on Civil Rights, *Education 1961 . . . Report* (Washington, D.C.: GPO, 1961), pp. 103–104; on Philadelphia, see Philadelphia Urban League, *A Proposal for Integrating Philadelphia Public Schools* (Philadelphia: The League, August 1964), p. 28; on New York City, see Annie Stein, "Containment and Control: A Look at the Record," *in* Annette T. Rubenstein (ed.), *Schools Against Children: The Case for Community Control* (New York: Monthly Review Press, 1970), p. 21.

67 *Report of the Special Committee on Nondiscrimination of the Board of Public Education of Philadelphia, Pennsylvania*, July 23, 1964, p. 18.

68 U.S. Commission on Civil Rights, *Civil Rights U.S.A.: Public Schools, Cities in the North and West* (Washington, D.C.: GPO, 1962), pp. 291–293.

69 U.S. Commission on Civil Rights, *Public Education, 1963: Staff Report* (Washington, D.C.: GPO, 1964), p. 122.

70 Citizens Committee, Berkeley Unified School District, *De Facto Segregation in the Berkeley Public Schools* (fall 1963), pp. 7, 9.

71 See C. A. Wennerberg, *Desegregation of the Berkeley Public Schools: Its Feasibility and Implementation: Appendixes to the Report* (Berkeley: Berkeley Unified School District, May 1964), pp. 32, 34, 74; and Ira Michael Heyman, *in* U.S. Commission on Civil Rights, *Civil Rights U.S.A.: Public Schools, Cities in the North and West, 1963, Oakland.* (Washington, D.C.: GPO, 1964), p. 63.

72 Committee on Race and Education, *Race and Equal Educational Opportunity in Portland's Public Schools* (Portland, Ore.: Board of Education, October 19, 1964), p. 163.

73 *Statement to the Bridgeport Board of Education on De Facto Segregated Public Elementary Schools* (Bridgeport: Bridgeport-Stratford Branch, NAACP, July 1964), p. 7.

74 *Youth in the Ghetto: A Study of the Consequences of Powerlessness and a Blueprint for Change* (New York: Harlem Youth Opportunities Unlimited, 1964), pp. 168, 194.

75 *Prospectus, Student Woodlawn Area Project (SWAP)* (Chicago: Ida Noyes Hall, University of Chicago, 1964), p. 1.

76 Coordinating Council of Community Organizations, *Handbook of Chicago School Segregation* (Chicago: CCCO, 1963), p. 33.

77 Massachusetts State Advisory Committee to the United States Commission on Civil Rights, *Report on Racial Imbalance in the Boston Public Schools* (Washington, D.C.: GPO, January 1965), p. 33.

78 Bert E. Swanson, *The Struggle for Equality: School Integration Controversy in New York City* (New York: Hobbs, Dorman, 1966), p. 13.

79 See, for example, Georg Iggers, *A Study of Some Tangible Inequalities in the New Orleans Public Schools*, 2nd ed. (New Orleans: Education Committee, New Orleans NAACP, 1963).

80 Stein, "Containment and Control," p. 32.

81 David Rogers, *110 Livingston Street: Political Democracy in the New York City Schools* (New York: Random House, 1968), p. 242; Aaron Brown, *Reflections on Seven Years of Experience on the New York City Board of Education* (New York: privately published, June 1, 1969), p. 16: "Some school administrators, less than enthusiastic over integration, often ignored Board directives and guidelines."

82 For a sketch of the background, see Harold M. Baron, "History of Chicago School Segregation to 1953," *Integrated Education*, 1 (January 1963).

83 U.S. Commission on Civil Rights, *Racial Isolation in the Public Schools: Appendices* (Washington, D.C.: GPO, 1967), pp. 4–5.

84 U.S. Commission on Civil Rights, *Public Education: 1963 Staff Report* (Washington, D.C.: GPO, 1964), p. 85.

85 See map, "Double-Shift, Cumulative Burden, 1950–1961," in Meyer Weinberg (ed.), *Integrated Education: A Reader* (Beverly Hills, Cal.: Glencoe Press, 1968), p. 91.

86 John E. Coons, "Report to the United States Office of Education on the Public Schools of Chicago" (draft copy, Cambridge, Mass., June 20, 1965), p. V-1.

87 *Integrated Education*, 1 (August 1963), p. 3. For data on boycotts, see *Integrated Education*, 2 (June-July, August-September 1964).

88 For quotations from the Senate hearings, see U.S. Congress, 88th, 1st session, Senate Committee on the Judiciary, *Civil Rights: The President's Program, 1963, Hearings . . . July 16–September 11, 1963* (Washington, D.C.: GPO, 1964).

89 For quotations from the House hearings, see U.S. Congress, 88th, 1st session, House of Representatives Committee on the Judiciary, Subcommittee No. 5, *Hearings: Civil Rights . . . Parts 1–4*, Serial No. 4 (Washington, D.C.: GPO, 1963–1964), II, pp. 1514, 1515, 1521, 1783, 1888, 1889, 2101.

90 *Congressional Record*, January 31, 1964.

91 *Ibid.*

92 Quotations from *Congressional Record*, January 31, 1964, p. 1483.

93 Quotations from *Congressional Record*, February 1, 1964, pp. 1526, 1547.

94 Fred T. Haley, "Tacoma Faces School Segregation," *Integrated Education*, 2 (April-May 1964), p. 28.

95 *Congressional Record*, February 6, 1964, p. 2197.

96 Gary Orfield, *The Reconstruction of Southern Education: The Schools and the Civil Rights Act* (New York: Wiley, 1969), p. 45.

97 *Congressional Record*, March 14, 1964, p. 5090; May 1, 1964, p. 9491.

98 Selz C. Mayo, "Social Change, Social Movements, and the Disappearing Sectional South," *Social Forces* (October 1964), p. 2.

99 *Congressional Record*, March 13, 1964, p. 5053.

100 See *Integrated Education*, 1 (August 1963), p. 46.

101 *Congressional Record*, April 3, 1964, p. 6628.

102 Iggers, *Study of Some Tangible Inequalities in the New Orleans Public Schools*, p. 14.

103 *Congressional Record*, April 18, 1964, p. 8086.

104 *Congressional Record,* June 4, 1964, p. 12257.

105 *Congressional Record,* April 3, 1964, pp. 6606–6607.

106 *Congressional Record,* June 4, 1964, p. 12257.

107 *Congressional Record,* March 30, 1964, p. 6304.

108 "The Allen Report on New York City Schools," *Integrated Education,* 2 (August-September, 1964), pp. 14, 18–19. This is a reprint of the entire report.

109 Urban League of Greater New York, "A Decade of New York Changes," *Integrated Education,* 2 (April-May 1964), p. 35.

110 "Allen Report on New York City Schools," p. 21; see also story by Fred Hechinger, *New York Times,* February 1, 1965.

111 See David Mallery, *Negro Students in Independent Schools* (Boston: National Association of Independent Schools, 1964).

112 *Congressional Record,* May 14, 1964, p. 10563.

113 *Congressional Record,* April 2, 1964, p. 6583.

114 *Congressional Record,* June 2, 1964, p. 12017.

115 Karl E. Taeuber and Alma F. Taeuber, *Negroes in Cities* (Chicago: Aldine, 1965), p. 4.

116 *Congressional Record,* March 26, 1964, p. 10563.

117 *Bell* v. *School City of Gary,* 213 F. Supp. 819 (1963).

118 *Briggs* v. *Elliott,* 132 F. Supp. 777 (1955).

119 *Congressional Record,* June 4, 1964, p. 12288.

120 Barney Sellers, "Appendix Background Material," in A. Philip Randolph Institute, *The Reluctant Guardians: A Survey of the Enforcement of Federal Civil Rights Laws,* PB 192 346 (Springfield, Va: Clearinghouse for Federal Scientific and Technical Information, December 1969), pp. 1–62.

121 Mrs. Ruby G. Martin to John Veneman, January 31, 1969, quoted in *ibid.,* pp. 1–65.

122 *Green* v. *County School Board of New Kent County,* 391 U.S. 430 (1968).

123 *Alexander* v. *Holmes County Board of Education,* 396 U.S. 19 (1969).

124 *Swann* v. *Charlotte-Mecklenburg County Board of Education,* 402 U.S. 1 (1971).

125 Robert C. Weaver, *Journal of Negro Education,* 21 (1952), p. 258.

126 Lerone Bennett, Jr., "Old Illusions and New Souths," *Ebony* (August 1971), p. 37.

127 U.S. Congress, 92nd, 1st session, Senate Select Committee on Equal Educational Opportunity, *Equal Educational Opportunity, 1971: Hearings,* Part 10, *Displacement and Present Status of Black School Principals in Desegregated School Districts* (Washington, D.C.: GPO, 1971).

128 Betsy Fancher, *Voices from the South: Black Students Talk About Their Experiences in Desegregated Schools* (Atlanta: Southern Regional Council, August 1970); Fancher, "Students Getting It Together: In Changing Schools Some Show How," *South Today,* 3 (July-August 1971), pp. 1, 7; John Egerton, "Report Card on Southern School Desegregation," *Saturday Review,* April 1, 1972; Robin Dorr, "Ordeal by Desegregation," *Integrated Education,* 10 (July-August 1972), pp. 34–39; Alabama Council on Human Relations and others, *It's Not Over in the South: School Desegregation in Forty-three Southern Cities Eighteen Years after Brown* (New York: NAACP Legal Defense Fund, May 1972).

129 Luther Munford, "Black Gravity: Desegregation in 30 Mississippi School Districts" (senior thesis, Princeton University, April 16, 1971), p. 156.

130 *NEA Task Force on School Desegregation in Louisiana* (Washington, D.C.: National Education Association, February 15–22, 1970); NEA Task Force III, *School Desegregation: Louisiana and Mississippi* (Washington, D.C.: National Education Association, November 1970).

131 Comptroller General of the United States, "Need to Improve Policies and Proce-

dures for Approving Grants Under the Emergency School Assistance Program," in U.S. Congress, 92nd, 1st session, House of Representatives Committee on Education and Labor, General Subcommittee on Education, *Emergency School Aid Act: Hearings* (Washington, D.C.: GPO, 1971), pp. 89–162; U.S. Congress, 92nd, 1st session, Senate Committee on Labor and Public Welfare, Subcommittee on Education, *Emergency School Aid, 1971: Hearings* (Washington, D.C.: GPO, 1971); American Friends Service Committee and others, *The Emergency School Assistance Program: An Evaluation* (Washington, D.C.: Washington Research Project, 1970).

132 See Commission on Professional Rights and Responsibilities, *Hyde County, North Carolina: School Boycott and the Roots of Conflict* (Washington, D.C.: National Education Association, September 1969), pp. 11–12.

133 *Integrated Education*, 7 (March-April 1969), p. 11.

134 See Commission on Professional Rights and Responsibilities, *Beyond Desegregation: The Problem of Power* (Washington, D.C.: National Education Association, February 1970). This study refers especially to problems in East Texas.

135 Munford, "Black Gravity," pp. ix–xi.

136 Mack H. Jones, *Black School Board Members in the Deep South* (Atlanta: Southern Regional Council, April 1970).

137 See Lillian S. Calhoun, "New York: Schools and Power – Whose?" *Integrated Education* (January-February 1969), pp. 11–35; Maurice R. Berube and Marilyn Gittell (eds.), *Confrontation at Ocean Hill–Brownsville* (New York: Praeger, 1969); Miriam Wasserman, "The I.S. 201 Story: One Observer's Version," *Urban Review* (June 1969); Rubenstein, *Schools Against Children;* Barbara Carter, *Pickets, Parents, and Power: The Story Behind New York City Teachers' Strike* (New York: Citation, 1971); Susan Fainstein, "The Movement for Community Control of Schools in New York City" (doctoral dissertation, Massachusetts Institute of Technology, 1971); Frances Gottfried, "A Survey of Parental Views of the Ocean Hill–Brownsville Experiment," *Community Issues*, 2 (October 1970), pp. 1–32; Ken King, "Attitudes and School Decentralization: A Survey of Community Group Leaders in New York's Three Experimental Districts" (doctoral dissertation, Teachers College Columbia University, 1971): Annie Stein, "Strategies for Failure," *Harvard Educational Review*, 71 (May 1971), pp. 158–204; Melvin Urofsky (ed.), *Why Teachers Strike: Teachers' Rights and Community Control* (Garden City, N.Y.: Doubleday, 1970); William R. Grant, "Community Control vs. Integration: the Case of Detroit," *Public Interest* (summer 1971); "Parents in the School: Community Control in Harlem," *This Magazine Is About Schools*, 4 (February 1970), pp. 72–109.

138 See Ruby Martin and Phyllis McClure, *Title 1 of ESEA: Is It Helping Poor Children?* (New York: NAACP Legal Defense Fund, 1969); National Advisory Council on the Education of Disadvantaged Children, *Title I, ESEA: The Weakest Link: The Children of the Poor* (Washington, D.C.: GPO, 1971); and *Educating the Disadvantaged Child: Where We Stand* (Washington, D.C.: GPO, 1972); School Finance Project, *Title I Comparability: A Preliminary Evaluation* (Washington, D.C.: Lawyers' Committee for Civil Rights Under Law, September 1972).

139 See, for example, with reference to Massachusetts: David K. Cohen and Tyll R. Van Geel, "Public Education," *in* Samuel H. Beer and Richard E. Barringer (eds.), *The State and the Poor* (Cambridge, Mass.: Winthrop, 1970), pp. 229–230; David K. Cohen, Walter J. McCann, Jerome T. Murphy, and Tyll R. Van Geel, *The Effects of Revenue Sharing and Block Grants on Education* (Cambridge, Mass.: Harvard Graduate School of Education, October 31, 1970), pp. 74, 79.

140 See, for example, Richard A. Berk and Alice Hartmann, "Race and School Funds in

Chicago, 1971," *Integrated Education*, 10 (January-February 1972), pp. 52–57; Jacob Landers, "Profiles of Inequality in New York City," *Integrated Education*, 11 (January-February 1973), pp. 3–14.

141 Owen M. Fiss, "Racial Imbalance in the Public Schools: The Constitutional Concepts," *Harvard Law Review* (January 1965), p. 584.

142 *Integrated Education* (December 1965, January 1966), p. 10.

143 Orfield, *Reconstruction of Southern Education*, pp. 198, 206.

144 For 1968 and 1970 data, see Table 16. For 1971–1972 data, see the court's ruling in *Adams* v. *Richardson;* John H. Pratt, "HEW Ordered to Defer Funds" *Integrated Education*, 11 (January-February 1973), p. 68.

145 U.S. Department of Transportation, *School Bus Task Force: Pupil Transportation Safety Program Plan* (Washington, D.C.: GPO, May 1973), p. 3.

Chapter 4. Mexican-American children: the neighbors within

1 Clark C. Gill, *Education in a Changing Mexico* (Washington, D.C.: GPO, 1969), p. 15. A possible exception lay in the fact that children of slave women were considered free. See Benjamin Keen, *The Aztec Image in Western Thought* (New Brunswick, N.J.: Rutgers University Press, 1971), p. 422. On the other hand, no evidence is cited by Soustelle in support of his statement that "no Mexican child of the sixteenth century, whatever his social origin, was deprived of schooling"; see Jacques Soustelle, *The Daily Life of the Aztecs on the Eve of the Spanish Conquest*, tr. Patrick O'Brian (London: Weidenfeld & Nicolson, 1961), p. 173. On the exclusion of slave and serf from schooling, see also James Lathrop Garrard, "A Survey of the Education of the Indians of Mexico as a Factor in Their Incorporation into Modern Mexican Society" (doctoral dissertation, University of Washington, 1956), p. 87.

2 Soustelle, *Daily Life of the Aztecs*, p. 22.

3 Keen, *Aztec Image in Western Thought*, p. 456.

4 Garrard, "Survey of the Education of the Indians of Mexico," p. 104.

5 Laurence Murrell Childers, "Education in California Under Spain and Mexico and Under American Rule to 1851" (master's thesis, University of California, Berkeley, 1930), fn. 1, p. 52.

6 *Ibid.*, p. 192. During the late 1860s and early 1870s, the government of Juarez enacted a law for compulsory public elementary education which had some effects in cities, and during the last twenty years of the century, the Mexican government sought to establish teacher-training institutions. The school law of 1891 made education obligatory, but on the eve of the Mexican Revolution, in 1910, two-thirds of the total population was illiterate, and rural education was almost completely neglected.

7 Treaty of Guadalupe Hidalgo, Article IX, as amended in the Senate and accepted by the Government of Mexico. See Hunter Miller (ed.), *Treaties and Other International Acts of the United States of America*, Vol. II (Washington, D.C.: GPO, 1931), p. 241.

8 Highly discrepant estimates for 1900 can be found in the literature. John Womack, "The Chicanos," *New York Review of Books*, 19 (August 31, 1972), p. 12, states 100,000; Rodman W. Paul, "The Spanish-Americans in the Southwest, 1848–1900," in John G. Clark (ed.), *The Frontier Challenge: Responses to the Trans-Mississippi West* (Lawrence: University of Kansas Press, 1971), p. 33, holds out for "several hundred thousand." The figure in the text is an estimate.

9 Carolyn Zeleny, "Relations Between the Spanish-Americans and Anglo-Americans in New Mexico: A Study of Conflict and Accommodation in a Dual-Ethnic Situation" (doctoral dissertation, Yale University, 1944, University Microfilm Order No. 66-7699), p. 281.

10 *Ibid.*, p. 287.

11 George I. Sanchez, *Forgotten People: A Study of New Mexicans* (Albuquerque: University of New Mexico Press, 1940), p. 23.

12 In 1966, New Mexico had a permanent common school fund derived from sale of land grants amounting to $239,088,287. See Gates, *History of Public Land Law Development*, p. 339.

13 Thomas Lloyd Miller, *The Public Lands of Texas, 1519–1970* (Norman: University of Oklahoma Press, 1972), pp. 115–116. From 1857 to 1970, income from school lands totaled $924,885,559.13; *ibid.*, p. 210.

14 Jorge C. Rangel and Carlos M. Alcala, "De Jure Segregation of Chicanos in Texas Schools," *Harvard Civil Rights–Civil Liberties Law Review*, 7 (March 1972), p. 312.

15 James Kilbourne Harris, "A Sociological Study of a Mexican School in San Antonio, Texas" (master's thesis, University of Texas, 1927), p. 8. Harris began teaching at the school in 1898 and later became its principal.

16 Rangel and Alcala, "De Jure Segregation of Chicanos in Texas Schools," pp. 41, 313, 342, 363.

17 Leonard Pitt, *The Decline of the Californios: A Social History of the Spanish-speaking Californians, 1846–1890* (Berkeley: University of California Press, 1966), p. 123.

18 Testimony of Jack B. Forbes, *in* U.S. Commission on Civil Rights, *Hearing Held in San Antonio, December 9–14, 1968* (Washington, D.C.: GPO, 1969), p. 29.

19 Herschel T. Manuel, *The Education of Mexican and Spanish-speaking Children in Texas* (Austin: Fund for Research in the Social Sciences, University of Texas, 1930), pp. 42, 97, 103, 68. Quotations cited are from pp. 72, 77, 79.

20 This was true in Crystal City; see Irene Castaneda, "Chronicle of Crystal City," *El Grito*, 4 (winter 1971), p. 50.

21 Harris, "Sociological Study of a Mexican School in San Antonio," pp. 45–46.

22 Paul S. Taylor, *An American-Mexican Frontier: Nueces County, Texas* (Chapel Hill: University of North Carolina Press, 1934), p. 195.

23 Albert T. Kaderli, "The Educational Problem in the Americanization of the Spanish-Speaking Pupils of Sugar Land, Texas" (master's thesis, University of Texas, 1940), p. 36.

24 Jay S. Stowell, *The Near Side of the Mexican Question* (New York: Doran, 1921), pp. 90, 92.

25 Eunice Parr, "A Comparative Study of Mexican and American Children in the Schools of San Antonio, Texas" (doctoral dissertation, University of Chicago, 1926), pp. 13–14.

26 Harris, "Sociological Study of a Mexican School in San Antonio," pp. 26–27.

27 Taylor, *An American-Mexican Frontier*, p. 273.

28 *Ibid.*, p. 211.

29 Testimony of Fermin Calderon, *in* U.S. Commission on Civil Rights, *Hearings Held in San Antonio, December 9–14, 1968*, p. 303.

30 Theodore W. Parsons, Jr., "Ethnic Cleavage in a California School" (doctoral dissertation, Stanford University, 1965), pp. 296–297. The preceding three paragraphs are taken from Meyer Weinberg, *Desegregation Research: An Appraisal*, 2nd ed. (Bloomington, Ind.: Phi Delta Kappa, 1970), pp. 258–260.

31 Mary Ellen Goodman and others, "The Mexican American Population of Houston: A Survey in the Field, 1965–1970," *Rice University Studies*, 57 (summer 1971), ERIC Number ED 060 997, p. 76.

32 Nephtale De Leon, *Chicanos: Our Background and Our Pride* (Lubbock, Texas: Trucha Publications, 1972), p. 46.

33 *Ibid.*, p. 58.

34 Parsons, "Ethnic Cleavage," pp. 207, 264, 271, 281.

35 Testimony of Sen. Joe Bernal, *in* U.S. Commission on Civil Rights, *Hearing Held in San Antonio, December 9–14, 1968,* p. 257.

36 Jose Vasconcelos, quoted in Francisco Armando Rios, "The Mexican in Fact, Fiction and Folklore," *El Grito,* 2 (summer 1970), p. 26.

37 See U.S. Commission on Civil Rights, *Mexican American Education Study,* 6 vols. (Washington, D.C.: GPO, 1971–1974). Vol. I, *Ethnic Isolation of Mexican Americans in the Public Schools of the Southwest;* Vol. II, *The Unfinished Education: Outcomes for Minorities in the Five Southwestern States;* Vol. III, *The Excluded Student: Educational Practices Affecting Mexican Americans in the Southwest;* Vol. IV, *Mexican American Education in Texas; A Function of Wealth;* Vol. V; *Teachers and Students: Differences in Teacher Interaction with Mexican American and Anglo Students;* Vol. VI; *Toward Quality Education for Mexican Americans.* An unpublished report prepared by the staff of the commission is "Research Methods Employed in the Mexican American Education Study," October 1971.

38 U.S. Bureau of the Census, *Selected Characteristics of Persons and Families of Mexican, Puerto Rican, and Other Spanish Origin: March 1972* (Washington, D.C.: GPO, July 1972).

39 Rangel and Alcala, "De Jure Segregation of Chicanos in Texas Schools," fn. 94, p. 723.

40 William Madsen, *Mexican Americans of South Texas* (New York: Holt, 1964), p. 107.

41 U.S. Commission on Civil Rights, *Mexican American Education Study,* Vol. III, pp. 14, 49.

42 *Ibid.,* p. 25.

43 Thomas P. Carter, *Mexican Americans in School: A History of Educational Neglect* (New York: College Entrance Examination Board, 1970), pp. 91, 204.

44 Theodore Andersson and Mildred Boyer, *Bilingual Schooling in the United States,* 2 vols. (Washington, D.C.: GPO, 1970), Vol. I, pp. 9, 53.

45 Jospeh F. Payne, "Race, Reading, and Poverty in Los Angeles," *Integrated Education,* 9 (November–December, 1971), p. 20.

46 Rangel and Alcala, "De Jure Segregation of Chicanos in Texas Schools," pp. 313–314.

47 Manuel, *Education of Mexican and Spanish-Speaking Children in Texas,* p. 70.

48 Taylor, *An American-Mexican Frontier,* p. 215.

49 See testimony of Dr. Fermin Calderon, whose father later became superintendent of the San Felipe schools, *in* U.S. Commission on Civil Rights, *Hearing Held in San Antonio, December 9–14, 1968,* p. 303.

50 Ralph Waddell Emerson, "Education for the Mexican in Texas" (master's thesis, Southern Methodist University, 1929), p. 46.

51 Taylor, *An American-Mexican Frontier,* p. 200.

52 *Ibid.,* pp. 237, 219.

53 *Mexicans in California: Report of Governor C. C. Young's Mexican Fact-Finding Committee* (San Francisco: California State Printing Office, October 1930), p. 177.

54 See testimony of Jack B. Forbes, *in* U.S. Commission on Civil Rights, *Hearing Held in San Antonio, December 9–14, 1968,* p. 33.

55 Simon Ludwig Treff, "The Education of Mexican Children in Orange County" (master's thesis, University of Southern California, 1934), pp. 21, 24, 25, 64–65, 133, 137.

56 For the practice in Ontario, California, see Mary M. Peters, "The Segregation of Mexican-American Children in the Elementary Schools of California: Its Legal and

Administrative Aspects" (master's thesis, University of California, Los Angeles, 1948), p. 42.

57 Jay Newton Holliday, "A Study of Non-Attendance in Miguel Hidalgo School of Brawley, California" (master's thesis, University of Southern California, 1931), pp. 51–52. For the data cited, see pp. 11–19.

58 Vesta Penrod, "Civil Rights Problems of Mexican-Americans in Southern California" (master's thesis, Claremont Graduate School, 1948), p. 69.

59 *Ibid.*, pp. 51–52.

60 Ruth D. Tuck, *Not with the Fist: Mexican Americans in a Southwest City* (New York: Harcourt, 1946), p. 185. The name of the city is given as "Descanso." From an analysis of census figures in the book, however, it is clear that "Descanso" is San Bernardino.

61 *Ibid.*, p. 186.

62 *Ibid.*

63 Victor Boyd Lehman, "A Study of the Social Adjustment of the Mexican-American in Chino and a Proposed Program of Community Action under School Leadership" (master's thesis, Claremont Colleges, 1947), pp. 30–31.

64 *Ibid.*, p. 99.

65 John Randle King, "An Inquiry into the Status of Mexican Segregation in Metropolitan Bakersfield" (master's thesis, Claremont Colleges, 1946), p. 59.

66 Robin F. Scott, "The Mexican-American in the Los Angeles Area, 1920–1950: From Acquiescence to Activity" (doctoral dissertation, University of California, 1971).

67 Emory S. Bogardus, *The Mexican in the United States* (Los Angeles: University of Southern California Press, 1934), p. 94.

68 Scott, "The Mexican American in the Los Angeles Area, 1920–1950," p. 169.

69 Most Rev. Robert E. Lucey, speech of July 20, 1943; cited in Scott, "The Mexican-American in the Los Angeles Area, 1920–1950," p. 14. Reference was to the Archdiocese of Dallas rather than the city proper.

70 Pauline Kibbe, *Latin Americans in Texas* (Albuquerque: University of New Mexico Press, 1946), pp. 228–229. See also John H. Burma, *Spanish-Speaking Groups in the United States* (Durham, N.C.: Duke University Press, 1954).

71 Testimony of Dr. Hector P. Garcia, *in* U.S. Congress, 92nd, 2nd session, House of Representatives Committee on the Judiciary, Subcommittee No. 5, *School Busing Hearings*, Part 3, Serial No. 32 (Washington, D.C.: GPO, 1972), p. 1515.

72 Lehman, "Study of the Social Adjustment of the Mexican-American in Chino," pp. 22–24.

73 Letter to *Valley Morning Star*, Harlingen, July 1947, quoted in Alonso S. Perales, *Are We Good Neighbors?* (San Antonio: Artes Graficas, 1948), p. 148.

74 Penrod, "Civil Rights Problems of Mexican-Americans in Southern California," p. 49.

75 *Ibid.*, p. 50.

76 Everett Ross Clinchy, Jr., "Equality of Opportunity for Latin-Americans in Texas: A Study of the Economic, Social, and Educational Discrimination Against Latin-Americans in Texas, and the Efforts of the State Government on Their Behalf" (doctoral dissertation, Columbia University, 1954), p. 138.

77 Affidavit dated March 4, 1947; quoted in Perales, *Are We Good Neighbors?* p. 148.

78 Emma Hall Gilbert, "Some Legal Aspects of the Education of Spanish-Speaking Children in Texas" (master's thesis, University of Texas, 1947), pp. 80, 90–91.

79 Isabel Work Cromack, "Latin-Americans: A Minority Group in the Austin Public Schools" (master's thesis, University of Texas, 1949), p. 25. See also Price Richard Ashton, "The Fourteenth Amendment and the Education of Latin American

Children in Texas" (master's thesis, University of Texas, 1949), pp. 26, 43, 54, for discussion of Austin.

80 Carlos I. Calderon, "The Education of Spanish-Speaking Children in Edcouch-Elsa, Texas" (master's thesis, University of Texas, 1950), p. 20. Calderon's work reproduces a number of photographs of the homeliest contrasts.

81 Sara Leonil Ramirez, "The Educational Status and Socioeconomic Backgrounds of Latin-American Children in Waco, Texas" (master's thesis, University of Texas, 1957), pp. 63, 66, 68.

82 Taylor, *An American-Mexican Frontier*, fn. 14, p. 201.

83 U.S. Commission on Civil Rights, "Research Methods Employed in the Mexican American Education Study," Appendix H, p. 6; and *Mexican American Education Study*, Vol. IV, p. 25.

84 U.S. Commission on Civil Rights, *Mexican-American Education Study*, Vol. IV, p. 14.

85 *Ibid.*, p. 15.

86 Gilbert, "Some Legal Aspects of the Education of Spanish-Speaking Children in Texas," p. 93.

87 John C. Hinsley, *The Handbook of Texas School Law* (Austin: Steck, 1938), p. 121; quoted in Gilbert, "Some Legal Aspects of the Education of Spanish-Speaking Children in Texas," p. 95.

88 *Vela* v. *Board of Trustees of Charlotte Independent School District* (Atascosa County); cited in Manuel, *Education of Mexican and Spanish-Speaking Children in Texas*, p. 83, and Gilbert, "Some Legal Aspects of the Education of Spanish-Speaking Children in Texas," p. 100.

89 Gilbert, "Some Legal Aspects of the Education of Spanish-Speaking Children in Texas," p. 244.

90 *Independent School District* v. *Salvatierra*, 33 S.W. 2nd 790 (1930), cert. den. 284 U.S. 580 (1931).

91 California Attorney General, Opinion 6735a, January 23, 1930, quoted in letter of Alfred E. Lentz, Legal Adviser, California Department of Public Instruction, to W. Henry Cooke, Claremont Graduate School, October 23, 1947; cited in Penrod, "Civil Rights Problems of Mexican-Americans in Southern California," pp. 53–54.

92 *School Code of the State of California* (Sacramento: California Department of Public Instruction, 1937), pp. 147–148; quoted in Penrod, "Civil Rights Problems of Mexican-Americans in Southern California," p. 54.

93 *Doss* v. *Bernal*, Superior Court of Orange County, No. 41466.

94 Penrod, "Civil Rights Problems of Mexican-Americans in Southern California," p. 47.

95 *Mendez* v. *Westminster*, 64 F. Supp. 544 (1946), aff'd 161 F. 2nd 774 (1947).

96 Rangel and Alcala, "De Jure Segregation of Chicanos in Texas Schools," p. 336.

97 Letter of October 18, 1946; quoted in Gilbert, "Some Legal Aspects of the Education of Spanish-Speaking Children in Texas," p. 104.

98 Texas Attorney General, Opinion No. V-128, April 8, 1947; quoted in Gilbert, "Some Legal Aspects of the Education of Spanish-Speaking Children in Texas," p. 105.

99 *Delgado* v. *Bastrop County*, U.S. District Court, Western District of Texas (1948), unreported; see *Gonzalez* v. *Sheely*, 96 F. Supp. 1004 (1951). Quotations are taken from the court's judgment in *Delgado*, reprinted in Ashton, "The Fourteenth Amendment and the Education of Latin American Children in Texas," pp. 57–58.

100 Ashton, "The Fourteenth Amendment and the Education of Latin American Children in Texas," p. 59.

101 Guadalupe Salinas, "Mexican Americans and the Desegregation of Schools in the Southwest," *El Grito,* 4 (summer 1971), p. 45; reprinted from *Houston Law Review,* 8 (1971).

102 Ashton, "The Fourteenth Amendment and the Education of Latin American Children in Texas," pp. 148–151.

103 Guadalupe Salinas, "Mexican-Americans and the Desegregation of Schools in the Southwest: A Supplement," *El Grito,* 4 (summer 1971), p. 63. Emphasis in original.

104 Testimony of Dr. Hector P. Garcia, *in* U.S. Congress, *School Busing Hearings,* Part 3, p. 1511.

105 Alfred Perez, *in* California State Advisory Committee to the U.S. Commission on Civil Rights, *Education and the Mexican American Community in Los Angeles County* (Washington, D.C.: U.S. Commission on Civil Rights, April 1968), p. 5.

106 A number of such actions in Texas were reported in *Integrated Education* (July-August, 1969), p. 76; (January-February 1970), p. 73; (March-April 1970), p. 65; (July-August 1970), p. 61; (September-October 1971), p. 64; (July-August 1972), p. 33.

107 See letter of Supt. Jack P. Crowther to members of the Los Angeles Board of Education, *in* U.S. Congress, 91st, 2nd session, Senate Select Committee on Equal Educational Opportunity, *Equal Educational Opportunity: Hearings,* Part 4, *Mexican American Education* (Washington, D.C.: GPO, 1971). In this source later school board actions relating to each of the demands are noted.

108 Oscar Zeta Acosta, "The East L.A. 13 vs. the L.A. Superior Court," *El Grito,* 3 (winter 1970), p. 13.

109 *Integrated Education,* 6 (July-August 1968), p. 4.

110 Testimony of Jose V. Uriegas, *in* U.S. Congress, *Mexican-American Education,* pp. 2469–2470.

111 Testimony of Jose A. Cardenas, *ibid.,* p. 2461.

112 Testimony of Jesus J. Rubio, *ibid.,* p. 2497.

113 Martin H. Gerry, *Cultural Freedom and the Rights of La Raza,* March 3, 1972, p. 4 (mimeographed). At the time of writing, Gerry was assistant director for special programs of the Office for Civil Rights, U.S. Department of Health, Education, and Welfare.

114 *Cisneros* v. *Corpus Christi Independent School District,* 324 F. Supp. 599 (1970).

115 *U.S.* v. *Texas Education Agency,* 467 F. 2d 848 (1972).

116 Testimony of Carlos Vela, *in* U.S. Congress, *Mexican American Education,* p. 2556.

117 *Ibid.,* p. 2555.

118 *U.S.* v. *State of Texas,* Civil Action No. 5281 (E.D., Tyler Div.), Order of December 6, 1971.

119 "Discrimination and Denial Due to National Origin," *Integrated Education,* 8 (July-August 1970), p. 53.

120 J. Stanley Pottinger, "Equality for Spanish-Surnamed Students," *Integrated Education,* 10 (November-December 1972), p. 52.

121 *Integrated Education,* 9 (November-December 1971), p. 61.

122 *Integrated Education,* 10 (January-February 1972), p. 67.

123 Rangel and Alcala, "De Jure Segregation of Chicanos in Texas Schools," p. 384.

124 An earlier report by the U.S. Office of Education assembled data about Mexican-American education drawn from the Coleman Report of 1966; see George W. Mayeske, "Educational Achievement Among Mexican Americans," *Integrated Education,* 6 (January-February 1968), pp. 32–37. See also Carter, *Mexican Americans in School.*

125 Basic data in U.S. Commission on Civil Rights, *Mexican American Education Study*, Vol. I, p. 17.

126 *Ibid.*, p. 23.

127 U.S. Commission on Civil Rights, *Ethnic Isolation of Mexican Americans in Public Schools in the Southwest* (Washington, D.C.: GPO, April 1971), pp. 41, 45, 48, 53.

Chapter 5. Indian-American children

1 National Congress of American Indians, "Economic Development of the American Indian and His Lands," *in* U.S. Congress, 91st, 2nd session, Joint Economic Committee, Subcommittee on Economy in Government, *Toward Economic Development for Native American Communities: A Compendium of Papers*, Vol. II (Washington, D.C.: GPO, 1969), p. 411.

2 William H. Veeder, "Federal Encroachment on Indian Water Rights and the Impairment of Reservation Development," *in* U.S. Congress, *Toward Economic Development for Native American Communities*, Vol. II, p. 467.

3 U.S. Congress, 90th, 1st and 2nd sessions, Senate Committee on Labor and Public Welfare, Special Subcommittee on Indian Education, *Indian Education: Hearings*, Part 1 (Washington, D.C.: GPO, 1969), p. 305.

4 *Ibid.*, pp. 48, 50.

5 Charles A. Eastman, *Indian Boyhood* (Garden City, N.Y.: Doubleday, 1911), p. 4. Originally published in 1902.

6 George A. Pettitt, *Primitive Education in North America* (Berkeley: University of California Press, 1946), p. 89.

7 Eastman, *Indian Boyhood*, p. 51.

8 See Alfonso Ortiz, "American Indian Philosophy: Its Relation to the Modern World," *in Indian Voices: The First Convocation of American Indian Scholars* (San Francisco: Indian Historian Press, 1970), pp. 9–17.

9 Arthur E. Allen, "The Education of the New England Indians During the Colonial Period" (master's thesis, Brown University, 1962), p. 41.

10 Martha E. Layman, "A History of Indian Education in the United States" (doctoral dissertation, University of Minnesota, 1942), p. 102.

11 Felix S. Cohen, *Handbook of Federal Indian Law* (Albuquerque: University of New Mexico Press, 1971), p. 51. Originally published in 1942.

12 Layman, "History of Indian Education in the United States," p. 123.

13 Virgil J. Vogel, *This Country Was Ours: A Documentary History of the American Indian* (New York: Harper & Row, 1972).

14 Cohen, *Handbook of Federal Indian Law*, p. 240. See also Robert F. Berkhofer, Jr., "Protestant Missionaries to the American Indians, 1787 to 1862" (doctoral dissertation, Cornell University, 1960), p. 86, for comments on the financial motivation of missionaries.

15 F. S. Cotterill, *The Southern Indians: The Story of the Civilized Tribes Before Removal* (Norman: University of Oklahoma Press, 1954), p. 226.

16 *Ibid.*, pp. 228–229.

17 Layman, "History of Indian Education in the United States," p. 137.

18 Lillie Duvall Henshaw, "A History of the Cherokee Tribal Schools Since the Civil War" (master's thesis, University of Oklahoma, 1935), p. 8.

19 Layman, "History of Indian Education in the United States," p. 141.

20 Angie Debo, *The Rise and Fall of the Choctaw Republic*, 2nd ed. (Norman: University of Oklahoma Press, 1961), pp. 45, 62–63.

21 Layman, "History of Indian Education in the United States," p. 146.

22 Debo, *Rise and Fall of the Choctaw Republic*, pp. 61–62.

23 Caroline Leola Davis, "The History of the Schools and the Educational Develop-

ment in the Chickasaw Nation" (master's thesis, University of Oklahoma, 1935), p. 45.

24 See Robert F. Berkhofer, Jr., *Salvation and the Savage: An Analysis of Protestant Missions and American Indian Response, 1787–1862* (Lexington: University of Kentucky Press, 1965), p. 141; and *Liberator*, September 22, 1854. For a Choctaw defense of the measure, see *Liberator*, December 1, 1856.

25 U.S. Office of Indian Affairs, "A Brief Statement on the Background of Present-Day Indian Policy, 1938," *in* Cohen, *Handbook of Federal Indian Law*, p. 28.

26 Annual message to Congress, December 3, 1901; quoted in Vogel, *This Country Was Ours*, p. 193.

27 Davida Woerner, "Education Among the Navajo: An Historical Study" (doctoral dissertation, Columbia University, 1941), p. 15.

28 See "Navajo–U.S. Treaty of June 1, 1868: The Complete Text," *Indian Historian*, 1 (spring 1968), pp. 35–37.

29 Woerner, "Education Among the Navajo," p. 20.

30 Allan Hulsizer, *Region and Culture in the Curriculum of the Navajo and the Dakota* (Federalsburg, Md.: Stowell, 1940), p. 1.

31 Thomas J. Morgan, Commissioner of Indian Affairs, 1889; quoted in *ibid.*, p. 44.

32 *Ibid.*, p. 68.

33 Gertrude Golden, *Red Moon Called Me: Memoirs of a Schoolteacher in the Government Indian Service*, edited by Cecil Dryden (San Antonio: Naylor, 1954), p. 153; Woerner, "Education Among the Navajo," p. 104.

34 Books by three Hopis, born between 1890 and 1898, are prime sources: *Sun Chief: The Autobiography of a Hopi Indian*, edited by Leo W. Simmons (New Haven: Yale University Press, 1942); Polingaysi Qoyawayma (Elizabeth L. White), *No Turning Back: A True Account of a Hopi Indian Girl's Struggle to Bridge the Gap Between the World of Her People and the World of the White Man* as told to Vada F. Carlson (Albuquerque: University of New Mexico Press, 1964); and *Me and Mine: The Life Story of Helen Sekaquaptewa as told to Louise Udall* (Tucson: University of Arizona Press, 1969). Hereafter these will be cited as *Sun Chief*, *No Turning Back*, and *Me and Mine*.

35 *Me and Mine*, p. 11.

36 *Ibid.*, p. 97.

37 *Sun Chief*, p. 99.

38 *No Turning Back*, p. 29.

39 *Me and Mine*, p. 93.

40 *Ibid.*, p. 105.

41 *Ibid.*, p. 134.

42 *Sun Chief*, p. 99.

43 *Ibid.*, p. 134.

44 *Me and Mine*, p. 14.

45 *Ibid.*, p. 128.

46 *Ibid.*, p. 144.

47 *No Turning Back*, p. 49.

48 *Ibid.*, p. 69.

49 *Ibid.*, p. 127.

50 *Me and Mine*, p. 248.

51 Stephen R. Riggs, *Mary and I: Forty Years with the Sioux* (Chicago: Holmes, 1880), p. 35; see also p. 56.

52 Vogel, *This Country Was Ours*, p. 58.

53 "Sioux Treaty of 1868," *Indian Historian*, 3 (winter 1970), pp. 13–17. The treaty was not ratified and proclaimed until February 1869.

54 Statement by Rt. Rev. Bishop W. H. Hare; quoted in C. C. Painter, *Extravagance, Waste and Failure of Indian Education* (Philadelphia: Indian Rights Association, March 1, 1892), p. 14.

55 William M. Kizer, "History of the Flandreau Indian School, Flandreau, South Dakota" (master's thesis, University of South Dakota, 1940), p. 15.

56 Milo C. Johnson, "The History of Education on the Fort Peck Reservation from 1885 to 1935" (master's thesis, University of Minnesota, 1937), pp. 70–71.

57 Charles A. Eastman, *From the Deep Woods to Civilization: Chapters in the Autobiography of an Indian* (Boston: Little, Brown, 1917), p. 125.

58 *Ibid.*, p. 103.

59 John C. Ewers, *The Blackfeet: Raiders on the Northwestern Plains* (Norman: University of Oklahoma Press, 1958), p. 219.

60 Robert E. Howard, "A Historical Survey of the Formation and Growth of Education on the Blackfeet Indian Reservation, 1872–1964" (master's thesis, Western Montana College of Education, 1965), p. 9.

61 *Ibid.*, pp. 11, 12, 20; and Ewers, *The Blackfeet*, p. 284.

62 Irene M. Alvstad Berven, "History of Indian Education on the Flathead Reservation" (master's thesis, Montana State University, 1959), p. 41.

63 *Ibid.*, p. 42.

64 *Duwamish et al. Indians* v. *United States*, 79 C. Cls. 588 (1934), pp. 585–586.

65 James Lynn Pester, "The History of Indian Education in the State of Washington" (master's thesis, University of Washington, 1951), pp. 113, 121, 131, 144, 151, 160, 171, 176, 183, 191.

66 *Ibid.*, pp. 39, 122.

67 *Ibid.*, p. 153.

68 Sherburne F. Cook, *The Conflict Between the California Indian and White Civilization*, Vol. III; *The American Invasion, 1848–1870* (Berkeley: University of California Press, 1943), p. 5.

69 Treaty of September 18, 1851; quoted in Robert F. Heizer and Alan F. Almquist, *The Other Californians: Prejudice and Discrimination under Spain, Mexico, and the United States to 1920* (Berkeley: University of California Press, 1971), pp. 222–223.

70 *Ibid.*, p. 46. On Indian slavery, see also Jack D. Forbes, *Native Americans of California and Nevada* (Berkeley: Far West Laboratory for Educational Research and Development, 1969), p. 56.

71 U.S. Congress, 33rd, 1st session, House of Representatives Committee on Indian Affairs, Report No. 167, 1854 (serial set No. 744).

72 Alice C. Fletcher, *Indian Education and Civilization* (Washington, D.C.: GPO, 1888), pp. 220, 222, 226, 231, 239. (U.S. Congress, 48th, 2nd session, Senate, Executive Document No. 95, serial set No. 2264.)

73 Jack D. Forbes, "The Native American Experience in California History," *California Historical Quarterly*, 50 (September 1971), p. 241. Also Heizer and Almquist, *The Other Californians*, p. 62.

74 Forbes, *Native Americans of California and Nevada*, p. 78.

75 Henshaw, "History of the Cherokee Tribal Schools," pp. 33, 35.

76 Cullen Joe Holland, "The Cherokee Indian Newspapers, 1826–1906: The Tribal Voice of a People in Transition" (doctoral dissertation, University of Minnesota, 1956), p. 508.

77 See Henshaw, "History of the Cherokee Tribal Schools," p. 121; and Abraham E. Knepler, "Education in the Cherokee Nation," *Chronicles of Oklahoma*, 21 (December 1943), p. 401.

78 Debo, *Rise and Fall of the Choctaw Republic*, pp. 96–97.

79 *Ibid.*, p. 237.

80 *Ibid.*, p. 242.

81 *Ibid.*, p. 285. The official was John D. Benedict.

82 Davis, "History of the Schools and the Educational Development in the Chickasaw Nation," p. 118.

83 The following material on Alaska is reprinted from Meyer Weinberg, *Race and Place: A Legal History of the Neighborhood School.* (Washington, D.C.: GPO, 1968).

84 Cohen, *Handbook of Federal Indian Law*, fn. 86, p. 406.

85 Joseph Engasongwok Senungetuk, *Give or Take a Century: An Eskimo Chronicle* (San Francisco: Indian Historical Press, 1971), p. 189.

86 33 Stat. 619, January 27, 1905. In 1917, the law was amended to read "white *and colored* children and children of mixed blood"; 39 Stat. 1131, March 3, 1917.

87 *Davis* v. *Sitka School Board*, 3 Alaska 484 (1908).

88 *Crawford* v. *District School Board for School District No. 7*, 137 Pac. 218 (1913).

89 *Jones* v. *Ellis, School Board* (of Ketchikan), 8 Alaska 147 (1929).

90 See Jeannette P. Nichols, *Alaska* (New York: Russell & Russell, 1963, reprinted), fn. 169, p. 102, for beginning of school; Clarence Hulley, *Alaska, 1841–1953* (Portland, Ore.: Binford & Mort, 1953), p. 206, for closing.

91 See Ted C. Hinckley, "The Presbyterian Leadership in Pioneer Alaska," *Journal of American History* (March 1966), pp. 745–746.

92 Hulley, *Alaska, 1841–1953*, pp. 309, 319.

93 Hulsizer, *Region and Culture*, p. 311.

94 James E. Officer, *Indians in School: A Study of the Development of Educational Facilities for Arizona Indians* (Tucson: Bureau of Ethnic Research, University of Arizona, 1956), pp. 31, 61.

95 Gledea S. Sanders, "The Educational Development of the Cheyenne and Arapaho Indians upon the Reservation," (master's thesis, Oklahoma A&M College, 1933), p. 32.

96 Earl Old Person, "Indians as Human Beings," *Integrated Education*, 5 (April-May 1967), p. 19.

97 Cohen, *Handbook of Federal Indian Law*, p. 241.

98 *Ibid.*, p. 242.

99 Harry A. Kersey, Jr., "Educating the Seminole Indians of Florida, 1879–1969," *Florida Historical Quarterly*, 49 (July 1970), p. 26.

100 Cohen, *Handbook of Federal Indian Law*, fn. 65, p. 242.

101 *In re Petition of Can-ah-couqua for Habeas Corpus*, 29 Fed. 689–690 (1887).

102 Cohen, *Handbook of Federal Indian Law*, fn. 62, p. 242.

103 *In re Lelah-puc-ka chee*, 98 Fed. 433 (1899).

104 *Ibid.*, 435.

105 *Peters* v. *Malin*, 111 Fed. 244 (1901).

106 Pratt to Rep. H. L. Dawes, April 4, 1881; quoted in Richard Henry Pratt, *Battlefield and Classroom: Four Decades with the American Indian, 1867–1904*, ed. by Robert M. Utley (New Haven: Yale University Press, 1964), p. 266.

107 *Sun Chief*, p. 157.

108 Treaty of May 6, 1828; cited in Cohen, *Handbook of Federal Indian Law*, fn. 25, p. 239, emphasis added.

109 Layman, "History of Indian Education in the United States," pp. 384–385.

110 Golden, *Red Moon Called Me*, p. 83.

111 Albert H. Kneale, *Indian Agent;* quoted in Maxine Wakefield Hagan, "An Educa-

tional History of the Pima and Papago Peoples from the Mid-Seventeenth Century to the Mid-Twentieth Century" (doctoral dissertation, University of Arizona, 1959), p. 81.

112 Forbes, *Native Americans of California and Nevada*, p. 74.
113 *Me and Mine*, p. 247.
114 Eastman, *From the Deep Woods to Civilization*, p. 25.
115 Golden, *Red Moon Called Me*, p. 88.
116 William T. Hagan, *The Sac and Fox Indians* (Norman: University of Oklahoma Press, 1958), p. 250.
117 Golden, *Red Moon Called Me*, p. 17.
118 Erwin F. Mittelholtz, "A Historical Review of the Grand Portage Indian Reservation with Special Emphasis on Indian Education" (master's thesis, University of South Dakota, 1953), p. 94.
119 Pester, "History of Indian Education in the State of Washington," p. 177.
120 *Sioux Tribe of Indians* v. *United States*, 84 C. Cls. 28 (1936).
121 *Ibid.*, p. 37.
122 *Duwamish et al. Indians* v. *United States*, 79 C. Cls. 530 (1934).
123 See Cohen, *Handbook of Federal Indian Law*, fn. 157, p. 377.
124 Pester, "History of Indian Education in the State of Washington," p. 133.
125 *Piper* v. *Big Pine School District*, 193 Cal. 667 (1924).
126 *Dorothy Sunrise* v. *District Board of Coche Consolidated School District No. 1, Comanche County;* cited in Ila Cleo Moore, "Schools and Education among the Kiowa and Comanche Indians (1870–1940)" (master's thesis, University of Oklahoma, 1940), p. 79.
127 Forbes, *Native Americans of California and Nevada*, p. 83.
128 Robert J. Murray, "History of Education in the Turtle Mountain Indian Reservation of North Dakota" (master's thesis, University of North Dakota, 1953), pp. 23, 26, 38–46.
129 Maud Drain, "The History of the Education of the Creek Indians" (master's thesis, University of Oklahoma, 1928), p. 104.
130 Lloyd E. Blauch, *Educational Service for Indians* (Washington, D.C.: GPO, 1939), p. 52.
131 See U.S. Congress, *Indian Education: Hearings*, Part 1, p. 98.
132 *Ibid.*, Part 1, p. 94.
133 *Ibid.*, Part 5, p. 2015.
134 Anne M. Smith, *Indian Education in New Mexico* (Albuquerque: Institute for Social Research, University of New Mexico, 1968), p. 16.
135 Comptroller General of the United States, *Administration of Program for Aid to Public School Education of Indian Children Being Improved* (Washington, D.C.: GAO, May 28, 1970), p. 37.
136 Peterson Zah, "Indian Education in Public Schools: An Indian's View," *in* U.S. Congress, 91st, 2nd session, Senate Select Committee on Equal Educational Opportunity, *Equal Educational Opportunity: Hearings*, Part 2, *Equality of Educational Opportunity: An Introduction* (Washington, D.C.: GPO, 1970), p. 894.
137 For later criticism by the Navajo tribe, see "Statement of Navajo Education Division," *in* U.S. Congress, 92nd, 2nd session, Senate Committee on Interior and Insular Affairs, *Comprehensive Indian Education Act: Hearings* (Washington, D.C.: GPO, 1972), pp. 409–413.
138 NAACP Legal Defense and Educational Fund with the cooperation of the Center for Law and Education, Harvard University, *An Even Chance* (New York: NAACP Legal Defense and Educational Fund, 1971). Quotations are from pp. 7, 26, 53.
139 See "Statement of Navajo Education Division," p. 409.

140 Howard, "Historical Survey of the Formation and Growth of Education on the Blackfeet Indian Reservation, 1872–1964," p. 25.

141 Earl Old Person, "Indians as Human Beings," p. 20.

142 Blauch, *Educational Service for Indians*, p. 124.

143 Senungetuk, *Give or Take a Century*, p. 176.

144 George I. Sanchez, *"The People": A Study of the Navajos* (Lawrence, Kans.: United States Indian Service, 1948), p. 26.

145 *Ibid.*, p. 38.

146 Hulsizer, *Region and Culture*.

147 Ruth Underhill, *The Navajos*, rev. ed. (Norman: University of Oklahoma Press, 1967), p. 246.

148 Kay Bennett, *Kaibah: Recollection of a Navajo Girlhood* (Los Angeles: Westernlore Press, 1964), pp. 226–227.

149 David Aberle, "A Plan for Navajo Economic Development," *in* U.S. Congress, *Toward Economic Development for Native American Communities*, Vol. I, p. 267.

150 Taylor McKenzie, "What the Navajo Needs," *Integrated Education*, 8 (July-August 1970), p. 30. Reprinted from the *Navajo Times*, April 23, 1970.

151 Aberle, "Plan for Navajo Economic Development," p. 274.

152 Jack Frederick and Anna Gritts Kilpatrick (eds.), *The Shadow of Sequoyah: Social Documents of the Cherokees, 1862–1964* (Norman: University of Oklahoma Press, 1965), p. viii.

153 Chapman J. Milling, *Red Carolinians*, 2nd ed. (Columbia: University of South Carolina Press, 1969), p. 381.

154 Albert L. Wahrhaftig, *The Cherokee People Today* (Tahlequah, Okla.: Carnegie Corporation Cross-Cultural Education Project, University of Chicago, 1966), p. 826.

155 Murray L. Wax, *Indian Americans: Unity and Diversity* (Englewood Cliffs, N.J.: Prentice-Hall, 1971), p. 107.

156 *Ibid.*, pp. 118, 128.

157 *Ibid.*, p. 115.

158 U.S. Congress, *Indian Education: Hearings*, Part 2, p. 567.

159 *Ibid.*, p. 575.

160 *Ibid.*, pp. 1986–1987.

161 Margery G. Caspar, "The Education of Menominee Youth in Wisconsin," *Integrated Education*, 11 (January-February 1973), p. 47. See also Deborah Shames (ed.), *Freedom with Reservation: The Menominees Struggle To Save Their Land and People* (Madison, Wis.: National Committee to Save the Menominee People and Forests, 1972).

162 U.S. Congress, *Comprehensive Indian Education Act: Hearings*, p. 191.

163 Estelle Fuchs and Robert J. Havighurst, *To Live on This Earth: American Indian Education* (Garden City, N.Y.: Doubleday, 1972), p. 352.

164 See *Indian Voices*, pp. 65, 31; Wolfgang Mueller, *The Cheyenne River Sioux Reservation, South Dakota* (Chicago: National Study of American Indian Education, December 1969), p. 19; Theodore R. Humphrey, *Browning, Montana: Blackfeet Indian Reservation, Montana* (Chicago: National Study of American Indian Education, n.d.), p. 4; and P. Michael Galvan, "The Ohlone Story," *Indian Historian*, 1 (spring 1968), p. 12.

165 Cohen, *Handbook of Federal Indian Law*, p. 122.

166 Forbes, *Native Americans of California and Nevada*, p. 83. On the general features of the colonial system of governing American Indians, see two articles by the Cherokee scholar, Robert K. Thomas: "Colonialism: Classic and Internal," and "Powerless Politics," *New University Thought*, 4 (winter 1966–1967), pp. 37–44,

44–53. See also Donald L. Burnett, Jr., "An Historical Analysis of the 1968 'Indian Civil Rights' Act," *Harvard Journal on Legislation*, 9 (May 1972), pp. 557–626.

167 Rupert Costo, *in Indian Voices*, pp. 284, 287. See also Costo, "The American Indian Today," *Indian Historian*, 1 (winter 1968), pp. 4–8, 35.

168 Earl Old Person, "Indians as Human Beings," p. 20.

169 U.S. Congress, *Indian Education: Hearings*, Part 4, pp. 1254, 1256. Emphasis in original.

170 *Ibid.*, p. 1232. See also Janice Jennie Weinman, "Local Control Over the Schools in Two American Indian Communities: A Preliminary Examination of Structural Constraints and Internal Control Attitudes," 2 vols. (doctoral dissertation, Harvard University, 1970), ERIC No. ED 060 988, a study of Santa Clara and San Juan Pueblos, New Mexico; Indian Education," *Inequality in Education*, No. 7 (1971) entire issue; and Donald A. Erickson and Henrietta Schwartz, "What Rough Rock Demonstrates," *Integrated Education*, 8 (March-April 1970), pp. 21–34.

171 U.S. Congress, *Comprehensive Indian Education Act: Hearings*, p. 291.

172 Peter McDonald to Sen. Clinton Anderson, April 6, 1972; cited in *ibid.*, p. 408.

173 Solomon Cook, *in Indian Voices*, p. 148.

174 See for example *Integrated Education*, 10 (November-December 1972), p. 20.

175 Stan Steiner, *The New Indians* (New York: Dell, 1968), p. 235.

176 Larry M. Perkins, *Pawnee, Oklahoma* (Chicago: National Study of American Indian Education, January 1970), fn. 1, p. 13.

177 U.S. Congress, 91st, 1st session, Senate Committee on Labor and Public Welfare, Special Subcommittee on Indian Education, *Indian Education: A National Tragedy – A National Challenge* (Washington, D.C.: GPO, 1969), Report No. 91-501, p. 60.

178 See Robert L. Bennett, "Commentary on the Testimony Before the Senate Subcommittee on Indian Education," May 21, 1969, *in* U.S. Congress, *Indian Education: Hearings*, Part 2, p. 1483.

179 Oglala Sioux Tribe, "An Appraisal of the Pine Ridge Education Program, Pine Ridge, S. Dak." *in* U.S. Congress, *Indian Education: Hearings* Part 4, p. 1270. For a different analysis of schools on the reservation, see Murray L. Wax, Rosalie H. Wax, and Robert V. Dumont, Jr., "Formal Education in an American Indian Community," *Social Problems*, 11 (spring 1964), pp. 1–126. (This study is reprinted in Part 4 of the *Indian Education: Hearings*, pp. 1313–1444.)

180 Comptroller General of the United States, *Opportunity to Improve Indian Education in Schools Operated by the Bureau of Indian Affairs* (Washington, D.C.: GAO, April 27, 1972), p. 6.

181 *Ibid.*, p. 11.

Chapter 6. Puerto Rican children

1 Manuel Maldonado-Denis, *Puerto Rico: A Socio-Historic Interpretation*, tr. Elena Vialo (New York: Vintage, 1972), p. 58.

2 *Puerto Rican Public Papers of R. G. Tugwell, Governor* (San Juan: Service Office of the Government of Puerto Rico Printing Division, 1945), p. 154.

3 Ricardo E. Alegria, *in* U.S. Congress, 89th, 2nd Session, Senate Document 108, *Status of Puerto Rico: Hearings*, Vol. 2, *Socio-Cultural Factors in Relation to the Status of Puerto Rico*, (Washington, D.C.: GPO, 1960), pp. 251, 266.

4 Maldonado-Denis, *Puerto Rico: A Socio-Historic Interpretation*, p. 227.

5 See especially Ricardo E. Alegria, "Cacicazgo Among the Aborigines of the West Indies" (master's thesis, University of Chicago, 1947), and Jessie Walter Fewkes, *The Aborigines of Puerto Rico and Neighboring Islands* (Washington, D.C.: GPO, 1907).

6 Juan Jose Osuna, *A History of Education in Puerto Rico*, 2nd ed. (Rio Piedras, P.R.: Editorial de la Universidad de Puerto Rico, 1949), p. 8.

7 *Ibid.*, p. 47.

8 R. De Villafuerte (pseud.), *The Americanization of Manuel de Rosas* (New York: Vantage, 1967), p. 25.

9 Edward J. Berbusse, *The United States in Puerto Rico, 1898–1900* (Chapel Hill: University of North Carolina Press, 1966), p. 141.

10 Henry K. Carroll, *Report on the Island of Porto Rico: Its Population, Civil Government and Currency; with Recommendations* (Washington, D.C.: GPO, 1899), p. 794.

11 Quoted in Gildo Masso, "The Growth of the School System of Porto Rico Under the American Administration" (master's thesis, University of Chicago, 1922), p. 58. General Davis was commanding officer in Puerto Rico from May 9, 1899, to May 1, 1900.

12 *Ibid.*, p. 231. In January 1901, $200,000 was given to Puerto Rico by the U.S. government to be used for schools. This money, however, was taken from the customs duties paid by Puerto Ricans; see *ibid.*, p. 54.

13 Henrietta Yurchenco, ¡*Hablamas! Puerto Ricans Speak* (New York: Praeger, 1971), p. 55.

14 Julian H. Steward and others, *The People of Puerto Rico* (Urbana: University of Illinois Press, 1956), p. 253.

15 Masso, "Growth of the School System of Porto Rico Under the American Administration," p. 239. Actual figures were $13.61–$21.24 in 1901 and $15.39–$49.11 in 1918.

16 Victor S. Clark, *Porto Rico and Its Problems* (Washington, D.C.: Brookings Institution, 1930), p. 566.

17 Lloyd E. Blauch, assisted by Charles F. Reid, *Public Education in the Territories and Outlying Possessions* (Washington, D.C.: GPO, 1939), p. 111.

18 Clark, *Porto Rico and Its Problems*, p. 86.

19 *Ibid.*, p. 279.

20 International Institute of Teachers College, Columbia University, *A Survey of the Public Educational System of Porto Rico* (New York: Bureau of Publications, Teachers College Columbia University, 1926), p. 48.

21 Osuna, *History of Education in Puerto Rico*, p. 135.

22 Aida Negron de Montilla, *Americanization in Puerto Rico and the Public School System 1900–1930* (Rio Piedras, PR.: Editorial Edil, 1971), pp. 47–48.

23 *Ibid.*, pp. 181, 183.

24 Bailey W. Diffie and Justine W. Diffie, *Porto Rico: A Broken Pledge* (New York: Vanguard Press, 1931), p. 206.

25 Negron de Montilla, *Americanization in Puerto Rico*, pp. 103, 118, 119.

26 *Ibid.*, pp. 134–141.

27 *Ibid.*, p. 192.

28 Teachers College, *Survey of the Public Educational System of Porto Rico*, p. 93.

29 Ana Maria O'Neill, *in* U.S. Congress, *Status of Puerto Rico: Hearings*, Vol. 2, p. 179.

30 Ismael Rodriguez Bou, "Significant Factors in the Development of Education in Puerto Rico," *in* United States–Puerto Rican Commission on the Status of Puerto Rico, *Status of Puerto Rico: Selected Background Studies* (Washington, D.C.: GPO, 1966), p. 161.

31 Franklin D. Roosevelt to Jose M. Gallardo, April 8, 1937; quoted in Osuna, *History of Education in Puerto Rico*, pp. 376–377.

32 Thomas G. Mathews, *Puerto Rican Politics and the New Deal* (Gainesville: University of Florida Press, 1960), p. 319.

33 Leila Sussman, "Democratization and Class Segregation in Puerto Rican Schooling: The U.S. Model Transplanted," *Sociology of Education,* 41 (1968), p. 325.

34 Basic data in Oscar Emilio Porrata, "Retardation in the Elementary Urban Schools of Porto Rico" (master's thesis, University of Chicago, 1934), p. 4.

35 Basic data in Angeles Pereles Cafouras, "The History of Elementary Education in Puerto Rico under the American Government 1898–1951" (master's thesis, Indiana University, 1951), p. 36.

36 Jose C. Rosario, *The Development of the Puerto Rican Jibaro and His Present Attitude Towards Society* (San Juan: University of Puerto Rico, 1935), p. 87.

37 Osuna, *History of Education in Puerto Rico,* p. 501. Emphasis added.

38 Rodriguez Bou, "Significant Factors in the Development of Education in Puerto Rico," p. 212.

39 See Blauch, *Public Education in the Territories,* pp. 113–127, 130. The data supplied in this source permit only an estimate to be made.

40 *Puerto Rican Public Papers of R. G. Tugwell,* p. 54.

41 Luis Nieves Falcon, *Recruitment to Higher Education in Puerto Rico, 1940–1960* (Rio Piedras, P.R.: Editorial Universitaria Universidad de Puerto Rico, 1965), p. 209.

42 For above data, see Candido Oliveras, Secretary of Education of Puerto Rico, *in* Francesco Cordasco and Eugene Bucchioni (eds.), *The Puerto Rican Community and Its Children on the Mainland: A Source Book for Teachers, Social Workers and Other Professionals,* 2nd ed. (Metuchen, N.J.: Scarecrow Press, 1972), p. 249; George L. Wilber and W. B. Back, "Rural Poverty in Puerto Rico," *in* President's National Advisory Commission on Rural Poverty, *Rural Poverty in the United States* (Washington, D.C.: GPO, 1968), p. 143. For slightly later data, see Henry Wells, *The Modernization of Puerto Rico: A Political Study of Changing Values and Institutions* (Cambridge, Mass.: Harvard University Press, 1969), p. 177; Kal Wagenheim, *Puerto Rico; A Profile* (New York: Praeger, 1970), p. 7; Dorothy Dulles Bourne and James R. Bourne, *Thirty Years of Change in Puerto Rico: A Case Study of Change in Puerto Rico: A Case Study of Ten Selected Rural Areas* (New York: Praeger, 1966), p. 57; Nieves Falcon, *Recruitment to Higher Education in Puerto Rico, 1940–1960,* p. 171. See also Osuna, *History of Education in Puerto Rico,* pp. 493–494, 497.

43 Nieves Falcon, *Recruitment to Higher Education in Puerto Rico, 1940–1960,* p. 172. Erwin H. Epstein, "National Identity and the Language Issue in Puerto Rico," *Comparative Education Review,* 11 (June 1967), reprinted in Epstein (ed.), *Politics and Education in Puerto Rico: A Documentary Survey of the Language Issue* (Metuchen, N.J.: Scarecrow Press, 1970), p. 146.

44 For private schools, see Wagenheim, *Puerto Rico: A Profile,* p. 203; Epstein, "National Identity and the Language Issue in Puerto Rico," pp. 146, 240; Sussman, "Democratization and Class Segregation in Puerto Rican Schooling," p. 336; Gordon K. Lewis, *Puerto Rico: Freedom and Power in the Caribbean* (New York: Monthly Review Press, 1963), p. 240.

45 Nieves Falcon, *Recruitment to Higher Education in Puerto Rico, 1946–1960,* p. 44.

46 J. Cayce Morrison, *The Puerto Rican Study, 1953–1957: A Report on the Education and Adjustment of Puerto Rican Pupils in the Public Schools of the City of New York* (New York: Board of Education, 1958), pp. 3, 171; Jacob Landers, *Improving Ethnic Distribution of New York City Pupils* (New York: Board of Education, May 1966), p. 47.

47 Robert M. Coleman, "A History and Evaluation of the New York University Workshop: Field Study in Puerto Rican Education and Culture, 1948–1967" (doctoral dissertation, New York University, 1969), pp. 51, 58.

48 Morrison, *Puerto Rican Study*, p. 184.

49 Coleman, "History and Evaluation," p. 58.

50 Deby Kirschenbaum, "The Non-English Speaking Puerto Rican Child in the New York City Public School System" (master's thesis, Bank Street College of Education, 1957?), pp. 31–32.

51 Herman Badillo, quoted in *Puerto Ricans Confront Problems of the Complex Urban Society: A Design for Change*, Community Conference Proceedings, April 15–16, 1967 (New York: Human Resources Administration, n.d.), p. 15.

52 Morrison, *Puerto Rican Study*, p. 84.

53 See Antonia Pantoja, *in* U.S. Congress, 91st, 2nd session, Senate Select Committee on Equal Educational Opportunity, *Equal Educational Opportunity: Hearings*, Part 8, *Equal Educational Opportunity for Puerto Rican Children* (Washington, D.C.: GPO, 1970), p. 3693; Anna Conogliaro, *in* Paul L. Tractenberg (ed.), *Selection of Teachers and Supervisors in Urban Schools Systems* (New York: Agathon, 1972), p. 662; Martin B. Dworkis (ed.), *The Impact of Puerto Rican Migration on Governmental Services in New York City* (New York: New York University Press, 1957), p. 37.

54 Morrison, *Puerto Rican Study*, p. 84.

55 Kirschenbaum, "The Non-English Speaking Puerto Rican Child in the New York City Public School System," p. 33.

56 Dr. Nathan Jacobson, principal of PS 191, quoted in Sarah K. Chartock, "A Descriptive Study of the Programs Undertaken by the Riverside Neighborhood Assembly to Further Democratic Integration on the West Side of Manhattan" (doctoral dissertation, New York University, 1957), p. 40.

57 Dworkis, *Impact of Puerto Rican Migration*, p. 32.

58 *Ibid.*

59 Helaine Ruth Messer, "The Puerto Rican Student in the New York City Public Schools: 1945–1965" (master's thesis, Columbia University, 1966), p. 113.

60 Morrison, *Puerto Rican Study*, p. 243.

61 Robert M. Willis, "An Analysis of the Adjustment and Scholastic Achievement of Forty Puerto Rican Boys Who Attended Transition Classes in New York City" (doctoral dissertation, New York University, 1961), pp. 211–212.

62 Morrison, *Puerto Rican Study*, pp. 239–241. On the lack of implementation of the Puerto Rican Study, see Joseph P. Fitzpatrick, *Puerto Rican Americans: The Meaning of Migration to the Mainland* (Englewood Cliffs, N.J.: Prentice-Hall, 1971), p. 147; Messer, "The Puerto Rican Student in the New York City Public School," p. 113; Herman Rodriguez, "Some Problems of Bilingualism in Acculturation of Puerto Ricans in New York City" (master's thesis, City College of New York 1965), p. 73; "Instruction for Non-English Speaking Puerto Rican Pupils in New York City Public School System," February 10, 1971, memorandum for Sen. Jacob Javits, *in* U.S. Commission on Civil Rights, *Hearing Held in New York, February 14–15, 1972* (Washington, D.C.: GPO, 1973), p. 631; Hector Vazquez, *in* U.S. Congress, *Equal Educational Opportunity: Hearings*, Part 8, pp. 3732–3733.

63 Center for Field Research and School Services, *An Evaluation of Teaching English as a Second Language in the Public Schools* (New York: School of Education, New York University, September 1969), pp. 7–8.

64 Willis, "Analysis of the Adjustment and Scholastic Achievement of Forty Puerto Rican Boys," pp. 204–205.

65 Gertrude A. Robinson, "A Case Study of Puerto Rican Children in Junior High School 65, Manhattan, New York City" (doctoral dissertation, New York University, 1956), p. 394.

66 Ada Stambler, "A Study of Eighth Grade Puerto Rican Students at Junior High School 65, Manhattan, with Implications for Their Placement Grouping, and Orientation" (doctoral dissertation, Columbia University, 1958), p. 70.

67 Frank Negron, *in* U.S. Congress, *Equal Educational Opportunity: Hearings*, Part 8, p. 3764.

68 *Ibid.*; for subsequent quotations, see pp. 3771, 3770.

69 Madeline Rivera, *in* U.S. Commission on Civil Rights, *Hearing Held in New York*, p. 51; for subsequent quotations, see pp. 59, 60.

70 Morrison, *Puerto Rican Study*, pp. 75, 128.

71 Elena Padilla, *Up from Puerto Rico* (New York: Columbia University Press, 1958), p. 64

72 *A Study of Poverty Conditions in the New York Puerto Rican Community* (New York: Puerto Rican Forum, 1970), p. 22.

73 Calculated from data in EQUAL, *Research for Action*, Bulletin No. 2, February 15, 1967.

74 U.S. Commission on Civil Rights, Staff Report, "Demographic, Social, and Economic Characteristics of New York City and New York Metropolitan Area," *in* U.S. Commission on Civil Rights, *Hearing Held in New York*, p. 246.

75 Hector Vazquez, *in* U.S. Congress, *Equal Educational Opportunity: Hearings*, Part 8, p. 3731.

76 See "The Public Educational System of Puerto Rico: Accomplishments and Unsolved Problems," *ibid.*, p. 3902; also Wagenheim, *Puerto Rico: A Profile*, p. 201.

77 Joan T. England, "The Puerto Ricans: Melrose School and Community, New York City" (master's thesis, Hunter College, 1958), p. 29.

78 J. J. Osuna, "Report on Visits to New York City Schools," *in* Cordasco and Bucchioni (eds.), *The Puerto Rican Community and Its Children on the Mainland*, p. 239.

79 Kirschenbaum, "The Non-English Speaking Puerto Rican Child in the New York City Public School System," p. 31.

80 Eugene Bucchioni, "A Sociological Analysis of the Functioning of Elementary Education for Puerto Rican Children in the New York City Public Schools" (doctoral dissertation, New School for Social Research, 1965), p. 147.

81 Patria Cintron De Crespo, "Puerto Rican Women Teachers in New York: Self-Perception and Work Adjustment as Perceived by Themselves and by Others" (doctoral dissertation, Columbia University, 1965), p. 87.

82 Amalia Betanzos, quoted in *Puerto Ricans Confront Problems of the Complex Urban Society*, p. 358.

83 Chartock, "Descriptive Study of the Programs Undertaken by the Riverside Neighborhood Assembly," pp. 39, 103.

84 *Ibid.*, p. 92.

85 Sara R. (Schenck) Levy, quoted in Coleman, "History and Evaluation of the New York University Workshop," p. 233.

86 Dan Wakefield, *Island in the City: The World of Spanish Harlem* (Boston: Houghton Mifflin, 1959), p. 150.

87 Padilla, *Up from Puerto Rico*, p. 272.

88 Carmen Arroyo, *in* U.S. Congress, *Equal Educational Opportunity: Hearings*, Part 8, p. 3776.

89 Patricia Cayo Sexton, *Spanish Harlem* (New York: Harper & Row, 1965), p. 50.

90 Richard J. Margolis, *The Losers: A Report on the Puerto Ricans and the Public Schools* (New York: Aspira, May 1968), p. 8.

91 *Ibid.*, p. 5.

92 Connecticut Advisory Committee to the U.S. Commission on Civil Rights, *El Boricua: The Puerto Rican Community in Bridgeport and New Haven* (Washington, D.C.: GPO, January 1973), p. 18.

93 Attendance statistics, Massachusetts Advisory Committee to the U.S. Commission on Civil Rights, *in* U.S. Commission on Civil Rights, *Hearing Held in New York*, p. 557; see also Sylvia Herrera Fox, *in* U.S. Congress, *Equal Educational Opportunity: Hearings*, Part 8, p. 3723.

94 Morris Raphael Cohen, *A Dreamer's Journey: The Autobiography of Morris Raphael Cohen* (Glencoe, Ill.: Free Press, 1949), p. 70.

95 Selma Cantor Berrol, "Immigrants at School, 1898–1914" (doctoral dissertation, City University of New York, 1967), pp. 99, 217–218.

96 Frank V. Thompson, *Schooling of the Immigrant* (New York: Harper & Row, 1920), pp. 118–119.

97 Moses Rischin, *The Promised City: New York's Jews, 1870–1914* (Cambridge, Mass.: Harvard University Press, 1962), p. 200. For data on New York City and Chicago see Berrol, "Immigrants at School," p. 120; and U.S. Immigration Commission, *The Children of Immigrants in Schools*, Vol. 32 (Washington, D.C.: GPO, 1911), p. 612.

98 Berrol, "Immigrants at School," p. 64.

99 Quoted in Columbia University, Bureau of Applied Social Research, *The Puerto Ricans of New York City* (New York: Puerto Rico Department of Labor, n.d.), p. 47.

100 See, for example, Berrol, "Immigrants at School," p. 128 and *passim;* testimony of Dr. Jacob B. Zack, *in* U.S. Commission on Civil Rights, *Hearing Held in New York*, p. 138; and relevant sections in Rischin, *Promised City*, and Charles S. Bernheimer, *The Russian Jew in the United States* (Philadelphia: Winston, 1905).

101 Samuel T. McSeveny, "Ethnic Groups, Ethnic Conflicts, and Recent Quantitative Research in American Political History," *International Migration Review*, 7 (spring 1973), p. 27.

102 Meyer Weinberg, "A Yearning for Learning: Blacks and Jews Through History," *Integrated Education*, 7 (May–June 1969), p. 27.

103 Data in U.S. Immigration Commission, *The Children of Immigrants in Schools*, Vol. 32, p. 612.

104 U.S. Commission on Civil Rights, *Hearing Held in New York*, pp. 238–239. For New York City, see *A Study of Poverty Conditions in the New York Puerto Rican Community*, p. 25.

105 *Ibid.*, pp. 336–338, 626.

106 Philip Kaplan, quoted in Tractenberg, *Selection of Teachers and Supervisors in Urban School Systems*, p. 201.

107 Dr. John P. King, quoted in Tractenberg, *Selection of Teachers and Supervisors in Urban School Systems*, p. 96.

108 See *Chance* v. *Board of Examiners et al.*, 458 F2d. 1167 (1972).

109 *Liberator*, February 13, 1863.

110 Carroll, *Report on the Island of Porto Rico*, p. 619.

111 Padilla, *Up from Puerto Rico*, p. 59.

112 Argelia Maria Buitrago Hermanet, "Ethnic Identification of Puerto Rican Seventh Graders" (doctoral dissertation, University of Massachusetts, 1971), p. 237.

113 Maria Teresa Babin, *The Puerto Ricans' Spirit: Their History, Life, and Culture*, tr. Barry Luby (New York: Collier, 1971), p. x.

114 U.S. Commission on Civil Rights, *Hearing Held in New York*, p. 631.

Chapter 7. Guarded preserve: black students in higher education

1 Crummell, *Attitude of the American Mind Toward the Negro Intellect,* p. 12.
2 See *Liberator,* April 15, 1834; July 19, 1834; November 5, 1836; August 4, 1837; July 30, 1841.
3 William J. Watkins, *Our Rights as Men* (Boston: Roberts, 1853), p. 9.
4 *Liberator,* July 5, 1834.
5 Billington (ed.) *A Free Negro in the Slave Era,* p. 74.
6 Ronald Takaki, "Aesculapius Was a White Man: Antebellum White Racism and Male Chauvinism at Harvard Medical School," paper read at the American Historical Association annual meeting, December 1971.
7 Victor Ullman, *Martin R. Delany: The Beginnings of Black Nationalism* (Boston: Beacon, 1971), p. 115.
8 W. E. Bigglestone, "Oberlin College and the Negro Student, 1865–1940," *Journal of Negro History,* 56 (July 1971), p. 198. See also report by William C. Nell, *Liberator,* October 10, 1856.
9 Frederick Rudolph, *The American College and University: A History* (New York: Knopf, 1962), p. 281. See also Oscar Handlin and Mary F. Handlin, *The American College and American Culture* (New York: McGraw-Hill, 1970), p. 27.
10 Horace Mann Bond dealt with this aspect of the mission colleges in at least four places: *Education of the Negro in the American Social Order,* pp. 359–361; "The Evolution and Present Status of Negro Higher and Professional Education in the United States," *Journal of Negro Education,* 17 (summer, 1948), p. 225; *in* Jessie P. Guzman (ed.), *The New South and Higher Education* (Tuskegee, Ala.: Tuskegee Institute, 1954), pp. 78–79; and "The Origin and Development of the Negro Church-Related College," *Journal of Negro Education,* 29 (summer 1960), p. 222.
11 Charles H. Thompson, "75 Years of Negro Education," *Crisis,* 45 (July 1938), p. 204.
12 Seymour Harris, *A Statistical Portrait of Higher Education* (New York: McGraw-Hill, 1972), p. 931.
13 Kelly Miller, quoted in *New York Age,* June 27, 1936.
14 Bond, *Education of the Negro in the American Social Order,* p. 361.
15 W. E. B. Du Bois and Augustus G. Dill (eds.), *The College-Bred Negro American* (Atlanta: Atlanta University Press, 1910), p. 12.
16 James W. McPherson, "White Liberals and Black Power in Negro Education, 1865–1915," *American Historical Review,* 75 (June 1970), pp. 1380–1385.
17 W. E. B. Du Bois, "Reason in School and Business," *Crisis,* 21 (November 1920), p. 6; see also Du Bois, "The Dilemma of the Negro," *American Mercury,* 3 (October 1924), p. 182.
18 Clarence A. Bacote, *The Story of Atlanta University: A Century of Service, 1865–1965* (Atalanta: Atlanta University, 1969), pp. 24, 30, 47.
19 Bond, "A Century of Negro Higher Education," p. 190.
20 *Ibid.* See also Bacote, *Story of Atlanta University,* p. 107; *Crisis* (October 1912), p. 270; and *Crisis* (December 1911), p. 53.
21 *Crisis* (March 1913), p. 218.
22 Booker T. Washington, "A University Education for Negroes," *Independent,* 68 (March 24, 1910), p. 618. See, however, Louis R. Harlan, *Booker T. Washington: The Making of a Black Leader 1856–1901* (New York: Oxford University Press, 1972), p. 275.
23 George N. Rainsford, *Congress and Higher Education in the Nineteenth Century* (Knoxville: University of Tennessee Press, 1972), p. 102.
24 *Ibid.,* p. 99.

25 Lurline Mahan Lee, "The Origin, Development, and Present Status of Arkansas' Program of Higher Education for Negroes" (doctoral dissertation, Michigan State College, 1955), p. 130.

26 Rainsford, *Congress and Higher Education in the Nineteenth Century,* p. 100.

27 Gates, *History of Public Land Law Development,* p. 27.

28 Bond, "A Century of Negro Higher Education," pp. 191–192.

29 See data in James A. Colston, "State Financial Support of Higher Education in Georgia from 1932 to 1949 with Specific Reference to Higher Education for the Negro" (doctoral dissertation, New York University, 1958), p. 46.

30 John S. Brubacher and Willis Rudy, *Higher Education in Transition: A History of American Colleges and Universities, 1636–1968,* rev. ed. (New York: Harper & Row, 1968), p. 79; John Sekora, "Murder Relentless and Impassive: The American Academic Community and the Negro College," *Soundings,* 51 (fall 1968), p. 257.

31 John W. Davis, "The Negro Land-Grant College," *Journal of Negro Education,* 2 (July 1933), p. 319.

32 Dwight Oliver Wendell Holmes, *The Evolution of the Negro College* (New York: Teachers College Columbia University, 1934), p. 152. Another source, however, reports twelve college-level students in the sixteen black land grant colleges; see Ambrose Caliver, *Education of Negro Teachers* (Washington, D.C.: GPO, 1933), p. 3.

33 Charles H. Houston, "Cracking Closed University Doors," *Crisis,* 42 (December 1935), p. 364.

34 Green Venton Curry, "Changes in Segregation Practices in Collegiate Institutions in Kentucky Since Modification of the Day Law" (master's thesis, Fisk University, n.d.), p. 9.

35 See Arthur S. Miller, *Racial Discrimination and Private Education: A Legal Analysis* (Chapel Hill: University of North Carolina Press, 1957), p. 23.

36 Data in W. E. B. Du Bois (ed.), *The College-Bred Negro* (Atlanta: Atlanta University Press, 1900), p. 42.

37 Harris, *Statistical Portrait of Higher Education,* p. 942.

38 Du Bois, *College-Bred Negro,* p. 29. See also Bigglestone, "Oberlin College and the Negro Student, 1865–1940," p. 198.

39 Du Bois and Dill (eds.), *College-Bred Negro American,* p. 42.

40 Mary Church Terrell, *A Colored Woman in a White World* (Washington, D.C.: Ramsdell, 1940), p. 41.

41 Du Bois, *College-Bred Negro,* p. 106.

42 W. E. B. Du Bois, "A Negro Student at Harvard at the End of the 19th Century," *Massachusetts Review* (1969–1970), p. 443; Lawrence R. Veysey, *The Emergence of the American University* (Chicago: University of Chicago Press, 1965), p. 92; Nell Painter, "Jim Crow at Harvard: 1923," *New England Quarterly,* 44 (1971), pp. 627, 632; Eslanda Goode Robeson, *Paul Robeson Negro* (London: Gollancz, 1930), p. 35. For Cornell, see *Crisis* (July 1913), p. 129; for Columbia and Chicago, *ibid.,* p. 132; for Yale, Du Bois, *College-Bred Negro,* p. 11; for Princeton, Du Bois, "John Howard," *Chicago Defender,* May 10, 1947; for Harvard, Mary Church Terrell, "Americans Black and White," *New Student,* 2 (February 24, 1923), p. 2. The author married one of these graduates. See also "Jim Crow at Harvard: 1923," p. 632, and see editorial in *New York Age,* April 23, 1921.

43 Veysey, *Emergence of the American University,* p. 271.

44 Paul Pierce, "Negro Alumni of the Colleges of Iowa," *in* Du Bois and Dill, *College-Bred Negro Americans,* p. 26; Charles Greenwood and Theresa Greenwood, "Some Historic Aspects of Hoosier Education of the Negro," *ISSQ (Indiana Social Studies Quarterly),* 17 (spring 1964), p. 57.

45 *Crisis* (August 1928), p. 278.
46 For discussion of Catholic colleges and universities, see George K. Hunton, *All of Which I Saw, Part of Which I Was: The Autobiography of George K. Hunton* (Garden City, N.Y: Doubleday, 1967), p. 20; W. E. B. Du Bois, "Negroes in College," *Nation*, 122 (March 3, 1926), p. 230; Richard J. Roche, *Catholic Colleges and the Negro Student* (Washington, D.C.: Catholic University of America Press, 1948), pp. 79, 90; *Crisis* (August 1931), p. 262.
47 *Crisis* (August 1927), p. 190.
48 *Crisis* (September 1932), p. 298.
49 Herbert L. Seamans, "Policies and Practices Regarding Minority Groups in Selected Colleges and Universities" (doctoral dissertation, Stanford University, 1947), p. 176.
50 *Crisis* (August 1930), p. 263.
51 *Crisis* (August 1928), p. 260.
52 Ina Corinne Brown and others, *National Survey of Higher Education of Negroes*, Vol. II (Washington, D.C.: GPO, 1942–1943), pp. 79, 83.
53 U.S. President's Commission on Higher Education, *Higher Education for American Democracy*, Vol. II, *Equalizing and Expanding Individual Opportunity* (New York: Harper & Row, 1948), p. 26.
54 *Ibid.*, fn. 1, p. 29.
55 "Breaking Down the Barriers of Discrimination in Higher Education," *School and Society*, 67 (February 14, 1948), p. 118.
56 Raymond Walters, "The Cincinnati Meeting of the Association of American Colleges," *School and Society*, 67 (January 31, 1948), p. 83.
57 David S. Berkowitz, *Inequality of Opportunity in Higher Education: A Study of Minority Group and Related Barriers to College Admission* (Report to the Temporary Commission on the Need for a State University, 1948), pp. 136, 143, 191; copies of letters from these principals are on pp. 191–194.
58 Data in George D. Wilson, "Developments in Negro Colleges During the Twenty Year Period, 1914–15 to 1933–34" (doctoral dissertation, Ohio State University, 1935), p. 78.
59 *New York Age*, August 3, 1935.
60 Du Bois and Dill (eds.), *College-Bred Negro American*, pp. 60–62.
61 Charles S. Johnson, *The Negro College Graduate* (Chapel Hill: University of North Carolina Press, 1938), p. 80.
62 Ambrose Caliver, *A Personnel Study of Negro College Students* (New York: Columbia University, 1931), p. 17.
63 W. E. B. Du Bois, "The Hampton Strike," *Nation*, 125 (November 2, 1927), p. 471.
64 Brown and others, *National Survey of Higher Education of Negroes*, Vol. II, p. 45.
65 Wilson, "Developments in Negro Colleges During the Twenty Year Period, 1914–15 to 1933–34," pp. 101, 105.
66 Caliver, *Education of Negro Teachers*, p. 30.
67 Ambrose Caliver, *Secondary Education for Negroes*, Bulletin 1932, No. 17 (Washington, D.C.: GPO, 1933), p. 35.
68 William Pickens, *The New Negro* (New York: Negro Universities Press, 1969, reprinted), p. 215. Published originally in 1916.
69 Kelly Miller, *The Everlasting Stain* (Washington, D.C.: Associated Publishers, 1924), p. 177.
70 W. E. B. Du Bois, "Pechstein and Pecksniff," *Crisis* (September 1929), p. 313. See also W. E. B. Du Bois, "The Tragedy of 'Jim Crow,'" *Crisis* (August 1923), p. 171.

71 Brown and others, *National Survey of Higher Education of Negroes*, Vol. II, p. 61.

72 Frank Bowles and Frank A. Costa, *Between Two Worlds: A Profile of Negro Higher Education* (New York: McGraw-Hill, 1971), p. 83.

73 Frank A. DeCosta, "The Tax-Supported College for Negroes," *Journal of Educational Sociology*, 22 (February 1958), p. 266.

74 Andrew Brimmer, "The Economic Outlook and the Future of the Negro College," *Daedalus*, 100 (summer 1971), p. 559.

75 Bowles and Costa, *Between Two Worlds: A Profile of Negro Higher Education*, pp. 142–144. See also Alan L. Sorkin, "A Comparison of Quality Characteristics of Negro and White Private and Church-Related Colleges and Universities in the South," *College and University*, 46 (spring 1971), pp. 199–210.

76 John A. Centra, Robert L. Linn, and Mary Ellen Parry," Academic Growth in Predominantly Negro and Predominantly White Colleges," *American Educational Research Journal*, 7 (January 1970), p. 97.

77 Gwendolyn Midlo Hall, "Rural Black College," *Negro Digest*, 18 (March 1969), pp. 61–65.

78 Terrell, *Colored Women in a White World*, p. 61.

79 Arthur J. Klein (ed.), *Survey of Negro Colleges and Universities* (Washington, D.C.: GPO, 1929), p. 48.

80 *Ibid.*, p. 144.

81 *Ibid.*, p. 397.

82 *Ibid.*, p. 720.

83 *Ibid.*, p. 475.

84 Harry W. Green, "Higher Standards for the Negro College," *Opportunity*, 9 (January 1931), p. 11.

85 Klein, *Survey of Negro Colleges and Universities*, p. 246.

86 *Ibid.*, p. 345.

87 *Ibid.*, p. 724.

88 *Crisis* (June 1912), p. 62; H. H. Hazen, "Twenty-Three Years of Teaching in a Negro Medical School," *Social Forces*, 12 (1933), pp. 572–573.

89 *Crisis* (July 1913), p. 117.

90 St. Clair Drake, "The Black University in the American Social Order," *Daedalus*, 100 (summer 1971), pp. 833–874.

91 Malcolm O'Leary, "Accreditation of Negro Colleges and Secondary Schools by the Southern Association of Colleges and Secondary Schools" (master's thesis, Catholic University of America, 1965), pp. 12, 18.

92 *Ibid.*, pp. 22, 55. See also Leland Stanford Cozart, *A History of the Association of Colleges and Secondary Schools, 1934–1965* (Charlotte, N.C.: Heritage Printers, 1967).

93 Brown and others, *National Survey of Higher Education of Negroes*, Vol. II, p. 18.

94 Winifred L. Godwin, "Southern State Governments and Higher Education for Negroes," *Daedalus*, 100 (summer 1971).

95 A. Gilbert Belles, "Negroes Are Few on College Faculties," *Southern Education Report*, 4 (July-August 1968), p. 23.

96 W. E. B. Du Bois, "Segregation in the North," *Crisis* (April 1934). Another source reports that in 1936 three Negro M.D.s were employed by white universities; see Michael R. Winston, "Through the Back Door: Academic Racism and the Negro Scholar in Historical Perspective," *Daedalus*, 100 (summer 1971), p. 695.

97 Belles, "Negroes Are Few on College Faculties," p. 23.

98 *Ibid.* Cf. Taylor, "Negro Teachers in White Colleges," p. 370, who refers to "some 40 Negro scholars" in 1947. For a listing of black faculty by name and field of

specialization, see R. B. Atwood, H. S. Smith, and Catherine O. Vaughn, "Negro Teachers in Northern Colleges and Universities in the United States," *Journal of Negro Education,* 18 (fall 1949), pp. 564–567.

99 James Allen Moss, "Negro Teachers in Predominantly White Colleges," *Journal of Negro Education,* 27 (fall 1958), p. 451; and Moss, "The Utilization of Negro Teachers in the Colleges of New York State," *Phylon,* 21 (spring 1960), p. 63.

100 Moss, "Utilization of Negro Teachers in the Colleges of New York State," p. 69.

101 Fred G. Wale, "Chosen for Ability," *Atlantic Monthly,* 180 (July 1947), p. 82.

102 Horace Mann Bond, "The Negro Scholar and Professional in America," *in* John P. Davis (ed.), *The American Negro Reference Book* (Englewood Cliffs, N.J.: Prentice-Hall, 1966), p. 544.

103 Personal communication in possession of the present writer. For a characterization of the racial beliefs of Ogburn and two colleagues, Robert E. Park and Ellsworth Faris, see O. C. Cox, "Introduction," *in* Nathan Hare, *The Black Anglo-Saxons* (New York: Collier, 1970), p. 28.

104 Roger M. Williams, *The Bonds: An American Family* (New York: Atheneum, 1971), p. 127. In 1972, when Professor Davis received an award from an educational organization that once excluded Negroes from membership, he was reported as citing "the racial bigotry in the big universities especially in the period when he came to the University of Chicago." See *Chicago Defender,* June 13, 1972.

105 F. L. Marcuse, "Some Attitudes Toward Employing Negroes as Teachers in a Northern University," *Journal of Negro Education,* 17 (winter 1948), p. 19. This survey was conducted under the auspices of the Cornell University Branch of the NAACP.

106 David M. Rafky, "Wit and Racial Conflict Among Colleagues," *Integrated Education,* 10 (January-February 1972), p. 39.

107 *Columbia University Affirmative Action Program, April 10, 1972.*

108 See "Affirmative Action in Higher Education: A Report by the Council Commission on Discrimination," *AAUP Bulletin,* 59 (June 1973), pp. 178–183.

109 Loren Miller, quoted in *Crisis* (August 1927), p. 187.

110 For New York University and Temple University, see *Crisis* (August 1928), p. 263; for Butler University, see *Crisis* (August 1930), p. 263.

111 Johnson, *Negro College Graduate,* p. 121.

112 For University of Cincinnati, see *Crisis* (January 1932), p. 466; for Northwestern University, see Johnson, *Negro College Graduate,* p. 326.

113 For Colgate-Rochester, see Elizabeth Yates, *Howard Thurman: Portrait of a Practical Dreamer* (New York: Day, 1964), p. 63; for Butler University, see Bigglestone, "Oberlin College and the Negro Student, 1865–1940," p. 215.

114 For Hamline, see Anna Arnold Hedgman, *The Trumpet Sounds: A Memoir of Negro Leadership* (New York: Holt, 1964), pp. 16–17; for University of Pennsylvania, see Leslie Pinckney Hill, "The State Teachers' College at Cheyney and Its Relation to Segregation in the North," *Journal of Negro Education,* 1 (October 1932), p. 413; for Oberlin, see Bigglestone, "Oberlin College and the Negro Student, 1865–1940," p. 217.

115 Brown and others, *National Survey of Higher Education of Negroes,* Vol. II, pp. 80, 84.

116 Berkowitz, *Inequality of Opportunity in Higher Education,* p. 89.

117 See Arthur G. Falls, "The Search for Negro Medical Students," *Integrated Education,* 1 (June 1963), pp. 15–19; "Prominent Black Medical Professor Rips Medical School Ban on Black Students," *Muhammad Speaks,* March 7, 1969, p. 5; and Melvin Cole, "Black Students and the Health Sciences," *Integrated Education,* 8 (January-February 1970), pp. 50–58.

118 Jim Hightower, *Hard Tomatoes, Hard Times: The Failure of the Land Grant College Complex* (Washington, D.C.: Agribusiness Accountability Project, 1972), p. 18.

119 Davis, "Negro Land-Grant College," p. 324. See also Wilson, "Developments in Negro Colleges During the Twenty-Year Period, 1914–15 to 1933–34," p. 355.

120 Hightower, *Hard Tomatoes, Hard Times*, p. 133.

121 Francis C. Sumner, "Environic Factors Which Prohibit Creative Scholarship Among Negroes," *School and Society*, 22 (September 5, 1925), p. 295.

122 Du Bois, "The Negro Scientist," p. 317; ftn. 1, p. 310.

123 Winston, "Through the Back Door," p. 678.

124 *Crisis* (February 1915), p. 168.

125 For Arkansas AM&N, see Lee, "Origin, Development, and Present Status of Arkansas' Program of Higher Education for Negroes," p. 132; for University of Missouri and Lincoln, see Robert M. Sawyer, "The Gaines Case: Its Background and Influence on the University of Missouri and Lincoln University 1936–1950" (doctoral dissertation, University of Missouri, 1966), p. 161.

126 Butler A. Jones, "Law and Social Change: A Study of the Impact of New Legal Requirements Affecting Equality of Educational Opportunities for Negroes Upon Certain Customary Official Behavior in the South, 1938–1953" (doctoral dissertation, New York University, 1955), pp. 108–109.

127 National Advisory Committee on Education, *Federal Relations to Education*, Part I, *Committee Findings and Recommendations* (Washington, D.C.: National Capitol Press, 1931), p. 113.

128 *University of Maryland* v. *Donald T. Murray*, 169 Md. 478 (1936).

129 Charles H. Houston, "Don't Shout Too Soon," *Crisis*, 43 (March 1936), p. 91.

130 *Gaines* v. *Canada et al.*, 305 U.S. 337 (1938).

131 Sawyer, "The Gaines Case," pp. 293–294.

132 Carey McWilliams, "Racial Dialectic: Missouri Style," *Nation*, 160 (Feburary 24, 1945), pp. 208–209.

133 For relevant court decisions during the *Gaines* era, see Jessie P. Guzman, *Twenty Years of Court Decisions Affecting Higher Education in the South, 1938–1958* (Tuskegee, Ala.: Tuskegee Institute, 1960); M. M. Chambers, *The Colleges and the Courts, 1941–45* (New York: Carnegie Foundation for the Advancement of Teaching, 1946); Chambers, *The Colleges and the Courts, 1946–50* (New York: Columbia University Press, 1952).

134 Jones, "Law and Social Change," pp. 290–318.

135 Houston, "A Challenge to Negro College Youth," p. 15.

136 *Pittsburgh Courier*, January 1, 1949; quoted in Wendell Jones, "The Negro Press and the Higher Education of Negroes, 1933–1952," (doctoral dissertation, University of Chicago, 1954), p. 58.

137 Jones, "Law and Social Change," p. 306.

138 Louis L. Redding, "Desegregation in Higher Education in Delaware," *Journal of Negro Education*, 27 (summer 1958), p. 256.

139 Jones, "Law and Social Change," p. 318.

140 Curry, "Changes in Segregation Practices in Collegiate Institutions in Kentucky," p. 21.

141 *Sweatt* v. *Painter*, 339 U.S. 629 (1950).

142 Bond, "Evolution and Present Status of Negro Higher and Professional Education in the United States," p. 231.

143 B. R. Brazeal, "Some Problems in the Desegregation of Higher Education in the 'Hard Core' States," *Journal of Negro Education*, 27 (summer 1958), p. 357.

144 James A. Hedrick, "The Negro in Southern Graduate Education" (doctoral dissertation, North Texas State College, 1954), p. 232.

145 Brown and others, *National Survey of Higher Education of Negroes*, Vol. II, pp. 88–89.

146 *Crisis* (August 1931), p. 262; *Crisis* (August 1930), p. 262; Herbert Crawford Jenkins, "The Negro Student at the University of Iowa: A Sociological Study" (master's thesis, State University of Iowa, 1933), pp. 18, 29. Information on Dickinson College relates to 1930; that on the State University of Iowa, to 1933.

147 *Crisis* (September 1918), pp. 240–241.

148 Rose Henderson, "Negro Education at Columbia," *Southern Workman*, 61 (July 1932), p. 306. See, however, Langston Hughes, *The Big Sea: An Autobiography* (New York: Knopf, 1940), pp. 81–82.

149 Benjamin E. Mays, *Born to Rebel: An Autobiography* (New York: Scribner, 1971), p. 65.

150 *State ex rel. Weaver v. Board of Trustees of Ohio State University*, 126 Ohio St. 290, 185 N.E. 196 (1933); quoted in Charles S. Mangum, Jr., *The Legal Status of the Negro* (Chapel Hill: University of North Carolina Press, 1940), pp. 113–114.

151 University of Michigan, see *Crisis* (November 1930), p. 383; *Crisis* (December 1931), pp. 427–428. For Oberlin, see Bigglestone, "Oberlin College and the Negro Student, 1965–1940," p. 211; for a generally critical statement by a black alumna about Oberlin at this time, see Terrell, *Colored Woman in a White World*, p. 45. For State University of Iowa, see Jenkins, "Negro Student at the University of Iowa," p. 18.

152 For World War I Harvard, see Painter, "Jim Crow at Harvard: 1923," p. 627. For Knox and Lowell, see *New York Age*, June 24, 1922.

153 For Bruce letter to Lowell, see Painter, "Jim Crow at Harvard: 1923," p. 628; for Lowell and Bruce responses, see *New York Age*, January 20, 1923; for Harvard University resolution, see Painter, "Jim Crow at Harvard: 1923," p. 634. A variant reading of the resolution is reproduced in *New York Age*, April 4, 1923.

154 Brown and others, *National Survey of Higher Education of Negroes*, Vol. II, pp. 88–89.

155 For Ohio State University, see *Crisis* (August 1930), p. 264. For University of Michigan, see Oakley Johnson, "Three Planks for President," *New Student*, 7 (March 21, 1928), p. 3.

156 James P. Comer, *Beyond Black and White* (New York: Quadrangle, 1972), p. 32. For Rutgers University, see Emily Alman, "Desegregation at Rutgers University," in Rhoda Goldstein (ed.), *Black Life and Culture in the United States* (New York: Crowell, 1971), p. 212. For University of Chicago, see August Meier and Elliott Rudwick, *CORE: A Study in the Civil Rights Movement 1942–1968* (New York: Oxford University Press, 1973), pp. 28, 185. For Northwestern University, see "Black and White at Northwestern University," *Integrated Education*, 6 (May-June 1968), p. 34. See also Oliver Wendell Markley, "Having a Negro Roommate as an Experience in Intercultural Education" (doctoral dissertation, Northwestern University, 1968), p. 15.

157 For University of Michigan, see William H. Boone, "Problems of Adjustment of Negro Students at a White School," *Journal of Negro Education*, 2 (1942), p. 478.

158 For State University of Iowa, see Jenkins, "Negro Student at the University of Iowa," pp. 14, 45.

159 Jerry Davis and Kingston Johns, Jr., "Changes in the Family Income Distribution of Freshmen," *Community and Junior College Journal*, 43 (December-January 1973), p. 27; Panel on Financing Low Income and Minority Students in Higher Education, *Toward Equal Opportunity for Higher Education* (New York: College Entrance Examination Board, 1973), p. 33.

160 Panel on Financing Low Income and Minority Students in Higher Education, *Toward Equal Opportunity for Higher Education*, p. 252.

161 Thomas Sowell, *Black Education: Myths and Tragedies* (New York: McKay, 1972), p. 43.

162 George Harris, quoted in *Financing Equal Opportunity in Higher Education* (New York: College Entrance Examination Board, 1970), p. 18.

163 Carl A. Fields, "Black Students in a White University," in *ibid.*, p. 35.

164 Murray Milner, Jr., *The Illusion of Equality* (San Francisco: Jossey-Bass, 1972), p. 67.

165 Ridgely Torrence, *The Story of John Hope* (New York: Macmillan, 1948), p. 98.

166 Cyrus Adler, *I Have Considered the Days* (Philadelphia: Jewish Publication Society of America, 1941), p. 30.

167 *Crisis* (January 1912), p. 99; *Crisis* (December 1913), p. 63; *Crisis* (January 1914), p. 117.

168 George Fishman, "Paul Robeson's Student Days and the Fight Against Racism at Rutgers," *Freedomways*, 9 (summer 1969), p. 228.

169 Jenkins, "Negro Student at the University of Iowa," p. 32.

170 One such exception was George Gregory, captain of the Columbia College basketball team, who stood six feet four inches tall; *Crisis* (May 1930), p. 166.

171 Frank Marshall Davis, "What a Negro Thinks About," *New Student*, 6 (March 16, 1927), p. 4.

172 Paul Rettig Mackey, "A Survey of Negro Participation in Intercollegiate Athletics in American Co-racial Colleges and Universities" (master's thesis, Ohio State University, 1940), pp. 41, 51, 55.

173 Jenkins, "Negro Student at the University of Iowa," p. 32.

174 For University of Kansas, see *Crisis* (August 1928), p. 187. For University of Cincinnati, see *Crisis* (August 1930), p. 263. For State University of Iowa, see Jenkins, "Negro Student at the University of Iowa," p. 30.

175 Beth Janet Shapiro, "The Black Athlete at Michigan State University" (master's thesis, Michigan State University, 1970), p. 11.

176 *Ibid.*, p. 39.

177 Robert L. Green, Joseph R. McMillan, and Thomas S. Gunnings, "Blacks in the Big Ten," *Integrated Education*, 10 (May-June 1972), p. 36.

178 Du Bois, "Negroes in College," p. 229.

179 *Crisis* (January 1927), p. 133. Emphasis in original. The correspondent of this information in the magazine commented: "Readers should bear in mind that Kent rests in the Klan belt."

180 Jenkins, "Negro Student at the University of Iowa," p. 29.

181 Brown and others, *National Survey of Higher Education of Negroes*, Vol. II, p. 88.

182 Mays, *Born to Rebel*, p. 99.

183 For University of Illinois, see G. James Fleming, "The Going Is Rough but They Make It," *Crisis*, 43 (August 1936), p. 232. For Northwestern University, see *Crisis* (February 1937), p. 43. For University of Kansas, see *Crisis* (August 1927), p. 187. For Oberlin, see Bigglestone, "Oberlin College and the Negro Student, 1865–1940," p. 216; Jenkins, "Negro Student at the University of Iowa," p. 30.

184 Langston Hughes, "Simple Discusses Colleges and Color," *Phylon* (December 1949), p. 400.

185 Comer, *Beyond Black and White*, pp. 33–34.

186 Will Braxton Scott, "Race Consciousness and the Negro Student at Indiana University" (doctoral dissertation, Indiana University, 1965), pp. 38, 50.

187 Don C. Bennett, "Segregation and Racial Interaction," *Annals of the Association of American Geographers*, 63 (March 1973), p. 57.

188 Aaron M. Bindman, "Participation of Negro Students in an Integrated University"

(doctoral dissertation, University of Illinois, 1965), p. 146; *Dallas Morning News*, October 11, 1968. See also issue of October 23, 1968.

189 U.S. Commission on Civil Rights, *Equal Protection of the Laws in Public Higher Education* (Washington, D.C.: GPO, 1960), p. 170.

190 Calvin Trillin, *An Education in Georgia: The Integration of Charlayne Hunter and Hamilton Holmes* (New York: Viking, 1964), p. 83.

191 Lee, "Origin, Development, and Present Status of Arkansas Program of Higher Education for Negroes," p. 150.

192 William Curtis Helton, "Characteristics, Performance, Problems and Successes of Negro Graduate Students Enrolled in Five Predominantly White State Colleges in Tennessee, 1963–1965" (doctoral dissertation, University of Tennessee, 1966), pp. 60, 62.

193 On student attitudes, see Nolen Eugene Bradley, Jr., "The Negro Undergraudate Student: Factors Relative to Performance in Predominantly White State Colleges and Universities in Tennessee" (doctoral dissertation, University of Tennessee, 1966), pp. 58–59.

194 For New York colleges, see Charles V. Willie and Arline Sakum McCord, *Black Students at White Colleges* (New York: Praeger, 1972). For Tennessee, see *Chattanooga Times*, May 23, 1972. The figures in Varner's comment relate to fall 1970 enrollment.

195 Allen B. Ballard, *The Education of Black Folk: The Afro-American Struggle for Knowledge in White America* (New York: Harper & Row, 1973), p. 4.

196 For Indiana University, see Comer, *Beyond Black and White*, p. 34. For Washington University, see Horace Mitchell, "The Black Experience in Higher Education," *Counseling Psychologist*, 2 (1970), p. 30.

197 For Harvard University, see Martin Kilson, "Blacks at Harvard: Crisis and Change," *Harvard Bulletin*, 75 (April-June 1973), p. 25 (emphasis in original), and Derrick Bell in *ibid.*, p. 45.

198 For Boston, see Ione Dugger Vargus, "Revival of Ideology: The Afro-American Society Movement" (doctoral dissertation, Brandeis University, 1971), p. 90. For New England, see William J. Wilson, "The Quest for Meaningful Black Experiences on White Campuses," *Massachusetts Review* (Autumn 1969) p. 739. For Columbia University, see Hilton Clark, "The Black Ivy League: Some Personal Observations on an Apathetic Negro," *Black Student*, 1 (spring 1966), p. 16. See also Kenneth B. Clark, "The Negro Student in Northern Interracial Colleges: An Overview," *ibid.*, p. 6.

199 For Texas, see Guzman, *Twenty Years of Court Decisions*, p. 22. For North Carolina, see *Frazier* v. *Tennessee Board of Higher Education*, 240 F. 2nd 689 (1957), *cert. denied*, 353 U.S. 965 (1957). See also Jack Greenberg, *Race Relations and American Law* (New York: Columbia University Press, 1959), pp. 260–267.

200 *Integrated Education* (September-October 1968), p. 11.

201 Leon E. Panetta and Peter Gall, *Bring Us Together: The Nixon Team and the Civil Rights Retreat* (Philadelphia: Lippincott, 1971), p. 130.

202 For Southern University, see Klein, *Survey of Negro Colleges and Universities*, p. 390. For New Orleans, see Sen. Frederick L. Eagan, *Louisiana Weekly*, January 27, 1968.

203 H. Rap Brown, *Die, Nigger, Die!* (New York: Dial, 1969), p. 39.

204 *New Orleans Times-Picayune*, April 18, April 21, May 15, 1969.

205 Panetta and Gall, *Bring Us Together*, pp. 330–331.

206 Tim Thomas, "The Student Movement at Southern University," *Freedomways*, 13 (1973), p. 22.

207 *Chicago Sun-Times*, July 11, 1973.

208 Student statement, *New Orleans Times-Picayune,* April 7, 1973; NAACP, "Louisiana Resolution Asks Merger of Colleges," *Crisis,* 80 (February 1973), p. 66.
209 *Los Angeles Times,* June 9, 1973.
210 Klein, *Survey of Negro Colleges and Universities,* p. 223. For University of Florida, see *Chicago Defender,* February 19, 1966; U.S. Department of Health, Education and Welfare, Office for Civil Rights, *Racial and Ethnic Enrollment Data from Institutions of Higher Education, Fall 1970* (Washington, D.C.: GPO, 1972), p. 193.
211 For statement by state board of regents, see *New York Times,* May 19, 1968. For FAMU president's comments, see *Miami Herald,* October 5, 1969.
212 *Miami Times,* April 16, 21, 1970. For college desegregation in Florida, see John Egerton, *Black Public Colleges: Integration and Distintegration* (Nashville, Tenn.: Race Relations Information Center, June 1971), pp. 15–26; *St. Petersburg Times,* November 12, 1972; *New York Times,* June 27, 1973.
213 *Arkansas Gazette,* August 9, 1969.
214 Panetta and Gall, *Bring Us Together,* p. 321.
215 *Arkansas Gazette,* January 21, 1972.
216 *Arkansas Gazette,* February 11, 1972.
217 *Arkansas Gazette,* February 3 and May 23, 1972.
218 *Philadelphia Bulletin,* February 26, 1969.
219 Charline F. H. Conyers, "A History of the Cheyney State Teachers College, 1837–1951" (doctoral dissertation, New York University, 1960), p. 254.
220 *Ibid.,* p. 269.
221 Bond, "A Century of Negro Higher Education," p. 192.
222 Pennsylvania Human Relations Commission, August 12, 1971, press release.
234 John P. Davis, "Unrest in the Negro Colleges," *New Student,* 8 (January 1929), p. 14.
235 For Tuskegee Institute, see Horace R. Cayton, *Long Old Road* (Seattle: University of Washington Press, 1964), p. 192. For Fisk, see W. E. B. Du Bois, "Fisk," *Crisis,* 28 (October 1924), p. 252.
236 See Herbert Aptheker, "The Negro College Student in the 1920's: Years of Preparation and Protest: An Introduction," *Science and Society,* 33 (spring 1969), p. 161.
237 Francis J. Grimke, "Lincoln University," *Crisis,* 23 (August 1926), pp. 196–197; Hughes, *The Big Sea,* pp. 307–308. See also Williams, *The Bonds: An American Family,* p. 159.
238 Langston Hughes, "Cowards from the College," *Crisis,* 41 (August 1934), pp. 226–228.
239 William Pickens, "Types of Southern Schools," *Crisis,* 44 (March 1937), p. 91.
240 Hylan Lewis discussed this point in a personal communication with the author.
241 Miles Wolff, *Lunch at the Five and Ten: The Greensboro Sit-Ins: A Contemporary History* (New York: Stein & Day, 1970), p. 59.
242 Joseph Fichter, *Graduates of Predominantly Negro Colleges* (Washington, D.C.: GPO, 1967), p. 211.
243 See Anthony M. Orum, "Negro College Students and the Civil RIghts Movements" (doctoral dissertation, University of Chicago, 1967), p. 122; Fichter, *Graduates of Predominantly Negro Colleges,* p. 5; Matthews and Prothro, "Negro Students and the Protest Movement," pp. 381, 401.
244 For North Carolina A&T, see Wolff, *Lunch at the Five and Ten,* pp. 67–69. For Tuskegee, see James Forman, *Sammy Younge, Jr.: The First Black College Student to Die in the Black Liberation Movement* (New York: Grove, 1968), p. 43; Kathleen Neal (Cleaver) quoted in *ibid.,* p. 45.

245 Lawrence B. de Graaf, "Howard: The Evolution of a Black Student Revolt," *in* Julian Foster and Durward Long (eds.), *Protest! Student Activism in America* (New York: Morrow, 1970), p. 322.

246 Wolff, *Lunch at the Five and Ten*, p. 119.

247 For South Carolina State College, see Jack Nelson and Jack Bass, *The Orangeburg Massacre* (New York: World, 1970), p. 98. See also Cleveland Sellers, *The River of No Return: The Autobiography of a Black Militant and the Life and Death of SNCC* (New York: Morrow, 1973), pp. 217–219. For Jackson State, see William Winn and Ed Williams, *Augusta, Georgia, and Jackson State University* (Atlanta: Southern Regional Council, June 1970), p. 48.

248 Forman, *Sammy Younge, Jr.*, p. 281. See also Julius Lester, "The Current State of Black America," *New Politics*, 10 (spring 1973), p. 11.

249 J. Saunders Redding, *On Being Negro in America* (Indianapolis: Bobbs-Merrill, 1951), p. 43.

250 Loren R. Miller, "College," *Crisis*, 33 (January 1927), p. 138.

251 See *Crisis* (May 1914), p. 9; (July 1920), p. 145; (April 1927), p. 130; and Jenkins, "Negro Student at the University of Iowa," pp. 5, 6.

252 Du Bois, "Negroes in College, p. 230; Jesse A. Reed, Jr., "Black Eye for Campus Liberalism," *Crisis*, 44 (August 1937), p. 237; and Seamans "Policies and Practices Regarding Minority Groups in Selected Colleges and Universities," p. 134.

253 Edyth Hargrave, "How I Feel as a Negro at a White College," *Journal of Negro Education*, 11 (1942), p. 486. See also William H. McClendon, "Which College: White or Negro?" *Crisis*, 41 (September 1934), pp. 264–265, and reply by H. C. Jenkins, *Crisis* (November 1934), p. 345.

254 E. Frederick Morrow, "Nordic Education for the Negro a Curse or a Boon?" *Opportunity*, (January 1931), p. 12.

255 *Crisis* (July 1922), p. 110.

256 Edmund W. Gordon, "Programs and Practices for Minority Group Youth in Higher Education," *in Barriers to Higher Education* (New York: College Entrance Examination Board, 1971), p. 111.

257 Ballard, *Education of Black Folk*, pp. 72–73.

258 W. E. B. Du Bois, *Chicago Defender*, September 13, 1947.

259 Lamar P. Miller, "An Analysis of Objectives of Institutes and Departments of Afro-American Affairs," *in* Edgar G. Epps (ed.), *Black Students in White Schools* (Worthington, Ohio: Jones, 1972), p. 90.

260 George Napper, *Blacker Than Thou: The Struggle for Campus Unity* (Grand Rapids: Erdmann, 1973), p. 80. See also Vargus, "Revival of Ideology," p. 171.

261 Kenneth B. Clark, "Higher Education for Negroes: Challenge and Prospects," *Journal of Negro Education* (summer 1967), p. 202; Clark, "A Charade of Power: Black Students at White Colleges," *Antioch Review*, 29 (summer 1969), p. 146.

262 John Egerton, "Inflated Body Count," *Change* (July-August 1970), p. 13; Robert H. Berls, "Higher Education Opportunity and Achievement in the United States," *in* U.S. Congress, 91st, 1st session, Joint Economic Committee, *The Economics and Financing of Higher Education in the United States: A Compendium of Papers* (Washington, D.C.: GPO, 1969), p. 181; and Panel on Financing Low Income and Minority Students in Higher Education, *Toward Equal Opportunity for Higher Education*, p. 23.

263 *Harvard Bulletin*, 75 (June 1973), p. 46, and Eddie Williams, Jr., in *ibid.*, p. 44.

264 *Washington Post*, May 19, 1973.

265 John Egerton, "High Risk," *Southern Education Report*, 3 (March 1968), pp. 5, 14.

266 Gene I. Maeroff, "A Kind of Higher Education," *New York Times Magazine*, May

27, 1973, p. 17; Leland L. Medsker and Dale Tillery, *Breaking the Access Barrier* (New York: McGraw-Hill, 1971), p. 19; and *Report on Higher Education* (The Newman Report) (Washington, D.C., GPO, 1971), p. 58.

267 Andrew L. Goodrich, Lawrence W. Lazotte, and James A. Welch, "Minorities in Two-Year Colleges: A Survey," *Community and Junior College Journal*, 43 (December 1972–January 1973), p. 29.

268 Dorothy M. Knoell, *People Who Need College: A Report on Students We Have Yet to Serve* (Washington, D.C.: American Association of Junior Colleges, 1970), p. 181.

269 William Trombley, "Colleges' Minority Aid Deficient, Study Says," *Los Angeles Times*, March 9, 1970. See also Harry Kitano and Dorothy Miller, *An Assessment of Educational Opportunity Programs in California Higher Education* (Sacramento: Joint Legislative Committee, Feburary 1971).

Chapter 8. Higher education for other minorities

1 For Dartmouth, see, "U.S. and Many Colleges Try to Recruit Students Among Indians," *New York Times*, May 11, 1973; Robert D. Kilmarx, *Bulletin*, Dartmouth College, 52 (June 30, 1972), p. 2. For Harvard, see Samuel Eliot Morison, *Harvard College in the Seventeenth Century*, Part I (Cambridge, Mass.: Harvard University Press, 1936), pp. 341, 354, and fn. 2, p. 357; Layman, "History of Indian Education in the United States," pp. 71, 359. Recent controversy has surrounded the contemporary application of the provisions and sections related to Indian students; see *Harvard Crimson*, March 11, 12, and 18, 1973.

2 Layman, "History of Indian Education in the United States," p. 52.

3 Ortiz, "American Indian Philosophy," p. 11.

4 Eastman, *From the Deep Woods to Civilization*, p. 65.

5 Berven, "History of Indian Education on the Flathead Reservation," pp. 64–65.

6 Howard, "Historical Survey of the Formation and Growth of Education on the Blackfeet Indian Reservation, 1872–1964," pp. 51–52.

7 Fuchs and Havighurst, *To Live on This Earth*, p. 260.

8 U.S. Department of Health, Education, and Welfare, Office for Civil Rights, *Racial and Ethnic Enrollment Data from Institutions of Higher Education, Fall 1970* (Washington, D.C.: GPO, 1972), *passim*.

9 Data in *ibid.*, pp. 6–12, and U.S. Department of Health, Education, and Welfare, *Education Directory 1968–1969*, Part 3, *Higher Education* (Washington, D.C.: GPO, 1968), pp. 22–55.

10 W. Roger Buffalohead, Ponca, *in Indian Voices*, p. 161.

11 See the differing viewpoints of Adolph Dial and David K. Elisades, "The Lumbee Indians of North Carolina and Pembroke State University," *Indian Historian*, 4 (winter 1971), p. 23, and Randall Ackley, "Pembroke State University," *Indian Historian*, 5 (summer 1972), p. 44.

12 Phil Kelly, quoted in U.S. Congress, 90th, 1st and 2nd sessions, Senate Committee on Labor and Public Welfare, Special Subcommittee on Indian Education, *Indian Education: Hearings*, Part 1 (Washington, D.C.: GPO, 1969), p. 483.

13 See Julie Smith, "A 'Vanishing American' Fights Back," *Navajo Times*, July 3, 1969; C. W. Charles, "A Tutoring-Counseling Program for Indian Students in College," *Journal of American Indian Education*, 1 (May 1962), pp. 10–12; Emmett Oliver, "Indians at College: 1971," *College of Education Record* (University of Washington), 37 (May 1971), pp. 81–82; Eddie F. Brown, "Guidance and Counseling of the American Indian College Student," *American Indian Culture Center Journal*, 3 (fall–winter 1971–72), pp. 28–29. See G. D. McGrath *et al.*, *Higher Education of Southwestern Indians with Reference to Success and Failure*

(Arizona State University, 1962), and Alphonse D. Selinger, *The American Indian Graduate: After High School What?* 1968, ERIC No. 026 165. For Black Hills State College, see Bud Mason, Arikara-Mandan, *in Indian Voices,* p. 170; and U.S. Department of Health, Education, and Welfare, *Racial and Ethnic Enrollment Data from Institutions of Higher Education, Fall 1970,* p. 96. For Indian studies, see Jack D. Forbes, "Native American Studies," *in* Robert A. Altman and Patricia O. Synder (eds.), *The Minority Student on the Campus: Expectations and Possibilities* (Boulder: Western Interstate Commission for Higher Education, November 1970), pp. 159–171; Brian Anderson, "Department of Indian Studies at 'U' Struggles Through Infancy," *Minneapolis Tribune,* January 24, 1971 (University of Minnesota); Ray Baldwin Louis, "Are Indian Studies and Programs Really Working?" *Navajo Times,* May 17, 1973; Buffalohead, *in Indian Voices,* p. 162.

14 Ruth Ann Douglas Fogartie, "Spanish-Name People in Texas with Special Emphasis on Those Who Are Students in Texas Colleges and Universities" (master's thesis, University of Texas, 1948), p. 62.

15 Manuel, *Education of Mexican and Spanish-Speaking Children in Texas,* p. 106.

16 Carey McWilliams, *North from Mexico: The Spanish-Speaking People of the United States* (Philadelphia: Lippincott, 1949), p. 286.

17 Data in Richard Roy Renner, "Some Characteristics of Spanish-Name Texans and Foreign Latin Americans in Texas Higher Education" (doctoral dissertation, University of Texas, 1957), pp. 78–79, 121, 123, 137, 176.

18 Herschel T. Manuel, *Spanish-Speaking Children of the Southwest: Their Education and the Public Welfare* (Austin: University of Texas Press, 1965), p. 59.

19 Richard I. Ferrin, Richard W. Jonsen, and Cesar M. Trimble, *Access to College for Mexican Americans in the Southwest* (New York: College Entrance Examination Board, July 1972), p. 19.

20 Zeleny, "Relations Between the Spanish-Americans and Anglo-Americans in New Mexico," pp. 298, 306; Nancie L. Gonzalez, *The Spanish-Americans of New Mexico: A Heritage of Pride,* rev. ed. (Albuquerque: University of New Mexico Press, 1969), p. 111.

21 United Mexican American Students at UCLA, "Retention of the Chicano Student as a Comprehensive Program Unit of the Mexican American Student Organization," *in* Manuel H. Guerra and others, *The Retention of Mexican American Students in Higher Education with Special Reference to Bicultural and Bilingual Problems,* May 1969, p. 5, ERIC No. ED 031 324. For San Fernando State College, see Rodolfo Acuña to present writer, May 17, 1973. For University of Texas, see *Integrated Education* (January-February 1968), p. 11.

22 Acuña letter.

23 Nick C. Vaca, "The Black Phase," *El Grito,* 2 (fall 1968), p. 47.

24 *Integrated Education* (November-December 1969), p. 58.

25 See Harry Kitano and Dorothy Miller, *An Assessment of Equal Opportunity Programs in California Higher Education* (San Francisco: Scientific Analysis Corporation, February 1970).

26 "Opening Academic Doors," *Agenda* (fall 1973), p. 8.

27 Manuel P. Servin, "The Post World War II Mexican American, 1925–1965: A Non-Achieving Minority," *in* Servin (ed.), *The Mexican-Americans: An Awakening Minority* (Beverly Hills, Cal.: Glencoe Press, 1970), pp. 156–157.

28 According to Dr. Alonzo Atencio, assistant dean of the medical school of the University of New Mexico; see *Albuquerque Journal,* May 5, 1973.

29 *New York Public Schools Staff Bulletin,* March 17, 1969.

30 David Rosen, "Open Admissions at the City University of New York: A Case Study," *in* Rosen, Seth Brunner, and Steve Fowler, *Open Admissions: The Prom-*

ise and the Lie of Open Access to American Higher Education (Lincoln: Nebraska Curriculum Development Center, University of Nebraska, 1973), p. 85.

31 Ballard, *Education of Black Folk*, ch. 7.

32 Gene I. Maeroff, "C.C.N.Y. at 125, Seeing Change in Student Body," *New York Times*, March 23, 1972.

33 Sussman, "Democratization and Class Segregation in Puerto Rican Schooling: The U.S. Model Transplanted," pp. 335, 341.

Chapter 9. To educate all the children of all the people

1 William W. Ellsworth, *Liberator*, September 27, 1834.

2 *Liberator*, November 30, 1849.

3 William J. Watkins, *Liberator*, August 19, 1853.

4 See W. E. B. Du Bois, "Fifty Years After," preface to *The Souls of Black Folk* (New York: Fawcett, 1961), p. xiv.

5 This paragraph is taken from M. Weinberg (ed.), *W. E. B. Du Bois: A Reader* (New York: Harper & Row, 1970), p. xvi.

6 R. R. Wright, Jr., quoted in *New York Age*, December 28, 1935.

7 Brimmer, "Economic Outlook and the Future of the Negro College," p. 549; Drake, "Black University in the American Social Order," p. 858.

8 Jack Elinson, Paul W. Haberman, and Cyrille Gell, *Ethnic and Educational Data on Adults in New York City, 1963–1964* (New York: School of Public Health and Administrative Medicine, Columbia University, 1967), p. iv.

9 Calvin Trillin, "U.S. Journal: Atlanta, Settlement," *New Yorker*, 49 (March 17, 1973), p. 105.

10 David L. Child to Effingham L. Capron, July 27, 1835; quoted in *Liberator*, August 15, 1835.

11 For offerings in courses in black life and history since 1921, see Nick Aaron Ford *Black Studies: Threat or Challenge?* (Port Washington, N.Y.: Kennikat Press, 1973), p. 52.

12 *Liberator*, August 22, 1856.

13 *Liberator*, August 21, 1857.

14 See Michael J. Schultz, "The Desegregation Effort of the National Education Association," *Integrated Education*, 8 (March-April 1970), pp. 37–44.

15 *Liberator*, August 21, 1846.

16 *Liberator*, August 2, 1844.

17 Arthur R. Jensen, "How Much Can We Boost I.Q. and Scholastic Achievement?" *Harvard Educational Review* (winter 1969). Cf. A. G. Davey, "Teachers, Race and Intelligence," *Race*, 15 (October 1973), pp. 195–211.

18 Sherwood L. Washburn, "The Study of Race," *in* Melvin M. Tumin (ed.), *Race and Intelligence* (New York: Anti-Defamation League of B'nai B'rith, 1963), pp. 54–55.

Bibliography

Bibliography

This bibliography consists of two parts: ten reference works that make up a general introduction to the literature of the subject of this book and a listing of references cited in this book. The latter are arranged under five headings: Afro-American Education, Mexican-American Education, Indian-American Education, Puerto Rican Education, and Black Higher Education.

General

American Indian Historical Society (comp.), *Index to Literature on the American Indian, 1970* (San Francisco: Indian Historian Press, 1971)

American Indian Historical Society (comp.), *Index to Literature on the American Indian, 1971* (San Francisco: Indian Historian Press, 1972)

Berry, Brewton (comp.), *The Education of American Indians: A Survey of the Literature* (Washington, D.C.: GPO, 1969). (U.S. Congress, 91st, 1st session, Senate Committee on Labor and Public Welfare, Special Subcommittee on Indian Education)

McPherson, James M., and others (comps.), *Blacks in America: Bibliographical Essays* (Garden City, N.Y.: Doubleday, 1971)

Miller, Elizabeth W., and Mary L. Fisher (comps.), *The Negro in America: A Bibliography*, 2nd ed. (Cambridge, Mass.: Harvard University Press, 1970)

Padilla, Ray, "Apuntes Para la Documentacion de la Cultura Chicana," *El Grito*, 5 (Winter 1971–1972), 3–46

Porter, Dorothy B. (comp.), *The Negro in the United States: A Selected Bibliography* (Washington, D.C.: GPO, 1970)

Schatz, Walter (ed.), *Directory of Afro-American Resources* (New York: Bowker, 1970)

Vivo, Paquita (comp.), *The Puerto Ricans: An Annotated Bibliography* (New York: Bowker, 1973)

Weinberg, Meyer (comp.), *The Education of the Minority Child: A Comprehensive Bibliography of 10,000 Selected Entries* (Chicago: Integrated Education Associates, 1970)

Afro-American education

Alabama Council on Human Relations and others, *It's Not Over in the South: School Desegregation in Forty-three Southern Cities Eighteen Years after Brown* (New York: NAACP Legal Defense Fund, May 1972)

"The Allen Report on New York City Schools," *Integrated Education*, 2 (August-September 1964)

American Friends Service Committee and others, *The Emergency School Assistance Program: An Evaluation* (Washington, D.C.: Washington Research Project, 1970)

419

Angelou, Maya, *I Know Why the Caged Bird Sings* (New York: Random House, 1969)

Aptheker, Herbert (ed.), *A Documentary History of the Negro People in the United States* (New York: Citadel, 1951)

Arkansas Advisory Committee to U.S. Commission on Civil Rights, *Public Education in Arkansas, 1963: Still Separate and Still Unequal* (Washington, D.C.: GPO, September 1963)

Armstrong, Charles F., "A Letter from Springfield," *Integrated Education*, 1 (April 1963)

Armstrong, Robert G., "A Reply to Herbert Wechsler's Holmes Lecture 'Toward Neutral Principles of Constitutional Law,'" *Phylon*, 21 (fall 1960)

Bagwell, William, *School Desegregation in the Carolinas* (Columbia: University of South Carolina Press, 1972)

Baron, Harold M., "History of Chicago School Segregation to 1953," *Integrated Education*, 1 (January 1963)

Bassett, John Spencer, *Slavery in the State of North Carolina* (Baltimore: Johns Hopkins Press, 1899)

Beer, Samuel H. and Richard E. Barringer (eds.), *The State and the Poor* (Cambridge; Winthrop, 1970)

Bell, Howard H., *A Survey of the Negro Convention Movement, 1830–1861* (New York: Arno Press, 1969, reprinted)

Bennett, Jr., Lerone, "Old Illusions and New Souths," *Ebony* (August 1971)

Berk, Richard A., and Alice Hartmann, "Race and School Funds in Chicago, 1971," *Integrated Education*, 10 (January-February 1972)

Berube, Maurice R., and Marilyn Gittell (eds.), *Confrontation at Ocean Hill–Brownsville* (New York: Praeger, 1969)

Bickel, Alexander M., "The Civil Rights Act of 1964," *Commentary* (August 1964)

Billington, Ray Allen (ed.), *A Free Negro in the Slave Era: The Journal of Charlotte L. Forten* (New York: Collier, 1961)

Blake, Jr., Elias, "The Track System in Washington, D.C." *Integrated Education*, 3 (April-May 1965)

Blascoer, Frances, *Colored School Children in New York* (New York: Public Education Association of the City of New York, 1915)

Blumenfeld, Ruth, "Children of Integration" (doctoral dissertation, University of Pennsylvania, 1965)

Bond, Horace Mann, "The Negro Common School in Oklahoma," *Crisis* (July 1928)

Bond, Horace Mann, "Self-Respect as a Factor in Racial Advancement," *Annals*, 140 (1928)

Bond, Horace Mann, *Social and Economic Influences on the Public Education of Negroes in Alabama, 1865–1930* (Washington, D.C.: Associated Publishers, 1939)

Bond, Horace Mann, "The Present Status of Racial Integration in the United States, with Especial Reference to Education," *Journal of Negro Education* (summer 1952)

Bond, Horace Mann, *The Education of the Negro in the American Social Order* (New York: Octagon, 1966, reprinted)

Bond, Horace Mann, *Black American Scholars: A Study of Their Beginnings* (Detroit: Balamp, 1972)

Bremner, Robert H., and others (eds.), *Children and Youth in America: A Documentary History*, Vol. I, *1600–1865* (Cambridge, Mass.: Harvard University Press, 1970)

Brown, Aaron, *Reflections on Seven Years of Experience on the New York City Board of Education* (New York: privately published, June 1, 1969)

Bullock, Henry Allen, *A History of Negro Education in the South: From 1619 to the Present* (Cambridge, Mass.: Harvard University Press, 1967)

Calhoun, Lillian S., "New York: Schools and Power – Whose?" *Integrated Education* (January-February 1969)

Carter, Barbara, *Pickets, Parents, and Power: The Story Behind the New York City Teachers'* *Strike* (New York: Citation, 1971)

Carter, Robert L., "The Warren Court and Desegregation," *Michigan Law Review*, 67 (1968–1969)

Catterall, Helen (ed.), *Judicial Cases Concerning American Slavery and the Negro*, I (Wash., D.C.: Carnegie Institution, 1936)

Cayton, Horace R., *Long Old Road* (Seattle: University of Washington Press, 1964)

Citizens Committee, Berkeley Unified School District, *De Facto Segregation in the Berkeley Public Schools* (fall 1963)

Clarana, José, "The Schooling of the Negro," *Crisis* (July 1913)

Clark, Septima Poinsetta, *Echo in My Soul* (New York: Dutton, 1962)

Cohen, David K., Walter J. McCann, Jerome T. Murphy, and Tyll R. Van Geel, *The Effects of Revenue Sharing and Block Grants on Education* (Cambridge, Mass.: Harvard Graduate School of Education, October 31, 1970)

Cohen, David K. and Tyll R. Van Geel, "Public Education," *in* Samuel H. Beer and Richard E. Barringer (eds.), *The State and the Poor* (Cambridge, Mass.: Winthrop, 1970)

Coleman, Jr., J. Winston, *Slavery Times in Kentucky* (Chapel Hill: University of North Carolina Press, 1940)

"Colored Teachers in Charleston Schools," *Crisis* (June 1921)

Commission on Professional Rights and Responsibilities, *Hyde County, North Carolina: School Boycott and the Roots of Conflict* (Washington, D.C.: National Education Association, September 1969)

Commission on Professional Rights and Responsibilities, *Beyond Desegregation: The Problem of Power* (Washington, D.C.: National Education Association, February 1970)

Committee on Race and Education, *Race and Equal Educational Opportunities in Portland's Public Schools* (Portland, Ore.: Board of Education, October 29, 1964)

Comptroller General of the United States, "Need to Improve Policies and Procedures for Approving Grants under the Emergency School Assistance Program," *in* U.S. Congress, 92nd, 1st session, House of Representatives Committee on Education and Labor, General Subcommittee on Education, *Emergency School Aid Act: Hearings* (Washington, D.C.: GPO, 1971)

Connery, Robert H. and Richard H. Leach, "Southern Metropolis: Challenge to Government," *Journal of Politics* (February 1964)

Coons, John E., "Report to the United States Office of Education on the Public Schools of Chicago," draft copy (Cambridge, Mass., June 20, 1965)

Bernice Cooper, "An Analysis of the Reading Achievement of White and Negro Pupils in Certain Public Schools of Georgia," *School Review* (winter 1964)

Coordinating Council of Community Organizations, *Handbook of Chicago School Segregation* (Chicago: CCC, 1963)

Coulter, E. Merton, *The South During Reconstruction, 1865–1877* (Baton Rouge: Louisiana State University Press, 1947)

Crummell, Alexander, *The Attitude of the American Mind Toward the Negro Intellect*. The American Negro Academy Occasional Papers, No. 3 (Washington, D.C.: The Academy, 1898)

Currivan, Gene, "Harlem Catholic Schools Cool to Transfers," *New York Times*, December 9, 1963

Dabney, Lillian G., *The History of Schools for Negroes in the District of Columbia, 1807–1947* (Washington, D.C.: Catholic University of America Press, 1949)

Dalfiume, Richard M., "The 'Forgotten Years' of the Negro Revolution," *Journal of American History*, 55 (June 1968)

Dancy, John C., *Sand Against the Wind: The Memoirs of John C. Dancy* (Detroit: Wayne State University Press, 1966)

Daniel, W. A., "Schools," *in* T. J. Woofter, Jr. (ed.), *Negro Problems in Cities* (Garden City, N.Y.: Doubleday, 1928)

Dann, Martin E. (ed.), *The Black Press, 1827–1890: The Quest for National Identity* (New York: Putnam, 1971)

Davidson, Basil, *The Growth of African Civilization: A History of West Africa, 1000–1800*, 2nd ed. (London: Longmans, 1967)

Davis, Arthur P., "I Go to Whittier School," *Phylon*, 21 (1960)

Davis, William R., *The Development and Present Status of Negro Education in East Texas* (New York: Teachers College Columbia University, 1934)

Day, Noel, "The Freedom Movement in Boston," *Integrated Education*, 2 (December 1964–January 1965)

Delany, Martin R., *The Condition, Elevation, Emigration, and Destiny of the Colored People of the United States Politically Considered* (Philadelphia: privately published, 1852)

Donnan, Elizabeth (ed.), *Documents Illustrative of the History of the Slave Trade to America*, Vol. II (New York: Octagon, 1969, reprinted)

Dorr, Robin, "Ordeal by Desegregation," *Integrated Education*, 10 (July-August 1972)

Drake, St. Clair and Horace R. Cayton, *Black Metropolis: A Study of Negro Life in a Northern City*, Vol. I (New York: Harper & Row, 1962)

Du Bois, W. E. B., "A Negro Schoolmaster in the New South," *Atlantic Monthly*, 83 (January 1899)

Du Bois, W. E. B. (ed.), *The Negro Common School* (Atlanta: Atlanta University Press, 1901)

Du Bois, W. E. B., "The Negro South and North," *Bibliotheca Sacra*, 62 (July 1905)

Du Bois, W. E. B., "Reconstruction and Its Benefits," *American Historical Review* (1909–1910)

Du Bois, W. E. B., "The Hosts of Black Labor," *Nation*, 116 (May 9, 1923)

Du Bois, W. E. B., "The Tragedy of 'Jim Crow,'" *Crisis* (August 1923)

Du Bois, W. E. B., "The Negro Common School in Georgia," *Crisis* (September 1926)

Du Bois, W. E. B., "The Negro Common School, Mississippi," *Crisis* (December 1926)

Du Bois, W. E. B., "A Negro Nation Within the Nation," *Current History*, 42 (June 1935)

Du Bois, W. E. B., "Does the Negro Need Separate Schools?" *Journal of Negro Education* (July 1935)

Du Bois, W. E. B., "Reconstruction, Seventy-Five Years After," *Phylon*, 4 (1943)

Du Bois, W. E. B., "Education," *Chicago Defender*, October 19, 1946

Du Bois, W. E. B., "The Negro Since 1900: A Progress Report," *New York Times Magazine*, November 21, 1948

Du Bois, W. E. B., "Race Relations in the United States, 1917–1947," *Phylon*, 9 (1948)

Du Bois, W. E. B., "We Rejoice and Tell the World. . . . But We Must Go Further," *National Guardian*, May 31, 1954

Du Bois, W. E. B., *Black Reconstruction in America* (New York: Russell & Russell, 1962, reprinted)

Du Bois, W. E. B., "Two Hundred Years of Segregated Schools," *Jewish Life Anthology, 1946–1956* (New York: Jewish Life, 1956). Reprinted *in* Phillip S. Foner (ed.), *W. E. B. Du Bois Speaking: Speeches and Addresses, 1920–1963* (New York: Pathfinder Press, 1970)

Du Bois, W. E. B., "The United States and the Negro," *Freedomways* (1971)

Dunbar, Leslie W., "Reflections on the Latest Reform of the South," *Phylon* (fall 1961)

Duster, Alfreda M. (ed.), *Crusade for Justice: The Autobiography of Ida B. Wells* (Chicago: University of Chicago Press, 1970)

Easton, H., *A Treatise on the Intellectual Character and Civil and Political Condition of the Colored People of the United States; and the Prejudice Exercised Towards Them. . . .* (Boston: Isaac Knapp, 1837)

Egerton, John, "Report Card on Southern School Desegregation," *Saturday Review*, April 1, 1972

Ehle, John, *The Free Men* (New York: Harper & Row, 1965)

Evers, Charles, *Evers.* (New York: World, 1971)

Evers, Mrs. Medgar, *For Us, the Living* (Garden City, N.Y.: Doubleday, 1967)

Fage, J. B., *A History of West Africa: An Introductory Survey*, 4th ed. (London: Cambridge University Press, 1969)

Fainstein, Susan, "The Movement for Community Control of Schools in New York City" (doctoral dissertation, Massachusetts Institute of Technology, 1971)

Fajana, Ade, "Educational Policy in Nigerian Traditional Society," *Phylon*, 33 (spring 1972)

Fancher, Betsy, *Voices from the South: Black Students Talk About Their Experiences in Desegregated Schools* (Atlanta: Southern Regional Council, August 1970)

Fancher, Betsy, "Students: Getting It Together: In Changing Schools Some Show How," *South Today*, 3 (July-August 1971)

Fiss, Owen M., "Racial Imbalance in the Public Schools: The Constitutional Concepts," *Harvard Law Review* (January 1965)

Flake, Tom, "Expenditures: Dollars on a Treadmill," *in* Patrick McCauley and Edward D. Ball (eds.), *Southern Schools: Progress and Problems* (Nashville, Tenn.: Southern Education Reporting Services, 1959)

Fleming, Walter L., *The Sequel of Appomattox* (New Haven: Yale University Press, 1920)

Fleming, Walter L. (ed.), *Documentary History of Reconstruction* (Gloucester, Mass.: Peter Smith, 1960, reprinted)

Foner, Eric, *Free Soil, Free Labor, Free Men: The Ideology of the Republican Party Before the Civil War* (New York: Oxford University Press, 1970)

Foner, Philip S. (ed.), *The Life and Writings of Frederick Douglass*, Vol. II, *Pre-Civil War Decade, 1850–1860* (New York: International, 1950)

Forman, James, *The Making of Black Revolutionaries: A Personal Account* (New York: Macmillan, 1972)

Foster, Marcus, *Making Schools Work* (Philadelphia: Westminster, 1971)

Fox, Stephen R., *The Guardian of Boston, William Monroe Trotter* (New York: Atheneum, 1970)

Franklin, John Hope, *From Slavery to Freedom*, 2nd ed. (New York: Knopf, 1956)

Franklin, John Hope, "Jim Crow Goes to School: The Genesis of Legal Separation in the South," *South Atlantic Quarterly*, 58 (spring 1959)

Franklin, John Hope, *Reconstruction: After the Civil War* (Chicago: University of Chicago Press, 1961)

Franklin, John Hope, *The Free Negro in North Carolina, 1790–1860* (New York: Russell & Russell, 1969, reprinted)

Frazier, E. Franklin, *The Negro in the United States* (New York: Macmillan, 1949)

Freehling, William W., "The Founding Fathers and Slavery," *American Historical Review*, 77 (February 1972)

Friedman, Leon (ed.), *Argument: The Oral Argument Before the Supreme Court in Brown v. Board of Education of Topeka, 1952–55* (New York: Chelsea House, 1969)

Fry, Charles L., *American Villages* (New York: Doran, 1926)

Fuchs, Estelle, *Pickets at the Gates* (New York: Free Press, 1966)

Fuller, Edmund, *Prudence Crandall: An Incident of Racism in Nineteenth-Century Connecticut* (Middletown, Conn.: Wesleyan University Press, 1971)

Gates, Paul W., *History of Public Land Law Development* (Washington, D.C.: GPO, November 1968)

Gates, Robbins L., *The Making of Massive Resistance: Virginia's Politics of Public School Desegregation, 1954–1956* (Chapel Hill: University of North Carolina Press, 1964)

Gottfried, Frances, "A Survey of Parental Views of the Ocean Hill-Brownsville Experiment," *Community Issues*, 2 (October 1970)

Granger, Lester B., "Race Relations and the School System: A Study of Negro High School

Attendance in New Jersey," *Opportunity* (November 1925)

Grant, William R., "Community Control vs. Integration: the Case of Detroit," *Public Interest* (summer 1971)

Green, Constance McL., *The Secret City: A History of Race Relations in the Nation's Capital* (Princeton: Princeton University Press, 1967)

Greenberg, Jack, *Race Relations and American Law* (New York: Columbia University Press, 1959)

Greene, Lorenzo J. *The Negro in Colonial New England, 1620–1776* (New York: Columbia University Press, 1942)

Haley, Fred T., "Tacoma Faces School Segregation," *Integrated Education*, 2 (April-May 1964)

Hansen, Carl F., "A Defense of the Track System," *Integrated Education*, 2 (June-July 1964)

Harding, Vincent, "Black Radicalism: The Road from Montgomery," *in* Alfred F. Young (ed.), *Dissent: Explorations in the History of American Radicalism* (DeKalb: Northern Illinois University Press, 1968)

Harlan, Louis R., *Separate and Unequal: Public School Campaigns and Racism in the Southern Seaboard States 1901–1915* (Chapel Hill: University of North Carolina Press, 1958)

Harlan, Louis R., "Desegregation in New Orleans Public Schools During Reconstruction," *American Historical Review* (April 1962)

Harris, N. Dwight, *The History of Negro Servitude in Illinois and of the Slavery Agitation in That State* (Chicago: McClurg, 1904)

Hawkins, Mason A., "*Colored High Schools*," *Crisis* (June 1911)

Hedgman, Anna Arnold, *The Trumpet Sounds: A Memoir of Negro Leadership* (New York: Holt, 1964)

Helper, Rose, "The Racial Practices of Real Estate Institutions in Selected Areas of Chicago" (doctoral dissertation, University of Chicago, 1958)

Herrick, Mary J., "Negro Employees of the Chicago Board of Education" (master's thesis, University of Chicago, 1931)

Herrick, Mary J., *The Chicago Schools: A Social and Political History* (Beverly Hills, Cal.: Sage, 1971)

Hersberg, Theodore, "Free Blacks in Antebellum Philadelphia: A Study of Ex-Slaves, Freeborn, and Socio-Economic Decline," *Journal of Social History*, 5 (Winter 1971–1972)

Hershaw, Lafayette M., *The Status of the Free Negro Prior to 1860*, Papers of the American Negro Academy (Washington, D.C.: The Academy, 1916)

Heyman, Ira Michael, *in* U.S. Commission on Civil Rights, *Civil Rights U.S.A. Public Schools: Cities in the North and West, 1963, Oakland.* (Washington, D.C.: GPO, 1964)

Hickock, Charles T., *The Negro in Ohio, 1802–1870* (Cleveland: Williams, 1896)

Holt, Rackham, *Mary McLeod Bethune: A Biography* (Garden City, N.Y.: Doubleday, 1964)

Holtzclaw, William H., *The Black Man's Burden* (New York: Neale, 1915)

Hope, John, "Negro Suffrage in the States Whose Constitutions Have Not Been Specifically Revised," *The Negro and the Elective Franchise*, American Negro Academy, Occasional Papers No. 11 (Washington, D.C.: The Academy, 1905)

Hoyt, Homer *The Structure and Growth of Residential Neighborhoods in American Cities* (Washington, D.C.: GPO, 1939)

Hunton, George K., *All of Which I Saw, Part of Which I Was: The Autobiography of George K. Hunton* (Garden City, N.Y.: Doubleday, 1967)

Iggers, Georg, *A Study of Some Tangible Inequalities in the New Orleans Public Schools*, 2nd ed. (New Orleans: Education Committee, New Orleans NAACP, 1963)

Integrated Education (1963–1973)

Interuniversity Social Research Committee, Chicago Metropolitan Area, *Militancy for and Against Civil Rights and Integration in Chicago: Summer 1967* (Chicago: Community and Family Center, University of Chicago, August 1, 1967)

Jackson, Luther Porter, *Free Negro Labor and Property Holding in Virginia, 1830–1860* (New York: Atheneum, 1969, reprinted)

James, Weldon, "Buildings and Equipment: Too Many Pupils, Too Few Dollars," *in* Patrick McCauley and Edward D. Ball, (eds.), *Southern Schools: Progress and Problems* (Nashville, Tenn.: Southern Education Reporting Services, 1959)

Johnson, Charles S., *The Negro in American Civilization* (New York: Holt, 1930)

Johnson, Charles S., *Negro Housing* (Washington, D.C.: President's Conference on Home Building and Home Ownership, 1932)

Johnston, James Hugo, *Race Relations in Virginia and Miscegenation in the South, 1776–1860* (Amherst: University of Massachusetts Press, 1970)

Jones, Butler A., "Law and Social Change: A Study of the Impact of New Legal Requirements Affecting Equality of Educational Opportunities for Negroes Upon Certain Customary Official Behavior in the South, 1938–1953" (doctoral dissertation, New York University, 1955)

Jones, Edgar L., "Transportation, From Bare Feet to White Bucks," *in* Patrick McCauley and Edward D. Ball (eds.), *Southern Schools: Progress and Problems* (Nashville, Tenn.: Southern Education Reporting Services, 1959)

Jones, Mack H., *Black School Board Members in the Deep South* (Atlanta: Southern Regional Council, April 1970)

Kaplan, John, "Segregation Litigation and the Schools, Part III, The Gary Litigation," *Northwestern University Law Review* (May-June 1964)

Kelly, Alfred H., "The School Desegregation Case," *in* John A. Garraty (ed.), *Quarrels That Have Shaped the Constitution* (New York: Harper & Row, 1964)

King, Ken, "Attitudes and School Decentralization: A Survey of Community Group Leaders in New York's Three Experimental Districts" (doctoral dissertation, Teachers College Columbia University, 1971)

King, Jr., Martin Luther, "'Let Justice Roll Down,'" *Nation*, March 15, 1965

Klingberg, Frank J., *The Appraisal of the Negro in Colonial South Carolina: A Study in Americanization* (Washington, D.C.: Associated Publishers, 1941)

Knowles, Lawrence W., "Kentucky," *in* U.S. Commission on Civil Rights, *Civil Rights U.S.A. Public Schools: Southern States, 1962.* (Washington, D.C.: GPO, 1962)

Landers, Jack, "Profiles of Inequality in New York City," *Integrated Education*, 11 (January-February 1973)

Landry, Lawrence, "The Chicago School Boycott," *New University Thought* (December 1962–January 1964)

Lefcourt, Robert (ed.), *Law Against the People: Essays to Demystify Law, Order, and the Courts* (N.Y.: Random House, 1971)

Lewis, Hylan, "Innovations and Trends in the Contemporary Southern Negro Community," *Journal of Social Issues*, 10 (1954)

The Liberator (1831–1865)

Logan, Rayford W., "Educational Segregation in the North," *Journal of Negro Education* (January 1933)

Logan, Rayford W., *The Negro in American Life and Thought: The Nadir, 1877–1903* (New York: Dial, 1954)

Lucas, Lawrence E., "Response to 'Harlem Catholic Schools Cool to Transfers,'" *Interracial Review* (March 1964)

Mabogunje, Akin L., "Urbanization and Change," *in* John N. Paden and Edward W. Soja (eds.), *The African Experience*, Vol. I, *Essays* (Evanston, Ill.: Northwestern University Press, 1970)

Mackler, Bernard, "Grouping in the Ghetto," *Education and Urban Society* (November 1969)

Mackler, Bernard, "Up from Poverty: The Price of 'Making It' in a Ghetto School," *in* A. Harry Passow (ed.), *Opening Opportunities for Disadvantaged Learners* (New York: Teachers College Press, 1972)

Mallery, David, *Negro Students in Independent Schools* (Boston: National Association of Independent Schools, 1964)

Mangum, Jr., Charles S., *The Legal Status of the Negro* (Chapel Hill: University of North Carolina Press, 1940)

Marshall, Thurgood, "An Evaluation of Recent Efforts to Achieve Racial Integration in Education through Resort to the Courts," *Journal of Negro Education* 21 (1952)

Martin, Ruby and Phyllis McClure, *Title I of ESEA: Is It Helping Poor Children?* (New York: NAACP Legal Defense Fund, 1969)

Massachusetts State Advisory Committee to United States Commission on Civil Rights, *Report on Racial Imbalance in the Boston Public Schools* (Washington, D.C.: GPO, January 1965)

Mayo, Marion Jacob, "The Mental Capacity of the American Negro," *Archives of Psychology*, 28 (November 1913)

Mayo, Selz C., "Social Change, Social Movements, and the Disappearing Sectional South," *Social Forces* (October 1964)

Mayo, Selz C. and C. Horace Hamilton, "The Rural Negro Population of the South in Transition," *Phylon* (summer 1963)

Mays, Benjamin E., *Born to Rebel: An Autobiography* (New York: Scribner, 1971)

McPherson, James M., *The Struggle for Equality: Abolitionists and the Negro in the Civil War and Reconstruction* (Princeton: Princeton University Press, 1964)

McPherson, James M. (ed.), *The Negro's Civil War: How American Negroes Felt and Acted During the War for the Union* (New York: Vintage, 1967)

Meier, August and Elliott Rudwick, "Negro Boycotts of Jim Crow Schools in the North, 1897–1925," *Integrated Education*, 5 (August-September 1967)

Meier, August and Elliott Rudwick, *From Plantation to Ghetto*, rev. ed. (New York: Hill & Wang, 1970)

Meredith, James, *Three Years in Mississippi* (Bloomington: University of Indiana Press, 1966)

Miller, Hunter (ed.), *Treaties and Other International Acts of the United States of America*, Vol. II (Washington, D.C.: GPO, 1931)

Miller, Kelly, *The Everlasting Stain* (Washington, D.C.: Associated Publishers, 1924)

Miller, Kelly, "Is the Color Line Crumbling?" *Opportunity* (September 1929)

Miller, Loren, *The Petitioners: The Story of the Supreme Court of the United States and the Negro* (New York: Pantheon, 1966)

Ming, William R., "The Elimination of Segregation in the Public Schools of the North and West," *Journal of Negro Education* (summer 1952)

Moody, Anne, *Coming of Age in Mississippi* (New York: Dial, 1968)

Moore, Jr., Howard, *Brown v. Board of Education:* The Court's Relationship to Black Liberation," in Robert Lefcourt (ed.), *Law Against the People: Essays to Demystify Law, Order, and the Courts* (New York: Random House, 1971)

Morehead, Richard M., "Special Services: Lunchrooms, Libraries and Learning," in Patrick McCauley and Edward D. Ball (eds.), *Southern Schools: Progress and Problems* (Nashville, Tenn.: Southern Education Reporting Services, 1959)

Morris, Willie, *Yazoo: Integration in a Deep-South Town* (New York: Harper & Row, 1971)

Moses, Robert, "Mississippi: 1961–1962," *Liberation*, 14 (January 1970)

Moton, Robert Russa, *Finding a Way Out: An Autobiography* (College Park, Md.: McGrath, 1969, reprinted)

Munford, Luther, "Black Gravity: Desegregation in 30 Mississippi School Districts" (senior thesis, Princeton University, April 16, 1971)

Murray, Pauli (ed.), *States' Law on Race and Color* (Women's Division of Christian Service, the Methodist Church, 1951)

Murray, Pauli, *Proud Shoes: The Story of an American Family* (New York: Harper & Row, 1956)

Muse, Benjamin, *Ten Years of Prelude: The Story of Integration Since the Supreme Court's 1954 Decision* (New York: Viking, 1964)

NAACP, *Brief for Appellant in Nos. 1, 2, and 4 and Respondents in No. 10 on Reargument, Supreme Court of the United States*, October term, 1953

Nabrit, Jr., James M., "An Appraisal of Court Action as a Means of Achieving Racial [Integration] in Education," *Journal of Negro Education*, 21 (1952)

National Advisory Council on the Education of Disadvantaged Children, *Title I: ESEA – The Weakest Link: The Children of the Poor* (Washington, D.C.: GPO, 1972)

NEA Task Force on School Desegregation in Louisiana (Washington, D.C.: National Education Association, February 15–22, 1970)

NEA Task Force III, *School Desegregation: Louisiana and Mississippi* (Washington, D.C.: National Education Association, November, 1970)

New Jersey Board of Education, *Annual Report . . . for the Year Ending June 30, 1920* (Trenton: State of New Jersey, 1921)

New Jersey State Temporary Commission on the Condition of the Urban Colored Population, *Report . . . to the Legislators of the State of New Jersey . . . 1939* (Trenton: The Legislature, 1939)

Oak, Eleanor O., "The Illegal Status of Separate Education in New Jersey," *School and Society* (May 21, 1938)

O'Connor, Ellen M. (ed.), *Myrtilla Miner: A Memoir* (Boston: Houghton Mifflin, 1885)

Orfield, Gary, *The Reconstruction of Southern Education: The Schools and the 1964 Civil Rights Act* (New York: Wiley, 1969)

Palmer, James M., *Mississippi School Districts: Factors in the Disestablishment of Dual Systems* (State College: Social Science Research Center, Mississippi State University, August 1971)

"Parents in the School: Community Control in Harlem," *This Magazine Is About Schools*, 4 (February 1970)

Parker, Majorie Holloman, "The Educational Activities of the Freedmen's Bureau" (doctoral dissertation, University of Chicago, 1951)

Peltason, Jack W., *Fifty-Eight Lonely Men: Southern Federal Judges and School Desegregation* (New York: Harcourt, 1961)

Philadelphia Urban League, *A Proposal for Integrating Philadelphia Public Schools* (Philadelphia: Philadelphia Urban League, August 1964)

Pickens, William, "Colored Student Discouraged in Mixed Schools," *New York Age*, February 18, 1922

Pierce, Truman M. and others, *White and Negro Schools in the South: An Analysis of Biracial Education* (Englewood Cliffs, N.J.: Prentice-Hall, 1955)

Pitman, Dorothy E., "Reactions to Desegregation: A Study of Negro Mothers" (doctoral dissertation, University of North Carolina, 1959)

Pratt, John H., "HEW Ordered to Defer Funds," *Integrated Education*, 11 (January-February 1973)

Prospectus, Student Woodlawn Area Project (SWAP) (Chicago: Ida Noyes Hall, University of Chicago, 1964)

Quarles, Benjamin, *The Negro in the Civil War* (Boston: Little, Brown, 1953)

Quarles, Benjamin, *Black Abolitionists* (New York: Oxford University Press, 1969)

Quillin, Frank U., *The Color Line in Ohio: A History of Race Prejudice in a Typical Northern State* (Ann Arbor, Mich.: Wahr, 1913)

Reddick, L. D., "The Education of Negroes in States Where Separate Schools Are Not Legal," *Journal of Negro Education* (summer 1947)

Reid, Whitelaw, *After the War: A Southern Tour, May 1, 1865, to May 1, 1866* (New York: Moore, 1866)

Report of the Special Committee on Nondiscrimination of the Board of Public Education of Philadelphia, Pennsylvania, July 23, 1964

Rice, Lawrence D., *The Negro in Texas, 1874–1900* (Baton Rouge: Louisiana State University Press, 1971)

Richards, Leonard L., *"Gentlemen of Property and Standing": Anti-Abolition Mobs in Jacksonian America* (New York: Oxford University Press, 1970)

Rivera, Ramon J., Gerald A. McWorter, and Ernest Lillienstein, "Freedom Day II in Chicago," *Integrated Education,* 2 (August-September 1964)

Robinson, Glen, "Man in No-Man's Land," *in* Don Shoemaker (ed.), *With All Deliberate Speed: Segregation-Desegregation in Southern Schools* (New York: Harper & Row, 1957)

Rogers, David, *110 Livingston Street: Political Democracy in the New York City Schools* (New York: Random House, 1968)

Rogers, Jeanne, "Nation's Showcase?" *in* Don Shoemaker (ed.), *With All Deliberate Speed: Segregation-Desegregation in Southern Schools* (New York: Harper & Row, 1957)

Rose, Willie Lee, "'Iconoclasm Has Had Its Day; Abolitionists and Freedom in South Carolina," *in* Martin Duberman (ed.), *The Antislavery Vanguard: New Essays on the Abolitionists* (Princeton; Princeton University Press, 1965)

Russell, John H., *The Free Negro in Virginia, 1619–1865* (Baltimore: Johns Hopkins Press, 1913)

Sarratt, Reed, *The Ordeal of Desegregation: The First Decade* (New York: Harper & Row, 1966)

School Finance Project, *Title I Comparability: A Preliminary Evaluation* (Washington, D.C.: Lawyers' Committee for Civil Rights Under Law, September 1972)

Schuyler, George S., *Black and Conservative: The Autobiography of George S. Schuyler* (New Rochelle, N.Y.: Arlington House, 1966)

Sellers, Barney, "Appendix Background Material," *in* A. Philip Randolph Institute, *The Reluctant Guardians: A Survey of the Enforcement of Federal Civil Rights Laws.* PB 192 346 (Springfield, Va.: Clearinghouse for Federal Scientific and Technical Information, December 1969)

Sellers, James Benson, *Slavery in Alabama* (University: University of Alabama Press, 1950)

Shapiro, Herbert, "Afro-American Responses to Race Violence During Reconstruction," *Science and Society,* 36 (summer 1972)

Sheldon, Eleanor B., James R. Hudson, and Raymond A. Glazier, *Administrative Implications of Integration Plans for Schools: Open Enrollment in New York City* (New York: Russell Sage Foundation, 1963)

Shuttlesworth, Fred L., "Birmingham Revisited," *Ebony* (August 1971)

Simms, Ruth P., "The Savannah Story: Education and Desegregation," *in* Raymond W. Mack (ed.), *Our Children's Burden: Studies of Desegregation in Nine American Communities* (New York: Random House, 1968)

Simpson, James, report to the Friends, *Liberator,* August 11, 1865

Southern School News (1954–1964)

Sowell, Thomas, *Black Education: Myths and Tragedies* (New York: McKay, 1972)

Spear, Allen H., *Black Chicago: The Making of a Negro Ghetto, 1890–1920* (Chicago: University of Chicago Press, 1907)

Stampp, Kenneth M., *The Era of Reconstruction, 1865–1877* (New York: Knopf, 1965)

Statement to the Bridgeport Board of Education on De Facto Segregated Public Elementary Schools (Bridgeport: Bridgeport-Stratford Branch, NAACP, July 1964)

Steel, Lewis M., "Nine Men in Black Who Think White," *New York Times Magazine,* October 13, 1968

Stein, Annie, "Containment and Control: A Look at the Record," *in* Annette T. Rubenstein (ed.), *Schools Against Children: The Case for Community Control* (New York: Monthly Review Press, 1970)

Stein, Annie, "Strategies for Failure," *Harvard Educational Review,* 71 (May 1971)

Stephenson, Gilbert T., *Race Distinctions in American Law* (New York: Appleton, 1910)

Stride, G. T. and Caroline Ifeka, *Peoples and Empires of West Africa: West Africa in History 1000–1800* (London: Nelson, 1971)

A Study of the Problems of Integration in New York City Public Schools since 1955 (New York: Urban League of Greater New York, September 1963)

Swanson, Bert E., *The Struggle for Equality: School Integration Controversy in New York City* (New York: Hobbs Dorman, 1966)

Swanson, Ernst W. and John A. Griffin (eds.), *Public Education in the South: Today and Tomorrow: A Statistical Survey* (Chapel Hill: University of North Carolina Press, 1955)

Swift, Fletcher Harper, *A History of Public Permanent Common-School Funds in the United States, 1795–1905* (New York: Holt, 1911)

Swift, Fletcher Harper, *Federal and State Policies in Public School Finance in the United States* (Boston: Ginn, 1931)

Sydnor, Charles S., *Slavery in Mississippi* (New York: Appleton, 1933)

Taeuber, Karl E. and Alma F. Taeuber, *Negroes in Cities* (Chicago: Aldine, 1965)

Tarry, Ellen, *The Third Door: The Autobiography of an American Woman* (New York: Guild Press, 1966)

Taylor, Alretheus Ambush, *The Negro in the Reconstruction of Virginia* (Washington, D.C.: Association for the Study of Negro Life and History, 1926)

Taylor, Susie King, *Reminiscences of My Life in Camp with the 33rd United States Colored Troops Late 1st S.C. Volunteers* (New York: Arno Press, 1968, reprinted)

Thomas, Jesse O., *My Story in Black and White: The Autobiography of Jesse O. Thomas* (New York: Exposition, 1967)

Tindall, George Brown, *South Carolina Negroes, 1877–1900* (Columbia: University of South Carolina Press, 1952)

Traxler, Harrison Anthony, *Slavery in Missouri, 1804–1865* (Baltimore: Johns Hopkins University, 1914)

Trelease, Allen W., *White Terror: The Ku Klux Klan Conspiracy and Southern Reconstruction* (New York: Harper & Row, 1971)

Trowbridge, J. T., *The South* (Hartford, Conn.: Stebbins, 1866)

Turner, Edward Raymond, *The Negro in Pennsylvania: Slavery, Servitude, Freedom, 1639–1861* (New York: Negro Universities Press, 1969, reprinted)

Urban League of Greater New York, "A Decade of New York Changes," *Integrated Education*, 2 (April-May 1964)

Urofsky, Melvin (ed.), *Why Teachers Strike: Teachers' Rights and Community Control* (Garden City, N.Y.: Doubleday, 1970)

U.S. Commission on Civil Rights, *Education 1961: Report* (Washington, D.C.: GPO, 1961)

U.S. Commission on Civil Rights, *Civil Rights U.S.A.: Public Schools, Cities in the North and West* (Washington, D.C.: GPO, 1962)

U.S. Commission on Civil Rights, *Civil Rights U.S.A.: Public Schools, Southern States 1962* (Washington, D.C.: GPO, 1962)

U.S. Commission on Civil Rights, *Hearings Held in Memphis, Tennessee, June 25–26, 1962* (Washington, D.C.: GPO, 1962)

U.S. Commission on Civil Rights, *Civil Rights '63* (Washington, D.C.: GPO, 1963)

U.S. Commission on Civil Rights, *1963 Staff Report, Public Education* (Washington, D.C.: GPO, 1964)

U.S. Commission on Civil Rights, *1964 Staff Report on Public Schools* (Washington, D.C.: GPO, 1964)

U.S. Commission on Civil Rights, *Report on Apprenticeship* (Washington, D.C.: GPO, 1964)

U.S. Commission on Civil Rights, *Racial Isolation in the Public Schools: Appendices* (Washington, D.C.: GPO, 1967)

U.S. Commission on Civil Rights, *HEW and Title VI* (Washington, D.C.: GPO, 1970)

U.S. Commission on Civil Rights, *Southern School Desegregation 1966–67* (Washington, D.C.: GPO, July 1971)

U.S. Commissioner of Education, *History of Schools for the Colored Population in the District of Columbia* (Washington, D.C.: GPO, 1871)

U.S. Commissioner of Education, *Special Report of the Commissioner of Education on the Improvement of Public Schools in the District of Columbia, 1871*, Part II, *Legal Status of the Colored Population in Respect to Schools and Education in the Different States* (Washington, D.C.: GPO, 1871)

U.S. Congress, Joint Select Committee to Inquire into the Conditions of Affairs in the Late Insurrectionary States, *Testimony* (13 vols.) (Washington, D.C.: GPO, 1872)

U.S. Congress, 88th, 1st session, House of Representatives Committee on the Judiciary, Report 914, Part 2, December 2, 1963, *Civil Rights Act of 1963* (Washington, D.C.: GPO, 1963)

U.S. Congress, 88th, 1st session, House of Representatives Committee on the Judiciary, Subcommittee No. 5, *Hearings . . . Civil Rights . . .* Parts 1-4, Serial No. 4 (Washington, D.C.: GPO Office, 1963–1964, II)

U.S. Congress, 88th, 1st session, Senate Committee on the Judiciary, *Civil Rights: The President's Program, 1963, Hearings . . . July 16–September 11, 1963* (Washington, D.C.: GPO, 1964)

U.S. Congress, 92nd, 1st session, Senate Committee on Labor and Public Welfare, Subcommittee on Education, *Emergency School Aid, 1971, Hearings* (Washington, D.C.: GPO, 1971)

U.S. Congress, 92nd, 1st session, Senate Select Committee on Equal Educational Opportunity, *Equal Educational Opportunity, 1971: Hearings*, Part 10, *Displacement and Present Status of Black School Principals in Desegregated School Districts* (Washington, D.C.: GPO, 1971)

U.S. Department of Health, Education, and Welfare, Office of Civil Rights, "Much Better Than They Expected," *Integrated Education*, 8 (January-February 1970)

U.S. Department of Transportation, *School Bus Task Force: Pupil Transportation Safety Program Plan* (Washington, D.C.: GPO, May, 1973)

U.S. Housing and Home Finance Agency, *Our Nonwhite Population and Its Housing: The Changes Between 1950 and 1960* (Washington, D.C.: GPO, July 1963)

U.S. Immigration Commission, *The Children of Immigrants in Schools*, Vol. 30 (Washington, D.C.: GPO, 1911)

van der Berghe, Pierre L., "Major Themes in Social Change," in John N. Paden and Edward W. Soja (eds.), *The African Experience*, Vol. I, *Essays* (Evanston, Ill.: Northwestern University Press, 1970)

Voegeli, Jacque, *Free but Not Equal: The Midwest and the Negro During the Civil War* (Chicago: University of Chicago Press, 1967)

Walker, Thomas Calhoun, *The Honey-Pod Tree: The Life Story of Thomas Calhoun Walker* (New York: Day, 1958)

Washington, Booker T. and W. E. B. Du Bois, *The Negro in the South* (Philadelphia: Jacobs, 1907)

Washington, Nathaniel Jason, *Historical Development of the Negro in Oklahoma* (Tulsa: Dexter, 1948)

Wasserman, Miriam, "The I.S. 201 Story: One Observer's Version," *Urban Review* (June 1969)

Watters, Pat and Reese Cleghorn, *Climbing Jacob's Ladder: The Arrival of Negroes in Southern Politics* (New York: Harcourt, 1967)

Weinberg, Meyer, "De Facto Segregation: Fact or Artifact?" *Integrated Education*, 1 (April 1963)

Weinberg, Meyer (ed.), *Integrated Education: A Reader* (Beverly Hills, Cal.: Glencoe Press, 1968)

Weinberg, Meyer, *Race and Place: A Legal History of the Neighborhood School* (Washington, D.C.: GPO, 1968)

Weinberg, Meyer, *Desegregation Research: An Appraisal*, 2nd ed. (Bloomington, Ind.: Phi Delta Kappa, 1970)

Weinberg, Meyer, "Schooling and the New Parenthood," *Journal of Negro Education*, 40 (summer 1971)

Wennerberg, C. A., *Desegregation of the Berkeley Public Schools: Its Feasibility and Implementation: Appendixes to the Report* (Berkeley: Berkeley Unified School District, May 1964)

Wharton, Vernon L., *The Negro in Mississippi, 1865–1890* (New York: Harper & Row, 1965, reprinted)

White, Arthur O., "Mid-Nineteenth Century Movement for Desegregated Schools in Six Northern Communities," *Integrated Education*, 10 (November-December 1972)

White, Walter, *A Man Called White: The Autobiography of Walter White* (New York: Viking, 1948)

Wiley, Bell Irvin, *Southern Negroes, 1861–1865*, 2nd ed. (New York: Rinehart, 1953)

Wilkerson, Doxey A., *Special Problems of Negro Education* (Washington, D.C.: GPO, 1939)

Williams, Robin M., Jr., and Margaret W. Ryan (eds.), *Schools in Transition: Community Experiences in Desegregation* (Chapel Hill: University of North Carolina Press, 1954)

Wilson, Charles H., Sr., *Education for Negroes in Mississippi Since 1910* (Boston: Meador, 1947)

Woodson, Carter G., *The Education of the Negro Prior to 1861*, 2nd ed. (Washington, D.C.: Associated Publishers, 1919)

Woodson, Carter G., *Early Negro Education in West Virginia* (Institute: West Virginia Collegiate Institute, 1921)

Woodson, Carter G. (ed.), *The Mind of the Negro as Reflected in Letters Written During the Crisis of 1800–1860* (Washington, D.C.: Association for the Study of Negro Life and History, 1926)

Woodson, Carter G., *The Rural Negro* (Washington, D.C.: Association for the Study of Negro Life and History, 1930)

Woodson, Carter G., *The African Background Outlined: Or Handbook for the Study of the Negro* (New York: Negro Universities Press, 1968, reprinted)

Woofter, Jr., Thomas Jackson, *Negro Migration* (New York: Gray, 1920)

Woofter, Jr., Thomas Jackson (ed.), *Negro Problems in Cities* (Garden City, N.Y.: Doubleday, 1928)

Workman, Jr., W. D., "The Deep South," in Don Shoemaker (ed.), *With All Deliberate Speed: Segregation-Desegregation in Southern Schools* (New York: Harper & Row, 1957)

Wright, Harry K., *Civil Rights U.S.A. Public Schools: Southern States 1963, Texas.* (Washington, D.C.: GPO, 1964)

Wright, Richard R., *A Brief Historical Sketch of Negro Education in Georgia* (Savannah: Robinson, 1894)

Wright, Richard, *Black Boy* (New York: Harper & Row, 1945)

Wynes, Charles E. (ed.), *The Negro in the South Since 1865* (University: University of Alabama Press, 1965)

Wynn, Neil A., "The Impact of the Second World War on the American Negro," *Journal of Contemporary History*, 6 (1971)

Youth in the Ghetto: A Study of the Consequences of Powerlessness and a Blueprint for Change (New York: Harlem Youth Opportunities Unlimited, 1964)

Zitron, Celia Lewis, *The New York City Teachers Union 1916–1964* (New York: Humanities Press, 1968)

Cases

Adams v. *Richardson,* 480 F. 2d 1159 (1973)

Alexander v. *Holmes County Board of Education,* 396 U.S. 19 (1969)

Bell v. *School City of Gary,* 213 F. Supp. 819 (1963)

Briggs v. *Elliott,* 132 F. Supp. 777 (1955)

Brown v. *Board of Education of Topeka,* 347 U.S. 483 (1954)

Brown v. *Board of Education of Topeka,* 349 U.S. 294 (1955)

Bryant et al., v. *Barnes, Tax Collector,* 106 So. 116 (1925)

Chandler v. *Ferris,* 1 Harrington 454 (1834)

Civil Rights Cases, 109 U.S. 3 (1883)

Clark v. *The Board of Directors,* 24 Iowa 272–273 (1868)

Claybrook v. *Owensboro,* 16 Fed. R. 302 (1883)

Cumming v. *County Board of Education,* 175 U.S. 545

Fisher v. *Hurst,* 333 U.S. 147

Gray v. *University of Tennessee,* 342 U.S. 517

Green v. *County School Board of New Kent County,* 391 U.S. 430 (1968)

Josiah Hughes v. *Samuel Jackson,* 12 Md. 450 (1858)

Jeffries v. *Ankeny et al.,* 11 Ohio 372 (1842)

Jumper v. *Lyles,* 77 Okla. 57 (1919)

Lewis v. *Henley et al.,* 2 Ind. 335 (1850)

McLaurin v. *Oklahoma State Regents,* 339 U.S. 637 (1950)

McNeese v. *Board of Education of Cahokia, Ill.,* 373 U.S. 668 (1963)

Missouri ex rel. Gaines v. *Canada,* 305 U.S. 337

Needles et al. v. *Martin,* 33 Md. 609 (1871)

People v. *McFall,* 26 Ill. App. 319 (1886)

People ex rel. Joseph Workman v. *Board of Education of Detroit,* 18 Mich. 419 (1869)

Pierce v. *Union District School Trustees,* 46 N.J. 26 (1884)

Puitt v. *Commissioners,* 94 N.C. 519 (1886)

Roberts v. *The City of Boston,* 5 Cushing 209 (1850)

Sipuel v. *University of Oklahoma,* 332 U.S. 631 (1948)

State v. *Albritton,* 98 Okla. 160 (1923)

Swann v. *Board of Education of Charlotte-Mecklenburg County,* U.S. (1971)

Sweatt v. *Painter,* 339 U.S. 637

Thacker v. *Hawk et al.,* 11 Ohio 38 (1842)

Turner v. *Keefe,* 50 F. Supp. 647 (1943)

U.S. v. *Jefferson County Board of Education,* 380 F. 2d 385 (1967)

Van Camp v. *Board of Education of Logan,* 9 Ohio St. 415 (1859)

Mexican-American education

Andersson, Theodore and Mildred Boyer, *Bilingual Schooling in the United States,* 2 vols. (Washington, D.C.: GPO, 1970)

Ashton, Price Richard, "The Fourteenth Amendment and the Education of Latin American Children in Texas" (master's thesis, University of Texas, 1949)

Bogardus, Emory S., *The Mexican in the United States* (Los Angeles: University of Southern California Press, 1934)

Broadbent, Elizabeth, "The Distribution of Mexican Population in the United States" (doctoral dissertation, University of Chicago, 1941)

Burma, John H., *Spanish-Speaking Groups in the United States* (Durham, N.C.: Duke , University Press, 1954)

Calderon, Carlos I., "The Education of Spanish-Speaking Children in Edcouch-Elsa, Texas" (master's thesis, University of Texas, 1950)

California State Advisory Committee to the U.S. Commission on Civil Rights, *Education and the Mexican American Community in Los Angeles County* (Washington, D.C.: U.S. Commission on Civil Rights, April 1968)

Carter, Thomas P., *Mexican-Americans in School: A History of Educational Neglect* (New York: College Entrance Examination Board, 1970)

Castaneda, Irene, "Chronicle of Crystal City," *El Grito*, 4 (winter 1971)

Chavez, Dennis, "The Good Neighbor Policy and the Present Administration," in Alonzo S. Perales, *Are We Good Neighbors?* (San Antonio, Tex.: Artes Grafica, 1948)

Childers, Laurence Murrell, "Education in California under Spain and Mexico and under American Rule to 1851" (master's thesis, University of California, Berkeley, 1930)

Clinchy, Jr., Everett Ross, Equality of Opportunity for Latin-Americans in Texas: A Study of the Economic, Social, and Educational Discrimination Against Latin-Americans in Texas, and the Efforts of the State Government on Their Behalf (doctoral dissertation, Columbia University, 1954, University Microfilm Order No. 8633)

Craig, Richard B., *The Bracero Program: Interest Groups and Foreign Policy* (Austin: University of Texas Press, 1971)

Cromack, Isabel Work, "Latin-Americans: A Minority Group in the Austin Public Schools" (master's thesis, University of Texas, 1949)

De Anda, Diane, "Chicanito in Checkmate," *Edcentric* (October-November 1971)

De Leon, Nephtale, *Chicanos: Our Background and Our Pride* (Lubbock, Tex.: Trucha Publications, 1972)

"Discrimination and Denial Due to National Origin," *Integrated Education*, 8 (July-August 1970)

Emerson, Ralph Waddell, "Education for the Mexican in Texas" (master's thesis, Southern Methodist University, 1929)

Galarza, Ernesto, *Spiders in the House and Workers in the Field* (Notre Dame, Ind.: University of Notre Dame Press, 1970)

Galarza, Ernesto, "The Mexican-American Migrant Worker: Culture and Powerlessness," *Integrated Education*, 9 (March-April 1971)

Galarza, Ernesto, *Barrio Boy* (New York: Ballantine, 1972)

Garrard, James Lathrop, "A Survey of the Education of the Indians of Mexico as a Factor in Their Incorporation into Modern Mexican Society" (doctoral dissertation, University of Washington, 1956)

Gerry, Martin H., *Cultural Freedom and the Rights of La Raza*, March 3, 1972

Gilbert, Emma Hall, "Some Legal Aspects of the Education of Spanish-Speaking Children in Texas" (master's thesis, University of Texas, 1947)

Gill, Clark C., *Education in a Changing Mexico* (Washington, D.C.: GPO, 1969)

Gonzalez, Nancie L., *The Spanish Americans of New Mexico: A Heritage of Pride*, rev. ed. (Albuquerque: University of New Mexico Press, 1969)

Goodman, Mary Ellen and others, "The Mexican American Population of Houston: A Survey in the Field, 1965–1970," *Rice University Studies*, 57 (summer 1971), ERIC Number ED 060 997

Grebler, Leo, Joan W. Moore, and Ralph C. Guzman, *The Mexican-American People: The Nation's Second Largest Minority* (New York: Free Press, 1970)

Griffith, Beatrice, *American Me* (Boston: Houghton Mifflin, 1948)

Harris, James Kilbourne, "A Sociological Study of a Mexican School in San Antonio, Texas" (master's thesis, University of Texas, 1927)

Hinsley, John C., *The Handbook of Texas School Law* (Austin, Tex.: Steck, 1938)

Holliday, Jay Newton, "A Study of Non-Attendance in Miguel Hidalgo School of Brawley, California" (master's thesis, University of Southern California, 1931)

Integrated Education (1971–1972)

Kaderli, Albert T., "The Educational Problem in the Americanization of the Spanish-Speaking Pupils of Sugar Land, Texas" (master's thesis, University of Texas, 1940)

Keen, Benjamin, *The Aztec Image in Western Thought* (New Brunswick, N.J.: Rutgers University Press, 1971)

Kibbe, Pauline R., *Latin Americans in Texas* (Albuquerque: University of New Mexico Press, 1946)

King, John Randle, "An Inquiry into the Status of Mexican Segregation in Metropolitan Bakersfield" (master's thesis, Claremont Colleges, 1946)

Lehman, Victor Boyd, "A Study of the Social Adjustment of the Mexican-American in Chino and a Proposed Program of Community Action under School Leadership" (master's thesis, Claremont Colleges, 1947)

Madsen, William, *Mexican Americans of South Texas* (New York: Holt, 1964)

Manuel, Herschel T., *The Education of Mexican and Spanish-Speaking Children in Texas* (Austin: Fund for Research in the Social Sciences, University of Texas, 1930)

Matthiessen, Peter, *Sal Si Puedes: Caesar Chavez and the New American Revolution* (New York: Dell, 1971)

Mayeske, George W., "Educational Achievement Among Mexican Americans," *Integrated Education*, 6 (January-February 1968)

McWilliams, Carey, *North from Mexico: The Spanish-speaking People of the United States* (Philadelphia: Lippincott, 1949)

Meier, Matt S. and Feliciano Rivera, *The Chicanos: A History of Mexican Americans* (New York: Hill & Wang, 1972)

Mexicans in California: Report of Governor C. C. Young's Mexican Fact-Finding Committee (San Francisco: California State Printing Office, October 1930)

Miller, Hunter (ed.), *Treaties and Other International Acts of the United States of America*, Vol. II (Washington, D.C.: GPO, 1931)

Miller, Thomas Lloyd, *The Public Lands of Texas, 1519–1970* (Norman: University of Oklahoma Press, 1972)

Oxnam, G. Bromley, *The Mexican in Los Angeles* (Los Angeles: Interchurch World Movement of North America, June 1920)

Paar, Eunice, "A Comparative Study of Mexican and American Children in the Schools of San Antonio, Texas" (doctoral dissertation, University of Chicago, 1926)

Parsons, Jr., Theodore W., "Ethnic Cleavage in a California School" (doctoral dissertation, Stanford University, 1965, University Microfilms Order No. 66-2602)

Paul, Rodman W., "The Spanish-Americans in the Southwest, 1848–1900," in John G. Clark (ed.), *The Frontier Challenge: Responses to the Trans-Mississippi West* (Lawrence: University Press of Kansas, 1971)

Payne, Joseph F., "Race, Reading, and Poverty in Los Angeles," *Integrated Education*, 9 (November-December 1971)

Penrod, Vesta, "Civil Rights Problems of Mexican-Americans in Southern California" (master's thesis, Claremont Graduate School, 1948)

Perales, Alonso S., *Are We Good Neighbors?* (San Antonio, Tex.: Artes Graficas, 1948)

Peters, Mary M., "The Segregation of Mexican American Children in the Elementary Schools of California: Its Legal and Administrative Aspects" (master's thesis, University of California, Los Angeles, 1948)

Pitt, Leonard, *The Decline of the Californios: A Social History of the Spanish-speaking Californians, 1846–1890* (Berkeley: University of California Press, 1966)

Pottinger, J. Stanley, "Equality for Spanish-Surnamed Students," *Integrated Education*, 10 (November-December 1972)

Ramires, Sara Leonil, "The Educational Status and Socioeconomic Backgrounds of Latin-American Children in Waco, Texas" (master's thesis, University of Texas, 1957)

Rangel, Jorge C. and Carlos M. Alcala, "De Jure Segregation of Chicanos in Texas Schools," *Harvard Civil Rights–Civil Liberties Law Review*, 7 (March 1972)

Rios, Francisco Ramando, "The Mexican in Fact, Fiction, and Folklore," *El Grito*, 2 (summer 1970)

Rodriguez, Armando, "Mexican American Education: Today," *Integrated Education*, 8 (September 1970)

Romano, Octavio Ignacio, "Goodbye Revolution, Hello Slum" *El Grito*, 1 (winter 1968)

Romano, Octavio Ignacio, "The Historical and Intellectual Presence of Mexican-Americans, *El Grito*, 2 (winter 1969)

Rubel, Arthur J., *Across the Tracks: Mexican Americans in a Texas City* (Austin: University of Texas Press, 1966)

Salinas, Guadalupe, "Mexican Americans and the Desegregation of Schools in the Southwest," *El Grito*, 4 (summer 1971). Reprinted from *Houston Law Review*, 8 (1971)

Salinas, Guadalupe, "Mexican-Americans and the Desegregation of Schools in the Southwest: A Supplement," *El Grito*, 4 (summer 1971)

Sanchez, George I., *Forgotten People: A Study of New Mexicans* (Albuquerque: University of New Mexico Press, 1940)

Sanchez, George I., "History, Culture, and Education," *in* Julian Samora (ed.), *La Raza: Forgotten Americans* (Notre Dame, Ind.: University of Notre Dame Press, 1966)

Scott, Robin F., "The Mexican-American in the Los Angeles Area, 1920–1950: From Acquiescence to Activity" (doctoral dissertation, University of Southern California, 1971, University Microfilms Order No. 71-27,955)

Soustelle, Jacques, *The Daily Life of the Aztecs on the Eve of the Spanish Conquest*, tr. Patrick O'Brian (London: Weidenfeld & Nicolson, 1961)

Stowell, Jay S., *The Near Side of the Mexican Question* (New York: Doran, 1921)

Taylor, Paul S., *Mexican Labor in the United States: Racial School Statistics, California 1927* (Berkeley: University of California Press, 1929)

Taylor, Paul S., *An American-Mexican Frontier: Nueces County, Texas* (Chapel Hill: University of North Carolina Press, 1934)

Treff, Simon Ludwig, "The Education of Mexican Children in Orange County" (master's thesis, University of Southern California, 1934)

Trillingham, C. C., "Status of 'Segregation' in School Districts Served by the Office of County Superintendent of Schools," *in* Vesta Penrod, "Civil Rights Problems of Mexican-Americans in Southern California" (master's thesis, Claremont Graduate School, 1948)

Tuck, Ruth D., *Not With the Fist: Mexican Americans in a Southwest City* (New York: Harcourt, 1946)

U.S. Bureau of the Census, *Selected Characteristics of Persons and Families of Mexican, Puerto Rican, and Other Spanish Origin: March, 1972* (Washington, D.C.: GPO, July 1972)

U.S. Commission on Civil Rights, *Hearing Held in San Antonio, December 9–14, 1968* (Washington, D.C.: GPO, 1969)

U.S. Commission on Civil Rights, *Mexican American Education Study*, 6 vols. (Washington, D.C.: GPO, 1971–1974)

U.S. Congress, 91st, 2nd session, Senate Select Committee on Equal Educational Opportunity, *Equal Educational Opportunity: Hearing Part 4, Mexican American Education* (Washington, D.C.: GPO, 1971)

U.S. Congress, 92nd, 2nd session, House of Representatives Committee on the Judiciary, Subcommittee No. 5, *School Busing: Hearings*, Part 3, Serial No. 32 (Washington, D.C.: GPO, 1972)

Vazquez de Knauth, Josefina, "Mexico: Education and National Integration," *in* Walter Laquer and George L. Mosse (eds.), *Education and Social Structure in the Twentieth Century* (New York: Harper & Row, 1967)

Womack, John, *Zapata and the Mexican Revolution* (New York: Vintage, 1968)

Womack, John, "The Chicanos," *New York Review of Books*, 19 (August 31, 1972)

Zeleny, Carolyn, "Relations Between the Spanish-Americans and Anglo-Americans in New Mexico: A Study of Conflict and Accommodation in a Dual-Ethnic Situation" (doctoral dissertation, Yale University, 1944, University Microfilms Order No. 66-7688)

Zeta Acosta, Oscar, "The East L.A. 13 vs. The L.A. Superior Court,"*El Grito*, 3(Winter, 1970)

Cases

California Attorney General Opinion 6735a, January 23, 1930, quoted in letter of Alfred E. Lentz, Legal Adviser, California Department of Public Instruction, to W. Henry Cooke, Claremont Graduate School, October 23, 1947, *in* Vesta Penrod, "Civil Rights Problems of Mexican-Americans in Southern California" (master's thesis, Claremont Graduate School, 1948)

Cisneros v. *Corpus Christi – Independent School District*, 324 F. Supp. 599 (1970)

Delgado v. *Bastrop County*, U.S. District Court, Western District of Texas (1948), unreported

Doss v. *Bernal*, Superior Court of Orange County, No. 41466

Gonzales v. *Sheely*, 96 F. Supp. 1004 (1951) *in* Price Richard Ashton, "The Fourteenth Amendment and the Education of Latin American Children in Texas" (master's thesis, University of Texas, 1949)

Hernandez v. *Texas*, 347 U.S. 475 (1954)

Independent School District v. *Salvatierra*, 33 S.W. 2nd 790 (1930) cert. den. 284 U.S. 580 (1931)

Lopez v. *Seccombe*, 71 F. Supp. 769 (1944)

Mendez v. *Westminister*, 64 F. Supp. 544 (1946) aff'd 161 F. 2nd 774 (1947)

Salazar v. *State*, 193 S.W. 2nd 212 (1946)

Sanchez v. *State*, 181 S.W. and 87 (1944)

Texas Attorney General, Opinion No. V-128, April 8, 1947, *in* Emma Hall Gilbert, "Some Legal Aspects of the Education of Spanish-speaking children in Texas" (master's thesis, University of Texas, 1947)

Indian-American Education

Aberle, David, "A Plan for Navajo Economic Development," *in* U.S. Congress, 91st, 2nd session, Joint Economic Committee, Subcommittee on Economy in Government, *Toward Economic Development for Native American Communities: A Compendium of Papers*, Vol. I (Washington, D.C.: GPO, 1969)

Allen, Arthur E., "The Education of the New England Indians during the Colonial Period" (master's thesis, Brown University, 1962)

Bennett, Kay, *Kaibah: Recollections of a Navajo Girlhood* (Los Angeles: Westernlore Press, 1964)

Bennett, Robert L., "Commentary on the Testimony before the Senate Subcommittee on Indian Education," May 21, 1969, *in* U.S. Congress, 91st, 1st session, Senate Committee on Labor and Public Welfare, Subcommittee on Indian Education, *Indian Education: 1969, Hearings,* Part 2, *Appendix* (Washington, D.C.: GPO, 1969)

Berkhofer, Jr., Robert F., "Protestant Missionaries to the American Indians, 1787 to 1862" (doctoral dissertation, Cornell University, 1960)

Berkhofer, Jr., Robert F., *Salvation and the Savage: An Analysis of Protestant Missions and American Indian Response, 1787–1862* (Lexington: University of Kentucky Press, 1965)

Berven, Irene M. Alvstad, "History of Indian Education on the Flathead Reservation" (master's thesis, Montana State University, 1959)

Blauch, Lloyd E., *Educational Service for Indians* (Washington, D.C.: GPO, 1939)

Burnett, Jr., Donald L., "An Historical Analysis of the 1968 Indian Civil Rights' Act," *Harvard Journal on Legislation,* 9 (May 1972)

Caspar, Margery G., "The Education of Menominee Youth in Wisconsin," *Integrated Education,* 11 (January-February 1973)

Cohens, Felix S., *Handbook of Federal Indian Law* (Albuquerque: University of New Mexico Press, 1971; originally published 1942)

Comptroller General of the United States, *Administration of Program for Aid to Public School Education of Indian Children Being Improved* (Washington, D.C.: GAO, May 26, 1970)

Comptroller General of the United States, *Opportunity to Improve Indian Education in Schools Operated by the Bureau of Indian Affairs* (Washington, D.C.: GAO, April 27, 1972)

Cook, John R., *The Border and the Buffalo: Untold Story of the Southwest Plains* (Chicago: Lakeside Press, 1938)

Cook, Sherburne F., *The Conflict between the California Indian and White Civilization*, Vol. III, *The American Invasion, 1848–1870* (Berkeley: University of California Press, 1943)

Costo, Rupert, "The American Indian Today," *Indian Historian*, 1 (winter 1968)

Cotterill, F. S., *The Southern Indians: The Story of the Civilized Tribes Before Removal* (Norman: University of Oklahoma Press, 1954)

Davis, Caroline Leola, "The History of the Schools and the Educational Development in the Chickasaw Nation" (master's thesis, University of Oklahoma, 1935)

Debo, Angie, *The Rise and Fall of the Choctaw Republic*, 2nd ed. (Norman: University of Oklahoma Press, 1961)

Drain, Maud, "The History of the Education of the Creek Indians" (master's thesis, University of Oklahoma, 1928)

Early, Kenzie to Louis R. Bruce, January 1971: reprinted in *Americans Before Columbus* (January–July 1971)

Eastman, Charles A., *Indian Boyhood* (Garden City, N.Y.: Doubleday, 1911; originally published 1902)

Eastman, Charles A., *From the Deep Woods to Civilization: Chapters in the Autobiography of an Indian* (Boston: Little, Brown, 1917)

Erickson, Donald A. and Henrietta Schwartz, "What Rough Rock Demonstrates," *Integrated Education*, 8 (March–April 1970)

Ewers, John C., *The Blackfeet: Raiders on the Northwestern Plains* (Norman: University of Oklahoma Press, 1958)

Fletcher, Alice C., *Indian Education and Civilization* (Washington, D.C.: GPO, 1888) (U.S. Congress, 48th, 2nd session, Senate, Executive Document No. 95, serial set No. 2264)

Forbes, Jack D., *Native Americans of California and Nevada* (Berkeley; Far West Laboratory for Educational Research and Development, 1969)

Forbes, Jack D., "The Native American Experience in California History," *California Historical Quarterly*, 50 (September 1971)

Frederick, Jack and Anna Gritts Kilpatrick (eds.), *The Shadow of Sequoyah: Social Documents of the Cherokees, 1862–1964* (Norman: University of Oklahoma Press, 1965)

Fuchs, Estelle and Robert J. Havighurst, *To Live on This Earth: American Indian Education* (Garden City, N.Y.: Doubleday, 1972)

Galvan, P. Michael, "The Ohlone Story," *Indian Historian*, 1 (spring 1968)

Golden, Gertrude, *Red Moon Called Me: Memoirs of a Schoolteacher in the Government Indian Service* (San Antonio, Tex.: Taylor, 1954)

Hagan, Maxine Wakefield, "An Educational History of the Pima and Papago from the Mid-Seventeenth Century to the Mid-Twentieth Century" (doctoral dissertation, University of Arizona, 1959)

Hagan, William T., *The Sac and Fox Indians* (Norman: University of Oklahoma Press, 1958)

Heizer, Robert F. and Alan F. Almquist, *The Other Californians: Prejudice and Discrimination under Spain, Mexico, and the United States to 1920* (Berkeley: University of California Press, 1971)

Henry, Jeannette, "The American Indian in American History," *in Indian Voices: The First Convocation of American Indian Scholars* (San Francisco: Indian Historian Press, 1970)

Henshaw, Lillie Duvall, "A History of the Cherokee Tribal Schools Since the Civil War" (master's thesis, University of Oklahoma, 1935)

Hinckley, Ted C., "The Presbyterian Leadership in Pioneer Alaska," *Journal of American History* (March 1966)

Holland, Cullen Joe, "The Cherokee Indian Newspapers, 1826–1906: The Tribal Voice of a People in Transition" (doctoral dissertation, University of Minnesota, 1956, University Microfilms Order No. 22, 491)

Howard, Robert E., "A Historical Survey of the Formation and Growth of Education on the Blackfeet Indian Reservation, 1872–1964" (master's thesis, Western Montana College of Education, 1965)

Hulley, Clarence, *Alaska, 1841–1953* (Portland, Ore.: Binford & Mort, 1953)

Hulsizer, Allan, *Region and Culture in the Curriculum of the Navaho and the Dakota* (Federalsburg, Md.: Stowell, 1940)

Humphrey, Theodore R., *Browning, Montana: Blackfeet Indian Reservation, Montana* (Chicago: National Study of American Indian Education, n.d.)

"Indian Education," *Inequality in Education*, No. 7 (1971), entire issue

Johnson, Milo C., "The History of Education on the Fort Peck Reservation from 1885 to 1935" (master's thesis, University of Minnesota, 1937)

Kersey, Jr., Harry A., "Educating the Seminole Indians of Florida, 1879–1969," *Florida Historical Quarterly*, 49 (July 1970)

Kizer, William M. "History of the Flandreau Indian School, Flandreau, South Dakota" (master's thesis, University of South Dakota, 1940)

Knepler, Abraham E., "Eighteenth Century Cherokee Educational Efforts," *Chronicles of Oklahoma*, 20 (1942)

Lamar, Howard R., *Dakota Territory, 1861–1889: A Study of Frontier Politics* (New Haven: Yale University Press, 1956)

Layman, Martha E.," A History of Indian Education in the United States" (doctoral dissertation, University of Minnesota, 1942)

McKenzie, Taylor, "What the Navajo Needs," *Integrated Education*, 8 (July-August 1970) (Reprinted from *Navajo Times*, April 23, 1970)

Me and Mine: The Life Story of Helen Sekaquaptewa (Tucson: University of Arizona Press, 1969)

Milling, Chapman J., *Red Carolinians*, 2nd ed. (Columbia: University of South Carolina Press, 1969)

Mittelholtz, Erwin F., "A Historical Review of the Grand Portage Indian Reservation with Special Emphasis on Indian Education" (master's thesis, University of South Dakota, 1953)

Moore, Cleo, "Schools and Education among the Iowa and Comanche Indians, 1870–1940" (master's thesis, University of Oklahoma, 1940)

Morison, Samuel Eliot, *Harvard College in the Seventeenth Century*, Part I (Cambridge, Mass.: Harvard University Press, 1936)

Mueller, Wolfgang, "The Cheyenne River Sioux Reservation, South Dakota" (Chicago: National Study of American Indian Education, December 1969)

Murray, Robert J., "History of Education in the Turtle Mountain Indian Reservation of North Dakota" (master's thesis, University of North Dakota, 1953)

NAACP Legal Defense and Educational Fund with the cooperation of the Center for Law and Education, Harvard University, *An Even Chance* (New York: NAACP Legal Defense and Educational Fund, 1971)

National Congress of American Indians, "Economic Development of the American Indian and His Lands," *in* U.S. Congress, 91st, 2nd session, Joint Economic Committee, Subcommittee on Economy in Government, *Toward Economic Development for Native American Communities: A Compendium of Papers*, Vol. II (Washington, D.C.: GPO, 1969)

"Navajo–U.S. Treaty of June 1, 1868: The Complete Text," *Indian Historian*, 1 (spring 1968)

Nichols, Jeannette P., *Alaska* (New York: Russell & Russell, 1963, reprinted)

Officer, James E., *Indians in School: A Study of the Development of Educational Facilities for*

Arizona Indians (Tucson: Bureau of Ethnic Research, University of Arizona, 1956)

Oglala Sioux Tribe, "An Appraisal of the Pine Ridge Education Program, Pine Ridge, S. Dakota," *in* U.S. Congress, 90th, 1st and 2nd sessions, Senate Committee on Labor and Public Welfare, Special Subcommittee on Indian Education, *Indian Education: Hearings*, Part 4 (Washington, D.C.: GPO, 1969)

Ortiz, Alfonso, "American Indian Philosophy: Its Relation to the Modern World," *in Indian Voices : The First Convocation of American Indian Scholars* (San Francisco: Indian Historian Press, 1970)

Painter, C. C., *Extravagance, Waste and Failure of Indian Education* (Philadelphia: Indian Rights Association, March 1, 1892)

Perkins, Larry M., "Pawnee, Oklahoma" (Chicago: National Study of American Indian Education, January 1970)

Person, Earl Old, "Indians as Human Beings," *Integrated Education*, 5 (April-May 1967)

Pester, James Lynn, "The History of Indian Education in the State of Washington" (master's thesis, University of Washington, 1951)

Pettitt, George A., *Primitive Education in North America* (Berkeley: University of California Press, 1946)

Porter, Kenneth Wiggins, *The Negro on the American Frontier* (New York: Arno Press, 1971)

Pratt, Richard Henry, *Battlefield and Classroom: Four Decades with the American Indian, 1867–1904* (New Haven: Yale University Press, 1964)

Qoyawayma, Polingaysi (Elizabeth L. White), *No Turning Back: A True Account of a Hopi Indian Girl's Struggle to Bridge the Gap between the World of Her People and the World of the White Man* (Albuquerque: University of New Mexico Press, 1964)

Riggs, Stephen R., *Mary and I: Forty Years with the Sioux* (Chicago: Holmes, 1880)

Sanchez, George I., "The People": *A Study of the Navajos* (Lawrence, Kan.: United States Indian Service, 1948)

Senungetuk, Joseph Engasongwok, *Give or Take a Century: An Eskimo Chronicle* (San Francisco: Indian Historian Press, 1971)

Shames, Deborah (ed.), *Freedom with Reservation: The Menominee Struggle To Save Their Land and People* (Madison, Wis.: National Committee to Save the Menominee People and Forests, 1972)

"Sioux Treaty of 1868," *Indian Historian*, 3 (winter 1970)

Smith, Anne M., *Indian Education in New Mexico* (Albuquerque: Institute for Social Research, University of New Mexico, 1968)

"Statement of Navajo Education Division," *in* U.S. Congress, 92nd, 2nd session, Senate, Committee on Interior and Insular Affairs, *Comprehensive Indian Education Act, Hearings* (Washington, D.C.: GPO, 1972)

Steiner, San, *The New Indians* (New York: Dell, 1968)

Sun Chief: The Autobiography of a Hopi Indian (New Haven: Yale University Press, 1942)

Tax, Sol and Sam Stanley, "Indian Identity and Economic Development," *in* U.S. Congress, 91st, 2nd session, Joint Economic Committee, Subcommittee on Economy in Government, *Toward Economic Development for Native American Communities: A Compendium of Papers*, Vol. I (Washington, D.C.: GPO, 1969)

Thomas, Robert K., "Colonialism: Classic and Internal" and "Powerless Politics," *New University Thought*, 4 (winter 1966–1967)

Underhill, Ruth, *The Navajos*, rev. ed. (Norman: University of Oklahoma Press, 1967)

U.S. Congress, 33rd, 1st session, House of Representatives Committee on Indian Affairs, Report No. 267, 1854 (serial set No. 744)

U.S. Congress, 90th, 1st and 2nd sessions, Senate Committee on Labor and Public Welfare, Special Subcommittee on Indian Education, *Indian Education: Hearings*, Part 1 (Washington, D.C.: GPO, 1969)

U.S. Congress, 91st, 1st session, Senate Committee on Labor and Public Welfare, Special

Subcommittee on Indian Education, *Indian Education: A National Tragedy – A National Challenge*, Report No. 91-501 (Washington, D.C.: GPO, 1969)

U.S. Office of Indian Affairs, "A Brief Statement on the Background of Present-Day Indian Policy," 1938, *in* Felix S. Cohen, *Handbook of Indian Law* (Albuquerque: University of New Mexico Press, 1971)

Veeder, William H., "Federal Encroachment on Indian Water Rights and the Impairment of Reservation Development," *in* U.S. Congress, 91st, 2nd session, Joint Economic Committee, Subcommittee on Economy in Government, *Toward Economic Development for Native American Communities: A Compendium of Papers*, Vol. II (Washington, D.C.: GPO, 1969)

Vogel, Virgil J., *American Indian Medicine* (Norman: University of Oklahoma Press, 1970)

Vogel, Virgil J. (ed.), *This Country Was Ours: A Documentary History of the American Indian* (New York: Harper & Row, 1972)

Wahrhaftig, Albert L., *The Cherokee People Today*, tr. Calvin Nackedhead (Tahlequah, Okla. Carnegie Corporation Cross-Cultural Education Project at the University of Chicago, 1966). Reprinted in U.S. Congress, 90th, 1st and 2nd sessions, Senate Committee on Labor and Public Welfare, Special Subcommittee on Indian Education, *Indian Education: Hearings*, Part 2 (Washington, D.C.: GPO, 1969)

Wax, Murray L., *Indian Americans: Unity and Diversity* (Englewood Cliffs, N.J.: Prentice-Hall, 1971)

Wax, Murray L., Rosalie H. Wax, and Robert V. Dumont, Jr., "Formal Education in an American Indian Community," *Social Problems*, 11 (spring 1964). Reprinted in U.S. Congress, 90th, 1st and 2nd sessions, Senate Committee on Labor and Public Welfare, Special Subcommittee on Indian Education, *Indian Education: Hearings*, Part 4 (Washington, D.C.: GPO, 1969)

Weinman, Janice Jennie, "Local Control Over the Schools in Two American Indian Communities: A Preliminary Examination of Structural Constraints and 'Internal Control' Attitudes," 2 vols. (doctoral dissertation, Harvard University, 1970), ERIC No. ED 060 988)

Woerner, Davida, "Education Among the Navajo: An Historical Study" (doctoral dissertation, Columbia University, 1941)

Zah, Peterson, "Indian Education in Public Schools: An Indian's View," *in* U.S. Congress, 91st, 2nd session, Senate Select Committee on Equal Educational Opportunity, *Equal Educational Opportunity. Hearings*, Part 2, *Equality of Educational Opportunity: An Introduction* (Washington, D.C.: GPO, 1970)

Cases

Anderson v. *Mathews*, 174 Cal. 537 (1917)

Crawford v. *District School Board for School District No. 7*, 137 Pac. 218 (1913)

Duwamish et al. Indians v. *United States*, 79 C. Cls. 530 (1934)

In re Lelab-Puo-Ka Chee, 98 Fed. 433 (1899)

In re Petition of Can-ah-couqua for Habeas Corpus, 29 Fed. 689-690 (1887)

Jones v. *Ellis, School Board* [of Ketchikan], 8 Alaska 147 (1929)

Peters v. *Malin*, 111 Fed. 244 (1901)

Piper v. *Big Pine School District*, 193 Cal. 667 (1924)

Quick Bear v. *Leupp*, 210 U.S. 50 (1908)

Sing v. *Sitka School Board*, 7 Alaska 616 (1927)

Sioux Tribe of Indians v. *United States*, 84 C. Cls. 28 (1936)

State v. *Wolf*, 145 N.C. 449 (1907)

Puerto Rican education

Alegria, Richardo E., "Cacicazgo Among the Aborigines of the West Indies" (master's thesis, University of Chicago, 1947)

Babin, Maria Teresa, *The Puerto Ricans' Spirit: Their History, Life, and Culture,* tr. by Barry Luby (New York: Collier, 1971)

Badillo, Herman, "The United States and Puerto Rico," *Congressional Record,* May 4, 1971. Reprinted in *Rican,* 1 (winter 1972)

Baer, Werner, *The Puerto Rican Economy and United States Economic Fluctuations* (Rio Piedras, P.R.: University of Puerto Rico, n.d.)

Berbusse, Edward J., *The United States in Puerto Rico, 1896–1900* (Chapel Hill: University of North Carolina Press, 1966)

Bernheimer, Charles S. (ed.), *The Russian Jew in the United States* (Philadelphia: Winston, 1905)

Blauch, Lloyd E., *Public Education in the Territories and Outlying Possessions* (Washington, D.C.: GPO, 1939)

Bourne, Dorothy Dulles and James R. Bourne, *Thirty Years of Change in Puerto Rico: A Case Study of Change in Puerto Rico: A Case Study of Ten Selected Rural Areas* (New York: Praeger, 1966)

Bucchioni, Eugene, "A Sociological Analysis of the Functioning of Elementary Education for Puerto Rican Children in the New York City Public Schools" (doctoral dissertation, New School for Social Research, 1965)

Buitrago, Hermanet, Argelia Maria, "Ethnic Identification of Puerto Rican Seventh Graders" (doctoral dissertation, University of Massachusetts, 1971)

Carroll, Henry K. *Report on the Island of Puerto Rico: Its Population, Civil Government, Commerce, Industries, Production, Roads, Tariff, and Currency: With Recommendations* (Washington, D.C.: GPO, 1899)

Center for Field Research and School Services, *An Evaluation of Teaching English as a Second Language in the Public Schools* (New York: School of Education, New York University, September 1969)

Chartock, Sarah K., "A Descriptive Study of the Programs Undertaken by the Riverside Neighborhood Assembly To Further Democratic Integration on the West Side of Manhattan" (doctoral dissertation, New York University, 1957)

Chenault, Lawrence R., *The Puerto Rican Migrant in New York City* (New York: Columbia University Press, 1938)

Cintron De Crespo, Patria, "Puerto Rican Women Teachers in New York: Self-Perception and Work Adjustment as Perceived by Themselves and by Others" (doctoral dissertation, Columbia University, 1965)

Clark, Victor S. and associates, *Porto Rico and Its Problems* (Washington, D.C.: Brookings Institution, 1930)

Cochran, Thomas C., *The Puerto Rican Businessman: A Study in Cultural Change* (Philadelphia: University of Pennsylvania Press, 1959)

Coleman, Robert M., "A History and Evaluation of the New York University Workshop: Field Study in Puerto Rican Education and Culture, 1948–1967" (doctoral dissertation, New York University, 1969)

Columbia University, Bureau of Applied Social Research, *The Puerto Rican of New York City* (New York: Puerto Rico Department of Labor, n.d.)

Connecticut Advisory Committee to U.S. Commission on Civil Rights, *in* U.S. Commission on Civil Rights, *El Boricua: The Puerto Rican Community in Bridgeport and New Haven* (Washington, D.C.: GPO, January 1973)

Cordasco, Francesco and Eugene Bucchioni (eds.), *The Puerto Rican Community and Its Children on the Mainland: A Source Book for Teachers, Social Workers, and Other Professionals,* 2nd ed. (Metuchen, N.J.: Scarecrow Press, 1972)

Cruz, Monclova, Lidio, "The Puerto Rican Political Movement in the 19th Century," *in* United States–Puerto Rico Commission on the Status of Puerto Rico, *Status of Puerto Rico: Selected Background Studies* (Washington, D.C.: GPO, 1966)

Diffie, Bailey W. and Justine W. Diffie, *Porto Rico: A Broken Pledge* (New York: Vanguard Press, 1931)

Donohue, Frances Marie, "A Study of the Original Puerto Rican Colony in Brooklyn, 1938–1943" (master's thesis, Fordham University, 1945)

Dworkis, Martin B. (ed.), *The Impact of Puerto Rican Migration on Governmental Services in New York City* (New York: New York University Press, 1957)

England, Joan T., "The Puerto Ricans: Melrose School and Community, New York City" (master's thesis, Hunter College, 1958)

Epstein, Erwin H., "National Identity and the Language Issue in Puerto Rico," *Comparative Education Review*, 11 (June 1967). Reprinted in Epstein (ed.), *Politics and Education in Puerto Rico: A Documentary Survey of the Language Issue* (Metuchen, N.J.: Scarecrow Press, 1970)

EQUAL *Research for Action*, Bulletin No. 2, February 15, 1967

Fewkes, Jesse Walter, *The Aborigines of Puerto Rico and Neighboring Islands.* Twenty-fifth Annual Report of the Bureau of American Ethnology, 1903–1904 (Washington, D.C.: GPO, 1907)

Fitzpatrick, Joseph P., *Puerto Rican Americans: The Meaning of Migration to the Mainland* (Englewood Cliffs, N.J.: Prentice-Hall, 1971)

"Instruction for Non-English-Speaking Puerto Rican Pupils in New York City Public School System," February 10, 1971. Memorandum for Senator Jacob Javits, *in* U.S. Commission on Civil Rights, *Hearing Held in New York, February 14–15, 1972* (Washington, D.C.: GPO, 1973)

International Institute of Teachers College, Columbia University, *A Survey of the Public Educational System of Porto Rico* (New York: Bureau of Publications, Teachers College Columbia University, 1926)

Kirschenbaum, Deby, "The Non-English Speaking Puerto Rican Child in the New York City Public School System" (master's thesis, Bank Street College of Education, 1957?)

Koss, Joan Dee, "Puerto Ricans in Philadelphia: Migration and Accommodation" (doctoral dissertation, University of Pennsylvania, 1969)

Landers, Jacob, *Improving Ethnic Distribution of New York City Pupils* (New York: Board of Education, May 1966)

Lewis, Gordon K., *Puerto Rico: Freedom and Power in the Caribbean* (New York: Monthly Review Press, 1963)

Maldonado-Denis, Manuel, *Puerto Rico: A Socio-Historic Interpretation*, tr. Elena Vialo (New York: Vintage, 1972)

Margolis, Richard J., *The Losers: A Report on the Puerto Ricans and the Public Schools* (New York: Aspira, May 1968)

Masso, Gildo, "The Growth of the School System of Porto Rico Under the American Administration" (master's thesis, University of Chicago, 1922)

Mathews, Thomas G., *Puerto Rican Politics and the New Deal* (Gainesville: University of Florida Press, 1960)

McSeveny, Samuel T., "Ethnic Groups, Ethnic Conflicts, and Recent Quantitative Research in American Political History," *International Migration Review*, 7 (spring 1973)

Messer, Helaine Ruth, "The Puerto Rican Student in the New York City Public School: 1945–1965" (master's thesis, Columbia University, 1966)

Seplowin, Virginia Montero, "Training and Employment Patterns of Puerto Ricans in Philadelphia" (doctoral dissertation, University of Pennsylvania, 1969)

Morrison, J. Cayce, *The Puerto Rican Study, 1953–1957: A Report on the Education and Adjustment of the Puerto Rican Pupils in the Public Schools of the City of New York* (New York: Board of Education, 1958)

Negron de Montilla, Aida, *Americanization in Puerto Rico and the Public School System 1900–1930* (Rio Piedras, P.R.: Editorial Edil, 1971)

Nieves Falcon, Luis, *Recruitment to Higher Education in Puerto Rico, 1940–1960* (Rio Piedras, P.R.: Editorial Universitaria, Universidad de Puerto Rico, 1965)

Osuna, Juan Jose, *A History of Education in Puerto Rico*, 2nd ed. (Rio Piedras, P.R.: Editorial de la Universidad de Puerto Rico, 1949)

Osuna, Juan Jose, "Report on Visits to New York City Schools," *in* Francesco Cordasco and Eugene Bucchioni (eds.), *The Puerto Rican Community and Its Children on the Mainland: A Sourcebook for Teachers, Social Workers, and Other Professionals*, 2nd ed. (Metuchen, N.J.: Scarecrow Press, 1972)

Padilla, Elena, "Puerto Rican Immigrants in New York and Chicago. A Study of Comparative Assimilation" (master's thesis, University of Chicago, 1947)

Padilla, Elena, *Up From Puerto Rico* (New York: Columbia University Press, 1958)

Pareles Cafouras, Angeles, "The History of Elementary Education of Puerto Rico under the American Government 1898–1951" (master's thesis, Indiana University, 1951)

Porrata, Oscar Emilio, "Retardation in the Elementary Urban Schools of Porto Rico" (master's thesis, University of Chicago, 1934)

Puerto Rican Public Papers of R. G. Tugwell, Governor (San Juan: Service Office of the Government of Puerto Rico Printing Division, 1945)

Puerto Rican Research and Resources Center, *Puerto Rican Migration: A Preliminary Report* (Washington, D.C.: U.S. Commission on Civil Rights, n.d.)

Puerto Ricans Confront Problems of the Complex Urban Society: A Design for Change. Community Conference Proceedings, April 15–16, 1967 (New York: Human Resources Administration, n.d.)

Robinson, Gertrude A., "A Case Study of Puerto Rican Children in Junior High School 65, Manhattan, New York City" (doctoral dissertation, New York University, 1956)

Rodriguez, Herman, "Some Problems of Bilingualism in Acculturation of Puerto Ricans in New York City" (master's thesis, City College of New York, 1965)

Rodriguez Bou, Ismael, "Significant Factors in the Development of Education in Puerto Rico," *in* United States–Puerto Rican Commission on the Status of Puerto Rico, *Status of Puerto Rico: Selected Background Studies* (Washington, D.C.: GPO, 1966)

Rosario, Jose C., *The Development of the Puerto Rican Jibaro and His Present Attitude Towards Society* (San Juan: University of Puerto Rico, 1935)

Senior, Clarence and Donald O. Watkins, "Toward a Balance Sheet of Puerto Rican Migration," *in* United States–Puerto Rican Commission on the Status of Puerto Rico, *Status of Puerto Rico: Selected Background Studies* (Washington, D.C.: GPO, 1966)

Sexton, Patricia Cayo, *Spanish Harlem* (New York: Harper & Row, 1965)

Silen, Juan Angel, *We, the Puerto Rican People: A Story of Oppression and Resistance*, tr. by Cedric Belfrage (New York: Monthly Review Press, 1971)

Stambler, Ada, "A Study of Eighth Grade Puerto Rican Students at Junior High School 65, Manhattan, With Implications for Their Placement, Grouping, and Orientation" (doctoral dissertation, Columbia University, 1958)

Steward, Julian H. and others, *The People of Puerto Rico* (Urbana: University of Illinois Press, 1956)

A Study of Poverty Conditions in the New York Puerto Rican Community (New York: Puerto Rican Forum, 1970)

Sussman, Leila, "Democratization and Class Segregation in Puerto Rican Schooling: The U.S. Model Transplanted," *Sociology of Education*, 41 (1968)

Thompson, Frank V., *Schooling of the Immigrant* (New York: Harper & Row, 1920)

Tractenberg, Paul L.(ed.), *Selection of Teachers and Supervisors in Urban School Systems* (New York: Agathon, 1972)

Tugwell, Rexford Guy, *The Stricken Land: The Story of Puerto Rico* (Garden City, N.Y.: Doubleday, 1947)

Tugwell, Rexford Guy, "Foreword," in Thomas Mathews, *Puerto Rican Politics and the New Deal* (Gainesville: University of Florida Press, 1960)

U.S. Commission on Civil Rights, *Hearing Held in New York, New York, February 14–15, 1972* (Washington, D.C.: GPO, 1973)

U.S. Congress, 89th, 2nd session, Senate, Document No. 108, *Status of Puerto Rico: Hearings*, Vol. 2, *Socio-Cultural Factors in Relation to the Status of Puerto Rico* (Washington, D.C.: GPO, 1966)

U.S. Congress, 91st, 2nd session, Senate Select Committee on Equal Educational Opportunity, *Equal Educational Opportunity: Hearings*, Part 8, *Equal Educational Opportunity for Puerto Rican Children* (Washington, D.C.: Government Printing Office, 1970)

U.S. Immigration Commission, *The Children of Immigrants in Schools*, Vol. 32 (Washington, D.C.: GPO, 1911)

Villefuerte, R. De, *The Americanization of Manuel de Rosas* (New York: Vantage, 1967)

Wagenheim, Kal, *Puerto Rico: A Profile* (New York: Praeger, 1970)

Wakefield, Dan, *Island in the City: The World of Spanish Harlem* (Boston: Houghton Mifflin, 1959)

Wells, Henry, *The Modernization of Puerto Rico: A Political Study of Changing Values and Institutions* (Cambridge, Mass.: Harvard University Press, 1969)

Wilber, George L. and W. B. Back, "Rural Poverty in Puerto Rico," in President's National Advisory Commission on Rural Poverty, *Rural Poverty in the United States* (Washington, D.C.: GPO, 1968)

Willis, Robert M., "An Analysis of the Adjustment and Scholastic Achievement of Forty Puerto Rican Boys Who Attended Transition Classes in New York City" (doctoral dissertation, New York University, 1961)

Yorchenco, Henrietta, ¡*Hablamas*! *Puerto Ricans Speak* (New York: Praeger, 1971)

Black higher education

Adler, Cyrus, *I Have Considered the Days* (Philadelphia: Jewish Publication Society of America, 1941)

"Affirmative Action in Higher Education: A Report by the Council Commission on Discrimination," *AAUP Bulletin*, 59 (June 1973)

Alman, Emily, "Desegregation at Rutgers University," in Rhoda L. Goldstein (ed.), *Black Life and Culture in the United States* (New York: Crowell, 1971)

Anthony, Earl, *The Time of The Furnaces: A Case Study of Black Student Revolt* (New York: Dial, 1971)

Aptheker, Herbert, "The Negro College Student in the 1920's: Years of Preparation and Protest: An Introduction," *Science and Society*, 33 (spring 1969)

Atwood, R. B., H.S. Smith, and Catherine O. Vaughn, "Negro Teachers in Northern Colleges and Universities in the United States," *Journal of Negro Education*, 18 (fall 1949)

Bacote, Clarence A., *The Story of Atlanta University: A Century of Service, 1865–1965* (Atlanta: Atlanta University, 1969)

Badger, Henry G., "Statistics of Negro Colleges and Universities, Students, Staff, and Finances, 1900–1950," *Statistical Circular*, No. 293 (Washington, D.C.: Federal Security Agency, April 1951)

Ballard, Allen B., *The Education of Black Folk: The Afro-American Struggle for Knowledge in White America* (New York: Harper & Row, 1973)

Barlow, Bill and Peter Shapiro, "The Struggle for San Francisco State," in James McEvoy and Abraham Miller (eds.), *Black Power and Student Rebellion* (Belmont, Cal.: Wadsworth, 1969)

Battle, William E., "The Desegregated All-White Institution: The University of Oklahoma," *Journal of Educational Sociology*, 32 (February 1959)

Belles, A. Gilbert, "Negroes Are Few on College Faculties," *Southern Education Report*, 4 (July-August 1968)

Bennett, Don C., "Segregation and Racial Interaction," *Annals of the Association of American Geographers*, 63 (March 1973)

Berg, Ernest H. and Dayton Axtell, *Programs for Disadvantaged Students in the California Community Colleges* (Oakland: Peralta Junior College District, 1968)

Berkowitz, David S., *Inequality of Opportunity in Higher Education: A Study of Minority Group and Related Barriers to College Admission* (Report to the Temporary Commission on the Need for a State University, 1948)

Berls, Robert H., "Higher Education Opportunity and Achievement in the United States," *in* U.S. Congress, 91st, 1st session, Joint Economic Committee, *The Economics and Financing of Higher Education in the United States: A Compendium of Papers* (Washington, D.C.: GPO, 1969)

Bigglestone, W. E., "Oberlin College and the Negro Student, 1865–1940," *Journal of Negro History*, 56 (July 1971)

Billington, Ray Allen (ed.), *A Free Negro in the Slave Era: The Journal of Charlotte L. Forten* (New York: Collier, 1961)

Bindman, Aaron M., "Participation of Negro Students in an Integrated University" (doctoral dissertation, University of Illinois, 1965)

"Black and White at Northwestern University," *Integrated Education*, 6 (May-June 1968)

Bond, Horace Mann, "The Evolution and Present Status of Negro Higher and Professional Education in the United States," *Journal of Negro Education*, 17 (summer 1948)

Bond, Horace Mann, "The Origin and Development of the Negro Church-Related College," *Journal of Negro Education*, 29 (summer 1960)

Bond, Horace Mann, *The Education of the Negro in the American Social Order* (New York: Octagon, 1960, reprinted)

Bond, Horace Mann, "A Century of Negro Higher Education," *in* William W. Brickman and Stanley Lehrer (eds.), *A Century of Higher Education* (New York: Society for the Advancement of Education, 1962)

Bond, Horace Mann, "The Negro Scholar and Professional in America," *in* John P. Davis (ed.), *The American Negro Reference Book* (Englewood Cliffs, N.J.: Prentice-Hall, 1966)

Boone, William H., "Problems of Adjustment of Negro Students at a White School," *Journal of Negro Education*, 11 (1942)

Bowles, Frank and Frank A. Costa, *Between Two Worlds: A Profile of Negro Higher Education* (New York: McGraw-Hill, 1971)

Bradley, Jr., Nolen Eugene, "The Negro Undergraduate Student: Factors Relative to Performance in Predominantly White State Colleges and Universities in Tennessee" (doctoral dissertation, University of Tennessee, 1966)

Brazeal, B. R., "Some Problems in the Desegregation of Higher Education in the 'Hard Core' States," *Journal of Negro Education*, 27 (summer 1958)

"Breaking Down the Barriers of Discrimination in Higher Education," *School and Society*, 67 (February 14, 1948)

Brimmer, Andrew, "The Economic Outlook and the Future of the Negro College," *Daedalus*, 100 (summer 1971)

Brown, H. Rap, *Die, Nigger, Die!* (New York: Dial, 1969)

Brown, Ina Corinne and others, *National Survey of Higher Education of Negroes*, Vol. II (Washington, D.C.: GPO, 1942–1943)

Brubacher, John S. and Willis Rudy, *Higher Education in Transition: A History of American Colleges and Universities, 1636–1968*, rev. ed. (New York: Harper & Row, 1968)

Caliver, Ambrose, *A Personnel Study of Negro College Students* (New York: Columbia University, 1931)

Caliver, Ambrose, *Education of Negro Teachers* (Washington, D.C.: GPO, 1933)

Caliver, Ambrose, *Secondary Education for Negroes*, Bulletin 1932, No. 17 (Washington, D.C.: GPO, 1933)

Cayton, Horace R., *Long Old Road* (Seattle: University of Washington Press, 1964)

Centra, John A., Robert L. Linn, and Mary Ellen Parry, "Academic Growth in Predominantly Negro and Predominantly White Colleges," *American Educational Research Journal,* 7 (January 1970)

Chambers, M. M., *The Colleges and the Courts, 1941–45* (New York: Carnegie Foundation for the Advancement of Teaching, 1946)

Chambers, M. M., *The Colleges and the Courts, 1946–50* (New York: Columbia University Press, 1952)

Clark, Hilton, "The Black Ivy League: Some Personal Observations on an Apathetic Negro," *Black Student,* 1 (spring 1966)

Clark, Kenneth B., "The Negro Student in Northern Interracial Colleges: An Overview," *Black Student,* 1 (spring 1966)

Clark, Kenneth B., "Higher Education for Negroes: Challenge and Prospects," *Journal of Negro Education* (summer 1967)

Clark, Kenneth B., "A Charade of Power: Black Students at White Colleges," *Antioch Review,* 29 (summer 1969)

Cobb, W. Montague, "Not to the Swift: Progress and Prospects of the Negro in Science and the Professions," *Journal of Negro Education,* 27 (spring 1958)

Cole, Melvin, "Black Students and the Health Sciences," *Integrated Education,* 8 (January-February 1970)

Colston, James A., "State Financial Support of Higher Education in Georgia from 1932 to 1949 with Specific Reference to Higher Education for the Negro" (doctoral dissertation, New York University, 1958)

Columbia University Affirmative Action Program, April 10, 1972

Comer, James P., *Beyond Black and White* (New York: Quadrangle, 1972)

Conyers, Charline F. H., "A History of the Cheyney State Teachers College, 1837–1951" (doctoral dissertation, New York University, 1960)

Coombs, Orde, "Barber-Scotia College," *Change,* 5 (May 1973)

Cooper, Theodore Bernard, "Adjustment Problems of Undergraduate Negroes Enrolled at Indiana University" (doctoral dissertation, Indiana University, 1952)

Cox, O. C., "Introduction," *in* Nathan Hare, *The Black Anglo Saxons* (New York: Collier, 1970)

Cozart, Leland Stanford, *A History of the Association of Colleges and Secondary Schools, 1934–1965* (Charlotte, N.C.: Heritage, 1967)

Crummell, Alexander, *The Attitude of the American Mind Toward the Negro Intellect*, The American Negro Academy, Occasional Papers, No. 3 (Washington, D.C.: The Academy, 1898)

Curry, Green Venton, "Changes in Segregation Practices in Collegiate Institutions in Kentucky Since Modification of the Day Law" (master's thesis, Fisk University, n.d.)

Davis, Frank Marshall, "What a Negro Thinks About," *New Student,* 6 (March 16, 1930)

Davis, Jerry and Kingston Johns, Jr., "Changes in the Family Income Distribution of Freshmen," *Community and Junior College Journal,* 43 (December-January 1973)

Davis, John P., "Unrest in the Negro Colleges," *New Student,* 8 (January 1929)

Davis, John W., "The Negro Land-Grant College," *Journal of Negro Education,* 2 (July 1933)

DeCosta, Frank A., "The Tax-Supported College for Negroes," *Journal of Educational Sociology,* 22 (February 1958)

deGraaf, Lawrence B., "Howard: The Evolution of a Black Student Revolt," *in* Julian Foster and Durward Long (eds.), *Protest: Student Activism in America* (New York: Morrow, 1970)

Drake, St. Clair, "The Black University in the American Social Order," *Daedalus,* 100 (summer 1971)

Du Bois, W. E. B., "Reason in School and Business," *Crisis*, 21 (November 1920)

Du Bois, W. E. B., "The Tragedy of 'Jim Crow,'" *Crisis* (August 1923)

Du Bois, W. E. B., "The Dilemma of the Negro," *American Mercury*, 3 (October 1924)

Du Bois, W. E. B., "Fisk," *Crisis*, 29 (October 1924)

Du Bois, W. E. B., "Negroes in College," *Nation*, 122 (March 3, 1926)

Du Bois, W. E. B., "The Hampton Strike," *Nation* 125 (November 2, 1927)

Du Bois, W. E. B., "Pechstein and Pecksniff," *Crisis* (September 1929)

Du Bois, W. E. B., "Negro Fraternities," *Crisis* (June 1934)

Du Bois, W. E. B., "Segregation in the North," *Crisis* (April 1934)

Du Bois, W. E. B., "The Negro Scientist," *American Scholar*, 8 (1939)

Du Bois, W. E. B., "John Howard," *Chicago Defender*, May 10, 1947

Du Bois, W. E. B., "Race Relations in the United States, 1917–1947," *Phylon*, 9 (1948)

Du Bois, W. E. B., "A Negro Student at Harvard at the End of the 19th Century," *Massachusetts Review* (1959–1960)

Du Bois, W. E. B. and Augustus G. Dill (eds.), *The College-Bred Negro American* (Atlanta: Atlanta University Press, 1910)

Egerton, John, "High Risk," *Southern Education Report*, 3 (March 1968)

Egerton, John, *State Universities and Black Americans: An Inquiry Into Desegregation and Equity for Negroes in 100 Public Universities* (Atlanta: Southern Education Foundation, May 1969)

Egerton, John, "Inflated Body Count," *Change* (July-August 1970)

Egerton, John, *Black Public Colleges: Integration and Disintegration* (Nashville, Tenn.: Race Relations Information Center, June 1971)

Engs, Robert F. and John B. Williams, "Integration by Evasion," *Nation*, 209 (November 17, 1969)

Falls, Arthur G., "The Search for Negro Medical Students," *Integrated Education*, 1 (June 1963)

Fichter, Joseph H., *Young Negro Talent: Survey of the Experiences and Expectations of Negro Americans Who Graduated from College in 1961* (Chicago: National Opinion Research Center, November, 1964)

Fichter, Joseph H., *Negro Women Bachelors: A Comparative Exploration of the Experiences and Expectations of College Graduates of the Class of June 1961* (Chicago: National Opinion Research Center, January 1965)

Fichter, Joseph H., *Graduates of Predominantly Negro Colleges: Class of 1964* (Washington, D.C.: GPO, 1967)

Fields, Carl A., "Black Students in a White University," in *Financing Equal Opportunity in Higher Education* (New York: College Entrance Examination Board, 1970)

Fishman, George, "Paul Robeson's Student Days and the Fight Against Racism at Rutgers," *Freedomways*, 9 (summer 1969)

Fleming, G. James, "The Going Is Rough but They Make It," *Crisis*, 43 (August 1936)

Fleming, G. James, "Desegregation in Higher Education in Maryland," *Journal of Negro Education*, 27 (summer 1958)

Folger, John K., Helene S. Astin, and Alan E. Bayer, *Human Resources and Higher Education* (New York: Russell Sage Foundation, 1970)

Forman, James, *Sammy Younge, Jr.: The First Black College Student to Die in the Black Liberation Movement* (New York: Grove, 1968)

Foster, Julian and Durward Long (eds.), *Protest! Student Activism in America* (N.Y.: Morrow, 1970)

Godwin, Winifred L., "Southern State Governments and Higher Education for Negroes," *Daedalus*, 100 (summer 1971)

Goodrich, Andrew L., Lawrence W. Lazotte, and James A. Welch, "Minorities in Two-Year Colleges: A Survey," *Community and Junior College Journal*, 43 (December-January 1973)

Gordon, Edmund W., "Programs and Practices for Minority Group Youth in Higher Education," in *Barriers to Higher Education* (New York: College Entrance Examination Board, 1971)

Green, Harry W., "Higher Standards for the Negro College," *Opportunity,* 9 (January 1931)

Green, Robert L., Joseph R. McMillan, and Thomas S. Gunnings, "Blacks in the Big Ten," *Integrated Education,* 10 (May-June 1971)

Green, Robert L. and others, "The Admission of Minority Students: A Framework for Action," *Integrated Education,* 9 (March-April 1971)

Greenberg, Jack, *Race Relations and American Law* (New York: Columbia University Press, 1959)

Greenwood, Charles and Theresa Greenwood, "Some Historic Aspects of Hoosier Education of the Negro," *ISSQ (Indiana Social Studies Quarterly)* 17 (spring 1964)

Grimke, Francis J., "Lincoln University," *Crisis,* 32 (August 1926)

Guzman, Jessie P. (ed.), *The New South and Higher Education* (Tuskegee, Ala.: Tuskegee Institute, 1954)

Guzman, Jessie P., *Twenty Years of Court Decisions Affecting Higher Education in the South, 1938-1958* (Tuskegee, Ala.: Tuskegee Institute, 1969)

Hall, Gwendolyn Midlo, "Rural Black College," *Negro Digest,* 18 (March 1969)

Handlin, Oscar and Mary F. Handlin, *The American College and American Culture: Socialization as a Function of Higher Education* (New York: McGraw-Hill, 1970)

Hargrave, Edythe "How I Feel as a Negro at a White College," *Journal of Negro Education,* 11 (1942)

Harlan, Louis R., *Booker T. Washington: The Making of a Black Leader 1856-1901* (New York: Oxford University Press, 1972)

Harris, George, in *Financing Equal Opportunity in Higher Education* (New York: College Entrance Examination Board, 1970)

Harris, Patricia Roberts, "The Negro College and Its Community," *Daedalus,* 100 (summer 1971)

Harris, Seymour E., *A Statistical Portrait of Higher Education* (New York: McGraw-Hill, 1972)

Haynes, M. Alfred, "Problems Facing the Negro in Medicine Today," *Journal of the American Medical Association,* 209 (August 18, 1969)

Hazen, H. H., "Twenty-three Years of Teaching in a Negro Medical School," *Social Forces,* 12 (1933)

Hedgman, Anna Arnold, *The Trumpet Sounds: A Memoir of Negro Leadership* (New York: Holt, 1964)

Hedrick, James A., "The Negro in Southern Graduate Education" (doctoral dissertation, North Texas State College, 1954)

Helton, William Curtis, "Characteristics, Performance, Problems, and Successes of Negro Graduate Students Enrolled in Five Predominantly White State Colleges in Tennessee, 1963-1965" (doctoral dissertation, University of Tennessee, 1966)

Henderson, Rose, "Negro Education at Columbia," *Southern Workman,* 61 (July 1932)

Hightower, Jim, *Hard Tomatoes, Hard Times: The Failure of the Land Grant College Complex* (Washington, D.C.: Agribusiness Accountability Project, 1972)

Hill, Leslie Pinckney, "The State Teachers' College at Cheyney and Its Relation to Segregation in the North," *Journal of Negro Education,* 1 (October 1932)

Hofstadter, Richard and C. DeWitt Hardy, *The Development and Scope of Higher Education in the United States* (New York: Columbia University Press, 1952)

Holmes, Dwight Oliver Wendell, *The Evolution of the Negro College* (New York: Teachers College Columbia University, 1934)

Houston, Charles H., "Cracking Closed University Doors," *Crisis,* 42 (December 1935)

Houston, Charles H., "Don't Shout Too Soon," *Crisis,* 43 (March 1936)

Hughes, Langston, "Cowards from the College," *Crisis*, 41 (August 1934)

Hughes, Langston, *The Big Sea: Autobiography by Langston Hughes* (New York: Knopf, 1940)

Hughes, Langston, "Simple Discusses Colleges and Color," *Phylon* (December 1949)

Hunton, George K., *All of Which I Saw, Part of Which I Was: The Autobiography of George K. Hunton* (Garden City, N.Y.: Doubleday, 1967)

Huson, Carolyn F. and Michael E. Schiltz, *College, Color, and Employment: Racial Differentials in Postgraduate Employment Among 1964 Graduates of Louisiana Colleges* (Chicago: National Opinion Research Center, July 1966)

Jackson, Donald W., "Some Reflections on the Movement," *Black Student*, 1 (spring 1966)

Jaffe, A. and Walter Adams, *American Higher Education in Transition* (New York: Bureau of Applied Social Research, Columbia University, April 1969)

Jay, William, *Condition of the Free People of Color, 1838* (New York: Arno Press, reprinted 1969)

Jenkins, Herbert Crawford, "The Negro Student at the University of Iowa: A Sociological Study" (master's thesis, State University of Iowa, 1933)

Johnson, Charles S., *The Negro College Graduate* (Chapel Hill: University of North Carolina Press, 1938)

Johnson, Oakley, "Three Planks for President," *New Student*, 7 (March 21, 1928)

Jones, Butler A., "Law and Social Change: A Study of the Impact of New Legal Requirements Affecting Equality of Educational Opportunities for Negroes Upon Certain Customary Official Behavior in the South, 1938–1953" (doctoral dissertation, New York University, 1955)

Jones, Mack H., "The Responsibility of the Black College to the Black Community: Then and Now," *Daedalus*, 100 (summer 1971)

Jones, Wendell Primus, "The Negro Press and the Higher Education of Negroes, 1933–1952" (doctoral dissertation, University of Chicago, 1954)

Kahn, Roger, *The Battle for Morningside Heights: Why Students Rebel* (New York: Morrow, 1970)

Katz, Jerry Martin, "The Educational Shibboleth: Equality of Opportunity in a Democratic Institution, the Public Junior College" (doctoral dissertation, University of California at Los Angeles, 1967)

Katz, Jerry Martin, Donna F. Gold, and Elliot Jones, "Equality of Opportunity in a Democratic Institution: The Public Junior College," *Education and Urban Society*, 5 (May 1973)

Kilson, Martin, "Blacks at Harvard: Crisis and Change," *Harvard Bulletin*, 75 (April and June 1973)

Kitano, Harry and Dorothy Miller, *An Assessment of Educational Opportunity Programs in California Higher Education* (Sacramento: Joint Legislative Committee, February 1971)

Klein, Arthur J. (ed.), *Survey of Negro Colleges and Universities* (Washington, D.C.: GPO, 1929)

Knoell, Dorothy, *People Who Need College: A Report on Students We Have Yet To Serve* (Washington, D.C.: American Association of Junior Colleges, 1970)

Lee, Lurline Mahan, "The Origin, Development, and Present Status of Arkansas' Program of Higher Education for Negroes" (doctoral dissertation, Michigan State College, 1955)

Long, Herman H., "The Status of Desegregated Higher Education in Tennessee," *Journal of Higher Education*, 27 (summer 1958)

"Louisiana Resolution Asks Merger of Colleges," *Crisis*, 80 (February 1973)

Lykes, Richard Wayne, "A History of the Division of Higher Education, United States Office of Education, From Its Creation in 1911 Until the Establishment of the Department of Health, Education, and Welfare in 1953" (doctoral dissertation, American University, 1960)

Mackey, Paul Rettig, "A Survey of Negro Participation in Intercollegiate Athletics in American Co-racial Colleges and Universities" (master's thesis, Ohio State University, 1940)

Maeroff, Gene I., "A Kind of Higher Education," *New York Times Magazine,* May 27, 1973

Mangum, Jr., Charles S., *The Legal Status of the Negro* (Chapel Hill: University of North Carolina Press, 1940)

Marcuse, F. L., "Some Attitudes Toward Employing Negroes as Teachers in a Northern University," *Journal of Negro Education,* 17 (winter 1948)

Markley, Oliver Wendell, "Having a Negro Roommate as an Experience in Intercultural Education" (doctoral dissertation, Northwestern University, 1968)

Matthews, Donald and James Prothro, "Negro Students and the Protest Movement," *in* James McEvoy and Abraham Miller (eds.), *Black Power and Student Rebellion* (Belmont, Cal.: Wadsworth, 1969)

Mays, Benjamin E., *Born to Rebel: An Autobiography* (New York: Scribner, 1971)

Mays, Benjamin E., "Does U.S. Seek Integration or Black Liquidation?" *Chicago Defender,* June 2, 1973

Mays, Benjamin E., "My View," *Chicago Defender,* June 23, 1973

McClellan, Frank, "A Black Student's Reaction to the Present System of Financial Aid," *in Financing Equal Opportunity in Higher Education* (New York: College Entrance Examination Board, 1970)

McClendon, William H., "Which College, White or Negro?" *Crisis,* 41 (September 1934)

McPherson, James W., "White Liberals and Black Power in Negro Education, 1865–1915," *American Historical Review,* 75 (June 1970)

McWilliams, Carey, "Racial Dialectic: Missouri Style," *Nation,* 160 (February 24, 1945)

McWorter, Gerald, "Tragedy at Southern U.: Accident or Political Assassination?" *Edcentric,* No. 22 (March 1973)

Medsker, Leland L. and Dale Tillery, *Breaking the Access Barrier* (New York: McGraw-Hill, 1971)

Meier, August and Elliott Rudwick, *CORE: A Study in the Civil Rights Movement 1942–1968* (New York: Oxford University Press, 1973)

Miller, Arthur S., *Racial Discrimination and Private Education: A Legal Analysis* (Chapel Hill: University of North Carolina Press, 1957)

Miller, Kelly, *The Everlasting Stain* (Washington, D.C.: Associated Publishers, 1924)

Miller, Lamar P., "An Analysis of Objectives of Institutes and Departments of Afro-American Affairs," *in* Edgar G. Epps (ed.), *Black Students in White Schools* (Worthington, Ohio: Jones, 1972)

Miller, Loren R., "College," *Crisis,* 33 (January 1927)

Milner, Jr., Murray, *The Illusion of Equality* (San Francisco: Jossey-Bass, 1972)

Mitchell, Horace, "The Black Experience in Higher Education," *Counseling Psychologist,* 2 (1970)

Moody, Anne, *Coming of Age in Mississippi* (New York: Dial, 1968)

Morrow, E. Frederick, "Nordic Education for the Negro a Curse or a Boon?" *Opportunity* (January 1931)

Moss, James Allen, "Negro Teachers in Predominantly White Colleges," *Journal of Negro Education,* 27 (fall 1958)

Moss, James Allen, "The Utilization of Negro Teachers in the Colleges of New York State," *Phylon,* 21 (spring 1960)

Napper, George, *Blacker Than Thou: The Struggle for Campus Unity* (Grand Rapids, Mich.: Erdmans, 1973)

National Advisory Committee on Education, *Federal Relations to Education,* Part I, *Committee Findings and Recommendations* (Washington, D.C.: National Capitol Press, 1931)

Nelson, Jack and Jack Bass, *The Orangeburg Massacre* (New York: World, 1970)

O'Leary, Malcolm, "Accreditation of Negro Colleges and Secondary Schools by the Southern

Association of Colleges and Secondary Schools" (master's thesis, Catholic University of America, 1965)

Orum, Anthony M., "Negro College Students and the Civil Rights Movements" (doctoral dissertation, University of Chicago, 1967)

Owens, George A., *in* U.S. Congress, 91st, 2nd session, Senate Committee on Labor and Public Welfare, Subcommittee on Education, *Higher Education Amendments of 1970: Hearing*, Part 2 (Washington, D.C.: GPO, 1971)

Painter, Nell, "Jim Crow at Harvard: 1923," *New England Quarterly*, 44 (1971)

Panel on Financing Low Income and Minority Students in Higher Education, *Toward Equal Opportunity for Higher Education* (New York: College Entrance Examination Board, 1973)

Panetta, Leon E. and Peter Gall, *Bring Us Together: The Nixon Team and the Civil Rights Retreat* (Philadelphia: Lippincott, 1971)

Payne, William, "The Negro Land-Grant Colleges," *Civil Rights Digest*, 3 (spring 1970)

Peirce, Paul, "Negro Alumni of the Colleges of Iowa," *in* W.E.B. Du Bois and Augustus G. Dill (eds.), *The College-Bred Negro American* (Atlanta: Atlanta University Press, 1910)

Pennsylvania Human Relations Commission, August 12, 1971, press release

Pickens, William, "Types of Southern Schools," *Crisis*, 44 (March 1937)

Pickens, William, *The New Negro* (New York: Negro Universities Press, 1969, reprinted)

"Prominent Black Medical Professor Rips Medical School Ban on Black Students," *Muhammad Speaks*, March 7, 1969

Rafky, David M., "Wit and Racial Conflict Among Colleagues," *Integrated Education*, 10 (January-February 1972)

Rainsford, George N., *Congress and Higher Education in the Nineteenth Century* (Knoxville: University of Tennessee Press, 1972)

Redding, J. Saunders, *On Being Negro in America* (Indianapolis: Bobbs-Merrill, 1951)

Redding, Louis L., "Desegregation in Higher Education in Delaware," *Journal of Negro Education*, 27 (summer 1958)

Reed, Jr., Jesse A., "Black Eye for Campus Liberalism," *Crisis*, 44 (August 1937)

Report on Higher Education (The Newman Report) (Washington, D.C.: GPO, 1971)

Robeson, Eslanda Goode, *Paul Robeson Negro* (London: Gollancz, 1930)

Roche, Richard J., *Catholic Colleges and the Negro Student* (Washington, D.C.: Catholic University of America Press, 1948)

Rothbart,, George S., "Ivory Tower or Modern Building?" *in* Arlene Kaplan Daniels, Rachel Kahn-Hut, and associates, *Academics on the Line: The Faculty Strike at San Francisco State* (San Francisco: Jossey-Bass, 1970)

Rudolph, Frederick, *The American College and University: A History* (New York: Knopf, 1962)

Sarratt, Reed, *The Ordeal of Desegregation: The First Decade* (New York: Harper & Row, 1966)

Sawyer, Robert M., "The Gaines Case: Its Background and Influence on the University of Missouri and Lincoln University 1936–1950" (doctoral dissertation, University of Missouri, 1966)

Scotford, John R., "The New Negro Education," *Christian Century*, 45 (January 12, 1928)

Scott, Will Braxton, "Race Consciousness and the Negro Student at Indiana University" (doctoral dissertation, Indiana University, 1960)

Seamans, Herbert L., "Policies and Practices Regarding Minority Groups in Selected Colleges and Universities" (doctoral dissertation, Stanford University, 1947)

Sekora, John, "Murder Relentless and Impressive: The American Academic Community and the Negro College," *Soundings*, 51 (fall 1968)

Sellers, Cleveland and Robert Terrell, *The River of No Return: The Autobiography of a Black Militant and the Life and Death of SNCC* (New York: Morrow, 1973)

Shapiro, Beth Janet, "The Black Athlete at Michigan State University" (master's thesis, Michigan State University, 1970)

Sorkin, Alan L., "A Comparison of Quality Characteristics of Negro and White Private and Church-Related Colleges and Universities in the South," *College and University*, 46 (spring 1971)

Sowell, Thomas, *Black Education: Myths and Tragedies* (New York: McKay, 1972)

Stephan, A. Stephen, "Desegregation of Higher Education in Arkansas," *Journal of Negro Education*, 27 (summer 1958)

Sumner, Francis C., "Environic Factors Which Prohibit Creative Scholarship Among Negroes," *School and Society*, 22 (September 5, 1925)

Takaki, Ronald, "Aesculapius Was a White Man: Antebellum White Racism and Male Chauvinism at Harvard Medical School," paper read at the American Historical Association annual meeting, December 1971

Taylor, Ivan E., "Negro Teachers in White Colleges," *School and Society*, 65 (May 24, 1947)

Terrell, Mary Church, "Americans Black and White," *New Student*, 2 (February 24, 1923)

Terrell, Mary Church, *A Colored Woman in a White World* (Washington, D.C.: Ramsdell, 1940)

Thomas, Tim, "The Student Movement at Southern University," *Freedomways*, 13 (1973)

Thompson, Charles H., "75 Years of Negro Education," *Crisis*, 45 (July 1938)

Thurman, Howard, "The New Heaven and the New Earth," *Journal of Negro Education*, 27 (spring 1958)

Torrence, Ridgely, *The Story of John Hope* (New York: Macmillan, 1948)

Trillin, Calvin, *An Education in Georgia: The Integration of Charlayne Hunter and Hamilton Holmes* (New York: Viking, 1964)

Trombley, William, "Colleges' Minority Aid Deficient, Study Says," *Los Angeles Times*, March 9, 1970

Ullman, Victor, *Martin R. Delany: The Beginnings of Black Nationalism* (Boston: Beacon, 1971)

U.S. Commission on Civil Rights, *Equal Protection of the Laws in Public Higher Education* (Washington, D.C.: GPO, 1960)

U.S. Department of Health, Education, and Welfare, Office for Civil Rights, *Racial and Ethnic Enrollment Data from Institutions of Higher Education, Fall 1970* (Washington, D.C.: GPO, 1972)

U.S. President's Commission on Higher Education, *Higher Education for American Democracy*, Vol. II, *Equalizing and Expanding Individual Opportunity* (New York: Harper & Row, 1948)

Vargus, Ione Dugger, "Revival of Ideology: The Afro-American Society Movement" (doctoral dissertation, Brandeis University, 1971)

Veysey, Lawrence R., *The Emergence of the American University* (Chicago: University of Chicago Press, 1965)

Wale, Fred G., "Chosen for Ability," *Atlantic Monthly*, 180 (July 1947)

Walters, Raymond, "The Cincinnati Meeting of the Association of American Colleges," *School and Society*, 67 (January 31, 1948)

Washington, Booker T., "A University Education for Negroes," *Independent*, 68 (March 24, 1910)

Watkins, William J., *Our Rights as Men* (Boston: Roberts, 1853)

White, Robert Melvin, "The Tallahassee Sit-Ins and CORE: A Nonviolent Revolutionary Movement" (doctoral dissertation, Florida State University, 1964)

Wilkins, Roy, "Blacks Begin to Question the Goings-On in Negro Education," *Los Angeles Times*, July 19, 1973

Williams, Roger M., *The Bonds: An American Family* (New York: Atheneum, 1971)

Willie, Charles V. and Arline Sakum McCord, *Black Students at White Colleges* (New York: Praeger, 1972)
Wilson, George D., "Developments in Negro Colleges During the Twenty Year Period, 1914–15 to 1933–34" (doctoral dissertation, Ohio State University, 1935)
Wilson, William J., "The Quest for Meaningful Black Experiences on White Campuses," *Massachusetts Review* (autumn 1969)
Windham, Douglas M., *Education, Equality and Income Redistribution: A Study of Public Higher Education* (Lexington, Mass.: Heath Lexington Books, 1970)
Winn, William and Ed Williams, *Augusta, Georgia and Jackson State University* (Atlanta: Southern Regional Council, June 1970)
Winston, Michael R., "Through the Back Door: Academic Racism and the Negro Scholar in Historical Perspective," *Daedalus*, 100 (summer 1971)
Wolff, Miles, *Lunch at the Five and Ten: The Greensboro Sit-Ins: A Contemporary History* (New York: Stein & Day, 1970)
Woodson, Carter G., *The Education of the Negro Prior to 1861*, 2nd ed. (Washington, D.C.: Associated Publishers, 1919)
Yates, Elizabeth, *Howard Thurman: Portrait of a Practical Dreamer* (New York: Day, 1964)

Cases

Adams v. Richardson, 356 F. Supp. 92 (1972)
Berea College v. Kentucky, 211 U.S. 45 (1908)
Booker v. Tennessee Board of Higher Education. 240 F. 2nd 689 (1957), cert. denied, 353 U.S. 965 (1957)
Frasier v. Board of Trustees of the University of North Carolina, 134 F. Supp. 589, aff'd, 350 U.S. 979 (1956)
Gaines v. Canada et al., 113 S.W. 783 (1937)
Gaines v. Canada, 305 U.S. 337 (1938)
Lincoln University v. Hackman, 295 Mo. 118 (1922)
State ex rel. Bluford v. Canada, Registrar of University of Missouri, 153 S.W. 14 (1941)
State ex rel. Weaver v. Board of Trustees of Ohio State University, 126 Ohio St. 290, 185 N.E. 196 (1933)
Sweatt v. Painter, 339 U.S. 629 (1950)
University of Maryland v. Donald T. Murray, 169 Md. 478 (1936)

Newspapers

African World
Arkansas Gazette
Atlanta Journal
Austin American
Baltimore Afro-American
Birmingham News
Chattanooga Times
Chicago Defender
Dallas Morning News
Houston Post
Lost Angeles Times
Louisiana Weekly
Miami Herald
Miami Times
Muhammad Speaks
Nashville Banner
New Orleans Times-Picayune
New York Age
New York Times
Philadelphia Bulletin
Saint Petersburg Times
Washington Post
Washington Star

Indexes

Name Index

Subject Index